"Hear, my son, your father's instruction,
And do not forsake your mother's teaching;
Indeed, they are a graceful wreath to your head,
And ornaments about your neck."
                                        (Prov. 1:8–9 NAS)

"Behold, children are a heritage from the Lord,
The fruit of the womb is a reward.
Like arrows in the hand of a warrior,
So are the children of one's youth.
  Happy is the man who has his quiver
  full of them."
                                        (Ps. 127: 3–5)

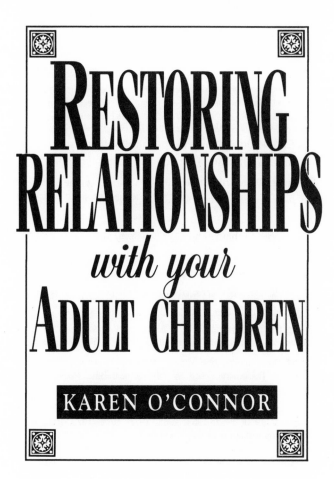

RESTORING RELATIONSHIPS

with your

ADULT CHILDREN

KAREN O'CONNOR

THOMAS NELSON PUBLISHERS
NASHVILLE

Published in Nashville, Tennessee, by Thomas Nelson, Inc.

Unless noted otherwise, Scripture quotations are from THE NEW KING JAMES VERSION. Copyright © 1979, 1980, 1982, Thomas Nelson, Inc., Publishers.

Scripture quotations noted KJV are from The Holy Bible, KING JAMES VERSION.

Scripture quotations noted NIV are taken from the HOLY BIBLE, NEW INTERNATIONAL VERSION®. Copyright © 1973, 1978, 1984 by International Bible Society. Used by permission of Zondervan Bible Publishing House. All rights reserved.

The "NIV" and "New International Version" trademarks are registered in the United States Patent and Trademark Office by International Bible Society. Use of either trademark requires the permission of International Bible Society.

Scripture quotations noted NASB are from THE NEW AMERICAN STANDARD BIBLE, Copyright © 1960, 1962, 1963, 1968, 1971, 1972, 1973, 1975, 1977 by The Lockman Foundation and are used by permission.

Library of Congress Cataloging-in-Publication Data

O'Connor, Karen, 1938–
    Restoring relationships with your adult chldren / Karen O'Connor.
        p.   cm.
    Includes bibliographical references.
    ISBN 0-8407-3443-3 (hc)
    1. Parent and adult child—United States.   2. Parenting—Religious aspects—Christianity.   I. Title.
    HQ755.86.035   1993
    306.874—dc20   93-26168
                                                                                                CIP

Printed in the United States of America

1 2 3 4 5 6 7 — 98 97 96 95 94 93

To

Julie,

Jim,

and Erin

with my love

CONTENTS

INTRODUCTION

"I'm selfish," said the soft-spoken brunette in the second row. "I've kept my son from realizing his adult responsibilities because I wanted to be needed and I didn't want him to suffer. That's being selfish. Isn't that a terrible thing to admit?"

"It sounds human to me," the speaker responded. "Human beings have flaws. That one's as good as any," she added with a twinkle in her eye.

About thirty of us had gathered one Saturday morning in San Diego to listen to local therapist Rebecca Cutter speak on the topic, "Empty Nest or Golden Opportunity?"[1]

I was particularly struck throughout the morning by the reminder that parents are human. We have flaws and character defects like anyone else. Some of us are pleasers. Some are rescuers. Others are manipulators, critics, or victims. Still others grieve a loss we cannot seem to recover. Sometimes those flaws create a crisis in our relationships. And sometimes our relationships are in crisis because of what our children do. We may carry burdens that belong to them. They may carry burdens that belong to us. Either way, there is no such thing as perfect parenting. It doesn't exist.

"I feel so much better after listening to you," said Midge, from the back of the room. "It's tough being a parent, but now that I look back, I did a pretty good job raising eight kids alone from the time my youngest was four—considering I'm human, that is!"

Some parents talked fondly of the relationship they have with their grown children. Many were proud of the people their sons and daughters had become. Others said they were clearly in transition—mourning the loss of contact and control in the lives of their children. Some said they still had a tendency to rescue their sons and daughters—often foregoing important needs of their own.

A few admitted the freedom they feel in having the house to themselves and a routine that centers around their own interests for a change. Others indicated they wished they had done things differently—had had more time, more money, more patience, more humor, more enthusiasm for their child-rearing days.

I also heard something else in the room—something that lay behind the words and the whispers and the chuckles of recognition. I heard a longing for a second chance—a chance to be closer, more intimate, more connected to their children. A chance to be needed again, to cook a favorite meal for a hungry boy, to shop with a young daughter for a special dress, to hang out together and laugh and talk, to hear their footsteps and voices and the familiar thump of the basketball against the garage door—one more time.

The harsh reality, however, is that those days are over. Our children have grown up. They are adults now. Most live on their own. And those still living with parents relate to us in a different way than when they were youngsters under our custody and influence.

We cannot go back. We cannot redo what we did. But there is reason for rejoicing even amidst the pain and regret. We can, with God's help, restore our relationships with our adult children. If we but ask, He will give us a second chance—an opportunity to heal our brokenness by learning to relate to our grown children in a new and special way, a way that's more sensitive than assertive, more spiritual than custodial, more nurturing than managing.

Just as we had to feel our way the first time around, we must learn and grow and feel our way now as we confront the problems between us and begin the process of restoration with our children. This time we are better equipped, more experienced, older, hopefully wiser, and indeed more willing to make the important changes necessary for the healing of those troubled or distant relationships.

In this book you will read the stories of parents like you—

men and women who are grieving, or are at least deeply concerned, about their relationships with their adult children. These parents want to do something to fix them or change them. They're mothers and fathers who want to make a fresh start but aren't sure how to make it happen.

This book will help you get started. My own experience, as well as observation and conversations with other parents, has provided the incentive for writing on this topic. I have been in great pain over my children at various times in their adolescent and adult years. For a long time I carried guilt and shame for decisions I made that contributed to their problems.

Through therapy and prayer, however, I now see that I was actually a pretty good mother—all things considered. Like you, I did the very best I knew how to do at the time. I made a lot of mistakes. But today I know more. I understand more and I want to bring that knowledge and understanding into my relationships with my three adult children and two step-children.

Several years ago I took hold of the second chance God gave me. It began when my youngest child moved in with my second husband and me when she was eighteen. It was the beginning of a whole new season in my life with her. Later on, the results of that time together led to a new season with my son and oldest daughter, as well. I now live in the fruit of that experience. My daughters have since married, and my son, who is single, lives with a roommate. I don't ever take that healing for granted. I am aware of this gift of time, contact, and the sharing of our thoughts and feelings—whatever they may be. And I thank God for it everyday.

As you read this book, I pray you will discover and take hold of the second chance God has for you, and that you will give yourself permission to acknowledge your weaknesses, reach for God's leading, and use the tools available for restoring your relationships.

To help you accomplish this I have divided the book into four parts. In Part One, I focus on why parents want and need restoration.

In Part Two you will meet a number of parents—some still in pain, some now in the healing process—all of whom are slowly rebuilding their relationships with their adult children. As you read their personal stories, I hope you will see yourself more clearly, gain insight into your parenting years, accept yourself, and commit to using the newfound awareness as part of your restoration process.

Part Three will look at recovery. I'll share five practical and spiritual steps, what each means, and how they can help you restore your troubled relationships.

Part Four will offer hope and help for living a healthy Christ-centered life as an individual and in your relationships with your children.

Finally, my wish is that you realize that a healthy relationship is not something your children bestow on you, but rather an opportunity you choose for yourself. With God's help, it will bring about the promise of Scripture, "You will also decree a thing, and it will be established for you; And light will shine on your ways" (Job 22:28 NASB).

PART ONE

Second
Chance—
Not
Last Chance

Chapter One

IT'S NOT TOO LATE TO BEGIN AGAIN

"I really blew it this time," said Margaret, looking pale and scared as she sat across from me at a corner table in our favorite café. "I can hardly talk about it." I watched as she folded and unfolded the paper napkin in front of her. "I did everything wrong—from the minute I walked into Greg's apartment until the moment I left. He'll never forgive me this time. I practically lost my voice I was so angry."

Margaret continued talking between hurried sips of coffee. "He knows how I feel about his life-style. Yet he hasn't done a thing to change it. I don't get it," she said, anger bubbling just below the surface. "Can you believe it? He's twenty-nine years old and he's still working minimum-wage jobs—when he works, that is. He has no comprehension of what it takes to make it in today's world."

Margaret ran a nervous hand through her auburn hair. "He lives hand-to-mouth. Half the time he doesn't know where he'll be sleeping let alone what he'll eat. And his friends are just as bad. They let him sleep on the couch or on the floor when he's between jobs. He's even slept in his car and had to take a shower at the beach. It's so degrading. It's tearing me apart."

My heart ached for her. I could feel her anger and disappointment.

"I let him have it," Margaret continued, her voice escalating. "I couldn't hold my tongue another minute. But this time I went too far. I know it. I can feel it."

Margaret stopped for a moment, took in a deep breath, then looked up. She reached across the table and took my hand. "I'm so sorry," she said suddenly. "I haven't let you get a word in. I'm sure you didn't come here to listen to me go on about Greg."

She was right. That hadn't been our plan. But I could tell she was still full of emotion from their confrontation the day before. "It's okay," I said. "You sound pretty upset. I can relate, believe me."

"You can?" she asked, a touch of relief in her voice.

I nodded. "Sometime I'll tell you my story."

She continued, but her words faded, as memories of my son flashed through my mind. I recalled a time when he had lived in his car for months, when he struggled with inappropriate roommates, unpaid bills, illness, and poor eating habits. There was even a time when he withdrew from family contact for nearly two years. I had been beside myself with worry and guilt—yet there was nothing I could do to change it.

For months I carried his pain with me twenty-four hours a day. I felt responsible for his choices. If only his father and I hadn't divorced. If only I hadn't moved to another city, we would have seen more of one another. If only I had taught him how to manage money better and set up housekeeping. A million "if onlys" flooded my mind. My stomach churned as familiar feelings surfaced.

Suddenly I felt Margaret touching my hand. "Is anything wrong?" she asked softly.

"I'm sorry, I'm off in my own little world," I said. "I was thinking about my son. Your sharing touched some sore spots. I can understand your hurt, I really can."

Margaret lowered her eyes and a faint smile crossed her lips. "Thanks for listening," she said. "I needed to get this off my chest." She took another breath.

"Please, if you can put up with me a little longer, I'd like your advice. The part that really worries me is when I lost my temper. I did something I swore I'd never do. I compared him to his father. I told him that if he didn't get a hold of his life he'd end up a deadbeat, broke and alone just like his dad."

Margaret clasped and unclasped her hands. "That wasn't fair.

I know it. His father left us when Greg was eight and there's a lot of hurt still inside him. I didn't mean to sound so cruel. I just want him to pay attention more—to realize that it could happen to him. But it didn't come out right."

Margaret grabbed a tissue from her purse, blotted her eyes, and wiped her nose.

"How did he react when you blew up?" I asked.

"He screamed at me—as if he hated everything I stood for. He told me to shut up and stop running his life. It was frightening. I can still feel his contempt."

"Have things always been like this between you and Greg?"

"No. That's why I'm so upset. I feel like we're strangers. I don't know how to talk to him anymore. He seems so stubborn, so determined to do things his way."

"What was he like as a little boy?" I asked.

"He was sweet and compliant. That's the word—compliant," she said. "A real nice boy. We were so close then. His dad was gone a lot during those early years, so Greg and I did things together. He liked the special meals I fixed for us, and I loved cooking for him. And we decorated his room together—a sports theme, you know, soccer and baseball and football stuff. I can still remember this terrific wallpaper I picked out. I surprised him with it. Everyone who saw it remarked on it."

My stomach began to churn. I remembered a similar situation with my kids. When we moved to a new house I took a strong hand in choosing wallpaper and furniture and accessories for their rooms. I felt so proud of myself for being interested and excited about it. It wasn't until years later that my daughters told me they wished they'd had more to say about the choices. Some of the things they really didn't like. I felt terrible.

Then I thought about my son and how I struggled to get him to do his homework at his new desk that I picked out. And I remembered how important it was to me to have order—my order in their space. I didn't simply teach and model good habits. I imposed my standards without much input from them.

I couldn't help but wonder if Margaret's standards for her son had failed for similar reasons. It sounded as if Greg, the little boy, submitted to everything his mother wanted because he needed her. He needed her companionship, her approval, her love—as all children do. But Greg, the adult child, on his own now, is just plain fed up. Maybe he doesn't even know he's fed up. Maybe my son got fed up too. Maybe the only way he could tell his dad and me that he was hurting was to drink, grow marijuana in the backyard, and finally live in his car.

Maybe Greg, like my son once did, is making a statement about himself and about his mother. Maybe his refusal to be responsible is his way of fighting back.

BATTLE FATIGUE

Could it be that parents of adult children now face just another battle in the same war we've been waging since their childhood? We had more power then so we got our way more often. Today, our adult children have power of their own. The power to remind us of our mistakes, our ego trips, our critical and manipulative behavior. They're bigger now, older, and sometimes wiser than we are. They have something to tell us—and I am seeing—perhaps for the first time—how important it is to really listen.

I recalled the times when I was so absorbed in my own hurt and anger following my divorce from my children's father, that I couldn't get past my own pain. I remember getting in my car and driving mile after mile down the freeway. No destination in mind. Just driving. Trying to put as much distance between me and the house and my feelings as I could.

My children needed my comfort, but I had little to give. And none for myself. I felt like an open sore. They needed me to listen, but I didn't have the ears to hear, so intense was the sound of my own fear and rage. They needed me to be there for them, but I couldn't even be there for myself. As much as I was separated from them I was separated from myself.

These and other incidents haunted me for years. I wondered if I could ever make up for those lost moments, and in some cases, lost years. I wondered if my children could ever forgive me. They not only lost their father when he left us, but they nearly lost me, as well. I simply could not face the future alone with three children.

"I feel better now that I've talked about it," said Margaret. Her words startled me back to the present. "But now you look sad. Did I do that?"

"I do feel sad," I replied. "But it's all right. It's part of the healing we both need. If we don't acknowledge our shortcomings, how can we make amends and start again?"

"Start again? Do you really believe there can be a second chance?" Margaret asked, focusing intently on each word. "I mean Greg's twenty-nine years old. He'll never be my little boy again."

"If I didn't believe it, I couldn't go on," I said just as intently. "I remember hearing a sermon once—at a time when I was on the brink of despair—about our God of a second chance—and a third and a fourth or more, if need be. He never turns His back on us. I have to believe that if we want another chance to rebuild our relationships, He'll make it possible. I feel it happening in my life and I know it can happen for you too."

"I don't have a clue what to do next," said Margaret, as she drained her coffee cup. "That's what I wanted to ask you about. What do you think I should do? I've said I'm sorry a million times, but we always get into it again. I mean it when I say it, but then I see him living like that and I can't keep my mouth shut." Margaret sat back for a moment, tears welling in her eyes. "If only he knew how much it hurts me to see my only child living like some derelict."

"I'm wondering if it hurts him too."

"Do you think so?" she asked. "It must. But he won't admit it. I think he'd rather die than agree with me."

"You sound as if you're to blame."

"I feel I am. What kind of a mother am I? I gave him everything I could think of—and not just material things. I spent time with him. We read together and played games and went places. I took him to church and Sunday school and summer camp—experiences that mattered. And he turns out like this. I must have done something wrong."

Margaret hit a responsive chord in me once again. I realized that I blamed myself too—for everything from poor grades in school to the kind of people my children dated to their housekeeping habits.

"But Margaret, wait a minute. If we take all the blame for what doesn't work then shouldn't we take all the credit for what does work? And if we do that, aren't we robbing them of their individuality? Our kids aren't us. We're part of each other but we're still individuals. They have interests and talents and priorities and habits that are entirely their own—some of which we'll be proud and some we aren't going to like."

Margaret suddenly looked solemn. "You're right. I realize I've been through this with my own mother," she said, rolling her eyes heavenward. "She had a fit when I married Ted. She said he'd never make a decent husband. And when it turned out to be true she blamed herself for not getting through to me. That's just one example in a long list of decisions throughout my life where I felt incapable of making a wise choice without her input."

Margaret's mother took responsibility for her victories, as well. "When I won a piano competition in high school," she added, "Mother let everyone know that my talent came directly from her."

Margaret lowered her voice. "She's been dead for five years. I'm wondering if I'm still trying to prove something to her. Seeing Greg like this makes it worse. If my mother were here she'd probably be telling me how to handle him, since she'd hold me responsible for all his decisions. Now I wonder if I'm as worried about Greg as I say I am, or if I'm more worried about what my mother would think."

Margaret slapped her right hand on the table and the spoon jumped. We both laughed. It was a moment of realization for each of us. "This is terrific," she said. "I don't know what I'm going to do with all these new insights, but I'm going to do something! All of a sudden I feel so free."

"Me too," I said. "This has been some morning." I glanced at my watch. "It's eleven. I've got to get back to my writing."

"I've got to run too. I have an appointment at 11:30." Margaret stood up, pulled on her jacket, and gave me a hug. "Thanks for listening—and sharing. I needed that. And I'm going to remember the topic of that sermon—about God giving us more chances. I want to believe that. I love Greg. I'm his mother, for heaven's sake, not his judge."

"Hey, thank you too. You gave me a lot to think about," I said and returned her hug.

GOD OF A SECOND CHANCE

As I drove home that morning, I was overcome with the idea of a second chance, and what that could mean to other parents like Margaret and me—mothers and dads who longed for the opportunity to restore a troubled or broken relationship with their adult children.

And I was filled with the reality of God's love for me and for Margaret and for all parents. A love so powerful that He sent His only Son to die for our sins. He didn't hold us to the law, He didn't judge us or manipulate us. He loved us and gave us a second chance through Jesus Christ. What an awesome gift! Surely, I thought, that same God wants to redeem our parenting.

COURAGE TO COMMIT

Talking about a second chance, however, can be quite different from living it. It doesn't take much to push our "guilt" button.

Pick up any parenting manual and the Contents alone will set it off.

the importance of healthy self-esteem
communication—the key to close relationships
strategies for effective discipline
respecting your child's privacy
teaching your children to establish boundaries

Multiply the number of new volumes by the number of years we've been parenting and the total can be overwhelming. Plenty of material to keep us in self-doubt and deadly self-critcism.

I can think of ways I've failed in every one of these areas. Probably you can too. But the moment the thoughts cross our minds, we're faced with a choice—allowing the accompanying feelings of guilt and remorse to consume us or looking to our God of a second chance.

One of the most important realizations is recognizing that we cannot do it alone. Through the years, I have been helped to see, through prayer and therapy and support groups, that I am not my emotions. I have feelings, but I am not synonymous with them. I am not my hurts. I am not my past failures. I am not my regret.

What an important distinction. When we merge with our feelings we cannot see where they end and where we begin. We show ourselves to others through the glass of fear, the window of anger, the pool of doubt. Our children cannot relate to us because we have vanished. Only our limiting beliefs and emotions are left. To be with someone under those conditions is to see through a glass darkly.

Does that mean we should ignore our character defects and chalk up every failure to being human? Or set aside our emotions to the point of not feeling anything? Of course not. We need to pay attention to our emotions, experience them, and express them. They are real. They are ours.

We must also acknowledge our shortcomings. They are real. They are ours. And like our feelings, our shortcomings are not who we are.

NO MORE IDOLS

Parents who are serious about experiencing a second chance must be willing to go all out—to bring down the idol of protocol (dinner at Mom and Dad's every Thursday night because that's the Johnson way), to call off fake conversations (where you disclose only what is safe), to give up control and meddling (in the guise of care and concern).

It also requires that we become realistic about the differences between us and our children. To start with there are at least two to three decades of differences—in age, life experience, viewpoint, interests, beliefs, life-style. There is nothing to be gained and everything to be lost by trying to get them to see things our way.

Think about Margaret and Greg for a moment.

She wanted to contribute. He saw it as control.

She wanted to help. He saw it as interference.

She wanted to share. He saw it as meddling.

She wanted to correct. He saw it as an attack.

Margaret and Greg completely missed one another. Remember Margaret's earlier statement regarding her mother's influence, "I felt incapable of making a wise choice without her input."

And during their confrontation Greg told his mother to "shut up," and stop "running my life." He said he wanted to live his own life, not the one she wanted for him.

Here are two precious people who love one another, each one trying to tell the other what he or she needs and wants, yet bound by the unfinished business of the past.

Margaret admitted that she may still be trying to prove to her mother her ability to make wise decisions—in this case that she was a good mother and raised a son successfully. And Greg, in his way, is trying to accomplish the same thing in his life—to prove to his mother that he can make wise decisions about his life-style without her help.

Neither one is having much success. Margaret is modeling her insecurity in her relationship with Greg. And Greg, picking up that insecurity, is struggling with decisions because he feels continually watched and advised. If he's not able to break this cycle now, he's likely to watch history repeat itself in the lives of his children.

Instead of talking through their fears together—sharing the deep feelings that are there, they are relating through a veil of resistance. She's resisting his unwillingness to do things her way, and he's resisting her unwillingness to let him do things his way.

None of us is exempt from this behavior. As we try to perfect our parenting (which is not even possible) by advising and suggesting and judging, our adult children, in turn, try just as hard to prove to us that they're okay and don't need our help, thank you very much! For many families these patterns stay in place for years.

Is there a way out? I believe there is. That is the focus of this book—to explore the possibilities for parents to restore their troubled relationships with their adult children.

What does it take to bring that about? First of all, it takes courage—courage to confront the problem that exists. Second, it requires a real commitment to the process. Relationships don't break down overnight and they don't become restored in a matter of hours either. And third, it takes conviction—the conviction of our belief that this is something God would have us do and that it has His blessing.

I believe that restoring relationships with your adult children includes the willingness to:

1. Recognize (and rejoice in) the differences between you and your children. My parents have been good examples of this. Recently my mother called to tell me about an award my brother had received. She was so proud to share every detail of the ceremony, his acceptance speech, and her own feeling of pride and gratitude for his talents. "I don't know how he does it," she said. "He just gets up there and the words flow." My mother admits that public speaking would be difficult for her.

Later in the week I received a copy of the evening's program and a note attached to it that said, "We continue to rejoice in the accomplishments of our children."

My parents recognize the differences between us and them, and they take delight in them. They may not feel called to speak or write or teach, as their children do, but their attitude has encouraged and blessed us.

2. Trust that they want restoration as much as you do. When things go wrong between adult children and parents, the parents often feel they are the only ones who want to make things right. My friend Jan, for example, said her daughter is so abrupt on the phone that she feels like an intruder everytime she calls. "We aren't close anymore," Jan said. "I feel as though I have to choose every word carefully before my time is up."

Later Jan disclosed that she calls her daughter early in the morning or around dinner time because she's sure to reach her then. I got to thinking about that. Perhaps Jan's daughter is not feeling distant at all. It's just that her mother calls at inconvenient times and doesn't ask first. I often call my daughter, Julie, around the same times, but we can rarely have an in-depth conversation then.

In the morning mothers are often preparing breakfast and lunches; some are rushing off to work, school, or the sitter's. And at night a similar scene takes place with dinner, baths, bedtime stories. Generally, such times are fine for a quick call to set a date or share some vital news. But if we want a longer visit, we need to plan ahead.

Rob said he and his daughter have been at odds ever since she dropped out of college. But now she's a successful hairdresser, owns her own business, and is doing well. He said he no longer feels upset about the past. He had wanted her to have the advantage of a college education but she chose, instead, to go to beauty shcool.

"It seems she's still trying to justify her choice," he shared at a support meeting for parents. "I'm fine with what she's doing, now that I see she's happy. I want to get together with her and have lunch once in awhile. We work less than two miles apart. But she makes excuses. And she seems to use every opportunity to make little digs about people with college educations."

Someone in the group asked if he had ever apologized for the pressure he put on her about going to college and if he told her how proud he is that she's doing so well in her own business.

Rob looked incredulous. "Well, no I haven't. Isn't it obvious that I'm proud of her? I tell everyone I know about her shop and how successful she is for someone 35. I've even sent her customers from my office. What more does she want?"

Other members of the group shared their viewpoints and before the end of the evening, Rob began to see that his pride and acceptance were known to others, but not necessarily to his daughter. He realized that she needed to hear it from him—in words. And probably, she'd also appreciate an apology for pressuring her about college.

It seemed apparent to everyone but Rob that his daugher wanted restoration as much as he did—but she was waiting for him to make the first move.

3. Believe that confrontation does not equal destruction.   Many parents believe that confrontation equals destruction. If they tell the truth or share their honest feelings, they're afraid the relationship will fall apart. I feared that outcome for years— until a situation arose with one of my children where I had to take a stand for myself—and in so doing the wall that separated us came tumbling down. We were no longer bound by the structure that had dictated our communication and behavior with one another for so long. We were then free to create something new.

It was a long and scary process for both of us. We handled much of our communication through letters, until the powerful feelings subsided and we could risk being together in person on a new and different ground. This was a particularly difficult time for me because I saw a need and an opportunity to be a parent—to let my child know that her lashing out had crossed my personal and parental boudaries—something I was entirely unaccustomed to doing. Most of my life has been devoted to pleasing others at my expense. I valued being nice over being real. I valued being popular over being a responsible parent.

Now I know that confrontation does not equal destruction. If anything, it can break ground and provide a foundation for a new and truly staisfying realtionship for both parent and child.

But the ultimate benefit of that process came some months later when my daughter was able to share how much she had longed for the childlike freedom as a child and teenager to complain, with abandon at times, and to know that I could take it—without monitoring the way in which she did it. I'm sure I too often turned away from her strong feelings because I was uncomfortable with them.

But in that moment I realized at a deep and profound level how important the freedom to complain would have been for her emotional development—how, in fact, that had been the very thing I had longed for when I was growing up. My parents probably had never had that freedom either.

For decades the importance of respect for elders took precedence over a child's need and right to experiment with and learn about his emotions in a safe and accepting environment.

4. *Look at your own behavior, thereby giving your children permission to look at theirs.* Many parents of adult children have spent two to three decades devoted to serving, monitoring, caring for, laughing with, and weeping over their children during a lifetime of development and growth. Those years require a deep commitment to these offspring. It is difficult, sometimes impossible, to make room for self-reflection during those intense parenting years.

Later, however, most of us pay a high price for that unbalanced way of life. Our children grow up and leave and a big piece of ourselves leaves with them. We wait for their phone calls, invitations, family gatherings, eager to be in touch with them again. Some of us feel lost, without purpose or meaning, unless we are involved in their life in some way. Others just mark time, unable to fill the emptiness.

But this time could be one of the most fruitful seasons of your life. Now you can look after yourself—spend time with yourself—reach out for those activities and experiences you've always wanted but never had time or resources for.

This can be a time for self-reflection, support groups, journal-writing, going back to school, taking piano or ballet lessons, hiking or backpacking, enrolling in a self-help class. It's a time for getting to know you—on a myriad of levels.

And it is one of the most important gifts you can give your children because as you model self-care, you give them permission to care for themselves. As you demonstrate the value of learning and changing and growing as a person, you help them see that same value for themselves.

For me this season has been the richest one yet. I am gradually eliminating behaviors that have kept me separate from other people. I have begun to value honesty over niceness, the importance of listening over giving advice, the gift of being there for another over doing something. It's been a painful journey. It's never easy or pleasant to look within, but it is deeply satisfying to come right up to those emotional barriers and get over them. Ultimately it is freedom of the best kind.

I am also overcoming physical and mental barriers to goals I've had for decades. To date, I've backpacked in the wilderness at 10,000 feet. I've written over thirty books, realizing a lifetime dream of being a published author, lectured to groups of a thousand people, knowing that public speaking is a human being's number one fear, learned to make great vegetarian meals, after having been raised on beef and potatoes, and bought and paid for a car on my own after years of leaving that task to the men in my life!

5. Face your flaws and failures with humility—and humor. Eve's kids love to tease her about her cooking. "It's been a sensitive area for years," she said. "My mother hated to cook and so do I. My son said he learned to cook in self-defense so he wouldn't starve to death. I don't think the situation was that bad, but to hear him tell it, you'd think my kids stood in soup lines. Let's just say I wasn't very imaginative."

Eve said she felt like a failure for years because she brought store-bought cookies to school bake sales. She used canned chile instead of making it from scratch. She ordered birthday cakes from the bakery while some mothers in her neighborhood created a cake that could have won first prize at a bake-off.

"Today that doesn't seem like much of a problem." said Eve, now sixty-two. "So many parents work outside the home that most probably take advantage of shortcuts. But in my day, I was an odd duck. I had the time but I just didn't like using it in that way. I still don't. I'd rather read a good book."

Eve admitted that after her children grew up and left home, she felt guilty about this area of her parenting. "Nutritious meals and mothering just seem to go together," she said. "And wouldn't you know it? One son's a chef and the other married a great cook."

Two years ago Eve took a big risk. She joined "The Over the Hill Gang," to try some new activities with people her age. First she went on a cross-country ski trip for beginners. Then she "took the biggest risk of all. I enrolled in a cooking class with a friend I met in the group. It has been such a kick," she said with a chuckle.

"I just did Thanksgiving dinner for the entire gang—my two sons, their wives, and our three grandchildren–and I must tell you, it was a smash hit. It was worth every minute of it to see the look on my sons' faces. My youngest son, Joel, the chef, told me as he was leaving that I was the greatest mom in the world. It wasn't the food that mattered, it was that I was willing to look at myself and laugh and to try something new."

Eve's story impressed me with how much we give our children when we first give to ourselves.

6. *Create a new blueprint for relating; don't simply patch up the old.* Most of us get stuck protecting, promoting, or defending our behavior instead of looking at what doesn't work, why it doesn't work, and what we can do to get it working!

Parents who take a second chance are willing to toss out the old plans and draw up new ones. And in some situations you can do this with your children.

Harold shared that he got tired of being the social director for his family. "I was always the one to arrange the dinner dates, get the theatre or football tickets, plan the family picnic on Labor Day. During the last few years I got the feeling that something wasn't working. Our get-togethers were becoming a ritual.

"My oldest son would show up late and go home early and didn't have much to say while there. My daughter told me once she didn't want to tie up so many Sunday afternoons. And my wife was sick of battling the beach crowds every Labor Day."

Harold looked up with a gleam in his eye. "I think they were trying to tell me something. But we had done things this way for so long it never occurred to me to do it any other way." As Harold notice the gradual decline in his family's interest and participation, he felt unappreciated and hurt. "But then I began to see that I was just as tired of organizing these outings as they were of attending them," he said.

Harold called a "family meeting"—"the kind we used to have on Sunday nights when the kids still lived at home." He told them what he noticed and how he felt. And in a playful tone, he asked if anyone would like to take up the role of social director, because he felt it was time for some fresh ideas.

"I can't tell you what this has done for our family," he said. "The pressure is off. No one took my place, by the way. They didn't want the job any more than I did. We decided to leave things open. If a game comes up and someone wants to go, he or she can invite the others. No expectations. We're going to treat each other like the adults we are. And we've given up the annual Labor Day picnic. My wife was right. It's a hassle at the beach. We decided to get together for a picnic or holiday meal a few times a year. We'll take turns being the host."

Harold said suddenly everyone is involved—him, his wife, his son and daughter—even the grandkids. "We have a new plan— one that's flexible and one that everyone can be part of. I wish I would have thought of it sooner."

7. Look to God—not yourself—as the source of the healing. The most comforting aspect of restoring our relationships—but one we can easily overlook if we're used to doing things for ourselves—is the fact that God is in charge. He is in the business of healing people. He wants restoration even more than we do. And He will direct our paths if we'll listen and obey.

As it says in the Book of Ecclesiastes, "To everything there is a season, A time for every purpose under heaven . . .

A time to plant, And a time to pluck what is planted . . .

A time to break down, And time to build up . . .

A time to embrace, And a time to refrain from embracing . . .

A time to keep silence, And a time to speak" (Eccl. 3:1–8).

God knows that time and purpose better than we do. And He will make them clear to us if we ask Him.

Restoring relationships with our adult children is not for the weak. It is not for people who are unwilling to look within. It is for individuals of courage, commitment, conviction—people who want no less than all that God has for them and for their children.

Chapter Two

WHY PARENTS WANT AND NEED RESTORATION WITH THEIR ADULT CHILDREN

Why do parents want to restore their relationships with their adult children? Why do so many want to try again—especially when there is a history of pain and avoidance? Most of us want to be reunited because we love our children, and it hurts—sometimes unbearably so—to be emotionally separated from them. Even those who hold grudges admit they do not want to die without being reconciled to their children.

As family therapist Rebecca Cutter phrased it, "There is nothing your children can do to keep you from loving them."[1] And I would add to that, "There is nothing you can do to keep you from loving them." Parents and children of every age are inexplicably bound to one another. I believe this close bond is part of God's plan for families. When there is a break in that tie, I believe it is His will for us to be reconciled one to another. And I believe that is why hurting parents long for restoration.

They want to forgive and to be forgiven. Katherine's eyes flooded with tears as she talked about the day she had punished her young son for soiling a white shirt. "I made him stay home from the music recital," she said just above a whisper, as her hands busily folded and unfolded the small square of paper in front of her. "That was nearly forty years ago," she added, "but I can't get it out of my mind. Louis was to be first violin that night. It was such an honor. He was only in sixth grade at the time. I'll never forget the look on his face when I told him the concert was off."

Lost in the memory of that awful day, Katherine looked away for a moment and then began to sob. "I have lived with regret over that all my life," she said.

"Have you told Louis how you feel?" I probed.

"No, I'm afraid to bring it up," she said. "I'm afraid he'll hate me all over again." Then like a frightened child she added, "But I don't want to die without his forgiveness."

They want to be free of guilt and shame. Jeanette, a forty-four year old single mother is filled with guilt and shame over an experience she had more than twenty years ago. She became pregnant in high school and gave up the baby for adoption. Later she married and gave birth to another child—her daughter, Dawn. "We grew up together," said Jeanette with a wistful note in her voice. "We've been best friends, especially since her father died when she was only seven. We tell each other everything—well, almost everything. She doesn't know about my pregnancy. How can I tell her?" she wondered aloud. "I feel ashamed for keeping this secret all these years. What will she think of me, especially since I've made such a big deal out of the sacredness of marriage and family life?" Jeanette wiped her eyes and took in a deep breath. "She has a sister and she doesn't even know it. And what if that daughter tries to find me someday? It could happen. I might even want to find her. I want so much to tell Dawn, yet I'm scared to death that things will never be the same between us again."

They want to participate in their children's lives. Bruce said he's tried everything he can think of to stay close to his son and family, "but they don't reciprocate," he said. "I've offered to help with yard work, take the kids to the park, have 'em over for a barbecue—and things like that—family things, you know." He stopped a moment and adjusted his baseball cap. "But it doesn't seem to be any use. It was better when Molly was alive. She took care of that sort of thing. I'm not too good at it, I guess," he said frowning. "I feel like I'm in the way."

As Bruce talked I was struck by his longing to be needed and wanted. I wondered if perhaps he wasn't smothering his son and wife—with gifts and ideas and even with his presence.

They want to make up for the past in whatever way possible. Hank said he was so busy building his accounting practice during the '60s that he didn't spend much time with his daughter or son. "I left that to my wife," he said with a sheepish grin. "But now I'd do anything to make it up to them. My son's on a baseball team at work and I try to go to as many games as I can. I like the guys to know he's my boy, but if I make too big a fuss he gets embarrassed. My daughter too. Matter of fact, she wrote me not too long ago telling me she'll always be my daughter but she's not my little girl anymore and she wishes I'd quit treating her as if she were. Boy that hurt, let me tell you. I thought they'd be happy I was taking an interest in their lives after I messed up years ago."

They want to feel understood and loved. "My daughter just doesn't get it," Lorraine said, as she looked around the prayer circle. "I want her to understand that I'm not on my last legs yet. If I have the money to travel, then I think I should be able to. She thinks I should save more—in case I need medical care or a nursing home in my old age. I can't think about that now."

Jane, an attractive woman in her mid-sixties, nodded in agreement. "I know what you mean," she added. "My son treats me as if I'm the child and he's the parent. Drives me crazy," she added between clenched teeth. "I don't need his advice—just a little understanding and love. He reminds me of my husband. He always looked after me as though I couldn't make it to the corner without him."

Many parents, driven by these desires, continue to suffer because they don't know how to bring about a healing. They have allowed pride, guilt, and often the pain of their own past to get in the way. Some need to back off and make a commitment to their own lives. Others need to tell their children to back off.

Still others feel it is their children's place to come to them. These parents want restoration, but it's the best kept secret on the planet! No one knows what's in their hearts and on their minds—least of all their grown children.

Hurting parents not only have wants. They also have deep needs regarding their adult children. As parents age, the blessing of family is even more important, particularly as material possessions, personal health, career, and other things of the world begin to fade.

They need to be right with their children before God. Martin, a man in his mid-fifties died of cancer last year. During his long illness prior to his death, he recommitted his life to Jesus Christ. Following that event, he told his friend Henry, "I couldn't stop thinking of my one daughter, Melanie. I kept seeing her face—as a toddler and then in school and later when she graduated. I didn't treat her right," he admitted. "She wasn't quick like her sister or like me. She didn't want to play tennis. She had trouble in school. I know I favored Maureen over Melanie. How can I ever make things right between us? And how can I face the Lord with this?"

Henry shared that one afternoon Martin asked him to stop by so he could 'confess' his wrongs. "It was a profound event," said Henry. "I've never witnessed anything like it. Later Martin met with Melanie and acknowledged all the ways he had hurt her. Melanie shared after his death that those few moments made all the difference to her. "Finally we were at peace with each other," she had said. "I knew my dad loved me, and I knew when he died that he'd be with the Lord."

They need to be set free of grudges and grievances. Some people carry their grievances to the grave. They'd rather be right than happy. They'd rather hold onto their pride than hold onto their children. Darrell's son and daughter-in-law no longer attend the Lutheran church—the denomination that his family had been faithful to for generations. For a variety of reasons, Darrell's son and his wife chose a different path. "We still love the Lord," his son told him in the midst of a huge argument about church attendance. "But we feel led to move in a new direction."

For years Darrell held a grudge against his son. But during a recent illness, his son came to the hospital to pray for him; Darrell was so moved, he asked for and received his son's forgiveness.

They need to be liked and supported. According to Rachel, her only daughter, who is single and middle-aged, is distant and reserved. "She's not a spontaneous person," said Rachel. "She's always been structured. She needs to plan ahead. It would be out of the question for me to pick up the phone and suggest a spur-of-the-moment outing. When we're together I feel stifled. I can't be myself. She thinks I'm entirely too impractical for a person my age and she seems annoyed by everything I say. I guess I want her to like me!"

They need to express their love and support. Hector and Anna reared a family of eight children in a Hispanic section of Los Angeles during the '40s and '50s. Today, the couple, both in their late seventies, admit they were too strict. "We didn't say 'I love you' enough," said Anna. "Now when I see all the little ones—grandchildren and the great-grandchildren running around, I just pick them up and put kisses all over their faces. 'I love you, I love you,' I tell them over and over. But I didn't do that with our kids," she said looking at her husband pensively.

"You were a good mama," Hector reassured her as he patted her wrinkled brown hand. "It was me with the problem. I drove a taxi everywhere—anywhere I could make some money. So many kids to take care of," he said. "No time for fun with them. Most of the time they were asleep when I came home."

"But now we're old," said Anna, taking up the conversation again. "I need to say the words, 'I love you' before it's too late. And they need to hear me say it."

They need to live in the freedom that healing brings. The McMasters have seen a miraculous change in the lives of close friends who went to their estranged son and invited him back into the family fold. "He was like the Prodigal in the Bible," said Bert. "Everyone who knew him could see that he wanted to come home. He had lived on the streets, abused drugs, drank too much. You name it, he did it. He'd call friends of the family from time to time, you know, just to check up and see how his folks were doing."

"We wished he'd call and talk to them," said Irene. "We even told him what a difference it would make, but he just couldn't do it. Then one Saturday he stopped by our place, and I took a risk and called his parents. They came right over. Makes me cry just thinking about it. It was as if each one was waiting for the other one. His mother, Loretta, came through the door and if she could have picked him up she would have. His dad stood back for a minute and then he broke down and threw his arms around his son. And I knew right then they'd be a family again."

GAMES PARENTS PLAY

Hurting parents also want and need a healing of their relationships so they can rid themselves of the deadly mind games, "If Only" and "Not Enough," that perpetuate the estrangement.

By continually demeaning themselves and expecting more than humanly possible, such parents keep the focus on themselves and off the relationship. And no one gets nurtured in such a state. Mothers and fathers talk about their guilt and shame but don't deal with it, and their sons and daughters, weary of the self-deprecating monologues, distance themselves. Everyone loses.

Perhaps you've indulged in a round or two yourself. Does any of the following self-talk sound familiar? I wasn't . . .

- committed enough
- loving enough
- encouraging enough
- helpful enough
- attentive enough
- firm enough
- permissive enough
- understanding enough
- spiritual enough
- consistent enough

Enough is enough of that self-defeating game. Who among us has ever had enough, or been able to give enough of anything?

Who wouldn't benefit from more love, praise, help, consideration, encouragement? What parent, in retrospect, wouldn't long to have been more loving, more appreciative, more fun, more selfless, more caring, more understanding, more accepting?

Just as deadly, is the game called "If Only." One white-haired great grandmother I know has dedicated her life to this pastime. Dialogue for this game goes something like this.

> If only I had been more fun.
> If only I had been more creative.
> If only I had been less of a disciplinarian.
> If only I had been more available.
> If only I had been more wise.
> If only I had been more affectionate.
> If only I had been less involved with myself.
> If only I had been more spiritual.

Enough is enough of that game too. Obsessive thoughts of this kind do nothing toward restoring our relationships with our adult children. In fact, they do just the opposite. The more we focus on what we didn't do, the more self-pitying we become, turning inward to a point where we have no creative energy to put toward the healing process and toward an understanding and resolution of the real emotion. But you can be set free of these guilt-producing mind games, as you will discover in later chapters.

Many of us create and nurture our own pain by remaining unwilling to release our children to their lives, their choices, their decisions, and their consequences. And we project our hostile feelings of:

Guilt Roger, for example, spent years berating himself for not having encouraged his daughter's musical ability. She quit piano lessons in high school after her teacher approached her sexually. She told Roger what happened, but instead of protecting his daughter by confronting the teacher, he dismissed the incident by telling her he was right after all—there was no future for her in music.

Years later he continued to carry feelings of guilt—misdirected as they were—over having discouraged his daughter's desire for a career in music. His real guilt, however, uncovered in counseling, was over not protecting her, and as a result, encouraging her to abandon the one thing she really wanted to do. Since that discovery he has gone to his daughter and shared his remorse and asked for forgiveness.

Jealousy   Angela said she noticed she was jealous of her sixteen-year-old daughter's looks. "She has the olive complexion I've always wanted," said Angela as she stared at a recent family photo. "I feel self-conscious when I'm with her. She gets a great tan in the summer. She doesn't have to worry about freckles. And she has the wavy hair in the family. She seems to have gotten the best of both sides. I wasn't so lucky."

As we talked further, it seemed Angela's jealousy had deep roots. She remembered feeling jealous of her sister when they were in high school. "She too had the looks I would have killed for," said Angela half-laughing. "My gosh, I'm doing the same thing all over again," she suddenly admitted. "My poor daughter. I feel terrible. I'm her mother, not her peer. I feel as though I owe her an apology. I should be affirming her looks not being jealous of them."

Disappointment   "Ron doesn't even try to do things my way," said Jim, an exasperated fifty-five-year-old executive, speaking about his thirty-year-old son. "If I ran my business the way he runs his life, I'd be bankrupt in a minute. I don't get it," he added. "You'd think he'd want to make something of himself. I've all but given him the firm. He knows it's his—for the asking. I want to retire early, and I'd like nothing better than to see him at my desk. But he won't settle down, finish school, and make a commitment."

I remember thinking at the time how unlike his own father Jim was. His dad had been a policeman in a large inner city precinct—the last place Jim ever wanted to work. In fact, he had told my husband and me with pride that he felt great having broken the family pattern. I couldn't help but wonder if his father was disappointed in him for not donning his policeman's hat.

Embarrassment   Les is a quiet man, proper in dress and manners, reserved and somewhat critical by nature. He admits that he is easily embarrassed—especially by his adult daughter who is loud, confrontational, and "very opinionated," according to Les. "She's just like my mother," he said with disdain. "She thinks nothing of jumping into a conversation and airing her views even if no one asks. I can't believe a daughter of mine could turn out so completely opposite of what I hoped for."

Les shared a bit about his early home life. His mother was forever marching in demonstrations, signing petitions, phoning or writing her opinions to the legislators. "She was no lady," said Les, as a small smile curled his thin lips.

"She sounds like a fascinating person to know," I said.

"Fascinating. Now that's a good word for my mother," he replied. "She was certainly that—but at the time I would have said embarrassing. Other kids had regular moms who stayed home, made cakes for the bake sale, or taught Sunday School. My mom didn't do any of those things. She said life was too short to spend over a stove. She'd rather buy cookies and use her valuable time to make a difference in the state of the world."

Les seemed unaware of how much of his unfinished business with his mother was being reflected in his relationship with his daughter.

Competition   Carolyn's youthful appearance belies her age. At 45 she looks ten years younger. She and her twenty-five-year-old daughter Sue are often mistaken for sisters. Carolyn admits to feeling competitive with her daughter. Both have done some modeling and are conscious of their figures and appearance. As Sue struggled to lose some weight before an important fashion show, Carolyn went on a crash diet for two weeks and dropped five pounds—"weight I didn't need to lose," she said. "It's almost as though I'm trying to outdo my daughter—show her what I can do at forty-five that she can't do at twenty-five. I think it's kind of sick. I realized the other day that my mother competed with me a lot when I was a kid. We both took ballet lessons. She bought clothes like mine and worked hard on looking good. She loved it when people thought we were sisters. Now the same thing is happening to Sue and me and it's creating a lot of stress in our relationship."

Anger   Walt is angry with his married daughter. "She won't listen to reason," he shared with a deep sigh. "I advanced her a down payment on a condo and bought her a car after college—to help her get started—but she's the most ungrateful person I've ever known. She's been in two car wrecks. She's behind in her mortgage payments, and she's totally irresponsible with money. She seems to think I'll take care of her if anything goes wrong. I'm really upset about this, but I don't know what to do. Our relationship is all about money—her expecting and me resisting and then giving in. I hate it. I raised her better than that."

IT'S NOT ALL BLACK OR WHITE

Some parents, like Walt and Ron, see everything their children do as a direct reflection on the way they reared them. They take the blame for what doesn't work or they blame the children for not holding up the family name or tradition. And they also take the credit for what they like and approve of. But relationships aren't that simple. Children are God's gift to us. They are on loan. At best, parents are stewards—for a time.

We aren't responsible for every past or present choice. And we aren't responsible for every victory and defeat. Our children reflect us—in appearance, perhaps, in mannerisms, in talents and preferences. But they aren't us. They are individuals, as we are, and they have thoughts and feelings and ideas and dreams that are unique to them.

From the many people I've spoken with and from my own experience as a parent and step-parent I see the truth of this over and over. My kids are not just like me, and I am not just like my parents.

As we recognize the truth of this, however, it's also important to look at the reality of our heritage. The sins and flaws of the father (and mother) are passed from generation to generation until someone is willing to turn and face them, expose them, and root them out. Many parents have unworkable, unsatisfactory, and even destructive relationships with their adult children because they are living out the failures of their past, and their parents' treatment of them. What has been heaped on them they are now heaping on their children, often without realizing it.

EXPOSING THE ROOTS

As Carolyn, Ron and Angela discovered as they talked, much of the trouble in their troubled relationships could be traced to their own childhoods and the way they related to their families. Carolyn remembered her mother competing with her. Ron recalled his dad demeaning his choices, and Angela relived her memories of being jealous of her sister.

I believe insights about our early years are important for all parents. For it is here that the foundation of our lives was laid. It is here that we first saw an image of ourselves—through the reflecting pool of our parents' eyes, the tone in their voices, the attitude of their hearts, the selection of their words. If they were angry or frustrated or abusive, what were we to think of ourselves? Not much.

On the other hand if they smiled when we made baby sounds, changed our diapers and fed us when we cried, and cuddled us when we were frightened, we were likely to feel valued, worthy, and loved. And if we were treated well on a fairly consistent basis over the years, then we had a good chance of growing up with a healthy self-image—a realistic picture of our strengths and weaknesses.

For parents to be a healthy mirror for their children, however, they needed to feel healthy about themselves. And many did not—and still don't. The mirror held up to them as children was likely cracked and in some cases, shattered. Hence, your parents passed on to their children, and you in turn, to your children, the same distorted image.

There are no perfect parents. If there were, we wouldn't need God. So we don't look at the past to escape personal responsibility or to place blame on former generations. But rather we look at it in order to illuminate and understand our own present behavior so we can eliminate or change what doesn't work.

SELF-IMAGE AND BROKEN RELATIONSHIPS

In his sensitive and insightful book, *Healing For Damaged Emotions*, author David Seamands names low self-esteem as the most powerful psychological weapon used against God's people.[2] Feelings of inferiority, inadequacy and self-doubt plague us all, though individuals have different ways of expressing them. Some wear the mask of self-pity. Others parade in a gown of grandiosity. Still others hide in the cloak of denial.

But however it is manifested, low self-esteem or more accurately, a distorted self-image, damages, even ruins, relationships. When you don't think much of yourself, you're not likely to think much of other people either. Pretty soon you see them through the same critical eye you see yourself.

When you foster negative thoughts, negative feelings follow, and when you feel inadequate and unable, your self-talk reflects this state of mind and heart.

"I can't do anything right."

"What's the matter with me anyhow?"

"I'm nothing to them. They just walk all over me."

"What's the use? I can't please them no matter how hard I try."

Think about the people in your life who practice this dialogue. Do you enjoy their company? Do they inspire and encourage you, or do you feel depressed and discouraged in their presence?

People who feel badly about themselves drain everyone around them as they try desperately to get from others what no human being can give them and what they cannot give to themselves. They even close off the gifts God has for them because they cannot imagine being worthy of such love and goodness.

Such persons are often spiritually stifled, unable and often unwilling to allow the Lord to lead them out of the wilderness of self-doubt and self-deprecation. They pray for a miracle of healing, but they don't cooperate with the healer!

From there it is only a short fall to the depths of spiritual depression where a person not only doubts God's love for him but also begins to doubt God's presence.

But God doesn't make junk! And He doesn't make cracked pots. "Yes, I have loved you with an everlasting love" (Jer. 31:3).

FROM INSIGHT TO COMPASSION

Rebecca Cutter does a lot of work with parents and adult children in her marriage and family practice in San Diego. "The children usually come into therapy first," she said. "Then they bring their parents."

As the children raise their unresolved issues from the past, Cutter offers both the parents and the adult child the opportunity, within the safety of the setting, to express his or her viewpoint and feelings. That process alone can contribute to a major healing of one's self-esteem. Each person gets to share out loud, without criticism or comment, his or her memories, and the deep feelings that accompany them.

"How do you know who to believe?" I asked.

"I believe both sides," said Cutter. "Both viewpoints are valid. Each one is telling the truth as he or she sees it, and I think it's important that those perceptions and feelings get expressed and are acknowledged by the other person."

Cutter emphasized the value and importance of both parties really listening. "I believe parents when they tell me they did what they thought was right. I believe that they did everything they thought they could do. And then we talk about the difference between what they actually did and what their children suggest they could have done.

"And finally, we talk about how the parents grew up, the messages and modeling they received from their parents, because you can only pass on what you know. If they didn't get the nurturing they deserved, they couldn't have passed it on to their children."

Cutter shared an example from her practice. One client, a physician, was raised in an extremely rigid environment with very little opportunity to express himself. "From his point of view, life was comprised of working, eating, and sleeping, and not much else," said Cutter. "When he talked about this with his parents they saw their parenting as very loving. They claimed they had made sure he was safe within the confines of the rules they were comfortable with. In no way did they see any of it as negative. But their son now feels that this rigidity is the reason he can't express himself and have fun."

To help him bridge the generational gap Cutter suggested that he ask his father to tell him three stories from his (the father's) boyhood. All of the stories, as could be expected, had to do with being good and working hard. It was easy to see how the father had simply passed on to his son the values he had been raised with.

"Before an adult child blames or criticizes the parents," said Cutter, "it's really important to get those stories from previous generations." Such stories provide insight which can lead to understanding and then to compassion—for one's parents and one's self.

But what if a child was raised in an alcoholic home? I wondered. Or was sexually, verbally, or physically abused? Perhaps that child also learns that the offending parent was similarly abused when he or she was young. What then? My questions mounted. Some forms of abuse are so extreme that they're almost impossible to get over. How does one, for example, forgive or express compassion for a molester? I shared my concerns with Cutter.

For a moment, she looked away in thought, then continued. "I differ a little bit from some counselors," she said, "in that I don't think forgiveness is required." It may be the goal. "But for some people to forgive a particular act, would require that they give up too much of themselves."

Of course this could work both ways. The parent of the adult child may also have deep grievances that include behavior that is such an outrage that forgiving and healing seem impossible. Perhaps one of your children has embezzled funds from your family business in order to support a cocaine habit. Or maybe your daughter has been an irresponsible parent and you have now assumed the task of raising her children. Or perhaps a child of yours has even made an attempt on your life or at least threatened you with physical violence. These are enormously difficult things to deal with. Forgiveness may seem impossible. Perhaps you agree with Rebecca Cutter—that some actions simply do not require forgiveness because the personal cost is too great.

For a Christian, however, I believe forgiveness should always be the goal. But I also know from my own experience, that we cannot force the process. It's extremely important to allow ourselves the freedom—with God's leading and protection—to express our outrage and deep pain in a setting that is safe, where we can be heard, understood, and loved through it. But ultimately, I believe that forgiveness is an act of the will, not a by-product of our emotions, though we may experience forgiveness, after we've been able to give full vent to our feelings in a safe place. To forgive another is really an act of kindness toward ourselves. In forgiving another, we actually release ourselves from the burden of bitterness. I will talk more about this important aspect of healing relationships in a later chapter.

PAST ABUSES

If you have been an abusive parent in some extreme way, you may be overwhelmed with guilt. Or if you are a parent who has suffered extreme abuse at the hands of one of your children, you may be consumed with rage. Or you may be a parent whose spouse abused one or more than one of your children during their youth, and you have just recently found out about it.

Memories of incidents from your past or information about the culture at the time you were growing up, or during the years you were parenting your children, are vitally important to your eventual healing. If you were abused as a child, for example, you can gain insight into how and why you abused your children and you can get the help you deserve. Or if your spouse hurt your children, that information as well, can be the turning point in your growth process and the eventual restoring of your relationships with your adult children.

One fifty-eight-year-old woman, a client of Rebecca Cutter, recently found out that all four of her children were sexually abused throughout her marriage. The adult children are now blaming her, wanting to know why she didn't protect them from their father.

"When I met with her," said Cutter, "I asked her to take me back to 1953 and to talk about what it was like to be taking care of four children under eight years of age and living on the margin of poverty. How much was on television about incest? Were there any books or magazine articles on this topic in those days? No. There was no information then, at least not available to the general population."

Does this excuse the mother or invalidate the tremendous damage the father inflicted on his children? No, but understanding the circumstances she faced and the lack of information available, she can at least begin to feel some compassion for herself. She simply did not know.

She wasn't looking for incest. She didn't know about it. And as a result she couldn't have detected it or seen it. At the time, her children didn't tell her, probably out of fear, and certainly their father wasn't going to admit it to her.

Some parents, however, are aware of incest or other abuse to their children and they don't do anything about it because of their own fear and low self-esteem. They too, of course, need help in understanding their behavior and in time, how to forgive themselves and seek forgiveness from their children.

Yet families deserve, even need, to talk about such things whenever they arise, even if they do not surface until later in life. Sometimes this occurs when adult children are looking for family patterns or reasons for certain troubling behavior or feelings of their own. Being willing to hear each other out creates the space for understanding, for compassion, and for forgiveness. In situations where the event was so intense, and emotions run high, the wisest course of action may be to see a professional counselor together, or alone and then together.

Cutter feels that when a parent can show some compassion for herself—in this case, the mother simply didn't know—she is in a better position to have compassion for her children. She can then begin to understand how they must have suffered, and to express her regret, her sorrow, and her comfort. She might even tell them now, as adults, how sorry she is that she didn't know about the abuse at the time, and that if she had known, she is certain she would have protected them.

It's amazing how much lasting healing can occur when people share their deep regrets and tell one another how they would like to have behaved. Just expressing the desire for change helps parents relieve themselves of the guilt they feel when their children come to them with grievances.

"You can't judge your past with present information," said Cutter. "You simply didn't know. Unless of course you really did know something was wrong and you went ahead anyway."

Equally important to being there for yourself is being willing to listen to your children—how it felt for them to be the victim of the things you didn't know.

Another of Cutter's clients had parents who were both physicians. "All of her economic needs were met, but emotionally she felt neglected. Neither her mother nor father was available," said Cutter. "Today she notices that she cannot have intimate relationships with anyone because as a child there was no emotional tending—no one-on-one. She was raised in an emotional desert by a live-in maid."

When the three meet in counseling, Cutter said the only thing the parents hear is, "You weren't there for me." Yet, they're likely to be thinking, but you went to the best schools and you had the best food and the best clothing.

"It was very important to this woman," said Cutter, "for them to hear about her childhood from her perspective. And it was important for me to help them see that she's speaking heart language. She's really saying, 'I didn't feel valued for who I am. I felt taken care of, but not valued. I don't think you saw me or heard me.'

"Unfortunately, as an adult she now goes to extremes to get people to see and hear her and it doesn't work. It gets in her way."

THE SANDWICH GENERATION

Today's parents of adult children are, as Cutter put it, something like middle management. "You can't get it right from above, and you can't get it right from below either."

When I began looking at my life, I found some of this to be true. I ran as fast I could, and learned all I could, in order to stay a step or two ahead of my children so I'd be prepared when they assaulted me with their memories. I smile at the thought now because there's something poignant and funny about it, but at the time it was anything but humorous. I was in deep pain. I wanted so much to understand them, to hear their feelings, and to make amends, but at the same time, I was trying to understand my own process—the way I was raised and the unaddressed issues I had with my parents. I really did feel like the filling in a sandwich—pressed in from both sides.

Cutter said she works "with a lot of ignorance" when she is counseling parents of adult children. And there is no judgment in her voice when she says it. It is simply a fact. Today we live in a recovery-oriented and information-glutted society. Thirty, forty, fifty years ago these resources didn't exist.

"When any of us talks with our parents," she said, "we are two generations away from them and then two more generations away from our own children. Each of us is having to switch back and forth, and it's not easy."

Cutter is not above the same problems in her own life. Today, at age 49 she has two grown daughters. During her mid-thirties she returned to school for a graduate degree in counseling. "I was a single parent during that time," she said. "I was on welfare for a time. Other times I worked two jobs and went to school at night. I remember taking one of my daughters from one daycare to another because I was gone so long."

"Did you feel guilty?" I asked.

"Not until much later. In fact, it hit me again the other day," she said reflectively, "as I packed up one of my daughter's childhood things. She got married a couple of months ago. I found a little branch or stick that she had painted on at camp one year. It said, 'Remember me?' Imagine," Cutter said, incredulously. "How could I forget my own child? But then I realized that there were times when she literally wondered if I'd forget to come home at night. At that time I was trying to survive—trying to help all of us survive. But now when I look back I have to say she was a latchkey kid. She missed a lot—even though today she's a neat young woman. She really knows how to take care of herself."

Then returning to her early parenting years, Cutter shared an example of what she would now call 'borderline negligence.' "When Anna was about five I remember coming home exhausted one night, as most single parents do, too tired to cook, too tired to do anything. I walked into the house and saw that she was hungry. So I asked with a big smile, 'What do you want for dinner? Would you like cold spaghetti, and I stressed the word cold or would you like hot spaghetti, I asked, frowning deeply and emphasizing the word hot.

"Of course she chose cold spaghetti. I was manipulating her. I was negligent. I realized my mother never would have served me a cold meal. I have guilt about that incident—even though my daughter and I can laugh about it now—but I also have to have some compassion for myself, especially when I look at what else was going on in my life at that time. I was a single parent with two young children, working as a maid, and going to school at night."

What happens if Anna someday confronts her mother with that incident and admits that she felt manipulated? Is it enough for Cutter to plead her case—single parenting, working as a maid, going to school at night—and stop there? She could do that and her daughter might even accept it, but a parent who truly wishes to restore those broken parts must also be willing to really hear the child's heart. And Cutter would be quick to admit that.

She may have had her reasons for doing what she did, and they may even be valid, given the situation and the circumstances, but nevertheless, her daughter, like all children, deserves to be listened to. Healing takes place when both parties can emerge from a discussion feeling heard, understood, and loved. That doesn't mean they have to agree. It doesn't mean they have to give up their point of view. It means, simply, that they heard and acknowledged one another.

Perhaps that recognition and acceptance is the most important realization we can have as we restore our relationships with our adult children and accept the healing God has for us.

But before we look at restoration, I'd like you to meet some of the courageous parents who have agreed to share their experience—parents who are working to overcome behavior and beliefs that block communication, block confrontation, block friendship, block intimacy, block spontaneity, and block spirituality— parents who are in pain, but also in the process of hope and healing.

PART TWO

*Parents
in Pain—
Parents
in Process*

Chapter Three

THE
PLEASER

66 **K**aren, guess what?" Rita shouted as she ran across
the parking lot and up the steps to the early morning
aerobics class we both attended. "Connie had a baby
girl this morning," she said, as we walked inside. "Hal just
called. He was ecstatic. Everything's fine. I'm so relieved." Rita
gulped a mouthful of water from the cooler and slung a towel
over her shoulder. "I can hardly wait to see them. I'm flying up
to San Francisco this afternoon."

"Hey, that's terrific," I said with pleasure. "Welcome to the
grandmother's club. It's the best," I added with the assurance
of a veteran.

Rita and I weren't close friends—mostly exercise buddies. I
saw her briefly a few times a week during aerobics. But we hit it
off, perhaps in part, because we were in the same season of life.
We shared details about our families and careers, compared
notes as we planned our daughter's weddings, and she had been
a patient listener as I talked about my grandchildren. Now she'd
have a chance to get even with me.

"SO HARD IT HURTS"

As I reflect on our relationship now, however, I suspect
that I had more in common with Rita than at one time I realized
or would even admit. Rita was a parent I've come to recognize
as a pleaser—someone who dedicates herself to pleasing others

in order to satisfy her own need to be liked and needed.

I know it can be dangerous to label people. None of us is a one-dimensional being. But for purposes of this section of the book, I'm going to zero in on six of the most common categories of behavior I've observed in myself and in other parents of adult children. Parents who are in pain—and in process—in their relationships.

Rita herself admitted that she loved her kids "so hard, it hurts." She wanted so much for things to be good between them that she often overlooked her own well-being in order to keep the peace that she perceived they shared. In fact, she took pride in the way she handled both her son and daughter. It was evident as she told me her plans for her visit to her daughter's house. "I'm taking two weeks off work," she said proudly. I was surprised. I knew she worked as a freelance bookkeeper and two weeks without pay would surely make an impact on her income.

"They need me," she said. "If I don't stay, Hal would have to take off work, and they can't afford that." Then, as if reading my thoughts, she added, "I can always get a couple of extra jobs next month. Besides I don't need the money as much as they do."

It sounded logical on the surface, but I noticed an intensity in her voice that was almost alarming. I could hear the struggle for perfectionism and the strong desire to please them, no matter what the cost to her. This decision, like previous ones she had shared, was made with little or no regard for herself.

She had bought her son a new car at a time when her own car was more than ten years old. She had won a free ticket to Hawaii and instead of enjoying the trip herself, she gave it to her daughter for a birthday present, "because she's always wanted to go to Hawaii," Rita had explained. I remembered her telling me at the time, "This probably sounds nuts, but I get a bigger kick out of doing little things for my kids than I do for myself."

Little things—wow! A car and a trip to Hawaii. Yet I could relate to her more than I wanted to. I had loaned my son money for a used car during a year when my own savings account was pretty slim and then let him out of the loan a year later. And I had noticed that shopping for clothes with my daughters or for my grandchildren was more fun than buying things for myself.

"NO PROBLEM. I'M EASY!"

In recent years, during the course of my recovery, I've taken a closer look at my motives. Did I have a hidden agenda? Was I a pleaser? Or did I simply offer honest help within the boundaries of wisdom and prudence? I'm not sure. My hunch is that pleasing my children had a lot to do with my choices then.

Today, however, though I may still buy them some clothing or treat them to a meal, I'm not driven by it. I am now conscious of my motives. I make sure it's something I want to do. I make sure I have a spending plan in mind. And I check my comfort level. My goal is to share or give because I truly want to, not because I have to in order to feel good about myself or to be popular with them. But that's been a long time coming.

A pleaser, unlike the critic, looks good on the surface. The pleaser's motto is, "No problem. I'm easy." The other person always comes first. Pleasers would rather melt into the ground than make a fuss or draw attention to themselves in an unpleasant way. I once took great pride in letting my children or husband choose the restaurant, the movie, the outing. I had my preferences but I rarely voiced them convincingly because I derived my happiness from their happiness and I was proud of the fact that I could blend in easily.

One day, however, I discovered how unsettling this behavior can be to others. While shopping with my youngest daughter I noticed that she stopped several times to ask how we were doing financially. "Is this okay?" she asked hesitantly. "I'd like the shoes but are they too much? Have we reached your limit yet?"

I realized that her questions not only showed genuine concern and care for me, which I appreciated, but they also may have resulted from my not being specific about the amount of time and money I had to share. She couldn't fully enjoy the outing if she were unsure of the boundaries. And if I was more concerned about pleasing her than being realistic, then I harmed us both.

Today, I decide on a limit ahead of time and let her know it so she can have it in mind as we shop. We're then free to enjoy our time together, with less of the focus on shopping, and more on just being together. And I have found it freeing. It's pleasing—in a healthy way. But I can't tell you how difficult it was to arrive at that place. I've been a pleaser for as long as I can remember. Perhaps you too, can relate to this behavior or to some of the traits listed below.

COMMON CHARACTERISTICS OF A PLEASER

1. Pleasers generally create child-centered families as their children are growing up. Unless they recognize and change their behavior they continue the practice even with their adult children. Years ago, for example, Peggy gave a key to her house at the beach to each of her four grown sons. "I told them they're welcome anytime," she said. "And they took me up on it," she added half-laughing.

They drop by whenever they want to, often without letting her know ahead of time, and sometimes bring a friend or two along. Peggy is shy by nature and admits she's always been a pleaser. But now she's fed up with her lack of privacy and doesn't know how to change the situation without alienating her sons.

"They love the beach, and it's like coming home to them," she said in their defense. "But I'm not the young mom they once had. I can't afford all the food it takes to feed them, and I don't have the energy to cook for such a crowd."

I could hardly believe her story. I found myself getting angry for her. "How old are these kids of yours?" I asked in mock sarcasm. "They sound like a bunch of overgrown teenagers."

"That's it," she said, her pale blue eyes brightening at the thought. "They do act like teenagers around me. We always had a houseful when they were growing up. Four sons and usually a couple of strays, as well," she said referring to the extra boy or two who rounded out their dinner table each night.

Peggy is 65 now and her sons, ranging from 32 to 40, are still the center of her life. And the two who are married have children of their own who are now learning by example, that Grandma is always available for anything and everything.

**2. Pleasers would rather be popular than respon-
sible.** I've met parents who've gone into debt in order to help
their children maintain the indulgent life-style they were accustomed to as youngsters.

One retired fireman and his wife, a former secretary, spent
more than half their combined pensions financing everything
from ballet lessons to summer camp for their grandchildren so
their daughter won't have to work full-time.

Fred and Paula are very popular with their granddaughters,
to be sure, but their daughter resents their gifts because she
feels robbed of the opportunity to parent her own children and
to make her own decisions. At the same time she has become
dependent on them financially which creates even more
resentment.

3. Pleasers need the approval of their adult children.
Marion can't make a move without calling her son and daughter-
in-law for advice. They know everything about her—the state of
her finances, the condition of her lawn, the results of her latest
blood test. She says she's terrified of making a mistake or
creating a problem for them.

When I spoke with Marion I was struck by her high-pitched,
childlike voice, although she is a woman of over sixty years of
age. She smiled and giggled often as she shared one story after
another of how "silly" and "stupid" and "crazy" she is when it
comes to making important decisions.

Her father had taken care of her totally after her mother died
when she was a toddler. Later, she went right into a marriage to
a naval career officer who also managed every aspect of her life.
When he died, Marion turned to her only son for the guidance
she suddenly lacked.

"I have no one else," she confided. "And besides, he seems
to like taking care of me."

**4. Pleasers crave attention, though they hide from
it.** Robert has been a caretaker all his life. It started when, as
a child, he began covering up for his alcoholic mother. It continues today, as he manages every detail of his home and yard,

even though he is married to a perfectly healthy woman. Robert shops for food and gifts, cooks, gardens, plans parties and pays the bills. There isn't anything this man can't do. It's incredible to watch him. He has his hand on everything. And everything is in perfect order.

At the same time he has high blood pressure, nagging headaches and an inability to sit still and read a book, watch a movie, or attend a church service without fidgeting, making notes, or whispering to his wife about some future project in the works.

The one thing Robert doesn't have is the gratitude and affection of his adult children. "They act as if I don't exist," he said with disappointment in his voice. "I could use a hand painting the patio cover," he added, pointing to the wooden structure through the family room door. "But do you think my son would offer to give up one of his precious weekends? Not on your life. His golf game comes first. Always has."

"Maybe he doesn't know you need his help," I ventured cautiously. "Did you ask him?"

"No!" he shot back. "He's got two eyes. If he can't see it for himself, no use in my telling him. It really hurts to have a grown son who'd rather play golf than help his father."

His logic eluded me. Robert was clearly dying for his son to notice him, to thank him for all he did, to pay attention to him, to offer his help. But my hunch is that this desire is one of the best-kept family secrets.

I met his son Matt a few weeks after talking with Robert. He was a pleasant, easy-going fellow who spoke fondly of his dad and all that his father had done to make their home a special place when he was growing up. It was clear that he had no idea of the intensity of his father's resentful feelings.

5. Pleasers believe, at some fundamental level, that unless they control themselves and others through pleasing, they will die. This sounds like a pretty dramatic statement but according to Rebecca Cutter, control is the bottom line issue for parents whose attention is more child-centered than self-centered. They are terrified of losing their relationship with their children—dishonest, hurtful, or childlike as it may be.

The cost to themselves is of no consequence. Their behavior is rooted in survival.

HOW PLEASING AFFECTS YOUR RELATIONSHIP WITH YOUR ADULT CHILDREN

Pleasing may appear to be the least offensive form of parental behavior. The pleaser, compared to the critic, for example, is a hands-down winner. The pleaser is "nice," generally reserved, polite, caring and helpful. Pleasers not only want to please but also to be pleasing. They want their children to like them, to accept them, to be proud of them, to enjoy them. Preserving the status quo is of utmost importance to the pleaser. However, that result often comes at great cost to the relationship.

Pleasing Blocks Communication. Joe discovered that his new daughter-in-law loved fresh flowers—especially tulips. A few weeks later, he brought her a pot of freshly-planted yellow and purple tulips for her birthday. She was thrilled. Her husband Paul, Joe's son, was not! He had planned a similar surprise for his wife, but his dad beat him to it. Paul approached his father later, wanting to share his strong feelings of anger and jealousy. "I wanted him to know that he had overstepped his boundaries," Paul told me. "She's my wife, and I think I should be the one to give her flowers. He could at least have checked with me first."

But when Paul spoke with his dad, Joe was incredulous. "Hey, relax. I was just being nice, thinking of what would make her happy. Come on. Let's have some iced tea and a round of Ping-Pong."

Joe's determination to do what he perceived as pleasing blocked his son's need for important communication. And he blocked himself from receiving an important truth.

Pleasing Blocks Confrontation. Pleasers, more than anyone, avoid confrontation with their children. Generally, fear is at the base of it. Fear of change. Fear of rejection. Fear of being misunderstood. Fear of losing the relationship. So when a son or daughter approaches them with a controversial issue having to do with parenting, financial help, discipline, or religious differences, pleasers will usually duck behind the nearest bush. Or they'll try to please their way out of it by telling a joke, sharing a new recipe, suggesting a walk, or a game of cards.

The adult child on the receiving end is left frustrated, angry, and bound up with no outlet. On the rare occasion when the pleaser does listen, he or she usually does not comment, leaving the adult child feeling abandoned and unacknowledged.

Pleasing Blocks Friendship.   One of the real joys of being the parents of adult children is the opportunity it offers for genuine friendship. Most mothers and fathers agree that hanging out with and talking with their children, without the burden of disciplining or overseeing them, is one of the great rewards awaiting us all.

Midge agrees. "Today I can say that my son and I are good friends," she said. "But that has not always been the case. My pleasing has gotten in the way on more than one occasion. I remember one incident in particular when he pointed out a jacket in a store window and said he really liked it. A friend might have acknowledged the remark and perhaps added that it would look good on him and he hoped he'd be able to buy it. End of subject. But not me. I had to make his desire my project. This would really please him, I thought. So before we got to the end of the block, I faked some excuse about having to make a phone call and instead dashed back to the store, bought the jacket, and arranged to have it mailed to his apartment as a surprise."

Midge says she now sees how destructive such a response can be. "I'm not even sure he really wanted it. It might have been a random remark, the kind of thing we say when we're window shopping. What I'm concerned about now is the fact that my pleasing took complete charge over my reasoning. I was not a good friend to him. I was a compulsive pleaser."

Pleasing Blocks Intimacy.   This may sound like a dichotomy. How can being nice, being pleasant, and wanting to help, block intimacy? Wouldn't such a person also welcome a deep, close, and personal relationship with loved ones? He or she probably would. But in practice, intimacy and pleasing are mutually exclusive. To be intimate with someone assumes the ability and the freedom to be one's self—to be pretty much who we are—in a relationship rather than who someone else would like us to be. It also means we allow others to do the same.

But pleasers are generally not aware of their core self. Pleasing is not a factor of their being. It is an assumed or learned behavior that they use to survive. As I mentioned earlier, parents who exhibit distancing behaviors such as pleasing or manipulating, criticizing or avoiding, in their relationships with their adult children do so because at some deep level they believe they have to in order to go on living. People who are preoccupied with survival do not think about intimacy. They may not even know what it is.

I do not say this lightly or without compassion. I know what it is to survive on pleasing. Even now, after years of success in counseling, I find myself having to assess my agenda on a regular basis. Am I taking off a day of work to attend my granddaughter's birthday celebration because I really want to be there or because I want to please my daughter?

Am I talking on the phone late at night with my son because I welcome his confiding in me about an important decision he's facing and want to support him, or am I stuck in pleasing and, therefore, afraid to end the conversation at an appropriate time for me?

These are challenging questions. Each of us who has spent a lifetime developing the art of pleasing others must deal with our own version of them. We must also spend some time looking at the roots of our behavior. If the custom in your family was to "keep the peace at any price" then you will probably value appearances over connection, performance over intimacy. I'm not saying that's bad or good, just that it may be a fact. It may be something that you've never given much thought to before.

But now suddenly you may feel something lacking in your relationship with your children. You may not be sure what it is but you know that something is in the way. If this is true, consider how your desire to please may be the source of your own pain.

Pleasing Blocks Spontaneity. Laura said she'd love to feel spontaneous with her mother but she can't. "Mom's such a pleaser that I don't know when she's telling the truth and when she's lying," said Laura. "I asked her for a small loan once and she wrote me a check on the spot. Later I found out from my aunt that she was down that month and it was a real imposition for her to loan me that money. I felt terrible, and I couldn't relax till I paid her back."

Another time Laura invited her mother on the spur of the moment for a walk on the beach and a picnic lunch. After they walked about a mile, her mother had to turn back. She had sprained her knee earlier that week, and the doctor had recommended that she stay off it for several days.

The mother's eagerness to please took over her common sense. The result was a spoiled outing and hard feelings on the part of her daughter. Now Laura admits that she's reluctant to be spontaneous with her mother because she can't count on her to be honest.

Pleasing Blocks Spirituality. Compulsive pleasing stands between us and God. There's no way around it. Scripture abounds with God's word to parents. "Train up a child in the way he should go, And when he is old he will not depart from it" (Prov. 22:6). "Fathers, do not provoke your children, lest they become discouraged" (Col. 3:21). "That they may set their hope in God, And not forget the works of God, But keep His commandments" (Ps. 78:7). But those of us who have made pleasing a way of parenting, cannot be faithful to God's plan for us. Parenting requires some tough choices and difficult decisions— two things that pleasers back away from naturally. It also calls for selfless love, at times, and abundant nurturing. It demands personal sacrifice. And most important, it requires a willingness to foster the love and leading of the Lord in the lives of our children through our own modeling, even when they are adults and out from under our daily influence.

When our attention is focused on being popular we cannot be truly good, responsible parents. And when God's Word and God's leading become faint sounds in our ears, we are more vulnerable to the ways of the world. We lose our spiritual sensitivity. We begin to lean on our own understanding rather than on God's. From there it is easy to put off communing with God and worshiping with fellow believers. Pleasing then takes the place of praying.

PLEASING AS A FORM OF CONTROL

No one would suspect Ethel, an eighty-three-year-old soft-spoken mother of eight to be guilty of control. She stands just barely over five feet and weighs under 100 pounds. She's sweet, kind, loving, quiet by nature and has a great sense of humor. Yet Ethel has every one of her eight children and her husband of sixty years under her thumb. She pleases her way into every situation, and always has. "I don't remember my mother ever raising her voice," said her eldest son, Sam. "She is the most pleasant person you'd ever want to know. But she drives me crazy. I don't know what she's thinking. I don't know how to really talk to her. I don't know how she feels about me. We all have our own issues with her," said Sam, referring to his younger brother and six sisters.

"She controls us by being sweet, putting us first, deferring her own needs. But sometimes it makes me mad. I feel as if I'm always walking on eggs around her. I don't know what she thinks or what she wants. It's always been that way."

Ethel controls her family by controlling herself, by keeping her emotions in check, her needs and wants unknown, and her wishes and desires unspoken. As a result, her children feel impotent around her—unable to express their true selves for fear of upsetting or offending this woman who has made a career of being sweet and pleasant—and very unreal.

PORTRAIT OF A PLEASER

"I was the pleaser in my family," said fifty-one-year-old Gail, a tall brunette with soft eyes and a warm smile. "I was the oldest and that was my role. I became a mediator for my mother who was an alcoholic, always trying to make peace, especially when she attempted suicide numerous times."

In addition to dealing with her mother's dysfunction, Gail had to contend with her father's terrible temper, a trait which she claims she inherited from him and often displayed. Today, however, she is not in touch with that side of her personality. "Now it takes a lot to make me angry," she said. "Some people tell me I don't get angry enough. I'm too nice. They think I'm in denial. Maybe I am."

When Gail talked about her ex-husband, I heard bits of anger, and a lot of hurt in her voice, though both were guarded. She feels upset that he shows almost no interest in their children and doesn't contact them even when he's in town. Perhaps that's one reason why Gail gives so much of herself to her children even when it's not easy or maybe even wise.

Gail has two children, a son twenty-eight, and a daughter twenty-four. And she has two grandchildren under three years of age. She's been divorced for about ten years and still finds it a challenge to live alone. "Turning fifty was difficult," she confided, "especially being alone. I'd like to get married again."

Gail misses what she calls "the family feeling." Few women worked outside their homes when she was growing up and she, too, stayed home when her children were young. "I liked being with my kids," she said, "baking for them, playing with them, and looking forward to hearing about their day at school."

Today Gail works in a dentist's office, "and I don't have time to bake anymore," she said laughing.

Then reflecting on the past she continued, "I miss those early days. I miss holding my children and mothering them. Their father was absent a lot during those years and after our divorce he's been around even less. I'm the only source of family my children have," she added. "But even when my husband and I were living together, I went to most of the kids' games, meetings, and school programs by myself."

Today Gail feels she has a pretty solid relationship with both of her adult children, though she admits her pleasing, at times, has been harmful.

For example, while her son-in-law was out of work for several months, he and Gail's daughter and their baby moved in with Gail temporarily—but then stayed for two years. "They had nowhere else to go," she admitted. "I'm their only family. What else could I do? I couldn't desert them."

But Gail learned quickly that "two women can't occupy the same house at the same time." The problem escalated when Gail realized that her daughter "expected" her "to cook and clean" just as she had always done. "She still saw me as 'Mom,'" Gail said, "even though she was now married."

One way Gail coped was to take a four-day vacation up the coast of California as a gift to herself on her fiftieth birthday. "It was wonderful," she said. "I spent a lot of time praying, worshiping, reading, and relaxing. And I wrote in a journal some of the things I was feeling and dealing with. It was a powerful experience. I received many new insights about my life during that time."

As Gail adjusted to having her daughter and family around, she became aware of her daughter's mood swings. "She has bottled up a lot of hurt and resentment," Gail said. "She's very volatile. It takes almost nothing to set her off. She told my sister that if her marriage fails, she knows it will be her own fault because she's such a difficult person to live with."

At the same time, Gail acknowledged that her daughter has a "sweet and beautiful side," as well. They moved out after her son-in-law joined the Army and today they live overseas. Gail admits that today she and her daughter have a much better relationship. "We're enjoying sharing the mothering process," she said.

Gail smiled and laughed easily when she spoke about her adult son. He's single and spends a lot of time with her. "We bowl and do a lot of social things together," she said. "And we have dinner at least once a week. He seems to enjoy going places with me, and I like that."

Gail feels free to express her love to both of her children and they do the same with her. She claims that she learned to stop being a pleaser when she devoted more time to developing her spiritual life. She now looks to the Lord for the acceptance she once sought from pleasing others. And with her life on a more balanced footing now, she is free to pursue some of her desires, such as drawing closer to the Lord. Prayer is a big part of her daily agenda. Like most parents I spoke with, Gail admitted that she would not have survived all the hurt and pain of the last twenty-five years without the Lord's presence and guidance.

LETTING GO OF PLEASING

Like Gail, you may see how your pleasing has interfered, at least in part, with your relationship with your adult children. But you've been doing it for so long you may not even know how entrenched the behavior is and more important, how to let it go. The first and most important step before change of any kind can occur is to admit the problem and then to become willing to release it, to be transformed, as the apostle Paul says, by the renewing of your mind.

We'll look at more specific steps to recovery in the last section of the book, but you can begin now, even as you continue reading, to adopt some new ways of thinking, as well as new and healthier ways of relating to your children. Consider these first steps an experiment. Pray about what you wish to do. Ask for guidance, and then notice God's gentle nudges, reminders, and whispers.

Pay attention to your intuition, to what feels right, to what seems appropriate. I believe God expects us to use our common sense as well as His wisdom. "He grants good sense to the godly—His saints—He shows how to distinguish right from wrong, how to find the right decision every time." (Prov. 2:7–9 TLB)

Words to Consider, Actions to Take

• With God all things are possible, so ask Him for wisdom as you turn away from pleasing, and then practice new ways of relating to your adult children.

• We are stewards of our children, not owners. Release yourself from the need to control through pleasing. Consider the benefits to both of you when you honestly communicate your needs and wishes, even as you listen to theirs.

• Nothing is forever except the love of God. Look at your children for who they are—human beings with virtues as well as vices, none of which is too big for God to redeem.

• The testing of your faith brings about patience. Embrace patience over pleasing. Give yourself permission to lean on God's understanding of each situation rather than your own.

• God will never leave you nor forsake you. Give Him your fear of change, fear of rejection, fear of not being enough.

LOOKING WITHIN

Parents who identify themselves as pleasers can relate to many of these statements.

1. I anticipate and try to meet the needs of my adult children without checking with them first.

2. I notice my need for my children's approval.

3. I defer my own preferences in order to please my adult children.

4. I spend more time, money, and emotional energy on my adult children than I spend on myself.

5. I feel responsible if my adult children are deprived in any way.

6. I feel more in control of my life when I am pleasing my children.

7. I please my adult children without considering the consequences to myself.

8. I am aware that pleasing has become a way of life for me in all of my relationships.

Chapter Four

THE RESCUER

In the late 1980s a friend introduced me to a book entitled, *Women Who Love Too Much* after I confided in her some of the problems I was struggling with in my marriage.[1] After reading Robin Norwood's book, I learned that the trouble I faced was deeply rooted in me, not in my husband.

Following the author's suggestions for recovery, I joined a support group at my church, and later went into private Christian counseling. It was during this time of discovery that I realized that the symptoms of "loving too much" sprang from the child within me—a young girl still very much in need. What I was doing had little to do with love as I now know it.

I gave to others what I desperately wanted them to give me—time, money, attention, support, love, and help. And I gave without much thought to whether it was appropriate or inappropriate, right or wrong, good or bad, helpful or hindering, wanted or unwanted. I didn't know about such things as co-dependence, where an individual depends on or enmeshes with a person who abuses a substance such as alcohol or drugs.

And I didn't know what it meant to be part of an environment where, according to Robin Norwood, "children are to some extent damaged in their ability to feel and relate"[2] due to family members who drink, diet, spend, clean, use drugs, or money in an addictive way, or where other disruptive events such as terminal illness or disease processes "prevent honest contact and intimacy in a family."[3] I had a lot to learn. I am still learning.

But as I uncovered the truth about my motives and began to delve into my past for the roots of my emotional neediness, I realized that I was attempting to take care of myself the only way I knew how. I assumed that if I took care of others first, they would return the favor. This behavior, as I have since learned, is very common in people who have experienced emotional deprivation in their early years.

Rescuing had become a way of life. To me it was the kind and loving thing to do. It never occurred to me that I was doing for others—including my children—what they could and should do for themselves. I was quick to do the dinner dishes if my kids had homework. I paid the bills because my husband, in my opinion, put them off too long. I shopped for birthday gifts and cards on behalf of my husband and children. I accepted overnight guests when I was in no shape to have them. I volunteered for everything that came along from being a leader of a Camp Fire Girls group, to school library aid and choir singer. I kept a "perfect" house, cooked nutritious meals, and sewed and did needlepoint in my "spare" time.

Today I feel overwhelmed just thinking about all that I did, whirling through lives like a Kansas tornado, wreaking havoc on everyone in my path, including myself.

Now that I have some insight and healing, however, I am aware of how dishonest I often was. Though I appeared to be putting others first, I was actually thinking of myself more than I want to admit. I needed to feel needed in order to validate my life, to make sense out of what I didn't understand, and because I often felt that I knew more than others, what was best for them and how to provide it. How ignorant—and how arrogant! But that was me—back then.

SUPER PARENTS

In recent years, I've been blessed to discover that I'm not alone. It's been a great relief! Other mothers and fathers have confided in me that they are attracted to and involved with sons and daughters who most need them. They may complain about bailing a child out of jail, covering a grown daughter's car payment, or paying for private schooling for their grandchildren, but they still do it.

At some level they must. It doesn't feel right to let their children face and solve their own problems. In a sense, they are still picking up their kids' toys, wiping their faces, and making school lunches. They have not been able to distinguish between parenting a young child and being the parents of a grown man or woman who must take responsibility for his or her own life.

And the payoff? It could be that rescuing and helping, particularly when they take on compulsive proportions, provides more opportunities to avoid looking closely at one's own life situations that need attention. It also helps assuage guilt and gives some of us a sense of purpose. "If it weren't for my kids, I'd just as soon end it all," said one lonely older woman who saw life as one negative event after another.

Unfortunately, the family is fertile soil for this troubling behavior. Women are especially prone to rescuing, since traditionally, as mothers, nurses, secretaries and teachers, we are the nurturers and care-givers. It is almost impossible for those of us who identify with rescuing to turn away a person in need.

Typically, we do not ask questions, assess the situation, weigh it, or pray about it. We simply respond to the stimuli. A son needs money. We write a check. A daughter sees a dress she wants. We buy it for her. A grown child needs a place to live. We let him move back home rent free. We set aside our vacation time to baby-sit our children's children. We pay off gambling debts, co-sign for loans, and give advice when no one asked for it.

As long as we focus on our children, we can put off looking at ourselves. The harder we try to help them, the more in need we become, for we are trying to give to others what we don't even have for ourselves.

We continually attempt to draw water from an empty well and then wonder why we're not appreciated and acknowledged as much as we'd like to be. Perhaps you will identify with some of the characteristics that are common among parents who rescue their children.

COMMON CHARACTERISTICS OF A RESCUER

1. Rescuers create a home where their children are denied the opportunity to experience a full range of emotions. Because their own emotions were largely unmet when they were growing up, rescuers are often frightened of feelings, especially when expressed strongly by a young child. Rescuers tend to "hush" their children, give them food and toys and other things to distract them from crying or from showing anger or from being too loud or demanding.

Millicent said that she tended to follow her mother's patterns when she was raising her two sons. "Their feelings frightened me," she said. "They were typical little boys, making loud noises, running endlessly up and down the stairs, crying at the top of their lungs when they got hurt, punching one another when they were angry. I couldn't stand it. I constantly interfered, hushing and rescuing them from working things out."

Reflecting on her own childhood, Millicent continued reflectively. "I was raised by a delicate mother who gave birth to me in her early forties. I now realize that I was too much for her. I don't think she had the physical strength or the emotional energy for a baby or a young child, even though in some ways I know she and my father thought of me as a special blessing."

Millicent remembers fighting with a playmate over a toy, much as her sons did when they were young. She says her mother stepped in and rescued her from hurt feelings. She took the toy away from the other child and sent the little girl home. "She did that sort of thing a lot," said Millicent.

"I realize I've done the same thing with my children," she said. "I'd rather be the savior than let them experience normal interactions with others."

2. Rescuers discourage their children from experimenting. They rarely ask questions or help their children work through a situation that might lead to valuable skills, such as learning to put a puzzle together, or preparing a small meal, tying a shoe, making one's bed, or earning money for a desired item. They generally finish these tasks for the child at the slightest sign of inability. Such children usually grow up feeling less than normal in terms of everyday skills.

Ralph shared that he discouraged his boys from science experiments because of the potential danger. He envisioned them being electrocuted or poisoned or harmed in some permanent way. "I've always been cautious," he said. "My dad was killed in a chemical accident. I guess that has a lot to do with my fears."

Gina said she interfered with her children's desire to try new things because she was fixated on keeping them neat and clean. Those were standards her mother had passed on to her. Today, as the mother of three adult daughters, Gina sees how her rescuing mentality has influenced their lives. "Two are unmarried and live together," she said, "and lead very simple, predictable lives. The oldest blames me for her fear of people and fear of work. She was the brightest of the three but she never realized her potential. Maybe I did control them too much."

Gina's third daughter is married and works in the military. "She chose a safe path too," said Gina, "but she has earned her college degree and seems content."

3. Rescuers are inclined to take responsibility for their children's triumphs and failures.   Since they are uncomfortable with failure (perhaps due to not being helped through their learning processes as children) they rescue their children before they too fail.

They also want so much for their children to be victorious that they "force" a triumph or a win by filling in where the child is unable or not yet ready. A father who wants his son to impress others with his woodworking skills may help the boy complete a project he could have done on his own. As the child grows up he is likely to become dependent on his father to finish for him what he never learned to complete by himself. The father continues to rescue his son—even into his thirties and forties.

A mother may rescue a daughter from potential unpopularity (something the mother may have endured when she was an adolescent) by inviting her daughter's friends over to the house, planning parties, and generally managing the girl's social life.

Keith remembers when he was eleven, wanting to participate in a fund-raiser for school by selling raffle tickets to the neighbors. "My dad wouldn't hear of it," said Keith. "He told me that no son of his was going to go begging door-to-door. He bought all five books himself and then couldn't understand why I was disappointed. It felt as if he did all the work for me."

4. Rescuers have a desperate need to remain prominent in their children's lives. Bill talked about how he helps his adult children by giving them a check each month. "I figure I don't need it as much as they do. You know, dental bills, car repairs, it's always something in a young family. Besides it's nice to be needed. My dad was never around much when I was a kid. I made sure that wasn't going to happen to my kids. If something goes wrong they know who they can come to. I'll always be there."

Emily baby-sits for her two grandchildren two days a week while her daughter works part-time at the family dry cleaners. "My daughter talked about day-care but I told her I couldn't bear it," said Emily. "No grandkids of mine are going to some stranger's house while I'm still alive."

Bill and Emily, eager to remain important to their adult children, insure their prominence in their son's and daughter's lives by rescuing them from situations and decisions that have nothing to do with them. It is more comfortable to invest their money and time in their adult children than to invest it in themselves.

5. Rescuers believe, at some fundamental level, that unless they control themselves and others through rescuing, they will die. Control is once again the core issue. Rescuers are driven to take charge in some way—through giving, withholding, spending, care-taking, managing or other assorted behaviors. They want to avoid painful consequences, unpredictable experimentation, and risk-laden results at all costs. So even if they understand intellectually that it is better for their adult children to handle their family budget without interference, or to work through a marital problem without interruption, such parents cannot follow through physically and emotionally. They enter into the situation and try to rescue their children or fix the problem.

The cost to themselves—and even to the relationship—never enters their mind. Their behavior is rooted in survival. They must rescue or they cannot live with themselves.

HOW RESCUING AFFECTS YOUR RELATIONSHIP WITH YOUR ADULT CHILDREN

Like the pleaser, the rescuer may appear at first glance, as one who is caring, generous, helpful. Rescuers want to keep their children from hurting themselves. How could anyone fault them for that? The desire is commendable. None of us wants to see our children in pain. But acting out that desire is something else.

Does our rescuing behavior stop our children from experiences that are essential to their development? Are we playing God in their lives? Are we taking on the task of deciding what's best for them when we don't even always know what's best for ourselves?

What might have been wise interference in the life of a young child, (holding hands while crossing a busy street, keeping away from electrical outlets, teaching swimming safety) is generally unwise when such managing continues in the lives of adult children who are now responsible for their own choices and decisions. But parents who believe their very survival depends on rescuing their children from pain cannot think about that.

Rescuing Blocks Communication.   Alex claims his relationship with his college-aged daughter is superb. Couldn't be better, to hear him tell it. "I don't know why people make such a fuss about communication gaps between the old and the young," he said laughing. "Therese and I are best friends. I told her the lines are open between us. No blocks here. Just tell me what you need and I'll handle it." That's the problem, according to Alex's wife. He manages and fixes. He doesn't discuss situations with her, ask questions, or share a related experience from his own life. He takes over.

For example, he doesn't want his daughter to work while going to school because he's afraid the distraction will take away from her grades and goals.

She, on the other hand, studying for a degree in library science, wants to work part-time in the university library. She told her mother it would be a great opportunity to test out the field. "When she approached her dad on this," said his wife Lynn, "he brushed her off, telling her if it was the money she wanted, no problem, he'd raise her monthly allowance. He told her she'd be out in the world soon enough, no need to rush it."

Lynn took a deep breath and sat back in her chair. "Imagine how discredited she must feel. He sees work as pain and struggle, always has. He can't imagine Therese wanting to work before she has to. So he jumped in and tried to rescue her from the pain he envisions. He has not talked it over with her. Maybe if he shared his feelings, they'd come to a better understanding of one another."

Alex may go on proclaiming the attributes of open communication with one's grown children, but in the meantime his words are empty to the one person he seems so sure of—his daughter.

Rescuing Blocks Confrontation. Rescuers do anything to avoid confrontation. They see no reason for it. They are into the solution even before the problem is fully communicated. I know this from my own experience. I remember a time when my youngest daughter confronted me with her pain over my inability to simply listen to her feelings without trying to rescue her.

Even as the words fell from her mouth, I was already sweeping them up and fixing them. I quickly explained, apologized, and denied as fast as I could, and then launched into a major monologue about a particular time in my life when such and such happened.

Then as I heard myself talking and really looked at the expression on her face, something suddenly snapped within me. I saw that I was doing the very thing she had just confronted me with. I was once again dismissing her feelings by attempting to rescue her with a "feel better" story from my past. I stopped in mid-sentence and told her what had just occurred. Her facial expression changed immediately. She had just been heard—by me, her mother—perhaps for the first time.

Rescuing Blocks Friendship. Rescuers don't have much room in their lives for friendship with their children, because their main focus is preventing and handling crises to avoid feeling out of control. One who lives life as a sentry on duty doesn't make friends easily. They are more comfortable protecting than relating.

Rescuers would rather save their drowning child from icy waters than play with them in the shallow water at the edge of the shore.

Rescuers would rather buy their teenager a new car than shop for a used one that they could fix up together.

And rescuers, as parents of adult children, would prefer to give their sons and daughters a down payment for a new house, putting their own finances in jeopardy if necessary, than listen to their children's plan for making the purchase on their own.

Mai-Lee had always dreamed of how she and her daughter (the only girl in a family of six children) would spend time as adults swimming, sewing, cooking and looking after her grandchildren together. But now she claims she doesn't know how to enjoy her leisure time.

"I spent so many years protecting my children during the Communist invasion in Vietnam and later when we fled to Thailand that I don't remember how to have fun. I must learn again. But it is difficult. I want to spare my daughter any more pain. She has been through enough. My sons, they can take care of themselves, but my daughter is like a young flower. I want to protect her."

Rescuing Blocks Intimacy. Those who rescue deny themselves the opportunity to get to know their children at a deep and intimate level. They are so concerned with keeping peace, controlling emotions, and putting out fires that they have no time for developing deep and lasting intimacy. Such a person is more of a watchdog than a wise and loving parent.

Fathers and mothers who rescue their children from financial disasters, divert painful communications, and avoid honest expressions of emotion, throw up a wall between themselves and their children. When the relationship becomes too intense, the rescuer puts on his helmet, grabs his weapon, and rides into battle, believing he is doing something noble and good.

Maybe, however, all that is needed is a heart-to-heart talk or some quality time in the company of one another. But the rescuer doesn't stop long enough to find out what's really needed. He or she has mounted the horse and is riding off to the front lines before the conflict has been fully verbalized.

I remember such a time in my life. My son, a young adult at the time, was living in his car for a period of weeks while he was still in his father's custody. When I heard about it, I was beside myself with guilt and worry. Was he eating? Did he have enough money? Did his father know about this? We were divorced at the time, and I was living in a city about 100 miles away from my son.

My first thought was to jump in my car and charge up to Los Angeles and rescue him. I had it all planned in my mind. I'd put him in my car, bring him back to my home, fix a room for him, prepare some nourishing meals, and nurture him back to health and well-being. Then I'd help him get a good job and we'd all live happily ever after. I wanted so much to be the heroine—to make up for some of the ways in which I had neglected him in the past.

But thanks to the Lord's leading I made an appointment with a counselor at my church and spoke with her before going ahead with my plan. She helped me see that this was a situation between my son and his father. To rush up there and rescue him might look good on the surface and might have felt good to my son who was probably pretty ragged at this point. And it certainly would have made me look good to others and feel good inside. But was it the wise and right thing to do? I prayed about it first—and I didn't go. It became clear to me that my interference at that time could easily disrupt a process between my son and his father that God had His hand on.

In that moment I knew that the most loving thing I could do was stay out of something that was none of my business. I needed to examine my motives, to drop any self-satisfying desires I might have, and finally to stand by and allow my son to struggle through a painful, yet very important passage in his life.

I could let him know that I loved him, that I was praying for him, that my home was open to him, but that's all. The rest was up to him—and the Lord.

Does that mean we should never help or reach out? Of course not. But there are no set guidelines to follow. I believe we must look at each situation separately, assessing it based on past behavior, present needs and future consequences. I generally pray and seek the counsel of someone I trust before making weighty decisions regarding my children.

Rescuing Blocks Spontaneity. Spontaneity is one of the great joys of life. It is an attitude and an aspect of the art of living that needs encouragement and opportunity. Have you ever considered getting up one morning and simply following your heart for the remainder of the day? Perhaps you'd eat cold lasagna for breakfast, run barefoot in the surf, make paper flowers and give them to a friend, take a nap under a big shade tree, or give yourself permission to just be.

Like me, you may like the idea, but you can't imagine being that spontaneous for that long a time. And to be spontaneous with your children would create even more of a challenge. Rescuers are hard pressed to be that free. They are more inclined to at least heat the cold lasagna for their children, have beach sandals nearby in case they cut their feet on a jagged rock or piece of glass, purchase real flowers instead of fake ones, and insist on taking a nap in a bed in order to protect one's back. Is it any wonder that the rescuer is not someone whose grown children are eager to have around.

Rescuing Blocks Spirituality. I realize that I have played God in the life of my children on more than one occasion. When they've expressed a need I was right there trying to handle it for them, fix it, solve it. I didn't pray about it first. I didn't ask God whether or not I was to play a part in the solution. I just saw a need and tried to fill it.

Today, thank God, I have more wisdom. I'm aware that God

can work things out in the lives of my children without any help from me, just as God works in my life without always using my parents. This has been an important element in my maturing process as a Christian.

A need in the lives of my adult children does not necessarily imply a call on me. It might. But it might not. And I won't know that unless I ask God first.

But I do know that if I continue to lean on my own understanding, offer man-made solutions, and give pat answers to complex problems, I will be seriously interfering with my spirituality as well as that of my children. They need to go to God as much as I do. Only Jesus can really save them.

RESCUING AS A FORM OF CONTROL

Parents who rescue are parents who control. They get into the problem and they create a solution. They also enjoy taking credit for what they do. Monty is such a person. He loves to talk about his adult son and the messes he gets into that only Monty can fix. Monty is a large man with an imposing presence. He has a deep voice, a hearty laugh, and an enormous ego. To hear him tell it, his son Len, a man of thirty-five, is about as capable as a ten-year-old. I doubt that Monty would have it any other way.

He loves to talk about the time Len totalled his car, botched a job interview, and fell in love with a woman who cheated on him. But Monty came to the rescue. He bought Len a new car, gave him a job at his pipe-fitting plant, and introduced him to "a solid girl who'll make him a good wife."

I don't know how Len feels about all this, but Monty thrives on it. He appears to control everyone and everything in his path. He's a one-man rescue squad.

PORTRAIT OF A RESCUER

"I'm a rescuer," said Mary, knowingly. "Anyone who needs help, I help—at my own expense."

It's been a challenge to let go of this behavior, even though she realizes it has cost her many of her own dreams. At one time Mary enjoyed such nontraditional jobs as roofer, landscaper, construction worker. More recently she has worked as a custodian but is now unemployed as she recovers from a work-related accident.

"I never wanted to be a typical homemaker," she said . "I wanted to go where there was more challenge and more money. But all of that contradicts what I do now," she said soberly. "And I face this turmoil everyday."

Now in her late forties, Mary lives at home with her twenty-five old son who has AIDS. "He's functioning," she said, "but he's depressed and in pain much of the time. There is a part of me that feels responsible for this," said Mary.

"For a time I paid his bills out of my guilt over a bad marriage to his father. Then when he was on drugs I was in denial and rescued him again. At one time he owed me a lot of money. But now I hold him responsible for half the rent. Even though he's sick he can work, and he does have a job."

Mary admitted that this arrangement is better for both of them. He needs to be accountable, and she needs to release him to live the life of an adult. On a practical level, now that she's unemployed, she needs him to carry his share of the financial responsibilities.

The most challenging aspect of parenting has been her lack of preparation. "My parents were not good role models," said Mary. "I came from a heavily dysfunctional family. My mother drank. Basically, she was a good person but she made a wrong choice in marrying my father. He was a policeman, a tough man who provided no emotional support. I was raised like a boy," she said. "I carried a lot of responsibilities that were not appropriate for a child."

Mary has since turned to her son for support. She said they've been close from the time he was a little boy. "I was always my son's closest friend and confidante. And he was my sounding board," she said, admitting that she may have told him too much at times.

Mary is committed to improving her life and her relationship with her son, despite the obstacles they face with his health and her unemployment. She realizes that her rescuing behavior has been harmful. It's a constant challenge to know when to help and when to back off. She has taken classes in parenting and "tough love" seminars. "I realize now there is only so much anyone can do for another—even your own children. You can't make someone else change. You can only change yourself," something Mary is committed to in her own life. "When someone says 'no' it means 'yes' to me," she said. "I'm a fighter."

CAROL'S STORY

Carol, an attractive, warm, and bubbly woman in her early fifties said she "woke up about ten years ago" and since then has been on a path of self-improvement. "I'm now open to anything," she said. "I want to be aware. I realized that I was doing with my kids some of the same things my mother did with me. I remember a time when my daughter wanted to stay overnight at a friend's house. I told her, 'No, you have a bed here. This is your home.' Then I suddenly realized that's what my mother had said to me when I was a child. I didn't want to copy her."

Mothering was Carol's whole world for many years as she raised her children alone. She and her second husband have six adult children between them, four from her first marriage and two from his. "For the most part, they are responsible, good people," she said. "I really like them all."

Today, however, after years of being a mother, she admits it's a challenge to "turn off those skills and to let go of being a mother hen." Her youngest son, now eighteen years of age, would like it if she did! "He's doing a lot of partying right now," she said, "and I fear that I'll lose communication with him. He's not smiling as much as he used to."

In the past Carol might have tried to force a change, or initiate a conversation that would result in advice-giving, but now she knows from experience with the other children that the best thing to do is "open my ears and close my mouth. I know my kids want to feel that I believe in them, that they can live their lives responsibly."

Carol looks back with some embarrassment over her years of rescuing her children. "I know I overdid a lot of things," she said. "For example, I did the footwork for my kids when they should have done it themselves. I remember when one of my sons was looking into colleges. He needed help finding the right resources. But I didn't just help him, I did the entire thing for him. I'm like that," Carol added.

When one of her children expresses a need, she's been quick to respond with an idea, a book, a thought, a piece of advice. It's a cycle that's difficult to break, even though Carol admits she's working on it.

She also said she has been one to replace things for her children that are broken or worn out and to "block the reality of consequences." In other words, they haven't always had to deal with difficult results because Carol has been there to rescue them. "I hate to see them make mistakes," she said, "or get lost. I have a tendency to want to help make things easier for them."

Carol's greatest current challenge is her relationship with her twenty-two-year-old daughter who has moved back home and is now pregnant. "She has been in counseling for years," said Carol. "I believe she really enjoys the attention. I know she resents my sharing my attention with others. She's been depressed since she was fourteen, and is still hanging on to her rage against her father."

Carol believes that her daughter "loves to hate." She also has a very difficult time letting go of things. "She hangs on to stuff like clothes, an old quilt and so on. She has a lot going on in her mind. And she has a lot of things from the past to deal with—an abortion, drug abuse, irresponsible choices, school problems. Today, however, she's back in school and maintaining a 4.0 grade point. She wants to become a teacher."

Carol admits that their relationship is as fragile as an eggshell, but she also feels more hopeful than ever before, because Carol is now taking care of herself, seeking more balance, and adding to the quality of her own life and her marriage.

She depends on God for the help she needs in letting go of her children, especially her daughter. "She's in your hands, Lord. I pray that everyday," said Carol, "and I know He's there for me. I have my own dialogue with God. He looks after me. I wouldn't be where I am without Him."

LETTING GO OF RESCUING

Perhaps rescuing has been a problem in your life. Maybe your parents rescued you so it is the only behavior you've known. Or like Mary, perhaps they weren't there when you really did need them, so you've made a vow to always be there for your children—perhaps to the extreme.

Letting go of destructive behaviors is not easy. It takes time. It takes commitment. It takes understanding. We cannot lean on our own understanding in this area anymore than we can in any other area of our lives. Only God can save others. The most we can do is offer a hand when guided to do so. And of course we can pray. More on that powerful tool in a later chapter.

One of the first ways to break yourself free from rescuing is to acknowledge, as Mary did, that there is only so much one person can do. We cannot change another human being, even our sons and daughters.

Look back over your life and pay attention to all the ways in which you have enabled and rescued your children. Has it really made any difference?

One of the most important gifts we can offer them is believing in them, and then stepping aside and providing the room for them to make their own choices and decisions.

And in the meantime we can begin to pour our creative energy into our own lives, trusting God to bring all things together for good, as He promised.

Words To Consider—Actions To Take

• "Now choose life, so that you and your children may live and that you may love the Lord your God, listen to his voice, and hold fast to him" (Deut. 30:19–20 NIV).

What does it mean to "choose" life? I believe it means that we are to intentionally line up with God as we know and understand Him. He is the God of life—life here on earth and life everlasting. Choosing life may include for you, turning your will and your life over to His care in a conscious way, seeking Him through prayer and meditation, listening for His guidance for your behavior, and holding onto Him as a small child would hold onto a loving parent. It may include letting go of your expectations, your way of doing things, your agenda for yourself and your adult children, and discovering what God has for each of you.

• Think about how your rescuing behavior has intensified the conflict between you and your children. Examine these areas of your life and notice the opportunities you now have to "choose life" anew. As God speaks to you in response to prayer, through other people, or books, sermons, lectures and by other means, look for specific steps you can take to interrupt your rescuing behaviors and to focus on what brings life to *you*.

• Remember that to move a mountain all we need is faith as small as a mustard seed. Ask God for that faith. He is faithful to give us what we ask for in faith. He will meet you where you are spiritually, emotionally, and physically. You may have only enough strength to say, "Help!" but it's a start. God will take it from there. And bear in mind that faith is a *daily* walk. It often requires trusting and believing in a process and in results that are largely unseen and unknown. But if you are to break the destructive pattern of rescuing, you must be willing to start where you are—perhaps unknowing and unseeing—at least for now.

• Change starts with being willing. Declare your willingness today. Then watch for opportunities where you would ordinarily rescue your children and instead, release them and the situation into the care of God. He may have you play a part in the solution and He may keep you entirely out of it. But you won't know unless you commune with Him about it.

• God will uphold you with His righteous right hand. What more support could anyone want? The King of the universe is our Father. He will not withhold any good thing from us if we but ask. Ask Him to help you overcome compulsive rescuing.

LOOKING WITHIN

Parents who identify themselves as rescuers can relate to many of these statements.

1. I confuse love and pity and tend to feel more "loving" toward my children when they need my help.

2. I feel it is my duty as a parent to take care of whatever they cannot handle.

3. I am afraid of losing the love of my children so I rescue them from their pain in order to win their affection.

4. I feel guilty if my children need help and I don't provide it.

5. I tend to avoid dealing with my own life issues by rescuing my children.

6. I am unlikely to trust God when I believe I have a workable solution.

7. I am more sensitive to my children's pain than I am to my own.

8. I feel better about myself as a parent when I rescue my children.

Chapter Five

THE VICTIM

Author and talk show host, Rich Buhler, in his ground-breaking book on victimization, *Pain and Pretending*, (Thomas Nelson Publishers) defines the word "victim" in this way. "A victim is a person who has experienced destruction at the foundation of who that person is and in a way that has caused significant hindrance in the living of life."[1]

From his ministry to thousands of callers on his nationally syndicated radio show, "Table Talk," he now believes that "the great majority of significantly hurting people in our culture and in our churches are dealing with the lingering effects of victimization."[2]

Buhler acknowledges that to an extent, we are all victims. No one can go through life without being hurt, disappointed, tormented or bruised in some way. But as he points out in his book, the key words in his definition are "destruction," "foundation" and "hindrance." I'd like to spend a moment discussing each one and then showing how they relate to broken relationships.

DESTRUCTION

As you look at your own life, consider the kinds of pain you've suffered. Perhaps you were deeply disappointed over losing an important ball game when you were in Little League or when you were overlooked for the leading role in a school play.

You may have dealt with profound pain and loss over the

untimely death of a loved one. Or you may have been overwhelmed by pain and rage resulting from someone who physically abused or sexually violated you.

Obviously not all pain and loss are the same. Nor do they all make the same imprint on our lives. Hurt and disappointment over losing a competition or pulling a poor score on a test can be considerable, but generally it is the kind of pain that prompts us to practice more and work harder. In some cases it can actually be a gift in disguise.

But the pain of being overwhelmed by another human being who intended to cause harm is different. If someone violated you physically or sexually, you carry the imprint of that experience on your soul. The consequences continue to affect you and your children, whether you're aware of it or not. It does not go away with a mere decision to protect one's self more effectively the next time.

FOUNDATION

Destructive pain of this kind, suffered during the formative years, has the most significant and longest-lasting effect. This is the time in a person's life when his opinion of himself is being shaped through people, events, circumstances, feelings, and experiences. This opinion then, becomes the basis of a lifelong self-image, influencing the person's decisions about self, other people, work, society, even God.

The earlier it occurs in life the more it becomes a part of the person's foundation as a human being. This is an important truth to realize because the way we deal with pain in later life is directly related to and deeply affected by how we experienced it as a child.

If, as children, we learn to accept the ups and downs of life as a normal part of living, we are more apt to move with the flow as adults, knowing that "this too shall pass." But if we experienced destruction at our very foundation, then as adults, we are likely to feel overpowered and paralyzed by pain.

HINDRANCE

When guilt, fear, low self-esteem, rage, and anger continually impede a person's ability to live life in a meaningful way, he or she probably has been victimized in some way. The key word here is continually. Everyone experiences bouts of fear and anger over the course of life, but the victim is hindered by them. There appears to be no way out of the maze of broken relationships, short-lived jobs, and compulsive behaviors with food, money, sex, alcohol, or other substances.

Not all victims are totally dysfunctional, however. Many function brilliantly in one or two areas and fall down in others. Some manage to hold all parts of their lives together for a matter of months and then suddenly everything falls apart.

VICTIMS AS PARENTS

Victims attract victims. And marital partners who are victims tend to produce more victims. You may recall from an earlier chapter Rebecca Cutter's important point, "You can't pass on what you don't have." It is also true that you cannot help but pass on what you do have. Just as you learned from your parents, your children will learn from you.

If you did not receive what you needed mentally, emotionally, physically, and spiritually, then you cannot successfully provide that for your children, try as you might.

Love and affection are the most obvious and fundamental emotional human needs. When these are neglected, children grow up feeling that something is wrong with them. That they are defective in some way, or else they would be loved. Many then spend their lives trying to get the love and affection they crave. Their behavior can range from the overzealous (showing off, forcing friendships, helping in the extreme) to the bizarre (compulsive talking and laughing) and even to the criminal (kidnapping, extortion, rape, murder).

Both the victimized and the victimizer experience destruction at the foundation of who they are. For whether we perpetrate the abuse or are the recipient of it, we are violated at the very foundation of our personhood.

Destruction that occurred at the foundation of who you are and is causing hindrance in living your life will not be overcome quickly. It will take time and courage, and a commitment to yourself and to the healing process. Awareness, however, is a key element to change—change and healing for yourself that will also produce change and healing for future generations in your family.

But before you can make that commitment you may wish to look at the common characteristics of a victim to see if they pertain to you.

COMMON CHARACTERISTICS OF A VICTIM

1. Victims are often emotionally closed. Because they have experienced destruction at the core of their lives, victims live "on guard." As parents, many are serious, hard-working, quiet, and emotionally controlled. They may love their children, but have difficulty expressing that love.

Thirty-year-old Tanya spoke about her mother with tears in her eyes. "My mom was continually terrorized by her alcoholic father when she was a child. She never knew what to expect. When he drank he hit her, and during his brief periods of sobriety he ignored her. She has never sought any kind of help. She doesn't trust anyone. She married my father, who had been a childhood neighbor. He was the only person who treated her kindly. But their marriage has not been good. My mother is an extremely private person. I know that's been hard on my dad."

Tanya said she and her two brothers dealt with the consequences of her mother's victimization throughout their childhoods. It hasn't changed much since then. "My mother and I have never been close," she said. "When I tried to talk to her about my feelings or get her advice about boys and school and usual things a kid wants to talk over, she would look worried and uncomfortable. She took me to the library a lot and looked for books that would answer my questions."

Tanya's mother is now sixty years old and in poor health. "When I try to talk to her about her past and to tell her that help is out there, she changes the subject or gets angry and walks away. She says the past is the past and she doesn't want to talk about it. She doesn't seem to realize how much her pain is hindering her own life and her relationship with my brothers and me."

2. Victims are dedicated to safety and tend to over-protect their children. Their fear of being overpowered physically or emotionally causes many victims to stifle their children's natural curiosity and experimentation. They would rather be safe than sorry, and as a result, they often pass on their fears.

Rudy said his mother had grown up in Germany during World War II and lived in terror for years. Those fears have stayed with her even though she has lived in America for over fifty years.

"She kept us close to her at all times," he said, speaking of himself and his two older brothers. "I felt like a prisoner sometimes. Other kids could go out after supper in the summer and play ball, but we weren't allowed to leave our front yard unless my mother was with us. Sometimes she'd take us to a game and then we could play. But only on those rare occasions. For years she walked us to school, brought us home for lunch, then took us back in the afternoon."

Rudy's father did not interfere. "He told us our mother had been scared as a child and we had to understand her ways. I didn't see why our lives had to be so different from everyone else's. We didn't live in Germany, and the war was over. But no one seemed to care how we felt," Rudy added, frowning in thought.

"There were times when I hated her. She didn't seem to understand that she was doing to us what her father had done to her. Of course he had good reason to protect his children. There was a war going on outside their house."

3. Victims view parenting through the lens of fear. Margo is such a parent. She admits that she is afraid of everything—people, new places, unfamiliar routines, unexpected events. To her, parenting is a process that is filled with fearful experiences. She worries about everything from her health to the weather to how her grandchildren will survive in a violent world.

She grew up in the overcrowded home of a maternal aunt after her parents were killed in a boating accident when she was five. "I never felt secure after that," she said. "My aunt and uncle had four kids of their own and I saw myself as a burden."

No one showed her how to deal with life crises. Instead, she was scolded, shamed, and ignored. She was made to feel that she was the crisis. Those feelings carried over into her relationship with her children. And today, as the parent of adult children, she realizes that she alienates her daughter with her constant warnings. She wants to stop giving advice but feels compelled to interfere when she sees things she doesn't approve of.

4. Victims have difficulty trusting, even their loved ones. Adults who have been violated sexually, or physically mistreated in some other way, find it almost impossible, without professional help, to trust. They are often private, passive individuals who prefer to remain in the background. Jeff's mother is such a person. She was often beaten and verbally shamed by a strong-willed father who ruled his home like a drill sergeant.

When Jeff attempts to draw out his mother's feelings with questions or to inquire about her past, she avoids the topic, offers him some food, or sits passively with arms folded, waiting for the "inquisition" as she calls it, to end. "I feel as though there's a lifetime of experiences and emotions locked up inside her, and she's not about to trust anyone—even me—with the key.

"We can have some fun together," he said. "I take her out for dinner a couple of times a month and she comes to some of my soccer games and seems to enjoy them. But we never talk about anything important. It's mostly a surface conversation."

Jeff says that one of his friends complains that his mother still treats him like a kid, offering advice that is neither needed nor wanted. But Jeff claims he's almost jealous of the attention his friend receives. "I'd faint if my mother ever meddled in my life." Then smiling, he said, "I think I'd like it."

5. Victims control their world and their children through passive, negative behavior. Will told his grown daughter Marsha that when he retired she could find him in front of the television set and that's where he planned to stay. He grew up in an alcoholic home, often fending for himself and his sister, and is now dedicated to withdrawing from the world he knows. "I've seen enough of this ugly world," he told her. He's been retired for a year now, and other than a short walk for a haircut or a few groceries, he hasn't left the house.

"It's as though he tuned out life and tuned in sitcoms," she said. "He's always been a negative person, even when my mother was alive, but it's gotten worse as he's grown older."

Marsha and her husband have played right into his hands. "We invited him to live with us," she said, "but he refused." His daughter calls him daily, drives him to the few doctor's appointments he has, and asks him to dinner weekly, but he rarely comes.

"I'm so worried about him," she confided. "I'd feel better if we could get him under our roof. I know it would be hard, but at least I'd know he was eating well and had us close by for emergencies."

Marsha admitted that her dad has always controlled the family with his negative attitude. "I guess I'm used to it," she said. "Sometimes I just want to shake him and say, 'Look you're not the only human being on this planet with problems,' but then I see how little he has going for him and I back off."

HOW BEING A VICTIM AFFECTS YOUR RELATIONSHIP WITH YOUR ADULT CHILDREN

Victims are used to being violated, discounted, even discarded by others, so it's little wonder that they have troubled relationships with their grown children.

The problems can come from either the parent victim or the adult child. Parents who will not face their past issues of victimization are a source of continued pain for their children. Control, irrational fears, worry, a negative attitude, depression, and misplaced guilt keep the parent stuck in his own world, focusing on his needs, his desires, his opinions.

There is little room for the needs or wishes of anyone else, including his children. This parent has probably grown up believing that to survive he had to take care of himself. So he continues to play out that belief even decades after the disabling event occurred, all the while denying that he needs help in dealing with its effects.

On the other hand, parent victims who are willing to face past issues and get into treatment are sometimes dismissed by an adult child who feels his mother or father is dwelling on the past unnecessarily. In cases like this, the adult child probably inherited the same dysfunctional patterns and may feel threatened by the parent who wants to break the system and get well. I think it's important for parents to recognize that they are not always the perpetrators of the brokenness. Adult children who are victims can also make life difficult for their parents.

Being a Victim Blocks Communication. Communication implies the give and take of information, feelings, opinions, ideas. It includes active listening as well as speaking. Victims, however, who have lived in fear and shame for many years, are rarely able to communicate in a way that nurtures another person. They are generally stuck in their patterns of self-indulgent behavior and have difficulty embracing others, even members of their own family whom they love.

Reba complains about her adult son never listening to her. "He hurries in and out of here like there's a fire," she said. "I want him to visit a little bit." But Reba's idea of a visit is a one-sided monologue, according to her son, Sid. She asks a question and then answers it for herself. She may ask him about work and before he can reply she swats the air with her hand and launches into a self-deprecating statement about how he probably doesn't want to talk to her about such things because she wouldn't be able to understand him anyway. She follows that with a sermon on the old days and how people had simple jobs then and they didn't fly all over the world trying to earn money. They worked hard and then came home to their families. They had time for their mothers and fathers.

What is Sid supposed to do with that? He's just been scolded for not being a caring son. What adult child would want to spend time with such a person, even if she is his mother? But victims usually cannot see outside their own world. His mother is blind to her controlling patterns.

Being a Victim Blocks Confrontation. Victims also stay clear of confrontational issues with their children. They cannot accept honest feedback. They cannot express honest feelings. So when there is a confrontational situation in the family, they avoid it or override it with self-pity, or guilt-inducing statements to the other person.

Jane, for example, claims that her mother continually undermines her authority in front of her young children. When it's their bedtime she tells them they can have an extra half hour for storytime. She knows Jane does not permit the children to eat anything but fruit between meals. Yet she sneaks them crackers and chips anyway.

When Jane has brought up the subject, her mother waves her away as though she were a child. "She tells me I'm too rigid and no fun and that my children will grow up hating me for not letting them be normal."

Imagine the devastating effect this has on Jane and the confusing message this sends to her children.

Jane's mother is clearly violating her daughter's home and family life and is absolutely unwilling to be told about it. Jane may have no other choice but to take a long vacation from the relationship. This will deprive her of her mother's companionship, the children of their grandmother, and her mother of a relationship with all of them. And all because her mother is unwilling to be confronted about her violating behavior.

Being a Victim Blocks Friendship. One of the great blessings of relating to our adult children is friendship. The time for active parenting is behind us. Our sons and daughters have made it. We can now enjoy them as friends. For the victim, however, this is another area of challenge. Most victims have spent years in isolation, even when they lived with other people. They have learned to protect themselves, fend for themselves, and generally look out for their own welfare.

Victims either attempt to befriend everyone in sight because they are so needy, and thus drive people away. Or they clam up and don't allow anyone in, which intensifies their feelings of isolation. In the life of a victim, even one good friend is a rare commodity.

Flo did the former. When I met her she had been in a wheel

chair for a number of years, the result of an unfortunate accident. She was not only a victim of her physical state by then, but she was an emotional victim, as well, having been abused continually by her overbearing father. She was one of the most needy individuals I've ever known.

Shortly after we met she began sending me notes and cards and phoning me often to express how grateful she was that God had brought me into her life. She had been looking for a close friend all her life and she was sure I was the one.

I panicked. I did not feel "chosen." In fact, I felt smothered whenever I was with her. Yet I did not want to add to her already intense feelings of rejection. For awhile I discounted my own needs and emotions and spent a lot of time with her. But her needs soon overwhelmed me and I backed off rather suddenly. A couple of years ago I received a printed notice from her family. She had died following an illness, as I recall. I wondered if her death was as lonely an experience as her life had been. I felt truly sorry that I had been unable to be there for her in the way she had hoped.

As I now reflect on that relationship, I'm struck by two things: the ways in which victims prey on others, including their children, and the way they set themselves up for abuse or neglect. Flo lived with her youngest son who, in exchange for room and board and help with school tuition, drove her around, took care of the house, and generally looked after her needs. He was in his early thirties at the time I met them.

But during the couple of years I knew her, I watched her son's resentment surface and grow, until he got up the courage to move out. Flo had never been treated for her victimization, so well into her fifties she was still acting out the hurt and rejection and shame of the past. The opportunity for friendship with her son—who may have stayed on if she had respected him as an adult—and with me, had passed her by.

Being a Victim Blocks Intimacy. Victims are usually in such need themselves, they find it difficult to reach out to others in a way that produces warmth, vulnerability, and true intimacy. Many see life as a war zone and every encounter a skirmish at the very least and a battle at the most. Life is to be endured, not lived. Adult children are managed or ignored, depending on the grievances they hold against them, but never enjoyed.

Bart is a victim. He was raised in an orphanage in the Midwest, turned to alcohol as a teen, and has struggled with compulsive drinking most of his life since then. His two adult sons keep their distance. Their dad is so unpredictable that they don't want to risk exposing themselves or their families to his behavior.

Bart has sought intimacy through three marriages, all of which ended in divorce. He has lived a flamboyant lifestyle, spending money wildly and taking the family on extravagant trips, all in the hope that he could get close to someone. What he doesn't see is that one can't buy or create intimacy. It is something that springs naturally from two people who love, respect, and want to be together.

Being a Victim Blocks Spontaneity. Harold, a man of about 70, approached me after a church service one Sunday. He had read an article I had written on the importance of being there for friends and family. In addition to sending a card or gift for a wedding, graduation or birthday, I encouraged readers to be there, to be willing to see that their presence is more important than their presents.

With a twinkle in his eye, he needled me about how my article had caused him to break a custom he had practiced most of his adult life. This sounded serious. What had I done? He plowed on, unconcerned about my reaction.

He had been "feuding," as he put it, with his oldest son since the boy had left home at age seventeen. He was now thirty-seven. For the past twenty years, Harold had refused to go to any family gatherings where his son would be present. He said he had never "gotten on well" with his only brother either, so he had "a double good reason" to stay away. Harold had not only avoided family affairs, he avoided all social contact. He was suspicious of people, didn't like crowds, and was generally a recluse, living a life that was bound by ritual.

But when he read my article, something deep inside gave

way. He said he had never before thought about his presence as important. He had been more concerned with avoiding his son's and brother's presence. When he read that he could make a difference by showing up, by acknowledging those he had avoided for so long, he came alive. He told me that he suddenly saw for himself that being there is "at the very core of civility" as I had said in my article. Maybe, even for him, such an act could lead to a renewing of love and friendship and spiritual and emotional restoration, just as I had written.

His eyes glistened with tears as he continued to share the insights he had gleaned from the article, often quoting verbatim what I had written. It was very touching to be on the receiving end.

Here was a man who had been alienated from two of the most important people in his life, his only brother and his only son. He had blocked all spontaneity in his life because of the bitterness he held. But that day he took joy in telling me that he had jumped up out of his chair after reading the article and went straight to the phone, called his brother, and said, "I'll be there," in response to an invitation he had received earlier in the week. He ended the conversation by telling me that his son would be there too. "I have a lot of patching up to do," he said, "and the Lord willing, I plan to do it."

Being a Victim Blocks Spirituality. Being victimized by people usually leads to feeling victimized by God. Questions such as, "How could God let this happen to me?" "What kind of a god would let a child suffer the way I did?" can be healthy if we are really searching for understanding and struggling with pain and confusion. Blaming God, however, can stand in the way of receiving the healing God has for you. All roads to the Lord— prayer, worship, Communion, fellowship with believers—tend to shut down when we hold God responsible for man's decisions and actions. The Lord did not promise to keep all trouble away, but He did say He would be there with us as we walk through it. "Though I walk in the midst of trouble, You will revive me" (Ps. 138:7).

If ever anyone needed the love of God and the fellowship of

Jesus Christ, it is the victim. Only the Lord can heal us, restore us, transform us through the renewing of our minds so that we might be for our adult children a light on the hill.

BEING A VICTIM AS A FORM OF CONTROL

Victims use their victimization to control. They voice their anger, fear, fatigue, hunger, physical aches and pains, and mental anguish with such intensity that those around them respond without thinking.

Doug has only to wince and his grown daughter flies to his side. Is he tired, hungry, uncomfortable, afraid, she asks. What can she do to make him happy or safe or satisfied in some way, she wonders.

Martin uses his physical condition as a weapon in his relationship with his twin daughters. He also enjoys comparing the two, then telling each one separately that she's his favorite because she takes better care of him than her sister. Martin not only enjoys observing the conflict between the two women, but he reaps directly the benefits of their trying to outdo one another. As long as Martin is in control, he feels powerful. And when he feels powerful, he's content. Never mind the effect this destructive attitude and behavior continue to have on his children.

PORTRAIT OF A VICTIM

Anna, a soft-spoken eighty-six-year-old, has the loveliest large blue eyes I've ever seen. She is a person who has endured life rather than lived it. She worked hard, mothered hard, saved hard, prayed hard, and worried hard. The only thing she hasn't done is play hard.

But Anna made it possible for those around her to play, especially her sons and their families. When she's the hostess, there is always more food on the table than you can eat, tickets for a play or outing of some kind paid for ahead of time, reservations at a fine restaurant at least one night during your visit, and plenty of questions asked to be sure everyone is happy.

She wants to make certain her "kids"—two sons, fifty-five and fifty-eight—are fine and their families and friends are comfortable. Anna is someone I love very much. We always feel so well taken care of when she's in charge. But Anna rarely participates with us. She is so busy taking care of everyone else that she has little inclination left to join the fun.

Anna is a victim. She married at age 16 to get away from a family where she felt unwanted, ignored and abused. Her father, a tailor who emigrated from Germany when he was a young man, took care of others, often to the detriment of his own family. He extended so much credit to his customers over the years, his children often did without necessities. Her mother was an emotionally distant woman, as Anna remembers her.

"No one ever hugged or kissed me or held me," she told her oldest son. Her husband, Carl, also had a difficult childhood. His father died when Carl was an adolescent. Things were never the same for him after that.

Anna and Carl celebrated their 64th wedding anniversary this year. That's an accomplishment by anyone's standards, especially today where one in two marriages end in divorce. Yet, according to Anna, she and Carl never bonded. She has felt alone all her life despite being married. To feel alone in the presence of another, as many people know, is one of the most devastating emotional experiences one can have.

Today Anna and her husband live with their youngest son and his family in Nebraska. She acknowledges their kindness to her, but she also claims she's already lived longer than she expected or wanted to, and now she feels like a burden, something she never wanted for herself or her sons.

I'm not sure Anna has ever really wanted to live or ever had an opportunity to do so. She admits to a deep distrust of people, feels insecure most of the time, and she speaks in a negative manner about almost everything—even though she always wants the best for her family and does what she can to provide it. But nothing is ever enough. Anna believes she's not enough. Her hospitality is not enough. Her appearance, behavior, dress, actions, abilities—you name it—are never, ever enough in her eyes.

Denial, isolation, control, and misplaced guilt result in her feeling hopeless and helpless most of the time. She is completely out of touch with any personal power. Yet, at the same time, Anna, like most victims, has more power than she's likely to ever realize.

Victims, by definition, wield tremendous power. Spouses hover over them, fight with them, and live with them. Sons and daughters worry about them, help them, complain about them, and take them on. Grandchildren whisper behind their backs and tiptoe in their presence. Friends come, go, come again, offer advice, provide a listening ear. Victims manage to get attention any way they can. Yet they're still not happy because no amount of anything is ever enough.

"I never could think straight," says Anna when discussing a mistake she made. "I never did learn to cook right," she adds, while setting the table. "We're just small town people," she says of her new life in the city. "City people don't want us around."

After a visit to the local Seniors club, she reported how no one there said hello. "They're cold, unfriendly," she said. When I asked if she introduced herself to anyone, she appeared to be amazed by the question. Apparently it had not occurred to her to make the first move. She felt it was someone else's place to make her feel welcome. "We're old people. No one wants to put up with us."

You cannot win with Anna. She can outwit anyone when it comes to negative comments, character evaluations, personal criticism, or lifestyle analysis. She is a woman in intense personal pain, in great need of inner healing, yet believing that she is not worthy of the slightest care. Anna considers herself ineligible for life's blessings and feels guilty for her thoughts and feelings.

To be a victim is to be a dichotomy. The very thing she craves she pushes away. To be in relationship with a victim is to be in contention twenty-four hours a day. No amount of convincing, cajoling, comforting, or confronting will budge a victim from his or her self-appointed perch. Life is a burden, and no one is going to tell him or her otherwise.

LETTING GO OF BEING A VICTIM

You may be seeing some familiar patterns in yourself as you read about victims in this chapter. Perhaps you are remembering incidents in your childhood where you were shamed, blamed, and belittled. Or maybe you were violated spiritually or physically. Parents and teachers and others in authority may have caused you to feel guilty for expressing even your most basic needs for love and comfort, for food and clothing, for play, for sleep, for time alone.

Or perhaps someone in your home abused alcohol or money or food and you were the recipient of the mood swings that occurred during these addictive cycles. Maybe you grew up and began abusing these same substances to cover up your pain or to find favor with these fundamental people in your life.

Victimization can occur in a few moments. It can occur over a long period of time. Keep in mind that victims experience destruction at the foundation of who they are. And that destruction creates hindrance to the living of life.

If you feel this applies to you in some way, take a deep breath. It can be a pretty scary experience at first. Then acknowledge yourself for being willing to look at the truth about your life. Healing will not come quickly or easily, but it can come. Help is available. And the Lord will see you through it. We can count on His promise that He will never leave us nor forsake us. (Heb. 13:5)

Words To Consider—Actions To Take

• "Cast your burden on the Lord, and He shall sustain you" (Ps. 55:22). Bring your newfound awareness to Jesus and ask Him to lead you as you seek insight and healing for yourself so you can then move toward the healing you desire with your children.

• Think about the ways in which your behavior has influenced your children and how it has affected your relationship with them. Has your fear, your anger, your self-pity driven them away? Are you over-focused on your own needs, wishes, problems, and complaints? Make a list of the things you observe about yourself. If you feel at a loss in this area, think about what you observed about your parents. Then look through your own life for similar behaviors.

• In Psalms 127:3, we are told that our children are a heritage of the Lord. They are His gift to us. They are "like arrows in the hand of a warrior" (Ps. 127:4). Do we want to continue to give credence to beliefs and behavior that keep our children at a distance?

• "It is your Father's good pleasure to give you the kingdom" (Luke 12:32). Included in that kingdom is the love and fellowship of our children. It is God's pleasure to bring us into harmony with our sons and daughters. Meditate on that thought. God works with us to mend, restore, and rebuild those vital relationships.

• Victims tire easily. They are used to being overwhelmed and overpowered. But the Lord says, "let us not grow weary while doing good, for in due season we shall reap if we do not lose heart" (Gal. 6:9). Here, God is telling us that we are partners with Him in reaping the harvest of health He has for us in every area of our lives.

LOOKING WITHIN

Parents who identify themselves as victims can relate to many of these statements:

1. I often feel overwhelmed by people and by life experiences.
2. I feel unsafe in the world. I do not trust people.
3. I prefer being alone to being with others.
4. I feel alienated from my children. I see myself as a burden to them.
5. Nothing ever works out for me. I'm just a loser.
6. I feel tired most of the time.
7. I have trouble focusing on necessary daily tasks.
8. I use food, money, prescription medications, alcohol, or other substances to make myself feel better.

Chapter Six

The MANIPULATOR

"I'm right, don't you agree? I mean if he talked to you that way, wouldn't you defend yourself the way I did?" Jane enlists her daughter's support with such questions each time Jane has an altercation with her son, who she believes deliberately shuts her out.

Roberto uses a different tactic. "Who do you think you are? Acting like Miss High and Mighty. Who gave you a good home and food on the table all those years when you were growing up?" Roberto's adult daughter said that whenever she disagrees with her father, he loves to remind her of the simple beginnings he provided.

Arlene has a more beguiling, but no less destructive way of dealing with her thirty-year old son who lives about 500 miles from his parents' home. "Anthony, honey," she'll say, "Christmas won't be the same without you. I just can't get into the spirit unless all my children are around me at this special time."

If he persists in declining the invitation, she hauls out her big guns. "The others are coming," she'll stress. "You've just got to be here too—no matter what. I rarely ask a favor of you, honey. Surely you can grant me this one wish." And if he remains firm or wavers even a little bit, she pounces fast and hard. "The way my health is we never know when it might be our last holiday together."

Can Anthony resist her blows? Not easily and sometimes not

at all. His mother is smooth. She's swift. And she knows how and when to make her move. Anthony admits that he has yet to defeat her. "But it's coming to that," he said with deliberation, as if trying to convince himself.

Sound familiar? Maybe you've been on the receiving end of such blows. Your parents may have manipulated you during your earlier life, and now, you may use similar tactics with your adult children. Like all abusive behaviors, manipulation is hurting, humiliating, and at times downright destructive.

MORE THAN A DIFFERENCE OF OPINION

Harold Smith, in his book *You and Your Parents,* claims that, "Just as there is no such thing as an insignificant cancer cell, so there is no such thing as an insignificant insult."[1] Some adult children experience sudden physical and emotional stress just thinking about being with parents who manipulate them.

Colitis, diarrhea, migraine headaches, tension in the neck and shoulders are among the most common physiological reactions. Such conditions can last for days following a family visit. Children and mates of the wounded are also affected. They have to live with men and women who slam doors, bury themselves in bed, or who go over and over the hurtful dialogue.

Many parents who perpetrate such behavior are often shameless about it. They are totally unconscious of how damaging their remarks can be. Others know exactly what they're doing and go ahead anyway. Their interactions with their children are more than a simple difference of opinion. These cruel-spirited individuals intend to wound and they do. Their own lives may be so empty that the only excitement they experience centers on making others miserable, even if those people are their own children.

I don't believe this is the norm. But I think it's fair to acknowledge that such people do exist, and it's likely that they did not become this way in a vacuum. They were probably manipulated in a deeply hurtful way when they were growing up.

As you read this section you may be squirming a bit within. Perhaps you see yourself in these examples, and perhaps you also recall being the victim of manipulative parents. If your parents are still alive you may endure their manipulation even now.

MANIPULATORS BEGET MANIPULATORS

That is the case with Virginia, a sixty-year-old woman I spoke with. She continues to be manipulated by her eighty-five-year-old father who is bedridden in an extended care facility. His emotional power over Virginia is frightening. If even one day passes without her customary phone call or one week without the expected visit, he abuses her with words—choice words that he knows can always get to her.

One childhood experience in particular has haunted her through the decades, and her father seems to delight in bringing it up whenever he feels neglected. Virginia had been left in charge of her three-year-old sister one day while her mother walked to the neighborhood market. The child dashed into the street in front of their house to retrieve a ball, just as a milk truck was turning the corner. Neither the driver nor the child saw one another. She was struck instantly and died at the scene. Virginia has lived with the guilt of that experience everyday since.

"He loves to remind me that if I hadn't been so selfish and had been more attentive, my sister would not have died," said Virginia choking back tears. "And now if I don't pay attention to him he says he could die and it will be on my conscience." One can only imagine the layers of resentment, anger, and shame that have built up inside Virginia after decades of such abuse.

One of the sad results of this treatment, however, has been Virginia's tendency toward manipulating her own children. She promised herself she would never do to her sons what her father did to her. "Yet there are times when I know I do the same thing," she said, "maybe not to the same degree, but I do manipulate them," she admitted. "I've never been able to express my needs directly."

Little wonder, with a father who has never encouraged her to be a full person.

Perhaps you are now looking more carefully at your behavior

with your adult children, or at how your parents manipulated (or still manipulate) you with words and actions.

COMMON CHARACTERISTICS OF A MANIPULATOR

1. Manipulators have difficulty facing reality. Parents who manipulate their adult children generally operate in denial of what is true right now. They do not accept the fact that their sons and daughters have grown up. They try to hold onto them by cajoling, reminding, teasing, organizing, advising, and managing them in whatever way they can.

Randall's mother is a good example of someone who has difficulty facing reality. Her son has repeatedly asked her to call him Randall, not Randy, his childhood nickname. But she ignores his request claiming, "You'll always be Randy to me. You're my little boy, and I don't care who knows it." Then she goes into a long dissertation about how precious he is to her and how she just can't imagine not being able to use this "pet name."

Randall said he fumes everytime they're together because he knows she'll ignore his wishes and treat him like a child of seven or eight instead of the 37-year old adult son he now is. "My sister thinks I'm making too big a deal out of it. She says Mom's older and set in her ways, and since she's always called me Randy, why try to change her now."

But to Randall it's more than a difference in name preference. "This is a good example of how it's always been between us," he said. "She refuses to face reality. She's never taken me seriously at any point in my life. No matter how much I've talked to her or shown her why it's important to me for her to respect me as a person, she manages to twist the conversation in such a way that I look like the bad guy who is unappreciative of such a dedicated mother."

2. Manipulators have a problem expressing their needs directly. Marcy's mother is the champion manipulator according to this forty-year-old daughter. "It's impossible for her to ask for what she wants or to express her feelings honestly," Marcy said, sharing a recent example.

"Mom called last week to ask me if my son had received the

check she sent him for his birthday. Brad is nineteen and lives at college in another state, so I wouldn't necessarily know if he got the check or not. I told her I didn't know, then suggested she call him if she was concerned about it. "She made up some excuse about not wanting him to think she was looking for a thank you note. I knew right then that that was exactly what she was looking for. 'Mom, I can see why you would want to be thanked,' I said. 'If you remembered his birthday you deserve a thank you note.'

"She flat out denied it, saying she just wanted to be sure the check had arrived safely and she hoped I wasn't offended by her call. She certainly wasn't suggesting that I had raised him wrong by not instilling in him the importance of sending thank you notes."

Marcy laughed at that point and said, "If I hadn't had more savvy, I'd have taken her bait. But no more. I'm on to her manipulative comments. I simply told her that I hadn't taken anything she said personally, that I knew the incident with the check was between her and my son, and I hoped she'd get it cleared up to her satisfaction. Needless to say, the conversation ended pretty quickly after that."

3. Manipulators use guilt and shame to avoid personal responsibility.
Fred, who recently retired from a welding job, likes to remind his adult children of how hard he worked and sweated for them the past forty years. Two of his sons are certified accountants and his only daughter is a chemist. All three are grateful for the personal sacrifices he made to send them to college—an opportunity his parents could not provide for him.

"I wonder if he's jealous of us," his daughter said, with some reservation. "He seems proud of us on the one hand, but kind of resentful on the other—like our lives turned out and his didn't and he doesn't want us to forget it for a minute."

His son Emile said he feels reluctant to talk about his work with his dad because he always turns the conversation back to himself and how hard he worked and how little he had. He reminds me of the old Ford he drove for twelve years, and then refs to the fact that I get a new car every three or four years and on and on. We never get past what he did for us. I'm exhausted at the end of each visit. All I feel is shame and guilt—as if I'm responsible in some way for him not having the life he wanted." Fred is avoiding taking responsibility for the sacrifices and choices he made for his children. No one *made* him do anything.

4. Manipulators explode at the slightest sign of confrontation. "I don't have to sit here and listen to you run off at the mouth."

"Don't you talk to me like that, young lady. I'm still your mother."

"Don't tell me about your feelings. What do you know about pain? I'll tell you what—nothing—that's what."

"How dare you speak to me in that tone of voice. Respect. That's what you need. Respect for your elders. I raised you better than this."

Have you ever spoken this way to your children when you felt threatened by their advances? Or did your parents dismiss your strong emotion with similar phrases? No one likes to be confronted, but manipulators especially dislike it. They cannot handle confrontation because it challenges them to look at their own lives, to see where they have failed or wounded another human being. And when that other human being is one of their children, the pain of facing the truth is almost unbearable.

To be confronted requires courage and strength, the willingness to listen to another's point of view, and to hear and acknowledge his or her feelings without defending one's self or dismissing the other person. This is not easy for any of us, but it is almost impossible for the manipulator whose agenda is built on pretense.

5. Manipulators use the past to control present behavior. Rhonda was raised a Baptist but during her twenties she felt spiritually hungry and decided to investigate a new charismatic denomination in California where she had moved following her graduation from college. Her father has never let

her forget this "desertion." He has taken her decision as a personal attack against him. Now whenever anything in her life goes wrong, he brings up this decision and uses it to manipulate her. "He can't separate our relationship from my desire to make a wise decision for my own life," she said. "He told me that I've brought shame to past and present generations by divorcing myself from the Baptist tradition.

"He is so melodramatic it makes me sick. It's not as if I joined a cult or became an atheist," she said. "I'm still a Christian. I believe in Jesus Christ. I just feel more comfortable in a less traditional environment. I don't ridicule his choice. But he seems to think he's still the authority figure in my life, and if I don't do it his way then I'm a deserter."

Rhonda's father pouts, punishes her with silence, and embarrasses her in front of other family members by referring to her as a "Baptist basher" or a "crazy charismatic." According to Rhonda, her father is completely unwilling to release her to her own life. "I get the feeling that he feels guilty if I deviate in any way from the way he raised me—as though it's a direct reflection on him."

HOW MANIPULATING AFFECTS YOUR RELATIONSHIP WITH YOUR ADULT CHILDREN

Manipulation hurts everyone involved. Parents who don't get their way with a few well-chosen words usually escalate their tactics. They use repetition, silence, anger, verbal abuse, and brooding to wear down their opponent. Some even stoop to bribes. They give or withhold monetary and other rewards if they don't succeed.

After an encounter with such parents, adult children are worn down and exhausted. They feel frustrated, furious, and futile over the lack of respect they receive. Some vow never again to put themselves in a situation like this. Sometimes, weeks, months, even years go by without contact. Manipulative parents overwhelm. And adult child victims feel too vulnerable in their presence—so they withdraw rather than subject themselves to this mistreatment.

Manipulating Blocks Communication. "I've had to withdraw from my father at times," said Harriet. "Our lack of communication centers around two major themes: money and religion. He can't seem to resist advising me. I always feel on the defensive in our conversations. I'm once again the little girl who must explain why I spent my allowance on candy bars and why I was so bold as to accompany a friend to her church, which is different than mine."

Harriet is a thirty-seven-year-old mother of four with many years of experience raising a family, running a household, and starting a career in real estate. "When I speak to my father about money, though, I feel like a child," she said.

"Too often I give in and tell him more than I want to. But I also have to assume some of the blame. I don't speak up for myself soon enough."

I can relate to Harriet. My father and I have had some challenging conversations about the same topics. I've realized in recent months, however, that I cannot expect him or anyone to know my limits until I'm clear about them myself. I have a lot of work still to do in this area.

Manipulating Blocks Confrontation. One mother I know has not heard from her son in six months following an episode at a family dinner when the mother suggested he get into treatment for his weight problem. It would have been one thing if she had spoken to him privately and lovingly, expressing her concern about his health.

But instead she manipulated him by saying in her sweetest, most controlling voice while in the buffet line, "Honey, did Marie [his wife] tell you about the new program for overeaters at Hillside Hospital? I know you've been struggling with your weight. Not that it's any of my business. I realize you're a grown man. But then I put myself in your place and decided that if I had a problem and you knew something that could help me, I'd certainly want you to tell me about it."

John's wife, Marie, felt guilty by implication, when in truth she had nothing to do with it. Her mother-in-law had phoned her after seeing the hospital ad on television and suggested that she tell John about it. Marie declined, saying she was uncomfortable dropping hints. John knew he had a problem with food and she felt it was up to him to ask for help if he wanted it.

Notice how John's mother worked Marie into her monologue—another way to manipulate her son into taking an action that was none of her business.

Manipulating Blocks Friendship. Manipulative behavior is ultimately disrespectful and deceitful. Parents who continue to practice it keep their children from relating to them as friends. And everyone loses because of it.

"I would love to be close to my mother," said Marianne. "I'm so jealous when I see some of my friends with their moms. They garden or cook together. Some are in the same profession. One friend and her mother are flying to Mexico City next summer for a month. They both want to learn more Spanish. They're making plans now—like two friends. It's so neat to hear about it. I could never do something like that with my mother. She'd treat me like a little girl the entire time and then try to make it sound as if her concern is for my own good."

Manipulating Blocks Intimacy. Lloyd has a problem with intimacy. "He's about as far away from his feelings as the North Pole from the South Pole," said his sister. She has watched from the sidelines as her brother manipulates his way through life, constantly saying one thing but meaning another. "His life is filled with hidden agendas," she said. "He's the most lonely man I've ever known."

According to his sister, Lloyd makes jokes about everything. Nothing is off limits to his bizarre sense of humor. And when his only child, a grown daughter, cringes at the sound of one more rude or crude remark he accuses her of being uptight and no fun. He speaks to others about her while she is in the same room. "Crissy is such a stick. Look at her. Takes life so seriously. She certainly doesn't take after her dad. I just like to have a good time. What's wrong with that?"

Twenty-five-year old Crissy, on the other hand, as much as she hates her father's behavior, longs for some real contact with him, a warm hug, a tender embrace, a loving word, but he's so caught up being the family clown that no one can get close.

Manipulating Blocks Spontaneity. Wes has always lived "by the book." He eats, sleeps, exercises, does chores, even watches TV according to a rigid schedule that hasn't changed in years. His son Rex thought they would have more time together once his dad retired but nothing has changed in the three years since his father left his job as a mail carrier.

"If I ask him to go sailing or to meet me for lunch when I'm in his part of town, he can't handle it. He snaps at me about calling him at the last minute. I don't think of it that way. I'm just being spontaneous."

But as Rex talked on he revealed that his father has always maintained an inflexible schedule. Rex's mother once told her son that she could set her watch by Lloyd's habits. Breakfast at eight, newspaper at nine, lunch at twelve and so forth. When Rex and his brother were growing up, it was no different.

"We could never do anything as a family on the spur of the moment," he said, "like go to the beach or take a bike ride. And if we begged him to change his mind, he turned things around and accused us of being selfish. If it wasn't part of his agenda we couldn't do it. The only time I remember having fun with him was when he took us to a baseball game or to a gun show. Those were his hobbies, and we got to go along."

Manipulating Blocks Spirituality. Manipulators not only twist situations, circumstances, and words for their own benefit, they also manipulate the Word of God, often quoting Scripture out of context in order to control others.

Ruth said her mother prides herself on being a "prayer warrior" and "living by the Word." But she can't let it rest there. She has made a career of broadcasting her spiritual life to anyone who will listen. "Actually, she's a very wounded person," said Ruth. "She grew up in an alcoholic home and she's never come to terms with how devastating it was for her. She took refuge in her relationship with the Lord, but she's never sought counseling or healing for all that pain."

Ruth said her mother loves to spout Scripture to the annoyance of all her children. If something goes wrong in one of their lives, she's quick to say such things as "The Lord giveth; the Lord taketh away," or "Don't lean on your own understanding; lean on the Lord's."

It sounds as if Ruth's mother has had to construct an elaborate network of manipulative behaviors just to survive. The Bible has become one more weapon in her arsenal, designed to keep people and the pain they may produce—at a safe distance. The sad result is that manipulators like Ruth's mother, perhaps unknowingly, also keep themselves away from God at the same time.

MANIPULATING AS A FORM OF CONTROL

A manipulator is a master of control. If he doesn't like what someone said or the way he said it, he simply twists the words, the tone, or the delivery in such a way that makes him look good and the other person look bad.

If an adult child doesn't come home for a family event the manipulator controls his disappointment through accusation. "Our anniversary won't be the same without Jerry. But what does he care? He's always been a self-centered person and he hasn't changed."

Manipulators control their relationships with bribes. "I picked up some oranges at the farmstand. I know how much you like fresh-squeezed juice. When can you stop by to pick them up?" Nothing is beyond the control of a manipulator.

PORTRAIT OF A MANIPULATOR

Louise admitted that she was manipulated by her parents and she has sometimes manipulated her daughters. After listening to her story I could understand how this came about. Raised in a home with a retarded brother and a mother who had a long history of mental illness, Louise was never encouraged to express herself honestly. She learned at an early age to manipulate her environment and her parents in order to get her needs met.

"I remember my mother and father telling me one thing then doing another," she said. "For example, we'd go to the beach with the understanding that I could be home by a certain time for a date I had. But when we got there they'd try and keep me from going home. If I reminded them of their promise they'd manipulate the situation so I'd be the bad one—the one who broke the commitment."

Louise's mother also withdrew gifts and rewards in order to manipulate their relationship. "She beat me up emotionally for days on end," said Louise. "She gave me things, then took them away. I received a hope chest when I graduated from high school. But then she got mad at me for something I did and she took it away. To this day I never got it back. She still has it. That was a pattern with my mother. She never did what she said she'd do. So I learned not to count on her."

Louise said she lived her entire life in the negative lane. "My father never interacted with me. And my mother's happy moments were so brief I can hardly remember them. I clung to those few times when she acted normal. As I look back, I probably tried to make her normal all my life. I was forty years old before I realized she was really sick and I couldn't make her well."

Louise had such poor parent modeling that she relied on books and counseling when she became a parent herself after an early marriage. Today, as the divorced mother of two adult daughters, Marguerite, twenty-one, and Lynn, nineteen, and the grandmother of a two-year-old girl, Louise is coming to terms with her role as mother and her relationship with her children.

The process is ongoing. Lynn, the younger daughter, is in college and she and Louise are still healing the fracture in their relationship that occurred twelve years ago. Louise was divorced from her husband, and the two girls remained with him. It's been a slow and painful transition. They have not had the time together that Louise has wanted.

"After the divorce my girls lived with their dad because I was in no shape emotionally to be with them," she said. "Yet that loss is one I don't think I can ever replace. Not being there on a daily basis, seeing them grow up, and participating with them in little things at school and church were probably the most difficult times I ever faced.

"I look at that everyday. I have to deal with it and say, 'Okay that was the best I could do at that time.' But I don't feel I'll ever be totally healed from that loss. Rationally, I know I couldn't change it, but emotionally it still hurts. I was an absent parent and I see the results of that loss in their lives today. That part is really hard on me."

Louise said her pain is particularly restimulated when Marguerite and Lynn become involved in things she believes would not have been attractive if they had lived with her. Drugs, teen pregnancy, friends she didn't feel good about have all added to the pain in their relationships.

In addition, they didn't have the quality family time they deserved. "They never had a consistent family dinner because their dad was always working," she said. "They didn't gather around the table the way we did when we were all together. We've all lost."

Despite the loss, however, Louise admits that she enjoys her daughters more now than she did when they were young. "There was always conflict in my marriage," she said, "so it was difficult for me to enjoy being a parent. Today I understand what it means to be a mother, and I want to take an active part in their lives."

Louise, however, sees that trying to make up for lost time is another form of manipulating. "Those years are gone," she said solemnly. "I've had to adjust my thinking. I can't treat adult women like young children."

Her oldest daughter, Marguerite, came to live with her while she was expecting her baby and stayed on for two years. That time of togetherness held a mixture of blessing and pain for both of them. "I had to stop myself from going back to when she was nine and trying to pick up where I left off. It couldn't be done," said Louise. "She was nineteen by then and was about to have a child of her own. Looking at her as an adult but thinking of her as a little kid put me in a lot of confusion."

Louise recognizes now that some of the things she wanted to do for Marguerite had more to do with her own needs than what was best for her daughter. "I wanted us to have dinner together at least a few nights a week and I wanted her to help with household chores, but she was more interested in having her friends around. And she didn't know the first thing about being a mother."

Louise was continually confronted with the lack in her daughter's life—a lack that she believes would not have existed if she had been on board to parent her during the lost years. "It was hard for me to come home at night and see her friends there. She seemed to prefer them to me. I felt as though my home was no longer mine. That created conflict between us and we got in a lot of disagreements. Now that she and my granddaughter are living on their own I'm hoping that some of the things I said and did with her during our two years together will help her."

Despite the conflict between them, however, Louise admitted that it was difficult for her when Marguerite moved out. "I manipulated her into staying longer than she should have. I asked her if she was sure she wanted to leave. Was she ready? Was this the right time? Maybe the roommate she picked wasn't quite right for her and so on. I manipulated her into staying because of my inability to let her go. I tried to rescue her from making a mistake. But now I realize maybe that's what she needed to learn."

Louise's relationship with her younger daughter has also been filled with pain. For a long time she did not want to be with her mother because she wasn't used to her.

"She was only seven when her dad and I separated," said Louise. "I know I tried too hard with her. I wanted to mend the years we were apart. Maybe she felt I abandoned her. She hasn't experienced me as a mother in twelve years. At times I felt she had written me off. She may have been thinking I left her and now she'll take her own time to come to me. But since she's been away at college, she seems more interested in who I am. I notice as we talk and share that we're beginning to communicate a little better. She's in counseling now and so am I. I think she's beginning to understand what I've been through and that's been good for both of us."

In the midst of all this turmoil, Louise went back to school at night for two years and earned her B.A. She has since counseled other women who have experienced the pain of divorce and separation from their children, and she has been an encouraging example to me as my prayer partner and dear friend.

CORINNE'S STORY

"Manipulating and caretaking are my primary addictions," said Corinne, a sixty-three-year-old woman who sees herself as "a woman of God, a Christian woman, a woman in process. And I'm thankful for that," she added.

As the mother of two young men and two young women, Corinne has come up against a number of challenges that have led her to participate in a twelve-step program based on the model of Alcoholics Anonymous. "My healing process has focused mainly around my relationship with our sons," she said. "It's been very difficult."

By contrast, she has an honest, more open relationship with her daughters. "When I decided to get help," she said, "they weren't surprised. They were patient. They knew, as I did, that God wasn't finished with me yet."

But that was not the case with her sons. "I got into recovery," she said, "because I woke up one morning and realized I had a druggie living in our house. For years I didn't see my son this way. I thought he was cute and funny. His behavior was just part of his personality."

Corinne said he was able to laugh his way out of a bad situation, and she fell for it. But that day she was suddenly aware of the problem. "I knew there was something very wrong, and through a set of circumstances I discovered he was involved with drugs."

The family held an intervention where together with a professional counselor family members confronted him about his drug abuse and he agreed to go into treatment at the McDonald Center in La Jolla, California.

During Family Week at the Center, Corinne stood up and introduced herself as a co-dependent, someone who unwittingly supports or enables another person to practice a destructive habit. "I was uncomfortable with that label," she said. "I thought it was a joke, but then little by little as I gathered information, I realized I was part of the problem."

That new insight also led Corinne to look at some of the issues she had with her other son who was a workaholic. Manipulating, controlling and caretaking were part of the picture with that child, as well. "I used to excuse them away," she said. "'Isn't that mothering?' I'd ask myself. In fact, I thought I was the world's best mother. And I wanted my kids to prove it by performing just right."

Today Corinne speaks about her flaws with humility and candor. "It feels good, really freeing," she said, "to admit these things about myself. I used to see my life through a glass darkly. Now I can clearly see my motives and I can check them. They're God-driven now instead of Corinne-driven. I feel honest and human."

Corinne sees her relationship with her children today as a blessing. "We're friends," she said. "My son with the drug addiction is in total recovery now, after three relapses, and so our level of communication is more real. I consider it a privilege to have an adult relationship with him.

"Last year he and I walked over to the beach alone. I told him I had some things to say, and I wanted him to hear me out—not to interrupt or rescue me. He looked me straight in the eye and listened." Corinne used that occasion to tell her son how she had been wrong, how she had hurt him, and she asked his forgiveness. "It was a powerful experience," she said.

With a twinkle in her eye, she then confessed that "the very next day I jumped back into my Mom role and had a terrific temper tantrum right in front of him and his son. But then I had an opportunity to promptly admit I was wrong."

For Corinne, the twelve-step support program is "God-breathed. It's a way of life for me," she said. And she continues to need and draw on that support because there is "tremendous estrangement" in her relationship with her other son.

"He's a workaholic, and his wife is an overeater. Unfortunately, I made several attempts to 'fix her'—which was not my place. It was very badly advised. When I did make amends to both of them, they did not receive it well. They both decided to withdraw from our lives. My daughter-in-law told me she felt she had never measured up to my standards, and my son said he was tired of being kicked."

This has been an area of great pain for Corinne and her husband. And it has intensified because her husband, who is not in recovery, continues making unwelcome attempts at reconciliation. "They are choosing to distance themselves," she said, "and he won't accept it. They never respond, but he keeps trying. I told him that I wished he could accept it. They're making their own choice about this. I think we need to give them that freedom and trust God to work it out. But my husband looked at me and said, 'I am not a quitter!' That's where he's at in his life," said Corinne, "and I guess I have to let him do his thing."

Corinne's sadness was evident in her eyes as she spoke about her son and his wife. "They live quite close," she said, "yet they're rarely able to spend time with us and the rest of the family. I feel lonely, bereft, and hurt a lot over this. There are also two precious grandchildren involved."

Then as an afterthought, she added, "Maybe we expect too much. I don't know. We do see them on big holidays and we send birthday cards and Christmas gifts. But I don't feel as loved and cared about by them as I do with my other children. For example, this past summer I had a physical problem and then our anniversary came and went without any communication from them."

Corinne has attempted to talk about this with her son and daughter-in-law. "I told him I'm through mothering him, that I just want to be friends. I don't have to be his best friend, but I would like us to relate as adults. He said he wasn't sure, and she said she'd try." Meanwhile there has been little change in the relationship. "The end of that chapter hasn't been written yet," said Corinne, thoughtfully.

As she reflected on the past, she acknowledged that one of the most challenging aspects of those early years was "realizing we weren't a perfect family. We set ourselves up for this role— the Christian lighthouse of the west—and the community set us up too," she added. Then laughing at the absurdity she added, "And we bought into it!"

Corinne now sees the importance of turning to one's past for information about the present. "I started to get well when I began digging into my own family history," she said, "and came face-to-face with how my parents raised me." Unfortunately, her mother and father had died by then so she couldn't talk with them about her childhood. "I'm very covetous of people who can go back to their families and straighten out some gray areas," she added.

"It really helped me to realize my childhood family wasn't perfect either. We were the victims of other peoples' problems. My grandparents, for example, were kind of weird in their own way. And my parents were role models for me—both good and bad. I don't have to blame them. I just want to understand some things."

Corinne talked about her mother for a moment. "She was a master controller—a master," she said, emphasizing the last word. "My father was a passive person—to a point. He seemed to need my mother to control his life. He was the planner and the party person."

But Corinne says her mother was the one who taught her how to control her family. "She told me one time that my children were putty in my hands. Pretty heavy, don't you think?"

I agreed.

"I remember a time when she visited us when I was a young mother," said Corinne. "My first son was about a year old, and he had the most beautiful curly hair. She made a big scene about how we had to get those curls cut because she wanted him to be a man. I was only nineteen at the time and thought my mother knew best, even though I was seething with resentment. I knew she was trying to run my life but I didn't know how to change it.

"So the two of us marched that little boy to the barber shop and had his curls cut off. That is still a very sensitive subject with me—even today. But it also has given me insight into my controlling issues. My mother was a good model in many ways, but the control issue I lay right at her feet."

Corinne dug a little deeper and discovered that manipulation was perhaps her mother's only way out of a life where she felt stifled by her own parents.

"When I think of other parents who are in painful relationships with their children because of manipulation and control, I want to say, 'Face your own issues first.' I have found that as I work on my own life, the people around me have to face their issues."

Corinne acknowledged the many wonderful self-help books and support programs available now. "Our parents didn't have access to all this," she said. "And we didn't have this information when we were young parents. I honestly thank God for all of it," she said with a sigh of relief.

Corinne and her husband pray for their children daily and she prays alone during her morning walk. She also draws strength from reading daily meditations.

LETTING GO OF MANIPULATING

If you see yourself or your adult children in any of these scenarios you may be feeling a bit squeamish right now. Manipulating is not a behavior any of us likes to claim. I've caught myself in both camps at times—manipulating and being manipulated. It's a difficult cycle to break—especially for those of us who have been taught to keep our emotions in check, to be "nice," to avoid making a scene. This dishonest and destructive behavior crops up, often without thinking.

But if we're sincere in our desire to become aware of it and eventually to rid ourselves of it we can take some specific steps now.

Words To Consider—Actions To Take

• "You shall not steal, nor deal falsely, nor lie to one another" (Lev. 19:11). These are strong words. Perhaps you don't think of yourself as someone who steals or deals falsely with your children. But in truth, manipulating is a form of stealing and lying. And it is dealing falsely with another person. Manipulators use words and gestures and voice inflections to create a desired response.

Examine your motives. What are your children's weak spots? What buzz words do you use to get what you want? "Honey, please, just this once. Do it for me." "This could be our last reunion. You've got to come." Look in a mirror as you speak. Pay attention to the look in your eye, the way you use your hands, the tone of voice. Practice asking for what you want in a straightforward, nonmanipulative manner. And ask your children to stop you when they hear you resort to your old way of responding.

• "If any of you lacks wisdom, let him ask of God, who gives to all liberally and without reproach, and it shall be given to him" (James 1:5). What a beautiful invitation—even mandate—from the Lord. We do not have to depend on ourselves for the answers. We can and should ask for wisdom, and we will receive it. We do not have to continue to drive away our children with our manipulative behavior. God wants to heal us of it. He wants to restore our relationships. He will grant us the wisdom we need, if we but ask.

• "In quietness and confidence shall be your strength" (Isa. 30:15). When your children disagree with you, turn down an invitation, or object to some action you take, practice being silent for a moment—or more. Trust God to give you peace. Instead of trying to manipulate your children or the situation, just let it be. If your son cannot or does not wish to come home for Christmas, stop for a moment. Practice new behavior. Thank him for responding, express your love, and wish him a joyful day. End there. Avoid carrying on as you have in the past, choosing words and voice inflections to gain control and instill guilt.

If you disagree with or disapprove of some aspect of your children's life, practice keeping your opinion to yourself unless they ask for it. Be still and find your strength in the quietness.

LOOKING WITHIN

Parents who identify themselves as manipulators can relate to many of these statements:

1. I often blame my children for my own inadequacies.

2. I trivialize my children's actions and decisions without thinking about the consequences.

3. I avoid my children's confrontation because I fear their disapproval.

4. I have trouble expressing my feelings honestly and directly.

5. I use guilt and shame to get what I need and want.

6. I feel guilty and angry when my children appear to reject my values.

7. I believe my children owe me their respect.

8. I tend to dwell on the past and have difficulty living in the present.

Chapter Seven

THE CRITIC

I learned an important lesson about criticism in my early years as a freelance writer. A man I wrote for obviously liked my work. He hired me for a number of jobs. He rarely edited anything I turned in, and a script I wrote for an educational film he produced won an award at an international film festival. Yet, he had difficulty expressing in words the acknowledgement and appreciation I felt I deserved.

I asked him about it once. He smiled tentatively, then responded in a measured tone. "I don't want you to get a big head. If I tell you how good you are you might not continue working at a high level of performance. I prefer to talk about what doesn't work and how you can improve it." Then as an afterthought he added, "Besides if you're good, you're good. You don't need me to tell you."

True enough. The only kind of approval that really matters is what comes from within. If we don't know our own worth, no amount of persuading from the outside will make a difference. The same is true regarding criticism. If we know we did well, then comments to the contrary will not ruin our day. And if we know we can do better at something then no one can convince us otherwise.

In my opinion and experience, however, I believe this man failed to see an important truth. Criticism does not motivate. And you cannot motivate by withholding praise. It might keep someone under control. It might frighten a person. It might even bring temporary results. But criticism and disapproval do not encourage creativity, spontaneity, or true self-expression—whether the individual is a child in a family or an adult in the marketplace.

PULLING RANK!

Many parents run their homes like a military base camp. They share my former employer's conviction that if you spare the praise and pour on the criticism you'll turn out a nice, neat row of soldiers! This may even be true, but there's no predicting how those children will feel about themselves and about their parents, once they are out from under that authority.

Mothers and fathers who have reared their children in such suppressive environments often find themselves estranged from those same children after their sons and daughters grow up and move out. These children may have performed when they had to because the parent said so, but there is nothing to keep them under the parental finger once they are of age.

A parent with a critical spirit is one of the most difficult individuals to be in relationship with. Mothers and fathers who continually criticize, complain, challenge, and chide their children—of any age—stifle their sons' and daughters' self-expression at a very deep and personal level.

Contrary to what many of us have heard (perhaps from our own parents), criticism is not constructive. It is destructive. Children want to please, naturally. They want to perform well. They want to succeed. They look to their parents for the encouragement, modeling, and motivation they deserve and need as they are forming their personalities and their view of themselves and the world around them.

It is our job as parents to supply that lifeline. But too many of us have been raised on criticism ourselves and, like my former employer, are afraid to change the course set before us for fear our children will get "a big head," or become "too big for their britches" or "too self-satisfied."

What if they did? What if their intelligence did expand? What if they did outgrow their "britches"? What if they did feel satisfied with themselves? Is that bad? Isn't that part of the life process? Growing and outgrowing, experimenting and changing, enjoying the benefits of a satisfying job well done?

If you have been the victim of a critical parent or you recognize yourself as one who relies too much on criticism and too little on praise, then you may relate to one or more of the following characteristics.

COMMON CHARACTERISTICS OF A CRITIC

1. Critics look for what is wrong before seeing what is right.   A critic sees the trash on the beach before he looks at the ocean. He notices the chipped paint on a house before he sees the child playing with a dog in the front yard. He tells his son what he should do before acknowledging him for what he has already done.

Lawrence, a retired attorney, admits that he was quick to criticize his son when he was young, and slow to compliment him. He was bright, Lawrence admitted, but he didn't take school seriously. "He preferred the baseball diamond to the classroom," said Lawrence with a look of disgust. "I spent a lot of time with him on homework but he drove me crazy. He never responded the way I wanted him to."

I asked Lawrence how their relationship is now. "Shaky," he said. "He seems nervous around me. We don't have much in common. He's thirty, a manager of a sporting goods store, and still a baseball nut."

Lawrence seemed sad as he talked. "I have a lot of regrets about the way I handled him as a kid. I know I criticized him too much. I didn't go to many of his games. I figured if he wasn't going to take school seriously why should I support his baseball mania?"

"How do you feel about that now?" I asked.

"Not too great. I remember my dad criticizing me for always having my nose in a book, and I guess in a way I've done that with Todd about baseball. I could have supported him more. Maybe if I had he'd have tried harder in school."

2. Critics undermine rather than encourage creativity. Roger is a sixty-seven-year-old artist who has only recently been able to devote full time to his life-long dream of painting. He retired early and since then has spent eight and ten hours a day at his easel several days a week. He's taking lessons again and even volunteering as an art instructor in a nearby public school.

"I feel like a kid," he said, sharing some of the details about his new life. "I wish I had followed my heart forty years ago." Instead, Roger followed his father's heart and he became an accountant. His father never encouraged his talent for painting—calling it "a waste of a man's life." If you want to support a family and make it in this world, you need a real job his father had told him. Roger succumbed to the criticism. He enrolled in the university and eventually got his accounting degree.

He worked in the same firm in Philadelphia for forty years, painting on the side, on weekends, on his vacation—longing for the day when he could quit working with numbers and do what he loved.

Talk about waste! Here was a gifted man who changed the course of his life because his father criticized him. What power we have as parents. And how irresponsible we can be—often without realizing it.

3. Critics have difficulty accepting their children's individuality. Don lived in the shadow of his father, a surgeon, for many years. Like his dad, Don was good with his hands, talented with small tools, and precise in cutting, shaping, and fitting things together. But Don chose to be a car mechanic instead of a physician. Don's father never let him forget what a "foolish" choice he had made.

"I like cars," he said. "I always have. I think I knew from the time I was a little boy that I'd work with cars someday. But that's not good enough for my dad. He despises the fact that my hands are greasy, that my fingernails aren't as clean as his."

Don recalled how critical his father was while Don was growing up. "He had his heart set on me following his footsteps. I remember him pushing me to take science classes and to volunteer at the hospital. It wasn't for me. He couldn't accept that.

He wasn't just disappointed. He made me wrong. He openly criticized my choices."

4. *Critics express disapproval by withholding love.*
Jeremy's critical spirit was obvious the minute he started talking about his oldest daughter. It was clear that this forty-year-old woman had disappointed him again and again. She had married someone he didn't approve of, divorced two years later, abruptly quit her job as a nurse, and went off to Europe to pull herself together.

Jeremy had nothing positive to say about her. "She doesn't even try to see my point of view," he said angrily. "How can she expect me to love her when she so openly challenges my values?"

It was apparently unthinkable to Jeremy to love his daughter because of who she is rather than as a result of what she does.

5. *Critics see themselves as the expert.* Marta, a fifty-nine-year-old homemaker and part-time babysitter, grew up with a mother who would not leave her alone. "She picked at me all the time," said Marta. "Do this. Do that. No, you're doing it wrong. I felt helpless without my mother. I couldn't shop for clothes, or decide where to go or what friends to play with."

Marta now realizes that her mother "trained" her well. "I have that same critical nature," she said. "I'm addicted to perfection, and I know I'm critical of my children. Even in small things that are really none of my business. I can't stand the way my middle daughter keeps house. Her habits drive me crazy. I don't seem to be able to talk to her in a sane way."

HOW CRITICIZING AFFECTS YOUR RELATIONSHIP WITH YOUR ADULT CHILDREN

The critic always has a better way. A better way of raising children, keeping house, building a patio cover, playing a game, folding sheets, handling finances, entertaining friends. Critical parents who express these "better" ways to their grown children set themselves up for broken relationships. Their adult sons and daughters, no longer accountable to them, often choose to stay away or to limit contact. No one likes to be around a person—even if that person is one's parent—who finds fault, who is a self-proclaimed expert, who always has a better way.

Many critics are also unaware of the depth and breadth of their damage. They are so intent on pointing out what their children did wrong and how to correct it, that they lose sight of the deep wounds their words inflict on the spirit of their sons and daughters.

Criticizing Blocks Communication.

When people feel evaluated in the presence of another person—especially one of their parents—they cannot communicate effectively. They often feel ill at ease, jumpy, reticent—even verbally paralyzed.

Mitch says his dad has never had a conversation with him that didn't entail some criticism. "If he's not on my case," said Mitch, "then he's on someone else's. I figure I'm next, and I'm usually right," he added, laughing nervously.

Mitch said he's actually worked hard at trying to bring up a neutral subject, and it's not possible. "If we stop for ice cream, he has an opinion about how it could be tastier, more colorful, creamier, you name it. This guy has something to say about absolutely everything—and it's usually negative."

Criticizing Blocks Confrontation.

Parents who criticize usually believe they're right and everyone else is wrong. This attitude generally stifles opportunity for honest confrontation. If an adult child confronts such a parent, the mother or father grabs the weapon of criticism and launches an all-out attack. Such children become the target of the parent's critical abuse. They hear how disrespectful, ungrateful, and irresponsible they are to go after their mother or father who has never done anything but love them. It's a defense that is difficult to dismantle.

Edna sent her granddaughter Mindy a pair of ice skates and money for six months of skating lessons—without consulting her daughter and son-in-law first. Edna's daughter was very upset. "Naturally Mindy was thrilled and we didn't want to spoil her enthusiasm. But we both work so driving her to and from lessons would have to be worked out. She'd need skating shirts and other accessories. Frankly, we aren't ready for this right now. And besides Mindy is only seven years old."

But when Edna's daughter confronted her mother with her feelings over not being asked ahead of time, Edna verbally attacked her. "She missed my point entirely," said her daughter. "As usual, I came away from that exchange feeling like the bad guy one more time."

Criticizing Blocks Friendship. No one needs—or wants—a critic for a friend. Friendship and criticism don't mix. In fact, criticism generally keeps friendships from forming. It's one thing to invite honest feedback from people we respect and care about. It's another to be subjected to a barrage of critical advice and negative input on an ongoing basis. Parents who criticize miss the opportunity to be friends with their adult children. No one would deliberately choose a critic as a close companion.

Criticizing Blocks Intimacy. If criticizing blocks friendship, then it blocks intimacy, for sure. Who would trust his or her most private feelings and thoughts with one who is quick to find fault? Who would share one's deepest needs with a critic? Who would risk being fully human with a person who cannot allow for differences? The critic is a lonely person—having only his or her objections and critical thoughts as companions.

"My mother lived a lonely life," said Herb, "and she's going to die lonely. All she knows how to do is complain and criticize. Nothing is ever right as far as she's concerned. Most of my life I've worked my tail off trying to get her to see me and listen to me. I finally realized that it's never going to happen. She doesn't know me because she doesn't want to. She'd rather look at what I did wrong or what I didn't do at all, than find out who I am and what I'm all about."

Criticizing Blocks Spontaneity. Critics aren't generally the type of parents who pile the kids in the car for a spur-of-the-moment picnic. Neither are they people who like to walk in the rain, set out an extra chair for a last-minute dinner guest, or speak in front of a group without being fully prepared. And what's more, they have something critical to say about anyone who is able to do such things.

Jenny remembers her mother needing to be "warned" several days ahead of time if she wanted to invite a friend to dinner or to spend the night.

Criticizing Blocks Spirituality. Parents who criticize their children don't usually stop there. They also find a reason to keep God at bay. They're critical of church, the pastor, the Bible, any aspect of religious or spiritual nourishment that would keep them accountable for their behavior. They prefer to remain "above" it all.

Neither can the critical parent accept spiritual encouragement without suspicion. This mother or father will always find a way to sabotage his or her need for God—even at times of real crisis.

Garth said that to this day his dad continues to criticize his church membership. "He has never let up," said Garth. "He badgered my mom every chance he got when we were growing up, and now that she's gone I'm the target. He loves to remind me that he doesn't need a 'spiritual narcotic' to keep him going.

"I'll never forget the expression on my mother's face when he started in on her. I know it wore on her terribly, but she didn't let it stop her. She still went to church, and she prayed every morning no matter what was going on. We knew better than to disturb her during those times. I guess we knew she needed God's strength to get through the day." Then as an afterthought he added, "And the strength to live with my dad."

CRITICIZING AS A FORM OF CONTROL

The critic controls with criticism and negative evaluation. Children of a critical parent often suffer from low self-esteem, self-doubt, chronic fear, and other forms of emotional insecurity. As adults these children may continue to express their feelings of inadequacy in inter-personal relationships, in their careers, in decision-making.

Many adult children complain that as much as they despise their parent's critical nature, they also feel controlled by it.

They continue to look for the parent's approval, or hope for a word of encouragement.

PORTRAIT OF A REFORMED CRITIC

Ken says he is an "internal critic." He does not always verbalize his critical feelings to his grown children, but he admits that he often judges within.

Ken grew up with a critical father and became emotionally entangled with him. During his adult years, he discovered that he had made his father an "idol." "I constantly second-guessed myself," Ken said, "looking for my dad's approval."

When Ken realized how deep-seated this condition was he "released it to the Lord." His father, now in his eighties, "is just as critical and manipulative as ever," said Ken, sounding sad and frustrated. "He's cynical, pessimistic, and negative about everything. And he's no longer a Christian. It's tragic. But rather than argue as I once did, I just listen."

Ken said he sees the same scenario being played out in the relationship between his twenty-six-year-old daughter Tracy and her mother, Ken's former wife. "Her mother is vindictive, bitter, and a pathological liar," he said. "I can see how she has influenced my daughter. I sometimes catch Tracy in lies when we talk."

Ken admitted that his critical side emerges during some of their conversations. "For example, she's dating a man who is bisexual and HIV-positive," he said. "It's hard not to be critical of that." Tracy has also had a difficult time holding a good job and making friends in Chicago where she recently moved. "And she's not attending church right now," he added.

Even though Ken feels "somewhat critical" of her choices, he has only to look at his own early years to see that he made some unwise choices too. For years Ken was an alcoholic. His life became so chaotic that he contemplated suicide twice. Every aspect of his life revolved around alcohol. "I remember when the kids were young, before my divorce, I could only take the family to places where I knew I could get a drink."

Following his separation from his wife, Ken did not see much of his children from the time they were five and seven years of age until they were out of school. "I had almost nothing to do with raising them," he said softly. "Their mother hated me and did everything she could to create problems. For example, we'd arrange a trip for the kids. I'd send plane tickets and at the last minute she'd find some excuse for not sending them."

At one point both his children legally adopted their step-father's last name. "They told me they hated my name," said Ken. "That really hurt. I wrote them a letter expressing my disapproval. It was very painful, but they went ahead anyway." Ken said he knows his ex-wife was behind that move.

Despite Ken's return to sobriety and sanity around drinking and his rebirth in Jesus Christ, he still struggles with his inner critic. "I know I exhibited my father's behavior at times. If I didn't say it, I was thinking the same things he had verbalized to me."

Ken also sees the toll that separation and criticism has taken in his children's lives. "Tracy has had a problem with weight most of her life," he said. "She's a loner and has a co-dependent relationship with her mother."

Ken is not as certain about the effects on his 28-year-old son Doug. "He kept busy with sports and other activities while he was growing up," he said. "Maybe he didn't feel the loss of me as much as she did."

When Ken speaks of his current relationship with his children his voice turns warm and happy. "Tracy spent two months with me last summer," he said. "That's when we finally really talked. We walked and we talked for hours. I asked her forgiveness for all those years of drinking and the separation between us. It felt good to do that.

"At times she exasperated me. It wasn't always easy having her around. I don't approve of everything she's doing. But after she left I received a card from her telling me how great it was to get to know me." Ken admitted how wonderful that felt.

He said that he is learning, through God's grace and his own desire, to do things differently with his kids than his father has done with him, to "listen and reserve criticism. Now when Tracy and Doug ask, 'What do you think, Dad?' I give an example from my own life and then share the result." Ken hopes that they will learn from his experience, rather than from his advice.

Today he says he never sees them or talks to them without praying first. "I ask for wisdom and discernment. I would not attempt to do anything with my children without God being present," he added.

Ken admits that he's "just as fallible as anyone, but that with the Lord in my life, I know I can live a good life, be the best I can be, and take responsibility for my actions in a way I never did before I became a Christian."

Some of Ken's best times now are listening to his children, observing them, and being a part of their world as a loving, rather than as a critical parent.

BETTY'S STORY

"I tend to be critical by nature," said forty-eight-year-old Betty. To look at her you wouldn't think she was a critic. This petite woman with twinkly blue eyes and a welcoming smile sat across from me over hot muffins and coffee sharing parts of herself I had never known about before. Strong, brave, loving, committed. Yes, yes, yes and yes. But critical? It must have been part of her before I ever met her.

But she admits she is (or was) critical. Actually, she's in transition. Betty is working on dismantling that behavior. "As my children become adults I want to be an encourager," she said, "not a critic. I want to allow them the freedom to choose their own direction in life." But it's not easy. Betty said this new desire is quite different from her usual tendency toward criticism, which she learned at a very early age.

"My father is the critical parent in my life," she said. "And I learned that domineering and controlling behavior from him. I tend to have a personality much like his." Reflecting on the past, Betty admitted that criticizing and correcting were a strong part of her parenting in the early years.

But she is now trying to adopt more of her mother's qualities. "My mother is this very accepting, soft Mother Nature type. As kids we couldn't do anything wrong as far as she was concerned. Any idea we had she'd jump on the wagon and go right along with us. She always allowed us to be exactly who we were. And she had a very high level of tolerance. I've always yearned to be that warm, accepting person she is. Yet I'm not at all like her and I had a lot of conflict about it."

Betty said her father continues to be quite critical at times towards her and her children. "It's as though he has critical tapes recording messages in his brain," she said. "I imagine he learned this behavior at the knees of one of his parents. I believe his mother was that way. My father is a kind and sensitive man in his heart—even overly sensitive—but he doesn't seem to be aware of the destruction of his words."

In recent years Betty has set limits with him, "refusing to continue conversations where he slings words like arrows. That's new for me," she said, "because in the past I would take it, out of respect for him as my father. But now I know that I don't have to be abused by his words."

When Betty began talking about her children, her eyes lit up as she recalled the "very intimate, pure, unspoiled time" in her life when she breastfed each of her sons and her daughter. "I feel the mother-infant bond that formed during breastfeeding is the most important thing I gave them," she said.

By contrast, the most difficult aspects of motherhood were the ten years she spent as a single parent. Like so many other women in the same situation, Betty needed to run a household, work outside her home, and at the same time, meet her children's physical, educational, and emotional needs.

"The emotional area is probably where I felt the greatest challenge," she said. "Keeping that link with who they really are and helping them develop as persons was so difficult—especially when our only quality time together was at nine or ten o'clock at night when we were all tired and there were still a billion things to do before the next day."

Betty paused a minute, her eyes misting as she reflected on those days. "I feel some of that nurturing slipped through the cracks, especially with my daughter. As the youngest she just got swept up in the majority. If one of my sons had a soccer game or a school function, she went right along. I was trying to be both mother and father without any other support."

Betty was quick to admit her strengths as well as her weaknesses. "When the chips are down I can mobilize," she said. "I can take command of the helm and do so masterfully." But then looking at how that affected her children, she said, "But in the process what about that growing child in front of me?" She admitted that her ability to lead and mobilize sometimes got in the way of being there for her children.

"There were goodnight hugs and kisses and a bedtime story each night," she said, "but there was never enough time to talk through an issue. If they had something important to discuss that required a couple of hours of talking or holding, I'm sure I missed some of those. I was in there simply hitting the high spots."

Betty said that she really missed not having a partner to point out what she was doing wrong and to support her when she was falling apart. "One of my stress behaviors is rigidity," she said. "I take control. I set up the rules and the regulations and then expect my family to observe them. When there's mutiny I take charge of the ship. But I now see that along the way, I lost parts of the little child in each of my children."

Next, Betty talked about Brian, her middle child, and the brokenness they experienced for a number of years. The restoration of that relationship is still in process, she said, as she shared some of the deeply painful issues that stood between them.

"When he was born he was a very sensitive, affectionate, and twinkly-eyed baby," she said, smiling warmly as she recalled her little bundle. "From the beginning, he lived with great passion. He was always independent and self-reliant to an extreme. As a little boy he had frequent tantrums that completely baffled me."

Betty now believes that he was reacting to her dominant traits. "I had my rituals throughout the day," she said, "and when he didn't like something, we clashed. He was always ready to manipulate the environment, to take charge, and to control the people around him."

Brian manifested his resistance over the years through bouts of anger and rage—much of it directed toward his little sister. He was also prone to wide mood swings. "He could go from happy to sad in an instant, as though a dark rain cloud had just come over him. When he was about eleven years old I became concerned," she said. "His anger and rage were erupting all over the house. He slammed doors, threw things, and whenever I approached him about it, he'd keep me away by creating a scene that was so explosive I'd back off. That was his way of avoiding the issue. And he was good at it," she added. "That way we never talked anything out and he could escape his deeper feelings."

His depression, however, worried Betty more than the rage. "We saw a therapist," she said, "and after a year of therapy, he was "noticeably more buoyant and upbeat. That change lasted for the next few years. Then around age fourteen, coupled with puberty and other adolescent changes, Brian began to slip into depression and sadness again—sometimes for days at a time."

Betty asked him about going into therapy again, but this time he flatly refused. "I tried to talk to his father about it, but since he rarely saw Brian, he denied that he had a problem. He abandoned us when the children were young, so I'm sure he couldn't even consider that his son might have a problem because it would be a confrontation to him."

Meanwhile, Betty and her other son and daughter had to live with Brian's wrath. "He didn't want to contribute anything to our household," she said. "He withdrew and used our home for his own needs only. I became desperate."

Betty sought help next through two books: *Back in Control* and *Tough Love*. "After reading these books," she said, "I realized that as a parent, I had to set limits, for my sake, and for the sake of Brian's brother and sister. If we were to have a healthy home, I could no longer allow him to manipulate us for his own needs."

Shortly afterwards she went to him and told him that if he wanted to remain in their household he would have to become a participant. There were certain duties and responsibilities that went along with the privileges of being part of the family.

"If he didn't do them," she said, "then his message to me would be that he did not care to live with us. Well he poohpoohed me as he always had. But this time I was not going to back down. I told him to put away a number of items from a science fair that had been cluttering up our common living areas and to put his room in order. I had been asking him the same thing for three days with absolutely no response."

That day Betty gave him an ultimatum. Complete the job by noon or pack up and move out. At 12:00 P.M. he had done nothing. She went to his room and told him he had made his choice. He obviously no longer wanted to live with the family.

Brian looked at Betty in complete disbelief. He had not taken her seriously. "I told him to pack his things and be out by 1:00 P.M.," she said. Immediately he backed down and wanted to talk things out.

"I said I'd be happy to talk. I'd been trying to talk for months, but that wouldn't change the 1:00 P.M. deadline. So we talked for thirty minutes. We both became emotional. He cried. I told him I loved him and that I wanted to work things out. But I also knew that I could not let him use his tears to manipulate me one more time and squeak out of his responsibilities."

At 1:00 P.M. Betty said good-bye. Brian picked up his things and went out to the driveway. "I had no idea where he would go or what he was going to do." Betty's voice was low and solemn as she continued. "It was the one most difficult thing I ever did as a mother," she said. "And yet I knew that if I didn't set those limits, he would never look at his own issues, and he couldn't begin to heal."

Betty alerted Brian's dad about the event. And later that night he phoned back to say that Brian was staying with him. "I had to be willing never to see Brian again," she said, "because when you set limits and release a child under those circumstances, you don't know if he'll ever come back to you. I had to accept that possibility. It was so hard. He was only fourteen years old. It was definitely the lowest point in my time as a mother."

For the next nine months, Betty and Brian had almost no contact. "I had to let him reach out to me. I had already told him that I wanted a relationship with him but that it couldn't be abusive, as it had been."

Then in April of the following year, they saw each other at a family gathering at Betty's parents' home in Arizona. Her father had intervened, encouraging Brian to come, yet respecting whatever he wanted to do or not do regarding his mother. Following that event, they had some contact over the next three months.

Later that year—one full year after he had moved out of his mother's house—Brian returned. "At that point he actually thanked me for having confronted him and for holding the line," said Betty. "He admitted that his behavior had been destructive."

She noticed some improvement almost immediately, although their relationship still remained uncomfortable. "He did his chores and there was more communication than before but I also noticed him slipping back," she said. "He stayed for a full year, then decided to move back to his dad's for his final two years of high school. I think as he got older he wanted more freedom to come and go without being accountable to anyone. He knew that our family was close and that we all knew what was going on with one another."

Now that he's away at college, Betty said their relationship is more cordial and more giving—"as giving as Brian can be"—than before. But she is also aware through a series of events and feedback from others that he has a drinking problem.

"At one point, he actually came and told me about it," she said. "It's quite a step for Brian to come to his mother and say it with his own lips. I'm trying to keep a warm and open link between us. I want him to know that he can come to me with anything—no matter what the problem is or how serious it might be."

Betty said his dad will not participate in a family intervention or cooperate in any way. He continues to deny the problem exists, so Betty feels that until he comes around—since he is the primary parent in Brian's life—that her hands are tied, except to pray for her son and to remain open to talking with him.

Betty then turned her conversation to her other children. "The most painful part of dealing with my adult children," she said, "has just come up these last six months. My oldest son, now twenty-three, and my daughter, who is eighteen, are experiencing tremendous grief and pain over the loss of their father in their lives. It's been fourteen years since he left and yet now they are feeling that loss at a very, very deep level. My daughter has manifested her grief in depression. She's been in counseling for it, and I've spent hours and hours in tearful conversation about this with my older son."

It has been a very difficult time for Betty, as well. "It's so painful for me to see them hurting over this," she said, "something I can't change and that wasn't my doing. I want to protect them, yet I know they have to come to terms in their own way with this life issue. One of the most challenging aspects for me is to learn how to help them do that, and to encourage them to complete the issue with their father. Their grief has been going on for about eight months now. They know they need to talk to their dad, but they're both very afraid to do so."

At this point Brian does not seem to share that same sense of loss. Betty feels that perhaps his grief is not as strong because he lived with his dad for three years and "felt some of the fatherliness that the other two didn't experience at all."

Betty is still working through these issues with her children, but she has a new confidence now—one founded on her own gradual healing and recovery and her growing spiritual life. "I believe that God has a purpose for each of my children," she said. "I've tried to release them to Him and then pray that they will find Jesus as their Savior and follow His way."

Betty said she has also discovered that the best gift she can give her children is her own healed self. She now sees taking care of herself as the number one priority in her life. She encourages any hurting parents to do the same, to begin looking within, and to lead productive lives of their own so their children do not remain their only focus.

"I think it's important to reach out to them," she said, "but it's equally important to leave room for them to respond, and to reach out to us so they can take responsibility for part of the relationship."

With a chuckle Betty concluded by saying, "My kids beat me up a lot over the last twenty years, but it was good for me because they knocked off a lot of the rough edges! I wouldn't have walked this road without the challenges they provided. They have been such a big part of my growth."

DEANNA'S STORY

"When I got into recovery I realized that I had every one of the characteristics listed for adult children of alcoholics," said Deanna, a woman in her early fifties and the mother of three adult daughters. "My father was a rageaholic," she said. "I was the youngest of five children in my family, and I got the worst of it."

"But John Bradshaw's workshop on healing the inner child changed my life," she said emphatically. "I cried the whole time."

It was then she realized the depth of the emotional abuse she had endured as a child and it was after that workshop that Deanna joined First Presbyterian Church in San Diego and met people who became her "new family." She said she realized that she was "looking for people to be close to."

Up to that point, Deanna, like so many adult children of alcoholics, was a survivor. "I could always pull myself out of any situation," she said. But she also admitted that she leaned on alcohol for many years. After her divorce from her children's father, Deanna "went drinking once a week and got drunk. I was a controller and a critic," she readily admits, "and I know that damaged my children."

Deanna said she always had problems with men because she had not had a healthy relationship with her father. "The verbal and physical abuse in our home was very bad," she said reflecting on the past. "When we lived on a farm my mother was a slave, cooking, canning, and serving food to fifteen people—family and farm hands. And when we lived in the city my father wouldn't allow her to leave the apartment. He verbally abused everyone, and he physically abused her," said Deanna. "My mother was thirty-nine when I was born. She had been embarrassed to be pregnant so I know that I was shamed in the womb. She was a sweet woman, but she never really took care of me. She was just there."

Deanna's father died when she was in high school, and it was only then that she and her mother had any freedom.

Unlike her mother, who remained in bondage to a tyrannical husband her entire married life, Deanna wants "to be a good role model for my girls." She knows now that the only real gift she can give them is her own healed self so they will have the courage to seek healing for themselves.

Deanna is in a second career now as a business trust administrator for a San Diego bank. "I don't see my daughters as much as I'd like to," she said. "They have their own lives and I have mine."

She particularly misses contact with her middle daughter who is twenty-six years old. "She had a crisis during high school, and at that time decided to move in with her dad. She had wanted to be with him since she was two. She was a kid I thought I'd like to kill at times! But now I'd just like to put my arms around her and tell her how sorry I am for all the yelling and screaming."

But her daughter doesn't seem ready for a reconciliation. "Mom, don't lecture me," is a refrain Deanna still hears from her. "We haven't lived together in so long that she has no clue how much I've changed," said Deanna wistfully.

Despite that unfinished business, however, Deanna is going forward with her own life. "It's hard to verbalize my healing," she said with a lilt in her voice. "For the first fifty years I never knew my own feelings. In fact, I had to write them down initially first because I was so unsure of them."

Today, she focuses on what's right—with her and with her adult children—instead of criticizing what's wrong. For the past two years she has been pursing her spiritual life, spending time each day in personal prayer, saying the Lord's Prayer and the Serenity Prayer each morning, and reciting twenty affirmations that refute the negative and suppressive life she lived for so long.

"I can't even discuss all the wonderful things that have happened to me since I started my healing process," she said with humility. "I'm truly at a loss for words. My life really has changed completely."

LETTING GO OF CRITICIZING

Criticizing is one of the most difficult characteristics to release because it is such a deeply ingrained habit, one that is rooted in feelings of low self-worth. The critic appears self-righteous but he is actually attempting to better himself by belittling others. Critics are also convinced that they are right and others are wrong. They are unable to see how damaging their criticism is, believing that their opinion and judgment will actually make a difference for good.

But once a critic is willing to look into his past for the origin of this destructive habit he will usually discover that he too, was the victim of a critical parent. He can then recall how criticism has shaped his life and how limiting it has been.

When a person gains insight about his own victimization at the hands of a critic, he becomes more aware of how he is repeating that past. He may then be willing to give up the practice, to release his hold on those around him, and to embrace God's healing.

Words To Consider—Actions To Take

• "For whom the Lord loves He corrects" (Prov. 3:12). What a relief to read these words. The Lord will correct those He loves. And He surely loves our children even more than we do. It is not our place to continue to criticize and correct our adult children. They are on their own now and they are responsible for their choices. If you need to talk about something confrontational with your children, first put that conversation into the Lord's hands and then proceed only as He leads you.

• "A merry heart does good, like medicine, But a broken spirit dries the bones" (Prov. 17:22). Think of criticism as the product of a broken spirit. Listen and observe the critical spirit in others. Notice the effect it has on you. It is enough to dry up your bones, isn't it? Sometimes seeing and hearing our own behavior reflected in others will spur us to repent. I doubt that any parent wants to dry up the bones of his or her children.

• "Let your conduct be without covetousness" (Heb. 13:5). You may wonder what criticism has to do with covetousness. In many situations I believe that critical parents are actually envious of their children. Perhaps one of your adult children has succeeded where you have failed. Maybe your daughter is prettier, smarter, happier, or more mature than you were at her age and you feel jealous of her gifts so you criticize her. Are you threatened by your son's independence? Criticism might be just the weapon to keep him in tow.

These are not easy things to consider, but they may be true, and if they are then you have a choice about continuing this behavior or seeking the Lord's intervention so you can cast them out and begin the process of restoration.

• "Wait on the Lord; be of good courage" (Ps. 27:14). Critical parents are not courageous. And they are not known for waiting on the Lord. In fact, just the opposite. They use criticism to punish, exhort, and dominate their children. In a sense, they are playing God, rushing in with their ideas of what is right and just and good without considering the effects of their words and behavior, and without consulting the Lord about the part they are supposed to play in a particular situation.

If you see yourself in this role, decide now, with God's help, to be courageous. Like Ken, Betty and Deanna, put down the mantle of criticism and take up the mantle of encouragement.

Chapter Eight

THE GRIEVER

Three years ago I joined a grief support group for women. It has been one of the most significant steps of my life. At the time I entered the group I knew that I needed to do some deep emotional work around my former marriage and my relationship with my three children. I felt ready to do this work in a group setting where I could have the support and understanding of other women who were experiencing similar needs. What a gift this has proven to be. I have shared parts of myself with them that I have not shared with anyone else. These women have become so important to me that I'm not sure I'd be able to complete my grieving process without them.

Grief embodies anguish, heartache, heavy sorrow over loss. As the writer of Proverbs stated in chapter 17, verse 25: "A foolish son is a grief to his father." And in turn, a foolish father (or mother) is probably a grief to his (or her) son or daughter. I felt very foolish at the time I started my recovery. I knew I had been a grief to my children, and when some of their behavior was a grief to me, I grieved even more, because I felt responsible, by either my presence or my absence, for influencing some of their choices.

The grieving parent, aware of the loss in his life, longs for restoration. In some situations, the grief is overwhelming because it is too late—or appears to be too late—for restoration. "The griever," says Rebecca Cutter, "is full of remorse. Some parents try to restore or at least talk to their estranged children, but the children are too bitter and too disconnected. Grief is one of the most painful emotions a parent can feel."

In other cases, grief over what might have been lingers in a parent even after restoration has begun. The door may be wide open for communication, confrontation, and eventual healing, but the parent is filled with regret and sadness. He never wanted things to turn out this way, yet they have. Coming to terms with our limitations as human beings and then as parents, is perhaps one of the most difficult challenges we face. We're not perfect. Our lives aren't perfect. And our children did not turn out perfect. Yet how we tried to do otherwise. And how guilty many of us feel over the results. If only we had known then what we know now.

GOOD GRIEF

"Grieving is the most misunderstood and neglected growth process a person can go through," state John James and Frank Cherry, authors of *The Grief Recovery Handbook.* "Simply put, grief is a normal and natural response to loss. (It) is a conflicting mass of human emotion that we experience following any major change in a familiar pattern of behavior. Over time the pain of unresolved grief is cumulative. Incomplete recovery can have a lifelong effect on a person's capacity for happiness."[1]

Recovery means feeling better. "Recovery," say the authors, "is finding new meaning for living without the fear of future abandonment. Recovery is being able to enjoy fond memories without having them precipitate painful feelings of loss, guilt, regret, or remorse."[2]

Grief is a good thing. It is a normal response to loss. It is an essential part of the healing process. But to face and recover from a significant loss is not easy. It requires your careful attention, willingness, courage, and a series of steps outlined at the end of this chapter. But before we do that here is a list of characteristics that may help you look at your own grief process.

COMMON CHARACTERISTICS OF A GRIEVER

1. The griever experiences a loss of aliveness. As James and Cherry indicate in their book, our culture teaches us how to acquire, not how to lose. We learn how to build a family, amass wealth, create a business, gather friends. But most of us are unprepared for the loss of family, loss of wealth, loss of business, or loss of friends. The process of losing something or someone feels wrong and unnatural. Little wonder that grief is so often an unwelcome emotion. It saps our energy, leaves us feeling lifeless, depressed, and preoccupied with the past until we can embrace it and work through it.

2. The griever buries his/her feelings.   Sandy has a lot of grief over the loss of raising her two sons, who lived with their father following her divorce when the boys were four and five years of age. "I was totally unprepared to manage a home by myself," she said. "Suddenly I had to find a job, learn how to deal with money, and—" Her words trailed off as she looked away in tears. "But what's done is done. I can't change the past. That was twenty years ago. I have to go on and do the best I can."

As she talked, it became apparent that Sandy had not allowed herself to grieve the loss of those years. In fact, it was such a painful experience she could hardly acknowledge it. When her feelings came to the surface she did what most of us have been taught to do. She buried them under a barrage of cliches: "keep a stiff upper lip," "look for the good in the bad," "make the best of it," "what's done is done,"—none of which offered one iota of comfort or peace.

3. The griever fears future losses.   Allen has grieved the loss of his youngest daughter who died of leukemia at age fifteen. As a result he has hovered over his second daughter, now twenty-two, to the point of smothering the relationship. He continually reminds her to take care of herself and of how important she is to him. She carries the burden of his incomplete grief, feeling guilty if she doesn't check in with him, spend time with him each week, and so on. She knows that he is afraid of losing her, as well. His preoccupation with the loss of his first daughter has impaired his relationship with this daughter.

4. The griever is filled with regret. Clark talks about the past. It's almost impossible to carry on a conversation with him about anything in present time. At age seventy-eight he finds little joy in everyday life, perhaps because he is so full of regret. He regrets his marriage, the profession he chose, and most of all, the way he mistreated his son because of his own unhappiness. He is unwilling to enter any kind of counseling program or even read a book on the subject. Meanwhile, his regret has overwhelmed his son and kept him at a distance, intensifying Clark's sadness.

5. The griever tends to isolate himself/herself. It is easy to understand why people in grief often do not reach out to others. Most people do not know how to respond in a truly helpful way. Friends and family usually have sadness and sorrow in their own lives so they are uncomfortable when faced with someone else's grief. Their attempts at comfort are usually cloaked in messages that say in effect: grieve alone, replace the loss, give it time.

Whenever Marion brought up the subject of her painful relationship with her adult daughter she regretted it. "I needed to talk about it," she said, "but even my own mother couldn't hear me out. She continually reminded me that I had two other children to focus on, and why didn't I just get away for a few days and I'd probably feel better. Needless to say, I don't go to her for comfort."

HOW GRIEVING AFFECTS YOUR RELATIONSHIP WITH YOUR ADULT CHILDREN

According to Rebecca Cutter, grieving parents are generally more aware of their part in the conflict between them and their adult children than the critic or the manipulator. The very act of grieving suggests regret over loss, which is a good thing.

In your relationship with your adult children, however, unresolved grief can be an impediment. Some parents, eager to let their adult children know how sorry they are, burden them with self-pity, guilt, and preoccupation with the past.

Grieving Can Block Communication. I remember a time when my own grief nearly overwhelmed my oldest daughter. I was so focused on my regret that that's all I could talk about with her. It became my current obsession. It was as though I couldn't apologize enough. As I look back now I see that my self-absorption interfered with our communication. I remember her saying to me that she looked forward to having a "normal" give-and-take relationship with me—free of continual analysis and processing. I can see why! My remorse during the healing process was almost as much of a burden as my lack of awareness had been prior to it.

Grief deserves to be felt, to be talked about, to be worked through, and healed. But in my experience, our adult children are not the ones to go to with this process. I believe we need the safety and support of a grief group and/or the help of a private therapist who understands the process and can lead us through it.

Grieving Can Block Confrontation. Christine's daughter told her that she had mixed feelings about coming to her mother with her unresolved hurts over some childhood issues. "But I find it so hard to confront you," her daughter had said. "You tried to be a good mom, and most of the time you were, but I still hurt, and I want to be able to talk to you about these things."

Christine realized that her own grief over some of the same issues brought her to tears whenever the conversation turned to those events. Her daughter would then back off, afraid to add to her mother's pain. Meanwhile, neither one of them experienced the healing both wanted.

Grieving Can Block Friendship. A caring friend can be a great support during a grieving process. But when it comes to our adult children, grieving over them or over our own past behavior can strain the friendship we want to develop with them. I made the mistake of telling my children too much, of confiding in them too deeply, of divulging too much of my pain. I became a burden. They were grieving their own losses (their parents' divorce, new living quarters, economic changes, emotional setbacks) and my often inappropriate level of grief was more than they could respond to at the time. I needed to seek help from a professional source or a pastoral counselor so I could do the heavy emotional work outside of my relationship with them.

When I did make a commitment to get that help, I saw a difference in my relationship with my children almost immediately. They knew that I was being cared for by someone who could handle my grief. And that freed them to do their own emotional work. Our friendship now is stronger than ever because we do not tax one another with more than the relationship can bear.

Grieving Can Block Intimacy. Unresolved grief can also keep parents and adult children from being intimate. Parents who are filled with remorse are generally unavailable emotionally. They are steeped in their own pain, their own regret, their own past behavior. They often feel unworthy, unforgiving, and unhappy with themselves and with their lives. Adult children of such parents can feel trapped by the grief, yet be unable to express their true feelings, for fear of hurting the parent. In time, rage and resentment surface and may take the form of blaming and shaming—the enemies of intimacy.

Grieving Can Block Spontaneity. It's easy to see why someone in grief would not be spontaneous. For people in grief, it's all they can do to get out of bed in the morning. They feel depressed, are self-absorbed, have a low energy level, and in general, experience a low threshold of interest outside their own problems.

Keith said that for years he "went through the motions of living—sleeping, eating, working, watching TV, doing laundry, watching TV, and watching more TV." He said months would go by without leaving his house except for work and grocery shopping. "I slept the weekends away," he said. "My son would invite me to go fishing or to a ballgame—two things I normally love to do—and I'd turn him down. After a while he stopped asking me.

"I know I wasn't any fun to be around. The truth is it's hard to be around him and his kids. Every time I see him with my grandson, I remember Jason as a little boy and I feel so badly about how little time I spent with him. I worked like a nut in those years, and when I was home on weekends the yard and the garage and all the chores came first. It kills me just to think about it."

Grieving Can Block Spirituality. It's hard to praise God when our spirit is in grief. We may even want to rail against Him, wondering why we have to endure such pain. Actually that may be one of the healthiest things we could do for ourselves. God wants us to tangle with Him, to wrestle through our issues with Him, and to draw on Him as father. But a grieving parent is generally so steeped in regret and remorse that he does not feel worthy of God's compassion, or forgiveness, or grace.

As James, the apostle, says in James 1:5, "If any of you lacks wisdom, let him ask of God, who gives to all men generously and without reproach, and it will be given to him." If ever we need the love and understanding and fellowship of the Lord, it is during our times of grief.

GRIEVING AS A FORM OF CONTROL

It may seem inappropriate to even consider grieving in the same context as control. But from my own experience I see that we can. An individual may not be aware of what he or she is doing, but the results prove otherwise. Parents who do not face their grief and work through it tend to express it in a number of ways—continuing sadness, depression, inability to live in the present, preoccupation with one's self, introspection, lack of trust—to name a few. Over time, these behaviors have a wearing effect on others, particularly the person's children, who are likely to behave in one of two extremes. They may back away from the relationship so they won't become controlled by their parent's grief. Or they may become caught up in it, and in an effort to save or help the grieving parent, are likely to feel controlled by the grief.

Many hurting parents don't even realize the devastating effect their grief can have on their children. I am not making a case for stuffing our feelings or denying them. Quite the contrary. Grief is an important and necessary part of our emotional and spiritual makeup. It is a good and natural response to loss.

But when we do not deal with the grief—through prayer, talk therapy, journal-writing, etc.—then it will naturally overflow into our lives and the lives of those we love, potentially threatening rather than aiding the restoration of our relationships with our children and others.

PORTRAIT OF A GRIEVER

For years, Charles experienced this threat to his relationship with his son and daughter without realizing the cause. "I'm a sensitive person," he said as we talked. "I'm a fairly feeling person, but those feelings are more toward pain than toward joy. I think I'm able to sense other people's pain and sorrow quicker than my own. I'm just now, in my early sixties, learning about my feelings."

Charles wanted so much for his children to know how sorry he was for the past—a past that included separation from them, divorce from their mother, and years of drinking and self-indulgence as he tried to find meaning for his life—that he nearly drove them away emotionally. He could not stop trying to make up for lost time, lost parenting, lost opportunities. When he felt ready to discuss and heal the past, they weren't ready, and his eagerness appeared to frighten and alienate them.

Today Charles admits that if he had been more sensitive to the deeper issues—the roots or causes of his grief—he would have known better how to approach the subject of the past so it could be a safe and healthy experience for all of them.

Much of Charles' grief is wrapped up in memories of treasured times with his children when they were very young—experiences that were interrupted when he left his wife during the children's early years. His son was twelve and his daughter seven at the time they separated.

"One of my most joyful memories," said Charles with eyes misting, "and a very important time, was Saturday afternoons when I'd come into the house after a morning of working hard in the yard. I'd stretch out on the living room floor and the kids would curl up on my chest for a nap. It was a marvelous time of bonding. It was so special for my son that he's carried on that tradition with his three boys.

"Christmas was another big event in our home. We went all out with a huge tree filled with hundreds of lights and ornaments, house and door decorations—you name it. My son is also repeating that tradition with his family. It's nice to see it carried on."

Charles' greatest periods of grief surfaced after yearly visits with his children following his move from New York to California. He missed his daughter climbing on his lap for a story, the hugs and kisses, the relaxed evenings in front of the television or at a ball game together. "We've always been a physical family," he said.

"The most difficult part of my parenting years was being away from them physically. Even though I felt I had to leave their mother, there was still the feeling of responsibility that I did leave. There was guilt then, and regret now," he said somberly. "Today, my grief has less to do with guilt. It's more of a sorrowing over the loss."

Charles continued, his grief sometimes spilling into the conversation as he reflected on his past. "I was trying to grow and expand as a person," he said, commenting on his former marriage. "By contrast, my wife seemed to be shrinking. Our life together was in a malaise, and I didn't see any hope of it getting better. I felt hamstrung—like the elephant with a chain around its leg. I was growing bigger, yet I still felt as though I couldn't go anywhere. There was no growth in our marriage. And there was no real affection between us. I felt confined, suffocated, cheated and finally, angry."

Charles said that he was in such despair at times that everything he did had to be forced. "I felt as though I had an enormous hole inside of me. I was absolutely starving for someone to fill me up," he added. Then on second thought, he said, "I'm sure that hole was there before I got married, but the marriage exacerbated it."

Much of Charles' grief, he admitted, stemmed from his own

expectations of himself. He said that as a young man he had challenged himself to be "the best husband, the best father, and the best at my job"—expectations that he had already failed to meet before he was thirty years old. He discovered that to be the best dad, for example, would include staying in his marriage, being there for his children. And yet he could not do that.

"I knew that if I stayed I'd almost be surrendering my life," he said. "I realize now that in order to take care of myself it looked like I was being cruel to others, cheating them so that I could live. And when the others are your son and your daughter, well, it's a horrible price to pay. Yet I truly believe that if I had stayed in that marriage I wouldn't be alive today. I'm not saying that the marriage would have caused me to die, but since I wasn't nourished in it, the demands that were coming at me in my personal and professional life would have done me in."

Charles also acknowledged that if he hadn't left physically, then he knows he would have left emotionally. "In fact, I believe I did that long before I moved out," he said. "I'm sure I left my children emotionally, as well. They suffered because of it. Children often believe they cause the problems between their parents. That's a horrible burden for them. And it just isn't true."

Pausing for a moment, Charles collected his thoughts and then continued. "I believe there is a consciousness among Christians, and others too, that if you marry someone and then you leave, you're automatically a louse." Charles feels that his situation was compounded by the fact that his wife was deaf. He felt even more guilty for leaving someone with an impairment. Many of their friends and some family members viewed him as the guilty party. "But her deafness was not the problem," he said. "That was just the outward sign of an internal limitation of the person. I married her not really knowing who I was, so I certainly didn't know who she was. Did I love her? Based on what I knew about love then, I'd say yes. But today I'm not sure I'd call it love, knowing what I know now."

Charles is currently in a men's therapy group. He said it is a wonderfully safe and supportive environment for dealing with his unresolved grief—over his relationship with his children—and with the root of that grief, his relationship with his parents.

Charles admits that their grief with one another covered him like a heavy blanket throughout his childhood. He believes he absorbed their pain and carried it right into his adulthood, making choices based on that modeling.

Today Charles experiences the joy of having his daughter live within a mile of his home. She moved to the West Coast from New York three years ago. And his son, now married with a family of his own, lives within a forty-minute drive. "It's wonderful to have them physically closer after all the years of separation," he said with a satisfied smile. "At the same time, I don't feel I see them often enough. But little by little I'm learning to enjoy them as people, as friends whom I can sit down with and talk to. And I'm beginning to see that I don't have to try and make up for lost time or to be the dad I wasn't for so long. I want to be their dad now, in this moment—whatever that might be. I know they're going to make their mistakes just as I made mine. I don't have to save them. I believe they're from good enough stock that they'll do fine. They're going to be okay.

"The greatest challenge for me today is to give up guilt and to heal my grief. I've been overly concerned about the harm I've caused them by my absence and by modeling behaviors I wouldn't want them to copy. I was out of the house for so many years. I was also a victim, covering my pain with alcohol. I don't want them to take up this role. I have thought about what it's going to take for them to get over the hurts of the past. For their own sake and health, I believe they're going to need to get extremely angry someday. But right now I think they are running away from the pain just as hard as I did.

"I realize now that it's more important for me—today—to be all that I can be, to let my children see that even though I went to the bottom rung I came up again, and they can do the same. I want to parent my children now the way the Lord parents me."

Charles closed our conversation by commenting on the value of loss and the grieving he's done over that loss. He's actually grateful for it now. "Losses are vital to a person's growth," he said, "because without them human beings have a tendency to remain unchanged. I believe that the enormity of loss I experienced as a parent has made the value of my children that much greater. I take nothing for granted anymore."

JENNIFER'S STORY

Jennifer is fifty years old this year—a milestone in her life, she admits. It's been a full half century according to what she shared as we talked over fresh fruit and tea in her sunny backyard in Dallas, Texas.

As an attorney with a specialty in mediation, Jennifer often works with clients who have unresolved emotional issues and disputes with their adult children. She knows from her own experience how emotionally charged these relationships can become and she is dedicated to helping both parties come to a resolution that will be good for everyone concerned.

"Being a mediator is actually my third career," said Jennifer. "I was a trial attorney for ten years and before that I was a therapist. I've had a varied life and have lived in many different places. All of these experiences have broadened my perspective."

Jennifer is also the mother of a son, age twenty-five, and a daughter, age twenty-seven. She was married to her children's father for twenty years but was divorced ten years ago. That subject has been a difficult one for Jennifer to talk about. It's not something she ever dreamed possible.

"I was the kind of person who always wanted to have children," she said. "I loved to babysit. I had always wanted to have a large family, five or even ten children. It was one of the things I thought my husband and I had agreed upon.

"I enjoyed all aspects of being a mother. Probably the happiest time of my life was when my children were pre-schoolers. There was never a time when I didn't want to be with them. I just loved the years that I was able to stay home with them. Then, as they grew older and became more independent, I've loved becoming friends with them."

Jennifer sounded emotional as she turned to the challenges that were also part of her parenting years. "Certainly one of the biggest challenges was the fact that my son was born with birth defects," she said. "I was overjoyed when he was born. But the next day I was devastated to learn that he had a physical handicap. Even though I loved him dearly, there was a part of me that couldn't imagine ever being happy again. I remember hearing a poem one day about the importance of appreciating just an ordinary day. I wondered at the time if I would ever see an ordinary day again.

"Everything seemed like a struggle and there was so much sadness over what might have been," she said, as tinges of grief touched her voice. "I felt that somehow I had caused his problems. No doctor has been able to tell me the cause, but it was still hard to let go of those feelings."

Understandably, Jennifer wanted to make up to her son what nature had deprived him of. "But that meant bending over backwards for him, and I realize, in retrospect, that my daughter paid a high price for all the attention I had to devote to her brother's care. I feel very badly about that. I was trying so hard to make things right for him that I did not spend as much time with her as I wish I had."

Jennifer acknowledged that she had to drive her son to a doctor 100 miles away from where they lived at the time. She left her daughter behind with a sitter during those monthly or twice monthly appointments. Jennifer knows now that she did the very best she could, but she still grieves the loss of closeness she had with her daughter before her son was born.

Another experience of grief and pain was Jennifer's divorce from her children's father. "It was a horrible time of custody battles and arguments," she said. "We both loved our children very much, and we both wanted them with us. It was very, very hard to let go of my daughter when she chose to live with her father. It was probably one of the most painful things that has ever happened to me in my entire life. She was sixteen at the time."

I could hear the grief and sadness in Jennifer's voice even though that event transpired over ten years ago. "My son, fourteen at the time, chose to stay with me, and that created another set of problems with his father. We ended up having a court battle over that too."

Following the divorce, her husband would not talk to Jennifer or communicate with her in any way. "There was a period of many years," she said, "when he said a lot of horrible things about me to the children. It was very difficult for me. Even though I didn't want to get back together, I did want to have a relationship that allowed us to co-parent peacefully, as I had observed my brother and sister doing with their ex-spouses."

Last fall, Jennifer's ex-husband suddenly became terminally ill. When she heard this news, she had a strong desire to visit him and make peace. He resisted for several months. Then just two days before he died he consented to seeing her.

Jennifer smiled as she recalled their visit. "It was one of the most beautiful experiences of my life," she said. "I was finally able to apologize for any pain I had caused him. He asked my forgiveness too, as we talked about things we hadn't been able to discuss in ten years, especially regarding our son and some of his problems. It was such a healing," she said with joy in her voice.

But what brought peace and closure to her relationship with her ex-husband created an upset with her daughter. "It was as though she thought I was invading her territory," Jennifer said, reflecting on the fact that her daughter had lived near her father for the past ten years. "I had the feeling she wanted me to go back home and just fade away. There was a lot of tension between us at the funeral, and I still don't know what that was all about. For awhile after that I felt the strain even when we talked on the phone. Maybe part of it was her own grieving process. She had been very close to her dad, and his death must have been extremely difficult for her."

Jennifer said that recently things have started to soften between her and her daughter. "But I still feel the need to talk to her to find out what that was about, and for each of us to be able to say to one another whatever we need to."

Jennifer recalled another time of tension between them. It occurred one summer when her daughter came to Texas from Arizona where she had been living with her dad. "It was impossible for us to relax around one another and to communicate on a day-to-day basis," she said. "Finally, at one point we had a very unpleasant confrontation. She brought up some pretty harsh and negative things about me that her father had said."

But there was good in it too, Jennifer was quick to admit. "The wonderful thing about it was that it gave us an opportunity to clear the air and come to an understanding. I had a chance to defend myself, and she had a chance to tell me how she perceived things during the divorce."

Jennifer learned an important lesson from that experience. "Even though it was painful to have the confrontation, it was the one thing needed at the time. It was a very helpful step toward healing our relationship. I think we need to have an honest talk like that again, to share how we really feel."

Jennifer admitted that her own behavior has added to the tension at times. She says she's been too quick to visit her daughter whenever she has a need and to try and be there for her in every way. Now she sees wisdom in stepping back in order to gain some perspective, and to avoid becoming so enmeshed in a situation that she can't see clearly. "I use journal writing and short vacations as ways to gain that perspective," she said.

Jennifer has had a lot of loss in her life, and she referred again to the challenge it presents and the grieving that accompanies it. But she is learning how to deal with it, and about the importance of not using her children to satisfy her emotional needs.

"Letting go of them is something I've been working on for many years," she said, "but I've just recently been doing some work with codependency issues, and I'm realizing I have a certain degree of enmeshment with my kids. I used to think I was helping by being there for them in every sense of the word. But now I see that in many instances the healthier thing would be to let them become more independent."

Jennifer admitted, however, that with her son "it's a whole different set of circumstances. Because of his disabilities, he does literally need my help. But I'm trying to encourage him to be more independent and to find other people who can help him learn new skills. He now uses some of the support available from an organization designed to assist people with physical challenges gain independence." A helper comes out to the house a couple of times a week to work with him on finances and housekeeping.

"And I'm realizing that it's better for him to have an outside person teach him those skills. When I'm too involved he either fights me on it or wants me to take over and that will just keep him dependent on me. We both know it's very important for him to become independent."

Jennifer also reflected on some of the same challenges she faced in her relationship with her own mother. "I felt smothered around her at times," she admitted, "particularly in the years when we lived together, both while I was married and after I was divorced.

"She had a lot more money than I did so money was one way she could help me. In fact, for several years after she and her sisters got married, their parents continued to give each of them a $200/monthly allowance. They believed a woman should always have money of her own," Jennifer said, admitting that today the custom does sound a little peculiar.

Without God's help, she said she wouldn't be the mother she is today. "I have a strong spiritual conviction that if we put things in the hands of God, He'll bring the answers to us. I've had to do this over and over with my children," she said, "particularly with my son. If I worry about how he's going to survive in the world, I get absolutely scared. I have to entrust him to God and then have the faith that he will be taken care of. My son is a very happy person. He has a job, friends, and he can do many things for himself." Jennifer's faith has proven itself.

"The same for my daughter," she added. "I need to put her and our relationship in God's hands. And I need to continue praying about it and trust that I will get the help I need. For example, through prayer I feel I was led to the twelve-step recovery program I'm in now."

Without a moment's hesitation Jennifer finished up our conversation by sharing her strong maternal feelings for her children. "They'll always be the most important part of my life," she said with love in her voice. "No matter how much I back off, the caring will always be there."

I didn't doubt her for a minute.

MY STORY

I've had my own issues with loss and grief in my relationship with my adult children. Like most people I spoke with, mine too are rooted in the long-ago past of my childhood, but I didn't know that for a very long time.

Like Charles and Jennifer, I had always wanted to be a parent. I loved holding my children, cuddling and nursing them as infants, reading to them when they were toddlers, and having the privilege of staying home with them during their growing up years.

But I was a nervous mother, a perfectionist in most ways. I had an almost abnormal desire to do everything right. I remember lying in bed at night going over the day in my mind, hoping that I had done everything I possibly could for my son and two daughters. I wanted them to feel loved and cared for and happy. But little did I know then how often I missed the target.

I had married a man I was crazy about from the day I met him. I thought we were going in the same direction, eager for our life together as partners, as parents, as friends. But before our tenth anniversary it was clear that we did not share the same values or dreams. I began feeling completely alone in the marriage. He was consumed by his law practice and I was consumed by our home and children. For many years I had been too busy to notice the imbalance. But as the children got older and needed less of my time, I had more opportunity to see the void in my life.

By the time we were married just under twenty years, my husband had met someone he preferred. Shortly afterwards he moved out of our home. In the weeks that followed, I cried, screamed, ran, drove for hours, and sobbed myself to sleep each night. Then one day, I took a good hard look at the way things were, gathered every ounce of strength I had, and vowed that I would keep the kids and me together no matter what.

I had always been a survivor, a solution-oriented person who had a high tolerance for emotional pain. When things got tough in my life, like the bumper sticker says, I got going. This episode was not about to undo me.

But my resolve lasted only about two weeks. Suddenly,

unexpectedly, I fell apart completely. My health went. My mental stability failed me. My emotions broke free. I was a wreck. Only then did I realize that I had been running on empty for a long time. Everything in my life came to a screeching halt. I couldn't think, feel, decide, choose or plan. All I could do was cry. Grief flooded over me like a tidal wave. There were days when I thought I would drown in sorrow.

Over the next year and a half, my husband and I went back and forth two or three times—each one at my invitation—but we couldn't stay together. His heart was with the other woman and my heart was torn watching him bond with her. We separated one last time, divided up our possessions, made financial arrangements, dealt with custody issues and filed for divorce.

My son and youngest daughter remained in our family home with their father who returned there after we made our final settlement, and our oldest daughter and I moved to an apartment nearby until she left for college.

The grief from those lost years is with me still. And the consequences of their father's and my actions have left a deep imprint on the lives of our children. Each one, in varying degrees and ways, is now dealing with his/her own grief.

Today my son is thirty, and my daughters are twenty-six and thirty-two. It has taken nearly a decade to face and deal with the wreckage of our past. For a long time it was easy for them and for me to focus our blame on their father. After all, he's the one who took a walk! But a divorce is never that clean-cut. No one person is ever completely at fault.

As my children moved into adulthood, their deeper pain flared up. My youngest daughter expressed her grief through rebellion and reckless living as a teenager. My son buried himself in sports and pot. And my oldest daughter dealt with her pain by escaping overseas, first as a student, and then as a missionary.

I handled mine by moving to another city, away from the scene of past hurts, settling down to make a living—something I had never done before—and eventually remarrying.

I'll never forget the day I arrived in San Diego. I had cried all the way down the freeway from my former home in Los Angeles. I couldn't believe twenty years of marriage had come to this.

After I unpacked the last box, arranged my furniture, and hooked up my telephone, it suddenly hit me. What had I done? Moving to a strange city, living in an unfamiliar place, and most important, doing so without my children at my side.

Periodic visits with them were both precious and painful. I hated to see them end. I felt like the weekend parent who spoils them with Sunday brunch and movies and toys, but who misses out on the day-to-day events that will never pass this way again.

I coped by jumping on the merry-go-round of self-improvement seminars and workshops and new-thought churches that were prevalent during the 1980s. None of them was a waste. But neither did any of them have the answers I longed for.

Then in December of 1982 I had the most beautiful experience of my life one morning on the beach as I returned from my morning walk. I stopped to pray, as I often did, and in those few moments, I felt in a deep and personal way the Lord comforting me and assuring me that He was real. That He could be trusted. That He could be known in a personal way—in a way that could make a difference in my life. I gave my heart to Him that day.

Four years later my youngest daughter came to live with my second husband and me while attending junior college. During that time our relationship took an important turn. We were together once more under the same roof on a daily basis. I had experienced a lot of emotional and spiritual healing by then, so I knew that, finally, I had something to give her.

Those two years were the beginning of our restoration. They were times of turbulence, as she experienced long bouts of depression and grief. There were also sweet and loving times, marked by long walks along the ocean together, shopping for clothes, and laying by the pool, hours of talking and crying, and times of angry confrontation when she told me how she felt about the divorce, her feelings of being abandoned by me, and her fear of being alone. And it was a time of deep inner healing, as she began building a relationship with Christ. We attended church together regularly and those were very special times for both of us.

By the time she left for her last two years of college in Northern California, I felt our relationship had been restored and that regardless of what surfaced in the future, we'd be able to face it and deal with it. That has proven true.

Meanwhile, my oldest daughter was living overseas. Our relationship had always been good, I thought. She had been my closest confidant following my divorce. I realize now, however, that I leaned on her too heavily. It wasn't fair to ask her to listen to my grief when she had grief of her own.

Then two years ago, shortly after she and her family moved back to the United States from Morocco, her pain broke loose. Suddenly the reality of what she had come home to was right there—in front of her—in a way that she had not looked at before. Her father lived in one city. I lived in another. She did not have a family homestead to return to. There was no big backyard for her children to play in, no continuity from the past to carry her through the transition to her new life in the United States.

She let out her emotions in spurts at first. She took swipes at me, answered abruptly and abrasively much of the time, seemed angry whenever we were together. Then one Saturday it all came out—in a torrent. Accusations, fear, anger, hostility and deep, deep hurts. For the first time in my life with her I felt like the enemy. She seemed to hate me—for who I was, for what I had done, for what I had not done. I was a major disappointment and she let me know it.

Months passed after that. We exchanged letters and cards as we each attempted to let the other one know how we felt. It was one of the most painful experiences of my life. I grieved the loss of the daughter I had known and loved and been close to for nearly thirty years.

What I didn't realize at the time, however, was that we were on the brink of a new birth in our relationship. And we each needed time to look at one another afresh, in the light of our individual maturing process. I think we both realized that we hadn't been completely honest with one another. She admitted later that she had a very difficult time expressing anger toward me. Little wonder! I never invited it. The moment any of my children seemed unhappy I went into my "pleasing" mode.

I also had a terrible problem expressing anger toward her—

toward anyone for that matter. Much debris stood between us, and it all needed to be hauled away. It took time—months of letter writing, periods of silence, tentative communications as we shared little by little, and then a breakthrough when the Lord spoke privately to each one of us about the other.

She came to a deeper understanding of my pain, and I came to a deeper understanding of hers. Being able to express these insights to one another accelerated the healing process and opened us up in a new way to feeling the love that was there all along.

I learned how to listen to her feelings instead of fixing them, how to share without burdening her, how to remain her parent and become her friend, and how to acknowledge her point of view without feeling threatened.

Today, our relationship is real—not perfect. And because of that I'm excited about what's ahead. I can now relate to her as a whole person, rather than as a fearful, grief-stricken, guilt-ridden parent with a one-dimensional agenda.

And as for my son, well our relationship feels very warm and good to me. We've always been able to talk and to share honestly. He admits that he has yet to really confront the past and the pain of his dad's and my divorce. But he has been able to express some of his strong feelings toward me. He has raged at me, cried with me, shared the intense pain he feels in his relationship with his father. I treasure each of these moments, tough as they are to live through. They show me that his heart has not hardened. He knows that I love him. I know that he loves me and he has forgiven me. The consequences of my choices—to leave the family home, to move to San Diego, to remarry, to become a Christian—are there for us to deal with as we go forward. But the worst is over. We are moving into a new level of healed emotions, understanding and compassion—and most important to me, a deep and abiding friendship.

LETTING GO OF GRIEVING

Grieving, unlike manipulating or criticizing, is basically a healthy and good process and an appropriate one in response to loss. It can become a problem, however, when it impairs your relationships and impedes you from moving on with your life. Only you can decide when this is true for you, and only you can choose to recover from the loss. I want to stress, however, the importance of doing the deep emotional work, not simply being aware of it or talking about it.

I recommend reading *The Grief Recovery Handbook*, mentioned earlier in this chapter, and then joining a grief recovery workshop or therapy group. I believe it is essential to participate with other supportive people while going through the healing process. And if you can be in a setting with a professional facilitator who understands the process, so much the better. But even now, while you are reading this book, you can begin to let go spiritually and emotionally by looking at what God has to say to us when we are stricken with grief and guilt.

Words To Consider—Actions to Take

• "If we confess our sins, He is faithful and just to forgive us our sins and to cleanse us from all unrighteousness" (1 John 1:9). What an opportunity the Lord provides here. If we confess our sins He will forgive us. This one act alone can have a powerful healing effect on our lives. Grief can be lifted. Guilt can be dismissed—when we take responsibility for our wrongdoing, openly admit it, and then accept God's cleansing. Imagine the results such an experience could have in your relationship with your adult children. When they see you go to God with your grief, with your sin, and with your regret, they will be set free of the burden your pain has been for them.

• "As far as the east is from the west, so far hath he removed our transgressions from us" (Ps. 103:12). Not only does the Lord cleanse us from our unrighteousness, but then He removes them from us. He remembers them no more. So if your grief is tied to your transgressions against your children, bring them before the Lord and let Him remove them. He is the only one who can.

• "For if our heart condemns us, God is greater than our heart, and knows all things" (1 John 3:20). Grieving parents are often self-condemning, as well. They are quick to absorb the guilt of an unresolved relationship, finding fault with themselves and then displaying that pain in every facet of their lives. But God says that He is greater than our condemning hearts. He knows all things about us. He knows the truth about us, about our children, about our situation, and He can minister comfort to us in whatever way we need it.

LOOKING WITHIN

Parents who identify themselves as grievers can relate to many of these statements:

1. I tend to bury my feelings.
2. I avoid facing and dealing with losses.
3. I spend a lot of time regretting the past.
4. I believe that time heals all wounds.
5. I feel sad and lifeless much of the time.
6. I replace my losses as quickly as possible.
7. I have a problem with trust.
8. I have difficulty living in the moment.

PART THREE

*Restoring
Troubled
Relationships*

Chapter Nine

TELLING
THE TRUTH

"**A**ll of your relationships will improve 100%—absolutely," said the tall, smiling man at the front of the room, "if you commit to telling the truth."

The day I heard those words I was sitting in a large hotel room, one of a hundred or more participants in a weekend communication workshop. I was in deep pain at the time, facing a divorce I didn't want, after nearly twenty years of marriage, feeling disconnected from my children, estranged from my parents and siblings, and sick to my stomach most of the time. I was desperate. I needed some one, some thing, some idea to help me get a grip on my life.

I played his words over and over in my mind. Commit to the truth? What a startling statement. I already do tell the truth, I reassured myself. Don't most people? I mean how many people make a decision to lie to the people they love and care about?

But the more I thought about the instructor's words the more I realized how far from the truth I was. I hadn't told my husband the truth about my pain. I hadn't told my parents that I felt sick and scared, even terrified of what lay ahead for me as a single mother. I didn't share my grief, anger, anguish, or fear with my children in a responsible and honest way.

Was this lack of honesty the reason for so much brokenness in my life? I couldn't put aside the question. I left the workshop committed to finding the answer. During the years since, I discovered that dishonesty was at the root of all of my troubled relationships. I was to learn, however, that I didn't tell the truth because I didn't know what the truth was.

Before I could tell the truth, I had to recognize it. That began a long process of self-discovery through prayer, private therapy, and group support that has led me to where I am today, aware that honest self-disclosure is the first step in the process of restoring broken relationships.

THE HIDDEN TRUTH

It's one thing to know what to do, however, and another thing to actually do it. What a challenge it is to remain committed to the truth and to continually speak it—no matter what. Fear of rejection, hidden agenda, low self-esteem, false humility, righteousness, anger, pride, you name it—something is always ready to come between us and the truth. And to the degree that these blocks remain in place, our relationships suffer and deteriorate.

Only in the last couple of years have I discovered how unwilling and unable I was to tell the truth in my relationships with my adult children. I wanted so much to be loved, liked, and to be popular that I was afraid to risk letting my true self be known. I'm sure my son and daughters could feel the facade.

As God began the healing process in my life, however, I realized that I—not my children—had to make the first move. I was responsible for my feelings, my pain, my truth. They were responsible for theirs. If I wanted a healthy and loving relationship with them, then I had to take the steps to bring it about.

I realized that unless and until I was willing to commit to the truth, no lasting or meaningful recovery could take place. It was a frightening realization because it required more than mere lip service. I felt that God wanted me to be an active partner in the healing process, not just a passive recipient.

THE TRUTH ABOUT US

Telling the truth, I was to learn, is about being vulnerable in the moment. It's more than simply opening our minds. One can be open without being vulnerable. To be vulnerable is to speak from the heart, to share our feelings, to risk rejection and confrontation and anger—and to risk being fully loved, flaws and all.

This was a new experience for me. I had been about as far from my emotions as the east is from the west. No one had ever inquired about my feelings prior to my first experience in counseling, so I had a lot of catching up to do.

But in the months that followed I became acquainted with my emotional self. I learned to say, "I hurt," "I'm excited," "I want," "I need," "I'm afraid." The more I let myself be known, the more of me there was to know. And the better I felt—physically, spiritually, mentally and emotionally. And the more I knew, the less afraid I was. In fact, it was an unexpected relief to discover that I had a lot more in common with the human race than I had ever admitted. I was a person with the same hunger, fear, love and longing as everyone else. I didn't have to impress, compete with or outperform anyone. I didn't have to work at or pretend to be the perfect mother. I had already proven I wasn't.

All I really had to do was be me, and then do the very best I could with what I knew about myself at any moment. What a relief!

Does that mean that as parents we go to our children and dump on them every thought, idea and opinion we've ever had? No. What it does mean, however, is that we remain faithful to our feelings, that we pay attention to them, that we take responsibility for them, that we learn to trust them, and that we express them as openly and honestly as we can.

Our children want to hear from our hearts ("Pat, I feel nervous about you driving that old car. I think I'd die if anything happened to you and the kids") not our heads ("Pat, that car is a trap. What are you trying to do? Kill yourself and your kids?")

They don't need a lecture on how to drive, rear children, pray, work, eat and sleep. What they do want, I suspect, is to know that we love them and that we care.

THE TRUTH ABOUT GOD

Once we get to the truth about ourselves, we are on the way to discovering the truth about God, for without Him there can be no deep and lasting peace. That came home to me with sudden clarity one Sunday morning during a prayer circle at church. A woman in the group I'll call Nancy, lovingly encouraged one of the women to talk and cry about her fears and concerns.

Marlene was frantic about her son, Tom, who was living "from hand to mouth," as she described it. She said she had been unable to communicate with him in any way that would make a difference. He wasn't working. He had no permanent place to live, and even worse in her mind, he didn't seem to care.

"I don't know whether to fly to Dallas and rescue him, leave him alone to work out his pain in his own way, or drop the entire thing and get on with my own life," she said. She appeared to be overwhelmed by guilt and fear. I could relate to everything she said, for I had had similar worries about my son.

Marlene stopped talking and crying long enough to pull a handkerchief from her purse. Then Nancy moved across the room and sat beside her. She put an arm around Marlene and hugged her firmly.

"He's an adult now," Nancy said. "He must take responsibility for his choices. God is with him. Pray for him and love him. But put him in the hands of the Lord."

I knew she was speaking the truth. The truth for me and for Marlene and for every parent in that room. We too needed to put our children in the hands of the Lord. He said He would care for them, and He will—if we stop getting in the way.

"All your children shall be taught by the Lord; and great shall be the peace of your children" (Isa. 54:13).

"The Lord is good, a stronghold in the day of trouble; and He knows those who trust in Him" (Nah. 1:7).

These and other scriptures were suddenly made new to me in my experience—not simply as words on a page.

It was not necessary for Marlene or for any of us to confront our children over and over, to unburden our emotions on them, or to saddle them with our ideas and advice.

It was a precious moment in my life. At some point later on I was able to tell my son how at times I had wanted to rescue him, that I had felt responsible for his pain, that I had wished I could have been a better parent. In fact, we talked about those very things again last summer, nearly ten years after the original incident. It was a particularly sweet time for both of us. He told me what he had learned and how he had grown during that time, and I was able to confess my sorrow over the brokenness in our family.

REACHING FOR SUPPORT

You may have identified with many of the parents who shared their stories in the preceding chapters. Maybe you can relate to the sometimes compulsive urges to control your adult children by pleasing, manipulating, rescuing, grieving, criticizing or being a victim.

Perhaps you also found some comfort in the healing scriptures and the action points at the end of each chapter. But you may also wonder how can you make a consistent and lasting change in your behavior. What can you do to demonstrate to your children that you are serious about restoration?

"The first thing to do is nothing," says Dr. Pardington, quoted in *Streams in the Desert*. That may sound like contradictory advice in the face of a pressing need for change. But he carefully points out that if we use our human resources to figure out the answer we actually impede God's work. "When you run into a spiritual fog bank," he says, "don't tear ahead; slow down the machinery of your life—We are to simply trust God. While we trust, God can work."[1]

How true that has been in my experience and in the experience of many of the parents I spoke with. All of our own "doing" got us nowhere, but when we went to God first, steps were revealed.

Before we go to our children with the truth, I believe we must first take it to God. Talk to Him from your heart. Tell Him your feelings, your fears, your desire for restoration. Ask Him what part you are to play in the healing process.

I'm sure that God spoke to me that day as Nancy ministered to Marlene. On the natural level, rushing about and rescuing our children seems like the loving thing to do. But I believe the Lord has something else in mind. He wants us to lay down our physical parenting and take up parenting in the Spirit. I never would have come to that realization on my own. I was still too much of a pleaser, and I was grieving too much to make a wise decision.

While we are in the process of restoration, it's especially important to let God lead us because without His wisdom most of us are prone to rely on our old behavior—the very tactics that contributed to the brokenness in the first place. More of the same will not produce different results! But it's difficult to believe that when we are racked with fear and worry and guilt.

Once we face and tell the truth, however, I believe God will move in power, and show us the right way to go. He may lead you to a support group for parents where you can share your pain and be confronted. Or you may feel a nudge to go into a season of professional counseling. If you are a Christian, God will likely lead you to someone who shares your belief that Jesus Christ is the center of your life. This relationship will be an intimate one over a period of many months so it's important to seek someone you will feel comfortable with emotionally and spiritually.

If you are not a Christian, but you believe in God and practice a spiritual discipline, then I encourage you to choose a therapist who will respect your views and who specializes in family relationships.

You may also want to investigate a twelve-step program such as Co-dependents Anonymous (modeled after Alcoholics Anonymous) or the Christian support group, Overcomers Outreach, listed in the Supplementary Resources in the back of this book.

Consider restoration and healing a gift you are giving to your adult children, as well as to yourself. By taking inventory of your life and seeking support for the changes you wish to make, you are investing in yourself and in your relationship with your children. This is a process that requires nothing less than a full commitment. It may take months, in some cases, two or more years. But don't let the amount of time drive you away. Your patterns were formed over many years. And most of them were unconscious as you absorbed your parents' beliefs and modeled their behavior. It will take some time to undo them. But the actual path of restoration can be an exciting and satisfying one—even during the painful times of looking within. Like a dedicated hiker you will hit hills and valleys, but over all you'll be going up! And the higher you climb, the clearer the view, and the more of the big picture you will see.

The Bible says that God knows our every need even before we bring them to Him. And He promises to transform us by the renewing of our minds. What a wonderful promise. As we commit to change, He will lead us on the path we should go. And He will finish the good work He started. How blessed we are to have such support. No human being I have ever met could keep such promises.

SHARE THE TRUTH

As you continue reading you may be tempted to grab your Bible and shut out the world. You and God can handle this alone, thank you very much! This point of view, however, tends to separate us from people, often the very people we want to be reconciled with.

I believe God has made us social, as well as spiritual beings. He wants us to fellowship with one another, to pray together, and to learn from each other. In fact, God often speaks to us through other people. So avoid the "Lone Ranger" approach to restoration.

Many parents have discovered that the simple act of confessing the truth to a counselor, trusted friend, prayer partner, spouse, or group can relieve them of physical and emotional symptoms they have endured for years.

If you feel ready to embark on this journey, I urge you to stop for a minute now and make a commitment to the truth. Speak it, share it, write about it, and then take whatever steps the Lord puts in front of you so that you may enjoy the full measure of grace He has for you.

Chapter Ten

FORGIVING

During October of this year, our pastor, Mark Slomka, focused his sermons on the topic, "Your Past: Friend or Foe." It has been one of the most compelling series I've heard in many years.

"Every future has a past," he said, "and for all of us this includes: relationship with our parents, responses to disappointment, disapproval and pain, disempowering comments, relationships with our children, validation of our sexuality, a secure or insecure home life, enmeshment, or disengagement with others."

Slomka says that "whether we like it or not, God has given us the past as a gift to keep us oriented to our future." By closing the door on it, we hurt ourselves and those we love. If we let it, however, "the past can be our guide" to present understanding and future behavior.

Our past can also be our friend, he said, if . . .

• We remember that Christ died for our sins, as well as the sins committed against us.

• We repent of the choices we made that we didn't have to make. "Something else took the place of God's Word and His mercy in our lives at those times," said Slomka.

• We receive God's tender mercy through Jesus Christ. We can then enter the sanctification process—the process of becoming holy or being made clean. When we embrace this work of God in our lives we are set apart to fully enjoy the freedom, love and grace He has for each of us.

"For I know the thoughts I think toward you, says the Lord, thoughts of peace and not of evil, to give you a future and a hope" (Jer. 29:11).

How difficult it is for parents, however, to let go of the past, and to turn toward the bright future God has for them. It is so easy to get stuck in the past, to focus on it and to remain there, instead of using it as a tool for understanding and healing.

Forgiveness, a crucial step in restoring relationships with our adult children, is important because it so often relates to experiences and events that occurred in the past. Before we can truly forgive ourselves or another we need to look back to the hurtful episodes and remember them, repent of any thought, word, or action we used for harm and receive God's grace for healing. This process can occur in an instant of realization and repentance, or it can take place over time, as we move through the stages of forgiveness.

THE FOUR STAGES OF FORGIVENESS

Lewis B. Smedes discusses this process at length in his book, *Forgive and Forget: Healing the Hurts We Don't Deserve.*

Hurt You are pushed into this first stage of forgiveness when someone causes you "pain so deep and unfair that you cannot forget it." Herman remembers such a time from his past. His mother shut him out of the house when he was a little boy, about four years of age, because he had spilled something on her clean carpet. "She told me that if I couldn't abide by the rules in our home, then I wasn't welcome, and she pushed me out on the front lawn and closed the door. I'll never forget the terror I felt," he said. "I looked out at the world and wondered what would happen to me. Who would take care of me. I learned then that if I wanted to be safe I would have to do exactly what my mother told me to do."

That experience made an indelible mark on Herman's spirit. Even though his mother let him in again after she calmed down, he knew the extent of her rage and power and he never wanted to displease her again. "I am sorry and ashamed to admit," he said, "that as much as I vowed otherwise, I brought that same controlling behavior into my marriage and parenting. I was a terrible perfectionist and expected much more of my children than they could possibly deliver. My son and I have been estranged for years, and I'm sure my standards are at the root of it."

Hate You enter the second stage of forgiveness when you "cannot shake the memory of how much you were hurt, and you cannot wish your enemy well." Some people at this stage are so enraged by the memory that they want the other person to suffer as much as they are suffering.

Loretta knows what it's like to feel this kind of hatred. She is raising her adult daughter's two children because the woman is unfit to mother them. She has been a drug abuser since she was a teenager and is still unstable at the age of thirty-five. Her two girls are fourteen and twelve. They've been living with Loretta for the last ten years. She is now their legal guardian. "You should have seen the conditions they were living in before I took them," she said, in tears. "Just thinking about my daughter brings up so much anger. I believe I really do hate her," she said. "She not only ruined her own life but she ruined her kids' lives too. She had no right to do that."

Loretta also acknowledged that her own life has been undeniably altered as a result of her daughter's problems. She had looked forward to retirement, travel, free time to do what she wanted. Instead she is back where she was thirty years ago, making lunches, attending P.T.A. meetings, helping with Scouts and the soccer team.

"I love these two," she said, displaying a recent picture of her and her grandchildren. "But this child-rearing is for much younger women," she added, laughing. "I keep going because they need me, but it's hard. I think it would be easier if their mother had died. We would grieve and we would heal. But the way it is now, there is no closure—for them or for me. We never know when she's going to show up and make trouble. I never believed a mother could have such hateful thoughts about her own child, but I confess I have them."

Healing   In the third stage of forgiveness you are given new eyes to see the person who hurt you in a new light. "Your memory is healed. You turn back the flow of pain and are free again."

Maureen's hatred was toward herself. She couldn't bear to think about how much she had hurt her son when he was growing up. Her husband had died when she was in her twenties, and her son was two years old at the time. "I was little more than a kid myself," she said. "I had no clue how to be a parent. I left him with sitters constantly. I hated staying home. I was young and I wanted to live. I saw him holding me back."

Her eyes watered as she continued talking. "Then when he was about five he had a frightening accident. A neighborhood dog bit him and he was nearly blinded in one eye. That really brought me up short," she said. "Everything changed after that. I realized how important he was to me and how selfish I had been. That happened twenty years ago," she added. "It changed my life. For a long time I couldn't forgive myself. I think I overindulged him after that, you know, trying to make up for the past."

Maureen said she knew she couldn't change what happened but she also couldn't live with the guilt. She confided a lot in a friend at work and one day about a year later the woman invited her to church. "I figured what did I have to lose, so I went," said Maureen. "That was the day I got saved," she said proudly. "I really heard the Gospel, that Jesus had died for me, for my sins. I left church that day feeling a thousand pounds lighter. After that, I gradually started to see myself the way Jesus sees me, and I began to understand why I had done what I had done. I didn't change all at once, of course. But I did change. I still remember those horrible times, but I'm not hurting the way I did. And my son and I have a pretty good relationship now—at least, we're working at it. I told him to take his time. He has a lot to forgive me for."

Coming Together In the fourth stage of forgiveness, says Smedes, "you invite the person who hurt you back into your life; if he or she comes honestly, love can move you both toward a new and healed relationship." This stage depends on the other party as much as it depends on you. If he or she does not come back, or does not see his or her part in the brokenness, then you must be healed alone. Lucy and Hal are in this position. Both are in their seventies now, the parents of two sons, Ken and Will. Ken, the youngest, has been an alcoholic for years and is still drinking. He's been in and out of rehabilitation programs, but so far he has not remained sober for more than several months at a time.

"For years our life was a nightmare," said Lucy, weeping openly as she talked about this very painful relationship. Hal patted Lucy's hand and nodded in agreement as she talked.

"We don't know what went wrong," he said. "We thought we raised both boys the same. But they sure turned out differently."

Lucy had difficulty going into detail about their relationship. She said he had been a very aggressive and moody sort of person growing up. He became verbally abusive and physically intimidating during his teens. "He was always big for his age," she said. Then pointing to her own diminutive stature she added, playfully, "As you can see, I was no match for him."

"But that's not the worst of it," Hal said, taking up where his wife left off. "He stole from us—a few dollars at first—then silver and jewelry and larger bills as he could get them. Sometimes he just plain took them out of my wallet or Lucy's purse when we were sleeping. Other times he wormed his way back with tears and stories about how he was going to change if we'd just help him."

Lucy wiped her swollen eyes with a tissue. "We've tried to reach him," she said, "but it's no use. We've had to get on with our lives. I'm still sad when I think about him, but I know the Lord has healed Hal and me. We're not so obsessed anymore. We have a good life together," she said, smiling at her husband. "And we have another son who is wonderful to us. We are going on, doing the best we can. It's better now than it's been in years."

ALL PAIN IS NOT THE SAME

It hurts if an adult child makes fun of our cooking or driving skills. Or reminds us of an embarrassing episode in our lives. Or teases us about a choice of clothing or shoes. My youngest daughter, for example, loved to needle me about wearing a certain pair of red sandals that she couldn't stand. Yet at the time, they were a favorite pair of mine.

It's another thing, however, for a child to steal food or money or clothing or a car in order to keep a drug habit going.

Playful teasing between loved ones is part of the life of a healthy relationship. Theft, cheating, lying is not.

Some hurts we can express openly in the moment, forgive, heal, and go on. For example, I might tell my daughter that it hurts when she teases me about my shoes. She could apologize, and we could hug each other and go forward.

The hurt that results from a child who steals, lies, and cheats, however, is not so easily dealt with. I'm thinking about Lucy and Hal and the years of pain they've endured because of their son's addictive behavior.

WHY WE HURT OUR CHILDREN—WHY OUR CHILDREN HURT US

Because we think the other person deserves it.   Parents may want to punish their adult children with silence or disapproval, teach them a lesson, show them who's in charge. Adult children may want to hurt their parents as retaliation for past mistreatment, current grievances, unexpressed anger, willful determination to be right.

Because they can't help it.   Some parents and adult children hurt each other through substance abuse such as alcohol or debt or other abusive behavior. They are compulsive, out of control, self-absorbed. They just don't get it! They don't see the damage they do.

One of my friends braces herself everytime her mother comes to visit. Her mother is a compulsive talker. She fills every quiet moment with nervous chatter, commentary and unwanted advice. Here is a mother who longs for a close and loving relationship with her daughter and hasn't achieved it yet. She cannot see or hear what she is doing to keep that relationship from developing.

Because they have problems of their own. When parents are in pain they are usually blind to the challenges and conflicts their children face. And the reverse is equally true. Just as I hurt my son and daughters by being preoccupied with myself, my children at times could not see what I was going through because they were overcome with their own grief. None of this is a matter of right and wrong. It is simply one of the challenging and painful issues that are part of every relationship.

Because of their desire to help. Parents and adult children sometimes hurt one another more through good intentions than by any other means. They do for one another what the other could and probably should do for himself or herself.

Some parents, for example, keep adult children tied to them through money. Remember Jennifer, whose parents sent her a monthly allowance even after she was married?

And adult children often hurt their parents by overindulging them. One seventy-year-old woman said her son treats her like an invalid. He won't let her take public transportation because he fears she'll get mugged. And he wants to take over her finances because he's afraid she won't make wise decisions. "I feel like a child," she said. "I'm starting to lose confidence in myself, yet I don't know how to get through to him."

WHY FORGIVE?

Because, it works!

Forgiveness opens the way to restoration. "Will you forgive me for offending you?" Consider the power of those words. You state the hurtful action and then ask the other person to forgive you. Even if your child is the guilty party, you can open the door to healing by asking forgiveness for being angry or resentful. In most parent/adult child relationships, no one is completely innocent. Even the victim holds vicious thoughts about the victimizer and needs to be released from them—justifiable as they may be. Revenge is never an answer. An eye for an eye too often leads to a life for a life.

Forgiveness is an expression of love toward ourselves. In fact, it is the only way to be fair to ourselves. To hang on to hurt and anger and revenge is to inflict more pain on ourselves than we received in the first place. The wound festers and enlarges until it consumes us. We become the victims of the wrongdoing all over again—to a greater and greater degree.

To release the child who has hurt us by extending and receiving forgiveness is to turn our attention away from the pain and toward life, to free our mind from the sting of going over the incident again and again, and to disengage from wounding memories that can only intensify the hurt. To forgive another is an act of love on our own behalf. And if the other is set free in the process, so be it. He is not off the hook. He is still responsible for what he did. He will still have to answer to God.

Forgiveness is an act of obedience to God. To forgive is to walk with Christ. We forgive because he first forgave us. "And be kind to one another, tenderhearted, forgiving one another, even as God in Christ forgave you" (Eph. 4:32). Whenever you have difficulties forgiving yourself, your children, or God Himself, consider your part of the problem. Ask the Lord to expose your heart and to bring to light any ways in which you have contributed to the brokenness.

Forgiveness is a decision—not a feeling. We do not have to feel forgiving in order for it to be valid. It is enough to decide to forgive. The feelings will follow. But feeling good is not the only result to work toward. Those who forgive have a greater vision. They are looking forward to a restored relationship.

Decide now to forgive. The other person does not even have to be present for your decision to take effect. "When you release the wrongdoer from the wrong, you cut a malignant tumor out of your inner life," says Smedes. "You set a prisoner free, but you discover that the real prisoner was yourself."

Forgiveness is not concerned with past details. As you give and receive forgiveness, concentrate on restoring the relationship, on coming together, on putting the past behind. Forgiveness is not about setting the record straight. It's about letting go of emotional baggage, blame, shame, and the need to be right.

If you are sincere in your desire to forgive yourself and others, you will not waste time trying to reconstruct former conversations, explaining your position, accusing and counter-accusing, or assigning responsibility for who said what to whom when and where. Attempts to recreate past grievances often widen the gap between people instead of closing it. Focus on the relationship and your desire to restore it. Leave the rest to the Lord.

Chapter Eleven

PRAYING

Ilearned an important lesson about parenting and prayer one Sunday morning shortly after I had become a Christian. I joined a group of men and women in the church house who had gathered to pray for one another. I was depressed at the time, feeling helpless in my relationship with my son. He was estranged from us at the time and it was driving me crazy. I wanted to talk to him, to reach him with common sense and encouragement. If only I could do something, I thought.

I shared my fears with the group and asked for prayer and counsel, and suggestions from other parents who had a similar experience. I could hardly talk I was so upset. As my tears fell, one woman from the other side of the room came over to me and put a caring arm around my shoulder. I'll never forget what that meant to me.

"Your work in the flesh is over," she said softly. "All he needs now is your prayer—a mother's most effective tool," she added with a playful smile.

Relief coursed through me like a warm wind. You mean I don't have to do anything, I thought. Like run up to Los Angeles and rescue him? Or wire him money? Or send food? Or get him another car? Or look into a treatment program? You mean I could still be a good mother without doing something? It was a totally foreign concept. To think of prayer as a mother's most important tool was also a new idea. But I liked it. It felt right. I was eager to learn more about prayer and to practice praying—for my son, for my daughters, for myself as their mother.

LIFE CHANGING

Richard Foster, author of *Celebration of Discipline*, says that prayer "brings us into the deepest and highest work of the human spirit. Real prayer is life creating and life changing."[1] That has been my experience these last ten years as a Christian. I once read that a life without prayer is a life without power. No wonder the first forty-four years of my life were such a battle. I did not know how to use the weapon of prayer.

C.H. Spurgeon, renowned man of God, had this to say about prayer. "God's seasons are not at your beck. If the first stroke of the flint doth not bring forth the fire, you must strike again. God will hear prayer, but He may not answer it at the time which we in our minds have appointed—Hence the need of perseverance and importunity in supplication."[2]

Those words also ministered to me as a parent. How quickly I used to give up or give in when I didn't see results. That day I needed a timely lesson in the art of perseverance.

Theodore Cuyler said he does "not believe that there is such a thing in the history of God's kingdom as a right prayer offered in a right spirit that is forever left unanswered."[3] How comforting. Our God is a god of understanding and compassion. He listens and He responds.

And what did Jesus say about prayer when He walked this earth? "If you ask anything in My name, I will do it" (John 14:14). "And whatever things you ask in prayer, believing, you will receive" (Matt. 21:22).

What a powerful promise. Yet many parents do not have what they most desire in their relationships with their adult children. The strong words of James to the Christian believer may apply to mothers and fathers who still struggle to manipulate and control their children and themselves. "You ask and do not receive, because you ask amiss, that you may spend it on your pleasures" (James 4:3).

PRINCIPLES OF POWERFUL PRAYER

Parents who struggle with their own pleasures of pleasing, manipulating, rescuing, criticizing and other controlling behaviors, may find themselves unable to pray effectively because they are operating from a hidden agenda instead of from a clean heart. But you can change that emphasis by going to the Lord in your brokenness, as a child to a loving father. Acknowledge your need for Him.

Praise God. Acknowledge Him for who He is and for the opportunity to cooperate with Him in restoring your relationships with your adult children. Allow yourself to sink into His presence and to absorb His teaching on prayer and His promise to give you the desire of your heart. "But seek first the kingdom of God and His righteousness, and all these things shall be added to you" (Matt. 6:33).

Submit to His Authority. Ask Him to help you put aside your own thoughts, "good" ideas, decisions and plans, as well as the opinions of others, wise as they may be. Even though the Lord has given you a good mind and common sense, right now you want to be open to His mind, the fountain of wisdom.

Confess Your Sins. Tell the Lord what you've done to block restoration. Are you compulsive in trying to manage your children's affairs? Have you sinned against them by criticizing or rescuing them? Have you burdened them with your problems? Have you manipulated circumstances in order to produce the results you want? These are tough questions that we all need to answer for ourselves. Broken relationships are never one-sided. "Therefore if you bring your gift to the altar, and there remember that your brother has something against you, leave your gift there before the altar, and go your way. First be reconciled to your brother, and then come and offer your gift" (Matt. 5:23–24).

Come Against Evil. Bind the enemy from interfering in your relationship with your children. All power in heaven and on earth belongs to us in Christ Jesus. "Whatever you bind on earth will be bound in heaven, and whatever you loose on earth will be loosed in heaven" (Matt. 16:19). Pray for a hedge of protection around your motives, your desires, your needs and wants, and the results you hope for so that no evil will block the good that God has for you and your children.

Ask the Holy Spirit for Wisdom. "If any of you lacks wisdom, let him ask of God, who gives to all liberally and without reproach, and it will be given to him" (James 1:5). How simple and how comforting. All we have to do is ask and we will receive what we need.

The next step is to allow God to speak to you in the way He chooses. He may use Scripture, an impression on your spirit, another person, an inner voice, a dream or vision. If you remain open to the means, however, you will not miss it. I once heard that there is a direct link between yielding and hearing.

Let Go of the Results. Once you have placed your relationship in God's hands, and you have acted on the wisdom He provided, let go! God knows what you and your children need in order to be fully restored to one another. He knows the perfect time and place for the result to occur. Don't turn over your situation to the Lord and then monitor His actions! You can't watch a flower bloom. Yet how hard some of us try to do just that.

Prayers for our children are often painful because we discover that we don't want to let go. We may believe it is safer to cling to a familiar past than to trust in a new future. We can actually become attached to our own fear.

But God is not intimidated by our inadequacy. In fact, He embraces us in all our imperfections. So go to Him with your flaws. Offer Him your anger and fear, hate, bitterness, and disappointment. He will replace them with peace, trust, love, serenity, and contentment. And He will take on the responsibility of bringing about the perfect result.

Persist in Boldness. Pray daily for wisdom and strength, courage and protection, for yourself and your children. Hold fast to the Scriptures that build your faith. One of my favorites is Ps. 91:11–12, "For He shall give His angels charge over you, to keep you in all your ways. In their hands they shall bear you up, lest you dash your foot against a stone." Isn't that a great image? Angels keeping us in all our ways. How much God must love us—to protect us so completely!

Such protection will shore us up in tough times, providing the confidence to continue to pray with boldness and strength, knowing that God will deliver the right answer for us at the right time in the right way.

Rest in the Lord.   Just as a little child is content to spend time beside his mother or father, with or without conversation, each one quietly absorbed in work or play, so we also can fellowship in silent companionship with God. It is not necessary to always speak to God or hear from Him in order to have communion with Him. Being silent together is often sweeter than words. It is the Lord's pleasure to draw us away from the world and into His comforting arms as we await His direction for relationships. "Come to Me, all you who labor and are heavy laden, and I will give you rest" (Matt. 11:28).

DEVELOPING A HEART FOR PRAYER

One cannot pray earnestly for long without developing a heart for prayer. Soon you will pray as easily and as routinely as you eat and sleep. You will turn to God in prayer during times of pleasure as well as pain. Petitions and praises will quickly become one as you begin to truly believe that God only gives us what is right and good. As we make our requests known to Him, we can be thanking Him even before we experience the outcome.

I remember such a time in my life—a Saturday morning in late September a number of years ago when God taught me the art of praying with a grateful heart.

The painting crew had finished the day before and my husband and I were eager to get our home in order. As I began arranging the family photos I was suddenly lost in memories. Many of them I had not really looked at in years. I was startled by how much pain some of them evoked.

I held a photo of my oldest daughter and her family during a time when they lived as missionaries in Morocco. How much I had missed them. Then I studied pictures of my son and youngest daughter as teens—a time in their lives when we did not live together. More pain came up over all the precious days I had missed.

I turned to my husband. "This is more difficult than I thought it would be. But I'm still glad we're doing it."

"I'm glad too," he replied. "Maybe it takes an ordinary event like this to make us stop and think how much we have to be grateful for."

He was right.

The Lord had given us a second chance at so many things. He had restored my husband's career, brought each of our children through the trials of adolescence into adulthood, and helped us make peace with our pasts.

That day I saw a connection between prayer and gratitude that I had not seen before. I realized that pain and prayer open the door to true thanksgiving. It was in suffering that I began to see the truth about myself and about my relationship with my children. And it was the pain that led me to prayer for the Lord's healing.

Without pain and prayer, giving thanks could easily become a mere observance, a pious platitude, a paper pilgrim on the front door on a Thursday in November. Because of the pain, however, we can, like the apostle Paul, in all things give thanks, through prayer. (Eph. 5:20)

Charles Jefferson claimed that "gratitude is born in hearts that take time to count up past mercies."[4] Perhaps without planning to, that is what my husband and I had done that day. We began counting past mercies—and isn't this another form of prayer—and were made new by the gratitude that was born in our hearts.

If suffering opens the door to true thanksgiving, then to give thanks in prayer suggests a release from the prison of pain, a healing of one's heart, an enlargement of one's soul. King David cried out such a prayer of gratitude almost 3,000 years ago. "I will praise you, O Lord my God, with all my heart. . . . You have delivered my soul from the depths of Sheol" (Ps. 86:12–13). What a testimony of thanksgiving to the God he served. He praised God for setting him free through suffering.

What parent has not experienced the truth of this in his or her own life? The pain and sorrow of the past have been the cause of our enlargement—and if we allow it, the cause of true thanksgiving, as well.

"If I had not been divorced," one woman shared, "I would not have been able to pray as effectively as I can now for my own children and for other children and parents of divorce." Her experience had enlarged her compassion for her own family as well as for other broken families.

A man I spoke with gives thanks for his adult son born deaf. "At first I asked God, 'Why me? Why him?' but now I know why. The pain of his handicap has helped me to grow up, to pay attention to other people, to pray for them, and to be grateful for even the smallest things."

Pain and prayer do open the door to true thanksgiving. This truth is as old as humanity itself. Joseph had to wear an iron chain about his feet before he could wear a gold chain around his neck. If he had not first been Egypt's prisoner, he could not have been Egypt's governor.

Mary, the mother of Jesus, had to stand at the foot of the Cross and watch her son die a despicable death before she could experience the joy of His resurrection.

And the father of the prodigal son had to release his son to the sins of the world before he could run down the path and welcome him home.

No disaster or sorrow can be an unmixed evil if we carry it to God in thanksgiving and prayer. "Gratitude," as Faith Baldwin put it, "is a humble emotion. It expresses itself in a thousand ways, from a sincere thank you to friend or stranger, to the mute, upreaching acknowledgment to God—"[5]

For it is through prayer and thanksgiving that we experience the quieting presence of God, commune with Him on a personal level, and hear His guidance. If we are committed to restoring our relationships with our adult children, we will be committed to prayer and thanksgiving.

Chapter Twelve

BEING THERE

When I turned forty, my husband staged a surprise party for me. I'll never forget how I felt as I entered the restaurant and saw loving friends amid flowers and music and a large display of photographs that spanned my life. I hurried from one table to the next, greeting each guest. Then suddenly at the rear of the room I spotted a gentle smiling man with snow-white hair and a vibrant blue-eyed woman on his arm.

"Mom, Dad," I gasped. They had flown to Los Angeles from Chicago just hours before. I burst into tears at the sight of these two who, more than anyone else, had taught me that being there is the greatest gift we can give to our children.

Nearly ten years later I had an opportunity to be there for my youngest daughter as she went through an unbearable trial with a man she was engaged to marry. I remember holding her close as she slept and sobbed intermittently over a long weekend of talking and grieving.

At other times I've had the privilege of being there for my other children when no one would do but "Mom." I attended the home birth of two of my three grandchildren. I helped my son refurbish his wardrobe and set up his home office, and I've spent hours on the phone with him when he simply needed to talk. And a couple of years ago during a visit to my parents' home, I experienced a very poignant time with my own mother as she shared some painful memories from her past.

There have also been other times when I was not there for my children. They needed me to listen, and I talked instead. They shared an experience and I gave unwanted advice.

It is only now, in the afterglow of years of counseling and grief work, that I am able to see the great need for parents to be there for their children, to hold the advice unless they ask for it, to check the urge to pontificate or preach or patronize. In some ways what could be easier than simply being available? There is nothing to do.

On the other hand, nothing could be more difficult. For it is the act of just being that is so challenging for most people, especially parents. We want to fix, change, manage, and control our children, for whatever reason.

I see now that a parent's presence in the lives of his or her children can be a duty, in the highest sense. It is, in fact, something that we owe them and ourselves, whatever the cost. To be there—in person—for the solemn or joyous occasions in their lives makes a difference, not just for our sons and daughters, but for ourselves as well. For in giving our self, self is renewed.

When we are truly present for our adult children, important things happen to them and to us. We are renewed in love and friendship. We are restored emotionally and spiritually. We are refreshed mentally and physically. Being there is at the core of our relationship with them.

Today, however, with many generations scattered across the miles, parents of adult children still working, or perhaps traveling extensively, families do not come together as often as they did years ago when life was simpler and families lived closer to one another. We can let that remain an obstacle or we can commit to overcoming it.

Still other parents are indifferent, even cold, toward interaction with their adult children, feeling perhaps that they earned their freedom and they're now going to make the most of it. So they beg off, or send a check or gift instead.

But to ignore these opportunities to continue participating in the lives of our children is to refuse reciprocity. It is to drain the lifeblood out of the family network that sustains our being. For when we cease to exchange courtesies and condolences, gifts and celebrations, we cease to be present to one another and our relationships become sterile and of no value.

When, by contrast, we do sustain the caring gestures—the little remembrances, the thank-you notes, sharing food and exchanging gifts, we draw life and spirit from one another. These are gifts of the self, but the greatest gift of all is our presence. When being there costs us some effort, the effect can be moving indeed.

What occasions are most important for being there for our children? Weddings and birthdays head the list. Christenings, anniversaries, family holidays, and victory celebrations follow closely. But there are other less obvious ways to express our caring—like visiting your children when they are ill, taking care of grandchildren, walking through a difficult emotional trial with your adult child, or attending your son's or daughter's office baseball or soccer game when he or she least expects it.

How can you best give the gift of yourself to your adult children? Here are some suggestions:

Be positive. When your children do invite you to a celebration or a picnic, party or backyard cookout, do you immediately think of an excuse? You're too tired. The grandkids will be noisy. You're not as young as you used to be and they should know that. You don't get along with your son-in-law or daughter-in-law or you don't like crowds. Maybe you have special dietary needs and you don't want to mention them. The list could go on. If you're such a person, train yourself to say yes—anyway—instead of thinking up conflicts. Be there for your children. What better way to show you care than to show up.

My brother-in-law Harry's operating principle is "Never say no to any invitation!" This may not always be practical, but what a great attitude. And it's attitude that counts.

Think about your own patterns. Must you say no or could you just as easily work things out and find ways to accept invitations? Keep in mind your presence can be a greater gift than anything material you could send in your place. An invitation I once received said it all, "No presents, please. Just your presence!"

Be available. Sometimes it is difficult, but when we manage to be there for our children, to share the ups and downs of their adult lives, in spite of the inconvenience of travel, expense or schedule, we may be astonished at what a difference our presence can make. My mother, for example, flew from Chicago to California to be with me following the birth of my first two children—despite the fact that at the time she was working for my father in his home-based business and had a seven-year-old and a fourteen-year-old still living at home. But what a gift her presence was to me during those important passages in my life.

A friend of mine told me that she'll never forget the time her father flew from Hawaii, where he was on a special teaching assignment, to New York to attend her graduation from law school. "I never doubted his interest in my life after that," she said. "Just seeing him in the audience made it the best day of my life."[1]

Being there does not always entail long-distance travel or financial hardships, however. We can all think of other less complicated times that don't involve expensive flights or long drives. Times when just showing up could make all the difference, when getting there may require little more than a few steps to visit our nearby children, a couple of hours to attend a school play or piano recital that our grandchildren are in, or a few moments with a daughter or son who needs a bit of parental comfort from Mom or Dad.

Be responsible. Sometimes it may be necessary for you to miss a solemn or special event in the life of one of your children. You may feel sad or embarrassed about it so you make light of it or you don't mention it at all. Gradually, you notice a breach in your relationship. Don't let guilt compound your absence. If you didn't go to the ceremony you can still go to the person. Share your feelings about this with your son or daughter. It is amazing how restored you both will feel once you acknowledge the absence and deal with it.

The parents of one of my friends were not able to attend a family wedding because her father was recovering from emergency surgery. Instead of focusing on his pain and problems, however, he called his daughter and his granddaughter (the bride) and told them how disappointed he was to miss such a grand event. "My dad's call was so personal and so intimate," said my friend, "that it was almost as good as having him there. I could tell that he really was sad about not making it. As a result we scheduled a family get-together later in the year when my parents could stay for a week and have plenty of time to visit with my daughter and her new husband and relive the wedding with us through pictures."

Just as this father did, you can make sincere amends by phone or letter when you are not able to participate in person. Sharing your true feelings as he did, can almost make up for the fact that you couldn't be there.

Be fun to be around. Some adult children have to brace themselves for a visit from their parents. "My mother is no fun," said Jenny. "She's always shushing the kids, commenting on my cooking or straightening the pictures, making the beds, you know busying herself instead of joining in. The kids would love it if she'd play a game with them and I'd like her to sit down and just talk with me."

Marv's mother is just the opposite. "I don't know where she gets all her energy," he said. "If there's a party or a picnic or a game on the front lawn, she's either participating or cheering us on from the sidelines. She's always been that way. No matter what my brothers and I were up to as kids, she got into it with us. She's really a fun person to have around."

Not everyone is as bubbly and energetic as Marv's mother but every parent can be fun in his or her own way. What can you contribute to your relationship with your children that will enhance your enjoyment of one another? Could you share some family customs from your past? Teach your children and grandchildren a game or how to cook a special recipe? When they see you coming do they run from you or run to you? It's up to you to make a difference—by being fun to be around.

Be respectful. Many parents of adult children struggle with this issue. They continue to view their sons and daughters as kids who need to be reminded, cajoled, advised, managed, or manipulated instead of grown men and women who have lives of their own—who deserve their respect.

Annette gave her mother an extra key to her home—for emergency use only. "That was a mistake," said Annette. "My mother now drops in unannounced. It would be bad enough if she just showed up without calling first. But she lets herself in since she has the key. This has created some embarrassing moments for our family."

Annette has talked this over with her mother but it doesn't seem to make any difference. "She just brushes it off with a guilt-producing comment such as, 'Well I am your mother, for heaven's sake. It's not like I'm a stranger.'" Annette's husband wants to take back the key which Annette is certain will create an uncomfortable confrontation. "I'm not sure I'm ready for that," she admitted.

Lydia, a sixty-five-year-old mother and widow can't understand why her only son and his wife are so cool towards her. Those of us listening to her share the story, however, could see his side immediately. Lydia refers to him as "my little boy," even in front of business associates or neighbors. She slips him money for a haircut when she thinks he needs one and she frequently drops off bags of groceries without checking with them first. Lydia sees herself as a help—a loving mother and grandmother who "just wants to give the kids a hand." They see it as disrespect and meddling. Here is a woman who appears unable to "read" their signals or respect their privacy.

Be true to yourself. One of the most important gifts you can give your children is your true self—your special gifts, your personality, your unique viewpoint on life. I believe our children respond to that individuality even more as they grow older. They appreciate the special ways in which we express ourselves in our relationship with them.

My husband, for example, loves music and art and the theater. But he also enjoys hard physical work. His son can call on him to help install a fence or move furniture. And his daughter enjoys his company at a baseball game, a stageplay, or a sushi restaurant.

One man I spoke with said he and his dad have been growing roses together for thirty years. "He knows more about roses than anyone I can think of," said his son. "As I get older I notice how much I appreciate this part of our relationship. It's more than his knowledge. It's something that's hard to define. I guess you'd call it sensitivity to life. I've always felt safe around my dad and I want to be like that for my kids."

Some parents go to the other extreme. They are so concerned about being in the way or showing disrespect or upstaging their children by being too involved with grandchildren, that they disappear from the scene.

"I wish my mom and dad were more available," said one woman I spoke with. "I sometimes get the impression that they're afraid to be themselves with us."

Adjusting to our new roles as parents of grown children, in-laws, and grandparents is a tall order for most of us. And we are not likely to fill all of them perfectly. But I do believe that if we're sincere, open in our communication and willing to share our feelings, our children will respond in a positive and supportive way.

I believe they really do want our presence, our input, our help, and our wisdom. But at the same time they do not want to feel smothered or patronized or rescued. Perhaps the best way to strike the balance we all wish for is to talk things over. Ask your children what they want from you and tell them what you want from them. Be willing to acknowledge that you may both be breaking some new ground and, therefore, require an extra measure of patience with yourselves and with each other.

When in doubt about what to do in such situations, listen to your inner voice. What does your heart say, your conscience demand, your spirit require?

When it comes right down to it, there is no excuse good enough for not being there. No excuse, no matter how well rationalized can make up for these missed opportunities. We will never pass this way again. We have only this moment to act upon before it slips away forever.

Your sheer physical presence may be the most you can muster at times, but don't underestimate it, as so many have. It may be a minimum, but it can be a saving minimum. And you can always move on from there!

To be there with and for our children involves, ultimately, a willingness to take on our son or daughter's joy, sadness, or desperation. Such a sharing is much more than just fulfilling an obligation. Merely doing one's duty, results in little more than a hired hand at a common gathering. Cheerleaders and paid mourners could do as well.

But when parent and child enter into and devote themselves to being together for a shared purpose, whether a time of grief or a time of great joy, a special bonding occurs. They are suddenly free to touch one another heart to heart. For "it is only with the heart that we see rightly," said Antoine de Saint-Exupery. "What is essential is invisible to the eye." Jesus made it clearer still. "For out of the abundance of the heart his mouth speaks" (Luke 6:45).

Truly being there for our children is nothing less than the power of God sweeping through us, encouraging us, inspiring us to greater heights of love and community. And this is the plan of God Himself. For God is love, and he who abides in love abides in God.

Sometimes this spirit can be conveyed in the smallest gesture. Sometimes it takes only an honest heartfelt word to be truly "there" for another person.

Being there is one of the ultimate expressions of our love for our children. For the greatest gift we can bestow is the gift of self.

Chapter Thirteen

SHARING YOURSELF

"I feel as if I know the real you now," my daughter Julie said with joy in her voice during a recent phone conversation. As we reflected on how our lives had changed over the past decade since her dad and I had divorced, and since she had completed college, married, and become a mother herself, we also remarked on how each of us had grown up emotionally in the process.

I feel as if I finally know the real me, as well. Until about five years ago I was a person who had spent much of my life in total darkness about who I am. I talked too much and too fast, over-explained, apologized unnecessarily and stuffed my feelings rather than embrace and express them.

Today, after five years of private counseling, group therapy, lots of books and seminars, and much prayer and healing, I feel comfortable with myself in almost every way. It's been a long and arduous journey, as anyone who has walked this path can attest to, but it has been worth every step.

I'm no longer afraid of being overlooked, previously a life-long fear, or of being mistreated or dismissed in relationships. Those things simply do not happen anymore. And I am no longer a magnet for verbal abuse or emotional mistreatment. I can hold onto my serenity and hold up my head.

This may sound self-serving, but I don't mean it that way. It simply feels good to acknowledge the growth I've experienced and to recognize again the old truth that you can't fix anyone but yourself. As I look back, I'm so grateful for, at last, putting my energy where it could do the most good—into my own life.

POWER FAILURE

Most of us spend the majority of our lives trying to make a difference—in our homes, in our workplaces, in our families, and in our communities. To achieve these goals, advertisers and seminar leaders encourage us to become as powerful as we can be. Have it all. Do it all. Be all. We are urged to wear a power tie or a power suit. Drive a powerful car. Create powerful relationships. Associate with powerful people.

We must believe that power springs from without—rather than from within—so persistent are we in our desire to accumulate, impress, and achieve. Even in our own families. We spend time and money on stuff—lessons, vacations, possessions, events. Yet many parents, after a lifetime of such behavior feel as empty and powerless as they did at the start. And instead of living in the fruit of peaceful, mature relationships with our children, there is often misunderstanding and brokenness. We got lost in the process. We shared stuff—instead of ourselves.

I know I did. My children's father and I spent thousands of dollars buying gifts, toys, sports equipment, elaborate vacations, cars, music and tennis lessons for our son and daughters. We bought a big house, joined an expensive tennis club and took frequent trips from Tahiti to Mexico. And yet our marriage ended in divorce. And it was not until more than a decade later, when all the trappings had been stripped away, that my children could look me in the eye and really know who I am. There was nothing more to hide behind or to take the place of my self.

THAT'S POWER

Parents who make a difference do not hide their light under a bushel of toys and trips and trinkets. They don't waste their energy trying to avoid being themselves. They don't tire out trying to play a role that doesn't suit them.

Susannah Wesley, mother of nineteen children, prayed for two hours each day. Her son John founded The Methodist

Church in Great Britain and America. And her son Charles was a famous hymn writer in the Methodist Church. That's power.

Mary, mother of Jesus, told the Angel Gabriel, "Let it be to me according to your word" (Luke 1:38), when told she would become the mother of the Messiah. She had only herself to give, and she gave willingly. That's power.

Mary's humble cousin, Anna, was chosen to be the mother of John the Baptist—not for what she had acquired but for who she was. That's power.

What do these parents have in common? They were people true to their ideals—whether humbly accepting an invitation from God Himself or quietly doing what they knew was right.

TO BE OR NOT TO BE YOURSELF

That is the question—of the day, of the year, of the century, of a lifetime. We all want to make our lives count for something. We especially want to matter in the lives of our children of any age—but certainly in the lives of our adult children. Yet some of us doubt the value of being ourselves. We get caught up in doing and forget to be. Being, however, is an expression of authenticity—that elusive quality that proceeds from the center of one's life—yet is not self-centered.

We may not know how to express it, but we recognize it when we see it. And it is a power that is available to every one of us. To be authentic as a parent, we must first be authentic as individuals, men and women willing to:

Share without pretense.   This is not an easy thing to do. We all have issues with low self-esteem. We don't want our children to see our flaws, our weaknesses, our shortcomings. Most of the time we don't even want to look at them ourselves. Does that mean we have to lay out our every thought, word, and idea or fear further damage to our relationships with our adult children? I don't think so. In fact, I don't believe they want to know every aspect of our lives, anymore than they want us to know every part of their lives.

Sharing without pretense is not so much about what you share, as how you share it. It could be just as authentic to say,

"I'm not comfortable talking about that right now," as it would be to take a deep breath and plunge into a story you do wish to talk about. As long as you are being true to yourself in that moment, you are sharing without pretense.

Share personal secrets. I will always treasure a special time with my mother on a visit home a couple of years ago. She and I spent several hours one morning after breakfast going through family photo albums and sharing stories about the past. As she talked I sensed her growing emotion. Finally, she let down and the tears flowed. I held her close as she poured out the details of a life-changing event that still concerned her after nearly forty years. I had never heard the full story. But here we were, years later, talking about it, all of it, and it didn't seem so bad after all. In fact, I felt privileged to be invited into this very personal part of my mother's life.

"Do you think I'm terrible for having such thoughts?" she asked, looking at me through tear-filled eyes.

"Terrible! Oh no. Just the opposite," I exclaimed. Here was one of the most beautiful experiences of my life with my mother. I wouldn't have traded it for anything. I saw a vulnerable side of her that day that I hadn't seen before.

Share feelings. "I spoke with my dad last weekend, when I came into town from school," said Alberto, a university student who has not lived with his father since he was seven years old. "I had written him a letter asking for some time together. I have so many questions that only he can answer. I want to know why he left my mother and us kids. I want to hear his side of the story. And I want him to know how it feels to grow up without a dad. We only live a few miles apart, but I hardly ever saw him when I was growing up."

Alberto said their set visits over the years were just that— set. "We went to his house and we watched television while he worked in the yard or at his desk. He'd take us out to dinner or a movie and then we'd sleep over and he'd bring us back the next day. We had some fun times. I remember going to the mountains once, and he took us to miniature golf on our birthdays. It became a tradition. But we never really talked. That's what I missed. I feel like I don't know much about being a man."

Alberto is not alone in his desire—his need—to share with his father on a feeling level. So many young adults and older adults would like their parents to share their feelings with them. They don't want lectures, or explanations, or reasons. They want to know how their parents feel—about being a parent, about the challenges they face, about the problems that separate them or keep them in a superficial relationship.

Jamie said he would like to pry open his dad's mind and peer inside. "What was it like for him when Mom died," I wonder. "He still hasn't dealt with the emotional side of it, and it's been fifteen years. How did he feel having to raise four boys alone. I want to talk to him about my mother. Did he love her? Was he angry when she died? What are his fondest memories of her?"

Share flaws. Carmen is sick of hearing what she calls her dad's I-walked-ten-miles-in-the-snow-to-school stories. "No matter what he shares he always comes across smelling like a rose," she said. "I've never heard my dad tell on himself. It's like he has this image he can't let go of. He's been telling these stories for so long that I think he believes them. He thinks he's just about perfect and the rest of us have a ways to go to catch up with him."

One of the most endearing qualities in parents is honesty—the willingness to tell their children and their grandchildren the truth about themselves. They didn't live the perfect life. In fact, they made mistakes and plenty of them. The wonderful part of telling the truth is that our children can learn from us. They can see where we went wrong, the consequences we faced and what these behaviors cost us. Some of us lost marriages, careers, health. We don't want our children to follow in those footsteps, and yet many of us hide the truth from them—the very truth that might keep them from repeating the same mistakes.

Think about the friends in your life who mean the most to you. What is one of the things you most admire about these men and women? I'm guessing that it is their refreshing honesty—

their ability to tell on themselves. This is the quality that creates safety and intimacy in a relationship. As parents of adult children, we have the opportunity and I believe, even the duty, to create that closeness with our children. We must take the first step—by sharing our weaknesses as well as our strengths.

Share hopes and dreams. "I was in my mid-twenties before I ever knew my father's secret wish for himself," said Drew. "One day during a round of golf, we got to talking about what I was going to do with my life. I had recently gotten an M.A. but still hadn't found a job in my field. Dad grew real quiet for a moment and then asked if I ever thought about entering politics. I was totally surprised by the question. It had never entered my mind. Before I could answer, he said quietly, 'I always thought I'd make a fine senator.' I nearly flipped. I had never thought of my dad that way. He was a salesman—had been for the past twenty-five years."

In that moment, Drew realized that his dad had never fulfilled his dream for himself. "I really felt sorry for him," he said. "Later I told him how much that sharing meant to me. I could suddenly see that if I didn't take my life in hand, the same thing could happen to me. I'd wake up in twenty years at a job I didn't like, still dreaming about what I wanted to do."

Sharing our dreams and visions may not have the same impact on our children as Drew's father's did on him. Maybe it won't have any impact at all, in terms of their decisions for their own lives. But it will be an important contribution, nevertheless, because whenever we share the truth about ourselves we automatically restore an important part of our relationship with our adult children.

Share your vision for yourself. By the time we're parents of adult children some of us believe it's too late to create a vision for ourselves. What's done is done, we may think. Or I made my bed, I have to lie in it. There's no going back. Dreams and visions are for younger people.

But it doesn't have to be that way. One eighty-three-year-old mother I know said just a few weeks ago, "Life just keeps getting better each day." She has not surrendered her vision. She volunteers at the church office, visits the elderly in a convalescent home each week, and takes charge of an intercessory prayer chain at her church.

Another woman in her eighties is just the opposite. She wonders why she has lived so long. She feels useless, unhappy, and alone. She will not attend senior functions or become a foster grandparent or contribute anything to anyone except her complaints. She has no vision. And as the Lord says in Prov. 29:18 (KJV), "Where there is no vision, the people perish." When we do not continue to pursue a vision for our own lives how can we expect our children to create one for themselves. We are their models.

Let your children know what you envision for yourself—however simple or complex it is. Invite them to become your partners in helping you realize it and ask them to help you be accountable for it.

Share your vision for your children. I believe our adult children are also interested in hearing our vision for them. That doesn't mean we tell them what to do or how to do it, or that we exercise control over them or create guilt if they don't live up to it.

But it does mean that we take a step of faith and share with them the possibilities we see and some ideas for how to develop those possibilities. Imagine the healing that could occur between you if your sons and daughters knew that you even had a vision for them.

For example, my oldest daughter recently told me that she wants to write books for children. What a delight it is to anticipate another writer in our family.

As she shared her dream I was able to share my vision for her—that she would publish her first two picture books, creating a niche for herself in the multicultural market from her many experiences living abroad.

As my youngest daughter embarks on her career as a marriage and family counselor, I envision her ministering healing words and prayers to hundreds of individuals and couples, as a therapist who can truly relate to their pain.

And my son, who has built a strong freelance sales business is now ready to share his experience with others. I can already see the result unfolding, as he begins work on his dream of producing a workbook and tape series.

By sharing your vision for your children—in terms of personal, family, and career goals—you help them create a landscape that may be larger than they can presently see. This will give them something to reach for and the assurance that you, Mom or Dad, are cheering them on and keeping the faith for them. With that kind of support how can anyone not succeed? And with that kind of honest sharing, what troubled relationship would not move a long way toward healing?

PART FOUR

*Hope
For
A New
Season*

Chapter Fourteen

WHAT PARENTS WANT THEIR ADULT CHILDREN TO KNOW (and what adult children want their parents to know)

In 1986 the popular children's writer Judy Blume published a book for parents titled, *Letters to Judy: What Kids Wish They Could Tell You.*[1] As I looked through her book once again, while preparing to write this chapter, I was struck by the similarity of comments of the school-age children who wrote to Judy Blume, and those of the adult children and parents whom I interviewed for my book.

It seems that parents and children (adult or otherwise) are trying to communicate the same thing to one another—their love, and their genuine need to be heard and understood and respected by the other. A powerful thing when you think of it. Chronological age has little to do with the cry of the heart. We all want to be loved and listened to and we always have.

GENERATIONAL BAGGAGE

A boy of thirteen who says, "Nothing I do is good enough for my father. If I get all A's and one B, he says I could have had all A's if only I had tried harder,"[2] is likely to become a man of thirty who is still trying to please his dad—by moving to the top of the corporate ladder, or writing a best-selling book, or becoming a recognized accountant.

And a girl of nine who writes, "I have a problem that I cannot tell my mom about or she'll get mad. My sister is two years younger than me and she gets all the attention"[3] may still be in conflict with her mother over the same issue years later, long after she has left home to make a life of her own.

Problems that face us as parents of adult children or as adult children of older parents are rooted in those early years. And unless we deal with those forces from the past, we are doomed to repeat them. They don't just go away. In fact, they get worse as time goes on. We know from Scripture that our sins are passed on to succeeding generations (Ex. 20:5).

As parents who want to restore our relationships with our adult children, we need to look at both sides of the picture—the experiences that influenced and shaped us as individuals, and the experiences we passed on to our children.

We cannot expect or hope for true and lasting restoration and healing if we still carry generational baggage from the past. It infected us as children. And if untreated, we carry it to our children and infect them. But as we face and deal with the issues that are still plaguing us about our parents, through counseling, support groups, prayer, and other means covered in this book, we may be surprised to find that our issues with our own children (and theirs with us) will begin to clear up with less effort than we might have imagined. And herein lies the hope for a new season. Restoration starts within—within each one of us. We can work on ourselves as the healing process continues.

THE KID WITHIN

Like the children in Judy Blume's book, I believe there is a little kid in each one of us—no matter what our chronological age—still itching to tell our parents a thing or two. I also believe that's a healthy desire. Sometimes, however, the only way we can get it out is to tell it to someone who is neutral in our lives, like an author, or a counselor, or a trusted friend. That's the conclusion Judy Blume came to about her role in the lives of thousands of young readers.

"Why do kids confide in me?" she asked in the introduction to her book. "I've been trying to figure that out for years. I'm still not sure I understand completely, but I know that it's often easier to confide in someone you don't have to face at the breakfast table the next morning, someone who can't use anything you have to say against you."[3]

Most adult children do not have to face a parent at the breakfast table anymore, yet many are still afraid to express their true feelings to their mothers and fathers. Men and women of thirty, forty, fifty, even a couple of women in their seventies whose mothers are still alive, become frightened little children at just the thought of confronting a mother who has held them captive most of their lives. One woman, at age seventy-four still refers to her strong-willed ninety-something mother as "Mommy." Imagine the destructive imprint this unresolved issue in her life has made on her own children.

I doubt there is one among us who has not at one time or another yearned to communicate something to our parents that seemed impossible to get across. If we had the courage to say it, they might not have listened. And if we kept it to ourselves, we were often overlooked, ignored, or misunderstood. Therefore, most of us need a healthy partner to help us through the process. In some situations it may be wise to communicate to our parents directly and in some cases it may be an unwise thing to do. But one thing is certain. It is always healthy to communicate it—preferably to someone we can trust—because if we keep it bottled up inside we not only make ourselves sick, but we pass on that sickness to our children in the form of manipulation, rescuing, criticizing and pleasing. They, in turn, lash out at us and the cycle of abusive and hurtful behavior continues.

Educators, psychologists, counselors, and youth pastors have been telling parents for years that children need to be heard. They deserve to be listened to. I don't think anyone would argue with the fact that honest, open and heart-felt sharing is the basis for restoration and intimacy. We need to be able to speak—as well as listen, and to listen—as well as speak. With that in mind I have asked the parents I spoke with to share here some of the things they most want their children to know. And I have also asked adult children to share what they most want to say to their parents.

DEAR KIDS—
(What Parents Want Their Adult Children To Know)

"More than anything I want you to know that I love you."

Mom

"You've been telling me for years that you wish I would just believe in you and trust you—well I do. I finally hear what you've been trying to say. Thanks for hanging in there with me. My mother never trusted me, so maybe that's why I had a hard time trusting you."

Dad

"I want you to treat me like a friend, not a doormat. It's hard to spend time with you when I feel like a hired hand.
Time is running out. Could we start over? I miss you."

Mom

"Okay, I promise not to take you so seriously. And, you're right. I don't spend enough time with you. I'm going to change that starting today."

Mom

"I want you to know that I'm in recovery. That's real important to me. I make mistakes. But by being in recovery I'm putting my money where my mouth is. I'm working on it. I'm not finished yet. I want to become a total woman—spiritually, physically, and emotionally."

Mom

"I want you to know that I love you and accept you where you are. I'm here for you. I want to encourage you and make it safe for you to be with me. I know it hasn't been easy for you to have a father like me."

Dad

"I know you're okay, you're capable, and you can manage your own lives. I know that you want me to validate you and to respect you. How do I know that? Because that's what I wanted from my mom and dad. Well, you have that from me today and everyday from now on."

Dad

"I hope you know that I love you without reservation. And I hope that I've acknowledged my errors to you. I tried to. I also want you to know that based on what I know now, I never would have done what I did then."

Dad

"I value you. I thank God for you. It is only now, decades after I gave birth to each of you that I am truly aware of the precious gift you are in my life. I love you."

Mom

"You've been a gift to me. You've taught me. You've stretched me. You've worn me out at times! But you're the best thing that ever happened to me."

Mom

"I'm as fallible as anyone, but that's life. I also want to be the best I can be. I take responsibility for my own actions and I hope you will do the same."

Dad

"When I think of you, mostly I cry. What happened? We were such buddies. Now I feel as if you can't stand the sight of me. Can we please talk? You're my son. I'll do anything to make things right between us again."

Dad

"I love you and I will always be here for you. No matter how much I back off, the caring will always be there."

Mom

"I'm sorry I was so hard on you. I didn't listen enough. I worked too much. I wish I could start all over again."

Dad

"I want you to know that I'm changing and that I want to change. I'll always be your mother but I also want you to see me as a person."

Mom

"I wish you didn't live so far away. I'd like to take the kids to the park and take you out for lunch like I did when you were a little girl. Remember? You grew up too fast."

Mom

"It hurts to be set aside. I don't feel important to you anymore. I don't know what to do next. You say I don't listen to you. I don't feel you listen to me either.
We need help. I do love you but sometimes, like now, I don't feel it."

Mom

"I love you very much. It's a privilege to be your mother. And I want you to know that it's important to me that you feel you can come talk to me about any matter, any problem."

Mom

"I'm disappointed, I have to admit. You don't seem like one of us. I don't know how to relate to you. I don't understand your life, your thinking, your choices. I'm not sure I know you. But you're my child and I do love you."

Dad

DEAR MOM, DEAR DAD
(What Adult Children Want Their Parents To Know)

"Dad, can we agree to disagree? I feel your shadow over my life. I want to be me. Please let go of me, *please.*"

Sarah

"Mom and Dad, it's truly a tragedy that you never worked through the pain of your own childhoods. I'm angry that I didn't have a childhood. You used me. You expected so much of me, but at the same time you didn't believe in me. I craved to be accepted for who I was. My body, my mind—my moods. I'm also sorry for all the mistakes I made. I don't blame you anymore. I do love you. And I know that it's up to me now to give myself the love that I never had. But I can't help wonder where I would be today if I had had your backing."

Debra

"Mom, your fears aren't mine, okay? Please stop reminding me to take care and button up and watch out for crazy drivers."

DeeDee

"Mom and Dad, you've had it tough, I know. Now that I'm an adult I'm beginning to appreciate what you went through raising us, learning a new language, settling in a new country. Thanks for everything."

Lou

"Dad, I admire you so much. We don't talk often but when I think of what you went through to bring us to the United States from Vietnam I realize what a brave and unselfish person you are."

Kim

"Dad, when I think of you I cry—and scream. You have no idea who I am. You drank away my childhood and I hate you for it. I needed you. Why did you leave Mom and me for a bottle of booze? Why?"

Angie

"Mom, I'm really okay. You don't have to worry about me anymore. And you can quit sending me care packages, like I'm going to starve or something. It's nice to get a present but sometimes I feel as if you think I'm a charity case and I hate it. Send it if you just want to surprise me, but if you think I need it, then forget it, okay?"

Bob

"Dad, I hate the way we fight about religion. You act like you have the last word on this subject. I remember when I was a kid you never went to church, yet you wanted me to go with Mom. Now you go and I don't feel like it. How come you want me to do things according to your timetable?"

Reg

"Dad, it really hurts my feelings when you keep making references to my weight. I'm working on it, okay? I feel as if I can never please you. When I was a child it was my grades. Now it's my weight. What's next? I feel like telling you to take a hike and never come back. But the truth is I want you to love me for who I am not for what I look like or for what I do."

Laura

"Mom, I don't want to hear another word from you about how to raise my kids. Could you please give me credit for a few brains? And so what if I make mistakes?
I'm entitled! You made yours."

Mona

"Mom and Dad, we feel totally violated when you use the kids to get to us. We did not appreciate your telling Anita that you're going to buy her a pony. You never said a word to us about it. How do you think that makes us feel?"

Marie and Jim

"You cursed me when I told you we needed to move you into a nursing home. I know you don't believe me, but it nearly killed me to do it. Dad, you need professional care now. I wish you would listen to me. But what can I expect? You never have."

Rosemarie

In her work with parents and adult children in conflict, therapist Rebecca Cutter said that both sides want the same thing—each wants the other to know they are doing the best they can. "It's a lot easier for the adult children to get it," she said, "when the parent is in recovery, because they can see the manifestations of change and the desire for change, even if the parent still bugs them. But the real hard part is when the parent is entrenched in old behavior—and that is still the best he can do.

"He is simply unable to see that he could open a new door or see through a new set of eyes. The most deadly thing in these relationships," said Cutter, "is the need to be right."

Imagine the healing that would occur if parents and children gave up that need. If each one would hear the other, really hear and understand, and validate and respect. As a parent, you wouldn't have to agree with your son or daughter, take sides, disregard your own feelings, abandon your thinking, or change anything about your life—unless you wanted to. You would simply give up the need to convince, persuade or coerce your children into your way of thinking and seeing. It's letting go, not taking on. It's listening—and being willing to get the other person's communication.

Chapter Fifteen

WITH GOD ALL THINGS ARE POSSIBLE

"God doesn't really give us our children," wrote John White, in a provocative article about the importance of relinquishing our adult children, "He only loans them to us for a season."[1] As I read those words, I was suddenly reminded of a truth I had been quick to acknowledge intellectually, but very slow to absorb in my heart. That's right, I thought, as I let the words of his article seep into my spirit. Julie, Jim and Erin are on loan to me. At best, I am a caregiver, a steward—for a time.

The Bible reminds us in the Book of Ecclesiastes that there is a time for every purpose under heaven. The time is now, for parents who are recovering from hurtful relationships with their adult children to relinquish their sons and daughters to God. If we have done the vital inner work on ourselves that is so necessary to spiritual and emotional restoration, then relinquishing our children will be easier than we might expect. We will no longer feel compelled to use them as a means of working through the unfinished business of our past or as the focus of our desires for the future.

We will take our hands off our children, releasing them to the victories and defeats that are part of each life. We will trust God to guide and govern in ways that we could never understand or carry out on our own. And we will abandon our headstrong attitudes and actions that have so often blocked our children from the joyful homecoming that can only be experienced after a season as a prodigal.

Just as the Lord wept over our waywardness, we may at times need to weep over our wayward sons and daughters. We cannot save them. Only Jesus can. And wisely and mercifully, He allows them time and space and room to experience and experiment with the gift of life so that when they return they will be choosing to do so.

That doesn't mean that we abandon our children or neglect our responsibilities to them as parents and as role models. According to White, relinquishing "—means to release those controls that arise from needless fears or from selfish ambitions."[2]

Ah! Those needless fears—things we fretted about that never came to pass, and things that did occur, that fear and worry could do nothing to avert or change anyway. And the selfish ambitions—the desire for your son to join the family business, for your daughter to be a dancer, as you had always wanted to be. Or your wish for a child to grace your home with music so you coerced him or her to study the violin when you were the one who should have taken the lessons!

None of this is easy. But as Jesus promised in Mark 10:27, "with God all things are possible." Only with God is it possible to find hope for restoration. And only with God is it possible to relinquish not only our adult children, but an entire host of seemingly infallible beliefs associated with them.

The belief that you possess your children.   Some parents, like Corinne's mother, view their children, even when they are adults, as "putty" in their hands. They have raised their children to believe that the parents' needs, feelings, beliefs, and standards are the only ones that matter. Such a child emerges from childhood an emotional cripple, unable to separate his or her own identity from his or her mother's—just the way the mother wants it. In one extreme case I heard about a senenty-two-year-old single man who still lived at home with his parents who were in their late nineties at the time. He didn't move back home to care for them in their old age. He had never left!

If you struggle with feelings of possessiveness about your

children, ask the Lord to move powerfully in this area of your life. Ask Him to show you the roots of these beliefs and to pull them out so that you and your children can be freed from the deadly ties that bind child to parent in this unhealthy way. Each one of us comes into this world with nothing and we leave it with nothing, no matter how much we acquired while here. Our children were given to us. They are likely to remain here for many years after we are gone. Let's give thanks for the time we do have together, relinquish them, and leave the rest to God.

The belief that they are accountable to you. One of the most challenging beliefs to overcome as parents of adult children is the belief that our children are accountable to us. After so many years of looking after them, weeping over their physical and emotional hurts, seeing them through school, participating in their development and raising them according to what we saw as right and just, it is understandable that we do not easily relinquish the cord of accountability.

You may wish to tell your son just one more thing about becoming a father himself. You may long to take your daughter aside and advise her about the challenge of being a working parent. Or you may feel that whenever your adult children make a decision—from buying a house plant to buying a house, they should consult with you. After all, you have good sound wisdom for them, built on a lifetime of trial and error. And you have their best interests at heart. They could learn a thing or two from you—if they'd just pay attention! They probably could. But the important thing to remember is that they don't have to.

Ask the Lord to give you grace in these situations. It hurts—sometimes deeply—to watch your children make mistakes with money, with their children, with their relationships, with their careers—with God. It feels good when they seek your advice, your wisdom, your ideas. But since they don't always, and since some never will, you'll need the grace of God to relinquish them and to see you through those hurtful times.

The belief that they owe you thanks for all you've done. This is another big one to let go of. You clothed and fed them, gave them music and swimming lessons. You took them on vacations, sat up nights with them, rushed them to the hospital, and listened to their jokes. You helped with homework, volunteered in their classrooms, and threw parties and picnics to honor them. And what did you get for all your love and labor? "Not much," said one mother. "I haven't seen my son and his wife for six months and they live only thirty minutes away."

Another mother said she's still waiting for her daughter to talk about the good memories of her childhood. "She has no problem remembering all the things I did wrong," said Vera. "You'd think she'd have a little gratitude."

One would think that. And her daughter probably will feel grateful one day. But right now she apparently needs to work through her pain. That's hard on a parent. I know how it feels. You probably do too.

There is nothing inherently wrong with wanting our children to express their appreciation. They do have much to be grateful for—just as we do, but there is danger in holding onto a belief that says they have to. You may not only expect words of thanks, but you may expect them to repay you in some way—with their time, their money perhaps, or with a flow of compliments on what a good job you did.

If you fall into that thinking pattern, ask the Lord to release you from it. Ask Him to fill your heart with gratitude. Even if you came from an abusive family yourself, you have a lot to be thankful for. You made it. You survived. You still have the gift of life—to now live as you choose. Give your children permission to do the same. When they say "thank you," relish it and relinquish it.

The belief that you will always be a close family. One woman I spoke with said that being close to her children is all she wants. "I can't stand us to be cross with one another. I don't see any reason not to be loving. After all, time is running out," she added, referring to the fact that she and her husband are in their late seventies.

At the time we talked, however, she was distressed over her son who was estranged from the family for over a year and she wasn't sure why. "I don't understand it," she said tearfully. "We've never done a thing to alienate him."

I was struck by the fact that she had no room in her thinking pattern for her son to be anything but close to the family. And she was also quick to abdicate herself from any guilt. It apparently had not occurred to her that he might be going through a stressful time at work, with his own family, with his health. Who knows? Whatever the reason, he obviously needed to withdraw for a time.

If your children want to take some "time off," let them. Support them in finding themselves, or in working out a problem, or in healing past wounds. One of my friends released her daughter after a painful episode one day. Months went by with no communication from her daughter. Then unexpectedly she received a card for Mother's Day. More time went by with no contact. Then suddenly the daughter called and invited her parents to dinner at a restaurant—her treat. Their relationship is healing now. Wisely, her mother gave her daughter the gift of time and space when she most needed it. Just as God gave her mother the grace to relinquish her daughter.

The belief that they will live by your value system. I can't think of a greater heartache for parents than to observe their adult children living by a different set of values than those they were raised by. I remember times in my first marriage when my husband and my father would get into painful conversations about religion. My father was terribly hurt and angry that we had chosen to send our children to public school after having attended Catholic school ourselves.

Over the years, my father has told me how disappointed he is that the Catholic tradition and value system has stopped with me since I did not pass it on to my children.

During my thirties, I stopped going to church. That caused him more pain. I did not set out to hurt him. I did it for myself, because I needed to stop and examine my parents' beliefs, ask some important questions of myself, and find my own way. Without that passage I would not be the woman or the Christian I am today. And yet I don't doubt for a minute that my choices then and since have caused my father great grief. He has admitted it. The gulf between us in that area of our lives exists even today—over twenty years later.

Today I observe my son sorting out his beliefs, reading, asking questions, assessing his own spiritual direction. At this time, it is vastly different from mine. But I now have my own experience to draw on. I know what it feels like to disappoint a parent. I don't want to put that pressure on my son.

He has to find his own way in his own time. I know that. I've relinquished my belief that he has to live by my system of values—as dear as they are to me.

The belief that they will (and should) follow family traditions. I remember as a young wife and mother trying my best to follow the tradition my mother had modeled for the twenty-some years I lived at home. She served a beautiful prime rib dinner most Sunday afternoons that I can remember, complete with whipped potatoes, gravy, fresh vegetables, warm bread, and dessert. It was a weekly feast we all looked forward to.

But what had worked for her in the Midwest during the '40s and '50s didn't work for me in Southern California in the early 1960s. We were an outdoor family. We liked to ride our bikes, play tennis, and swim. A big meal in the middle of the day didn't fit our lifestyle or our appetites.

It was an incredible relief to me when one day I suddenly realized that I was not being disloyal to my mother by doing some things differently. I could appreciate her traditions and learn from them, but I didn't have to model every one.

I'm sure my mother wouldn't have cared one way or the other. That is something I put on myself. But not every parent is that lenient. Some feel offended if their children move to another town, leave the family business behind, home school their own children, or serve the homeless on Thanksgiving instead of joining the family, as generations have done before them.

If you struggle with the belief that your children should follow your traditions, ask the Lord to relieve you of that thinking.

Pray for the grace to relinquish your hold on their behavior. Set your children free—free to choose what is meaningful to them, to create traditions of their own, and free to return to many of those you taught them.

Chapter Sixteen

LOVE IS ALL THERE IS—AND IT'S ENOUGH

"All you really need from us now is our love," my mother said in a recent conversation. She was right. Though I often go to my parents for advice, I don't need it now in the same way I did when I was growing up. They had given me roots—and wings—and I have been flying on my own for some time.

But I never outgrew my need for their love, and as my mother made that statement, I realized it again. I also saw love as the most valuable gift I can give to my son and daughters. My years of parenting them as young children are over. But my love for them will never cease. In fact, it seems more vibrant than ever. And it is enough.

THE PIVOTAL FORCE

There's love, however, and there's love. Many of us, as we recognized in earlier chapters, have confused love with pleasing, grieving, manipulating, criticizing and rescuing. We give our children unwanted advice, pass on our fears, try to control their behavior, instill guilt and pout or shut down when we don't get our way—and we sometimes do it in the name of love.

"If I didn't love you so much I wouldn't worry like I do."

"I'm doing this because I love you."

"I'm your mother. I love you. Can't you just—"

"Your father loves you. That's why he—"

"If you'll take the advice of someone who loves you—" But love has nothing to do with guilt and worry and fear and punishment. In Paul's letter to the Corinthians (1:13), he says, among other things, that love is patient and kind and not jealous, that it does not take into account a wrong suffered, and that it never fails. That is a big commitment for anyone to live by. But it is especially challenging for parents who are in the process of restoring painful relationships.

I believe it's important, however, to reach for that commitment and to envision what it will be like when we are more able to live by Paul's words.

Love is patient. Parents who love with patience don't blow up or sulk if their children are late for a dinner date. They don't stop speaking to their son or daughter if he or she has to change an appointment or postpone a get-together. They share their feelings. They may ask questions, but they don't unload their upset in the name of love. And they are not compelled to straighten out their children with words and gestures and periods of self-imposed silence.

Love is kind. Parents who are kind remember that their children, like them, are human. They are still learning and growing and they make mistakes. They know instinctively that it doesn't work to discount, diminish, or demean their children with words, gestures, innuendoes, and facial expressions. On their birthdays and other special occasions, such parents express their love and attention in an individual way. They show their children that they are among the most important persons in their lives. They've taken the time to get to know them. And because they know them, they care deeply, and they make a point of saying so.

Love is not jealous. Even though most of our adult children are married with families of their own, or single and living away from us, a loving parent does not create or nurture a rift by expressing jealousy regarding his or her children's spouses or their children or their time. They don't object to their children having lives of their own. They respect their limits, enjoying what time they do have together, and living a full life of their own when they are not. Such parents don't drill their sons and daughters on why they weren't home when they called, or how they don't see them often enough. They don't jealously guard their relationships, afraid that other family members will take their place.

When their children talk excitedly about work, their spouses or their children and friends, loving parents are not jealous. They know there is room in the lives of their children to love more than one person.

Love does not take into account a wrong suffered. Parents who can express their love with confidence don't spoil the present by living in the past. They don't wear their pain like a badge of honor. And they don't hold their children hostage over actual or perceived hurts. They go to them and share and listen and ask to work through the trial together or get help from a third party when needed. They show by their own lives that to live today is healthier than to loiter in the past.

Love never fails. Such parents don't withhold their love until their adult children shape up, measure up, or live up to their standards or desires for them. Instead, their children learn through them that love is faithful, honest and loyal. Their boundaries are healthy. They continue to discover how they can communicate that truth in a loving and caring way.

When we live by this commitment, what response can you hope for from your children? By loving them you will have helped free them to love you more expressively. As a result, they will just naturally become more patient and kind when you are late, or make a mistake, or feel out of sorts. And they will just naturally want to spend more time with you because of who you are and what you have demonstrated.

They are likely to cheer you on in your own life rather than feel jealous of your victories. They will know there is plenty of room in your life for them.

They are also less likely to take into account a wrong suffered.

You'll see them become less touchy. And they will not be likely to get upset if you misunderstand one another or forget to keep a promise or bring up a past hurt.

They may even see your modeling as an opportunity to practice the same principles with their children and spouses. They will learn through experience that when parents love their children, they stand by them. They remain loyal to them. They believe in them. And they expect the best from them.

By meditating on Paul's words and committing to them in action, you will be teaching your children that love is all there is—and it's enough. Everything else will pass away—hurt feelings, forgotten appointments, misunderstandings, differing parental styles, friends, spouses, beliefs and practices we may not approve of will all pass away. But love will not pass away. And love will never fail.

Supplementary Resources

Books

Exposing the Myths of Parenthood by David Jeremiah with Carole C. Carlon. Word Books, 1988. The author exposes ten common myths of parenthood that have imposed guilt and unrealistic standards on parents and grandparents.

Facing Codependence by Pia Mellody et al. Harper & Row, 1989. A definitive guide to understanding the origins of codependence and the path to recovery by a nationally known authority on codependence.

Forgive & Forget by Lewis B. Smedes. Harper & Row, 1984. Helpful advice and practical steps about healing the hurts we don't deserve.

The Grief Recovery Handbook: A Step-by-Step Program for Moving Beyond Loss by John W. James and Frank Cherry. Harper & Row, 1988. An excellent resource on grief recovery by the co-founders of The Grief Recovery Institute.

Healing for Damaged Emotions by David A. Seamands. Victor Books, 1986. Helpful words and real-life illustrations about how God can restore emotional wholeness.

Love, No Strings Attached by Rich Buhler. Thomas Nelson, 1987. Straight talk about the difference between love and approval by the host of the nationally syndicated radio show, "Table Talk."

Pain and Pretending by Rich Buhler. Thomas Nelson, 1988. A significant work dealing with the importance of coming to terms with one's past.

What Did I Do Wrong? What Can I Do Now? by William and Candace Backus. Bethany House, 1990. Practical help for parents (of children of all ages) who think it's too late.

You and Your Parents: Strategies for Building an Adult Relationship by Harold Ivan Smith. Augsburg, 1987. For adult children of older parents on forging a relationship that works. Good insight for parents on the adult child's perspective.

Support groups

Overcomers Outreach
2290 W. Whittier Blvd., Suite A
La Habra, CA 90631
   Send a donation of $11.00 for postage and materials, which include literature describing this Christ-centered program and a format for establishing the Outreach in your church or area.

Codependents Anonymous (modeled after Alcoholics Anonymous)
   Check your local listings for the phone number of a group in your area.

NOTES

Introduction
1. Presentation by Rebecca Cutter, M.F.C.C. at Sharp Hospital, San Diego, California, February 29, 1992.

Chapter 2
1. From an in-person interview, Sept., 1992. Used by permission.
2. Seamands, David A., *Healing for Damaged Emotions* (Wheaton, IL: Victor Books, 1986).

Chapter 4
1. Norwood, Robin, *Women Who Love Too Much,* (New York: Pocket Books, 1985).
2. Norwood, 16.
3. Norwood, 15.

Chapter 5
1. Buhler, Rich, *Pain and Pretending,* (Nashville, TN: Thomas Nelson, 1988), 35.
2. Buhler, 34, 35.

Chapter 6
1. Smith, Harold Ivan, *You and Your Parents,* (Minneapolis, MN: Augsburg, 1987), 166.

Chapter 8
1. James, John and Frank Cherry, *The Grief Recovery Handbook,* (New York: Harper & Row, 1988), 3, 4.
2. James and Cherry, 7.

Chapter 9
1. Cowman, Mrs. Charles, *Streams in the Desert,* (Grand Rapids, MI: Zondervan, 1925, 1953, 1965), 310.

Chapter 10
1. From a series of sermons and study notes provided by Rev. Mark Slomka at Mount Soledad Presbyterian Church, October, 1992, La Jolla, California.
2. Smedes, Lewis B., *Forgive & Forget,* (San Francisco, CA: Harper & Row, 1984), 2.
3. Smedes, 2.
4. Smedes, 2.
5. Smedes, 2.
6. Smedes, 133.

Chapter 11
1. Foster, Richard, *Celebration of Discipline,* (San Francisco, CA: Harper & Row, 1978), 30.
2. Cowman, 352.
3. Selected.
4. Mead, Frank S., Ed. the *Encyclopedia of Religious Quotations,* (Old Tappan, NJ: Fleming H. Revell, 1965), 440.
5. Partnow, Elaine, *The Quotable Woman,* (Los Angeles: Crown Books, 1977), 239.

Chapter 12
1. Selected.

Chapter 14
1. Blume, Judy, *What Kids Wish They Could Tell You,* (New York: Pocket Books, 1986).
2. Blume, 12.
3. Blume, 16.
4. Blume, 1.

Chapter 15

1. John White, "Relinquishment of Adult Children," Equipping The Saints, Spring, 1991, 18.
2. White, 19.

THE AMERICAN THEATRE

The American Theatre

ETHAN MORDDEN

New York
OXFORD UNIVERSITY PRESS
1981

Library of Congress Cataloging in Publication Data
Mordden, Ethan
The American theatre.

Bibliography: p.
Includes index.
1. Theater—United States—History. I. Title.
PN2221.M66   792'.0973   81–676
ISBN 0–19–502959–3   AACR2

Printing (last digit): 9 8 7 6 5 4 3 2 1

Printed in the United States of America

To the "pretty and inept ingenue supporting John Barrymore" whom critic Percy Hammond spotted in a restaurant the morning after opening night, weeping as she read his review.

Preface

IT IS MY INTENTION to inquire into what is American in American theatre. In format, this is a straight chronicle, following the evolution of the American stage as art and industry from its beginnings to the present day. This is not an interpretive work; however, there are things to be learned. How has the native culture informed the material? What sort of stories, what kind of characters do Americans want from art? How have different eras—times of war, or the Great Depression—affected the writers' world views? How have free-market factors and the rival entertainment media affected the stage? Can elitist experimentalism coexist with mass-cult conventionalism?

For much of its early history, American drama regarded itself as a "useful" art, subservient to popular taste in all things, especially in its moral content. Shortly before 1900, certain theatre professionals began to question this usefulness. Audacious actor-managers and writers saw the possibilities in a stage independent of the cultural establishment, and used their platform to question some deeply rooted notions of the American social contract. Their aim was not political but artistic; they needed more room. Still, in seeking new stories to tell and new definitions for character, they entered a politics of art. Once useful in its benediction of middle-class ethics, the theatre now became useful in expanding or even attacking them. In a way, this volume is a report on the evolving purpose of theatre in America.

The purpose not only shifts from time to time, but also shows ambivalence in any given era. Like the American character itself, American theatre often finds itself torn between conflicting energies. It loves the excitement of the city yet fears its climate of upheaval. It swears by the status quo, yet continually experiments with schemes in the name of progress. It longs for nonconformist heroes, yet seeks a mystical oneness of oppressive community. It reveres tradition and order, yet delights in its anarchic impulses.

Most strikingly, it reduces parables of universal meaning to a protagonist whom it can admire or dislike, yet retranslates that protagonist back into an allegorical archetype. American drama is seldom ontological or metaphysical—it does not attempt to explain the nature of the universe or postulate an American role in it. American drama is personal and narrative. And the American public seems to want it so—it has almost invariably rejected instances of this philosophical kind of art in favor of stories about specific people: *Uncle Tom's Cabin, The Front Page, Show Boat, You Can't Take It with You, Carousel, A Streetcar Named Desire, Death of a Salesman*, and *Long Day's Journey into Night* are the types of play that Americans have chosen to be their classics.

Now, some of these works stretch to encompass an idea as well as a story. *Show Boat* tells of the transience of human lives and fashions, *You Can't Take It with You* of the need for imagination in a dully pragmatic world, *Death of a Salesman* of the empty promise of the Protestant-capitalist success formula. American audiences may get the messages, but I think they tend to experience and recall *Show Boat* for its sad picture of lovers separated because of Gaylord Ravenal's gambling, *You Can't Take It with You* for Grandpa Vanderhof's wiry composure, *Death of a Salesman* for the pathos of Willy Loman. Even *Our Town*, one of the few genuinely epic plays to enter the enduring American repertory, is widely mistaken to be a sketch of rural serenity when it is in fact a work of despairing sorrow. Hearing it described—its economical presentation, its whimsey and fantasy, its young love and touching early death—the average theatregoer might think it invitingly reassuring. But in performance, it makes spectators uneasy; its many careful smallnesses grow too big together, and in the end one leaves the auditorium deflated.

The war between works that flatter and works that deflate is the American theatre's major conflict, one that had to generate an alternative theatre culture in the 1910s (what we now call off-Broadway) simply to get a hearing for artists opposed to the appeasing usefulness of the established stage. Commercial Broadway quickly learned to initiate recruits from the alternative stages—O'Neill, Odets, and most recently Lanford Wilson have come to prominence in this way. But the union of the idealistic and the profit-making is touchy and haphazard, and there are times—the mid-1970s was one—when it totally falls apart. Each time (at least so far), a new purpose or another alternative stage is derived, and the stage revives somewhat from its recession.

I have made no attempt to include everything famous or colorful; even this relatively concise synopsis runs longer than I had planned. Its aim is to recount, simply, the events that have shaped the American scope in drama, tracing the progress of the art from idea to idea. I apologize for merely skimming the musical. That form needs a book of its own.

New York   E.C.M.
January 1981

The author has the pleasure of acknowledging, for the third time, the crucial guidance of editor Sheldon Meyer. As well, Vicky Bijur queried and corrected, and Dorothy Pittman stood by cheering.

Contents

THE AMERICAN THEATRE

1

Made in England I
circa 1700–1900

GOD, THERE WAS THEATRE THEN! The entire nation was a roaring network of playhouses brimming with actors and auditors—one-night stands, split weeks and open runs, repertory companies, farce "combinations," minstrel-Shakespeareans, tours "direct from Broadway" or heading there or merely routing about the outback, separate but equal. As the actress Minnie Maddern Fiske put it, "New York's just a stand." Cities that now mainly offer movies by way of popular art had live theatre in plenty in the nineteenth century, what with an "opera house" and two or three vaudeville palaces seconding the regular play auditoriums. The stage was a general passion.

There's still theatre today, but the roar has dulled, overawed by movies and television; once it was everywhere and the spice of life. Out on the circuit, from Jacksonville to Seattle, theatregoing—stories told and heard—was so important that people took to meeting the players at the train stations to escort them to their hotels, cheering as they went. Old actors didn't fade away in those days—they toured indefinitely in their roles of choice until their Big Moments, line and delivery, had imprinted themselves upon the memory of generations. "He stood just like this," they'd tell you, of the great Henry Miller as Sidney Carton in *The Only Way*, Freeman Wills' adaptation of *A Tale of Two Cities*. "Like this," they'd recall, doing it for you because they'd seen it so often, "with his hands locked behind him and head staring out at you in a sorry peace, one foot in hell and one eye on the balcony. We didn't dare take a breath. . . . 'It is a far, far better thing I do' . . . You should have seen him!"

The theatre had started here as an English profession—naturally enough, as we were an English colony. But the British stage tradition went back hundreds of years (though of course it suffered a serious disintegration during the Puritan era). The colonials had nothing indigenous to draw on, and those who were eager to inaugurate a few traditions often found themselves surrounded by contrary legislation. Worst of all, the early American acting companies were not only English but often second-rate English as well, since few London stars were willing to trade the security of town celebrity and comfort for an abrasive ocean voyage and a tour through the jungle.

Tracing the first days of theatre in America is not easy. The records are impromptu—chance mentions of some performance in a diary, legal chronicles (actors often played courts on morals charges), real-estate transactions, and the like. Historians specializing in the colonial period have unearthed evidence of a gradual emergence of thespian activity; generally, the picture is picturesque but not inspiring. Derivative, sporadic, quasi-amateur, and temporary as much because of popular apathy as official harassment, our colonial theatre lacked the broad cultural bases necessary for economic—which in turn allows for artistic—permanence.

Yet, somehow, theatre kept turning up in one city, in two cities, three, a tour. Chased out of here, a company resurfaced there. A paradigm for theatrical activity may be found in the misadventures of the troupe managed by David Douglass. It was, of course, a British company, organized in London and transplanted in 1751 to Jamaica, at the time a cosmopolitan place with lively recreational interests. Theatre did well there, but in 1758 Douglass happened to marry the widow of Lewis Hallam, the scion of a noted London theatrical family and one of the pioneers of the colonial theatre. (Theatre dynasties used to be a regular feature of the business, though since the passing of the three Barrymores—"the last of the Drews"—tradition no longer sustains itself through the genes.)

Douglass found that he had not only married a business partner, but also in his various in-laws inherited a seasoned company to combine with his own. America beckoned—the present Mrs. Douglass knew the territory, as it were—and they set off on tour in 1758, billing themselves, for tone, as "The London Company of Comedians." New York, their first destination, proved unfriendly. An old theatre in Nassau Street known to the Hallams had been converted to other use. Douglass promptly built his own theatre, but neglected to apply for an acting license first; when he finally did so, he was turned down. But actors in those days lived as much by their wits as by talent, and Douglass now proposed to carry on under the guise of running "an histrionic academy." The authorities saw through the scheme, but were sufficiently moved by Douglass' apology as to permit him a brief season, and, if only because of the publicity, this went over well.

The repertory was standard for the place and time: Farquhar's *The Beaux' Stratagem* and *The Recruiting Officer*, Nicholas Rowe's *Jane Shore*, John Home's *Douglas, Othello*, plus the customary comic afterpiece—all British. There were no native plays, neither by nor about Americans. When Douglass' short season drew to a close, he staged Colley Cibber's much-liked, hashed-up version of *Richard III*, designating it as "Positively the last Time of acting in this City." To the disheartened London Comedians, it might well have seemed so.

But they pushed on to Philadelphia, carefully obtaining permission to perform from the King's Governor. If Douglass' choice of plays is illustrative of the agenda of the day, so was the opposition of Philadelphia's Quakers, by no means the only group in the colonies to see some evil in drama. In fact, when Douglass constructed his own theatre in Society Hill, some two neighborhoods south of what was then "center city," petitions (fruitless, however) to close him down were circulated by Presbyterian, Lutheran, and Baptist leaders as well as by the Friends.

Witnessing the mobilization of the revolutionary spirit, Douglass renamed his troupe The American Company of Comedians, though they were still no more American than the entirely British plays they performed. They visited Maryland, Virginia, Rhode Island, building theatres wherever they went—for these structures were raised swiftly and cheaply on a simple wooden plan, without the slightest regard for lobby space, fire safety, or ventilation. Douglass even tried New York again, building yet another theatre, which stood where Nassau and Beekman Streets meet today. We've seen typical repertory and typical blue-nose resistance. Now we meet a typical audience in Douglass' advertisement offering a reward for information concerning "the Person who was so very rude to throw Eggs from the Gallery upon the stage last Monday, by which the Cloaths of some Ladies and Gentlemen in the Boxes were spoiled, and the Performance in some measure interrupted."

This is a fair picture of colonial theatre. Now, how did it grow, when it did become American? As Douglass noted when he blithely announced his cohort as the American Comedians, something local was going on, and with the repertory widening and English actors of quality chancing the American tour, we needed forms for self-expression that no visitor could give. Perhaps the American outlook in theatre begins to evolve with William Dunlap, once considered "the father of American drama." He was the first prolific writer and producer (or manager, as producers were called through the 1920s) of American plays, and his titles suggest a native's interest in native art: *The Modest Soldier; or, Love in New York* (unproduced), for instance, or *The Father; or, American Shandyism* (1789). Dunlap had no great gift, but he was on our side, and contributed a kind of jumping-off place for a native theatre community. He even sent over the first American dramatic export to London, *Tell the Truth and Shame the Devil*, in 1797. And, best of all, he helped erect a sense of continuity in his field with the first retrospective narrative, *The History of the American Theatre*, published in 1833.

If Dunlap's plays were not the kind that date gracefully, at least one of his contemporaries came up with a relatively immortal work that is still performed today. It furthermore has the distinction of being the first American play—written and acted by and about Americans, Royall Tyler's *The Contrast* (1787).* *The Contrast* identified a fundamental native character in the person of the unpolished, laid-back rural Yankee who with his good nature and horse sense shows up the swank slicks of the city. Thus the contrast of the play's title: downhome (American) roots versus social ambitions (Anglophilia). Tyler naturally preferred the former; true worth was to be found in gingham and rustic mottos, not in epigrams and "fashion." This set up a kind of spiritual charter for American drama, and for a century after *The Contrast*'s debut, characters named Jonathan Ploughboy or Jedediah Homebred inveighed across the footlights against the false idols of the mannered classes. Fops and fine ladies are the villains of *The Contrast* and people of simple virtues the favorites, with names as adjectival as any in Massinger or Sheridan: Billy Dimple, Colonel Van Titter, and Miss Pomonade, worshippers of urban chic, bear the brunt of Tyler's satire, while Colonel Manly and Maria Van Rough teach us what democrats ought to learn.

Amusingly, the play's servants mirror the lifestyles of their "betters," as in a scene in which the unscrupulous Dimple's Jessamy coaches Manly's Jonathan, an utter Yankee (though originally played by a Britisher, Thomas Wignell), in the hypocritical art of enjoying the theatre *à la mode*:

> JESSAMY: This is a piece written by Ben Jonson . . . the places where
> you must smile, look grave, or laugh outright are marked below the

---

* The record here is complicated. Possibly the first play written in America about anything at all was Thomas Godfrey's *The Prince of Parthia* (1767). And possibly the first play published in America—but never performed—was the work of a Briton, Robert Hunter's *Androboros*, in 1714.

line. Now, look over me. "There was a certain man"—now you must smile.

JONATHAN: Well, read it again; I warrant I'll mind my eye.

JESSAMY: "There was a certain man, who had a sad, scolding wife"—now you must laugh.

JONATHAN: Tarnation! That's no laughing matter, though.

JESSAMY: "And she lay sick a-dying"—now you must titter.

JONATHAN: What, snigger when the good woman's a-dying! Gor, I—

JESSAMY: Yes; the notes say you must. "And she asked her husband leave to make a will"—now you must begin to look grave—"and her husband said"—

JONATHAN: Ay, what did her husband say? Something dang'd cute, I reckon.

JESSAMY: "And her husband said, you have had your will all your lifetime, and would you have it after you are dead, too?"

JONATHAN: Ho, ho, ho! There the old man was even with her; he was up to the notch—ha, ha, ha!

JESSAMY: But, Mr. Jonathan, you must not laugh so. Why, you ought to have tittered *piano*, and you have laughed *fortissimo*.

When *The Contrast* premiered, in New York, Broadway was John Street, way downtown, and the theatregoers were largely leisure-class males. Theatre followed the *haut monde*, and the *haut monde* followed London—this imitation of life was what *The Contrast* sought to attack. Thus, Tyler's Colonel Manly utters a fifth-act curtain line fit for a democracy: "I have learned that probity, virtue, honour, though they should not have received the polish of Europe, will secure to an honest American the good graces of his fair countrywoman and, I hope, the applause of the public." The public loved it, especially the scenes with Jonathan, that plucky proletarian whose jib seemed cut right off the bark of the Liberty Tree. "Brother Jonathan," in fact, was the eighteenth-century equivalent of the term "Yankee," and of course it was the comedies, with their Jonathans and their sometimes incipiently anti-intellectual ethics, that best captured the native spirit; serious drama was then still too derivative of English models to deal with contemporary America.

By the turn of the nineteenth century, a stable theatre complex spread over the eastern seaboard. Perhaps it was too stable, too content with itself to consider experimentation. New York, Philadelphia, and Charleston were the towns especially known for drama, each with its resident companies and playwrights, and the public in these three cities exerted a fond but resolute opinion to keep the stage a popular institution, popular in the sense of currying their favor to survive. They wanted heroes to applaud, villians to disdain, and to be flattered with romance and cheered by comedy. The new American drama offered little variety of subject matter. Indian plays, Revolutionary War plays, and costume romances were the rule for drama, rural sitcom for comedy, with an occasional urban satire (often in the form of ballad opera, a primitive musical with the score drawn from folk tunes). Playwrights of the early 1800s did not usually specialize in genres; slapdash versatility made them equal to all occasions. For example, the poet and politician James Nelson Barker went from the *Contrast*-like comedy of *Tears and Smiles* (1807) to the topicality of *The Embargo; or, What News*, from that to one of the first of the Indian sagas, a ballad opera about Pocahontas called *The Indian Princess; or, La Belle Sauvage*, both in 1808, thence to *Marmion* (1812), a verse play adaptation from Sir Walter Scott, capping his career with another verse play on how Puritans like to smother individuality with a witch hunt, *Superstition* (1824)—we'll meet up with this theme again in good time.

Barker is considered one of the more gifted of the early American playwrights, and to his credit he was eager to synthesize a national worldview in his plays. But he, like all others, was bucking the public's conditioned response to favor English works, settings, style. Thus, on the eve of the War of 1812, when segments of popular opinion had grown strongly anti-British, Barker still had to express American outrage at British arrogance through the mouth of the Scottish King James IV in *Marmion*:

> How shall a free and gallant nation act?
> Still lay its sovereignty at England's feet—
> Still basely ask a boon from England's bounty—
> Still vainly hope redress from England's justice?
> No! by our martyred fathers' memories,
> The land may sink—but, like a glorious wreck,
> 'Twill keep its colours flying to the last.

Worse yet, when *Marmion* was premiered (in New York), it was announced as a London import—even to the actors! A fast success, it was then revealed to be the work of an American, and, according to a theatre legend, immediately lost its popularity. In fact, it survived to be one of the favorites of its era.

Playwrights mainly won popularity when their scripts offered prime opportunities for star turns by leading actors, thus becoming stock items in those actors' repertories. John Howard Payne, famed as actor and playwright (the two professions tended to blur in those days, what with writers' verbosity, actors' illiteracy, and the consequent interest in collaborative composition), set something of a standard for grandiose tragedy, *Brutus; or, the Fall of Tarquin* (1818). But one notes that this work, a mainstay of numerous American actors for decades, was first performed in London with Edmund Kean as Brutus. Kean, a legend, to put it mildly, toured America twice in the 1820s, polishing the already high luster of the British acting influence, that style, carriage, intonation—not to mention Kean's personal entailment on the style, incisively ferocious magnetism. Other Britishers rivaled Kean, such as the father-and-daughter act, Charles and Fanny Kemble, or Junius Brutus Booth, a supreme Lear and Shylock and a really dangerous Richard III. (His company found to their horror that Booth sometimes confused art with life in his fencing scenes.) Kean ruined his reputation in this country with a temperamental cancellation and was virtually hissed back to England, but Booth settled on a farm in Maryland and began to raise a theatrical dynasty. His acting sons, Edwin, Junius, Jr., and John Wilkes, then, were American pros with English genes, a novel turn in evolution. (The three brothers appeared together only once, in *Julius Caesar*; in any case, John Wilkes threw the Booth family, and the American acting community in general, into disrepute when he assassinated President Lincoln during a performance of Tom Taylor's comedy *Our American Cousin* at Ford's Theatre in Washington, D.C., one famous night in 1865.)

John Howard Payne offers a handy point of comparison to his contemporary, James Nelson Barker, partly because Payne emphasized the all-around thespian, where Barker was strictly a literary man: the business versus the paneled study. More striking is their different cultural climates. Barker, not all that concerned with show-biz pressures, wrote about what interested him; Payne wrote to please the public: wrote English. He spent much of his career abroad, after getting his start on the regular tour stops of the eastern seaboard—Philadelphia, Baltimore, Norfolk, Richmond, Charleston—in the days when theatre remained a touchy subject in many middle-class circles. It was a very different trade from what we think of today, with its scattered terrain, its local favorites unknown or disliked elsewhere, its spectacular foreign Keans and Kembles, its occasional fires and riots, its fluctuating reputation with state, religious, and cultural authorities, and its ill-assimilated hodgepodge of melodramas, tragedies, and comedies. Payne is the key to this old American theatre, not Barker; we look at Barker's small but varied output and think it admirably native, but it is really Payne's adaptations of British and, especially, French originals that fix the early nineteenth-century American stage for us. (*Brutus*, for instance, seems to have been based on five

earlier Brutus plays, including one by Voltaire *and* its British adaptation.)
Indians, puritans, and Francophile Philadelphia fops turn up in Barker's
plays. What were Payne's subjects?—*Richelieu, Ali Pacha, The Spanish
Husband, Thérèse.* Even when he set a melodrama in Baltimore, it had a
foreign ring to it: *The Italian Bride.* And for virtually all of Payne's contemporaries, the "truth" of alien adventure was the useful truth, laid in Carthage
or Castile, dedicated to revenge or madness, and unthinkable except in verse
or English mannerisms.

The stage made little effort to adapt to the prevailing informality institutionalized in Jacksonian democracy in the late 1820s and 1830s, but native-
born stars were challenging the visitors from London by the 1820s, sometimes
even in native-born drama. If James Henry Hackett won his spurs as Shakespeare's Falstaff, he became far better known in his Yankee guise as Colonel
Nimrod Wildfire (generally thought to have been modeled on Davy
Crockett) in James K. Paulding's *The Lion of the West* (1831), and as Rip
Van Winkle, a figure popular enough to be the subject of several different
plays. Our next homegrown star after Hackett, Edwin Forrest, may just have
been looking for a good script when he sponsored a five-hundred-dollar contest to stimulate American playwrighting, but he may well have been thinking of tradition as well—and of how much his future depended on the
negotiation of that tradition.

Forrest's prize—for the "best tragedy, in five acts, of which the hero . . .
shall be an aboriginal of this country"—went to John Augustus Stone's
Metamora; or, The Last of the Wampanoags (1829), one of the many
Indian sagas. Loosely derived from Shakespearean tragedy, this genre dealt
with Indian protagonists, noble as Othello—so noble that Mark Twain declared them to be "an extinct tribe which never existed." Going back to late
seventeenth-century New England, Stone told of the efforts of Metamora to
rouse his people to resist encroachments upon their territory: "Our lands!
Our nation's freedom! Or the grave!" Eloquent, bold, and inventive, Metamora nonetheless fails, though he movingly declares, "We are no more, yet
we are forever." It's a tremendous part, and Forrest played it for forty years,
but Stone, an unknown actor, won no fame and only the five hundred dollar
prize from his work: Forrest had purchased all the rights to *Metamora.* In
despair, Stone drowned himself in the Schuylkill River.

Even when purporting to cover American events or characters, this early
American drama craved exotics. (Comedy, at least, stayed down to earth—
but then that's what comedy is.) No real-life Indian would have found much
to recognize in *Metamora* or any of the many plays about Pocahontas. Yet

"Indian" theatre held the stage from about 1810 to 1845. A partial listing: *Onylda; or, The Pequot Maid, The Manhattoes, Eagle Eye, Sassacus; or, The Indian Wife*, and, of course, *Hiawatha*. Eventually, burlesques were mounted to exorcize the cliché, such as the early musical *Hiawatha; or, Ardent Spirits and Laughing Waters* (1856), with its noble savages Hianakite and Nukkleundah.

The Indian era coexisted with a romantic period, especially associated with authors and actors active in Philadelphia. This was an absurd interval in our progress toward native art, a borrowed time when the great and little of the European stage inspired a repertory of poetic romances set in faraway climes among faraway interests, painted with majestic love and duty, dressed in antique posh, lit with adultery, garrottings, and royal riot. The climax of the old American verse play was reached when George Henry Boker wrote *Francesca da Rimini* (1855), which lent a new meaning to the term "brotherly love," especially in Philadelphia. Boker's poetry would not hold up today, but his tale created a sensation at the time, and Francesca and her fatally amorous brother-in-law started turning up in assorted versions on a regular basis, like Rip Van Winkle and Pocahontas. Boker's remained the favored entry, however, and survived, fitfully, into the twentieth century.

Rarely, the wittier writers attempted to fuse the exotic with the everyday, as if attempting to develop a middle ground for drama, mindful of popular opinion but too highbrow to surrender to it unconditionally. A notable example was *Charles the Second; or, The Merry Monarch* (1824), a loose adaptation of a French original by John Howard Payne and Washington Irving. The authors wanted to have it both ways: costume romp and farce. They raised their curtain on Lady Clara saying to Rochester, "Yes, my lord, her majesty will have it, that you are the chief cause of the king's irregularities"—but there was a wonderful comic business about Captain Copp, an innkeeper who never quite gets to finish the only song he knows:

> In the time of the Rump,
> As old Admiral Trump
> With his broom swept the chops of the Channel;
> And his crew of Tenbreeches,
> Those Dutch sons of—

Irving brings us to another facet of the evolving American theatre, the critics. In the 1700s, cities were so small and the theatregoing audience so inbred that word of mouth kept shows running. But as the expanding newspaper picked up on the "feature" article, the theatre gossip/reporter/aesthetician emerged, and by the 1840s had a recognized function. No, he had two: to give his opinion of a production and to encourage the public to support it. Because he recognized only the former and the theatre industry recognized only the latter, theatre artists and critics have never got together.

As today, nineteenth-century critics were a diverse lot, numbering both informed and idiot journalists as well as literary men and theatre specialists. But if now the more insightful analysts seldom occupy power positions in the daily publications, the mid-1800s offered a field day for in-depth but relatively mass-market criticism in the grand tradition of the Pope-Addison-Steele debate on pastoral poetry in the old *Guardian* or Hector Berlioz' music columns in the *Revue Musicale*. These critics knew what they were up to, were often successful writers themselves, and tried to guide theatre folk toward art as well as the public toward a deserving show. The play reviewer and sometime poet Walt Whitman exercised his expansive visionary powers in the *Brooklyn Eagle* in the 1840s, fulminating against the star system and the English biases in genre and diction. "The drama of this country," wrote Whitman, "can wield potent sway to destroy any attempt at despotism—it can attack and hold up to scorn bigotry, fashionable affectation, avarice, and unmanly follies . . . New York City is the only spot in America where such a revolution could be attempted, too. With all our servility to foreign fashions, there is at the heart of the American masses there a lurking propensity toward what is original, and has a stamped American character of its own."

The source of that character getting stamped in impressionable young American minds—and not only in New York—may be found in McGuffey's Readers, used by possibly half the children in the nation's schools from the 1840s to 1900. The Readers didn't invent the Yankee, but they filled him out with golden rules and an informal Calvinism; growing up with the Readers meant accepting their way of dealing with life as *the* way, and seeing the home truths vindicated on the stage promised a cheery *déjà vu*, a ratification of one's opinions and experiences. That was the contract that the theatre made with its public, and no wonder that theatre critic and general dandy Washington Irving found "no play, however poor or ridiculous, from which I cannot derive some entertainment."

But what outrageous lack of imagination there was, never developing artistic concepts to compare with concurrent events in Europe, where Lenz, Büchner, and Kleist had already come and gone by 1850 and where Hauptmann, Strindberg, Chekhof, Ibsen, and Shaw were waiting in the wings. This free-market American threatre didn't merely lack direction but chose to lack it, for the spectators saw the theatre as a gambol—fancies, baubles, and fables—that ought to be less real than its customers, not more. No wonder five-act "Renaissance" tragedies went over so well: nothing could have been further from the truth.

But the occasional critic, like Walt Whitman, demanded more from the stage than escape, and every so often one of the minor companies would mount a work with an opinion about some contemporary incident or development. The Irish émigré actor C.S. Talbot wrote *Captain Morgan; or, The Conspiracy Unveiled* (1827) to promote anti-Masonic feeling; one Joseph M. Field contributed *Oregon; or, The Disputed Territory* (1846) to the American-Canadian boundary controversy in the Northwest; the Mexican War inspired a whole squadron of plays; and Thomas Nunn English's comedy *The Mormons; or, Life at Salt Lake City* offered a novel setting for the same old "city slicker outsmarted by the hicks" trope in that a New York politician arrives among the Mormons to try some eastern savvy on them and finds they know the scams better than he.

Before there could be an adult theatre—adult in terms of textual depth, naturalistic acting, and technological artistry—the stage would have to be taken seriously as a social presence, as a *reasonable* phenomenon of some authority in the propagation of a national identity. In this, the topical theatre had a hard time of it; it was thought sensational, reckless, good for business but bad for the industry. In general, the important managers refused to mount topical plays, leaving them to the local groups of the smaller cities— but comedy, being by its nature contemporary, capitulated immediately. And it seems that New York was where the topical revolution first took hold.

New York, by the mid-nineteenth century, had surpassed Philadelphia as the leading American theatre city. One reason was that New York became the nation's most populous city in this period; another was New York's situation as the terminal point-of-entry for European visitors, which made New York the site of all the major debuts and farewells; still another was the received American opinion on "the New York character," with his brashness, his lack of sentimentality, and his accent—all perfect material for the comic playwright. And there was a strictly thespian reason as well: a war among the leading Philadelphia managers in the late 1820s bankrupted most of them, and the unemployed actors poured into New York, where they were dismayed to find that the lush tragedies that were so popular in Philadelphia (and, on tour, in Baltimore and Washington, D.C.) were in the process of being elbowed aside by the New York school of farce, satire, and light verbal comedy.

Farce, no doubt, proved the most shocking to the uninitiated, though New York's distinctive timbre of underworld fun quickly established itself nationally. Typical products were the plays about New York's "b'hoys" or fire fighters, men of endless fascination to playwrights for their rude urchin's humor. Benjamin Baker's *A Glance at New York* (1848) viewed the anarchic internecine strife among the city's competitive fire-fighting brigades, incidentally introducing one of the most successful comic archetypes of the day, Mose the Fireboy. This was the joint creation of Baker and Francis F. Chanfrau, who played Mose in a replica of the fireman's outfit and a sometimes improvised stylization of his insouciance and aggressiveness. Mose inspired a series of spinoffs such as *Mose in California* and *Mose in China*; the first of them, *New York as It Is*, played simultaneously with *A Glance at New York* to keep up with public enthusiasm. Meanwhile, Philadelphia was beginning to catch on; while at the Arch Street Theatre on tour with *New York as It Is*, Chanfrau found a *Philadelphia as It Is*, featuring John Owens, a Britisher who specialized in Yankee parts.

Melodrama, too, assimilated the new mode for topical realism in an urban setting, though the plots themselves were by the very nature of the form bound to non-realistic devices and surprises. Typical of mid-nineteenth-century melodrama—but its most ingenious practitioner—was Dion Boucicault. Irish by birth, somewhat French in training, and continually active in England and the United States from the 1840s through the 1880s, Boucicault produced historical romances, domestic comedies, semi-social documents, mysteries, satires, and novelties. Whatever the public seemed to want at a given time, he could give them, and he gave so much that critics cite numerous works as his masterpiece, from his second play (produced when he was nineteen), the delightful *London Assurance* (1841), to the fiery *The Shaughraun* (1874), set during the Fenian Uprising of 1866.

Like most of the thespians of his period, Boucicault was an all-around theatre man; but he placed more importance on his playwright self than on his acting or producing. Because his plays were so irresistibly actable and so popular with audiences, he had a lot of power in his profession, and he exercised it to emphasize the playscript as inviolable entity. Nineteenth-century theatre was stock-company theatre, rotating a repertory of works night after night from town to town, always featuring a star or two as the main attraction. But Boucicault took to mounting a production of *one* of his scripts and sending that on tour, to play each town until it had exhausted all local business, whereupon it would move to the next town. This marked the beginning of the one-work, one-cast approach of the twentieth century, a warning to the imperious star player that the play was the thing.

As writer, Boucicault observed the conventions and dealt in character clichés much too often. And, like everyone else, he borrowed from other plays and from fiction when invention flagged. But he was vital. His settings had color, his acts had pace, his people caught one up in their affairs. His dialogue has dated as badly as that of his contemporaries, but it has verve. Consider the entrance of the villain in *The Octoroon; or, Life in Louisiana* (1859). Jacob M'Closky, the bad guy, a plantation overseer born in the north, interrupts the lazy breakfast of his *ancien régime* employers, complete with visiting young heiress and servant fanning a breeze. Boucicault leaves no doubt where everyone stands:

M'CLOSKY: Miss Dora, your servant.
DORA: Fan me, Minnie. (*Aside*) I don't like that man.
M'CLOSKY: (*Aside*) Insolent as usual. (*Aloud*) You begged me to call this morning. I hope I'm not intruding.
MRS. PEYTON: My nephew, Mr. Peyton.
M'CLOSKY: O, how d'ye do, sir? (*He offers his hand. George bows coldly. Aside*) A puppy. If he brings any of his European airs here, we'll fix him!

Based on Mayne Reid's novel *The Quadroon*, *The Octoroon* tells of Zoe, a mulatto beauty caught between heroic George Peyton and the vicious M'Closky. The question of race prejudice would seem to be an issue, but Boucicault concentrates on love, jealousy, and murder, and *The Octoroon* proved as successful with southern audiences as with those in the north. The two sections saw the same work from different angles: the northerners linked Zoe's personal tragedy (she takes poison) to the slavery system, while southerners delighted in hating M'Closky, a rat from Connecticut. Perhaps the most telling piece of business in the whole five acts is the use of a camera in the detection of M'Closky's murder of a young slave. The camera happens to be set up to shoot at the scene of the crime, and Boucicault directs M'Closky to pose motionless while he reads the important letter he has killed to intercept. M'Closky is ignorant of how a camera works—but the audience has been informed that it needs a few moments and a still subject to make a photograph. M'Closky is trapped in one of the great novelty surprises of mid-century melodrama, and considerations of slavery are left unheard.

Social polemic was not as interesting to theatre people or their public as character polemic. The question was not "What should life be like?" but "What are people like?" Thus, an outstanding early satire of this age recalls *The Contrast*, Royall Tyler's ancient confrontation of democratic innocence and European corruption. This new work was Anna Cora Mowatt's *Fashion; or, Life in New York* (1845). As in Tyler, Mowatt's characters bear names that tell what they're worth as people. Adam Trueman, a farmer, guards the author's belief in earthbound, anti-materialistic values; Mrs. Tiffany sounds the call of parvenu ostentation. Between them hover a parlor full of phonies—Snobson, a blackmailing accountant; Augustus Fogg, "a drawing room appendage"; T. Tennyson Twinkle, "a modern Poet." Though a comedy of manners, depending on the motion of smart writing, *Fashion* anticipates early twentieth-century farce in its screwball characters and involved plotting. Its grace and wit made it a rage of its day, and inspired a vogue for New York "society" plays written by women, some of them so lacking Mowatt's sardonic touch that they came as more as glorifications of fashion than arraignments. *Self* (1856), for example, by Mrs. H.L. Bateman, displayed too much confidence in billing itself as "an original New York comedy." Bateman was hopelessly dependent on the *Fashion* plan, yet lacked Mowatt's amused admiration for the fashion-despising Yankee. Actually, the New York comedies of manners had less popular success than the many informal proletarian farces imitative of the Mose comedies. As with the Revolutionary War and Indian dramas, so was there a host of plays on New York life—*The Mysteries and Miseries of New York*; *Adelle, the New York Saleslady*; *Young New York*; *The Fast Young Men of New York and Brooklyn*; and so on, mainly melodramas and comedies. Here, again, Dion Boucicault was right on the mark with *The Poor of New York* (1857), set during the Panic of 1837. Commentators have praised this last work for its certain sense of locale, but it is useful to note that Boucicault adapted it from a French original, *Les Pauvres de Paris*, and that the setting was changed in two revisions, *The Poor of Liverpool* and *The Streets of London*, with no apparent loss of resonance.

By about 1850, the stage had shown itself capable of adapting its inherited form to native use. In the wildly popular Mose the Fireboy, for example, it had an urban complement to the Yankee, just as roughhewn but contentious and racy where the Yankee moved open and easy. And like the Yankee Mose entered the characterological pantheon to inform such later developments as George M. Cohan's strutting style, James Cagney's intense movie rogues, and countless comic-strip heroes. The Yankee himself was in top form these years, as witness the extraordinary popularity of Solon Shingle, the shrewd downeast farmer of J.S. Jones' *The People's Lawyer* (1864). This character was so adaptable that actors played him both as a nimble youth and a doddering codger, and his refrain, "Jes' so," became a favorite catchphrase of the era.

The material was lively, then, and now seemed to be capturing the national spirit spontaneously. But those who ran the theatre cornered it as one does a market, and as soon as something vital came along, bang! the trap would close and the jobbery would commence: imitations sucked the life from new characters or forms, stars bought The Rights and kept them exclusive, playwrights' work was hashed and rehashed. And who ran the theatre? The star. Most kinds of plays depend to a great extent on magnetic personalities, but an essential difference between the star system then and now lies in the attitude of the stars themselves. Today they actively hunt for change and love to take chances; back then they limited themselves drastically. No one now would try to base an entire career on his or her four or five most grateful parts—many actors did, however, through the 1910s. (Even Katharine Cornell, who endlessly revived or toured in her two most famous roles, Shaw's Candida and Elizabeth Barrett in *The Barretts of Wimpole Street*, still sought regeneration in new work.) Modern actors inhabit a theatre world that has been transformed by the additional possibilities of film and television (either of which may preserve a star turn for posterity), and which is also more receptive to artistic and social change. Not only would no actor today want to play the same part over the years for decades; there is no need or desire to keep a play continuously available for that amount of time. But in the mid-nineteenth century, a static theatre style encircled the actors. American thespians had not even assimilated David Garrick's revolution in acting traditionally blood-and-thunder parts in quasi-naturalistic style, yet Garrick had put the stage through his changes one hundred years earlier. And, as the old-hat repertory limited the potentiality of playwrighting, the star system limited the development of acting, with its Big Moments and its relegation of secondary characters to the outback of the playing area (where they could not distract attention from the star).

The incredible proportion of this star worship is best demonstrated by New York's Astor Place Riot of 1849. Nowadays, that immediate area is distinctly "off-Broadway" (out of the big-money arena of the larger and more widely attended houses); at the time it lay right in the heart of the theatre district. The immediate cause of the riot was the rivalry between two tragedians, our own Edwin Forrest and the British William Macready. On an English tour in 1845, Forrest had suffered various humiliating rejections by both press and public, which he took to be Macready's doing, certainly to Macready's delight and possibly at his prompting. The rivalry exploded in feud when Forrest was hissed as Macbeth—at Macready's direction, he was certain—and Forrest in retaliation hissed Macready in the same role.

Four years later, both Forrest and Macready were playing New York, both as Macbeth the same night, Macready at the Astor Place Theatre. Forrest's friends planned a hostile demonstration, and halted Macready's Macbeth with a storm of catcalls and fruit. But this is not the riot yet. Macready promised to finish his Macbeth in a second performance, and it was that night, May 10, 1849, that the riot occurred. Irish-Americans may have used the Forrest-Macready feud as a pretext for an anti-British demonstration; in any case, the mob outside the theatre at the conclusion of Macready's performance went so berserk that police fired on the crowd, killing twenty-two and wounding thirty-six. Macready was smuggled to Boston and put on the first boat to England.

Without the magic names to head the bill—usually one male or female attraction, occasionally a pairing, but never more—no company could figure importantly in the business. But theatre outside the eastern cities could not always count on the star system to carry it. It is not surprising to learn that the blockbuster hit of the nineteenth-century provincial tour was neither Shakespeare nor *Fashion* nor *Hiawatha*, but *Uncle Tom's Cabin*—a play with numerous leading roles but no star part.

Harriet Beecher Stowe's novel appeared in New York as a play the very year of its publication as a book (after magazine serialization), 1852. The adaptation was run off something like over the weekend by an actor named Charles W. Taylor and quickly supplanted by others, but some of Stowe's abolitionist pleadings came through. Was this social drama? It wasn't too early for reformers to conceive of the stage as a progressive force to complement the newspaper editorial, but *Uncle Tom's Cabin*'s audiences didn't feel privy to a movement: they were there for a show. The press, however, was aroused. The New York *Herald* voiced fears that the play would turn the theatre into "the deliberate agent in the cause for abolitionism." But while Stowe's book had social impact, the play *Uncle Tom* excited little controversy among its customers, who were too busy counting the bloodhounds in the Ohio River chase scene to consider Stowe's theme. These bloodhounds became a byword of provincial stagecraft—the Wellesley and Sterling troupe plugged the significant item in their *Uncle Tom* as "the wonderful dogs, Sultan, Caesar, and Monarch, for which Buffalo Bill makes a standing offer of $5,000, or $3,000 for Sultan alone."

Taylor's *Uncle Tom's Cabin,* which didn't even have Topsy or Little Eva in it, flopped; New York welcomed what was to prove the durable version, by George L. Aiken, in 1853, after a premiere in Troy and a stopover in Albany.* Aiken hadn't included bloodhounds in his cast list, but then as a staple of touring companies the "Tom show"—a genre more than a play— was always ready to introduce some new piece of spectacle to draw the customers back in all over again. (As late as 1902, sixteen tent-show *Toms* were still out on the circuit.) Companies that skimped on the bloodhounds might put their all into the Levitation—Little Eva's death scene (still so vital as a cultural memory that it turned up in an early *Our Gang* comedy, with Eva hiked to heaven on a swing while Alfalfa, Buckwheat, and such waved goodbyes)—or into a really dynamic criminal element, led by the vicious overseer Simon Legree, or into the Allegory Tableau Finale, set in the hereafter: accompanied by saintly music, Little Eva looked more or less enchanted on a milk-white dove while her father and Uncle Tom knelt at her sides.

Uncle Tom's Cabin wasn't by any means the only melodrama featuring a sadistic villain and a pathetic child, but it must have been one of the few to include animals in the cast. More interesting to modern eyes than the bloodhounds, however, is Aiken's treatment of the slave girl Topsy, "de wickedest critter in de world" by her own reckoning, but soon transformed by the example of dear Little Eva. Biracial acting companies were unknown in those days, and the blacks in *Uncle Tom's Cabin* were played by whites in dark makeup. ("Blackface" is the precise term; so used was the public to the overemphasized features and impossibly black-and-white color scheme of the format that black actors themselves were expected to turn their natural endowment into the standard grotesquerie, a practice that didn't break down until the arrival of mixed casts on Broadway in the 1900s acclimatized the public to the natural look of Afro-Americans.) This was one reason why the quasi-documentary nature of Stowe's novel did not transfer to the stage: everyone in the *Tom* shows, in whichever of the many different adaptations, was white: a charade. Moreover, it doesn't take a folklorist to spot the lineage of midcult, non-racial comedy beneath the dialect in Topsy's lines:

TOPSY: Dar's somethin' de matter wid me—I isn't a bit like myself. I
     haven't done anything wrong since poor Miss Eva went up in de skies

---

* Aiken's *Uncle Tom's Cabin* was so popular for so long that Edwin S. Porter's early silent film version showed only the key scenes, letting his audience fill in the plot from their considerable experience of the play.

and left us. When I's gwine to do anything wicked, I tinks of her, and somehow I can't do it. I's getting to be good, dat's a fact. I 'spects when I's dead I shall be turned into a little brack angel.

OPHELIA: (*enters*) Topsy, I've been looking for you; I've got something very particular to say to you.

TOPSY: Does you want me to say the catechism?

OPHELIA: No, not now.

TOPSY: (*aside*) Golly, dat's one comfort!

Theatre was fun and even thrilling, then, but it was child's play. The maturing process was long and slow, but seeds were sown in the 1800s. The trick was not so much to import the graces of the European tradition or to imitate its radicals as to refine what was already at our disposal—to breed a more telling clarity out of our dramatic life-stock and to devise the formulas, and their antidotes, out of our forms.

There was, for example, the playwright Bronson Howard, sometimes cited as the first to fight hard to establish the essential rights and obligations of the author. Except for the poets of the Philadelphia school, this was not a great day for the author in the theatre; even Dion Boucicault's revolutionary national tours of a single play performed by a set cast (as opposed to stock-company repertory) came out of Boucicault's all-around thespian professionalism. Howard worked at a desk, though not in an ivory tower. Like Boucicault, he reached a wide public in a variety of modes. *Saratoga; or, Pistols for Seven* (1870) is a farce; *The Henrietta* (1887) a comic melodrama on love and intrigue along Wall Street; *Shenandoah* (1889) a dashing Civil War romance (not the source of the 1975 musical). Howard acceded to, even flattered, convention. *The Henrietta* scored an immense success; it seemed virtually unclosable. But convention dates badly when there is no urgency behind the writing, and, even in a revised version, a revival in 1913 entitled *The New Henrietta* proved that Howard was no classic. He had served a purpose: to affirm the position of the creator in a world of re-creators. But in the end his lack of originality sent him to the shelf.

Howard's contemporary James A. Herne was original. An actor and dramatist who courted unpopularity with critics, public, and his fellow thespians for his determination to put a little life—real life—into his work, Herne cited "Art for truth's sake" as his motto. He tested it in *Margaret Fleming* (1890), a psychological study of marital infidelity that, in the context of late nineteenth-century American theatre, is bold, even dangerous. Herne served as a kind of prelude to middle-period (realistic) Ibsen for American audiences, in that he respected formal conventions but dealt with controversial material. Herne's colleagues in the literary realist movement cheered him on—but were Americans ready to hear Margaret confront her unfaithful husband by questioning the sexist "double standard"? In the play's final scene, he returns to their home to beg her forgiveness. He had hidden himself from the world in shame, and she tells him, "Oh, you are a man—people will soon forget." Can she forgive him? She thinks forgiveness irrelevant. They have a family to maintain. But, she says, "Suppose I had been unfaithful to you?" This was not the cut of fare that Americans expected of the stage, though they accommodated themselves to Herne's realism is his *Shore Acres* (1893), a gentler piece in the then-neophyte genre of middle-class domestic comedy which was to flower in the 1920s and '30s.

Both Yankee and urban comedy remained a jumble. The former went into decline and the latter had a golden age, but neither form produced anything comparable to James A. Herne. The master of citified farce was Charles Hoyt, who penned countless knockabout farces throughout the 1880s and 1890s, peppering them with slang and song but giving them nothing of distinction in either plot or character. His biggest hit was *A Trip to Chinatown; or, An Idyl of San Francisco* (1891), one of the few of its kind not to be set in New York. Like all of Hoyt's farces, *A Trip to Chinatown* revolved around eccentric characters, spot "bits," disguises, silliness, and mischief upon mischief: in the show's central scene, young bloods and a widow from Chicago run into the hero's prim uncle in a restaurant. Percy Gaunt's score was a vaudeville of little reference to the action, but it contained an unusual amount of song hits, including "Reuben and Cynthia" (Reuben, Reuben, I've been thinking . . .), "The Bowery" (note the continuing fetish for New York), Charles K. Harris' story-ballad "After the Ball" (interpolated on a road tour), and a black pastiche, "Push Dem Clouds Away," a favorite in its day for its whimsical line, "Just push! Don't shove!" It was probably the score that made *A Trip to Chinatown* so successful; at 657 consecutive performances, it set a precedent for long runs on Broadway that was not surpassed till *Lightnin'* closed in 1921.

Hoyt's emphasis on the hustlers and coneys (the hustlers' dupes) of the gala urban jungle reflected the character of the theatregoing audience, and it was no accident that the theatre district nudged the Tenderloin in every city big enough to support one. Not till the 1860s would a "decent woman" have been seen in a theatre at all, and for many years after, the word "actress" betokened a woman whose older profession took in more than telephone scenes, soliloquies, and mistaken identity. In Manhattan the pleasure island was "Broadway," naturally, down around Astor Place and

Fourteenth Street in the late nineteenth century but soon to progress up to Forty-second Street, while sporting houses and saloons hugged the area just to the west. By 1901, when electricity turned Broadway into the Great White Way, the theatres stretched from Twenty-third to Forty-sixth Streets, then steadily chugged into plots north in the ensuing years, where they stand today. And the Tenderloin moved right along with them, offering a real-life cynicism that coexisted oddly with the often quite alien glamor of the American stage.

This glamor was superintended by the actor-manager, the traditional executive of the theatre community. The actor-manager combined the duties of today's producer, director, and star: he or she acquired the scripts, assembled the company, rehearsed the productions, and planned the tour. Until the 1890s, every lead player of any importance was either an actor-manager or related to one by blood or marriage, but at about this time certain theatre owners (the non-acting managers) moved to seize top power in the business. Oddly, this only added to the stars' glow: freed from behind-the-scenes work, actors became less like everyone else, a little fabulous. They seemed not so much toiling professionals as archons of magic.

Take Richard Mansfield, for example, one of the best-known stars of the late nineteenth century—known for his gallantry in heroic parts and for his quaintness as freaks. Somehow, Mansfield managed both. Short of stature but handsome and a brilliant actor, Mansfield personified elegance as he toured in Clyde Fitch's *Beau Brummel*, Rostand's *Cyrano de Bergerac*, Booth Tarkington's *Beaucaire*—yet he also excelled as the dual lead in *Dr. Jekyll and Mr. Hyde*. In the absence of the electronic media, stars weren't made overnight in the 1800s, but they could get discovered in a hurry; so it was with Mansfield, who had an uncanny gift for detailing the humanity in bizarre characters—rogues, hunchbacks, evil geniuses. Whatever he did, they loved; parts he occupied he owned—Beau George, the agile Beaucaire, his biting Baron Chevrial in *A Parisian Romance*—and his Big Moments were among the Biggest of the day, such as the aged Chevrial's crackly, whispered toast, "To Rosa . . . to Rosa," or Beau's casual great line, upon meeting a friend and the obese Prince of Wales after Beau and the Prince have quarreled: "Who's your fat friend, Sherry?"

Romances, adaptations from the novel, and Shakespeare were the meat of the great. Everybody's favorite actress Minnie Maddern Fiske launched her stardom in 1897 in a stage version of *Tess of the D'Urbervilles* to such acclaim that the show was sometimes sold out three weeks in advance, extreme for the time, while Eugene O'Neill's actor father James based his career very

largely on *The Count of Monte Cristo*, giving an estimated 6,000 performances throughout the land. Lesser actors, too, drove such vehicles, and
sometimes gifted actors rode the wrong ones while seeking the identity that
best suited them and their public together. E. H. Sothern, who was eventually
to team up with Julia Marlowe as the most famous Shakespearean couple of
the early 1900s, established an early primacy in swashbuckling parts—*The
Prisoner of Zenda, The Song of the Sword,* and *If I Were King*—after
abandoning a feckless light comic career as *Editha's Burglar* and *Captain
Letterblair.*

It was mostly through the sweeter blends of romance that this theatre
paid its bills. Not only Mansfield, Fiske, O'Neill, and Sothern, but every
one of their colleagues could have testified to the purity of the escapism that
they, sometimes or always, had to support, as role models for their public's
fantasies. *If I Were King's* heroine Katherine de Vaucelles explained it, to
her François Villon and to us, as well as anyone of her time:

> A woman may love a man because he is brave, or because he is comely,
> or because he is wise, or gentle—for a thousand, thousand reasons. But the
> best of all reasons for a woman loving a man is just because she loves him,
> without rhyme and without reason, because heaven wills it, because earth
> fulfills it (*taking his hand*), because his hand is of the right size to hold
> her heart in its hollow.

There is an awful hardness in that "just because," a toughness in the
innocence. Was theatre romanticizing real life or inventing a false romance
that life could not hope to realize? The Katherines de Vaucelles who inhabited the *If I Were Kings* had it easy; their Villons were always brave,
comely, and gentle because that was the type of hero that theatregoers came
to see. Not until the workers' theatre movement of the late 1920s and early
1930s did actors look and sound like people; years earlier, disciples of various
trends in realism had already learned to portray lives real enough to fail, as
they can in life.

If I Were King, even when new, referred to the costume romance of our
youth; more up-to-date in the same period was the more naturalistic, sometimes even modern-dress heroism of William Gillette, an actor who wrote
his own scripts so as not to have to compromise his image with someone else's
production of it. Here was an actor who knew what charisma was for—
Gillette could have drawn a chart. His two great turns as star and playwright
were *Secret Service* (1896) and *Sherlock Holmes* (1899), thrillers shocking
with explosive devices, sudden movements, matches struck in darkness.

Gillette's most famous role was Holmes, delivered in his signature persona of intense reserve heightened by rare outbursts of sentimental fatalism. This was the leading "crook play" of its day, workmanlike in plot and language, but the true grit in what Gillette had done for the character—his character, he, Holmes. (Not surprisingly, when London's Royal Shakespeare Company revived the work and brought it to New York in 1974 to be the smash of the season, most of the credit belonged to John Wood's consummately methodical Holmes, the persona again supreme.)

What was the point of melodrama in the late nineteenth century? Its rustic chivalry won it favor, but its focus was romance, because the audience Believed. Without that commitment, on both sides of the footlights, the show simply cannot play. This Royal Shakespeare *Sherlock* emphasized the Holmes-ness of the piece at a time when Doyle's detective was enjoying a revival of interest; but two years later, New York's little Phoenix Theatre found itself strapped for the romantic hardware needed for Gillette's other perennial, *Secret Service*—as did the audience. Love was the main dramatic premise for creators and public alike, the certain beauty of the day.

It should come as no surprise, then, that Gillette's spy drama *Secret Service* incorporated as much romance as cloak-and-dagger. Gillette had already produced a love-versus-duty Civil War thriller with a too-noble-for-words hero (no; Gillette found the words) in 1886, *Held By the Enemy*. But *Secret Service*, on the same theme, was his most accomplished play. Its big scene depends on the sending of a crucial telegraph message; the love plot between a southern girl and the intrepid Yankee spy (Gillette), not to mention the fate of the south, hung in the balance while the telegraph key clicked away, the spy and his adversary hurled curses at each other, the other characters swayed indecisively, and the audience forgot to breathe: Belief. Gillette also wrote in a pregnant meeting—in the dark, of course—between himself and his own brother, another spy, whom he must kill to preserve his cover. (Gillette being too noble to do it, the brother shoots himself.)

Good looks and easy passion were the keys to drama in the late nineteenth century. Even that national heroine and John Greenleaf Whittier's valiant crone Barbara Frietchie, who dared fly the Union flag when Stonewall Jackson passed by, became a "ravishing young creature who has more or less willingly upset the youth of the town" in Clyde Fitch's play of 1899 and particularly in Julia Marlowe's portrayal. *Barbara Frietchie* dispensed with Whittier's deathless "Shoot, if you must, this old grey head (but spare your country's flag, she said)" business: an old Mother Courage could not lure the customers the way Julia Marlowe could. Furthermore, Fitch took the liberty of killing Barbara off just before the final curtain; she dies clinging to the flag while the chorus sings "My Country, 'Tis of Thee," a beautiful death. It wasn't Whittier's Barbara, but it was appropriate theatre.

Comedy was chaotic and drama fantastic; both preferred standardized types of character to an individual idea. We arrive at 1900, and settle down in New York, just as the national theatre does, centralizing its sense of territoriality on New York and the taste of the New York public. The place is "The Street," Broadway, the time just prior to the investiture of an adult American theatre, circa 1900. And the action is the evolution of thematic and characterological possibilities that do not necessarily defer to popular notions on what is useful in art. This chapter has charted the acculturation of certain characters—the Yankee, the fashionable climber, the tragic Indian, the urban know-it-all—and certain genres—good-versus-evil melodrama, Indian tragedy, the New York comedy of manners, the New York "fireboy" farce. All these, and others, have grown out of a popular tradition and were produced specifically to appease the public. Almost nothing in this early American theatre attempts to impose a touchy theme or ambiguous character upon the customers; this would have invited financial ruin. Moreover, this would have run directly contrary to the very purpose of American theatre: to ratify popular beliefs in American culture and the American character.

Now, that purpose begins to change. The cultural critique of Shaw and Ibsen, the modern revolution in theatre stagecraft, and the emergence of a progressive leadership among the most influential actor-managers will transform the business. The universal popular audience will break up into separate publics looking for different things from theatre—including challenge. And the theatre will cast off its old identity as the unquestioning supporter of American life and love, viewed in a dream.

2

Clyde Fitch, Mrs. Fiske,
Shaw, and Barrie
Comedy: 1900–1915

IF TRAGEDY—LET US SAY, SERIOUS DRAMA—is the poetry of great persons and great possibilities, comedy is a crazy replica of the everyday. The human possibilities in comedy are modest, and comic characters make a peace with rather than defy fate or (in industrial-age drama) the System. More natural and elastic than serious theatre, American comic theatre effected its evolution more easily than American tragedy.

In a way, comedy had no need to evolve at all, because it would draw on the same ethical vocabulary that had made it spry from the start. As if in an unbroken line stemming from *The Contrast* and *Fashion*, Clyde Fitch's *The Climbers* (1901) indicted the materialism of urban vogue. *The Climbers* is actually more of a melodrama than a satire, but it is sometimes offered by writers as a starting point of modern American comedy, for its prolific author, a "dude prince" of his day, did make a pass at a kind of social comedy, emphasizing a central concept, some strained niceties of dialogue, and an upper-middle-class atmosphere, all of which point to the later more elegant art of S. N. Behrman and Philip Barry.

Fitch never got much play from the critics of his time, and his inspiration frequently took wing after trips to his producer's scenery warehouse to see what decor needed airing, but he helped set American social comedy on its feet. He caught the spectators with a workmanlike blend of joke, sentiment, and sensation, though sensation ran amuck in his adaptation from the French, *Sapho* (1901), when virile Hamilton Revelle carried fragrant Olga Nethersole to an upstairs bedroom for a shocker of an act curtain. "At last," he snorted; "so soon," she replied, as patrons gasped and called for their wraps. Public outcry was such that the police closed the show after four weeks and arrested Nethersole, but she was acquitted of the charge of corrupting public morals and released to give *Sapho* eight more weeks of sensual life, plus several revivals and the field day of whirlwind road tours.

What of Fitch the social commentator? "[His] preoccupation with the idea of successful Entertainment was a blemish on his work," wrote James Gibbons Huneker, eminent as a critic from 1891 to 1917. As Huneker saw it, "the sensitive predominates—delicacy, tact and a feminine manner in apprehending the meanings of life." Fitch's play were women's plays. It was they who held the spotlight, who ran the machinery, who were threatened by the conflict and saved in the climax—*Betty's Finish, The Stubbornness of Geraldine, The Girl with the Green Eyes, The Woman in the Case*. Fitch's men were either nice, solid guys, or vacillating bounders; none of his male leads, not even the Beau Brummell he dashed off for Richard Mansfield, could compare with Fitch's fearless, or gracious, or plangent heroines.

Fitch's plays played like burned toast without front-rank talent, even with the theatre-wise author staging most of the premiere productions himself. It was a Fitch play that made a star of Ethel Barrymore, as the opera singer Madame Trentoni in *Captain Jinks of the Horse Marines* (1901); typically, Trentoni's story requires her to tame a rakehell firefighter. The men had always to be tamed in a Fitch play, wheedled or tricked or somehow supervised. Critics assured their readers that Fitch's psychology was sloppy, but with an actress of charm at the helm it did not appear to matter—she would fill in Fitch's textual gaps with her personal truth.

Barrymore had truth to spare. Her husky voice—which led Ashton Stevens to dub her "Ethel Barrytone"—and her allure were very telling, but when *Captain Jinks* launched its tryout tour in Philadelphia's Walnut Street Theatre, the young debutante came down with a case of nerves. Philadelphia was her home town, home also of her famous acting family, the Drews, and a well-wisher in the gallery called out, "Speak up, Ethel, you Drews is all good actors!" The local reviews, however, were terrible. One woman critic caught on to the secret of Clyde Fitch in writing, "If the young lady who plays Madame Trentoni had possessed beauty, charm, or talent, this play might have been a success," but she missed the boat on Barrymore. When the show reached New York, first nighters were bowled over, a star was born for one of the longest limelight careers ever, and Philadelphia is still known as the town with the most obtuse critics.

But the best of Fitch's leading lady parts was that of a weak woman who needs supervision herself. Becky Warder, heroine of *The Truth* (1907), is a compulsive liar, testing the tolerance of her doting but square husband until their marriage dissolves and humiliation brings her around to genuine repentance. *The Truth* was not a New York hit, but it did offer a *locus classicus* of the Big Moment in one of the earliest of the century's uncountable "telephone scenes," wherein the favored actress must put on a happy front for the mouthpiece while her heart is breaking. The original Becky, Clara Bloodgood, hoped to reclaim the show's merit on tour, but, telephone scenes aside, her heart must truly have been breaking, or something, for she shot herself in her Baltimore hotel room one night just before curtain time, stunning her colleagues—who played many a death scene on stage but had never thought of playwrighting or -acting as having much to do with the truth.

Fitch's death, too, stunned the theatre world. The man who had mastered timing on stage bungled it in life on the eve of his greatest triumph, *The City* (1909). How weary he had grown of being rated a miniaturist creator of capricious women. Hadn't he created men as well—*Beau Brummell, Nathan Hale, The Bachelor?* And what about the lionhearted heroes of his American Revolutionary War play, *Major André* (1903), a dismal box-office failure but Fitch's personal favorite? *The City* was to be his masterpiece, and not just for its healthy contingent of males. This one had a serious theme, that endemic American attack on urban corruption, here focused on the disintegration of a small-town family living in New York. Only a few years later, Edgar Lee Masters, Sherwood Anderson, and others were to unveil skeletons in the country closets, but in 1909 echoes of *The Contrast* and *Fashion* were still reverberating, and the city was still the great American evil. *The Contrast* and *Fashion*, however, were comedies, chiding vogue; *The City* was a drama, hating it. True Fitch in style, it had its bit of sensation, when one of the principals, learning that he has inadvertently married his sister, brings down the second-act curtain shouting, "You're a Goddamn liar!" (Blanche Bates had already shocked the town with a God-less "damn" in David Belasco's *The Girl of the Golden West*, but she hadn't married her own sister.) *The City* scheduled for a fall opening, Fitch had sailed off to Europe, where he was seized with appendicitis and succumbed a few weeks before rehearsals for *The City* were to begin. John Emerson was brought in to direct in Fitch's place, but the Fitch-trained actors already had the hang of the author's style even as they labored to acquire it anew. Emerson did what he could, yet the cast seemed to be listening for Fitch; they were being directed by a ghost.

The City's premiere was emotionally exhausting for everyone in the Lyric Theatre building. Though it was already winter, sweat dribbled off foreheads onto evening clothes in the auditorium, actors had to collect themselves when they gained the wings, and the drama critic of the New York *Sun* fainted. Fitch would have been pleased with the hysteria provoked by his "Goddamn" line, and he would doubtless have come through with an elegant curtain speech (a standard frill of the day), for the play was a triumph. At 190 performances *The City* was the class smash of the season, and the critics convened in the morning papers to give their benediction. They called *The City* realistic—"as strong as a raging bull." Fitch had done it, not again, but at last.

If Fitch was as famous as his leading ladies, most authors were virtually anonymous outside the theatre community. They served the players with product, and "should" be prolific, seasoned professionals (many were former actors and most staged their plays themselves), and supporters of the status quo. The rare author who attempted to break through convention could simply be neglected, because managers and actor-managers had the muscle. But it was inevitable that the idealistic actor-managers would tire of convention themselves and encourage playwrights' ambitions; such a one was Minnie Maddern Fiske.

Mrs. Fiske (as she was billed) was justly adored by a tremendous national public as the incarnation of honesty and valor. The theatre is, inevitably, art by committee and compromise, but Mrs. Fiske struck bargains with no one on earth. Besides being possibly the greatest and most versatile actress of her day, she was a tireless foe of the theatre trust known as the Syndicate and an articulate champion of causes (she once had a man arrested for mistreating a horse). Armed with a crusading journalist for a husband, Harrison Grey Fiske, the editor of the unbearably reputable *Dramatic Mirror*, she ran her shows from top to bottom, poking her actors as one goads a slow-burning fire, charging around backstage to check on morale—once a reporter in Kansas City caught her drilling the ushers. Her husband took up the seamier side of things, such as securing a theatre, which for the country's loudest opponent of the Syndicate was no easy matter. Mrs. Fiske's company could tour the continent and never once see the inside of a decent playhouse. Frozen out by the monopoly, they converted barns, speaking halls, tiny vaudeville boîtes, and even lesser whatnots, raising up altars to a pioneer muse. One critic wrote, "for genius, all places are temples," but some temples are more equal than others. In her first season with *Becky Sharp* (1899), Langdon Mitchell's adaptation of *Vanity Fair*, Mrs. Fiske found herself, in the middle of winter, in the slums of Denver in a dime-a-seat house with a stage the size of a parlor. The stagehands had to remove the back of the theatre to fit in the second act ballroom set. Snow blew in, and the wind kept the women's hoopskirts busy—but Fiske and company made the magic.

Mitchell couldn't recapture much more than the spirit of Thackeray's original, but he wrote meaty parts for the principals, so *Becky Sharp* gave Mrs. Fiske her biggest triumph till then. New York clamored to see the show, and in the fall of 1899 it slipped into one of Manhattan's few non-Syndicate houses, the Fifth Avenue Theatre, which for some reason was located on Broadway at Twenty-eighth Street. ("Carriage parties," the program tells, "received at Twenty-eighth Street entrance.") *Becky* enchanted New York. However, except for the irascible, prudish, grand old man of the *Tribune*, William Winter, who loved it, the reviewers rejected both play and production. One writer left early and, assuming that the piece ended in the heroine's death, as plays sometimes will, wrote derogatively of Minnie's death throes. He should have read the book.

In those days, bad notices didn't matter too much, not least because the public knew that some critics were on the Syndicate payroll. (But Winter, an impossible curmudgeon who worked for starvation wages, was untouchable by bribe. H. L. Mencken dubbed him "the greatest bad critic who ever lived," and Harrison Grey Fiske said Winter could "unearth impurity from quotations of the stock market.") Syndicate pressure, however, did matter—another attraction had booked the Fifth Avenue Theatre, and the trust barred all the other houses, effectively hunting *Becky Sharp* out of Broadway. The Fiskes hied themselves to the Brooklyn Academy of Music for a week, then hit the road: New York's just a stand.

Becky was fluff to Minnie Maddern Fiske, who had played *Tess of the D'Urbervilles* and Ibsen's Hedda Gabler and Nora in *A Doll's House*. So she turned to *Becky Sharp*'s author, Langdon Mitchell, for a comedy with some point to it, some edge. And Mitchell gave her the most distinctive social comedy of the era, *The New York Idea* (1906), burnished with a bright swank. Minnie played Cynthia Karslake, charming but willful, separated from her husband because they "wrangled and jangled." Both still love each other, and the crux of the evening is how they will shed the rebound romances that they have assumed and get back together.

This New York idea is—well, as a visiting Englishman puts it in Act I, "New York is bounded on the north, south, east, and west by the state of Divorce." This was a timely subject in 1906, especially among the managing classes. President Theodore Roosevelt had been calling for a bulk population, fulminating at what he termed "race suicide," and the fluency with which moneyed couples were divesting themselves of their spouses had long been raising eyebrows. (Fiske herself had had to divorce her first husband, Legrand White.) *The Theatre* magazine in March of 1904 referred to Roosevelt's dictum in pointing out how few American actresses had troubled to become American mothers as well. The unsigned article, illustrated with such performers as could be drummed up to pose with infant progeny, claimed that "the American stage is as barren, comparatively, as is upper Fifth Avenue, the most beautiful and most childless thoroughfare in America."

The social setting of Mitchell's play really became prevalent in the 1920s: luxury-class decor and luxury-loving people divided into the selfish and the true in heart. Later, Philip Barry and S. N. Behrman would write of the wicked *haut monde* with a touch of sentiment, sophisticating American high comedy out of articulate wordplay, a breezy elegance, and a highly moralistic context trying to disguise itself as hedonism. Almost never, then or later, would our literate comedy—more or less engendered in *The New York Idea*—be truly adult enough to take its morality as it comes, to bend the behavioral code with an author's, as opposed to the audience's, conception.

(Is it too soon yet, in 1906, to speak of the ethics of a fully developed comic form? It is not, for the ethics have not changed much in all this time; a revival of *The New York Idea* at the Brooklyn Academy of Music in 1977, despite a thin production, held up quite well. The *sound* of it was dated, unavoidably. But the moral structure of the play accorded exactly with our contemporary marital comedy.)

Making it clear whom to root for, Mitchell made Cynthia and her husband those nimble, polished people one likes at first sight, and he created the perfect society vamp in his Vida Phillimore, heartless to a fault. "She's a man-eating shark," cries Cynthia to her husband, "and you'll be a toothsome mouthful!" But the vamps cannot win in popular theatre: the public wouldn't stand for it. In *The New York Idea*, Cynthia and her husband are reconciled in a cute plot twist barely one minute before the final curtain—it turns out that her divorce was declared invalid. "The good ended happily and the bad unhappily," Oscar Wilde once noted. "That is what fiction means."

The New York Idea's spoof of the divorce craze made some people nervous. The old *Life* magazine commented, "Gentlemen like Mr. Mitchell do not appreciate, perhaps, the power of the medium at their command, and therefore do not stop to think that they should be careful, very careful, how they use it, lest they should sow evil in minds not able to understand the good they intend." There was a catch-22 in all this: the theatre was an irresponsible medium, so overseers of public policy discouraged it from taking the learning steps toward responsibility. But without latitude, how was it to expand and find its form?

The New York Idea succeeded not as controversy but as diversion, but a social agitator was already working Broadway, George Bernard Shaw. Here was controversy. Shaw, of course, was not native but imported, brought in as early as 1894 with *Arms and the Man,* starring Richard Mansfield as Bluntschli, the "chocolate soldier" who prefers making love to making war, and with *The Devil's Disciple,* also with Mansfield, in 1897. In a land where the theatre was expected to mind its place, manners, and business, Shaw had impact. The rich verbiage and debunking of heroism in these two plays found ready support from the literati, but no play survives on elitist appeal alone. As the manager Charles Frohman put it, "great successes are made by the masses, not the classes." The masses took to Shaw. They lined up for *Candida* in 1903, with Dorothy Donnelly as the serene womanly archetype and Arnold Daly as the roiled young poet Marchbanks, and again for *You Never Can Tell* in 1905, also with Daly, who threw in a few of Shaw's one-acts and was beginning to hold the American monopoly.

By the time the manager Charles Dillingham stepped in with a wildly triumphant production of *Man and Superman* in 1905, it was clear that these iconoclastically conceptual comedies were to almost everybody's taste. Some critics ceased worrying about the sowing of evil in tender minds and started to ask why American playwrights lacked Shaw's dash. Never did the advocates of the innocuously beautiful theatre have so much to defend: the New York Public Library went so far as to put *Man and Superman* on the restricted list to preserve impressionable adolescents from the example of its feminist heroine Anne Whitefield and her Henri Bergson-derived Life Force, and a few pulpits thundered sermons of alarm. But this only added to the luster of a thinking theatre. Shaw was in, and Arnold Daly, our early Shaw specialist, was in with him, revolving his Shaw hits in repertory all over the Northeast.

Then Daly capped a five-bill Shaw season in the autumn of 1905 with *Mrs. Warren's Profession,* that profession being prostitution. This time, Shaw's new woman had gone too far for Broadway's taste (for England's too—its play censor, the Lord Chamberlain, wouldn't license a staging until the 1920s). Why should honest folk be put through what promised to be a defense of a criminal act when they could spend their time so much more . . . usefully . . . at Clyde Fitch's *Her Great Match* with the chaste beauty Maxine Elliott, or at Edward Peple's *The Prince Chap,* or, for that matter, at Shaw's own *Man and Superman,* which wasn't so blatant as *Mrs. Warren's Profession* in its mockery of contemporary society?

Word filtered in from Daly's New Haven tryout that *Mrs. Warren* was a touchy proposition, and the scheduled two-week stand in New York was sold out before the opening. "There is no worthy motive in any of his plays," stormed *The Theatre*. "Most of his characters are vile, with detestable views of life." Yet elsewhere in this very issue of the magazine one read an interview with the playwright himself that pleaded a stronger case for his work than any reactionary could against. "My plays advocate moral reform," stated Shaw. "I do not complain when [they] are withdrawn from the public libraries in the U.S., or when my plays are prohibited by the police. I simply tell the American people that they are making themselves ridiculous in the eyes of the civilized world."

The police did not disappoint Shaw. They closed *Mrs. Warren's Profession*, charging Daly and his leading lady Mary Shaw with disorderly conduct. Both, however, were promptly acquitted, and the play returned in 1907 in a vastly inferior production, dying quietly after three weeks. Not till Mary Shaw again played Mrs. Warren, in 1918, staging the show herself, did the script play as its author intended, morally instructive—and outraged, not outrageous.

However, most successful comedies of the time depended less on satire than on physical action, the familiar personae, and good-natured derision: low comedy. In the context of buffoonery, the great platform was burlesque, a spoof of some play or literary work—anything from Shakespeare to the latest midcult hit. Burlesque was lowdown comedy, and the aforementioned jeering version of *Hiawatha* in 1856 attests to burlesque's staying power, for fifty years later the form still held the stage. Nothing in New York at the turn of the century was more popular than Joe Weber and Lew Fields' lampoons of current attractions, largely extemporized and changed almost weekly. "Dutch" (= German-dialect, which is to say, Jewish) comedy was the pair's gimmick, and pathos and profundity were put through the meat-grinder regularly at their little Music Hall on Broadway and Twenty-ninth Street: Clyde Fitch's *The Stubbornness of Geraldine* turned up a short time after its premiere in a Weber and Fields' version, *The Stickiness of Gelatine*, and the Biblical epic *Quo Vadis?* surfaced, rent from toga to sandal, as *Quo Vass Is?* Nobody was safe from the team's dialect takeoffs; nobody wanted to be, for all New York frequented the Music Hall and to be lambasted there was to have achieved not notoriety but a loving ridicule and, incidentally, free publicity.

When not slicing into other people's creations, Mike (Weber) and Myer (Fields) introduced song-and-dance specialty acts or stood around in front

of an olio drop (a secondary curtain hung downstage near the footlights)
and purveyed their ethnic patter:

MYER: I come from a very rich family. Ve hadt a shoffer, a botler—
MIKE: Don't try to kidding me, Myer. I know how it vass you lived.
        Your family got t'rown oudt on the street so many times thadt your
        mother hadt to buy coitans vodt matched the sidevalk!

(The ghost of Mose the fireboy must have been looking over their shoulders.)

Burlesque was a lampoon-*cum*-variety show. Farce was better organized,
more solidly structured in its narrative, though like burlesque it did not use
language as a vehicle in itself. The point in farce was plot, pace, and eccentricity—strange characters, mistaken identity and disguise, bizarre twists,
crazy meetings, and all the traditions of slapstick. It had changed little from
Charles Hoyt's day, except that after 1900 it was less casually musical: farces
either became full-scale musical comedies or did without music altogether.

Later on, American farce was to rise above the screens, ladders, slamming
doors, and other physical manifestation, but the farces of the early 1900s
doted on ruckus. Our modern farce is often dated from George M. Cohan's
Seven Keys to Baldpate (1913), a mystery about a hack writer trying to
finish a story in one night while various oddballs intrude. The piece was all
noise (plus the inevitable but rather insufficient love plot), created to be
stamped and shot at the public in living boldface. This was by no means
the first of its kind, but its popularity made it stick out as a trend setter.
Certainly, it set one precedent in that previous mysteries always let the
audience—but not the characters—in on the deception. *Seven Keys to Baldpate*
seems to have been the first to deceive public and characters alike. And
Cohan was generous with his novelty: he also introduced the deserted inn
and the vindictive hermit in this work.

The critics were sour about *Seven Keys to Baldpate*, as they were about
everything Cohan did; they thought him a bad example for American youth.
His plays, they said, were rubbish, portraying American manhood as a jag-
time hot shot and manipulating the customers with heathen jingoism. He
was too slick for them, with an ego as extra as his platform shoes—but he
knew what most people liked in the way of entertainment and his "cheer up,
life's a joke" philosophy set a tone for the times.

The very essence of popular theatre, Cohan had luster in places the
diamond didn't know existed, rough places of a very man-in-the-street glow.
But this man *owned* The Street: they called him "The Man Who Owns
Broadway" from about 1905 to 1919, when the actors struck the managers

and actor-manager Cohan picked the losing, managerial side. Yes, he was arrogant and flashy, but this was an era of Coming Out in the culture, more and more the immigrant's urban era. Cohan's arrogance was his emblem, his way of distinguishing his sector of theatre from those of the Shakespeareans and rural sentimentalists. Disdaining makeup, playing himself in every role, winking at the crowd so they'd know he didn't take it seriously, he seemed to have come right in off the sidewalk in street clothes. They liked him for that: meet John Doe, born on "the fourth of July."

There was lighter, less pushy farce than the Cohan type, one given to more naturalistic settings and characters. Philip Bartholomae's *Over Night* (1911), for example, underplayed the zanies to spend some real time with its four principals, two mismated couples who are separated and remated in a more amenable alignment on a Hudson River cruise. But the thing just wouldn't sit still. *The Theatre* magazine assessed the method in its review of the play: "Anybody and everybody . . . must get busy and keep busy . . . there is something doing all the time." Even a quiet moment doesn't last long—at one point, when the action has settled down "over night" in a riverside hotel, the night clerk takes out his guitar, an insomniac guest wanders in in his nightshirt, and the two of them go into a routine of no relevance to the work at hand. This sort of anything-for-an-effect "business" (what we now call "shtick") may not sound much like naturalism, but at least *Over Night*'s main characters were played as much for their humanness as for sight gags or puns. It is interesting to note that the first revolution in naturalizing American musical comedy—the "Princess shows" of Jerome Kern, Guy Bolton, and P. G. Wodehouse—was effected by junking the stock figures of exotic "comic opera" (meaning operetta) and making musical adaptations of these ethnically low-key (if active) farces. *Over Night*, in fact, transmuted into the most impressively naturalistic of the Princess shows, *Very Good Eddie*, in 1915.

Far removed in tone from burlesque and farce was romantic comedy, craving nostalgia, sweet conventions, refinement. This is the applied, not descriptive stage, as beautiful as possible, bewildered by the everyday (unlike freewheeling urban comedy or the subtly shrewd Yankee shows). Louis N. Parker's *Pomander Walk* (1910) says all that need be said for this genre, from its wistful title through its cast of characters (Barbara Pennymint, the Honorable Caroline Thring, the Reverend Jacob Sternroyd, Sir Peter Antrobus, a lamplighter, a muffin man) right down to its several happy endings, all successful proposals of marriage spanning three generations. Oddly, *The Theatre* took it as a novelty for its delicate re-creation of a bygone era, as if the rest of the stage, in or out of modern dress, were actively engaged in scuttling the beautiful with life as lived: "The reversion to the simple, the elemental, even the romantic, comes as a delightful surprise." "Plays of purpose" was a term of derogation for as many commentators as it was others' salute to an author's intelligence. But the public, through Shaw, was whetting a taste for topical comedy, and would want more.

Until it arrived, however, there was always rural comedy, our oldest native form. More solidly put together than farce or burlesque but less tactful than Clyde Fitch or Langdon Mitchell, this was the arena of the Yankee and his relative stereotypes, the haunt of the folk and the family and the home town. In the early twentieth century, the best-known authors working this terrain tended to come from the Midwest; George Ade, once considered the nation's outstanding humorist, offers an instance, and brings us closer to wherever the roots of our public quality may lie than Cohan or Weber and Fields with their Manhattan-based humor. Ade's political satire *The County Chairman* (1903) crossed a local election with romance to raise an ethical question about campaign tactics. Ade's protagonist Jim Hackler is another Yankee, more fair-minded than educated and given to "quoting" Shakespeare with some license—as if the picture of a hero who really knew his poetry might challenge the dedicated lowbrow taste of segments of the American audience. In Jim Hackler's mouth, the Bard comes off like one of the old buzzards who lounge on the steps of the Courthouse, as here when he is heartening a hesitant young man to run for office:

> Well, my experience has been that a woman, if she's any good, don't fall in love with a quitter. You know what our old friend Bill says. Bill says, "There is a tide in the affairs of men, which, taken on the jump, leads on to fortune. But if you don't get aboard at the right minute you're liable to be a dead card all the rest of your life."

The County Chairman contained a good deal of artifice in its plot, but the important thing is that Ade's projection of county character made for the most vigorous colloquial texture in the era. Lyricism takes many forms, and we must consider what options face the poet in this democratic theatre, when he must satisfy the public's need for self-expression and yet do so in the rude, non-poetic terms that such a public can comprehend.

Ade wrote not just well but, like most of the dramatists of his day, often. Always, he seemed to be working out little commentaries on the basic American life (which at that time was not considered to include unassimilated immigrants, industrial workers, blacks, or city dwellers). Besides writing the books for numerous musical comedies, he followed the course charted by *The County Chairman* with such bucolic romps as *Just Out of College* (1905), *Father and the Boys* (1908), and the most durable of his plays, *The College Widow* (1904), a winsome piece set at a small school in the era when the big football game was the most pressing matter at hand. Here was another Kern Princess adaptation, farce into musical: *Leave It to Jane* (1917).

Comparable to Ade's tangent in general was *The Man from Home* (1908), a 496-performance hit by Booth Tarkington and Harry Leon Wilson. (496 performances in the early twentieth century was phenomenal. When *The Man from Home* closed, it held the record as the third longest-running non-musical attraction in Broadway's history, surpassed only by *The Lion and the Mouse* and *The Music Master*.) Here the Yankee proved unusually daring: rather than outsmart the (New York) slicker as before, he travels to continental Europe, so long associated in American popular art with decadence and oversophistication. Though they invariably were turned into cartoon idiots as immigrants in urban comedies, Europeans shown on their home turf were fortune hunters, gigolos, and assorted wastrels (except in musicals, which could not have lasted out a season without their princes and goosegirls). But however well-mannered, foreigners were no match for the stubborn virtue of the Yankee. In Europe, the Man from Home is the Good Guy from Common Sense.

Tarkington and Wilson had logged some time in collecting broadsides at Europe from traveling Americans, particularly the disoriented husbands, and they intended *The Man From Home* at least partly as a friendly satire on The Innocent Abroad—but instead the audience approved of the jingoistic bravado and casual one-upmanship. Missing the point entirely, they cheered for scenes such as this one between Daniel Pike, the man from Indiana, and a Frenchman:

PIKE: When you come right down to it, Colonel, I wouldn't trade our new State Insane Asylum for the worst ruined ruin in Europe—not for hygiene and real comfort.
LE BLANC: And your people?
PIKE: Well, we kind o' like each other.
LE BLANC: But you have no leisure class.
PIKE: No leisure class? We've got a pretty good-sized colored population.
LE BLANC: I mean no aristocracy.
PIKE: We haven't? You ought to see somebody from Boston traveling out west, if you don't think so.

This *man from home* was the usual roughhewn but perceptive rustic who uses folk humor and common sense the way the Count of Monte Cristo used his sword. Extricating an American girl from the clutches of rapacious English nobles, this gallant rube worked such a spell on the audience that the original Pike, a character actor named William Hodge, was suddenly invested with stardom as a romantic lead, interviewed, wondered at, and worshipped. As far as most theatregoers were concerned, those who spoke those lines *were* those lines. It was, for the time, a crazy kind of realism.

Ade and Tarkington weren't the only alternatives to the grouchy wisecracks of the city-based frolics, but they counted among the most potent at freeing the rural prototype from his identity as ne'er-do-well farmer. This was an increasingly industrialized age; Tarkington and Wilson took the Yankee to Europe, further widening his parameters, and the one and only George M. urbanized him countless times, as in *Broadway Jones* (1912), democratic (Jones) and know-it-all (Broadway) at once. Natural as he was in his roles, however, Cohan as author turned the crackle of New York into his personal cliché. The Ade-Tarkington school surveyed life more truly, meanwhile preparing the way for the genre known as domestic comedy and its extrapolation of the non-events of middle-class life. Even the titanic Eugene O'Neill connected with the Ade-Tarkington tradition if not with their technique when he wrote his domestic comedy, *Ah, Wilderness!*. Neither of the two older writers is properly comparable to O'Neill, of course—still, it was they, carrying on James A. Herne's work in the uncovering of an emotional leverage in the humdrum, who helped break ground for important work to come. The Midwest, circa 1900–1920, was their habitat. Don't patronize it; there is beauty there, too. Asked where they got their ideas, Ade and Tarkington might well have answered, like Satan unto the Lord, "from going to and fro in the earth, and from walking up and down in it."

But most comedies of the time were neither urban parades, nor depictions of Americana, nor sub-social tracts like *The New York Idea*. Most comedies were just comedies, hoping to be funny, to charm, to run. The titles speak, if not volumes, whole sentences on what was considered feasible in terms of character and situation: *The Chorus Lady* (1906), *The Rejuvenation of Aunt Mary* (1907), and *The Girl from Rector's* (1909) were typical hits of the decade, and one, *Brewster's Millions* (1906), embodies the wish fulfillment property of the stage with its tale of a young man faced with the problem of having to spend a million dollars in a single year (incidentally introducing an inside Broadway joke in the person of an actor in a tiny part billed pseudonymously as "George Spelvin," a handle assigned to walk-ons, corpses, and whatnots ever after).

These were American comedies, by us and of us, but the British theatre retained its attraction, and exports from London were a commonplace. The manager Charles Frohman had a close tie-in with Sir James M. Barrie, and dutifully requisitioned one hit after another for local viewing. "If it isn't British, it isn't a play," should have been Frohman's motto, though he was willing to present American authors who had established themselves. The prize in his collection of starry gems was Maude Adams, whose natural shyness perfectly accorded with Frohman's demand that the actors under his management nurture a mystery by hiding from the public. Adams didn't even like to give interviews. Slight of figure, easily startled, with the habit of catching words in her throat at sticky moments, the actress was favored with ripply ash-brown hair and large blue eyes in a plain-pretty face—just the "look" for Barrie's delicate light-comic romances. Frohman crowned Adams queen of the pixies in a rotation of Scottish whimsey—*The Little Minister, Quality Street, Peter Pan, What Every Woman Knows,* and *A Kiss for Cinderella.*

Lady Babbie in *The Little Minister* was the essence of Adams. A book of 1899, Lewis C. Strang's *Famous Actresses of the Day,* recalls her in the part: "She was dashing, careless and free as the tantalizing gypsy girl . . . graceful and spirited, serious and sympathetic," qualities that most likely defeated her Juliet, one of Adams' rare failures. But dash and spirit were just the ticket for Barrie's Peter Pan, the role for which Adams is most often cited, king of the pixies this time and haunting the memories of all who saw her. Adams' Peter was one of the touchstone events of the time, and after 223 performances in 1905–06, she repeated it in late 1906, 1912, and 1915, each time in Frohman's flagship, the Empire Theatre at Broadway and Fortieth Street, never missing a single performance.

The country's adoration of this woman in this role is indicative of something, especially given the newly intellectualized climate of the stage at the time. The year that *Peter Pan* debuted here, 1905, was the heyday of Clyde Fitch and George Bernard Shaw, and if *The New York Idea* was only just being written, the smash of the season was Charles Klein's *The Lion and the Mouse,* which amassed the unprecedented total of 686 performances largely on its indictment of monopolistic capitalism and on the rumor that Klein's character of an unscrupulous millionaire was modeled on John D. Rockefeller. But the new wave was as nothing when likened to Adams in her Barrie repertory; she was the figurehead, the memory of the era, sweep-

ing all before her, rivaling even the moist palpitations of the much-loved
David Warfield in David Belasco's *The Return of Peter Grimm* (1911),
coming back from the dead to save his niece from a bad-risk marriage.

Adams and Barrie of course incorporated nothing but escapism—in their
gentleness and fantasy and in her fragile warmth—and this is a form of
beauty. It is not the beauty of art, with art's compelling vision. But it was
no mere diversion, either. In such theatre, one escaped into an idyll but not
out of morality, for if Barrie's psychology is a form of massage, his life-code
is vital. These plays do not challenge—but that is not the point. One man's
escapism is another man's realism, or burlesque, or morality play. In the
early twentieth century, virtually all theatre was escapist in its urge toward
fun, shocks, and sweetness, but it also reflected the perspective of its audience. It had a legitimate cultural function: to provide not a vacation from
life's miseries, but a rationale for them. The public's belief in William
Gillette's unstinting chivalry, Mrs. Fiske's rectitude, and Cohan's optimism
was universal.

It was a *moral* escapism, then. But in yielding entirely to prevailing
American self-beliefs, it was static. Playwrights were like hired puppets permitted to work their own strings; they knew the rules and didn't dare refute
them. All Yankee Doodle Dandies were good; all sexually liberated women—
i.e., vamps—were evil; what every woman knows is how to cook and boss
(or be) a maid; all-night clerks can be counted on for a little moonlit shtick.
As in Restoration comedy, with its commentative names (Lady Wishfort,
Sir Fopling Flutter), one knew the players by the scorecard of types. And
the rigid morality was poorest in what a theatre needs most: ideas. All the
American stage could be reduced to one basic plot conflict, and it was not
that of man's unharnessable impulses versus man's need for societal law,
say, but of good guys versus bad guys.

In Paul Armstrong and Wilson Mizner's *The Deep Purple* (1911), this
good-versus-evil pattern was brought to the neatest of conclusions: a "man
from the west," notches on his gun and all, dispatches an oily blackmailer by
application of some old-fashioned self-reliance and a shot of his pistol—in
self-defense, be it admitted. But still the deck was stacked from the start of
the evening: same old good, same old evil. When the villain was felled, "No
murmurs of pity or regret were heard from the audience," wrote one critic;
on the contrary, the customers "experienced a pleasurable gratification." But,
he went on, "is the public eager to become participants in crime?"

The question is, rather, was the public eager to participate in any sort
of dialogue with playwrights: was it ready to repudiate the stagnant themes

it had adored since the days of Jedediah Homebred? Even *The New York Idea,* with its lightly satiric "new" comedy, had to bless the nice people and blast the vamp. But Shaw gave us the true new comedy, and Shaw was a hit. "Plays of purpose" would go over.

It is time to turn to serious drama, to see how it fared in the early 1900s. Consider its traditional purposes on the American stage, its Indian braves, Philadelphia exotics in verse, and Civil War lovers trapped on opposing sides. Consider what might replace them, what other characters and places. The public likes the look of novelty—but, so far, it has loved the substance of routine.

3

Belasco, the Western, and Realism

Drama: 1900–1915

PERHAPS THE FIRST PORTENT OF REVOLUTION in American drama comes in the work of David Belasco. Mainly a manager (meaning producer-director) but often a playwright as well, Belasco earned much fame in his lifetime as the "father of realism in American theatre." Even today, one occasionally hears an echo of this preposterous overstatement: actually, Belasco arrived on the scene shortly after others had launched the first experiments in naturalizing the stage. Realism in the mounting of American plays dates back to Steele MacKaye, an innovator in lighting and design; realism in writing belongs foremost to James A. Herne. Belasco's contributions consisted of 1. his adapting the forms of European quasi-naturalism to please the thrill-seeker, and 2. the detail work in his stage pictures, whose lifelike clarity was an impressive achievement. There is no doubt that Belasco was a great showman, but he was the father not of realism but of realistic effect. He was an effect himself, with his clerical collar, his mane of silvery hair (complete with forelock for tugging), and the delerious naiveté of his curtain calls, as here for Avery Hopwood's *The Gold Diggers*: "Ladies and gentlemen . . . [thoughtful pause] . . . I thank you for Mr. Hopwood . . . [humble pause] . . . I thank you for Miss [Ina] Claire . . . [radiant pause] . . . I thank you."

Belasco commenced his affairs on the west coast in the early 1860s as "Davido the Circus-Boy Wonder." He wrote his first script at the age of twelve (*Jim Black; or, The Regulator's Revenge*), played York to Charles Kean's Richard III in Canada at age thirteen, and knocked about the theatre learning the whole trade. He couldn't seem to break through to power—until he happened to work Pygmalion's magic on Caroline Dudley Carter after her mildly scandalous divorce from the palsied millionaire Leslie Carter, of Chicago's "little liver pills" family, turning Carter from the latest divorcée into an actress. Now it begins.

Mrs. Leslie Carter—as she was billed, to keep her celebrity credentials before the public—had no talent other than horseback-riding. But Belasco trained her so gruelingly that if she was crude and off-pitch in her first stints in comedy and operetta, she triumphed in Belasco's Civil War romance, *The Heart of Maryland* (1895), after a sudden retirement for further lessons from the master. Of this course of study, Carter later recalled: "Mr. Belasco would select a role, talk with me upon it, make suggestions, answer questions, and then leave me to work it out." Others thought the training somewhat less matey. Stories circulated of Belasco's screaming fits, his love of violence. He broke the woman down to nothing so he could own her outright when she at last Arrived.*

Belasco first came to notice as a trainer of actors. Then he grew popular as a writer of a certain kind of melodrama, emphasizing bloody horror and flamboyant characters in the style of Victorien Sardou. (For all his coaching of Carter and her successors, Belasco was quite a pupil himself, his hands forever in teacher's desk, taking things.) Later, his aptitude for spectacle emerged. For *The Girl of the Golden West* (1905), Belasco gave Broadway a blizzard and the dazzling vista of Cloudy Mountain with cabin lights shining in the distance. For a sleazy rented room in *The Easiest Way* (1909) he *bought* a sleazy rented room—gas fixtures, battered furniture, even the walls—and set it up at the Belasco Theatre. For *The Governor's Lady* (1912) he re-created the interior of a Childs Restaurant, even unto steaming coffee urns and flapping flapjacks. With Belasco, even the rehearsals had to be real: he once threw a tantrum at a run-through because a supposed jar of molasses turned out to contain maple syrup.

Let us examine, briefly, *The Darling of the Gods* (1902). Belasco collaborated with John Luther Long on this five-act Japanese melodrama-pageant, and though Long apparently wrote the dialogue after Belasco laid out the scenario, the master's touch is felt in the heavy Sardou pilferings that litter the script. In fact, *The Darling of the Gods* is Sardou's *La Tosca* in kimonos and tableaus, right down to the offstage torture of the hero (=Cavaradossi) that the corrupt war minister Zakkuri (=Scarpia) resorts

* It may be that Bruce Millholland, Ben Hecht, and Charles MacArthur had the Belasco-Carter partnership in mind when they wrote the several plays (Millholland initiated the idea) known as *Twentieth Century* and best remembered for Howard Hawks' 1934 screen version with John Barrymore and Carole Lombard.

to to force the heroine (=Tosca) to yield herself to him. There was little plot per se, but much extravaganza—pictorial colorations, pantomimes, musical interludes—and, fronting it all, the tender Yo-San, the outlaw Samurai whom she loves, and the war minister who destroys them. Melodrama though it was, *The Darling of the Gods* was not without its touching moments, but, as Arthur Hornblow, Jr., explained it in *The Theatre*, "the triumph belongs to the stage manager, the electrician, and the scene painter rather than to the the playwright." There were forty-five speaking parts and no end of extras— Gentlemen of Rank, Geisha Girls, Singing Girls, Heralds from the Emperor, Maids-in-Waiting to the Princess, Screen Bearers, Kago Men, Coolies, Retainers, Runners, Servants, Musume, Priests, Lantern Bearers, Banner Bearers, Incense Bearers, Gong Bearers, Jugglers, Acrobats, Torturers, Carp Flyers, Imperial Soldiers, and Zakkuri's Musket Men. Spectacle had been a regular feature on Broadway for over sixty years, but it was sheer size that had counted before—here was variety in the shading of Belasco's finicky, almost motor-driven orientalism, "a symphony of smells and sounds and color," in Hornblow's view, "while the Japanese retainers beat their heads on the floor to the accompaniment of strange Japanese music." The whole business cost $78,000 to mount and took nearly two years of touring to get out of the red in a day when the average play paid back its investment in a matter of weeks.

Belasco's showpiece was more a cycle of postcards than drama, but it did provide a certain excitement when he proposed it for the 1904 Louisiana Purchase Exposition at St. Louis, and the Syndicate barred the local theatres to him. They and he had been sparring for years; this, finally, meant war, ruinous war that had already been taken up by such actors as James O'Neill, Francis Wilson, Joseph Jefferson, Richard Mansfield (who gave in under fire), and of course the two Fiskes. Joseph Pulitzer's New York *World* had called the Trust "a peculiar abomination" back in 1897: "It aims not only to compel the public to pay what price the Trust pleases for its entertainment, but to decide arbitrarily what plays and what actors the public shall see." But now, in the seedtime of trust-busting, other journals warned the audience, so innocent of the word "industry" in the idea "theatre," to beware of monopolistic oppression.

The Trust got started in the late 1890s as a conspiracy of theater managers, a varied lot that took in grim little "Honest" Abe Erlanger as well as dapper Charles Frohman. When Belasco took the Syndicate to court— incredibly, he lost—theatregoers had a chance to think about the different kinds of person involved in theatre, perhaps for the first time. In the nineteenth century, "theatre" meant actor-managers and a few playwrights. But after 1900, the stage counted real estate dealers like Erlanger, producers like Frohman, and a diverse group of writers and actors. Belasco most clearly defines the theatre of his time; he wrote it, staged it, cast it, and, in court with the Syndicate, questioned its practices. Like Cohan and Mrs. Fiske, he was of the race, a true thespian. Frohman could only hire and fire actors; Belasco invented them. Long after he broke with Carter (for remarrying without saying "May I?"), he succeeded with such disparate models as the wispy Mary Pickford, the dusky Lenore Ulric, and the morbid David Warfield, a mediocre talent who could cry at will. Belasco discovered him stooging for Weber and Fields and turned him into a star who played only five roles for twenty-three years. (A sixth didn't go over and was quickly abandoned.) As Solomon in *The Auctioneer* (1901), as *The Music Master* (1904), or as Shylock in *The Merchant of Venice*, Warfield wore an invisible tag reading, "Made in Belasco," but he retired having amassed a fortune of twelve million dollars. Was it at Belasco's suggestion that Warfield turned down a thirteenth million for a contract to film *The Music Master?*

Probably the best of the Belasco stock company was Blanche Bates, a subtle actress who dealt in fragility—in *The Darling of the Gods* and Belasco and Long's one-acter *Madame Butterfly* (1900)—as well as tomboy pluck, in *The Girl of the Golden West*. As Minnie, the "Girl," she swore like a cowboy, won her bandit love in a poker game, saved him from a lynch mob, and rode off with him on a horse. Preposterous final lines awaited her at the conclusion of the saga: "Oh, my Sierras! Oh, my lovely mountains! Oh, my California!" Yet Belasco's melodrama was so expansive that anything less would have felt perfunctory. (Both *Madame Butterfly* and *The Girl of the Golden West* adapted nicely as operas by Giacomo Puccini; song, so to speak, hid latent in them.) But all of Belasco was preposterous, and those who learned to enjoy Shaw and Ibsen found that they had outgrown Belasco. They still went to his shows: because they were hungry for theatre. Yet ten minutes after they left they were hungry again. For a play.

Old-fashioned thrills and sentiment in a new-styled look: that was Belasco. That was popular theatre. If Belasco was realism, what was Henrik Ibsen? The Norwegian playwright, a contributor not only to modern realism but to modern symbolic fantasy as well, was introduced to America in Belasco's day: *Peer Gynt, The Master Builder, Rosmersholm, When We Dead Awaken, Little Eyolf,* and *The Pillars of Society* had all been staged in New York by 1910, some for very short runs. (*The Master Builder* lasted one night.) *Hedda Gabler* and *A Doll's House*, however, had caught on. The whole Ibsen canon horrified most opinion-makers. In the eyes of William

Winter, Shaw was a "man of very little importance." But Ibsen might actually "disrupt society" with his uprising wives, his nonconforming doctors and architects, his philosophizing trolls and—how dare the man?—venereal disease (in *Ghosts*). Theatregoers who gave Ibsen a hearing disgusted Winter, though not beyond description: "long-haired men and flat-chested she-goats of women" was his impression of the first-nighters at Mrs. Fiske's *Hedda Gabler*. This new school of playwrighting was bound to upend the theatre's simple purpose: "Since when did the theatre become a proper place for a clinic of horrors and the vivisection of moral ailments?"

This is just what the American theatre was to become—and its immediate prerequisite was the public's acceptance of perceptions that refuted their own. In mid-Belasco, as the genuine American realists and idealists started coming, the public felt again the shock with which they had first greeted Shaw and Ibsen. What were they to think of such an offering as Arthur Hopkins' *The Fatted Calf* (1912), concerning a girl driven to paranoia by suffocating parents, even with a sort-of happy ending? Melodrama had taught them other facts for life. They could accept a hortatory theatre, as in Augustus Thomas' *As a Man Thinks* (1911), an assault on racial and religious intolerance. But Thomas worked according to traditional guidelines for tone and structure, and his people behaved as people, in plays, were "meant to." Thomas aligned his terms with those of the public, while Hopkins had leaned too far in Ibsen's direction in the matter of character: they dripped real blood.

Thomas could have given Hopkins lessons in how to speak out without having to be heard—the gift of the day—for whether in a comedy like *The Earl of Pawtucket* (1903—note the typical democratic self-congratulation), in national bombast, as in *Alabama* (1891) and *The Copperhead* (1918), or in a novelty like his crime thriller about the powers of ESP, *The Witching Hour* (1907), Thomas captured the crowd.

Even around 1910, when productions of plays by such other foreign authors as Gerhart Hauptmann, Arthur Schnitzler, Maurice Maeterlinck, and Ferenc Molnar seconded the revisionism of Shaw and Ibsen, Broadway wished the avant garde away with the rusty revivals, the hygenic classics, the star parade, the downhome genres. More conspicuous than any *Fatted Calf* or Ibsen premiere were George M. Cohan, Maude Adams, and David Warfield, were Margaret Mayo's ridiculous farce *Twin Beds* (1914) and Ruth Chatterton's winsome stint as the orphan heroine of *Daddy Long-Legs* (1914), were H. B. Warner enlivening the already spirited doings of the crook play *Alias Jimmy Valentine* (1910) and George Arliss catching the life and breath of *Disraeli* (1911): were loud thrillers, fastidious fantasies, lavish helpings of good versus evil, and a determined strategy of non-inquiry.

A bittersweet autism informed Edward Sheldon's mad, sad *Romance* (1913), which serves as a useful paradigm for the conventional work of the period, even admitting that the "alas, my darling, we must part" salon piece was about to be retired forever (except in operetta). Sheldon's heroine, the opera singer Madame Cavallini, loves a dashing young rector, not wisely. "Your lips drop as the honeycomb," he tells her. "Your mouth is smoother than oil. But your feet go down to death, and your steps take hold on hell." Two minutes later, however, he takes another tack: "I thought I came here to save you, but I didn't. It was just because I'm a man and you're a woman, and I love you, darling . . . I love you more than anything in the world!" The hapless young minister of *Romance* nearly loses his soul while trying to save Madame Cavallini's; alas, they must part. Chastely, they do, leaving the minister to grow old alone. His ancient recollections frame the action, and after hearing his story, a young couple decide not to make his mistake, but to marry and live their own romance without further delay. As the opera singer, Doris Keane enjoyed a mild vogue, making a film of the play in 1920 only to be erased ten years later by Greta Garbo in the same role. This overbred tale better suited Hollywood or even the dressy London stage, where *Romance* played 1,046 performances compared to a mere 160 in New York.

The climate was shifting on Broadway. Take, for instance, the western, a potboiler of the late nineteenth century. In 1905, Edwin Milton Royle crystallized the form in *The Squaw Man*, an evening of good and bad guys, nasty rowdies in the saloon, and inscrutable, skulking Indians. The "squaw man" hero is an Englishman who takes the blame for someone's embezzlement and flees to anonymity and a new life in the American West, where he settles down with Nat-u-ritch, a laconic Indian woman. Nat-u-ritch saves the hero's life by shooting villainous Cash Hawkins, then delivers Act II's stirring curtain line, "Me killum"—but amid all the cliché, the play does make the point that the reasonably invincible hero can best fulfill his potential out on the lawless range, especially as he has extenuated the hubris of the loner in his devotion to Nat-u-ritch.

As with the roles that William Gillette wrote himself, a romantic involvement was considered not only pretty, but essential; there is such a thing as being too lone a ranger. The public admires self-reliance yet demands selfless love matches, and *The Squaw Man* obeys the rules. Royle has his hero marry Nat-u-ritch, only to dissolve the dream when the perhaps never entirely converted aristocrat decides to send their son (the future Earl of Kerhill) back to Britain, thereby ruining the simple life he has carved out of anarchy and wilderness. Apparently it never occurred to Royle that Nat-u-ritch might pick up a little English over the years, and the touching finale is conducted in pidgin. "Big White Father send for little Hal," the hero tells his wife, "says make him big Chief. Teguin cross wide waters, fire-wagon, fire-boat . . . Hal have heap cattle, heap ponies, pretty soon maybe so, *heap Big Chief!*" To which Nat-u-ritch replies, "Katch pah-si-du-way." At last, the woman kills herself in despair, adding the utmost in climax to a feverishly climactic story.

But now comes the reinvestment of form, if on a primitive level. Only a year after *The Squaw Man*, in 1906, William Vaughan Moody presented the nation with an adult western that exploited the psyche of virile self-determination not as a simple mandate for romance and gunplay but thematically—to explain what freedom feels like and where it comes from. Moody was an out-and-out amateur, with neither theatre nor even professional writing experience. Perhaps that's why he was able to avoid the clichés: he didn't know them. His play came to light in Chicago, whence Margaret Anglin and her troupe had roamed with *Zaza*, a version of Wilkie Collins' novel *The New Magdalen*. Someone sent Anglin a script about an eastern girl who, about to be raped by three bravos in a lonely Arizona cabin, makes a deal with one of them to save herself, leaves him and later returns, smitten. *A Sabine Woman*, Moody called it.

Anglin impulsively threw it into rehearsal, closed *Zaza*, and stunned Chicago with the power and psychological breadth of Moody's vision. The suspenseful first act, with its promise of gang rape, its fight-to-the-death among the three desperadoes, and its chilling finale with the girl limply riding off with her captor, hit the bullseye. But Act II and its central conflict of eastern security opposed to western freedom blew the roof off, earning fifteen curtain calls. With the final act yet to come, it was a given that *A Sabine Woman* would conquer New York as soon as Anglin took it there.

Then she remembered that she had made no deal with Moody for the rights to his play.

Warned about theatre sharpies, Moody, backstage, refused to sign anything; impatient with amateurs, Anglin declined to play Moody's third act. The stalemate was finally broken by University of Chicago law students and a Shubert Brothers attorney who happened to be in the house. Forty-five minutes later, Chicago got the rest of *A Sabine Woman*, in which the heroine succumbs to her barbarian of the plains and his way of life. "I guess every wife is paid for in some good coin or other," he snarls, and she tells him: "Teach me how to live as you do."

Revised, retitled *The Great Divide*, cast with Anglin and matinée idol Henry Miller and redirected by Miller, Moody's play was roasted by the critics in Washington and Pittsburgh, who were unprepared for a western that did not jibe with formula. At the last dress rehearsal in New York, the two stars indulged an ancient theatre tradition by having a scream session over the placement of a prop straw basket, but at the premiere all went well and both press and public were entranced. The New York *Sun* declared *The Great Divide* "so bold and vital in theme, so subtly veracious and un-affectedly strong in the writing, that it is very hard . . . to speak of it in terms at once of justice and of moderation."

Things were looking up. Now playwrights were to turn from the flat edge of the earth as painted on canvas drops to a real horizon, one less finite and less complacent—most importantly, one that made plot not an end in itself but the solution to a moral equation. In place of brother discovering he has married sister, Clyde Fitch-style, followed by an obscene curtain line and ripples of delighted horror in the auditorium, now it was *The Great Divide*'s Ruth Jordan discovering the regeneration of her life force in Stephen Ghent, the westerner who has not been exposed to society's sculpture, a free man. Suddenly, we understood what had attracted us to this character in less instructive, less self-comprehending westerns. Ruth Jordan's recognition was ours; and recognition is exhilaration.

If the western could be so neatly reintegrated, why not other forms as well? Eugene Walter gave new information on the "fallen woman" in *The Easiest Way* (1909)—this was the show referred to earlier as one of Belasco's exhibits in "realism," the one with the authentic shabby boarding house room in its second act, when the heroine, an actress with a past, is fighting poverty and a blacklist while waiting for her boyfriend to return to her. She shows courage and good sense in her fight, but her past has her pinned, and Walter's title is ironic: the actress does *not* take "the easiest way" (reversion to her life as a kept woman). It takes her. This was patently contrary to the requirements of public uplift; courage and a belief in one's own good intentions *should* win out. Boston was so offended by Walter's revision of the theatre's Sunday School morality that it banned the play. Even in New York the *Dramatic Mirror*'s rave notice (for the thrill of the performance) was tempered with disgust (for the author's message).

Walter's solid script and Belasco's solid sets made their point, but audi-

ences were especially drawn to the pathos of the final moments, and par-
.icularly to the penultimate line, spoken by the actress after her boyfriend
has walked out on her forever. Stunned at first, she suddenly rouses herself.
"Doll me up, Annie," she tells her maid. "Get my new hat, dress up my
body, and paint my face. It's all they've left of me."

"Yuh goin' out, Miss Laura?" chuckles Annie, and spectators gasped when
Laura answered, "Yes, I'm going to Rector's to make a hit and to hell with
the rest!"

It's a bluff, of course, and the actress ultimately breaks down for a
poignant finale, but even as the curtain was falling, women in the house
were wondering what sort of hit *they* might make in Rector's had they dared
to push through its revolving door to the hurly-burly carousing inside.
Rector's, Jack Churchill's, Shanley's, Louis Martin's Café de l'Opéra, Joel's
with its "lady orchestra," all in the Times Square area: this was Broadway
after respectable folk dispersed to Delmonico's or home. They passed through
the neighborhood, saw it, heard of its gaudy high life—did it never occur to
them that here and in other city districts was a world waiting to be dramatized, an environment of popular speech, vocations, politics, and such? It
had occurred to theatre people. Just before Eugene Walter looked in on the
System that oppresses independent women, Edward Sheldon wrote on slum
life—the whole life—gave his script to Mrs. Fiske, and turned a corner for
American drama, using the framework of melodrama to demonstrate what
Belasco's "realism" should have been all along: not the look of place, but
the *sense* of it.

Sheldon's play was *Salvation Nell*. It was 1909, a depression year. Foreign
authors supplied the more intrepid dramatic fare: Mrs. Patrick Campbell
gave a week of Arthur Symons' translation of Hugo von Hofmannsthal's
adaptation of Sophocles' *Electra*; Olga Nethersole and Vera F. Komisarzhefsky
dispensed continental repertory; the Irish National Theatre Company of
Dublin performed Yeats and Lady Gregory; Maude Adams plied her boyish
charm in a translation from the French called *The Jesters*; and August 18
brought two rival productions of Ferenc Molnar's *The Devil*. (Molnar had
sold the American rights to both Harrison Grey Fiske and Henry Savage.)

For strictly American theatre it was a run-of-the-mill year, then—except
for *Salvation Nell*. Sheldon had come out of George Pierce Baker's playwrighting workshop at Harvard, the famous English 47, with this tale about
a drudge of a girl who finds stability in the Salvation Army. Her love for an
unrepentant heel is uncomfortably sentimental in Sheldon's treatment; and

tough-but-loving Hallelujah Maggie of the tambourine brigade and tough-but-loving Myrtle Hawes of Madame Cloquette's bordello were poured from the mold. But Sheldon's grasp of setting is sharp. The folk who inhabit McGovern's Empire Bar on Christmas Eve fill the eye and ear with a relaxed naturalism—the cheap cigars and clay pipes, the "ladies' buffet," the buckets of beer to go, the ragged Italian musicians in corduroys and soft hats, the racist cracks, jokes and reproaches in immigrant dialect, lines spilled out on top of each other like ad libs. There were forty-one in the cast, and not a Belascoian gong-bearer in the lot. Sheldon even dispensed with the star entrance for Mrs. Fiske. "Call Nell to wash up them pickles," says the bar owner; seatholders nudged each other and got ready. But Mrs. Fiske had so completely redone herself as the washerwoman that most of the spectators didn't recognize her. There was also a novel bit, much commented on, when Mrs. Fiske cradled her drunken lover's head in her lap without a sound for eight minutes while the barflies carried the play behind them. *Salvation Nell* is not all crowd scenes, however, and when Sheldon had to close in on his principals he gave his heroine a rich ambiguity of personality and her lover a rude awareness of environmental pressures. "If I'm a thief," he shouts, "it's 'cause the Gawd yer always gassin' about's made things so I can't be anythin' else!"

All three of these crudely pivotal works—*The Great Divide, The Easiest Way,* and *Salvation Nell*—affirmed the new trend toward works emphasizing not melodrama's passionate people but the play of purpose's psychological people: yet all three are melodramas. Like Shaw and Ibsen, they enjoyed a popular success without having to curry popular favor, and thus helped clear the way for a beneficial schism in the industry that set ambition side by side with conservatism. The "good old" theatre would remain. But there would be a daring complementary theatre as well.

One has to understand how bizarre the nonconformist plays were thought to be in those days, how disloyal; also how profit-oriented the business was. There was no great notion of the "artistic success" then, as opposed to the box-office success, no sense of a work so worth mounting that one stages it regardless of its chances and praises its honesty, its literacy, its refusal to Love the public. Admiring a show for not loving its public was like admiring a person for not breathing.

American playwrighting is already improving now; obviously, public attitude needs improving, as does technique—acting, design, overall direction. But some theatre people thought us so advanced as it was that they attempted to establish a permanent repertory company in New York along the lines of Europe's great national theatres, trading off classics and new works night after night for an enlightened elite (plus, it was hoped, converts to the cause). They called it the New Theatre and planned it to institutionalize the public's as-yet uncommitted curiosity about "important" theatre.

The New Theatre, Broadway's first bid for international status, would not offer anything more important than had already been seen and heard along The Street at intervals. But it was Broadway's first self-consciously non-commercial theatre project, a first admission that worthy theatre might not necessarily pay a profit. Choosing a catalogue that ranged from Shakespeare and Sheridan to Pinero and Maeterlinck, with the attractions to change from night to night in true repertory style, general manager Winthrop Ames and his dramaturg John Corbin settled on a fixed acting ensemble beefed up with guest stars. With munificent support from a few philanthropists (mainly William K. Vanderbilt, John Jacob Astor, and Otto H. Kahn), the temple was raised on Central Park West at Sixty-second Street: a splendid Italian Renaissance palace of cool grey Indiana limestone, suited with columns, porticoes, and marble filigree, costing three million dollars and seating three thousand, with a horseshoe tier of boxes topped by two cavernous balconies. (The acoustics, not surprisingly, were poor.) For their debut, Ames and Corbin mounted a stupendous production of Shakespeare's *Antony and Cleopatra*, built around the great E. H. Sothern and Julia Marlowe.

But the opening, November 6, 1909, brought the laying of the biggest plush egg that Broadway had yet seen. "What could have induced the management to decide that Sothern and Marlowe were fitting exponents, mentally and physically, for the titular roles?," asked *The Theatre* in an article assessing that sad first season. "*Antony and Cleopatra* was an egregious error, so wonderfully beautiful in its failure, so gigantically gorgeous in its downfall that at its very inception the New Theatre received a setback that has dogged it ever since."

Bad judgment doomed the New Theatre. The plays put on leaned heavily to respectable mediocrity; few productions caught the required style, whether Elizabethan or *art nouveau*. Furthermore, revolving repertory is expensive to begin with, for the more engaging attractions must continually yield the stage to less highly prized items, and running costs are much higher than those of the one play-one staff-one theatre operation of the commercial stage. Three hundred and eighty-four persons drew a regular paycheck at the New, and even the triumphant second season opener, Maeterlinck's *The Blue Bird,* failed to repay its investment after a five-week open run in the gilded New cage and being set free at a Broadway house for a further ten weeks.

To succeed, a repertory troupe must fix a pattern of general excellence in all that it does, a *rhythm* of quality such that the public has the confidence to buy a ticket for any given night. Folks were cautious of the New's program: it was a "folly," and its bad press and poorer word-of-mouth prevented its turning a vision into an absolute. One couldn't even tell what was being given from one night to the next without consulting a detailed newspaper advertisement because the management neglected to put up any posters out front. (On the other hand, whoever went up to West Sixty-second Street in 1909 in the first place?)

This is hardly the spirit in which Europe's great theatre companies flourish; when they experiment with way-out fare or controversial staging concepts, the theatregoers give them a hearing, for a "failure" might well prove as interesting as any success. At the New, there was no leadership, no guiding beliefs. It was as if the directors had said "let there be art" and left it at that. But *which* art? Was the enterprise American or Anglo-American (as so many smaller, traveling groups were, since Galsworthy, not Fitch, had the swank)? Would it nurture a native authorship or work out a more generally Western will? Was it to sustain an acting troupe or wait on the availability of headliners? And what of its staging style?

In its mere two seasons of life, the New never attained the authority it had lost on that first embarrassing night of *Antony and Cleopatra.* There were further disasters and a few near misses, but almost nothing broke through to outright victory: Edward Knoblauch's (later Knoblock) *The Cottage in the Air* and Rudolph Besier's *Don* were comedies of no particular definition; Galsworthy's *Strife* (on the class war) lost effectiveness by an inapposite change of setting from England to America; *Twelfth Night* and *The School for Scandal* suffered deficiencies in casting; Arthur Wing Pinero's *The Thunderbolt* proved simply too British to tell here; an English adaptation of Thackeray, *Vanity Fair,* gathered its measly charms too desperately around the glow of the likewise English Marie Tempest; René Fauchois' "dramatic biography" *Beethoven* overplayed its orchestral accompaniment (including not just themes and snippets but whole symphonic movements, the *Coriolanus* overture as a prelude, and an absurd pantomime in which nine showgirl-muses impersonated the nine symphonies to a swelling medley in the pit). Besides *The Blue Bird*, only Maeterlinck's delicate *Sister Beatrice* and a lone native effort, Edward Sheldon's melodrama on race relations, *The Nigger*, won an all-around acclaim.

If few critics of the time decried the lack of an American bias in this, our first attempt at a not-very national theatre, it only illustrates the prevalent inferiority of American drama and the complacency of those who analyzed it. The New Theatre went bankrupt after two years without having argued a genuine alternative to the often squalid consumerism of The Street and without having offered more than a stab at founding a lasting home for American drama. Those great European companies so admired today took centuries of trying out and putting on before arriving at an aesthetic, but here the project was permitted to founder as soon as it failed to meet its market. With its management disbanded as of 1911, the house itself rented out, as the Century, to various takers—musicals, Shakespearean revivals, festival spectacles—and was torn down in 1929.

And yet, others of the day knew how to play repertory for profit; such ventures were not as rare then as they are today. Just when the New was wrapping up its second and final season with a last-ditch mounting of Maeterlinck's *Mary Magdalene* starring Olga Nethersole, some twenty blocks south in the heart of the theatre district at the Globe, Sarah Bernhardt and her strolling cohort gave a lesson in how to play classics—in French, by the bye—and get rich. In a four-week stand comprising Rostand's *L'Aiglon*, Sardou's *La Sorcière* and *La Tosca*, Daudet's *Sapho* (the original that Clyde Fitch adapted for Nethersole's court adventure) and Dumas' *La Dame aux Camellias*, Bernhardt packed them in. This was more show business than drama, perhaps, but what there was to know about making the ledger run black, Bernhardt had learned.

The Shubert brothers had undertaken to handle Bernhardt's American booking, and as they were enemies of the Syndicate, the "divine Sarah" and her Absolutely Guaranteed Last Farewell Performances played shantytown barns, skating rinks, and tents as Mrs. Fiske had before her. But the thousands came—as they had not done in the case of the New Theatre. With an acting ensemble, a bill that changed nightly, no steady place of business (sometimes from night to night), and performances in a foreign language, Bernhardt still made a fortune. And she watched the Shuberts like a hawk. Jerry Stagg's book on the Shuberts records brother Lee's opinion of the actress: "English she couldn't talk, English she couldn't pronounce, but boy, could she count in English!"

4

The Art Movement
1910–1920

THE EARLY YEARS OF THIS CENTURY took the United States from the often repressed self-expression of a transcontinental backwater to the aroused eloquence of a world power: from Herman Melville and Stephen Foster to Charles Ives and Gertrude Stein. The cultural transition was sudden and savage, and not everyone agrees on where to fix its dates, but it is undebatable that by the 1920s, American art was enjoying a riot of awareness, satire, tragedy, experimentalism, and epic that it had not known before. Dos Passos, Fitzgerald, Faulkner, Pound, Stevens, Crane, Ruggles, Gershwin, and their colleagues had somehow built up an energy of creative extrapolation—something had happened; what? One takes one's pick of themes: that the upheaval of war made us more appreciative of the value of a national artwork; that encounters with European art after centuries of isolation opened local minds; that the groundwork for artistic revolution had been laid in the early 1900s in numerous inconspicuous plots; that the horror of war and Wilson that voted landslide Republican tickets (Harding, Coolidge, Hoover) radicalized the artists; or that it was time.

This revolution was sparked to a great degree by European attitudes. In the last three decades of the nineteenth century, men such as Richard Wagner, Adolphe Appia, and George II, the Duke of Saxe-Meiningen—a composer-librettist, a designer, and a manager—laid the traces for a theatre of the future. They wanted to rid the stage of its artificiality (including artificial realism) and pull it into the subterranean truth of myth. Wagner wrote virtually sacramental operas, luring the spectator into a state of mystical understanding through the powers of music, story, folklore, decor, and mime in collaboration. He called it the *Gesamtkunstwerk* ("work of all the arts"). Appia experimented with flexible lighting technique that spilled "atmospheres" of light onto greyish, non-representational masses rather than onto painted sets. In less musical circles, Saxe-Meiningen trained his Meiningen Players as an *ensemble*, overthrowing the star system. Bringing the lead roles into his "collective personality of the group," junking the generic backdrops of the day (A Street; A Forest; Another Part of the Forest) to create a distinct scenic ambience for each work, and researching the past for historical verisimilitude, Saxe-Meiningen spent fifteen years touring Europe with his Players. He was like a preacher of art, a healer; his *Julius Caesar* in 1874 cured that play of generations' worth of ills inflicted by solipsistic actor-managers.

The aim in all this was unity, and the message of unified production would pass from hand to hand. Constantin Stanislafsky and Vladimir Nyemirovitch-Danchenko saw the Meiningers in Moscow, for example, and Stanislafsky in turn was to inspire the Group Theatre in New York in the 1930s. The major advocate of this new unity in the early twentieth century was Gordon Craig. As a Briton, Craig had clout in the Anglophile American theatre community. Son of the famed actress Ellen Terry and the architect and stage designer Edward Godwin, young Craig was an actor and designer himself, but also a theorist. In *The Art of the Theatre* (1905) Craig recommended deposing the actor-managers and their Big Moments in favor of a more organic concept: light and sound, color and movement, all would flow together, suggesting to the spectator the most profound and universal images. Craig was teaching supertheatre, and the person who would superintend such a production would be neither playwright nor actor nor manager but, like Craig, a stage director.

This was a new profession—new ideas call for new masters. On Broadway, when Craig's book was published, there were no "directors." David Belasco directed, Mrs. Fiske directed, Clyde Fitch directed. This was professionalism, but not invariably art, especially in the case of the directing actor. As Ronald Jeans once said, an actor-manager is "one to whom the part is greater than the whole." Craig called for *auteurs*, so to speak, to shape a production from an idea into a living mosaic, integrating all theatre functions in poetic synthesis. "The theatre," wrote Craig, "should not be a place in which to exhibit scenery, in which to read poems, or to preach sermons; it should be a place in which the entire beauty of life can be unfolded . . . the inner beauty and meaning of life."

Not only thespians, but dancers, painters, and composers responded to the call for unity; the line between drama and everything else in art began to dissolve. In 1911, Gertrude Hoffmann and her ballet troupe came to New York to disseminate the methods pioneered by Syergyey Dyagilyef's Ballet Russe in the homogeniety of theme, score, movement, and design. Hoffmann not only presented Dyagilyef's *Schehérazade* and *Cléopâtre*, but popularized her message by rendering Salome's Dance of the Seven Veils on the vaudeville stage. In 1912, the Deutsches Theater of Berlin came to New York with Max Reinhardt's *Gesamtkunstwerk* called *Sumurun*, an Oriental pantomime worked out on Craigist principles. Reinhardt thrilled the theatre community but scandalized the general public by ditching entirely the dialogue, direct lighting, and old-maid modesty that Americans had grown soft on. *Sumurun* offered musical commentary, atmospheric movement, and much sensuality. The New York *Times* complained of a "scene of Oriental wooing which would come as near justifying the ringing down of the asbestos curtain as anything which has been disclosed." In one of Saki's stories, an obdurate dandy named Clovis describes *Sumurun* less formally: "weird music, and exotic skippings and flying leaps, and lots of drapery and un-drapery. Particularly undrapery."

In the United States traditional stagecraft and the declamatory method of acting had kept the theatre distant and safe, pictures from a play. But just before and particularly after Gordon Craig, a cultivated technocracy reinvented the American theatre experience. Thus, the designer Lee Simonson, who inherited the new "art" stage working for the Theatre Guild in the 1920s and 1930s, tells how Guild directors collaborated with him: "The wheat field seen through the barn door of the last act of *The Powers of Darkness* resulted from Emmanuel Reicher's plea that somewhere the beauty of the outside world must break in on the moment of redemption." And again: "The brain storm in *The Adding Machine* was the result of a remark of [Philip] Moeller's—'If the whole scene could go mad; blood, you know, something to show what's happening inside the man. . . .'"

Not only production methods, but the structure of the playhouses themselves would join the revolution, as when Max Reinhardt borrowed the *hanamichi* (flower-way) of the Kabuki theatre, a runway for entrances and exits connecting the stage to the back of the house, for *Sumurun*. Wagner had to build his own theatre for performances of his *Ring* tetralogy and *Parsifal*; Craig, too, got impatient with received notions on what was prac-tical, and would lay blueprints for schemes that could not possibly be implemented. Once, offered the management of a company in Paris, Craig accepted on the condition that he could rehearse his premiere production in a closed house—for ten years.

As so often with seminal developments, it was the people in the profession who showed the first enthusiasm. Not all of them were enthralled, however. To many actors, revolution was just another job, and some of the old hands failed to make the transition and were edged off the scene in that way the theatre has of telling an actor that he or she is dead: nobody comes. But a great many theatre people reacted with wonder and interest. In their play *The Royal Family* in 1927, Edna Ferber and George S. Kaufman pictured a John Barrymore-like character excitedly reporting to his actor relations on a newfangled German epic he has just seen, the latest word in artistic revelation. "Of course," he tells them, "the great thing about the play is that it takes two nights to do it." In fact, the real-life Barrymore starred in just that sort of *Hamlet* in 1923, with the murky unit set of Robert Edmond Jones using the players as if their main purpose were the casting of larger and larger shadows.

Thespians, then, were the leading revolutionaries. Art was their world—"call that a world?" cries Goethe's Faust; his play, too, takes two nights—and it turned on a sense of community. "One man cannot produce drama," wrote George Cram Cook after an exploratory, communard system of theatre production in Provincetown, Massachusetts. "True drama is born only of one feeling animating all the members of a clan—a spirit shared by all and expressed by the few for the all. If there is nothing to take the place of the common religious purpose of the primitive group, out of which the Dionysian dance was born, no new vital drama can arise in any people." But the spirit was shared—not least because almost everyone of any standing in the theatre was living in New York. They exchanged reading lists. At parties, they read plays aloud. Designers and playwrights compared their visions of the unstageable pageants which they would force the theatre to stage if they had to tear it all down and build it anew. Fired by designers' descriptions of the theatre to come, playwrights who had been reading in imagism, espressionism, absurdism, and dada realized that Dionysus had entered Thebes and rushed off to help score the bacchanale.

With nods to Strindberg and Maeterlinck, these writers turned to symbolist fantasy and the dream play, such as Eleanor Gates' *The Poor Little Rich Girl* (1913) or Alice Gerstenberg's adaptation of Lewis Carroll's *Alice* books in 1915, filled with wish fulfillment and anxiety. *Alice in Wonderland* did not succeed (the public was not prepared for that until Eva Le Gallienne presented a less ferocious version in 1932), but Gerstenberg's popular one-act *Overtones* (1915), with its four women playing two characters—each seen in her surface and interior selves—did the trick, even making it in the lowbrow market of vaudeville. Sigmund Freud lectured at Clark University in Worcester, Massachusetts, in 1909 in the company of Carl Jung and Ernest Jones; a year later his *Three Contributions to the Theory of Sex* appeared in English. Still, revolutions take time. 1910 was also the year that Percy MacKaye's avant-garde *Anti-Matrimony* failed at the Garrick Theatre.

Anti-Matrimony was the first lampoon of the Freudian fad—not of Freud's teachings, but of those who glibly quoted them without comprehension. (As it happens, the author was the son of one of America's first innovators in dramatic realism, the forenoted Steele MacKaye, and thus the heir in a highly personal sense to all that the art movement hoped to accomplish.) "Neurasthenia, I understand," observes one of *Anti-Matrimony's* characters to a playwright, "is the foundation of tragedy." "Absolutely," replies Mac-Kaye's dramatist, whose own very modern tragedy contains "a morphine patient, an inebriate pastor, a suicidal doctor, a tubercular poet, a klepto-maniac, and some others." A modern tragedy calls for modern options: "Which do you prefer?" asks the playwright. "Death by paranoiac insanity or pistol shot?"

The choice was easy for many to make; violent death in popular drama of 1910 or so was devoted to the pistol shot. As for paranoiac insanity, the general public would have none of it, nor of even the less extreme sorts of Freudian drama. MacKaye would suffer another failure at the Garrick in 1911 with *The Scarecrow*, a gentle "tragedy of the ludicrous" drawn from Nathaniel Hawthorne's "Feathertop," about a scarecrow brought to life to pose as a nobleman until a magic mirror confronts him with his deformity of soul and destroys him. We of today may look back at Gerstenberg and MacKaye and note them as sentinels of revolution, but at the time these novelties were generally looked on not as advertisements for new ware but as simple novelties.

No one knew what was coming; it came that fast. No wonder the 1920s appear to have invented modernity overnight: it took little more than the decade of the 1910s, with its *Cléopâtre* and *Sumurun*, its Freudian awakening, its *Spoon River Anthology* and *A Dome of Many-Colored Glass*, its infamous art show at the New York Armory in 1913—Picasso, Rouault, Matisse, and Duchamp; not mere portent now, but art arrived—to prove that the entire creative world was in ferment.

It was in revolt against realism. Manneristic styles of all kinds rushed in as if in horror at the triviality that the realist revolution had created. True, there had been tremendous gains in the psychology of character, in topical penetration, in stage design. But there was also Belasco's steaming coffee urns and Fitch's "Goddamn." Realism in the wrong hands ended up as just a more excruciating form of pop, not the art truth that artists had been looking for. They sought a scope of expression, a romanticism of theatre, an alternate magic to life—not new trimming for pert beauty. Realism had not turned out useful after all. So the artists moved into fantasy.

Ironically, the theatre's most unmitigatedly popular form, the musical, found liberation in realism. In the first two decades of the century, the farce and burlesque of the 1800s combined with the informal musicality of such rag- and ballad-inspired songwriters as Cohan, Irving Berlin, and Jerome Kern to subvert the often dowdy faerie of "comic opera" (what we now call operetta). Confronting the Ruritanian charades of European émigrés like Ludwig Englander and Victor Herbert was a contemporary American show, real musical comedy, snazzy but plain. This form softpedaled romance and emphasized satire: Cole Porter, the Gershwins, and Rodgers and Hart came forth. Yet more ironically, operetta reasserted itself to share in the revolt against realism in the fabulous adventures of student princes and vagabond kings. If American drama was to reach amazing highs of thematic and char- acterological communication in the 1920s through resources of non-realism, so did the musical, in Kern and Hammerstein's *Show Boat* (1927), reach an apex of panoramic cultural poetry, playing human instability against the symbolic permanence of the Mississippi River.

The art world was in ferment, but so was the bourgeoisie. It was the Briton and Craig disciple Maurice Browne who coined the term "little theatre" in naming his small auditorium in Chicago's Fine Arts Building. His little didn't mean "not big" so much as "not Broadway" or "not pop," and the term "Little Theatre" caught on as the regional answer to the supremacy of New York and the show shops of The Street. In spaces similar to that occupied by Browne's Chicago Little Theatre, others took European theatre techniques to heart and mind: Mrs. Lyman Gale's Toy Theatre in Boston; Alfred G. Arnold's Little Country Theatre in Fargo, North Dakota; Samuel Eliot's Little Theatre Society in Indianapolis; the Vagabonds in Baltimore; the Hull House Players and the Donald Robertson Players, both also in Chicago; various other amateur and quasi-amateur groups in churches, schools, and settlement houses; and even a touring little theatre, Stuart Walker's Portmanteau Players. Their repertories sought out Molière, Strind- berg, Hauptmann. They developed a sense of style, carrying through a look and a feel all their own from work to work. They alerted each other to new achievements abroad, staying young. And they cut themselves off entirely from the regular run of Broadway's prefabricated concoctions set in living rooms or police headquarters.

The battle between commerce and art grew keener when Manhattan inherited its own little theatres in the mid-1910s—the Neighborhood Playhouse, a well-equipped 450-seat theatre on the lower East side financed by Alice and Irene Lewisohn; the Provincetown Playhouse, moved from Massachusetts to MacDougal Street with a historic staff that included John Reed, Robert Edmond Jones, Eugene O'Neill, George Cram Cook, and Cook's wife Susan Glaspell; and the Washington Square Players, operating out of the little Band Box Theatre on East Fifty-seventh Street.

Tending to evenings of one-acts and operating on tiny budgets (as Walter Pritchard Eaton had it, the Washington Square Players "laid a spell of suggestive visual beauty and haunting mood" in Maeterlinck's *Interior* on an outlay of $35.00), these three little theatre groups offered an alternative to establishment fare. This is where off-Broadway begins its history, as a scattered secondary "theatre district" dedicated to the principles of the art movement: imagination, honesty, unity of conception, and Craig's "inner beauty and meaning of life." It would be foolish to pretend that little theatres in any city could reeducate the people who herded to Fitch and Belasco, however. The art theatre ran a showcase for an elite of theatre people, well-wishers, and philanthropists. But out of the little theatre came the resolution to bring the art movement to the nation's main stages. Thus, while the Washington Square Players disbanded when the United States entered World War I, its members regrouped after the Armistice to form one of the most influential theatre companies in American history, the Theatre Guild.

The fledgling Guild installed itself in the Garrick Theatre on Thirty-fifth Street on an informal grant from Otto Kahn. Their opening entry was daring, a Spanish piece in *commedia dell'arte* style by Jacinto Benavente, translated as *The Bonds of Interest*, on April 19, 1919. Everyone did everything in the Guild's infancy; actors painted scenery, designers coached actors, the managing board harassed the stage director, and everybody screamed at everybody else. The cast of *The Bonds of Interest* took in both Edna St. Vincent Millay and the production's designer Rollo Peters as well as more conventionally professional actors such as Dudley Digges, Helen Westley, and Amelia Somerville, who wore the show's one attempt at Broadway glamor, an oilcloth hoopskirt faked to look like brocade by the application of radiator gilt. On opening night, Somerville and the gown melted into a chair under the heat of stage lights and nervous tension, and when Somerville rose to go, the chair came bobbing up with her. But lo, it was art.

The Bonds of Interest did not catch on, but the Guild's second offering did. This was St. John Ervine's dour Irish tragedy, *John Ferguson*. On opening night, the Guild's coffers held less than twenty dollars, but *John Ferguson*'s success secured the Guild's future and, incidentally, the upgrading of popular theatre on Broadway. Through its first-class foreign writers, its insistent O'Neill and Shaw, and its audacious production technology, the Guild helped force the art alternative upon mainstream theatregoing. *John Ferguson*'s success proved to be one of the great opening gambits in art's war with commercial inertia. Had Ervine's play failed, it would have meant—in Eaton's oft-quoted hypothesis—"the setting back of the theatrical clock in America."

This was only ten years after the New Theatre's abysmal failure to erect a permanent high- and middlebrow institution, and the climate was so different now that a New Theatre might well have gone over, badly managed though it was. Probably the main difference between the New and the young Guild was the latter's dependence on contemporary, even advanced, production styles, but this in itself—modern *theatre*—led to the main difference between the New's era and that of the Guild: modern playwrighting. Production science and composition are infinitely interconnected, and it seems that the pictorial technicians inspired the word men, and both in tandem then convinced the public to subsidize the new plan: situation and character to tell of the primitive drives and configurations that authorize human behavior, and design and acting to bring the images out.

A rash theatre inspired a bold drama. Thus, the bohemian world of early off-Broadway produced Eugene O'Neill. He was still engaged in working up a personal style in a series of short pieces on the subculture of sailors and their sea fever, unknown except by those who frequented the Provincetown Playhouse in Greenwich Village, when *Beyond the Horizon* arrived on Broadway in 1920 as his first full-length production.

The script had been urged on the producer John Williams by the critic George Jean Nathan, who wanted to review it, and by the actor Richard Bennett, who wanted to play one of the two leads, though Williams hoped to sign Lionel and John Barrymore. (Bennett was a veteran of maverick drama: when every producer in town refused to mount Eugene Brieux' play on venereal disease, *Damaged Goods*, in 1913, Bennett turned manager to get the work a hearing, underwriting the project with his fellow cast members.)

How different was *Beyond the Horizon?* Behavior in it was human, crude and huge and desperate—but the desperation came out of character, not out of plot dynamics. Then, too, O'Neill's writing was neither polished nor "natural." But the work holds together, because his language works for his concept. Too often in the past, writers who could plot had no gift for verbal communication, while the poets did not understand the dynamics of drama. In other words, one has on one hand the theatrical but trivial *Barbara Frietchie*, and on the other the beautifully written but turgid *Francesca da Rimini*. O'Neill brought language and rhythm together. True, he combined them effortfully. At times one could hear his technique at labor, as if seeing into a glass-backed watch; but he always wrote to disclose the truths behind the story, always going deeply in. Singlehandedly, he smashed convention— he had to, because convention was based on the old moral escapism and O'Neill set forth a new morality. He held that life is based on illusion, that these illusions are a necessary makeweight to bolster man's haphazard adjustment to the world but are ultimately wasteful and devastating. A menace of destiny controls the outcome, but it is a Christian rather than a classical destiny: the fault lies, as someone once wrote, not in our stars but in ourselves. Unlike our earlier heroes who were given as perfect in themselves and had only to act in order to win, O'Neill's characters are foiled by their own willing weaknesses, victims of ruinous "pipe dreams."

In *Beyond the Horizon*, two brothers trade dreams, disastrously. One, a free spirit, ties himself down to farming and family and degenerates; the other, a homebody, goes forth to nowhere. Interestingly, it is love that knots their impasse all the more tightly, the "boy meets girl" that will not carry the weight for this generation that it did earlier. Consumption finally kills the farmer, and guilt will destroy both his wandering brother and the girl between them. Augustus Thomas and Clyde Fitch would never have dropped their curtains on such messy—such unresolved—irony. O'Neill encompasses the realism idealized but not attained in the early 1900s, the realism of life-like psychology (as in Ibsen) that was overlooked in the admiration for Belasco's flapjacks.

Never one to underestimate the public's squeamishness, Williams offered *Beyond the Horizon* for one tryout matinée, but an enthusiastic response demanded an open run. This tallied at 111 repetitions, no mere *succès d'estime* but a profitable transaction, and with the Pulitzer Prize in hand and astounded cheers from the press, O'Neill and modern American drama were launched.

Oddly, considering O'Neill's background in the little theatre movement, the production itself was rather old-fashioned. Alexander Woollcott, in his *Times* review, found the sets "painted in the curiously inappropriate style of a German post card" and didn't even mention the director, Homer Saint-Gaudens. But this was early in the art revolution, and soon O'Neill's work would benefit from the attentions of Gordon Craig's director-kings. In his work at the Provincetown Playhouse, O'Neill had delved into the whole-shebang unity of the new art stage; by the time he bestowed such works as *The Hairy Ape* and *Marco Millions* on The Street, art had moved uptown with him. The opening moments of *The Hairy Ape*, set in the filthy, low-ceilinged forecastle of a ship, impressed with the vigor of its naturalism: in choking semi-darkness, half-naked seamen appeared, "shouting, cursing, laughing, singing," as O'Neill demanded in his text, "a confused, inchoate uproar swelling into a sort of unity, a meaning—the bewildered, furious, baffled defiance of a beast in a cage." And this is exactly the situation of the work's protagonist, Yank, an atavistic outcast so desperate to belong that he finally seeks fellowship in the ape's cage at the zoo, where his fellow animal crushes him to death.

Similarly, Lee Simonson's sumptuous Oriental settings for *Marco Millions* deliberately gave off an uncomfortable whiff of Main Street consumerism, for O'Neill intended to puncture the complacency of the American business-man in his Marco Polo. Further, in the proscenium-smashing outreach of art-movement directors, Rouben Mamoulian planned to bring the point home by having Alfred Lunt as Marco leave the stage at the end in costume to walk out with the spectators and fall into a limousine at the curb, a tired butter-and-egg man like the rest of them.

The art movement rehabilitated our native forms. Domestic comedy turned into *The Show Off*, melodrama into *Winterset*, farce into *The Front Page*, social comedy into *The Second Man*, satire into *Beggar on Horseback*. Now that Broadway is on the rise, we may see it turn giant. But first let's view the flesh and blood of the art, theatre people.

5

The Actors Versus the Managers
1919

THE 1920s, which brought the stage director into power, also made the playwright prominent as never before. Both could clearly be seen cresting the tide of the little theatre and art movements throughout the 1910s—but for the less well known actor, the going could be incredibly rough. His position, as stooge for stars and slavey for managers, had changed little over the years. Let one case define the actor's position in the business for the decades before and after 1900: in the hard winter of 1881–82, which coincided with a theatrical slump, a stranded actor named Harry Bascom tried to walk from New York to Boston, where he had relatives, and fell victim to frostbite so severe that one of his legs had to be amputated. Mr. Fiske's *Dramatic Mirror* drummed up support for Bascom, thus giving birth to the Actor's Fund of America. Private charity, then, might be counted on. But the industry had no official welfare procedures; what industry did, in those days? Show business differed from steel, coal, and manufacturing in its informal profit-sharing with the stars. But otherwise the theatre—meaning, by 1900, the managers—exploited its workers as heedlessly as any other concern. There was no guarantee of wages if a show folded, even for work already performed, and out on tour a trouper might be stranded halfway across the country if business gave out. Moreover, there was no pay for rehearsals or for extra performances (though musicians and stagehands had overtime clauses). The managers treated their employees with the same contempt they felt for the public. David Warfield said that "acting is what the audience thinks it is"; the managers might have said, "Theatre is what we say it is, and what it always was. And it will stay that way."

A typical turn-of-the-century manager was Charles Frohman, the Barrie fanatic, with his Cuban cigars, his stable of thoroughbred stars, his office so grandly upholstered that to be interviewed by Frohman was like sitting inside a wallet. Eugene Walter attained the sanctum, to read his *Paid in Full* to Frohman, but *Paid in Full* lacked glamor, Frohman demurred, and Walter spat on the producer's Persian carpet as he strode out. It was about as close to real life as Frohman ever got. He was the type of idol carver who insists that the public, not he, creates idolatry. "Over here," he once said, "we regard the workman first and the work second. Our imaginations are fired not nearly so much by great deeds as by great doers. There are stars in every walk of American life. It has always been so with democracies."

But the actors had made themselves matter by their deeds: act and actor were one. And many actors were prepared to take risks with the new material that Frohman disdained. The times had changed in the 1910s: if James O'Neill spent most of his career in cloak-and-dagger melodrama, his son Eugene was brought uptown from the little theatre to Broadway by an actor who believed in *Beyond the Horizon*. Even in 1919, after our first significant playwrights had begun to emerge, Frohman's brother Daniel defined the managers' position in a reactionary article in *The Theatre*. He wistfully named it "The Audience of Yesterday," recalling the "two prime requirements" for popular drama, "cleanliness and happy endings." Theatre to him was a romance comic book, not *Beyond the Horizon*. And this, the seedtime of the art movement, was an age of Frohmans, of Belasco and revivals of Clyde Fitch, of Al Woods and his malodorous sex comedies, of Cohan and his smartalecky Yankee dandies, of William Anthony Brady, a one-time prizefight manager who brought the savvy of the carny barker with him when he deserted the ring for the stage.

True, the public balked at "complicated" art as surely as the managers did, and supported the star system enthusiastically. Drama to them meant not the work of this or that author, but the work of Ina Claire, or Jeanne Eagles, or John Barrymore, or, nostalgically, Henry Miller's Sidney Carton in *The Only Way*— the doer, not the deed. George Jean Nathan documented this personality approach to theatre, noting how "the fame of Mary Anderson sprang less from her considerable ability as an actress than from her reputation for being a virtuous woman . . . and the fame of William Gillette less from his unmistakable dexterity in the fashioning of adroit farce and melodrama than from the report that he had consumption and took long walks at two A.M. in Central Park."

Few managers who sustained the star system contributed to the expansion

of the new, the post-Frohman theatre. Al Woods, who is credited with introducing "Hiya, sweetheart" jargon to Broadway, got rich sticking with the
like of the self-describing *Up in Mabel's Room* (1919), and, when last seen,
going down with the *Lusitania*, Charles Frohman was distinctly heard
quoting Barrie. Really. Obviously, the new theatre could only arrive if the
managers were replaced by more ambitious producers. And that is exactly
what happened—the word "manager" even began to fall out of style, as if
everyone realized that the person who would mount *Beyond the Horizon* or
Overtones had a calling different from the person who would mount *Madame
Butterfly*.

"Producers" inherited Broadway in the 1920s—men such as Winthrop
Ames, who had headed the New Theatre and built the Booth and Little
Theatres; Gilbert Miller, son of Henry, who took over Charles Frohman's
firm but opened it to younger writers; Arthur Hopkins, tirelessly producing
and staging masters from the charismatic Shakespeare to the still unknown
and unfriendly Hauptmann, a season of Ibsen with Nazimova, O'Neill's
Anna Christie, Philip Barry's early successes *Paris Bound* and *Holiday*, and
the first realistic war play, *What Price Glory?*; Sam H. Harris, George M.
Cohan's former partner moving into the new times with the new style of
musical, politically aware in *Of Thee I Sing* and *Face the Music*; Jed Harris,
a Machiavellian cyclone of brilliance and bitterness, who presented an inadvertent study in "before and after" in American playwrighting with two
smash hits—*Broadway*, the last of the oldtime crook plays, and *The Front
Page*, a viciously funny send-up of municipal corruption in the modern style.
So there were idealists among the theatre's management class as well as
among the actors.

What had become of the Syndicate? Astonishingly, it made its peace
with the Fiskes in 1909—and this after Harrison Fiske took a poke at Abe
Erlanger while strolling down The Street one evening when Honest Abe,
strolling up, let pass a dastardly crack at Minnie. Only one thing could
break the Syndicate's monopoly to the point where they would deal with the
Fiskes. Two things, really: Lee and Jake Shubert. The two Shuberts engaged
the Syndicate in a war to the death in every city that could support only one
major theatre—that theatre would be either the Trust's or the Shuberts'. The
confrontation promising a Shubert victory, the Trust threw open its auditoriums to Minnie to use her touring schedule as a crowbar on the Shubert vise.

The Shuberts, who came to control many Broadway houses just as the
national theatre scene was shrinking down to New York, the northeastern
tryout circuit, and tours of New York hits, are hard to categorize. Much of

what they did suggests the bad old days of the Frohman school; no revue was too smutty, no operetta too deranged for Lee's taste, and Jake (also known as J.J. for purposes of sophistication), who preferred the spoken stage, was no more deft. Yet Lee sometimes invested in worthy, even risky entries such as *The Children's Hour* and *The Green Bay Tree*, and even helped Winthrop Ames bring Max Reinhardt's *Sumurun* to town (though he screamed bloody murder when he saw how many orchestra seats would have to be sacrificed to the Kabuki-style runway).

Where do the Shuberts fit in, then? Perhaps they symbolize the shifting ethnic coloration of the business. Before 1900 it had been a WASP stronghold with some Jewish talent, especially in the managerial end. But the years just before and just after World War I saw the emergence of immigrant cultures into the national sensibility. Like the Hollywood moguls, the Messrs. Shubert asserted a certain underdog defiance in their dealings. They never kept a regular company of star actors in the Charles Frohman manner (mostly because no one could face working for them twice) and were forever suing somebody for libel or barring a critic from their theatres. From the flash success of Augustus Thomas' *Arizona* in 1900, booked into the Shuberts' first little Broadway niche, the Herald Square Theatre, to the one-night failure of their last official production, *The Starcross Story* in 1954, the Shuberts show the fluke continuity of The Street in a patchwork of repertory that could take in *Lulu's Husbands, The Student Prince*, and the Abbey Theatre Players of Dublin.

There was new art; there were new producers to believe in it and new actors and technicians to bring it to life. In short, the theatre was a new business. It was time to settle on a fair system of paying the actors for their part in it. As far back as 1896, an Actors' Society had been formed to correct abuses, but this came to nothing, and with renewed vigor, the Actors' Equity Association was founded in 1913. But Equity found itself trying to knock over a brick wall petitioning the Producing Managers' Association for free Sundays, no unpaid layoffs during Holy Week (Easter was and is the worst time of the year for business), a touring allowance for the road, a maximum of eight performances a week, and other securities.

Not only did the producers refuse to come to the bargaining table, but many of the leading actors thought a trade union demeaning and refused to help their colleagues. Even the times seemed wrong for dissension within the business, as the motion picture had begun to lure customers out of the theatres and into the picture palaces. A ridiculous peep show in the early 1900s, movies had advanced remarkably by 1913, telling full-length stories and developing their own star-personalities. Then, in 1915, came D. W. Griffith's *The Birth of a Nation*, and the heat of competition was on. Some of the biggest stage actors put in appearances before the camera—Mrs. Leslie Carter, James O'Neill, James K. Hackett, and Minnie Fiske among others gave film a try in the years before the war.

The more ambitious or pretentious producers saw no menace in the cinema: film just could not do what they were doing. But those who dealt in masscult theatre felt genuinely threatened, especially because movies were cheaper to go to. One thing all producers agreed on: the enemy film could be fought only in a united front of theatre people. But the insurgent actors held out for minimum rights, and their insistence reached the confrontation point in the summer of 1919, the ugly year of the famous "Red Scare" that had already seen strikes by harbor, railroad, and garment workers, and even a general strike in Seattle (the big steel and railroad strikes were yet to come). Equity had scheduled a meeting with the Producing Managers' Association, but in the event only Sam Harris showed up—and he refused to hear the actors out and sent them away.

So they struck.

The night of August 6, 1919, bewildered many a Broadway theatregoer. The walkout occurred within minutes of curtain time, but only twelve of some twenty shows were closed down (most attractions had shuttered, as was usual, for the warm weather). The next night saw the firing of the big gun: Frank Bacon walked out of Broadway's hugest hit, *Lightnin'*. That smashed the dam. Companies up and down The Street strode out of dressing rooms to play their grievances to the public milling around outside. Managers George M. Cohan and William Anthony Brady swore they'd conquer and prepared to go on themselves in, respectively, *The Royal Vagabond* and *At 9:45*, with the help of understudies. But the stagehands and musicians respected the picket lines, and Cohan and Brady, too, were closed. The canny Shuberts got an injunction to force the opening of *Those Who Walk in Darkness* as scheduled for August 14, but the stagehands eventually walked out of that one as well. Soon only the few shows produced by non-P.M.A. managers were playing, including Florenz Ziegfeld's latest *Follies* revue (until Eddie Cantor led some of the stars out) and the Theatre Guild's *John Ferguson*, the Guild being a highly democratic group and thus in Equity's sympathies. Before long, *John Ferguson* was the only play in town, and the producers were crying, "Starve the actors out!"

But the public was with the union, despite a widespread horror of strikes, and for every E. H. Sothern and Charles Coburn who repudiated the walkout, there was an Ethel Barrymore, a Marie Dressler, an Ed Wynn, a Lillian Russell, a W.C. Fields, a Florence Reed, a George Arliss, a Francis Wilson, leading parades, exhorting crowds, picketing theatres, and posing for photographs. By far the most notable participant in the strike was the king of Broadway, George M. Cohan, who sided with the manager half of his actor-manager being. He came up with a rival organ, the Actors' Fidelity League, inveigling David Warfield, Otis Skinner, Lenore Ulric, Frances Starr, and Sothern and Marlowe to join him. (Equity dubbed them "Fidoes.") Surprisingly, that staunch advocate of numerous reforms, Minnie Fiske, went with the managers. "Acting is an art," she decreed, "not a trade."

As the strike spread through the nation, the New York thespians maintained superb public relations with a series of once-in-a-lifetime vaudeville benefits at the Lexington Avenue Opera House. With emcees De Wolf Hopper and Marie Dressler, Shakespeare, stand-up comedy, song-and-dance persons, and the diffuse but avid efforts of the "Equity Dancers," a male chorus line, the whole thing was turning into a giant lark. Finally, it became clear that the actors must win, were winning, had won. Reason was on their side, the producers were losing a fortune, the show might as well go on—and Dorothy Parker pointed out what a service the union had performed in closing such stinkbombs as *Stranger in the House* and *Oh, What a Girl!*. The mammoth Hippodrome Theatre gave in first, dismantling its sign that promised "Nothing Doing Twice Daily at this Theatre" and ceding a raise of ten dollars to the chorus, upping their minimum to thirty-five dollars a week. On September 6, the new Equity contract was signed, and everything shot open.

A few friendships had been severed by the strike—Cohan in particular reviewed it with bitterness ever afterwards—but the upswing in activity that followed betokened a great future for all concerned. So generous was the settlement that for decades, even in the unstable 1930s, management-labor relations remained congenial, and Mrs. Fiske's fears of being drawn into a mobocracy proved groundless.

But more recent years have seen a change of heart among the satraps of Equity. The celebrity heroes of 1919's exuberant street jamborees and monster benefits have been replaced by the non-acting Uriah Heeps of union leadership, who are more inclined to power than a play and who swear to negotiate raises and other exactions with each succeeding contract irrespective of the state of the theatre's economy. Though Equity hasn't yet equaled the feather-bedding cannibalism of the musicians' union, it has a stunt or two to pull later on in the 1960s and 1970s. It won't be pleasant.

6

Popular Taste
The 1920s

AMERICANS TEND TO THINK OF THE 1920s as the vacation time of Al Capone, Calvin Coolidge, and Babbitt—three businessmen—when a charleston was danced and history stood still. But it was in many ways a revolutionary age, not least in the arts media and especially for the stage. With the little theatre established as the non-commercial alternative drama, with the art movement arguing for a more penetrating use of decor, and with actors trying to live up to the new styles in playwrighting, American theatre rethought its social contract with the public.

What was the purpose of theatre? Charles Frohman held out for the gentle flutter of Maude Adams in James M. Barrie. The so-called matinée maids looked for an inspiring murmur of the heart. The businessman loved leg. Winthrop Ames sought the truth of literate writing and alert stage direction, George M. Cohan the celebration of self, Florenz Ziegfeld spectacle and the specialty spot of a pathetic Bert Williams or elfin Marilyn Miller, the Theatre Guild the sensitivity of imported scripts in "artistic" productions.

Where did the average theatregoer stand, with his instinctive suspicion of the avant garde and his nostalgia for golden ages? He doesn't believe in anything in particular; he just knows what he likes. There is no moral ethic involved in preferring plays with a beginning-middle-end linear narrative and straightforward production to plays that wander through time on bare stages or through sets that collapse unnervingly while an actress is trying to look her best and remember her lines. It is the "average customer" who makes theatre go. And the average, it appears, opposes art.

But if much of Broadway in the 1920s resembles a faceoff between pop complacency and artistic progressiveness, many of Broadway's patrons end up enthralled by the latter. Art took them, osmotically, because the art revolution was partly a matter of infiltration. Art crept in with design and lighting; it rustled in newly revealing dialogue for old-fashioned plays; it reconstructed the star player's sense of involvement; it intimidated with the maturity of its ideas yet, once one got used to it, began to stimulate.

Of course, there were many open-minded theatregoers in New York, who had tired of Belasco, Cohan, and Tarkington and welcomed the new wave. The urge for art is involuntary and uncrushable, with its empirical data for sensuality, idealism, and degradation. Art told one so much that the taste for it could not be shaken even when it insulted one's optimism. A cause for the art buffs was something such as *Roger Bloomer* (1923), John Howard Lawson's study of a tormented Oedipal adolescent and an offering with none of that escapist reinforcement once held to be the very foundation of theatre. "There's something between us," Roger tells a sales girl working in his father's store. "We both hate my father."

Far more ingratiating to any taste was, say, John Colton's *The Shanghai Gesture* (1926), in which Florence Reed startled the town as Mother Goddam, the proprietor of China's biggest, meanest brothel; Goddam speaks in a pidgin monotone that hides lavish hatreds, and procures desirable girl-flesh for her clients and a corny revenge for the sake of Colton's plot. Here was violence and bitterness to match *Roger Bloomer*'s—but Lawson's piece had to be taken seriously, while *The Shanghai Gesture* was obviously meant to be fun. Not surprisingly, *Roger Bloomer* did not do well, while *The Shanghai Gesture* became a hit despite mixed notices.

By a coincidence, the two share a plot premise. Roger Bloomer has a father problem; Mother Goddam kills her daughter. Goddam's revenge is aimed at the noble British tai-pan, Sir Guy Charteris, who led her astray some twenty years before. She gets her inning by selling his kidnapped daughter in the manner of her profession, not realizing that this is her own long-lost daughter. Then, when all is revealed, Goddam's daughter dies in Goddam's arms; much horror, much despair. (There was despair of a different kind on the play's tryout tour in Newark and Atlantic City, when Goddam was played by that fading veteran of Belascoiana, Mrs. Leslie Carter.) Alexander Woollcott, for one, took *The Shanghai Gesture* in the correct way, reveling in its sleaze yet ridiculing it. His first-night report for the New York *World* captures the old style of theatre in its last days, when it had not

changed but its audience had: "The girls in Mother Goddam's establishment
. . . all kept turning out to be someone's long lost daughters. The identifi-
cations came so thick and fast, in what was fondly intended to be the climax
of the play, that my own respectful gravity was somewhat imperiled by
mutinous memories of a somewhat earlier seaport opus entitled *H.M.S.
Pinafore.*"

The camp horror of a Mother Goddam went over; the real-life horror of
Roger Bloomer's Father Goddam did not. Even when horror was played for
"real," as in a slightly menacing production of the English adaptation of
Dracula (1927), utilizing some art movement-derived scenic effects and a
post-Valentino sexual undertone, it remained more camp than horror and
thus no bar to amusement. Bela Lugosi enacted the Transylvanian count
with an absurd extra-heavy on the creepy-crawly; moreover, the producer
could not bring himself to allow too complete a view of the big seduction
scene in which Dracula tastes of the angelic Lucy Harker in his peculiar
way, opting for a gauze curtain at the moment of truth. Fifty years later,
when this same dramatization of Bram Stoker's novel was revived with a
prickle of ghoulish sexuality, it was still camp—a textured camp, sure enough,
spoof and non-spoof at once, but a fun trip all the same. Edward Gorey's
quaintly macabre design of Gothic arches and scuttering rats and Frank
Langella's reticent but intimidating vampire gave the old script a new look;
this time the seduction scene came off as a nocturne of lush carnality. The
culture was fifty years older then, and nobody fainted. However, some things
do not change, and Michael Cristofer's *The Shadow Box*, an honest look
at the final days of the terminally ill, ran far behind the essentially dishonest
Dracula in popular approval in 1976 as a *Roger Bloomer* ran behind a
Shanghai Gesture in the 1920s.

Popular taste was holding back. It knew how disturbing art can be—not
boring, not complicated, not anti-socially "highbrow," but disturbing: honest.
Art doesn't flatter. It teaches. Do most people want to take lessons? But how
bad could pop be on Broadway around 1920? As it happens, the biggest hit
of the time was the theatre's most famous example of lumpen excess, ama-
teurishly written and produced yet the hit—the fluke, perhaps?—of not one
season but nearly six seasons running. It may be the fluke of this entire
history: *Abie's Irish Rose*. Who can explain its fascination? Lame in its
comedy, faulty in its dialect humor, and staged with the deftness of a dribble
glass, this tale of a Jewish man and his Irish bride who at length reconcile
their warring fathers-in-law to the marriage was already a smash on the west

coast when its author, a former actress named Anne Nichols, brought it to New York in 1922—and contrary to tradition the reviews were not universally bad. The *Times* gave it a rather nice notice.

Abie's Irish Rose was not the first of its kind; the comparable *Potash and Perlmutter* (1913) ran 441 performances and held out for sequels like *Abe and Mawruss* (1915), likewise a hit. Nor was it the last, as the television sitcom *Bridget Loves Bernie* proved in the early 1970s. For much of its run, *Abie's Irish Rose*'s only service seemed to be provisioning of Robert Benchley's cute diatribes in the theatrical listings of the *New Yorker*: "An interesting revival of one of America's old favorites"; "People laugh at this every night, which explains why democracy can never be a success"; or "Where do the people come from who keep this going? You don't see them out in the daytime." In a way, *Abie's Irish Rose* did amount to a revival—of one of America's favorite theatre tropes, sentimental applesauce. Let's consult that notice in the *Times*: "The play has its little sermon that earned one of the heartiest bits of applause last night." Priest and rabbi, it appeared . . . had met "over there." "I gave the last rites to many Jewish boys," said the fighting chaplain. "And I to many of your Catholic lads," the Jewish chaplain replied. "We're all on the same road, I guess, even though we do travel by different trains."

An updated, extremely poor and shortlived revival of the show in 1954 exposed it as a shambles of dingy material. Yet for a decade after it closed it not only broke Broadway's long-run record at 2532 performances but beat the runner-up, *Lightnin'*, at a plurality of 1241. "What can be hoped of an art which must necessarily depend on the favor of the public," wrote a critic of the time, "—of such a public, at least, as ours? Good work may, does sometimes, succeed. But never with the degree of success that befalls twaddle and vulgarity unrelieved."

Thus spake Max Beerbohm some fourteen years before *Abie's Irish Rose* opened, of a situation peculiar neither to his Shaftesbury Avenue nor our Broadway. What is popular in drama? It is a good deal more than twaddle, especially when a vernacular mode of expression and demotic iconography can interpret popular lives. In a sense, *Ah, Wilderness!*, *Awake and Sing!*, and *Our Town* are examples of popular art. So is *Abie's Irish Rose*. The difference between them is that *Abie's Irish Rose* truly is vulgar twaddle. But more ticketbuyers saw *Abie* than saw the other three put together—which proves what? Is it possible that Anne Nichols clumsily and inadvertently hit upon something with greater resonance than O'Neill, Odets, and Wilder in their above examples? Or does masscult art simply rise to the top as a matter of course?

Before we condemn the show shops of Broadway, let's see what else went over big around this time. Wilder can help us out here. In the early 1940s, he defined an "average" theatregoer's preferences in his very odd play *The Skin of Our Teeth*. Non-realistic and unpredictable, this was the sort of work that would have worried popular taste in the 1920s, so at one point in the show Wilder has a shirty housemaid (and sometime vamp) named Sabina step out of character and complain to the audience about the author's impropriety. "I hate this play and every word in it," Sabina tells the public, leaning over the footlights—or, rather, where the footlights had been before the revolution in lighting technology did away with the cumbersome old floor lamps. "As for me, I don't understand a single word of it, anyway—all about the troubles the human race has gone through, there's a subject for you . . . Oh, why can't we have plays like we used to have—*Rain*, *Peg O'My Heart*, and *Smilin' Through* and *The Bat*—good entertainment with a message you can take home with you?"

Aha! Let's have those four again. *Rain*, *Peg O'My Heart*, *Smilin' Through*, and *The Bat*: racy melodrama, saccharine comedy, maudlin fantasy, and murder mystery, a reasonable cross-section of non-singing popular theatre circa 1920. *Peg O'My Heart* (1912), the oldest of the four, is the simplest; its tremendous international success attests to the universal attraction of the Cinderella story. J. Hartley Manners' comedy tells how an Irish-American girl, domiciled with stuffy Britishers, shows them up with her sincerity, pluck, and common sense (this Peg is a girl Yankee), not to mention falling heir to a huge inheritance and getting engaged to a handsome lord. Written for Manners' wife Laurette Taylor, *Peg* became so popular that it was never very long out of sight for about two decades after its premiere, and while Taylor's apparently quite wonderful wearing of the title role had a lot to do with the show's popularity, the many touring companies that traversed the nation (eight in the 1914–15 season alone) in the 1910s and 1920s didn't need Taylor. Nor was she on hand to lead Peg forth to such outposts as New Zealand and India, where it heartened one and all no less than in the Middletowns of America. It's a homey piece, with one set and nine characters (plus Peg's inseparable *vis-à-vis*, "a shaggy, unkempt, and altogether disgraceful-looking terrier" named Michael) and it tells homey things: love is better than wealth (even if Peg gets wealth in the end: because she doesn't need it), horse sense preferable to chic, and a humble origin "nicer" than a title.

Peg and Taylor were the *Peter Pan* and Maude Adams of their era, though Manners used none of Barrie's bizarre fantasy and though *Peter Pan* is still good for a run (in its 1954 musical adaptation) while *Peg*, despite an off-Broadway comeback in 1977, has retired. It succeeded for the same reason that comparable now-scampy, now-heartwarming pieces will always succeed. They console. They believe in themselves. One doesn't need utter naturalism or utter morality in one's entertainment to find truth there and take it, as Sabina says, home. The cellophane make believe of Allan Langdon Martin's *Smilin' Through* (1919), second of Sabina's four paradigm plays, won favor not because its thousands of more or less permanent admirers believed in its ghosts, but because they believed in the premise behind them, which is—stop the presses!—that love is stronger than death. "Make believe" literally means to *inspire*, not pretend, belief. *Smilin' Through* inspired both in spite and because of its mawkish sentimentality—this was one of the last of the grand old so-called "three handkerchief" plays. The setting is Scotland; Jane Cowl is murdered at her wedding by her bridegroom's rival. Years later, the bridegroom's niece and the murderer's son want to marry—and Cowl, from beyond the grave, begs her former lover to let the youngsters go ahead. It sounds impossible; no doubt it would be today—but you should have been there then.

Non-believers claimed that it was Cowl, not make believe, that made the show work, and certainly a star turn such as Taylor's Peg or Cowl's Moonyeen is an important factor in success. *Lightnin'* (1918) was another slim script that triumphed because of its star, Frank Bacon, a veteran of Yankee character parts who was known as "the old hokum bucket." Bacon wrote *Lightnin'* himself, with Winchell Smith, specifically to give himself a lead part for once in his life, and as Lightnin' Bill Jones, who runs a hotel perched on the Nevada-California border, Bacon utterly triumphed. There is no question that the entire evening belonged to Bacon the actor, not Bacon the writer.

But *Lightnin'* is exceptional. However invigorating the star turn, from Shakespeare to pop, it is the material that captures the public—as witness the decades' worth of tours, revivals, and film versions that kept *Peg O'My Heart* and *Smilin' Through* alive (*Lightnin'* disappeared when Bacon did). Take *The Bat* (1920), next on Sabina's bill of pop classics. This "who-dunit" had no stars, needed none. It's one of the thrillers set in an isolated mansion where lights flicker, knockings rap, sudden crashes and bashes pervade, and characters drop dead one by one while a cranky Englishwoman in mannish tweeds plays sleuth with a squad of Suspicious Types, each as likely to have dunit as another. Written by Mary Roberts Rinehart and Avery Hopwood, *The Bat* regaled the crowd much as *The Shanghai Gesture* would do: as a scrawny frolic. What it was was a "good show."

A good show—that's what the pop audience wants. But art, too, is a good show; it was only a matter of time till the average theatregoers figured it out. True, cunning *Peg*, treacly *Smilin' Through*, and that shock treatment *The Bat* taught them nothing they didn't know already. But the last of Sabina's pop foursome, *Rain* (1922), offers an instance of the old-fashioned play somewhat remodeled by newfangled conception. *Rain* was a seamy melodrama, with South Sea Isle rut to entice and a super star turn to cinch the deal—and *Rain* would have been unthinkable, half-baked, or closed by the authorities had it appeared before the revolution in the writing and staging of (and the public reaction to) American drama.

Adapted from W.S. Maugham's short story by newcomers John Colton and Clemence Randolph, *Rain* looked in on Joe Horn's general store in Pago Pago, where a blood-and-thunder minister determines to "save" the wayward and fascinating Sadie Thompson. Backed up by the missionary's colleagues, a few itchy Marines stationed on the island, and the usual natives, Sadie and the Reverend did not spare the earthy *frisson* so basic to "fallen woman" plays. But the authors second Maugham in their refreshing sympathy for Sadie's libertarian humanity. Edward Sheldon's *Romance* nine years earlier treated a similar situation to a lavender party in damask and dew, but *Rain* dealt so forthrightly with its subject that analysts were reminded not of *Romance* but of Eugene O'Neill's salty *Anna Christie*.

With the smoldering blonde Jeanne Eagels as Sadie—rude, raucous, and scared—*Rain* jumped theatregoers with a stinging elan. Of course the Reverend who starts by striving with Sadie's soul succumbs to her physical allure and ends by cutting his throat; of course. But if *Rain*'s authors were no great manipulators either of English words or psychological paradigms, they greatly helped the audience to broaden its own grasp of life's curiosities. Moreover, Eagels did more than smolder. She was frankly burning herself out onstage and off. Her philosophy was: "Never deny. Never explain. Say nothing and become a legend." Ambitious but unstable, Eagels eventually had to do some explaining to Actors' Equity on the subject of unprofessional conduct, got suspended, and made three last movies before disappearing from the scene. But Maugham himself claimed that no one else could approach her in the part.

Even given the essential integrity of a playwright's composition, one aspect of pop is its self-image as an entertainment "package," and few writers attempted to separate the thrust of the *Rain* text from that of Eagels' wildly instinctive portrayal. Script, cast, direction, and decor make a production—but a production *is* its star. Some writers did separate play and player at the time of the 1935 revival, when Tallulah Bankhead's lumbering, crotchety Sadie turned a vital adventure into a sorry artifact. Similarly, an underpowered off-Broadway production in 1972 drowned in 7 performances, though Madeline LeRoux's Sadie earned what read as grudging respect from reviewers. The script has dated; minor transitional works tend to. The point is that our old avatars of the pretty world in its pretty theatre box were becoming more individual as persons. The allure of Sadie Thompson, an unprecedentedly human "vamp," proved to all tastes, average as well as elite, that honesty was more gratifying than corn, and that escapism was not immoral, but the wrong morality.

Sadie was admired. She made it on her own, even if the minister almost convinces her and then, grabbing for her like any other man, almost destroys her. Like the heroine of Eugene Walter's *The Easiest Way*, heading to Rector's to make a hit, Sadie is trapped in a society ruled by ministers. In *Rain*'s closing moments, daunted by a meeting with the minister's shaken but forgiving widow, Sadie decides to move on: "I guess I'm sorry for everybody in the world . . . Life is a quaint present from somebody*—there's no doubt about that. (*A little sob works its way into her voice.*) It'll be much easier in Sydney." Obviously, she knows it won't be. Pop theatre was beginning to explore the psychology of independence.

The art people, waiting for popular taste to find a good show in their lean and hungry beauty of revelation, were doing poorish business, tending more to the "artistic success" (one or two months of break-even box office but flurries of enthralled discussion among the theatre community and admiring commentary from the more responsible critics) than to success. But note that at last they were speaking of artistic successes—an admission that good theatre might not be commercial theatre.

On the other hand, some theatre people feared that failure—any failure—

---

* A large percentage of the plays discussed in this book have been adapted for Broadway as musicals, often gaining a rich tonal definition in the cut of the score. The line asterisked above inspired composer Vernon Duke and lyricist Howard Dietz to fill out their *Sadie Thompson* (1944) with "Life's a Funny Present from Someone," an amiable schottische with self-deflating jokes.

was bad for business. Yes, it gave writers a hearing, occupied theatres, and employed actors and staff. But what if "bad" plays alienated customers and backers? What if art sabotaged pop—and, therefore, the business as a whole— by sending theatregoers to less highbrow precincts, such as the cinema? Conservatives had raged when Mrs. Fiske played Ibsen's *Hedda Gabler*; now, some two decades later, much that Ibsen and Fiske had promised for art was coming true.

For example: Elmer Rice's *The Adding Machine* (1923), an arraignment of the machine society. Rice's protagonist, Mr. Zero, is a hapless electron trapped in the collector current of industrial capitalism, an accountant who slaves for a drab, embittered wife and an unfeeling boss for twenty-five years until, replaced by a machine, he goes mad and stabs his employer. Rice set his tale in expressionism, a form of playwrighting that seeks out the psychological contiguities of a situation rather than its "natural" appearance. In expressionism, the sets and costumes are exaggerated, the lighting narrates, the dialogue babbles, all pitched to nightmare fantasy. There is no better example of the war between art and pop than *The Adding Machine*, for it held out for only 72 performances despite its intriguing blend of social criticism and technical experimentalism. Here was another credit to the Theatre Guild, which mounted Rice's text with daring stagecraft. The crime itself, when Zero, expecting a raise and promotion, is instead given his notice, was played on a revolving platform that slowly began to turn as the boss mouthed stylized banalities and the numerals that Zero had shuffled for a quarter of a century whirled around him and the lighting shifted to red. Sound effects aided this suggestion of exploding madness, and, just before the murder, the stage went black on a clap of thunder. (This was the business that *The Adding Machine*'s designer Lee Simonson referred to earlier when he was quoted as feeling like the director's partner—"If the whole scene could go mad . . .")

In its short heyday, expressionism struck some people as artificial and pretentious. But expressionism intends to be artificial; it is as overdrawn as Grosz. And it did, if nothing else, rejuvenate the old interior monologue, as in this excerpt form Sophie Treadwell's *Machinal* (1928):

Marry me—wants to marry me—George H. Jones—George H. Jones and Company—Mrs. George H. Jones—Mrs. George H. Jones—Dear Madame —marry—do you take this man to be your wedded husband—I do—to love honor and to love—kisses—no—I can't—George H. Jones—How would you like to marry me—What do you say—Why Mr. Jones I—let me look at your little hands—you have such pretty little hands—let me hold your pretty little hands—George H. Jones—fat hands—flabby hands—don't touch me—please . . .

This speech is delivered by *Machinal*'s heroine, who like Rice's Mr. Zero commits compulsive murder, a pawn of System. What could more aptly report on the psychological subtext of her story than this motor-driven concert of words, as pliant and fitful as the System is metallic and inexorable? There was a fulfilling vitality here, in the mind-opening writing and the quasi-cinematic productions—both Robert Edmond Jones' sets for *Machinal* and Simonson's for *The Adding Machine* invoked the grinding oppression of cogwheels and pistons that Treadwell and Rice suggest in their words.

Many found it a bitter caviar. In Moscow, the Chamber Theatre staged *Machinal* starkly with great success; New Yorkers didn't like it. Perhaps it was because Rice and Treadwell did not give them fully rounded characters to sympathize with, only an ideological position. And perhaps that is why Broadway supported Eugene O'Neill with such enthusiasm: O'Neill dealt exclusively in the ideology of character.

The 1920s was the age of O'Neill. *Beyond the Horizon* was followed by *The Emperor Jones* (1920), *Anna Christie* (1921), *The Hairy Ape* (1922), *All God's Chillun Got Wings* (1924), *Desire Under the Elms* (1924), *The Great God Brown* (1926), *Marco Millions* (1928), *Strange Interlude* (1928), and *Dynamo* (1929), all very much post-art movement in their staging concepts. The icon-breaker O'Neill had to answer to the authorities for undermining the spell of pop—both plays of 1924 were threatened with watch-and-ward interference, though only threatened. The public, however, found him thrilling; even his expressionism seemed human.

O'Neill was literally born on Broadway, at Forty-third Street, a son of the James O'Neill who barnstormed *The Count of Monte Cristo* into the memories of the nation. That was a time when heroes were purely valiant; O'Neill wrote mainly on the dark side—"the one eternal tragedy of Man in his glorious self-destructive struggle," as he himself described it. He noted the struggle for self-preservation as well: both *Marco Millions* and *Ah, Wilderness!* are comedies, and the whore-heroine of *Anna Christie* ends up in reasonably good shape attempting to make a new life for herself—attempting, not necessarily succeeding. Audiences and critics took *Anna Christie*'s carefully ambiguous finale for a happy ending, unready as they were for the rhythm of O'Neill. "A kiss in the last act," he ruefully observed, "a word about marriage, and the audience grows blind and deaf to what follows."

Anna Christie's misunderstood conclusion proves how conditioned the public was; plays about censured women ended either in disaster (*The Easiest Way*) or in happy marriage to a forgiving man (*The Truth*). O'Neill captured the more complex "resolutions" of life, where the solution to one problem might well entail a wholly new problem. Bizarre as it may sound, taking in and enjoying if not completely understanding *Anna Christie* enabled the public to understand the equally ambiguous *Rain*.

While extending the bounds of thematic realism, O'Neill strayed into the most fantastic modes of his time. He had helped make the art movement, after all, and the art stage rioted in mummery. O'Neill wants masks, weird costuming, poses, ghosts of yourself and others, spectacular lies, and shafts of light pinning a character to truth. Above all, he uses language—not well, but grandly. He had no gift for it; still he made it work. He was neither poet nor mimic. No one, in life, ever talked like an O'Neill character, but eternal tragedy and glorious self-destructive struggles don't call for the naturalist's tidy specimens. Sometimes building whole acts in strophic blocks culminating in verbal refrains, O'Neill used English symphonically; his *Leitmotiv*-like repetitions reflect a mastery of dramatic orchestration despite their awkward insistence. Even at the height of reputation, during rehearsals for *The Iceman Cometh* in 1946, O'Neill had to debate his textual organization with actors who wondered why they had to say the same thing so often. One of the company marked the repetitions of a particular statement in the script, then talked one of the producers into asking the author if he really wanted to make the point eighteen times. O'Neill answered, "I intended to be repeated eighteen times."

Someone who saw the theatre as a working out of life's mythic initiations, as O'Neill did, has a lot of unraveling to do—he must reach not only the elite audience, but the popular one as well. Who can respond to such mystery? Anyone. What mystery?—"The mystery any one man or woman can feel but not understand as the meaning of any event—or accident—in any life on earth. And it is this mystery," O'Neill wrote, "which I want to realize in the theatre." His scope was vast, but his variety was, too. And he made such demands on the acting pool that if the art movement hadn't already engendered advanced techniques in style and psychology in the profession, O'Neill would have had to open an acting school just to get his plays performed. Though he twitted his father about that lifetime career spent as the Count of Monte Cristo during a ridiculous, a pre-(Eugene) O'Neill, age, he respected his father's generation for their blind instincts for the vast, the mythic. Once he said of them, regarding a play of his that was withstanding all efforts to cast its major role, "The actors those days would not have understood my play but they could act it; now they understand it but can't act it."

For the authors of that age, however, he had nothing but contempt. When the grand old man of American drama, Augustus Thomas, paid a visit to O'Neill's playwrighting class at Harvard (the famous Baker workshop), O'Neill expressed disgust: "I was one of the hardest-working students of the lot. But . . . once someone started charting an Augustus Thomas play on the blackboard to show how it was built, I got up and left the room." O'Neill was the new psychology, the new realism, the new fantastic art. He preceded black playwrights of the 1960s in visualizing the race war in terms of sexual love-hatred in *All God's Chillun Got Wings*, wherein a white woman genuinely loves her black husband but cannot accept his blackness— or his ambitions as a law student—and attempts to destroy him. This is almost political. But a line from *The Great God Brown*, "What aliens we were to each other," captures the basic O'Neill condition, a broad and timeless worldview. The vastness of O'Neill is always humanistic, not political, and the ghastly marriage of white Ella and black Jim in *All God's Chillun* says as much about mankind as about American race relations.

There was to be no show-shop truckling from O'Neill. Thousands of authors might hole up in a hotel room just short of a premiere to decorate scripts with rewrites marked "Hit or Bust"; not O'Neill. Like Thornton Wilder and a very few others, when he wrote a play he did not sketch it, did not leave room for the personality of players, did not collaborate with popular opinion. We had to meet him on his say-so, learning the new American drama as he learned it. Much of his development was experimental and transitional, for the great O'Neill would not surface until after his prolific 1920s, in *Mourning Becomes Electra*, *The Iceman Cometh*, and *Long Day's Journey into Night*, one a decade in the 1930s, 1940s, and 1950s. Still, the varying quality of the earlier works marks our rite of very necessary passage, an explosion of genius from within a popular, a genius-fearing, medium.

O'Neill exploited popular forms when it suited him, as in the comic *Marco Millions*. Using the code jargon of the lodge fellow, O'Neill attacked the Babbitt: this Marco Polo takes his moxie and pep to thirteenth-century China, where Western materialism fails to comprehend or even notice Eastern poetry. There are no great O'Neill conflicts here. The beauteous Princess Kukachin adores Marco, but that Main-Streeting lumpkin has promised himself to some Venetian girl-next-door:

KUKACHIN: (*With an irony almost hysterical*) In the typhoon when a wave swept me from the deck, was it not you who swam to me as I was drowning?

MARCO: (*modestly*) It was easy. Venetians make the best swimmers in the world.

KUKACHIN: (*Even more ironically*) When the pirates attacked us, was it not your brave sword that warded off their curved knives from my breast and struck them dead at my feet?

MARCO: I was out of practice, too. I used to be one of the crack swordsmen of Venice—and they're the world's foremost, as everyone knows.

KUKACHIN: (*with a sudden change—softly*) And when the frightful fever wasted me, was it not you who tended me night and day . . . even brewing yourself the medicines that brought me back to life?

MARCO: (*with sentimental solemnity*) My mother's recipes. Simple home remedies—from the best friend I ever had!

O'Neill did give way, however, to nihilistic fury at one point. "Wisdom!" cries Kukachin's grandfather, Kublai Khan. "What good are wise writings to fight stupidity? One must have stupid writings that men can understand. In order to live even wisdom must be stupid." A judgment on popular taste? But the average theatregoer understood O'Neill's wisdom. His plays are long and emotionally exhausting, but one thing they are not is obscure.

By the late 1920s, O'Neill was the preeminent American dramatist, but *Strange Interlude* was called everything from splendor to swindle. Earlier, in *The Great God Brown*, O'Neill wrestled with split personality through the use of masks. In *Strange Interlude* he utilized endless interior monologues to unwrap his characters' covers. As one would deliver his innermost thoughts in expressionistic free-association, the others onstage would freeze—ludicrous to some, psychological lightning to others.

Strange Interlude followed the life of Nina Leeds (Lynn Fontanne in the original production, insisting for the rest of her life that she hadn't the remotest idea what she was supposed to be doing). Haunted by the death of her perfect lover, an aviator killed in World War I, Nina succumbs to promiscuity, takes a weak man for her husband, and then, to father a perfect son, borrows their best friend. Yet another weak man hovers nearby in her world, a father-surrogate, and roughly halfway through the evening, Nina kisses all three of them goodnight—her "big brother," her "father," and her lover—and exits in a shattering moment of horror such as Sardou might have envied.

"Nine Picturesque Acts" was the heading of Brooks Atkinson's *Times* review (a misprint for "picaresque," most likely), which amounted to a carefully enthusiastic critique despite reservations about the value of O'Neill's mouthy asides. But these strange interludes, weird though they were, were not as novel as what O'Neill demanded of his public in the way of stamina. One didn't attend *Strange Interlude*—one enlisted in it; the temptation to go AWOL during the one-hour dinner intermission must have tested some portion of the audience. Why? Wasn't it an absorbing evening of theatre, all the more interesting for its innovatively searching exploration of a distinctive woman's pathology? It was. But it was also the best publicized achievement of the art movement, one that no one with vulnerable cultural pretensions could afford not to witness. Critical taffy, word-of-mouth, the inexorability of the O'Neill output, and sheer artiness made *Strange Interlude* a Must See. Those who need to be In are more afraid to miss out on the latest Event than they are of having to sit through it, and most of O'Neill's later output profited from this phoney support. He never lost his box-office magic; but how much of it was the hocus-pocus of cultural consumerism? Looking back from the early 1950s, Eric Bentley called this inflation of O'Neill "cultural gas" (blaming much of it on O'Neill himself), while admitting the man's "historic function" in "helping the American theatre to grow up." O'Neill, said Bentley, gave the would-be highbrow

> profundities galore, and technical innovations, and (as he himself says) Mystery. . . . There is a large contingent of the subintelligentsia in the theatre world. They are seen daily at the Algonquin and nightly at Sardi's. They don't all like O'Neill, yet his "profound" art is inconceivable without them. O'Neill doesn't like *them*, but he needs them, and could never have dedicated himself to "big work" had their voices not been in his ears telling him he was big. The man who could not be bribed by the Broadway tycoons was seduced by the Broadway intelligentsia.

All the same, there is an immense energy in this middle-period O'Neill of the 1920s, between his incisive one-act plays of the sea and his later masterpieces. O'Neill amazes, yet he belongs very much to his era, fixing a type for us as much as Belasco did with his photographic "realism" in the early 1900s. Think of his family background, looped up in *The Count of Monte Cristo*'s boots; his early training in George Pierce Baker's English 47 at Harvard; his groundbreaking one-acts for the Provincetown group, first in Massachusetts and then on MacDougal Street, spearheading the little theatre movement, and finally taking the movement's countercultural ethics to Broadway as alternatives to establishment beauty. O'Neill and the public,

then, met head on. Thoughtful theatregoers no longer needed to patronize a
little theatre in a remote corner of town where actors proclaimed their art
like fanatics, self-conscious, rapt, pleading, angry, *when* will the world comprehend? The world was beginning to, and the little theatres became big.
Roger Bloomer fails. *The Adding Machine* fails. But the no less difficult
O'Neill succeeds. The public is as comfortable with O'Neill as it was with
Sophocles, Racine, Schiller. Popular taste attends the revolutionary new
American stage and behold: a good show. And what did the new theatre's
purpose turn out to be? It was to challenge Americans' notions on human
character.

This is not to say that Broadway had changed overnight; much of the
old remained. But along with the melodramas, farces, Ruritanian operettas,
and urban musical comedies, *Rain*'s 1922–23 season also featured the Moscow
Art Theatre on tour to catch the United States up on ensemble acting and
the precision of character, Karel Capek's *R.U.R.** (a dour look at a future
rebellion of the world's robot proletariat), no less than five Shakespearean
entries (including John Barrymore's Hamlet), all hitting or nearing the
100-performance mark, and the Theatre Guild's usual concentration of
European works, including Ibsen's *Peer Gynt* and Paul Claudel's *The Tid-
ings Brought to Mary*.

Broadway always had variety; now it has depth as well. In earlier years
we have only an occasional landmark to cite—a Shaw or Ibsen premiere,
The Great Divide's investigation of the anarchical American psyche as developed out west, *Salvation Nell*'s revision of the rhythms of urban melodrama. Now, in the 1920s, there is experimentation, invention, and sophistication in quantity amidst the throwbacks and standpatters. This is the era
in which *Abie's Irish Rose* vulgarizes domestic comedy—but also the era of
Rachel Crothers' insightful cultivation of the same terrain. Social comedy
at first seems to have gone no further than *The New York Idea* did way
back when—but suddenly, Philip Barry and S. N. Behrman appear. And note
the prevalence of European masters—the Theatre Guild *Peer Gynt* lasted
121 performances, no small reception for the supposedly forbidding Ibsen.

Peer Gynt's director was Theodore Komisarzhefsky, imported from Moscow to teach the Guild Staff his "non-objective synthesis," another term for
the unified concept production in which decor, lighting, and movement
conspire to express the essence of a work. (The most notable conspirator in

---

* The title stands for Rossum's Universal Robots. Capek coined the word "robot" from
the Czech word for work, *robota*.

Peer Gynt was Helen Westley, who went non-objectively off the deep end as the Troll King's Daughter.) Stanislafsky took in this *Peer Gynt* while in town with the Moscow Art Theatre. He wasn't impressed.

No matter: the artistic race was on. Even the old-hand producers were waking up to what turned out to be a *popular* demand for unhackneyed scripts. It was the oldtimer William Brady who presented the Capek brothers' "insect comedy," *The World We Live In*, that lively 1922–23 season, and one of the new breed, Brock Pemberton, helped things along with *Six Characters in Search of an Author*, Luigi Pirandello's bizarre "is it real? am I a play?" piece that spoofed the sentiments of many outdated thespians when Pirandello's theatre manager hustles the six crazies of the title off his stage and calls for *The Bride's Revenge*—"that's what the people want!"

On the contrary, some people wanted *Six Characters*, which went on 136 times (in the tiny Princess Theatre, albeit), and more than a few average theatregoers took the trouble to visit the Provincetown Playhouse to see Sholem Asch's implacable Jewish tragedy, *The God of Vengeance*. This high-strung work about a brothel keeper who fails to save his innocent daughter from The Life was something like a serious version of *The Shanghai Gesture*—too serious, for the police closed it and a jury trial declared it "vicious and immoral." But Asch's play was a work of power and honesty, certainly moral.

Traditions of free speech notwithstanding, the United States has not historically respected liberty in the theatre.* Thomas Forrest's ballad opera *The Disappointment; or, The Force of Credulity* was shuttered during rehearsals in Philadelphia in 1767 when somebody noticed that it satirized the attitudes of certain prominent Philadelphians, and similar incidents led year by year right up to the controversies over Shaw, Ibsen, and O'Neill. The authorities made no distinction between works of an obviously serious intent and works of sleaze, however, and the citizenry too often tolerated censorship without complaint. Even theatre people themselves occasionally tried to manipulate controversy to call attention to their work—more than a few charges of "indecency" and "immorality" were phoned in from producers' offices. Vice squads found it refreshing to hang out in theatres; and the public enjoyed hearing about the latest scrape. In sum, neither theatre people nor the nation as a whole recognized drama's part in the development—if nothing else the maintenance—of free expression as a universal right.

---

* The motion picture industry, too, spent the early 1920s fighting censorship. Unlike the stage, which quickly achieved more or less full liberty, Hollywood accepted prior censorship—its own, in the form of the Hays Office.

Avery Hopwood, who earned a fortune for his coyly salacious bedroom farces, typifies the misunderstanding in an article he wrote for *The Theatre* at the time of his *The Demi-Virgin* (1921), harried but not closed by blue-noses. "In a really comic play," Hopwood observed, "one is never conscious of the presence of Aphrodite. One cannot be amorous and laugh oneself to death." How natty Hopwood looks in his byline photo—legs crossed, left arm cocked at the hip, cigarette perched just so between thumb and fore-finger. What he meant was that sex comedy is arch and suave, not *hot*. He couldn't have been more wrong—had he never seen *The Taming of the Shrew*? But Hopwood knew what puts the popular into popular theatre. "Drama is a democratic art," he went on, "and the dramatist is not the monarch but the servant of the public."

Hopwood served and served again, sticking to golden rules that the public could applaud after enjoying an evening of "daring" demi-monde. Look at the plot of *The Gold Diggers* (1919): a conservative, middle-aged business-man tries to save his foolish nephew from showgirl Ina Claire and—surprise?—falls for her himself. But while Hopwood and the New York Society for the Suppression of Vice had at most an occasional tiff, Mae West's deliberately anti-sentimental comedies had to fight a very thorough suppression. But then, West passed her own rules for democratic art. Her gold diggers really were after gold, not true romance. They were as hard as the metal they coaxed of the men they ruined; Hopwood's gold diggers were good girls gone weak. West betrayed the illusion. She was dangerous. She got ten days in the workhouse and a five-hundred-dollar fine for having written and co-produced *Sex* in 1926.

That was a big year for the repression of theatre. While *Sex* showed every sign of becoming a major hit and censors were laying plans to silence West, Edouard Bourdet (translated by Arthur Hornblow, Jr.) provided a searching study of a woman's attraction to and horror of bisexuality in *The Captive*. Too searching. Avery Hopwood might have got away with it; his lesbian would have proved to be straight, after all. Bourdet's homosexuality was intolerably real—"Padlock Drama!" the headlines drooled. Later in the year, Mayor Jimmy Walker, whose corrupt administration was a padlock drama beyond Hopwood and West's wildest dreams put together, shook his finger in warning at an assemblage of leading producers. Three plays were raided that season; if the city's attorney-general Joab H. Banton had had his way, several others, including Philip Kearney's stinging transformation of Dreiser's *An American Tragedy*, would have been closed as well.

Censorship made little headway in New York, in the end. It reached a climax two years after *Sex* when West reopened her case with *Pleasure Man,* involving a rake's castration (offstage) and a party of drag queens (front and center) with names like The Cobra, The Bird of Paradise, and—from *The Shanghai Gesture,* instant camp—Mother Goddam. The entire cast was treated to a ride in a Black Maria after the second performance, but West was ultimately acquitted, and Banton and his kind had given up trying to "clean" the stage by 1929.

Still, an emphasis on popular taste—on a theatre meant to please—virtually invites state censorship: writers who reinforce rather than challenge pop attitudes make themselves hostage to those attitudes, and to the state that presumably passes and enforces the popular law. Art had to teach pop a significant lesson: freedom is won by defiance, not propitiation.

7

Genres
The 1920s

WITH THE ART REVOLUTION WON, the two American theatres—one traditional, one unpredictable—rode out the twenties together on a boom. From some 140-odd productions in 1919–20, the annual tally rose steadily through the decade to a high of 264 in 1927–28 (though failures outnumbered hits three to one). There was no one shaking his head and crying Where are the playwrights, where are the directors, where are the great actors, the playgoers? There was a shortage of nothing whatsoever.

One price we did pay for the rise of Broadway was the collapse of the rest of the theatre business. That "New York's just a stand" attitude that had encouraged the various American sections to find their own cultural voices had shrunk to a few fading signals along the most major circuits. All the rest, middle America, was dead wire. Chicago, which had rivaled New York around the turn of the century as a great theatre-producing center, was now just another booking stop, its great theatres pulled down and its artisans dispersed. Many reasons have been advanced for the collapse of The Road, but there really were only two: radio and film. It was easier to run a movie house than keep a theatre in operation; in terms of manpower alone, the difference in cost outlay was tremendous. Moreover, with movies cheaper to attend, fewer people were available to fill a talking theatre. Radio added to the problem, for while its sightless sound could not compete with theatre or film, it was there and for free, once one bought a receiver. Thus, when not staying home altogether, the public supported films, and theatres all over the nation converted into movie houses or simply closed up. Touring

companies of Broadway hits, local repertory groups, and vaudeville all suffered. Then when the Depression hit, the decline was aggravated.

The Road would never quite disappear (though vaudeville did go under
in the 1930s). But it lost its independence as a collation of regional companies and could no longer provide important economic backing for theatre
people. Thus, the centralization of the industry on New York and New
York tastes, a development lauched by the Trust when it seized control of the
nation's major auditoriums, was accomplished. As of 1925 or so, the intimate
communication between the theatre and a *national* public loses its nation-
hood; it becomes a contagion of New Yorkers.

This is, then, a last chance to take a cross-section of American dramatic
types before they lost their national flavor. First comes domestic comedy, once
among the most popular genres and now found more often on television,
though it has lasted into the 1970s in such guises as *God's Favorite*, *Gemini*,
and *On Golden Pond*. Domestic comedy belongs to the (usually small-town
and middle-class) family. Farce deals in plot and "characters"; high comedy
takes wit; social comedy holds to a theme. Domestic comedy needs no more
than an American home and its day in, day out.

Consider Frank Craven's smash hit *The First Year* (1920): "Strong
dramatic stuff can be spun out of the most insignificant and humble details
of our everyday existence," said Arthur Hornblow, Jr., in his review in *The
Theatre*. "A veritable crisis can be created by the nondelivery of the Sunday
papers, and a denouement seems latent in the inability of a hired girl to
come to work. . . . The story, the conflict, the suspense are all, in one sense,
thin as air, but, in another, they are as vital as drama can ever hope to be,
concerning as they do real people doing real things." *The First Year*'s tale of
a newly wedded couple making a go of it, hitting an impasse, and finally
recovering, was a pageant of dawdle and putter: what mattered in one's life
was made to matter on stage. Reading the script now, one finds nothing
particularly dramatic, but that in itself is the form's charm. Maxwell Anderson
tightened it slightly in *Saturday's Children* (1927), domestic comedy moved
to the city on a budget ("Saturday's children have to work for their living . . ."). Says Bobby, the new bride (Ruth Gordon), to her square husband:

> What we wanted was a love affair, wasn't it? . . . And what we got was a
> house and bills and general hell . . . I want my love affair back. I want
> hurried kisses and clandestine meetings, and a secret lover.

In *The First Year*, the spatting kids patched their marriage together, but
Anderson's couple rebel against the structure of marriage and elect to live

apart. For a final curtain, the husband sneaks into his wife's rented room to retrieve their romance in the form of an affair.

Our ancient comrade and likeness, the Yankee, was active these days, as father, gentleman caller, or neighborhood eccentric, still saving the day when wiser and more accomplished folk failed to. What new way is there to depict this coonskin homesteader? Booth Tarkington made a go of it in *Clarence* (1919), a zesty hit written for non-action, with Alfred Lunt as the apparent dope who solves everybody's problems and plays a mean saxophone.

The ultimate pro of the profession, Lunt mastered the saxophone from scratch for *Clarence*, except for one note that generally eluded him; later, he would shave his head for *The Guardsman*, grow a paunch for *Caprice*, starve into a wraith for *Meteor* (to look like Jed Harris), learn nightclub emceeing from Milton Berle for *Idiot's Delight*, and call a rehearsal of *The Taming of the Shrew* before the last two performances of the run because Friday night had been sloppy. He should have been too sophisticated for the title part of *Clarence*—but in the 1920s, one no longer played one's type in role after role. This, too, was new.

For his part, Tarkington was adept in charting the immense, tiny tribulations of midwestern life. His novel *Seventeen* made a humdinger of a comedy in 1918; Ruth Gordon played the visiting heartbreaker, Paul Kelly the lovestruck adolescent, nothing much happened: delight. The framework of such endeavors, bizarre as it sounds, is Chekhofian, though of course without the contrapuntal dialogue, depth of character, eliciting leanness of language, and odd tonal ambiguity of the Russian playwright. Then why compare them? The actor of a comprehensive repertory might tell us, for he or she would be bound to notice the similarity of tempo between our old domestic comedy and that much finer drama of Chekhof. The dynamic derives from a reverse of the formula for melodrama, wherein congruencies of plot impose themselves on congruencies of character. In domestic comedy, as in Chekhof, all action is subordinated to the effect of one focal situation on the interplay of personality. Let us not suggest that *Clarence* or the capable adaptation of *Seventeen* (not by Tarkington himself) or *The First Year* or any other such unaffected, disarming domestic comedy is our *Uncle Vanya*. We have no Chekhof. Yet this was a time when comedies with an inner purpose found both creative advocates and a willing audience.

Plotted comedies stood preeminent. Don Marquis' *The Old Soak* (1922) ran 423 performances on little more than the memory of the old Yankee-saves-the-day plot. Marquis, creator of the wonderfully whimsical *archy and mehitabel*, was not at his best here, though he touched a universal nerve when he had his protagonist threaten a villainous banker with blackmail and murder with sadistic nonchalance. But perhaps it was time to take a closer look at Yankee smugness.

George Kelly changed the trope in *The Show Off* (1924), showing the Yankee to be loud-mouthed, phoney, yet unbeatable—the sort of character that Bob Hope later brought off with guile and charm. Kelly's play is set in Philadelphia, where Amy Fisher adores the unbearably self-confident Aubrey Piper, and where Amy's tough mother would gladly see Piper boiled alive. Always watchful for a chance to expose Piper's innocent arrogance, Mrs. Fisher is blocked by an accident: Piper pulls off a deal that nets Amy's inventor brother a hundred thousand dollars, and the Fisher family settles down to a lifetime of adoring the show off. Mrs. Fisher takes the play's famous final line, a Cassandra trapped in Troy:

AMY: Aubrey, you're wonderful!
AUBREY: A little bit of bluff goes a long way sometimes, Amy.
AMY: Isn't he wonderful, Mom?
MRS. FISHER: (*after a long sigh*) God help me, from now on.

What about a Yankee woman for once: who were our heroines? It was quite an assortment. Some women were Bad or Loose: Florence Reed's Mother Goddam, the iron Madam Butterfly of Shanghai's hell quarter, or Pauline Lord's splendid Anna Christie, who shuffled onstage in her first entrance with a suitcase in hand and a bitter smile on her lips anticipating the next careless joke her real life would throw at her. Lenore Ulric's mulatto prostitute Lulu Belle died the death, but Jeanne Eagels' Sadie Thompson got to look into the heart of a man of God, and saw man. There was Rose McClendon's heartbreaking Goldie in Paul Green's *In Abraham's Bosom*, introducing many to the black woman's blues on her terms, however much through the edition of a white man's writing; and Lynn Fontanne's Nina Leeds in *Strange Interlude*, the archetypal Electra caught between several generations of father-brother-lovers. More raucously, there was Francine Larrimore's jiving Roxie Hart of *Chicago*, where truth is what the media make it. And there was Mae West, peaking between the notorious *Sex* and *Pleasure Man* with the milder *Diamond Lil*, and running her personal liberation movement not only in her outspoken persona but in her professionalism as actress, author, and director. Nowadays, a writer who stages his or her own plays—much less acts in them—is a rarity. But West was only upholding actor-manager tradition in conceiving and superintending her shows.

Perhaps most traditional of all were the scatterbrained charmers of farce, as in George S. Kaufman and Marc Connelly's *Dulcy* (1921), modeled after a character introduced in Franklin P. Adams' column "The Conning Tower" in the New York *Tribune*. Lynn Fontanne played the young wife who balls up her husband's and some other lives while spouting bromides as if they were epigrams of prodigious epiphany; "You know," she observed at one point, "sometimes I think I would lose my head if it wasn't fastened on."

Dulcy's producer, George C. Tyler, could have given the Shuberts lessons in cutting corners. Costuming wasn't thought to be one of the decisive tactics in the mounting of most modern-setting plays, and Tyler suggested that his leading lady select Dulcy's outfits off the rack in a department store basement. But Fontanne wouldn't have been caught dead without her style— even in a middle-class domestic comedy—and she ran up a bill at Bouillet Soeurs that almost gave Tyler a stroke. "You won't be happy," Fontanne told him, "until I walk on in a table cloth."

Fontanne had a point—women came to theatre to see such style as hers. Naturalism or even just unpretentiousness was useful to art but did nothing for the stage's role as showcase for glamor. What about the *fantasy* of theatre? Unfortunately for many, the Freudian writers took this over for their own purposes, coming up with archetypal women that almost nobody could recognize. In Sidney Howard and Edward Sheldon's "Freudian fairly tale" *Bewitched* (1924), Florence Eldridge played some six or seven versions of eternal woman—the protagonist's girlfriend, his mother, the goddess of love, and so on. In the vogue for Maeterlinckian somnambulism, the cast further included mysterious wanderers caught in illusory lighting, and theatregoers simply could not understand what was supposed to be going on.

However, theatregoers enthused for Freudianism in less fantastic formats. While they would not tolerate father-hating sons (the first night of the Abbey Theatre's performance of Synge's mock-patricidal *The Playboy of the Western World* in 1911 sparked a riot in New York as it had in Dublin), vicious mothers attracted them. George Kelly's Harriet, the protagonist of *Craig's Wife* (1925), and Sidney Howard's Mrs. Phelps, the grasping mother of *The Silver Cord* (1926), fascinated the public with their inadvertent destructiveness, though most ruthless of all was Rena Huckins in Lewis Beach's *A Square Peg* (1923). A robber baron limited by her sex to church guilds and her family, Mrs. Huckins has browbeaten her husband into living bits, and when she gets him off a charge of embezzlement, he shoots himself rather than spend another day with her. Rena's reaction to his suicide, very quietly spoken, replaced the hand-wringing hyperemotionalism of a bygone day: "Like that . . . all my work . . . gone."

It was as inevitable that the "Freudian" explosion of the 1920s detonate the great Mother symbol as it was inevitable that the social theatre of the 1930s go after Father capitalism. But some mothers of the 1920s were eating their families for breakfast or getting dragged into mythopoetic relationships with their sons. In Eugene O'Neill's *Dynamo*, Reuben Light established a love affair with his late mother by confusing her with the power of electricity to worship her in the form of a hydroelectric transformer. As an antidote, Harry Wagstaff Gribble and Wilton Lackaye ridiculed the romance between stepmother and stepson in O'Neill's *Desire Under the Elms* for their adaptation of a French frolic, *Oh Mama* (1925), and, reviewing *Your Uncle Dudley* (1929), a confrontation of domineering mother and indomitable Yankee, critic Robert Littel demanded a "closed season during which playwrights are not allowed to paint mothers black and then shoot them."

Rachel Crothers, however, reclaimed woman's originality and wisdom in a lively oeuvre that deserves to be better remembered, if only because it was so relevant—and successful—in its day. Crothers was an old pro by the 1920s; she had brought the women's movement to the stage as long before as in 1904, in *The Point of View*, and she framed a rebuttal to the mother-haters in *Mary the 3d* (1923), a look at the younger generation and an inquiry into the institution of marriage. Strange that one of the most enjoyable domestic comedies of the era should have questioned the wisdom of domestic comedy's one inviolate given, the eternal expedience of the nuclear family. But Crothers' gift was fairness, and her public could not discount her logic even when she assailed their ethics. Unlike some of her fellow playwrights, she spent satire but never hatred—and like Mae West, Crothers staged her plays herself.

As the title implies, *Mary the 3d* gives us three generations of Marys— cranky grandma, bewildered mother, and resilient flapper. In a flashback prologue, we see the two older Marys each on the eve of a rash marriage, girlish at a dance. They have invested too much romance in romance: "There has never been a love as great as this," cries Mary I, pressed in a suitor's arms, and "We must make it the most wonderful love that was ever in the world," echoes Mary II in comparable bliss.

But Mary III is not so blind; she proposes to spend a trial period in intimate contact with her men of choice. Her planned practice marriage (on a camping trip) of course throws the adults into an uproar, though ultimately she comes home unrehearsed, out of sympathy for her parents' feelings. While sneaking back into the house she overhears her folks engaged in a nasty quarrel and decides that marriage, even after a trial, is not what it's cracked up to be by its—victims. Looking at the situation with the awful rationality of the revolutionary, Mary III insists that her mother and father divorce, and does so on grounds that were not much heard again before the 1970s:

MARY: You mean you haven't any *money* without Father? That you and
        Granny are dependent on him? (*Mother nods.*) All that is so horrible—
        so disreputable!
MOTHER: *Mary!*
MARY: It *is!* It's *buying* things with you! . . . I shall have my own money.
        I'll *make* it. I shall live with a man because I love him and only as long
        as I love him. I shall be able to take care of myself *and* my children if
        necessary. Anything else gives the man a horrible advantage, of course.
        It makes the woman a kept woman.

Had *Mary the 3d* been written by almost anyone other than Crothers, all would have been put "to rights" by the finish. As it is, Mary III convinces Mary II to go off and learn her own truths—to evolve a woman's, not a wife's, usefulness. It is not marriage that Crothers attacks, but "what we've done with it." Amusingly, Crothers' spokeswoman Mary III, so sanely theoretical on others' lives, is about to go the way of her forebears as the curtain trembles. Using exactly the frame of reference we heard in the two prologue scenes, Mary III signs herself over, as the other Marys did, to the middle-class comic tragedy of American marriage. Girlish even without a dance, Mary tells her beau, "It is one of those great eternal passions that will last through the ages—isn't it, dear?" And the curtain falls.

Carrying on in the tradition fostered by *The Contrast* and *Fashion*, Crothers attacked the Freudian fad in *Expressing Willie* (1924), arraigning its phoney With It and secret conformity. "Free yourself," cries a hip painter, himself chained to a crushing lack of talent; "I'm reborn," explains a lifeless divorcée after undergoing psychotherapy. The evening's prize *mot* went to a bewildered anti-Freudian mother: "If we were all running around without any *suppressions*, we might as well have tails again." Reviewing *Expressing Willie* for the New York *Times*, John Corbin pointed up domestic comedy's peculiar asset, its heart: "Even while sides were still shaking with laughter, unaccustomed eyes took on the glamour of tenderness, of rapture at the perfection of humor that lies in perfect humanity."

Farce, on the other hand, had neither humanity nor heart. Structurally much like such early modern farces as Cohan's *Seven Keys to Baldpate*, farce in the 1920s took up "relevant" topics in irrelevant situation comedy. Thus, Aaron Hoffman's hit *Give and Take* (1923) pictured the disastrous, laugh-a-minute takeover of a factory by bumbling laborers as directed by the factory owner's son, pumped full of socialism at college, and as bailed out in the nick of time by an odd millionaire. Hoffman borrowed Red peril for shenanigans, not social demonstration; in another place and time he might have pictured the disastrous, laugh-a-minute takeover of a socialist factory by bumbling capitalists with no less verve.

Farce found a point of view in Ben Hecht and Charles MacArthur's *The Front Page* (1928), an edgy, satirical look at the interdependent corruption of big-city power machines. Callous itself, farce was ideally equipped to expose the callous officials and gin-blooded reporters, interested only in votes and scoops. It is notable that the concurrent *Gentlemen of the Press*, on the same subject, has vanished while *The Front Page* is a classic: *Gentlemen of the Press* was a melodrama. Farce managed it better, for farce, like officials and reporters, doesn't care. Farce was more cartoons than ideas, a kind of jazz, and its detachment contained its sordid subject. Hecht and MacArthur had written for Hearst in newspapers in Chicago, and while their lampoon is very, very funny, as a document of white-collar crime it is—or would be, in any form but farce—unpleasantly honest.

The authors' style recaptures the crude anarchy of the early American comic strip—the authority-baiting of the Katzenjammers, the delirious brick throwing of *Krazy Kat*'s Ignatz Mouse. *The Front Page*'s Chicago reporters inhabit their own world, with fretting wives, frantic editors, and hapless prostitutes on the outskirts and a marathon poker game in the center. Here's Murphy, of the *Journal*, calling in to the rewrite man while covering the eve of a condemned man's hanging:

> Ready? . . . Sheriff Hartman has just put two hundred more relatives on the payroll to protect the city against the Red Army, which is leaving Moscow in a couple of minutes. (*Consults the cards he has been handed*) Up a dime. (*Back to phone*) And to prove to the voters that the Red menace is on the square, he has just wrote himself four more letters threatening his life. I know he wrote them on account of the misspelling.

Even Chicago's ablest managing editor, Walter Burns, is an older, coat-and-tied version of the New York *World*'s historic comic-strip scamp, The Yellow Kid. As the authors describe him, Burns "is a Devil with neither point nor purpose to him . . . the licensed eavesdropper, trouble maker, bombinator, and Town Snitch, misnamed The Press."

Well staged by George S. Kaufman, *The Front Page* offered splendid opportunities for cameo parts, such as Dorothy Stickney's pathetic Clark Street tart Molly Molloy, but at the heart of the event were two scalawag newspapermen—Lee Tracy, setting up a career of brash city slickers that would last him through the 1960s, and Osgood Perkins, dapper and tack-sharp as the diabolical managing editor. Some of the play's elfin charisma derived from the chemistry of the two archetypes in opposition, the editor married to the news trying to hold on to the star reporter who wants to marry and settle down; strangely, while the first movie version of *The Front Page*, an early talkie, attempted to retain the original's quicksilver cynicism, a remake in 1940 called *His Girl Friday* scattered the tone by casting Rosalind Russell in the Lee Tracy part opposite Cary Grant—two cool numbers, certainly, but no Hildy Johnson or Walter Burns.

Hollywood's relationship with Broadway, especially once the sound era got going, bore heavily on some and lightened the burden of others. In the latter class were the authors, for the movies subsidized their careers via film rights to plays (often as eagerly sought when the shows bombed as when they hit: they were cranking cinema out by the yard in those days, and every little script helped), not to mention the disreputable but irresistibly lucrative sojourn in the film factories as screen writer. The stage producers saw Hollywood as cheat and assassin, yet at least some of Broadway's problems were pretty much the fault of its public and creators. Even before Jolson sang and Garbo talked, the *Herald Tribune*'s Percy Hammond wrote, "It isn't that the people who ought to be going to the theatre are going to the 'movies.' It is that the people who ought to be going to the 'movies' are going to the theatre. . . . Alienated by a small group of illiterati, [the intelligentsia] have not yet been taught to believe that there is a better element producing better plays."

Some of that better element abandoned Broadway for Hollywood; one such loss was that of Preston Sturges, celebrated for his part in Hollywood's era of populist satire, an American specialty that, on the stage, seems most telling in musical comedy (e.g., *Let 'Em Eat Cake*, *Pins and Needles*, *Finian's Rainbow*, *The Pajama Game*). Sturges' farce *Strictly Dishonorable* (1929) pictured nothing more than the chance dalliance of a shy maid from the suburbs and a quasi-caddish Italian singer in a Manhattan speakeasy (Sturges whimsically sets the rise of the curtain at exactly 11:41 P.M.). Absurdly casual, *Strictly Dishonorable* drew on farce's surrealistic caricature but avoided its manic plotting, creating a genre all its own: a fairy tale for grownups. Sadly, Sturges left for the West Coast shortly after the play finished its 557-performance run, to claim his element on film during the war years with *The Great McGinty*, *The Miracle of Morgan's Creek*, and *Hail the Conquering Hero*.

Melodrama was not so easily modernized as farce. Windy gallantry in period decor had fallen from favor, though a star turn could keep it alive. Lionel and John Barrymore, for (isolated) example, bellowed, cursed, and clawed the stage in an Italian item, *The Jest* (1919), translated by Edward Sheldon from Sem Benelli's insidious *La Cena delle Beffe* (The Dinner of Jests). Designed for color, light, and shade by Robert Edmond Jones, *The Jest* took Broadwayites back to Renaissance Florence, where brutal Lionel is king of bullies and gentle John must defend himself with his wits. The sight of Lionel driven mad because John cuckolded him and then tricked him into murdering his own brother made for a riveting curtain, and a bloodcurling scream that Lionel used in Act II was the talk of the town. But how many such evenings did the public need? A revival of the play six years later—without the Barrymores—flopped like a stone soufflé. The cloak-and-dagger days had ended.

In modern dress, good-versus-evil melodrama was petering out in the 1920s—the O'Neill school of better motivated, more articulate, and more reasonably lifelike scripts replaced it in works like *Beyond the Horizon* and *Anna Christie*. *Broadway* (1926), however, showed how much life was left in the form, if only under ideal circumstances. As a "realistic" free-for-all of gangsters, cops, and showgirls, it was all that the times could wish for—if by the times one means northeast-urban hustling America, the twenties that showed. Everyone in on *Broadway* was just getting started. The producer, Jed Harris, had two flops and no hits on his résumé when he mounted *Broadway*; two years later he was, next to Ziegfeld, the most famous producer in town (albeit an extremely disliked man).* Philip Dunning, who wrote *Broadway*'s first script (entitled *Bright Lights*—close, but not quite there), came up from carnivals and vaudeville into stage managing. George Abbott, who worked with Dunning on the rewriting, was still trying to decide whether he was going to make it as an actor, writer, or director, and *Broadway*'s backer Crosby Gaige had less professional experience than anyone. ("He seemed to have no feeling for the theatre," Abbott recalled in his memoirs. "In fact, I suspect that he got into it just to meet actresses.")

---

* Laurence Olivier reportedly modeled his Richard III after Harris.

Abbott became a major figure in America's lighter theatre, concentrating on farce and the rowdier types of musical comedy. He ended up a sometime producer, sometime author, sometime director, and sometime doctor for shows ailing in tryouts, but whether as originator or editor he perfected techniques for making a piece move (such as the jumpy "crossovers" he used in multi-scened musicals to keep something going downstage while stagehands rushed a new set into place behind a curtain). George Jean Nathan railed at Abbott's swift tempo, dubbing his style "hoptoad drama." But what did he expect farce to be, an adagio dance?

Broadway, staged by Abbott and Dunning, set the pace for hoptoad drama, sustaining a triangle love plot involving a hoofer, a shy "weenie" (chorus girl), and a hoodlum on non-stop smarts and lingo. (Sample line, one showgirl to another: "Listen, Personality—what difference does it make in this man's town where you get the sugar so long's so you got it?") American writers never worked harder to create a City of Satan than they did in characterizing New York and Chicago on the stage in the 1920s. In this *Broadway*, in *The Front Page*, and in Maurine Watkins' *Chicago*, city dwellers were lewd, vagrant, and amoral, hostless dybbuks screaming for gin and other fun.

Broadway was, of course, a smash. Set in the private party room of the Paradise Night Club, it cut romance, crime, sentiment, and jazz into a kaleidoscope of nightcrawling frenzy. *Broadway*'s romance belonged to the hoofer and his weenie, the crime was provided by a crew of Prohibition gangsters, who obliged with a shooting (in the back) right onstage in Act I, and for sentiment there was a showgirl who murders the head heavy to avenge her dead lover:

PEARL: Turn around, rat! I don't want to give it to you like you did him—in the back.
STEVE: For Christ's sake, don't!
PEARL: I'm giving you more chance than you gave him—I'm looking at you—and the last thing you see before you go straight to hell is Jim Edwards' woman, who swore to God she'd get you.
STEVE: (*Backing away*) Don't . . . don't kill me . . . don't—

She does, however; it's terrifically sentimental.

Jazz was omnipresent in *Broadway*, and added to the excitement of one murder by camouflaging it with the drummer's rim shots in a "battle" number. Romance, crime, sentiment, and jazz: that's late twenties melodrama for you. But melodrama so pure and obvious was not to go much further. A new vigor was cutting deeply into the backwardness of escapist entertainment, most deeply perhaps in *Rope* (1928), a melodrama without a vestige of pop veneer, melodrama turning into drama, combining the high-strung profile of the one with the thoughtful foundation of the other. David Wallace and T.S. Stribling adapted Stribling's novel *Teeftallow* into *Rope* as an indictment of small-town intolerance and mob rule, but it is interesting that the intolerance of their Irontown, Tennessee, was not racial but social, white on white; and the grim dialogue was not without its touches of gallows humor. *Rope*, in short, had a lot of personality: lynch-happy reformers, drunkards grinning Prohibition and their lives away, revivalists who'll damn your soul if you won't let them save it, and several victims. In its 31 ill-attended performances, *Rope* gave Broadway a new option in melodrama; but Broadway replied, Nothing doing.

Even conventional melodrama was having trouble, so what's a specialist to do? In *Icebound* (1923) Owen Davis gave the form sour but non-violent characters and won the Pulitzer Prize for supposedly having renovated melodrama along psychological lines. Did he, after all? *Icebound*'s New Englanders, imprisoned as much by their personal coldness as by the symbolic drifts building up at the door, won praise perhaps because they resolved their tale without shedding blood, as they doubtless would have in the Belasco era. *Icebound* was polite and mature, but hardly worth a major honor, even one constipatedly designed for a work that "shall best represent the educational value and power of the stage in raising the standard of good morals, good taste and good manners." But then few members of the Pulitzer advisory boards were regular theatregoers, and the professionals whose help they enlisted were often too outraged by past Pulitzer awards to assist. (George Jean Nathan took a poll of the high committee's theatregoing activities in 1940: the members had seen a yearly average of four plays, and the most frequently cited entry was Olsen and Johnson's slapstick revue *Hellzapoppin'!*.)

Even granted that the Pulitzer people didn't know much about drama, some of their awards looked so obtuse that they began to resemble Tony nominations of the mid-1970s, when survival panic and a dearth of deserving nominees robbed theatre awards of their meaning. Catcalls and curses greeted the Pulitzer presentation in 1924 to Hatcher Hughes' *Hell-Bent Fer Heaven* over George Kelly's vastly more intelligent *The Show Off*—not least because Professor Brander Matthews of Columbia University, which administers the award, overrode the nominating tribunal in favor of Hughes, one of his old students. Six years later, the committee topped that event and showed exactly the race of theatre it supported when it handed the prize to the musical comedy *Of Thee I Sing*—an unusually adult satirical musical, to be sure; a breakthrough in the form, in fact, for the touches of eloquent music theatre in George and Ira Gershwin's score. But that was the season of *Mourning Becomes Electra*.

The fact that the ordinary *Icebound* got the Pulitzer Prize and the awesome *Mourning Becomes Electra* didn't proves the inequity of some prize-giving in the first place. But besides that, what's so important about subduing melodrama, as *Icebound* did? Far better for the form was something openly melodramatic but, at least, alive—as was Elmer Rice's *Street Scene* (1929), no attempt to uplift the form but rather to exploit its thin texture to point up the jittery congestion of city life. It was odd, though, that Rice, who did so well by the newfangled expressionism in *The Adding Machine*, should bother with outdated melodrama in *Street Scene*; perhaps the possibilities for social criticism in his veristic melting-pot setting overcame his natural bent for experimentation.

A somewhat anthropological angle on the question of what makes a national culture stimulated yet another genre, the folk play. This was an art of regional people in dialect and custom; it dealt with midwestern and white and black southern life, viewing blacks as tragically striving for liberty (there is a sense of the old Indian drama here) and whites as natural comics, with their incompetent schemes to buy a used automobile or their glad recollection of the last ride of the "revenooer" who menaced the family still. Song—folk song, as a rule—helped authenticate the art, and the scope of the folk play was continuity, the epic of the people in their universality and endurance, the uncorruptible permanence of their ritual structures. The city, all transience and surprises, has no continuity. City settings suited spoofs of fashion or claustrophobic working-class realism, not recognitions of the origin and future of the race. Even when located in a city, as was *Porgy*, the folk play that later turned into George Gershwin's folk opera *Porgy and Bess*, the form took the pulse of *village* life as revealed in a Charleston ghetto.

In a way, the black folk plays were like a combination of melodramatic composition and art-movement presentation, which gave them a distinctive verbal-visual style all their own. White men wrote and staged them, but they marked a major social breakthrough in that they gave black actors opportunities far wider than those offered in the many black musical revues, where singing, dancing, and hambone comedy prevailed.* Outfitting a *Dixie to Broadway* (1924) or *Connie's Hot Chocolates* (1929) was easy: one toured

---

* Contrary to current revisionist romance, black self-satire was as stereotypically derisive as Gosden and Correll's *Amos 'n' Andy* sketches on radio.

the Harlem nightclubs and hired promising talent. But producers casting more serious endeavors often had to trawl their net through odd corners of the culture, into church choirs or black colleges.

The oppressive "blackface" makeup was moribund by the 1910s; black entertainers pursued their partial liberation in the 1920s in the sassy revues, which owed more to black vaudeville performing traditions than to those of the white stage. Such authenticity made the old white "blackface" specialists obsolete, and such instances as Rosetta Duncan's Topsy in a musical version of *Uncle Tom's Cabin, Topsy and Eva* (1924), and a turn by Tess Gardella (known professionally as Aunt Jemima) in the original cast of *Show Boat* (1927) climaxed this now unknown subgenre of theatre Americana.* Indeed, reviewers who, before the twenties, had been callous toward or simply not aware of racial emergence suddenly grew impatient with blackface comedy; nothing pained Chicago's critics more than *Topsy and Eva*'s ten-month run there in the face of their at first bored and later pained dismissals of its amateur score, of Rosetta Duncan's endless slapstick, and of sister Vivian Duncan's stealthy blonde innocence as Little Eva. Vastly more appealing to critical and informed lay taste were the serious black folk plays, though these did not invariably please the general public. Paul Green's *In Abraham's Bosom* (1926) and DuBose and Dorothy Heyward's *Porgy* (1927), both personal tragedies that suggested a panorama of racial tragedy, looked deeply into the viewpoint and voice of American black culture in the rigid South. The use of spirituals and work songs naturally added to the spell, as for example in a chain-gang tableau in Green's *Roll, Sweet Chariot* (1934), a moment of stunning visual creativity much discussed by theatre people. *Theatre Arts* magazine likened the play to Elizabethan drama, "weaving the individual stories into a pattern of character and action"—this, of course, is exactly the folk play's plan.

It proved less so in the white folk plays. Hatcher Hughes' *Hell-Bent Fer Heaven* (1924), the work that discredited the Pulitzer Prize by winning it, is a typical number, an overwrought tale of how a fifth-rate Iago, a born-again Bible-shouter, almost rekindles a defunct feud in the Carolina mountains. An unimportant but amusing melodrama, it worked less for any cultural depiction than for its quaint, cynical folk wisdoms. "I tell you," says one of Hughes' characters during the denouement, "religion's a great thing when the Lord's on your side!"

---

* Al Jolson and Eddie Cantor had grown too dependent on the blackface specialty to drop it, but by the 1930s they had carried it with them into film, and the stage was at last rid of it.

Despite the artistic and social idealism of the black folk play, it some-times ran ahead of its white counterpart—if only in New York—because of the Harlem fad. Taking their free ride on the town topic, the *bon ton* made *Porgy* a Must See. Such an attitude was good for business, but cheapened the event for others; certainly, such condescension clouded the issue of racial integration. Too many of *Porgy*'s spectators took the Heywards' tale as a portrayal of black laziness, superstition, and drug addiction—however sym-pathetic—when *Porgy*'s plan is to show how laziness, superstition, and drug addiction have become institutionalized by an oppression so fully developed that its victims can't even identify it as such. Ben Hecht impaled the Harlem-ite myopia on his pen: "My set has discovered something too marvelous for words. Negroes! Oodles and oodles of them! Big ones and little ones! Harlem, way this side of the zoo."

It was one of Hecht's set who, in 1930, argued the best-received case for the white-conceived black folk play, Marc Connelly, in *The Green Pastures*. Prompted by Roark Bradford's dialect Bible retellings, *Ol' Man Adam an' His Chillun*, and adhering faithfully to Bradford's Dixie mushmouth, *The Green Pastures* has fallen victim to racial touchiness since its immense first success, though today's easing of sensitivities might allow a timely revival or a musical adaptation. There was already much music in the show to begin with, for Connelly balanced a gently satiric picture of the southern black idyll of fish fries, plantation loafing, and musical piety with the solemn collaboration of the Hall Johnson Choir, whose part work in the indispen-sable spiritual added to the at times ecstatic quality of the evening.

Introduced by a bayou Sunday school class, *The Green Pastures* viewed the familiar Old Testament stories as many rural blacks might have viewed them. Said Connelly, "Unburdened by the differences of more educated theologians, they accept the Old Testament as a chronicle of wonders which happened to people like themselves in vague but actual places, and of rules of conduct, true acceptance of which will lead them to a tangible, three-dimensional Heaven . . . through an eternity somewhat resembling a series of earthly holidays." Thus, when the Sunday school teacher asks his little charges what they thought of their first lesson, on Genesis:

MYRTLE: I think it's jest wonderful, Mr. Deshee. I cain't understand any of it.

. . .

CARLISLE: What de worl' look like when de Lawd begin, Mr. Deshee?
DESHEE: How yo' mean what it look like?

MYRTLE: Carlisle mean who was in N'Orleans then.

DESHEE: Dey wasn't anybody in N'Orleans on 'count dey wasn't any N'Orleans . . . Dey wasn't any Rampart Street. Dey wasn't any Canal Street. Dey wasn't any Louisiana. Dey wasn't nothin' on de earth at all caize fo' de reason dey wasn't any earth.

As friendly to as awed by black survival, Connelly schemed what might have been too episodic a script (Adam and Eve, then Noah, then the Exodus, and so on) around one principal, de Lawd. A conflation of "good" white landowner and ·fundamentalist preacher, de Lawd strides through *The Green Pastures* as God of both wrath and love; eventually he comes to understand man and wills his own martyrdom to redeem the human race. Amid the affectionate spoofing, Connelly created a remarkably powerful miracle play, one that ranks with *Our Town* and very few others for profound cultural quest and cathartic wonder. As in *Our Town*, there is no focal story; effects central to discovery build and build, until at length the sense of commentary on an idea dissolves into the emotional experience of that idea on an almost mystical level. Even *New Yorker* readers were moved.

Those who saw Richard B. Harrison's titanic portrayal of de Lawd in the original production spoke of it rapturously ever after, with good reason. This former college teacher, who had lectured but never acted before, embodied to the nth degree the goodwill intended in Connelly's script that was later too glibly discounted in the reaction against his use of Jim Crow dialect. As teacher, Harrison's field was, bizarrely, speech—he also had to apply brown makeup to his light skin to appear Negro under the stage lights. But he lacked nothing that *The Green Pastures* needed to borrow; as John Mason Brown put it, "He was possessed of that rarest of mortal as well as theatrical virtues—a nobility which neither was, nor had to be, assumed. . . . So innately reverent, so alive with everything most wanted in religion was Mr. Harrison's Lawd that a 'ten-cent seegar,' given to him by a custard-maker, could become in his hands as natural and devout a holy offering as incense."

It is no act of patronization for Broadway to revere—and many did; it was that big a moment—a work as lightly comical in part as this one. Harrison's natural truth collided precisely with Connelly's perceived truth: actors matter. Read the text today; you'll enjoy it, but can you reckon what the commitment of actors and singing ensemble brought to the black-and-white of words? How easily Connelly's script might have overblown its cutesy brass; how it might have run short of urgency at the finale, when de Lawd, inspired by human heroism down on earth, conceives His role in the destiny of mankind, His burden, and gazes into the audience as The Crucifixion is invoked by an offstage voice and the choir bursts into "Hallelujah, King Jesus." The whole thing might have collapsed in preciosity; it didn't, and Harrison's weight was no little reason why. Such was the man's gravity—beauty—that almost no commentator has failed to cite his first entrance, heralded by Gabriel's "Gangway! Gangway for de Lawd God Jehovah!," as the Big Moment of the era.

Much less enthralling as sheer drama but infinitely more popular than the folk play was the higher comedy, that slightly disengaged arena of "topics" and fine language. This was "social" comedy, surprisingly similar in tone and shape to *The New York Idea* (whose topic, remember, burlesqued divorce and whose language spoke finely enough for 1906). A later chapter discloses Philip Barry and S. N. Behrman, the mikados of social comedy in the interwar years; for now let us drop in on Robert E. Sherwood's *The Road to Rome* (1927).

Always intrigued by social generalities, Sherwood undertook a liberal's progress in his work on Broadway, moving from anti-war polemics in apparently peaceful times to considerations and then advocacy of defensive action when totalitarian imperialism changed his mind about America's role on the world stage. O'Neill would never have written a *Road to Rome*: it is less about persons than about the way the world is and how it might be changed. *The Road to Rome* visits the city of the Caesars on the eve of its destruction by Hannibal and his invincible Carthaginians. Amytis, wife of Rome's babbitty leader, steals across enemy lines to talk Hannibal out of finishing his campaign. But Hannibal is a warrior hero—pillage, he says, is his job. No, replies Amytis. A hero's job is improving the world, not leveling it. Along with his pacifist argument, Sherwood provides the usual boy-meets-girl, letting Amytis share Hannibal's bed and making the most of Jane Cowl's personal magnetism as Amytis. In the end, he combines the part's star quality with the argument, letting Cowl win the public over to her "human equation":

HANNIBAL: The human equation does not interest me.
AMYTIS: Because you don't know what it is. If you could ever find it, you'd know that all your conquests—all your glory—are only whispers in the infinite stillness of time . . . and then you'll wish that all you've done could be undone. . . . Go out and destroy the wind, Hannibal. Destroy the stars, and the night itself—if you can. Then come back and kill me.

Sherwood cast *The Road to Rome* as a sex comedy with touches of historical spoof, and he conveyed his images so clearly that they were hard to miss. But at other times public and critics failed to "get" a show, so subtly were the old genres being transformed. *What Price Glory?* (1924), a lusty comedy-melodrama about Marines loving and fighting in the field, arrived during the literary antiwar drive of the post-Wilson era, when such novels as *Three Soldiers, All Quiet on the Western Front,* and *The Enormous Room* emphasized the brutality rather than the gallantry of Over There. Long thought of as a classic anti-war tract, *What Price Glory?* was on the contrary a jaunty torpedo shot from the armory of pulp fiction and fired by the powder of farce, neither for nor against war: about it.

What Price Glory?'s co-authors Laurence Stallings and Maxwell Anderson met in the offices of the New York *World,* where the idea for the play sprang from Stallings' recollections of glory and despair in the Marine Corps. He had lost a leg in World War I, and the resultant bitterness inspired a shattering novel, *Plumes,* which he dedicated "to an unknown soldier." Anderson was a pacifist, and it was his reforming zeal that put out a first draft of *What Price Glory?,* but by the time Stallings was through amending the script with Marine Corps jive, it was no longer quite the denunciation of war that Anderson had conceived. One senses the beating of great wings in this work, the challenge of combat and the thrill of male camaraderie—so much so that Anderson's censure of war is less intriguing than the sado-masochistic friendship of his and Stallings' principals, Captain Flagg and Sergeant Quirt. One can bet one's boots there was no one like Flagg or Quirt in the British World War I classic, R.C. Sheriff's *Journey's End,* a Broadway hit in 1929 and a tale of world-weary but defiantly radiant heroism.

What Price Glory? takes the American view of things, dangerous and romantic, never mistaking a fact for an ideal. It created a furor for its obscene dialogue, but its power and honesty defeated any would-be crusaders—this one they could not close. It was one of the most virile plays since the Elizabethan period, a far cry from the poetic peace-pleadings of the war novels. Its comedy alone would have sent it to the top, as witness Corporal Kiper discussing his wife back home:

> Ain't I signing the payroll for her every month? A twenty-dollar allotment, and she gives it to a fireman in Buffalo. Here I am saving democracy, and he's turning in a twenty-bell alarm the first of every month.

What Price Glory?'s curious charm mainly devolves on its two principals, Flagg and Quirt, brawny and unstoppable, yet oddly bashful. The significance of their ferocious black-and-forth bullying and their eagerness to have sex with the same woman was lost on almost everyone at the time, possibly including Anderson if not Stallings, but then the nature of platonic homosexual sublimation was still one of the country's best kept secrets. The play's oft-quoted final line, Quirt's "Hey, Flagg, wait for Baby!," embodies an arcane psychological transaction that audiences of 1924 might admire but never comprehend. They had a good time, though. A popular joke of the day pictured two dowagers in their orchestra seats after *What Price Glory?*'s final curtain.

"Well, Laeticia," says one, "shall we get the hell out of here?" and her companion replies, "Not till I find my Goddamn gloves."

8

Satirists
The 1920s and 1930s

HAVING FOUND A PURPOSEFUL VOICE, the theatre grew militant. Presenting their various cases, writers found melodrama, low and high comedy, naturalism and mannerism, and documentary equally useful, though the era is remembered mainly for two approaches, satire and the angry protest play.

American satire is too innocent; it always has been. American writers forgive too much. Rather than sustain a tradition in the bitter, cynical Juvenalian style of satire, American writers have specialized in the Horatian mode, applying the Protestant belief in human perfectability. The tolerant rib-poking of *The Contrast*, in which fashion is exposed as silliness, defines American satire; such a piece as Sheridan's *The School for Scandal*, in which fashion is exposed as evil, was popular here in *The Contrast*'s day, but inspired a few American successors. Indeed, American theatre comedy is typified better in burlesque than in satire; burlesque's dead-level innocence made it the most popular comic form in late nineteenth-century theatre, though oddly it resurfaced after some decades of neglect with a brand-new component of satiric sophistication. In the musical revue in the 1920s and '30s, in cabaret vaudeville in the 1950s, and on television ever since, refurbished burlesque has largely filled in for satire in the American popular arts.

Burlesque cut down the giants of literature and quasi-literature. The works of Longfellow, Sardou, Fitch, and such saw duty in rambunctious lampoons as much improvised in rehearsals as set down in script, as the irresistibly off-the-wall offerings of the Weber and Fields Music Hall attested to in an earlier chapter. But satire, as the Horatian-style Joseph Addison observed, must "pass over a single foe to charge whole armies," and beneath its abrasive humor is a morality aimed at reform. Burlesque would do anything for a laugh: a performer's medium. Satire had the consistency of purpose, and belonged to the writer.

If American satire is friendlier than a reformer's exorcism ought to be, Broadway's reason was less good nature than the obsequious prudence of the businessman. *The Lion and the Mouse* in 1905 made a hit with its arraignment of the money bosses in the person of John D. Rockefeller—but this was a popular issue of the day. Imagine how much less thrilled the customers would have been if the author had blamed not Rockefeller for being Rockefeller but industrial democracy for allowing a Rockefeller to happen.

"Satire is what closes Saturday night." With these words George S. Kaufman served himself and Broadway with an excuse for not going too far. Kaufman's plan let him put on a little irony while not truly engaging controversy: like giving candy to a baby. Where a moralist like Elmer Rice tuned expressionism in *The Adding Machine* to play a spectacular satire in the form of a psychological toccata, words hammering words till language threatens to dissolve, the practical satirists of commercial Broadway held back, assuring themselves that how far they went was as far as the public and *Variety* would tolerate their going. But as it happened, satire played way past Saturday night more often than Kaufman's joke suggests—in at least one case in a play by Kaufman.

Taking satire at its looser, "Broadway" definition as burlesque in words, we can cite Kaufman as The Street's most prolific and profitable satirist. So clever so often that his sallies were credited to Dorothy Parker—a real tribute—Kaufman embodies the self-unimportance of pop satire as aptly as Belasco did the hyperbole of sentimental/sadistic melodrama in the early 1900s. Like Belasco, Kaufman had his detractors. Even reviewers who saluted his premieres with rave reviews could turn high-hat in their Sunday columns ("Can Broadway Eat Its Cake and Have Satire, Too?"). Whatever they thought of Kaufman's style, it would have been irresponsible to pan the shows at their premieres, for they were funny, well-made, and sometimes neatly pointed. Of the nine plays that Kaufman wrote with Marc Connelly from 1921 to 1924, *Dulcy* was the most engaging, but their *Merton of the Movies* (1922) offered a prize look at the ersatz personae that Hollywood deals in. Using as their source a novel by Harry Leon Wilson (Booth Tarkington's *The Man From Home* collaborator), Kaufman and Connelly hit the same blend of satire and loving character comedy that the film *Hearts of the West* was to in 1975, taking a movie-struck innocent from the Midwest to Hollywood, where he plans to find himself as a cowboy hero. Merton, in but not exactly of the movies, is prototypal: nice, neither bright nor dumb but deluded, and charming (though of course he doesn't know it). Like George Kelly's show off Aubrey Piper, Merton will Get the Girl; but unlike Piper he is no bluffer, and must endure a ritual humiliation before he can deserve success. It seems that Merton's gunslinging screen incarnation, "Clifford Armytage," doesn't come off except as a spoof. At the debut of his first film, the audience hoots in delight and Merton runs away, but somehow he drags himself back and, shaken out of his fantasy world, accepts his new vocation in comedy.

Merton of the Movies observed the proprieties of Horatian satire, and the customers came running. But when Kaufman and Connelly really asserted themselves, the public still showed up. Diving into Juvenalian disgust in *Beggar on Horseback* (1924), the authors expressed the alienation of the artist in a philistine society, sensing in Warren Harding's "normalcy" an epoch of parochial materialism as rampant in art commodities as in automobile manufacture. This time, there were no half-measures—*Beggar on Horseback* even helped itself to some brutal expressionism to warn against the popular judgment of art as either financially profitable or useless.

Years later, people would approach Kaufman and say something like, "You know what work of yours should be revived?," and Kaufman would cut in with, "It's dated." Besides the expressionism, *Beggar on Horseback* needed the culture of the twenties too well to survive it. Without a Calvin Coolidge to debunk, who needs anti-Coolidge angst? (A revival of *Beggar on Horseback* at Lincoln Center in 1970 felt less dated than campy, but the two are often interchangeable.) The main thing is that *Beggar on Horseback* pulled off a pungent evening of satire and ran way past the first Saturday night.

The play was a reworking of a German original, Paul Apel's shocker of 1912, *Hans Sonnenstössers Höllenfahrt* (Jack Sun-Basher's Journey to Hell). Though America supposedly holds the monopoly on anti-intellectual materialism in the West, Apel found plenty of it in Germany, and so insulted the first-night public in Munich that they tried to silence the play with a ruckus, causing someone to get up and shout, "Es ist eine Roheit zu lachen!" (It's base to laugh!).

New York laughed at *Beggar on Horseback* in the right way. Kaufman and Connelly retained Apel's surrealist nightmare sequence, slanting it to attack assembly-line commercialism with spoofs of the famous American "know-how." The beggar is an idealistic composer who dreams that he kills his vapid fiancée for ripping up the manuscript of his symphony, slays her family as well, and is suddenly surrounded by six reporters calling for a statement; at that moment, newsboys raced down the aisles of the Broadhurst Theatre's orchestra to pass out copies of the *Morning-Evening-Evening-Morning*, containing a detailed story on the murders. The real-life audience naturally swiveled around to take this in, and when they turned back to the stage, the curtain had fallen on Part One.

Perhaps *Beggar on Horseback* was not as daring as everyone thought; certainly, its targets—midwestern boobs, industrialism, and midcult art manufacture—were universally accepted targets for ridicule among New Yorkers, and the composer's masterpiece, a lengthy ballet turn scored by Deems Taylor, turned out to be a devastating take-off on the fruitier junkets of the art movement. This was long overdue and something everyone could enjoy; in a way, it marked the first breath of clean air since *Sumurun*. Part Two, mainly comprising the hero's nightmare, was replete with such commentary. The conveyor-belt approach to masscult media was dispatched in a visit to the Cady Consolidated Art Factory. Tourists are guided as if in a zoo past a novelist, an artist, and a poet, all in cages conceiving for the time clock. The novelist, dictating to a stenographer, dries up in mid-sentence, and the secretary calmly takes up the story herself:

VISITOR: Was *she* writing it?
GUIDE: Oh, no! Sometimes she gets a little ahead of him, that's all . . . Forty-five minutes after he finishes a novel we have it printed and assembled and on its way to the movie men.

Beggar on Horseback's bourgeois-baiting wit typifies but is not exclusive to the American twenties. Throughout the twentieth century, art folk have condemned their local Babbitts for their soulless appetite and narrow worldview. But while the Babbitt is an international modern art stooge, he does foot the bills for the operas, plays, and novels that spoof and despise him. And that makes for a certain internal contradiction in the aesthetic of antibourgeois satire. One thing Babbitt must have noticed: nobody hates him on television.

How far can the stage go in lampooning a major segment of its public? All the Babbitt does it buy a ticket and peep like Tom—i.e., support the theatre. Kaufman asked, will he support playwrights' aggression as well? He himself preferred not to blast the public's self-image. Some found him brilliant, others a mere wag, with the result that his reputation is hard to place. He was a lot funnier than either S. N. Behrman or Philip Barry, the two leading satirists of Kaufman's era. Yet his scripts seem pat next to theirs. They were dramatists; he was a theatre man: as critic (for the *Times*), author, director . . . even actor in *Once In a Lifetime* (1930), playing a wry New York writer growing wryer by the minute in Hollywood. He knew, above all, how to make a play work. Perhaps that was what held him back from real eminence: audience gratification was too clear a matter for him to sabotage it with audacity. His topics, mostly, were cute and current. With Ring Lardner he dismissed popular song in *June Moon* (1929); with Moss Hart he axed the sell-out school of playwrighting in *Merrily We Roll Along* (1934), which unfolded its story in reverse, starting with a loud soirée of the pseudo-intelligentsia and ending with the later-to-be-corrupted playwright's optimistic valedictorian address at his college graduation ceremony; and on his own, a rare foray, he junked the "hiya, sweetheart" school of theatre producers in *The Butter and Egg Man* (1925). All three were hits, but in their friendly humor and rodeo pacing they lack *Merton*'s humanity and *Beggar*'s hellish clarity.

Few of Kaufman's post-1930s works equaled his early ones. In his prime, with Edna Ferber, he embraced the actor heroes of *The Royal Family* (1927) with tenderness and a finely controlled respect for the dynastic inevitability of the theatre. The play itself was overshadowed at the time by its apparent *à clef* models, the Drews and Barrymores (hotly denied by the authors, but Ethel never forgave them), and the resultant difficulties in casting. Yet for those theatre buffs who had sensed the urgent destiny of the acting profession across the footlights, there were moments to treasure in this picture of the great Cavendish family upholding the old ideals.

The most flamboyant of the Cavendishes is Tony (a patent runoff of John Barrymore, whatever the authors said), hiding out from reporters and a process server after his latest peccadillo in Hollywood, but the foundation of *The Royal Family* and the clan itself is ancient Fanny, eager to get back on the road after a crippling illness, more conscious than the others of the thrill and responsibility of stardom:

> Every night when I'm sitting here alone I'm really down there at the theatre! Seven-thirty, and they're going in at the stage door! Good evening to the door man. Taking down their keys and looking in at the mail rack. Eight o'clock. The stagehands are setting up. (*Raps with her cane.*) Half hour, Miss Cavendish! Grease paint, rouge, mascara! Fifteen minutes, Miss Cavendish! My costume! . . . More rouge! . . . Where's the rabbit's foot! . . .

Overture! . . . How's the house tonight? . . . The curtain's up! . . . Props! . . . Cue! . . . Enter! . . . That's all that's kept me alive these two years. If you weren't down there for me, I wouldn't want to live . . . I couldn't live . . . You . . . down there . . . for me . . . going on . . . going on . . . going on . . .

A sort of satiric domestic comedy-*cum*-farce, *The Royal Family* explained how the American theatre renews itself, goes on. The original cast was weak, as no actress with the requisite glamor was willing to play Julie Cavendish— "a walking ad," as Ina Claire put it (while turning it down) for Ethel Barrymore. Claire did the movie version, however, and the London staging in 1934, renamed *Theatre Royal*, offered Marie Tempest and Laurence Olivier. But not till 1975 did Broadway get a *Royal Family* cast to type, with Rosemary Harris' velvety Julie, Ellis Rabb's high-strung Tony, and Sam Levene's creampuff peddler of an old-style Broadway producer.

Ironically, by the 1970s the show business that the Cavendishes had known was gone, and the continuity implicit in the story seemed a hopeless fantasy, all the more so since the Fanny, Eva Le Gallienne, was just closing a lustrous career in a vanished profession—actress, stage actress, actress of great plays. The Big Moment quoted above proved electrifying in her hands, but the ovation that cheered her exit rang with loss, not just of Le Gallienne and her unflagging dedication as actress-manager, but also, perhaps, of theatre-going. Ferber always felt it a mistake that Fanny dies at the end of the piece: "We should have seen her starting off on her last road tour, vain, stage-struck to the end, gay and courageous." But how inappropriate this would have been for 1975. The road is gone, the Fanny Cavendishes are gone, and the kind of plays they prized—the old beautiful plays only sometimes alternated with Ibsenist subversion—are gone. Indeed, Kaufman, in his quiet way, helped kill them.

Kaufman's compromise with satire kept him successful. True, his and Hart's aforementioned *Merrily We Roll Along* did investigate the moral deterioration that may accompany an author's commercial success. But, as if the theme itself might prove too hard to take, they ran their plot backwards: novelty sells. Perhaps the work's retrospective, gaining in irony as the hero's cynical winter is progressively illuminated by his hopeful spring, was meant to point up the authors' lecture. Still, the evening wears itself out early on, the novelty relentless and the irony forced.

Later Kaufman-Hart was even less enterprising. Unlike *Beggar on Horse-back* and *Merton of the Movies*, the Hart collaborations depend entirely on comic timing and urbanity. Except for a nationalist epic in *The American*

Way (1939), a non-comic spectacle tracing the acculturation of an immigrant couple (Fredric March and his wife Florence Eldridge), the team favored domestic comedy, yielding one classic, *You Can't Take It with You* (1936); one deathless staple of the high-school repertory, *The Man Who Came to Dinner* (1939); and one very funny but not much liked look at city slickers in the country, *George Washington Slept Here* (1940).

Farce. That was the Kaufman-Hart ticket. In 1930, their first venture, *Once in a Lifetime,* told of three vaudevillians in Hollywood who cash in on the sound boom as elocution "experts." The authors chose the setting for spoof and pace (plus two love plots). Gags, not a viewpoint, shape the event. Movie producer on the sound revolution: "What did they have to go and make pictures talk for? Things were going along fine. You couldn't stop making money—even if you turned out a good picture you made money." Or this, from the producer's secretary: "I hate to go into the playwrights' room. It always scares me—those padded walls, and the bars over the windows."

A huge cast and numerous scenes—a rented room in New York, a pullman car en route to California, the watering hole of the film colony on stars' night out, a studio reception room, and "on the set"—made *Once in a Lifetime* a colorful package. But there is no real commentative sense here, and for the happy ending, the three principals become masters and mistress of the film world that the authors have taken such pains to ridicule. This is *happy?* It turns out that one of the three is so stupid, and movies so stupid, that his blunders work out as brainstorms. But if Hollywood is as awful as Kaufman and Hart paint it, shouldn't their sympathetic heroes and heroine catch on and evacuate? The play doesn't follow through with its own premise.

What do we want from farce then? An adult manipulation of the form's amazing resilience. Most of the modern absurdist theatre is farce or a variant of farce, and two of our most telling movie genres, the screwball comedy and the Marx Brothers burlesque, both evolved their character and rhythm out of farce. Did Broadway's satirists regularly capture the flavor of anarchic America as well as Groucho, Chico, and Harpo? Did they ever understand the American romantic ideal as well as the screwball comics, who taught that good looks, zany wit, and a free soul identify democracy's elite class? Broadway's satire might better be termed *semi-satire*: an amoral burlesque of diversions and wisecracks. Semi-satire is topical but not engrossed. It made Broadway appear smart without its having to think.

There was satire of a truer sort on Broadway, scarcer than Kaufman's genre but often just as successful. In the mid-twenties, an unknown writer named Maurine Watkins contrived an exposure of the media racket in

Chicago (1926). The title reverberates; so symbolic was that place in that time that Watkins might have been calling her play *Chaos* or *Sleaze*. Between the lines of a comic melodrama about an unscrupulous young woman's days in court, Watkins peeled away the tinsel of sentimental jury-pleading, faintings on the witness stand, and publicity tactics from a simple case of murder, showing how easy it is to get away with it if you know the steps of the dance.

Like Hecht and MacArthur, Watkins had seen service as a Chicago reporter; no doubt her experiences on the *Tribune* acquainted her with real-life models for the crafty lawyer Billy Flynn, the gullible "sob sister" columnist Mary Sunshine, the murderesses Go-to-Hell Kitty and Machine-Gun Rosie, plus Watkins' heroine Roxie Hart, "the Jazz Slayer." Roxie is guilty of first-degree murder—we've seen her in the act—but she's going to get off. Outlining his scheme to win public sympathy for her, Flynn coaches his client in how to earn friends and an undeserved acquittal. "The story of your life starts tomorrow in the *Star*," he tells her:

> "From Convent to Jail." I'll have my secretary write it tonight—signed with your name, of course . . . Here's the idea: beautiful Southern home— every luxury and refinement—educated at the Sacred Heart—parents dead —fortune swept away. Runaway marriage—you're a lovely, innocent child, bewildered by what has happened. Young, full of life, lonely, you were caught up by the sad whirl of life in a great city. I'll have a red hot picture of cabaret life—jazz stuff is always good.

Jazz stuff, whining and wild: jazz as will, tempo, identity . . . jazz as America. Watkins put jazz and Chicago together rather casually but other writers saw jazz as the key to a code of culture. John Howard Lawson used it to underscore his radical leftist polemic *Processional* (1925), billed as "A Jazz Symphony of American Life," and as much a potpourri of vaudeville tropes as an attack on capitalism. Laid in a West Virginia coal town, *Processional* set labor agitation against repressive "law and order," playing its Ku Klux Klansmen, token Jewish figures, minstrel-show blacks, and radical hero "Dynamite" Jim to the accompaniment of a jazz combo. Comparably, in *Chicago*, Roxie Hart's sobriquet "The Jazz Slayer" is star billing right off a theatre marquee, and she plays the court like a Fontanne to her lawyer's Lunt. She learns the rules well enough to advise her own successor in the production of jazz-crime at the play's final curtain: no sooner has Roxie been acquitted than shots ring out offstage and the police drag in the next Roxie Hart, Machine-Gun Rosie. Rosie refuses to cooperate with the cameramen, but Roxie sets her straight: "Come on, sister, you gotta play ball—this is Chicago! Pitchers!" And they pose for the Kodaks.

Two melodramas, *Five Star Final* and *Midnight*, both in 1930, blamed the newspapers for encouraging crime by building up the public's response to criminals. Angry plays, they lacked the self-congratulatory zing of *The Front Page* and the ugly exposure of *Chicago*. A close contender with Watkins' script as regards plot material was *The Trial of Mary Dugan* (1927), with Ann Harding as an implicated but reassuringly innocent *Follies* girl in the dock for the murder of her lover. A far less brilliant piece than *Chicago*, *Mary Dugan* ran twice as long because its heroine was played for sympathy—but then that was Watkins' thesis in the first place.

In contrast to Watkins' tough-talking *Chicago*, Philip Barry and S. N. Behrman based their careers on upper- or upper-middle-class settings, observing verbal niceties. Barry and Behrman wrote in an almost direct line from *The New York Idea*; Barry veered between high-fashion hit comedies and flop experimental dramas while Behrman stuck with light satire. Both men were motivated more by a curiosity about mankind than a need to instigate reform, and both were prized as carriage-trade laureates. A debonair age patronized them, the epoch of Noel Coward, the Lunts, Gertrude Lawrence, and of first nighters chattering in fur and velvet.

Philip Barry was at his best when assaulting the presumption of the philistine rich, as in *Holiday* (1928), which pitted a rising but vagrant young businessman against his stuffy fiancée and her pompous father. Materialists, they see only his aptitude for Wall Streeting. Luckily, Hope Williams was on hand as the fiancée's sister; she saw his soul. *Holiday* ends with the engagement over, the hero sailing off to Europe, and Williams dashing off to join him at the last second. Barry loved bohemians.

Of Barry's light comedies, *The Philadelphia Story* seems the most durable (not least in its dynamite movie version), but *The Animal Kingdom* (1932) may be his most fulfilled piece, breathless wtih the banter of the literary set. Again, Barry prefers the nonconformist to the straight: the protagonist, like Johnny Case in *Holiday*, is attracted to both a "safe" woman and a free spirit. Like Hope Williams in *Holiday*, he raced off at the final curtain for the unpredictable romance.

Fascinated by psychodrama (an improvised dramatization of one's drives and fears), Barry sought ways to express a grander psychology than light comedy was used to. But each time he suppressed his pop identity his following balked. *Hotel Universe* (1930), an evening-long one-actor, pictured a weird house party of disoriented Americans on a terrace in France, getting a pep talk from a psychoanalytic interloper and playing at word-association games and infantile regression. Broadway was respectful but not amused. "Mystic," the critics called it, "turbid," "vague," "off the deep end." But they treated Barry's even more difficult—but greatly superior—*Here Come the Clowns* (1938) with ignorant awe, some of them visiting it a second time to reassess it in their columns. *Here Come the Clowns* gathered the loose ends of the psychodramatic *Hotel Universe* plan into a tight knot of problem play, asking, as so many have, "What is truth?" Barry's trick here is to pose his question in a perfectly naturalistic—yet perfectly bizarre—frame. In this allegory that doesn't act like one, truth is sought in the lives of outcasts in the back room of a café adjoining a vaudeville theatre.

A select population frequents this café, for it is off limits to all but the theatre's performers. And yet: all the world's a stage, and the theatre—the Globe—is a microcosm. Like *Street Scene*, *The Iceman Cometh*, *The Time of Your Life*, the German *Grand Hotel*, and the British *Outward Bound* (an enticing curio: passengers on an ocean voyage turn out, skeleton crew, to have all died before the play begins and are on their way to the hereafter), *Here Come the Clowns* reveals in one spot at one time a human epic, all types and sizes, all hopes and despairs. "If the word 'Globe' means the world," Barry stated in a defense of his play after the discouragingly confused reviews appeared,

> I am afraid that is just what I mean . . . I feel that [the play's protagonist] Clancy is but one man ready and willing to go down in the battle with evil, which continues to be fought throughout the world; that all men should live and die fighting it. That it is infinitely better to die in the struggle than it is to live in fear or in the questionable security which follows any compromise with all these things in government and human society that we know in our hearts to be wrong.

This is very thirties—as we soon shall see. If the twenties brought us technique, the thirties taught us argument. The Freudians of the so-called "Theatre Guilt" era must have thrilled to Barry's psychodramatic set pieces in *Here Come the Clowns*, for the bulk of the show is a vaudeville tossed off by the characters as prompted by a gnomic "illusionist"—not, he insists, magician. "Magicians are interested primarily in deceptions," he announces. "I am interested only in truth. But truth is so often an illusion I must, you see, in truth call myself an illusionist."

Still, the stunts that he pulls fall out of a bag of psychological tricks, group therapy combined with variety show: a ventriloquist is urged to play identity games with his dummy; a midget, on the illusionist's knee, is made to confront another patient-performer in the café, who may be his son; a drunken press agent delivers a recitation on the existence of God. Each item on the bill adds to the central treatment of Clancy, the seeker, who at the point of death finds God in "the will of man." The public, partly, supported the experiment. Eighty-eight performances is not one of the historic long runs, but for one of Barry's alleged *faux pas*, it proves the growing curiosity in New York theatregoing.

What of Barry's colleague, S. N. Behrman? They shared the drawing-room setting, but Behrman's plays were less virile than Barry's. Like Fitch's, they leaned heavily on leading women. The crisp repartee at the heart of light comedy somehow didn't suit his male characters; a few of them sound like a Mother Abbess doing Ronald Firbank. Admittedly, neither Barry nor Behrman ever approached the whiplash gentility of the Noel Coward types (exhibited here in top form in *Private Lives*, *Design For Living*, and *Blithe Spirit*), yet their people have a squishy British feel about them. They had such *diction*, such transatlantic poise, emphasized by the swank folk attached to those parts—the Lunts, Ina Claire, Jane Cowl, Leslie Howard. When Barry turned his attention to the Skid Row of the world stage in *Here Come the Clowns*, he had no trouble with the vernacular, but Behrman laid some accidental perspective on his autograph when he based *Brief Moment* (1931) around the marriage of an airy dandy and earthy ex-showgirl. (Here was another example of Broadway's *à clef* reference to life, as Otto Kahn's son Roger Wolfe Kahn had not long before wed Hannah Williams, a more or less earthy ex-showgirl.) Habituated to Behrman's sculpted *mots*, theatregoers must have been shocked by the downbeat dialogue given to Francine Larrimore, a Belasco veteran and the gutsy Roxie Hart of *Chicago*, as the showgirl bride.

The Second Man (1927), Behrman's first Broadway hit, fixes his mode: a light gem, quaintly psychological and utterly suave. Behrman gave almost all of *The Second Man* to Alfred Lunt and a succession of entrances and exits to Lynn Fontanne as his bill-paying girlfriend, aided only by Margalo Gillmore as a fluttery temptress and Earle Larrimore as a doltish chemist who loves Gillmore badly enough to shoot at (and miss) his rival Lunt. The second man of the title was the nattering alter ego in Lunt's mind—"a cynical, odious person, who keeps watching me, who keeps listening to what I say, grinning and sophisticated, horrid." This "other" complicates his already distracted existence as a writer too proud to be a hack yet too third rate to be anything else. The problem is, how is one to spend his life?, and the answer is: with flair. "Life is sad," says Lunt. "I know it's sad. But I think it's gallant . . . to pretend that it isn't."

Though he laid a meaty "shall I write it?—shan't I?" role on Ina Claire in *Biography* (1932)—she doesn't, after all—Behrman felt inadequate working in bittersweet romance and spent the rest of the thirties fitting broader themes into the personal comic frame. Behrman did not fear being too "useful" (commercial). He feared not being useful (provocative) enough, and stated the crisis of literate social comedy—his own crisis—in *No Time for Comedy* (1939). Here, a Behrman-like playwright dreams up a holy terror of a serious work containing identity anxieties and death ritual. His wife, an actress famed for light parts, doesn't think his Freudian experiment works, and almost loses him to a *femme fatale* who encourages his serious bent. Perhaps the original production meant the audience to side with the wife from the start, for Katharine Cornell played her with irresistible wisdom, while Laurence Olivier as the playwright emphasized the character's insecurity. "I hate your detachment," Oliver tells Cornell. "I hate your destructive critical nature." It's Behrman confronting his career, his public, himself. "Don't throw away your charming gift, don't despise it!" cries Cornell. "Is it more profound to write of death of which we know nothing than of life of which we may learn something, which we can illuminate, if only briefly, with gaiety, with understanding?" Thus Behrman first attacked and then vindicated light comedy.

The musical had its say, too, to the constant surprise of reviewers who kept congratulating their readers that Americans lived in a society that made such wonders possible, not to mention legal. Actually, musical comedy has a long history of satiric commentary—Offenbach's *opéras bouffes* regularly spoofed high art, culture, and politics both verbally and musically—and since George S. Kaufman worked in the musical as well as spoken comedy it was inevitable that political lampoon enter the picture. Three works, early in the decade, set the tone, each a collaboration of Kaufman and Morrie Ryskind (the book) and George and Ira Gershwin (the score): *Strike Up the Band* (1930), *Of Thee I Sing* (1931), and *Let 'Em Eat Cake* (1933). The first (originally produced out-of-town in 1927) dealt with militarism, the second with machine politics, the third (a sequel to *Of Thee I Sing*) with a successful leftist revolution in the United States. *Strike Up the Band* hewed most closely to conventional musical comedy in structure; *Let 'Em Eat Cake* proved the most ambitious, with a tricky score and some extreme, even savage turns in the plot. *Of Thee I Sing* struck the best balance between commentary and diversion, and exercised a strong influence over later musicals, encouraging them to slash at politics at least in passing if not for an entire evening. The revue came in handy here: *As Thousands Cheer* (1933), a big-budget show with Marilyn Miller, Clifton Webb, and an Irving Berlin score, featured comic digs at Mahatma Gandhi, John D. Rockefeller, and Herbert Hoover, and even dared present Ethel Waters in one serious scene as the widow of a lynch mob's black victim, singing the ironic blues "Supper Time" as she set the table for dinner. Considering that the show's format comprised flashing newspaper headlines as premises for each of the sketches, and that each headline naturally promised either humor or sentiment, the appearance of UNKNOWN NEGRO LYNCHED BY FRENZIED MOB marks a significant moment in the redefinition of what was to pass as entertainment on the American stage. By comparison, the low-budget *Pins and Needles* (1937), an amateur show put on by the International Ladies Garment Workers Union, kept to a buoyant tone but played it hard-line for the union side in the class war. (Sample satiric dance number: "Doin' the Reactionary.") By further comparison, the Theatre Guild's too angrily outspoken "social revue" *Parade* (1935) closed quickly.

Though Brecht and Weill's *The Threepenny Opera* lasted a fast 12 performances in 1933, having violently offended most of the reviewers, an Americanized Weill lent his talents to a less ferocious reform work, Paul Green's *Johnny Johnson* (1936), in which an innocent idealist very nearly brings World War I to a halt by introducing laughing gas into a summit conference. Green's script and his bizarre song situations (an army captain's ironic meditation on rape; a pastiche number, "The Rio Grande," for a Texan in the trenches; two priests calling for God's assistance—one for the Allies and one for the Axis) really asked more of the public in the way of non-pop engagement than it could give. It was Kaufman who reestablished the mood for the politically minded musical in *I'd Rather Be Right* (1937), this time with an off-form Rodgers and Hart and with George M. Cohan impersonating Franklin D. Roosevelt. Considered extraordinarily daring in its day—the musical had burlesqued politics in general but never so blatantly kidded a major public figure—the show was very funny and totally innocuous. For example, Kaufman and co-author Moss Hart portrayed the President's struggle with the recalcitrant Supreme Court (the justices would pop out from behind bits of scenery every so often and cry, "Oh no, you don't!") but Roosevelt's controversial attempt to pack the court earlier that year with his deputies wasn't mentioned.

When Behrman sought social diagnosis in social teas and Barry alternated the same with symbolic rites of philosophical passage and the musical wavered between the Kaufman line and more insightful commentary, other writers and forms charged the social scene more patently. Much of the 1920s, we have seen, was spent in technical exploration: stagecraft. The 1930s were to introduce socially relevant themes. The trend has been in the offing in such entries as *The Adding Machine* and *Machinal* (phantasmagoric melodramas on the tyranny of System), *The Front Page* (farce on the corrupt union of municipal pols and the press), *Chicago* (satire on hype), and *The Road to Rome* (light antiwar comedy). Both art and social revolutions are related in their rejection of what the pop stage was offering—it was a small step to move from outlaw technique to outlaw ideas. "Going on . . . going on," cries Fanny Cavendish in *The Royal Family*; her sort will go on in Coward or Wilder or Brecht or modern-dress Shakespeare or Racine scored for jazz. But there was something unusual in the social revolution in theatre: for the first time, American writers regularly wrote in terms of archetypes rather than individual characters.

Perhaps the best early example of the willfully political stage is Maxwell Anderson and Harold Hickerson's *Gods of the Lightning* (1928), on the Sacco and Vanzetti murder case that began in 1920 with the arrest of two immigrant anarchists for the killing of a paymaster and his guard in South Braintree, Massachusetts, and which ended in 1927 with the pair's execution. In the twenties, the controversy among informed debaters centered not so much on the defendants' questionable innocence as on the partiality of the trial judge, Webster Thayer—it is necessary to assume the perspective of the times to understand Anderson and Hickerson's method, for in interpreting and fictionalizing while keeping to the factual outline of the case, they set a pattern for the genre of documentary theatre that has since become a force of disturbing magnitude in American culture, especially in the dangerously powerful medium of television. Genuinely documentary art, if such a thing is possible, prepares a kind of truth. However, documentary art, as here and almost everywhere else that we've known it, offers, as truth, opinion.

In Anderson and Hickerson's opinion, Sacco and Vanzetti had been railroaded—not by Judge Thayer's partisan interest, but by a repressive system through its enforcement agency, the police. Such theories are a commonplace in the suspicious 1980s; in 1928 the charge was flung acid, and since amidst the soapbox oratory and hypothetical exposé the authors wrote a remarkably exciting play, it is surprising that *Gods of the Lightning* did not run, on sheer melodramatic demonology if not hot topic. Agreed, its two anarchist defendants never quite impose themselves on the action, overshadowed as they are by numerous secondary characters and their own ideological polemic; also agreed, the love plot connecting one of the accused and a Sylvia Sidney type (played by Sylvia Sidney) is too reminiscent of the boy-meets-girl syndrome. Still, the show holds together as insightful naturalism and forceful protest.

Three acts cover the Sacco-Vanzetti days in miniature: Act I the arrest, Act II the trial, Act III the execution. The authors hedge on their documentary a little, using the fictional Macready and Capraro for their doomed heroes, and stating as fact that the state has framed the pair to silence them—the actual case provides no basis for the allegation. In the end, *Gods of the Lightning* is unacceptable as a "version" of the Sacco and Vanzetti case, but it admirably sets off the authors' libertarian fury. A character named Suvorin, entirely invented, speaks for them. "Uplifters, you are," Suvorin tells a bunch of union agitators, "reformers, dreamers, thinking to make over the earth. . . . The earth is old. You will not make it over. Man is old. You will not make him over. . . . Let us change the government, you say . . . I tell you there is no government—there are only brigands in power who fight for more power! Till you die! Till we all die! Till there is no earth!"

Such strong language seems the logical successor to *The Adding Machine*, *Roger Bloomer, Processional,* and *Rope,* and the next few years saw an explosion of protest theatre in New York. Again, the purpose of theatre had to be reinterpreted: now it was to open the channels of communication to spokesmen for the underclasses—and even to the underclasses themselves in the form of the workers' theatre. Inexperienced and perpetually broke, the workers' groups found on the stage the voice they had heretofore been denied in the community. Movies are expensive, and who reads books?—but the theatre was anyone's for the taking, nothing more than a free space, people to speak lines, and commitment. The workers seized the stage.

Around the country, anxiety over possible rioting led to sporadic censorship. But in New York there was not fear but excitement. Though the city authorities occasionally tried to sabotage a production that exposed the graft machine, they shrugged off the broader intent of the workers' theatre, which was to radicalize the citizenry on moral issues. Statist Oppression. The Corruption of Commercialism. Warmaking. Racism. The Role of a Militant Working Class. These were the themes of the workers' plays; soon enough, they were absorbed by writers working for the main stages on Broadway. For this if no other reason, the workers' theatre proved a tremendous breakthrough in the redefinition of what is useful in American playmaking.

There was more excitement than fear because most of the spectators at the workers' plays were not only workers but convinced advocates of the Marxist line on revolution or those in non-active sympathy with it. Those who were neither could be very uncomfortable—Otto Kahn, for instance. A habitual backer of non-commercial theatre organizations, whether establishment or leftwing, Kahn began to have second thoughts about his charity at a performance of the famous Group Theatre's second production, Paul and Claire Sifton's *1931—*. A love story played against archetypal representations of economic injustice, *1931—* closed with the cast marching inexorably forward like a homeless army; some of the actors clearly saw Kahn in the second-row, turning shades of white.

Great theatre can be impressive—but can it actually convert? As a moral force, it had long served as a custodian of established values; since the early 1900s, it had increasingly assumed adversary positions. The workers' movement hoped that their theatre might bear on the national philosophy, if only by radicalizing some fraction of the citizenry. Some nights, after an especially incendiary performance, the audience appeared so galvanized that some dreamers supposed that the revolutionary moment was within reach. That moment never came—and the question of whether or not the stage can convert a public on ideological grounds was not answered—because the workers' hard-line presentations alienated all but the *already* committed. Who was there to convert? Who was there, besides the few Otto Kahns, to inspire with fear? There was excitement because the communion of stage and house and was perfect; but it was perfect because everybody agreed.

The art revolution of the first postwar years was an incipiently political revolution as well, so one is not surprised to find the workers' theatre borrowing techniques from the art revolutionary's handbook—use of the "body language" of modern dance, mass chanting in geometric groupings, a bare stage, improvisatory rehearsals, direct address of the audience. The workers needed the three-dimensional mystery of art as much as a text. They were visionaries of a new theatre as well as a new order, though they wouldn't have thought themselves such. Like the adherents of the little theatre, they discredited the profit motive of Broadway; unlike them, they limited their bills to works relevant to the revolution.

The workers' purpose was, indisputably, Communist induction, but they knew the value of showmanship and contrived pageants on the tiniest budgets, for experienced theatre people collaborated with them, developing a unique theatre scene. The sketch, rather than any evening-length work, funded the workers' repertories at first. Sketches were portable, brief, relatively easy to cast, and therefore adaptable to the needs of speech rallies, union meetings, and skit nights. These were not true one-act plays, but telegrams enacted as harangues—here again the workers showed their roots in the little theatre era, for that was another great day for the short piece. Eugene O'Neill's and Susan Glaspell's one-acts dealt in character or thematic studies; the workers' sketches scorned such bourgeois folderol. Michael Gold's *Strike!* (1926), one of the first sketches written for one of the first workers' stage collectives, the Workers' Theatre, shows how it was done. The title is the work: in stark choral lecture, management confides its needs to exploit the workers, workers lament their hardships, an organizer recommends the solution—strike!—and the workers cohere in a mass to shout the point home.

Agitprop (=agitational propaganda), the term for this type of theatre, carries a negative reading that emphasizes its bullhorn shallowness. But this lean directness is exactly what its backers had in mind. John E. Bonn, director of the German-language Prolet-Bühne (Proletarian Theatre), in the late 1920s, defined the aim of agitprop: "Workers' Theatre today is the theatre of the class struggle. Its only purpose is reflecting (dramatizing) the class struggle and promoting (propagandizing) the class struggle . . . Workers' Theatre is for the exploited, bourgeois theatre is for the exploiters."

Agitprop, too, discovered the convenience of exploitation, as when Bonn's Prolet-Bühne borrowed the Scottsboro rape case of 1931 for its artful *Scottsboro!* sketch, building up a call for protest demonstrations in blocks of taut choral narration:

> In Scottsboro,
> In Scottsboro,
> Murder stalks the streets;
> In Scottsboro,
> In Scottsboro,
> Death haunts the cells.

The best known of the workers' groups' sketches was *Newsboy*, devised in the early 1930s by the elite Shock Troupe of the Workers' Laboratory Theatre on, all things considered, rather elaborate lines. Based on a poem by the Communist party's arts maven, V. J. Jerome, *Newsboy* blasted the American press for ignoring the more apropos stories on unemployment, racial intolerance, and political malfeasance for reports on crime, sports, and sex, and enlightened the characteristic rigidity of agitprop with a savage theatrical swank. Though nothing could have mattered less to its producers, *Newsboy* played as a compendium of post-art movement staging technique, melding mime, choral antiphony, illustrative interludes, pseudo-documentary quotations, and spectacle, and it owed as much to the montage effect in Syergyey Eisenstein's films as to the spur of dogma. The professional theatre people who caught a showing of it on its various appearances here and there praised its dramatic power—its "beauty" as theatre experience rather than its usefulness as sermon. Only one of numerous nameless characters, the newsboy of the title—"Love nest raided on Park Avenue! Extra! Marlene Dietrich insures legs for $50,000!"—takes a Candide's trip through the skit's fifteen or so minutes, learning that the real news takes in not love nests or legs but persecution of labor activists and lynchings. At the finale, a line of newspaper readers turns around one by one to display their source of news: *The Daily Worker*.

Who wrote *Newsboy*? Alfred Saxe coached the Shock Troupers who premiered the piece, and much of it does lift right off of the pages of Jerome's poem, but the play's specific authorship seems to be a matter of committee. Moreover, an investigation of *Newsboy*'s origin yields a confusion of texts, for as the working script passed from company to company (and at least one interloper known to record penned a same-only-different *Newsboy* for a meeting of the American League Against War and Fascism in 1938), alternate versions surfaced to cloud the issue. Who wrote *Newsboy*? Who wrote the workers' plays? Our outrage and solidarity, reply the workers. Anyone, reply the organizers; all are one. Nobody, reply the uptown critics, on their rare and generally condescending sorties into the tense off-Broadway of the radical left.

On the whole, nobody did write too many of the workers' plays. Committees ordered them, laid down the rules of purpose, colluded on plot and dialogue, staged them in chorus, analyzed them in talk sessions afterwards. Of course, the workers' sketches were meant from the beginning to serve as agitprop, nothing more. (Later, to avoid the stigma felt in the "prop" of propaganda, they were retermed "theatre of action.") But the transition from skit nights in rented halls for an audience of convinced workers to evening-length pieces in the mainstream theatre for a public that must be convinced proved difficult to accomplish, for Communist domination locked the radical theatre into doctrinaire positions; inescapably, the Party line allowed only slogan-plays with all the thematic substance of a picket sign. What writer could possibly open minds with such strictures as these wound around his pen?—the workers must always be heroes, the bosses always villains, without the slightest shade of character; heroes must consistently laud the Soviet Revolution and international agitation; all plays must deal exclusively with the class war. One sees the rub. Even so valiant and persuasive a work as

Anderson and Hickerson's *Gods of the Lightning* fails to satisfy the test, yet *Gods of Lightning* proves far more successful, both as entertainment and thesis, than the biggest works produced during the heyday of the organized radical theatre in the 1930s.

Unemployed, a sketch performed by the Workers' Laboratory Theatre in 1930, showed the true nature of the radical stage in denouncing the role of reformers. *Unemployed* didn't want a perfected democracy—that would obstruct the Communist march. Addressing a crowd of the alienated and jobless, the play's Party spokesman, a mechanical mouth, brands a minister and labor leader as stooges for capitalism. "Yes, I am an agitator," he cries. "I agitate for the defense of the Soviet Union, the only country in the world where there are no more exploiters, the only country in the world where the workers are free, the only country in the world where the worker rules." Critics in leftist periodicals contributed to this Communist-or-else bias by condemning non-Party radicalism for its independence. Covering I. J. Golden's *Precedent* (1931), a piece on the framing of the labor organizers Tom Mooney and Warren Billings, Sidney Ball fumed in *Workers Theatre* magazine that Golden "entirely neglects the treacherous role played by the AF of L, who assisted the bosses in railroading these militant leaders to jail."

The crippling organizational orthodoxy of the workers' theatre may be chalked up as a grievous loss not only to the culture, but to Broadway proper. Who knows what intriguing forms might not have developed there, given the often brilliant stage technique of the radical sketch, had its practitioners been willing to wrestle with an idea? Way back in the days of the muckrakers and the realistic social novel, Frank Norris outlined the need of naturalistic writers to overstate, enlarge as myth enlarges. Norris prescribed a superhuman energy to be dramatized in the clash of forces larger than the everyday in order to isolate the unseen agony of the everyday. This paradox of naturalism—fantasy seeking the realest truth—is just what such a work as *Newsboy* brought out. A just excitement welcomed the workers' theatre as theatre, but a just fear might well have doubted it as a medium of the people, for a stage of the free masses should not end up as an organ for Party dupes.

Even some full-length works that stood out in the non-commercial alternative of the workers' off-Broadway adhered to orders from the Comintern. The former expressionist-satirist and now eager Party-liner John Howard Lawson inaugurated the New Playwrights Theatre group with *Loud Speaker* (1927), an acrid lampoon of political reprobacy, personified in a candidate for governor of New York and backed up by Mordecai Gorelik's contentedly ugly set of steps and platforms. As in Lawson's *Processional* of two years before, a jazz combo aided the author's commentary on the tempo of American life, and a year after *Loud Speaker* Lawson dove deeper into jazz in *The International*, conceived for "jazz treatment with the dignified narrative strophe and antistrophe of Greek drama." Lawson, whatever his politics, did at least intend art of some kind, though leftist critics hated his "experimentalism" (i.e., unclear propaganda) and establishment critics couldn't grasp his wild gallimaufry of styles.

Shamefully, few analysts realized the significance of a "workers' theatre" exploding overnight in what is after all a culture designed to reflect the ambitions of us all. We *are* the masses, not to put too fine a reading on it; shouldn't this upsurge of workers' opinions have thrilled us?—talk about your folk plays! But no. Everyone immediately interpreted the movement, *used* it. Radicals held it responsible for Party palaver. Theatre people admired only its technical clarity. Moderates disliked its militancy—dainty Alexander Woollcott, first-nighter for the New York *World*, liked to call Lawson and his colleagues the "revolting playwrights." Possibly the only group that recognized the populist emergence in the workers' theatre was its audience, who were treated to a ticket-price scale far lower than that of the big houses along The Street. In rented halls or in the older auditoriums down around Fourteenth Street, abandoned when Broadway moved north, one paid thirty cents to $1.50 for radical theatre, half the cost for Kaufman and Hart or O'Neill, and the people seated near one might never have attended theatre before.

The workers found a new purpose for theatre: to dramatize social problems and urge solutions. Everyone was naive; everyone was bitter with experience. Everyone had ideals; everyone secretly believed that nothing could be done. Everyone had ambivalence—but not since the little theatres did the American stage have something huge and raw to develop. But the writing was *too* raw at first; luckily, some spokesmen emerged after 1930 with work of breadth and insight. George Sklar and Albert Maltz attacked the urban boodle machine in *Merry-Go-Round* (1932), basing their plot on a news item about a poor soul in Cleveland who witnessed a gangland slaying, got locked up as a material witness, and was found hanged in his cell, obviously a victim of the complicity between the authorities and the outlaws. Setting their play in New York, the authors incurred the wrath of Tammany Hall. Good notices in a downtown house encouraged *Merry-Go-Round*'s producers (two men, not a workers' group) to move the show to Broadway, but on the eve of reopening they found their theatre shuttered on an idiot technicality that could have closed—but didn't, of course—half the houses in town. It took the outrage of the press, the American Civil Liberties Union, the Dramatists' Guild, and front-line producers, plus a small fortune for trivial structural renovations on the part of the theatre owner, to get *Merry-Go-Round* a hearing.

Now comes a great breakthrough. The Theatre Union convened in 1932 on the energy of a variety of radical beliefs, on a hazy fiscal status, and on a manifesto "based on the interests and hopes of the great mass of working people." Scorning agitprop, the Theatre Union's executive board hoped to do what their predecessors had not done, create a *viable* theatre for the working class. What is viable? —the *question* of truth, not casehardened "socialist realism"; the justice of democracy as formulated in America, not the lie of totalitarian "paradise." As the Theatre Union produced it, the viable worked.

Sklar and Maltz wrote the Union's first outing, *Peace on Earth* (1933), on the raising of a college professor's activist consciousness during a workers' strike in protest of a sale of arms to foreign powers. With a clever sense of prophecy, the authors laid their scene a bit in the future, predicting what was to be the American government's solution to national Depression: war industry. Though Sklar and Maltz's protagonist grows into an activist of such righteous iconoclasm that he is framed on a murder charge and hanged, the authors pictured the danger of failing to dissent from mob action more than the safety in numbers. No one wants to end up like *Peace on Earth's* professor, awaiting execution for advertising one's anti-war principles. But, as the promoters of grisly projects like to say, you can't make an omelet without breaking eggs.

On the other hand, there is no such thing as a free lunch. *Peace on Earth* enjoyed a success, but one or even a few successes did not constitute a breakthrough in theatregoing. Wooing and maintaining a regular audience proved to be one of the most bothersome tasks of the social protest theatre in general, whether a "fancy" item by a name author in a big Broadway house or the less "attractive" presentations of the workers' theatre in their out-of-the-way little places. Broadway, except for the Theatre Guild's bulging subscription list, has always opted for the open-market sale, taking chances each time out. Workers' groups such as the Theatre Union hoped to stabilize a patronage by the season.

More easily hoped than done. When in 1930 the Theatre Guild produced a Soviet play on white imperialism, *Roar, China* (translated from the German from the Russian, and staged somewhat desperately with Chinese actors in Chinese parts who couldn't understand English), the radical Yiddish

newspaper *Die Freiheit* (The Freedom) offered to assume ticket sales for
a month's performances. But the Guild backed off, willing to mount propaganda but not to address it directly to an impressionable public. On the other
hand, the aforementioned workers' organization The New Playwrights Theatre culled their regulars from any and all sources, from the Ukrainian
Window Washers (workers but non-English-speaking) to the Doctors' Wives
(English-speaking but not workers).

The Theatre Union went about collecting an audience with a will. They
sent speakers around town to read from scripts, they stuffed mailboxes with
leaflets, and they managed to find works worth doing as theatre, something
not all their radical fellows could say for themselves. *Peace on Earth* gave
them some uneasy but tangible momentum in the public notice; their second
production, *Stevedore* (1934), put them over.

Stevedore, originally entitled *Wharf Nigger* and *On the Wharf*, was the
work of Paul Peters. Pitched in black vernacular to cover life on the docks
of New Orleans, it reflected labor's shifting position on the separation of the
American races, collating the tragic tale of a black framed on a rape charge
(to silence his racial and political militancy) with a what-is-to-be-done proposition: unity of all workers, black and white as comrades. Peters' script
looking a bit uneven, George Sklar polished it with him, and the result won
praise from radical critics as well as the mainline reviewers. Workers flocked
to *Stevedore* along with the more perennial theatregoers of The Street. Word
of mouth reached everyone in town: a good show. Thus is an audience
created.

Some analysts of the time held that *Stevedore*'s concluding scene, an
exhilaratingly nick-of-time "popular front" of white and black dockworkers
fighting off a white lynch mob, was mere melodramatic device. But that is
what melodrama does; it is why we single out certain plays as melodrama—
not to demote them necessarily, but to define their tone. *The Shanghai
Gesture* is demoted melodrama, lusty and shallow for the sake of cardboard
thrills. *Gods of the Lightning*, however, is melodrama for a purpose, to com-
press in non-poetic terms a set of urgencies that in life would take years to
accumulate. Novels and movies do this all the time; why not the stage, too?
As Frank Norris suggested, social realism must borrow from surrealism simply
to encompass its subject, which is the conflict not of individuals but of a
mass. That's big stuff: you've got to talk it big.

Along with certain Broadway-bound endeavors to be discussed shortly,
the Theatre Union made the breakthrough denied other workers' groups
because it put theatre ahead of propaganda. Especially given the Communist

eagerness to juice its propaganda machine on the currents of American racism, it seems strange that the Party's opinion makers did not attack *Stevedore* for its lack of Bolshevik plugola. Perhaps the general excitement about a hit show that blasted racism and played with an integrated cast to an integrated audience (an important novelty—black theatregoers tended to get shunted to the balcony) disarmed them. There were some holdouts. John Howard Lawson, recovering from his own oversight in experimenting with art-movement formalism in the 1920s, led the doubters: "It is absurd," he wrote some months after *Stevedore* opened, "for any writer to attempt to write about the class struggle in *general* terms. The Communist Party is playing a definite role in every strike, in every activity of the working class."

Never mind Lawson; his work had begun to rot after *Roger Bloomer* and *Processional*, anyway. The point here is that our American theatre has elaborated its structure as a useful art, specifically as a communicative link between the too easily disinherited working class and the poets, storytellers, moralists—choose your word—of the day. Until certain Broadway playwrights and the workers' theatre forced the situation to give, a kind of pop bottleneck had stopped up the flow of ideas. When Charles Frohman declared that "hits are made by the masses, not the classes," his masses were not *the* masses, but the mass of middle-class theatregoers. Lower than that on the socioeconomic scale Frohman did not care to look.

Such scattered but related innovations as Anderson and Hickerson's subversive documentary, *Gods of the Lightning*, the amateur professionalism of the workers' sketches, and the Theatre Union's ability to secure a public all helped consolidate the populist dialogue. So far, only one variable has ruled on them all—the good show. Theatre is theatre; and fear and excitement are part of it. The reason for the latter should be clear now, in the discovery that the stage is as much a communications medium as a beauty business, that alternatives to consumerism are available to anyone who can produce one. As for the fear, theatre is a powerful engine for social protest, bigger than it looks; one might well fear. Consider *Dimitroff* (1934), a short piece of agitprop by Elia Kazan and Art Smith designed to actuate protest on behalf of Ernst Thälmann and Ernst Torgler, two of the many German Communists arrested in connection with the Reichstag Fire of 1933. *Dimitroff* turned a corner for American drama in its hysterical finale, a canny elicitation of the mindless mass will. Addressing the audience, one of the characters turns his call for concerted action into a series of screams and responses promoted by plants in the house:

DIMITROFF: We must fight fascism with undiminished strength and courage! We must free our comrades! Free all class war prisoners!!!
AUDIENCE: Free all class war prisoners!!!
DIMITROFF: Free Torgler!!
AUDIENCE: Free Torgler!!
DIMITROFF: Free Thälmann!!
AUDIENCE: Free Thälmann!!

By far the most popular direction given by the militant theatre was "Strike!," which brings us to the movement's sole entry in the canon of classics, Clifford Odets' *Waiting for Lefty* (1935). One appreciates the sense of time and place in the tale that has Odets pounding out the script in one twenty-four-hour session under lock and key in some hotel room—*Waiting for Lefty* has just that air of *now before the desperation passes!* Everything about it belongs to the movement as it was, and its steadily gathered snowball of rage and recognition completes the voyage of this second off-Broadway of social protest so exactly that the era might have ended with this one work, as if to say, If this doesn't do it, nothing will. But *Lefty* did as much as any one work could have done for a genre that hangs on the outskirts of American theatre, the genre in which story and character are less important than theme. Americans want their themes to slip in *through* story and character, like a magic. Still, the portable *Lefty* was popular, not only at workers' meetings, but on Broadway, where it played on double-bills with Odets' *Till the Day I Die* and *Awake and Sing!*.

A taut one-act, *Waiting for Lefty* does not court but rather insults realism; its real is truer than life, more direct, meaner. Wherever it is played, the auditorium is the set: a meeting of a cabdrivers' union in a hired hall. We, the public, are the drivers. Thugs menace us in the aisles, for the union administration is as crooked as crooked gets, and Fatt, our evil president (in league with the bosses), addresses us in hopes of discouraging a projected strike. A special strike panel, the good guys, have called us here to vote; their chairman, Lefty, is inexplicably late. As we wait for him, we hear from the five other members of the panel.

This is the play part. As each of the five rises to speak, the lights dim down to a spot onstage and the members' separate moments of epiphany are enacted, events leading up to the strike vote. An actor, forced to hack a cab out of unemployment, gets the business from a callous producer. A Jewish doctor loses his job to hospital politics and anti-Semitism. A lab assistant goes under for refusing to take part in poison gas experiments. A tender young couple are parted by his low salary. A husband will lose his wife unless he reclaims his self-respect—"get wise," she tells him, "get your buddies together."

The tension generated by the actors to an obviously sympathetic house grew to immense proportions as the play proceeded on its premiere performance, a Sunday evening skit night put on by the League of Workers' Theatres. Gasps of belief crackled in the air. The connection between what the actors were doing and what the movement needed in the way of self-expression so energized the audience that we thought ourselves let in on the definitive realism possible in art. Drama, they were saying, is a weapon.

Like Godot, Lefty never shows up. Finally, we learn that he has been murdered, and the vote is demanded: "Christ, cut us up in little pieces," cries one of the drivers. "We'll die for what is right!, put fruit trees where our ashes are!" And he asks us, "Well, what's the answer?"

And on the show's legendary opening night, we rose in a body and hurled ourselves at that realism, to be one with it: "Strike!"

"Louder!"

We screamed, "Strike!"

And everyone on stage called "Again!" and we shouted it again, again, again, the way a mob shouts, off its head for war. The Nazis manipulated crowds into humanoid atavism in exactly this way at their rallies.

George S. Kaufman, Maxwell Anderson, Philip Barry, George Sklar and Albert Maltz, Clifford Odets, set the tempos for reform, each in his way. All of them entertained, and most of them have a lot in common. Plays as separately derived as Barry's *Hotel Universe* and Odets' *Waiting for Lefty* draw on aspects of art movement procedure that, in the 1920s, were considered inseparable, Freudian psychodrama (*Universe*) and spotlit anti-realistic naturalism (*Lefty*). How different was Broadway reform from worker reform? Were Broadway's semi-satirists so different from the writers of the workers' skits? Obviously, two very different audiences separate them (also, Broadway's was already mustered, whereas the workers had to find one), as does the profit motive (though the workers were working for the profit of power) and the different views on organization (Broadway's, unions and all, is tolerably loose; the workers were completely controlled by the Party). But more: the workers experimented with a ferocious performing style that frightened Broadway. In a way, the major difference between Broadway and the workers lies not in reform but in aesthetics. Though the workers approached their subjects from too general a position ever to capture a broad public, some of their dynamics for presentation stand as the most rigorous—

even beautiful—in our history. They were unique in mime, in choral dialogue, in neo-Classical "distancing." True, they thought themselves politicians, not artists. Art, to them, was only a means. Yet astute commentators, while respecting the workers' opinion about themselves, could not help but describe them in art-oriented similes. In 1931, the director of Vassar's Experimental Theatre, Hallie Flanagan, assessed the workers' theatre movement for *Theatre Arts* magazine:

> Unlike any art form existing in America today, the workers' theatres intend to shape the life of the country, socially, politically, and industrially. They intend to remake a social structure without the help of money—and this ambition alone invests the undertaking with a certain Marlowesque madness.

A Marlowesque madness—*just* the phrase. Keep your ears on those words; some seven or eight years hence, we'll wish that Flanagan had never uttered them.

9

"Ah, But Are They Her Own?"
The 1930s

THERE IS A PLAYWRIGHTS' THEATRE, a director's theatre, and an art theatre. The first, obviously, puts the greatest importance on text, the second on the concept and stylistic thrust of the production, and the last on organic collaboration, not only from theatre people, but from the audience as well, intent on the unfolding of art *in toto*. Broadway prefers the playwrights' theatre brought to life by scrupulously respectful directors and reasonably special performers—José Quintero's O'Neill, for instance. Broadway admires the directors' theatre, but only for limited-run events, such as a tour from abroad or in so-called "repertory"—Peter Brook's *A Midsummer Night's Dream* with the Royal Shakespeare Company or Andrei Serban's *The Cherry Orchard* at Lincoln Center. The art theatre is rare; it combines the integrity of the one with the individuality of the other. To an extent, the best of Broadway in the 1920s and 1930s was art theatre—and that mainly because the superstar director had not yet emerged in the popular consciousness and could not therefore call too much attention to himself.

On one level, however, it is all an actors' theatre; what do actors want? In 1928 and 1929, the chaotic implementation of the talkie drew hundreds of theatre actors to the sound stages. (Many of these were located not in Hollywood but in the New York suburbs, to allow performers to pursue stage and movie careers at once.) By 1930 and thereafter, acting broke up into two very separate sectors: separate economically (movies paid better), culturally (movies lacked elite cachet), professionally (stage acting demands more talent but drains less time), and personally (stage actors were free to plan their careers; film actors answered to the studio heads). Interestingly, newcomers in either sector had to launch themselves on the stage, for there was no other method of auditioning for Hollywood.

Once one arrived, however, those faithful to theatre and those who preferred cinema went their separate ways, and gave their respective publics two different ways of supporting them. Theatregoers were at once less gaga over and more personally liable to their favorites, because Broadway's use of mythmaking PR was not as extensive as Hollywood's. The stage actor might play parts so different that no mythic persona could ever be imagined for him or her; conversely, one's personal magnetism could be very telling. One moved slowly on Broadway; one earned praise. After years of light comedy, clearly out of her depth doing Shaw's Cleopatra as a Bedouin Zelda Fitzgerald in 1925, Helen Hayes found herself in serious drama, and began to gather a following when she played the heroine of Maxwell Anderson's *Mary of Scotland* (1933). No one was ready for the fire Hayes threw off in the confrontation scene for Mary and Elizabeth I, which Anderson couldn't resist writing, though the two women never met in life. Hayes snatched the scene for Mary and Scotland, seething with phoney humility, then affronted, then wild. "You have no heir!" she hissed. "A devil has no children." It was all Helen Mencken's Elizabeth could do just to stay alive.

Underheight for Mary, Hayes was just the size for England's most persistent monarch in a British script (banned in England, however), Laurence Housman's episodic but cumulatively intriguing *Victoria Regina* (1935), arguably Hayes' greatest part. From 1837 to 1897, she limned the changes in "Vicky's" life, getting dumpier in each scene till dental props, padding, and a wheelchair turned her into a pile of living dishrag in the final scene. Everyone commented on the transformation, but it was really Hayes' acting that brought it off.

Happy Hayes. Her marriage to Charles MacArthur at the time of his esteem as the co-author of *The Front Page* and their cheery home life in Nyack filled out the profile of the "nice woman under the greasepaint." It suited her and the roles she played. Hayes became one of the best-liked of her profession—not as adored as glamorous Ina Claire, nor as scrutinized as seductive Lynn Fontanne, but loved. Brooks Atkinson has pointed out that her Lucy Andree Ransdell (=Lyubof Andryeyevna Ranyefsky) in Joshua Logan's universally reproached Deep-South version of *The Cherry Orchard* as *The Wisteria Trees* in 1950 was supported by a public sympathetic to Hayes' loss of a daughter to poliomyelitis. It was a vote of confidence they would have made also for Katharine Cornell or Lillian Gish, but not perhaps for Tallulah Bankhead, Katharine Hepburn, and other "independent" women. The public needs to be kind, but it demands its compromises. Eva Le Gallienne, for one example, never consolidated a broad following because of her constant preference for classic repertory; a lot of theatregoers seldom if ever saw her.

In the 1930s, actors as drawing cards had more allure than the most distinguished playwrights or directors, excluding O'Neill. In 1937, for instance, one went to see Walter Huston's Othello, not to see *Othello* per se. Huston's carefully passionless reading of the role, however, confused those who had admired his lanky, informal (i.e., American) Dodsworth in the stage adaptation of Sinclair Lewis' novel three years before. The critics, in particular, were not amused. Goaded by adjectives like "colorless" and "impotent," Huston played one of the last evenings of the run in full cry. "I went forth," he later recalled, "like a madman. I hammed the part within an inch of burlesque; I ate all the scenery I had time and digestion for; I frightened the other actors, none of whom knew I had changed my characterization. And upon my soul the audience seemed to enjoy it." But it was a terrible performance, as terrible as Brian Aherne's swaggering romantic hero of an Iago was excellent (that is, given director and designer Robert Edmond Jones' unorthodox interpretation of the play). But then Aherne would have been awful in something like *Dodsworth*, which is most likely why he was best known as Robert Browning opposite Cornell's Elizabeth Barrett in *The Barrets of Wimpole Street*, in which the two of them toured around for eons.

Huston wasn't the only reputable actor to fail in one of the big roles. In 1936, Leslie Howard played Hamlet competitively with John Gielgud; the free-falling urbanity that had served Howard so well in the romantic comedies *Berkeley Square* (period) and *The Animal Kingdom* (modern-dress) does not equip a Hamlet. Furthermore, the Howard *Hamlet* production was underpowered in general, while the vivid Gielgud rendering, staged by Guthrie McClintic, boasted Lillian Gish's ethereally screwy Ophelia and Judith Anderson's Gertrude. Howard's *Hamlet* gave way after 39 performances; Gielgud smashed precedent with 132.

Technique was now a problem: if you didn't have it. Theatre had grown so diversely nuanced since the days when there were universally distinct styles for 1. tragedy, 2. melodrama, 3. drawing-room comedy, and 4. farce that actors who would have treaded water nicely in 1900 were drowning by 1930. Worse yet, naturalistic drama was being written—and produced—before acting teachers had developed an approach to it. Not till the formation of the Group Theatre in 1931 did the American acting ranks develop a practical theory—an ideology, really—on the performance of realistic drama.

Ironically, the least respectable genre was the one that had naturalism down first, the musical. But the natural style of Fred Astaire, William Gaxton, Bert Lahr, Bobby Clark, Marilyn Miller, Ethel Merman, and others such consisted almost entirely of projecting one's own personality, quite casually, through lines, songs, and dances that had been tailored to one's specific talents. There were no big roles in which to test oneself against the great portrayals of the past, for musical revivals tended to be second-rate affairs mounted mainly for provincial tours "direct from Broadway." True, the operetta, naturalistic only in its subsidiary comic characters, tended to expose singers' poor acting ability in the spoken scenes. But then, until *Show Boat*, operetta was meant and regarded as a kind of stunt in the first place, a dream that flew on musical wings—and the directness of *Show Boat*'s book scenes rendered the stunt obsolete. That seminal masterpiece catalyzed the reintegration of the musical as an organic entity, and by the 1940s most of the better shows no longer served as vehicles for the special qualities of a dancer like Astaire, a romancer like Gaxton, or a clown like Lahr or Clark. Specialists began to give way to singing actors who possibly danced, though as it happened the great Merman unexpectedly turned into exactly that for one of the better shows of the 1950s, *Gypsy*.

A theatre history must take show business into account, always. Theatre is never just "text"— but conversely show biz is more than manipulations of the celebrity image. When the great revolution in American theatre occurred in the 1920s, it did, it's true, call up a *literature* for the stage. O'Neill surfaced then, and Anderson, Barry, Behrman, Sherwood, Sturges, Wilder, and Odets came soon after. A script is a play. But *theatre*, the whole idea of drama, is a production—words, actors, a staging concept, a rhythm, a version, style. The 1920s collated these elements; every facet of creation and recreation now depended on all other facets. Thus, O'Neill could survey the general level of American acting in that decade and assess it as the weak link in the chain he was helping to forge, along with such others as Robert Edmond Jones and Lee Simonson (conceptual decor), Philip Moeller (the "whole idea" director), and the Theatre Guild (a producing organization responsive to new technique). "I feel very strongly about the matter of acting in this country," said O'Neill, "and in my opinion, it is impossible to carry on much further until the actors catch up."

Playwrights needed actors; actors needed playwrights. And both, often to their misfortune, needed directors. Today, the director is the overlord of Important Theatre, and his assaults on Chekhof, Shakespeare, Aeschylus, are what brings an audience into The Theatre. The 1920s is when he first came to power. Nothing like the unaffected, chivalrous George S. Kaufman nor the crotchety William Brady (who muttered to himself throughout run-throughs and saw directing as the business of keeping the actors from falling off the edge of the stage), unlike even the extreme Belasco, who wandered through life in a murderous trance but at least never spoke of subtexts or "emotional spaces"—unlike anything known before, these Svengalis sat their rehearsal desks like emperors, creating personal visions of *Uncle Vanya* and *Peer Gynt*. Philip Moeller, one of the Theatre Guild's busiest directors, was such a one. He fought bitterly with people like the Lunts, who knew their stuff and were not easily bullied—it has often been suggested that Moeller's failure as a playwright contributed to his willingness to embellish the scripts he staged. Out of town in Boston with S. N. Behrman's *Meteor* (1929), a second-rate play about a young businessman obsessed with power, Moeller rode the Lunts, sneered at Behrman, and dramatized himself with grouchings and hysteria. At one point both he and Behrman stomped out of the theatre with a third act not yet fully rewritten. Lunt turned to Guild manager Theresa Helburn. "We can't play tonight," he told her. "This play doesn't have an ending."

Artistic to the core, Helburn observed that the house was sold out, and they were too playing, so Lunt decided to extemporize a final speech, warning the stage manager to ring down the curtain when he got to a certain word. And what word would that be? Lunt thought for a moment. "Schlemiel," he answered. It must have been on his mind.

One of the things that keeps theatre nimble is the spontaneity of its collaborative pacts. While a big-name star holds the power in one production, a producer or director or author in another, in still others it is not agreed beforehand that everyone in the production knows (and assents as to) who holds the power. Within such ambiguity, a schlemiel may make trouble. Recently, a character in the musical *A Chorus Line* could recall a high school acting class in which the teacher led improvisational exercises which included such studies as imitating an ice-cream cone (viz., melting); the audience, few of whom had ever seen an acting class in operation, could smile—we know how wild that world can get. But, decades ago, directors and their methods were not so familiar even to many actors, and every so often somebody would balk. In 1937, the relentless Philip Moeller inaugurated rehearsals for Ben Hecht's *To Quito and Back* with one of his representational improvisations. He told Joseph Buloff, who was playing a South American revolutionary, that he was a bassoon. Leslie Banks, Moeller announced, was a clarinet. And Sylvia Sidney was on oboe. "Nuts," replied Sidney, or some word to that effect. "I'm just a girl in love with a man."

Only the superstar could challenge the director successfully, then and now. Stars might walk through a play of no account written, for the dismal fun of it, expressly for them; they might share the honors with a writer of merit; they might revive an old favorite or invest themselves in the pomp of the classic. But the star turn remained the center of Broadway-as-business. Until the very late nineteenth century, when the industry expanded so widely that there were more hit plays than there were prominent actors, virtually everything was a star vehicle. But the star system broke down at last, partly because playwrighting improved (and outstripped the limitations of the less gifted celebrities, creating gaps that could be filled by non-stars), partly because acting in general became more detailed and textually alert (and thus robbed the lazier personalities of their control), and partly because the dedication of actors like Mrs. Fiske kept throwing attention on theatre as (written) work of art. By the 1920s, the actors' theatre had accommodated itself to the playwrights' theatre.

Yet even as late as the 1930s, a theatre season was planned mainly around who was available to play the parts. Thousands of plays have come and gone, some of them for very profitable stays, having been written, produced, and acted by no one known. But these are the flukes, the *Abie's Irish Roses* and *Tobacco Roads*. One seldom read about them in the gala magazine pieces about what was promised for Broadway in the coming season; and when they closed, the theatre community felt almost glad to see them go.

Because they were not Big—not even the two cited above, still the second and third longest-running non-musical plays in Broadway history. The Big plans were laid by producers, theatre owners, important authors, and stars in a thousand informal conferences: an actor was free, and a script was found to contain him.

The exemplary stars of the early middle twentieth century were Alfred Lunt and Lynn Fontanne. Along with Tallulah Bankhead, the three Barrymores, and very few others, the Lunts upheld the "legend" aspect of stage acting; each season's plans invariably revolved around what the Lunts would be up to—and it was a given that whatever they played would last out the season and then take to the road. Helen Hayes and Katharine Cornell had too much dignity to become legendary, Ruth Gordon was too wonderfully informal, Katharine Hepburn too often in Hollywood, Eva Le Gallienne too inaccessible in her Ibsen. It was the Lunts that legend loved, and they knew it; early on, they realized that with his insatiable versatility and her spiced glamor, the pair of them would outsum their separate parts. Once their careers got going in the late 1920s, they worked only as a duo.

Short memories recall their idling in trifling sex comedies; actually, they played everything from farce to tragedy. Lunt was Trigorin to Fontanne's Irina in a Theatre Guild *Sea Gull*, Essex to her Bess in Anderson's verse play *Elizabeth the Queen*, and it might be that the oddly kiltered seriocomic tone that made their boudoir fun so special equally enlivened their rhythm for drama, as when they dovetailed their lines as if speaking a medley—a raffish effect in comedy, an added tension in drama. Trifling comedies? The Lunts even commissioned William Saroyan to write them one of his freeform fantasies; too bad Saroyan never came through. Years later, Lunt complained that he and Lynn were too seldom given the chance to do something other than seduce each other: "Why didn't Elia Kazan give us a crack at *Death of a Salesman*?" he asked. "Lynn and I would be as excited to play in one of these theatre-of-the-absurd plays as we were excited when we joined the Theatre Guild, only they called it 'art theatre' then."

The Lunts provided a kind of rallying point for theatre people in that they didn't abandon the stage for Hollywood at a time when virtually anyone who was asked to did so. They made only one film after sound came in, *The Guardsman** (and that based on their stage production), later turning down MGM's contract offer of just under a million dollars at the depth of the Depression. The Lunts were heroes: theatre people were ultra-sensitive about Hollywood, most obviously because of the economic impact ("Will the Screen Kill the Stage?"). The theatre community—thespians, journalists, and hangers-on—insisted that an actor sold out by going to Hollywood and then proceeded to lose all his talent in the preposterous cosmetics of making film. For proof, they would point to the often embarrassing performances movie actors would give when they returned to Broadway.

Some, like Clark Gable, Joan Crawford, and Cary Grant, never looked back at Broadway once they were discovered. Others, such as Bette Davis and Spencer Tracy, returned rarely. Some, however—Margaret Sullavan and Katharine Hepburn, for instance—made the Broadway sortie a regular event, with a polish that curdled the theory about Hollywood's ruining talent. In *The Royal Family*, Kaufman and Ferber took it for granted that their John Barrymore likeness can work in films for the high salaries while remaining

---

* They also contributed a silly cameo bit to *Stage Door Canteen* in 1943.

loyal in heart to the stage. (The real-life John Barrymore upended this perspective by making a seedy comeback on Broadway in *My Dear Children* [1940], larding a foolish script with reckless ad libs and pretty much playing himself, not well.)

Part of *The Royal Family*'s charm was its view of the nation's leading acting family as a bunch of children, dedicated but irresponsible. A decade later, Kaufman and Ferber changed their minds somewhat and wrote *Stage Door* (1936) to focus on the dedication, using an actresses' boarding house in New York as their scene and an idealistic ingenue as their protagonist. All the troubles known to unknown actresses were invoked—the discouraging rounds of producers' offices, the daring waylaying of a producer with résumé fixed, the grim waiting for a call as one's money runs out, the job that folds in a week, and especially the temptation of a screen career. One of *Stage Door*'s characters yields to that "temptation"—actually, it is what she wants in the first place. Yet at the play's end, her New York comeback is a disaster: Hollywood has stripped her of whatever acting potential she had. At the last minute, her part is handed to *Stage Door*'s heroine, who, despite her trying apprenticeship, had never broken faith with the stage.

The odd thing was that the heroine was played by Margaret Sullavan, herself returning to Broadway after four years on the Coast. Sullavan had not squandered her gifts in cinema; if anything, she was even more of a joy now than in her several mediocre roles on Broadway in the early 1930s (including taking over the ingenue role in *Dinner at Eight*) before she established her reputation. It gave everyone in New York who hated (and needed) Hollywood something to think about. Even odder was the transformation of *Stage Door* from a third-rate play into a first-rate movie (for Katharine Hepburn, Ginger Rogers, Eve Arden, Ann Miller, Lucille Ball, and others such) with bitchy dialogue that caught the energy of making it as the play never did. Hollywood may have been troublesome to New York, but it had certain qualities that no reasonable critic could deny.

Hepburn, too, had her Broadway comebacks, one of them a crucial one: *The Philadelphia Story* (1939). Her cinema moon had been waning badly, so she got Philip Barry to compose a smashing Broadway comedy around her considerable gifts—she must wear this play like ermine. And did. As the socialite divorcée engaged to Mr. Wrong, flirting with a reporter, but always loving her former husband, Hepburn was the top. Some critics scoffed, but *The Philadelphia Story* delighted the public. Such a treat as this, lightly oddball in the very heyday of madcap society comedy, would be just what Hollywood needed; and Hepburn made certain that she would play the lead by picking up the option on film rights for the play. It proved one of her most triumphant Hollywood parts.

The New York comeback was less common than the Hollywood exodus in the first place. Everyone, it seems, got started on The Street. Clark Gable won his Hollywood call for *Love, Honor and Betray* (1930); Henry Fonda for the first of the *New Faces* revues (1934); Barbara Stanwyck for a wildly popular backstage comedy, *Burlesque* (1927); Melvyn Douglas for the last Belasco production, *Tonight or Never* (1930), in which he met his real-life wife, Helen Gahagan; James Cagney and Joan Blondell both for *Penny Arcade* (1930); Joan Crawford, still in the kickline then, for another revue, *The Passing Show of 1924*; Bette Davis for *Solid South* (1930); Irene Dunne for her Magnolia in the first national tour of *Show Boat*; Miriam Hopkins for an unsuccessfully transnational mounting of Arthur Schnitzler's parochially Viennese *Anatol* (1931); Edward G. Robinson for *Banco* (1922), a silly evening of sex and gambling that even Alfred Lunt could not save; Robert Montgomery for his characteristic smoothy juvenile in *Possession* (1928); even the Marx Brothers, for a supremely chaotic musical, *Animal Crackers* (1928).

This was a period of immense expansion in Hollywood. How better to expand than by trawling the stage for adaptable star quality? But what was such quality made of? We are told that the camera "makes love" to certain people and rejects others, and that no one can tell beforehand how an actor will project (thus the customary screen test). Yet the camera developed a sometimes amazingly cosmopolitan taste, and some actors one might have thought least likely to adapt not only made the transition but made the camera their weapon—Paul Muni, for instance, admittedly under a pile of makeup in his many historical roles. Orson Welles, to pick another instance, was surely everything that Hollywood thought it didn't need when he sur-faced in the mid-1930s, unorthodox both as actor and producer—in 1937 he staged *Julius Caesar*, brilliantly, to parallel fascism in a menacing modern-dress production and an almost conversational delivery of the poetry, mean-while playing a diffident, bewildered Brutus out of sync with tradition. This and other Welles' activities were of course the talk of The Street, but could the movies use such a talent? Didn't Hollywood want "less" than Broadway; weren't movies still in that stage of exclusive popular appeasement that the theatre had shucked out of in the 1920s? What was "less" or "more" in acting? Welles' Tybalt in Katharine Cornell's *Romeo and Juliet* in 1934 went largely unnoticed except by theatre people. Brooks Atkinson mentioned it among "minor parts played with something better than minor authority";

can that have been all it was? John Houseman's first impression reveals more: "a monstrous boy—flat-footed and graceless, yet swift and agile; soft as jelly one moment and uncoiled the next." It could only have happened in the very beginning of his career, but Welles was simply outnumbered by star turns—Cornell's Juliet, Edith Evans' Nurse, Brian Aherne's Mercutio, and possibly Basil Rathbone's Romeo as well, over the hill for the ardent teen-ager, but Cornell was no flapper by then, either (and of course veteran Juliets, Cleopatras, Romeos, and Hamlets were a convention of the old, pre-Method theatre). Part of what a star is is what pollsters call "recognition," the final confirmation of a person's reach as character—judged not by talent or experience, but by fame itself. Welles didn't really have it till he released *Citizen Kane* in 1941—and even this fame was too individual, too radical, for Hollywood to admire.

Did Hollywood want fame as opposed to technique? Many film actors lacked the latter. But so did many stage actors. Anyway, what is technique? Lynn Fontanne once defined it as "saying things with truth a little louder than in a room and not bumping into people." Rubbish—and she knew it. No actress had more technique than Fontanne, who would time her pauses, angle her stares, shape an entire act with a precision worked up in many hours of rehearsal . . . who would even, once satisfied with these details in performance, vary them just that much to accord with the relationship made anew and differently with each audience. A certain house met a certain Fontanne.

Technique is an actor's capacity for control—the voice, the body, timing, movement. One's technique is not entirely unrelated to one's instincts but, importantly, not entirely dependent on them. Nor does technique fluctuate according to such natural endowments as looks, vocal tone, and so on. It is learned and developed.

It is also not necessary for popular success, nor a guarantee against popular distaste. Some of the most technically accomplished actors of this era—Osgood Perkins, Burgess Meredith, Helen Westley, for instance—never won much of a following. Hollywood, itself, was technique—or, rather, a collection of techniques, none of which the actor himself controlled. Cinema-tography, coaching, lighting—these were the techniques for manifestation in the movies, applied externally. But all the wizardry in Hollywood wasn't *live*.

This, Broadway wanted: something famous in the flesh. There is no denying the three-dimensional luster of a first-rate production of a first-rate play, as with the legendary *Uncle Vanya* that Jed Harris staged in 1930 with Lillian Gish, Osgood Perkins, and Walter Connolly. Perhaps this *Uncle*

Vanya has a musty sound today, telling of an alleged "grand old Broadway" that most theatregoers scarcely remember or miss. It was old-fashioned, "straight" Chekhof, done without reference to avant-garde acting technique or Moscow Art style (though the Russians' *Cherry Orchard* and *Three Sisters* remained a vivid study from their visit seven years earlier). On the other hand, let's not underestimate the grand old style. Gish's extraordinary performances in the silent films *The Wind* and *La Bohème*, still shown today, attest to an irreplaceable gift, one so startling that Gish had to be forced out of film work when sound came in and the bold, florid acting that took active part in rather than simply inhabited stories was retired for talky naturalism. Gish and her colleagues living this *Uncle Vanya* was something one couldn't find at the movies, and it stood high in the memories of a generation.

On the other hand, there were many regular theatregoers who wouldn't have bothered with an *Uncle Vanya* unless it were cast with stars on the order of Julie Christie, George C. Scott, and Nicol Williamson (as it was in 1973 at the Circle in the Square's uptown theatre under Mike Nichols' direction). To them, "live" meant not the quick rapport of work, presentation, and reception but the treat of watching a celebrity from close up. Vaudeville found a place for a ranking name, regardless of its qualifications as talent. Daredevils, divorcées, aquitted murderesses, and other geeks of the media midway would turn up on stages and be gawked at; people love to look. The theatre, too, showed its names off wherever possible. That, on the basest level, Broadway did have that Hollywood never had. Technique aside, Broadway was live.

All sorts of people fell into theatre who had no business being there. Perhaps the most extreme example of this practice is that of Alexander Woollcott, the actor. Best recalled today for his personality rather than his gifts, he was elfin loyalty to some, adolescent shrillness to others. Onstage, he was immortalized as Sheridan Whiteside in the Kaufman-Hart farce, *The Man Who Came to Dinner* (1939), in which Monty Wooley played a Woollcott who suffers a minor injury on a midwestern family's front stoop and stays on in a wheelchair to turn the household into a war zone of insults and riot. That was Woollcott the celebrity, fitting neatly into a semi-satire, and of course there was Woollcott the theatre critic, running up Pickwickian reviews for the New York *Times* in the early 1920s which were notorious for their fealty to his personal favorites. (Woollcott could be very funny, though, as in this capsule notice: "*Number Seven* opened last night. It was misnamed by five.") The peak of Woollcott's career of pouting and preening, however, was marked by his rather incredible transformation into Woollcott the actor. There were two Broadway roles, traced on Woollcott by S.N. Behrman, in *Brief Moment* (1931) and *Wine of Choice* (1938), plus a west coast tour of *The Man Who Came to Dinner*. Woollcott playing Whiteside is like Candida playing Katharine Cornell.

In *Brief Moment* (mentioned earlier as the play about the Pygmalion marriage of a nightclub singer and a drifting millionaire), Woollcott played Harold "Siggy" Sigrift, a miniature of himself, lolling on sofas and making moues:

> SIGRIFT: Let me tell you something about vitality, my chuck. It's fatiguing to live with. I lived with a girl once who had vitality. She wore me out. Nowadays I go in for languor.
> RODERICK: That's why you're so trim and athletic looking.
> SIGRIFT: What is this mania for flat stomachs, anyway? I think they're insipid.

Nominally, *Brief Moment* belonged to the playboy and his showgirl, but the show was really there for Woollcott. He was as rotten an actor as ever entered to a public's applause, but his job in *Brief Moment* was not to act but to be exhibited. After the play opened, on a free Sunday, Woollcott chanced to attend a benefit performance of the latest Lunt-Fontanne frolic, *Reunion in Vienna*, and decided that the Lunts' throwaway approach to certain lines held the secret of comic delivery. Back onstage in *Brief Moment*, Woollcott happily threw away his entire part; his colleagues a few feet from him couldn't hear their cues. The audience must have thought that he was doing his role in charades.

Social comedy in the hands of Behrman and his colleagues had developed remarkably from its antecedent in the days of Clyde Fitch and *The New York Idea*, but the tenets of pop held to a market ethic, and Woollcott's stints in *Brief Moment* and the more fully Woollcotted *Wine of Choice* were no less likely than the acting turns of boxers James Jeffries and James Corbett in earlier years, or the fruitless campaigns to get Charles Lindbergh before the movie cameras. Perhaps Charles Frohman was right about democracies preferring "the doer, not the deed"—it's actors they like, certain actors in particular, not something as inert as a script. Neither Behrman nor Barry, kings of social comedy, could fight it. So they joined it, tailoring parts to fit Hope Williams, Katharine Hepburn, the Lunts, and, as above, Woollcott. The playwrights' theatre had established itself and was dueling with the directors and *their* theatre, but on the most immediate level Broadway was still, as it had long been, a public's theatre, observing the strictures that bind any commercial event.

Actors were go-betweens, but they were also the whole show; and if Woollcott is a profane choice to close a chapter on theatre people circa 1935, that chapter mainly deals with the theatre's audience, lining up to see Woollcott! in a play! What does the public want? Theories on what draws them to the box offices do not hypothesize many people with a genuine hunger for theatre, driven by art. Actors, sometimes, *are* the play, plus a little technique. Thus, two matinee matrons overheard making up their minds about Lynn Fontanne at a performance of *There Shall Be No Night*— not, incidentally, one of the Lunts' excursions into boudoir chic:

"Her hands," says one of the women. "Oh, what lovely hands she has."

"Ah," replies the other. "But are they her own?"

10

"Griffith Used It. Lubitsch Used It. And Eisenstein's Coming Around to It" The 1930s

"IT IS NO USE TELLING THE TRUTH to people whose whole life is a lie," Lynn Fontanne announces in a Veronica Lake wig in Robert E. Sherwood's *Idiot's Delight*, in the middle of the 1930s. But Sherwood and his colleagues spent the decade telling the truth as they saw it, because, for once, the theatre was feeling and showing the times as much as any structure in the culture.

What the theatre felt most strongly was the economic crunch of the Depression: fewer productions each year, widespread unemployment (an old problem for theatre people, but worse now than ever), bankrupt producers, tight credit, shorter runs for the successful shows, half-filled and empty theatres. The season of 1929–30, most of which occurred after the Stock Market Crash, had seen the mounting of some 240 productions. (Most of the plans for that season had been drawn up, and the capital raised, in the preceding summer.) But in 1930–31, the tally dropped to 190, and continued to drop steadily thereafter, to a dazed total of 89 in 1938–39.

What the theatre showed most strongly was its new machinery for societal investigation. Drama was less zealously a business, a little more an initiation. A major feature of American drama in the 1930s was its interpretations and affirmations of the democratic system, in its obligations to Americans and the world. Sparked in part by the highly critical evaluations of the workers' theatre but perhaps even more by the initiative of professional theatre people, the profit-making stage addressed itself to politics.

Nothing proves this as powerfully as the 1930s careers of Philip Barry and S.N. Behrman. As we have seen, Barry made two valiant sorties into psychological grotesquerie at this time with *Hotel Universe* and *Here Come the Clowns*, but what is most striking about his defection from salon banter is the optimistic moral urgency about the latter play, its instruction "that all men should live and die fighting [the battle with evil]." Similarly, and more specifically with regard to the political situation in Europe, Behrman entered this battle in *Rain from Heaven* (1934). As so often before, the setting was a British house party; also true to Behrman's fashion (and light social comedy in general) was the casting of the vivacious Jane Cowl as the hostess, an attractive woman with strong liberal biases. Otherwise, Behrman was operating on new territory: to Cowl's graciously open house come refugees from totalitarianism—nazism and communism alike—and an American explorer and his industrialist brother, who plans to use the explorer's Lindbergh-like celebrity to prepare an Anglo-American fascist movement. Yes, there was dalliance, sentimental drollery, and delicate poesy (Cowl to her German lover: "I want my love to shield you from the odium of a graceless world") that would earn snickers from a modern audience if the play were revived in hip New York. But Behrman did make an effort to bend his work to a current—yet how universal—topic. He wanted to join the debate on what free men must do about tyranny. His answer: fight it. At curtain's fall, the Nazi's victim decides to leave Cowl to battle nazism at home; an unusually heroic ending for Behrman. In terms of comic composition, *Rain from Heaven* is vintage Behrman: for his second-act curtain, he has the Lindbergh likeness call the German refugee "a dirty Jew." Cowl is horrified, the German urbane ("This makes me feel right at home," he replies). Then Cowl gets off the zinger of the evening. "Please remember," she suavely tells the two anti-Semitic Americans, "Herr Willens is not only my lover, he is also my guest."

Some playwrights did not have to achieve politics, but were, so to speak, temperamentally born to it. Lillian Hellman enjoyed a sensational debut with *The Children's Hour* (1934), an indictment of the destructive power of slander. The play is often cited today as one of the early plays to deal with lesbianism, but unlike Edouard Bourdet's aforementioned *The Captive*, seen here in the previous decade, *The Children's Hour* is not about homosexuality, but about how uninformed public opinion too easily accepts an accusation as proof: about slander. A melodramatic fire in Hellman's script brought on a ferocious conclusion—one of the two libel victims comes to believe the accusation herself, and kills herself in despair. Brooks Atkinson, in his New York *Times* review, thought this a bit overdone, "a lamentable respect for the theatre" on the author's part. But that respect—too viciously subscribed to in Hellman's anti-capitalist view of a violent, successful strike in a midwestern industrial town, *Days to Come* (1936)—at length created one of the era's outstanding plays, *The Little Foxes* (1939). Pulling back from *Days to Come*'s sloganeering generalities, this one moved close up to individuals. Doubtless Hellman meant it as an arraignment of all capitalism, but it is a tribute to her talent as a dramatist that the piece works brilliantly as a study not in political system but human greed. No one, surely, could have been more aligned with the attitudes of the workers' theatre. Yet no play could be less like agitprop than this one.

The Little Foxes peered into a small town in the Deep South in 1900, when Ben and Oscar Hubbard and their sister Regina are scheming to build the district's first cotton mill—"to bring the machine to the cotton," brother Ben announces, "and not the cotton to the machine." The plan can make millionaires of them all, but each angles for a greater share, the intriguing eventually including thievery and even murder. Ultimately it is Regina who wins, getting a 75 percent share of the deal, but as Ben sees it, there's room for them all in the system. He explicates, in the work's one symbolic reference:

> The century's turning, the world is open. Open for people like you and me. Ready for us, waiting for us. After all, this is just the beginning. There are hundreds of Hubbards sitting in rooms just like this throughout the country. All their names aren't Hubbard, but they are all Hubbards and they will own this country some day. We'll get along.

The Little Foxes' success as theatre lies in Hellman's manipulation of evildoers and their doings; all the best parts in the play are written for scoundrels. Still, the script survives, as script, despite star players' most earnest attempts to turn it into their vehicle. The original production disciplined the usually erratic Tallulah Bankhead to the extent that her unbearably cold-blooded Regina was hailed as her debut as an actress of consistency rather than Personality, and the play proved itself all over again in Mike Nichols' 1967 Lincoln Center revival with Anne Bancroft, Margaret Leighton, and George C. Scott. Interestingly, there was bad feeling among the theatre community that Nichols had deliberately turned the work into a star show, though the public, less expert in such matters, enjoyed it for what it is, a superb melodrama about villainy.

That "we'll get along" in the speech quoted above, the smarmy rationale of the status quo, incited other writers less well remembered today than Hellman. In tone, they owed much to *Gods of the Lightning*—fury, "overwriting," violence, a quasi-documentary basis. An accountant might not call Sidney Howard's *Paths of Glory* (1935) "useful," for it lasted a mere three weeks on Broadway. However, this work (the source, along with Humphrey

Cobb's novel, of a cultist Stanley Kubrick film) exposed the evil genius of war as few works ever will—not the tragedy of death and destruction, but the self-serving righteousness of the military, never called to question before on American stages. Even an accountant might have cheered the runaway success of *The Last Mile* (1930), John Wexley's argument for prison reform that played as a gripping death-house thriller (and, incidentally, gave Spencer Tracy his ticket-of-leave for Hollywood as a brutal convict determined to escape). Wexley's bitter view of the proletarian condition, *Steel* (1931), did not go over, but his *They Shall Not Die* (1934) aroused all of Broadway for its fiery, partisan adaptation of the Scottsboro case.

Unlike the several Scottsboro sketches of the workers' theatre, which abstracted impressions of the case, *They Shall Not Die* set it naturalistically on stage, following the progress of the black men, framed on a rape charge in Alabama, from arrest to the first trial, just before the verdict (which is obviously going to be Guilty) is brought in. Utilizing something of what actually transpired in the real-life trial, Wexley thundered at the unequal system through his portrait of the defense attorney, played by Claude Rains:

> We're not finished. We're only beginning. I don't care how many times you try to kill this negro boy. I'll go . . . to the Supreme Court up in Washington and back here again, and to Washington and back again . . . if I have to do it in a wheelchair. And if I do nothing else in my life, I'll make the fair name of this state stink to high heaven with its lynch justice. . . . These boys, THEY SHALL NOT DIE!

Political awareness now led the public to look for a good theme as well as a good show, and authors called up the universal themes that serve any place and time, polishing off their opinions with prescriptions for specific action here and now. This was tricky to bring off, however, as most Americans were not comfortable with comprehensive prescriptions from their art on racism, war lordism, and the oppression of the working class. How appropriate were these themes to the ticket-buyers of Broadway and the public backing up Broadway's taste in road tours and film adaptations? Few Americans regarded themselves as racists; those who did didn't welcome lectures on its evils. Few Americans thought of warmaking as an American problem; we bailed out other nations' wars rather than started our own. (*Paths of Glory*, with its incompetent generals eager to spend lives in the line of "duty," would have been unthinkable if it had dealt with American generals. Novel, play, and film all turn on the brutality of the French military.) As for the problems of the working class, American audiences preferred a generalized populism to the strict Marxist separation of exploiters and exploited.

What were the successful universal themes of the decade? Human themes, as before. *Rain from Heaven* is not about anti-totalitarianism, but about making a moral commitment; *The Little Foxes* attacks greed more successfully than it does capitalism. The best drama remained drama, whatever its plot premise, which is why *The Little Foxes* and even the dated *Rain from Heaven* are still performed today while *They Shall Not Die* has vanished. And when it came to pleading the case of the underclasses, Sidney Kingsley's apolitical melodrama *Dead End* (1935) far outran the many propagandistic slum dramas of the decade. An urban cross-section, *Dead End* examined the inverted morality of society's outcasts, and amazed with its realism, in Kingsley's vernacular dialogue; in Norman bel Geddes' strikingly photographic setting of East River wharf, alley, gardened terrace, and tenements; and in the strongly individualized contributions of the forty-five actors (including the original set of "Dead End Kids," Gabriel Dell, Huntz Hall, Bobby Jordan, Billy Halop, Leo Gorcey, *et al.*).

Perhaps the development of the American city melodrama, from *Salvation Nell* in 1908 through Elmer Rice's *Street Scene* in 1929, needed a Great Depression to synthesize a morality of the humiliations of slum naturalism. Kingsley sympathizes with those whose have-nothing caste traps them in degradation and poverty, whose only clear way out is talent or crime. The easternmost end of Fifty-third Street as seen in *Dead End* is an Oz of great encounters: gangsters, shiftless teenagers, an out-of-work architect, neighbors, cops, and the rich are all in place, becoming what they were born to become. Life is stasis, but every little thing happens suddenly, as when Marjorie Main shuffled into view for a three-minute cameo as the mother of the local star hoodlum, a killer whom she hasn't heard from in years. This blasted slattern with a face of granite and a whine for language at first doesn't recognize her son, then bitterly cracks him across the face and slumps away. (Main's astonishing performance was preserved in William Wyler's 1937 film adaptation.) Less optimistic than plays like *Stevedore*, *Dead End* used the city as it is rather than the place it might more ideally be.

In the same season as *Dead End*, Maxwell Anderson wrote a completely different slum drama—a verse play called *Winterset*. Anderson invented an odd naturalism in this work, employing not only the poetry of words but poetic action to remove itself from reality while apparently belonging to it. Here, again, were the waifs, gangsters, and bullying police of *Dead End*, but here was a psychological and philosophical rhetoric unknown to melodrama. *Winterset* marked Anderson's second use of the Sacco-Vanzetti case in drama, but where *Gods of the Lightning* offered a "true-story" approach *Winterset* romanticized a possible aftermath. Even the scenery, by Jo Mielziner, added to Anderson's lifelike-yet-dreamy atmosphere, especially in the first set, waterfront sludge piled high under the arch of an immense bridge, the paradox of Urbantown: a derelict humanity cowering under technology. Everything in this play seemed at first glance vaguely real; everything in it soon turned out to be exactly fantastic.

This was a daring experiment, the artistic aspirations of the 1920s coupled with the hardline polemics of the 1930s. George Jean Nathan called *Winterset* "Gorki trying to dance with Maeterlinck," but the work is a stupendous achievement, bizarrely, beautifully written in an adaptable blank verse that accommodates the colloquial (says a terminally ill gangster, "Six months I get, and the rest's dirt, six feet") as easily as character writing and hard-core dramatic verse ("Now all you silent powers that make the sleet and dark . . . let the throw be ours this once . . . let fall some mercy with the rain"). Some reacted contemptuously to Anderson's lyrically ratiocinating characters; others were stunned by his eloquence. (The *New Yorker*'s theatre critic Wolcott Gibbs drew up a burlesque of Anderson's verse as it might been used to write *Uncle Tom's Cabin*. It's still funny today, but it also shows how little a critic respects creative talent; another play Gibbs didn't think much of is *Hamlet*.) One thing for sure: *Winterset* delivered a titanic evening of problem, aggravation, and resolution, Shakespearean echoes broadening its thrust. The crux of the plot is a meeting between the son of a man wrongly executed for murder and the judge who sentenced him, the son hunting for evidence to clear his father's name and the judge wandering the earth to jabber about the case to anyone who will listen. Their confrontation, Hamlet meets Lear, occurs in the house of a rabbi whose son witnessed the crime and knows who the real culprit is. Such a coincidence would have seemed preposterous in Odets or Kingsley, but *Winterset* inhabits another world, for all its veneer of realism, and the public of the 1930s accepted its oddities as easily as that of the 1800s accepted oddities of their time, out of that certain Belief in the *ethics* of the story (if not in the story itself).

Winterset arrived at the dead center of a decade marked by Anderson's astonishing prolificacy—he produced twelve plays in all, nine of them verse plays. The quality of the work was variable, but always fired by strong dramatic instincts, a great writer's gift, and a testy anarchism that could rip to the surface of a script like a monster reptile in a Mesozoic sea. Remember the Jeremiads of Suvorin in *Gods of the Lightning*—there you have, though he often hid it, your basic Anderson. Like many Americans in this decade, he found his worldview undergoing a development as the years wore on, a development neatly reflected in his plays. Until *Winterset*, historical re-enactions predominated—Elizabeth I of England, Mary of Scotland, and George Washington were Anderson's protagonists in the early 1930s. After *Winterset*, fantasy took over, along with a certain positivism to assuage the desperation. But, by then, Anderson was reaching for something: war.

A glance at the posters for *Elizabeth the Queen* (1930) and *Mary of Scotland* (1933)—Theatre Guild specials, the Lunts as Elizabeth and Essex and Helen Hayes as Mary, sets by the two champions of twenties art truth, Lee Simonson and Robert Edmond Jones—suggests the crusty luxury of Must See. But these are taut, not trendy, plays, confronting an ugly world that seems permanently resistant to improvement. "Till you die! Till we all die. Till there is no earth!" Matching Suvorin in tone, Fontanne as Elizabeth delivered a classic line of cynical disgust: "The rats inherit the earth."

The positive note that soon intruded into Anderson's point of view never quite overcame his distrust of public institutions, but it did eventually rise to the challenge faced by free men in the war to come. A non-verse play political satire, *Both Your Houses* (1933), pictured a Frank Capraesque populist hero vainly attempting to block the passage of pork-barrel legislation—but the author suggests that the days of unlimited graft are numbered. In *Valley Forge* (1934), Washington closed his saga like a gentle Solzhenitsyn, reminding the public of the vulnerability of democracy: "This liberty will look easy by and by when nobody dies to get it."

Then came *Winterset*, and it was clear that Anderson was working out a personal moral system, a play at a time. Eugene O'Neill had embarked on a huge nine-play cycle following the progress of an American family, and the now more frankly political Anderson also seemed to be collecting serial data on democracy: *The Wingless Victory* (1936) dealt with racism, *The Star-Wagon* (1937) with materialism, *High Tor* (1937) with the corruption of commercialization and the epic of historical dialectics, *Knickerbocker Holiday* (1938)—a musical with a score by Kurt Weill—with the authoritarian state, Roosevelt's as much as Stalin's and Hitler's, and *Key Largo* (1939) with selflessness as the free man's counteraction to evil.

Fantasy played a role here: *The Star-Wagon* uses a time machine, and *High Tor*'s cast of characters includes the ghosts of pre-colonial soldiers. More significantly, Anderson constantly veered between optimism and disbelief. *The Wingless Victory*, a resetting of the Medea tale set in Salem in

1800, told tragically of white racism and xenophobia, while *The Star-Wagon* delighted in its picture of a poor scientist who, having traveled back in time, gets the chance to make it in the marketplace as a sell-out—and refuses. A tragedy, then a comedy. Then, doubtful again, Anderson merged the two modes and shook his fist at all our societal organization and its greedy progress in *High Tor*, one of the strangest pieces ever to succeed on Broadway. This was another verse play, set on a mountain in New York (the tor of the title) that is, in a busy evening, owned by a loner, coveted by speculators, haunted by ghosts, crowded by bank robbers on the lam, and comprehended as ecological abstraction by an Indian. *High Tor* offered much comedy, some of it angry and some of it, in the persons of the two speculators, Biggs and Skimmerhorn, almost corny slapstick. *What* can Anderson have been moving into here? At the end, the loner decides to leave his beloved mountain and venture westwards, and the Indian gave his reading on the matter of mountains versus technology: "Nothing is made by men but makes, in the end, good ruins."

Anderson cheered up again in *Knickerbocker Holiday*, which proposed that the American spirit will never tolerate statism (not, at least, as embodied by Pieter Stuyvesant in old Manhattan; this is the role in which Walter Huston snorted, stomped, and, in a Big Moment of the musical rather than the spoken theatre, whispered his way through "September Song"). Anderson appeared to have reached a destination, after World War II began, in *Key Largo*. Like *Winterset,* this verse play courted the problem of poetic naturalism in the use of gangsterism in its plot; also like *Winterset*, with its Shakespearean echoes, *Key Largo* payed homage to an earlier work—in this case, Joseph Conrad's *Lord Jim*. To the audience, however, it was neither verse play nor literary homage so much as thriller about a coward who repeats his past to redeem a past mistake. As *Key Largo* ended, its protagonist McCloud (Paul Muni), mortally wounded, spoke of an Indian burial ritual in which a slain warrior is seated upright in his grave surrounded by his weapons. "That's very sensible," he concludes. "Very sensible."

Weapons to fight with. To fight racism, exploitation, statism, whatever an author called evil: that was the premise of the times. Like Anderson, Robert E. Sherwood made a voyage of discovery in the 1930s, seeking weapons. The antiwar preacher of *The Road to Rome* in the late 1920s, with his "human equation," began to probe more deeply into philosophical and political questions, and did not always find a ready answer. He was still the flamboyant, even boyish, showman, admiring innocence in his characters but expertise in the actors who played them—the Lunts, Raymond Massey, Leslie

Howard, Humphrey Bogart. No doubt it was the showman in Sherwood who cooked up a frothy romp in the style of Molnar for the Lunts to dally in, *Reunion in Vienna* (1931). But a more probing Sherwood sneaked some existential questions into a gunman-on-the-loose thriller, *The Petrified Forest* (1935). Howard played a gutless intellectual, Bogart the gunman, the two of them suggesting the confrontation between Europe's peace-loving but weak-willed democracies and bullying fascist states. What action is to be taken, Sherwood asked—have we the will to defend ourselves? As the curtain fell on *The Petrified Forest*, it seemed not. But in his next play, *Idiot's Delight* (1936), a more decisive Sherwood tackled the world situation directly, and if his questions concerning the will to action were not yet fully answered, he was clearly coming around to the heroic point of view.

A macabre comedy, *Idiot's Delight* perched high up in the Italian Alps in the art deco cocktail lounge of a sanatorium-turned-hotel. The view is spectacular: all Europe falls away below, roiling in the hours just prior to the start of the next war. The play's characters can see four countries from their eyrie; Sherwood sees more—the future (which was, anyway, only three years off at the time). An international miscellany is stranded in the hotel, and Sherwood builds his tension on three acts of confrontation politics: a German doctor working on a cure for cancer knows he will have to turn his attentions to the fabrication of new and invidious matériel mousetraps; a French pacifist denounces war and is dragged off and shot; a honeymooning English couple keeps a stiff upper lip; a French munitions industrialist remains aloof and impervious to insult; and American vaudevillian Alfred Lunt meets up with Russian beauty Lynn Fontanne . . . for the second time, he insists, the first being the night they spent together in the Governor Bryan Hotel in Omaha, Nebraska. She laughs. She finds that very amusing.

Ultimately, war does break out, and Fontanne is forced to remain, presumably at the cost of her life—but Lunt stays behind with her for the final scene. After all the international wrangling, the quasi-symbolic play of ideas on a mountain peak in central Europe, Sherwood threw doctrine to the winds and embraced romantic idealism, convincing some that he hadn't been able to conclude his argument. But perhaps that in itself was his plan, to topple reasoning with gallant fantasy. It seems right that Lunt and Fontanne close the play alone together (bellowing "Onward Christian Soldiers") while an incredible array of bombs, blasts, and assorted Blitzkrieg goes off around them. Lunt isn't just "her" hero—he is fascinated by her mystery. Did they or did they not spend that night in the Governor Bryan? She finally admits that they did—Room 974, she recalls—but we're never sure. Mystery is preferable to honesty: "It is no use telling the truth to people whose whole life is a lie."

Was life a lie? Maxwell Anderson appeared to think it was—a swindle, at any rate. But as he ended the decade certain of the need for armed defense of liberty, so did Sherwood, moving on from the sardonic glitter of *Idiot's Delight*, from its irresistible box-office lure of Lunt singing and dancing and Fontanne in blonde wig, to the austere *Abe Lincoln in Illinois* (1938). As one of Franklin Roosevelt's speechwriters, Sherwood might be accused of retailoring Lincoln's saga to hymn the New Deal; the charge does not hold up. Whatever parallels may be drawn between Lincoln and Roosevelt, Sherwood hewed closely to chronicle and made no allusions to current politics. (Indeed, he troubled to remind those who may have forgotten that Lincoln was fervently opposed to northern agitation for civil war, which hardly parallels Roosevelt's eagerness to involve the United States in World War II.) The south had threatened to secede if Lincoln were elected, and the play closes with Sherwood's hero leaving Illinois for Washington in February of 1861, president-elect of a divided nation. Which is to have priority, union or peace? From the rear end of his train, Lincoln makes a farewell speech; it is Sherwood's, his affidavit for active resistance. As delivered by Raymond Massey at the climax of a great performance of almost ghoulishly underplayed grandeur, this was one of the era's Big Moments, a dialogue between history and its heirs:

> I have heard of an Eastern monarch who once charged his wise men to invent him a sentence which would be true and appropriate in all times and situations. They presented him with the words, "And this too shall pass away." That is a comforting thought in times of affliction . . . and yet—(*suddenly speaks with quiet but urgent authority*) let us believe that it is not true! Let us live to prove that we can cultivate the natural world that is about us, and the intellectual and moral world that is within us, so that we may secure an individual, social, and political prosperity . . . which, while the earth endures, shall not pass away!

Still, the south of 1861 was hardly comparable to the totalitarians of 1938, and Sherwood had not yet openly acknowledged the enemy. Two years later, he got the chance: Russia's invasion of Finland in 1939 inspired a piece of outright propaganda and a call to arms, *There Shall Be No Night* (1940). The Lunts called off a much-needed vacation to play it, and Sherwood's progress from passive intellectualizing to battle position was completed. (History being even less orderly than the stage, Finland had thrown its allegiance to Hitler by the time the Lunts took the play to London. Sherwood simply moved the play from Finland assaulted by Germans to Greece assaulted by Germans.)

These two voyages, Anderson's and Sherwood's, are paradigmatic for this decade of American theatre, positive with suggestions on improving the human situation at home and around the world. This was quite a change from the gleeful debunking of American mores in the 1920s, but then the times were different. *Stevedore, Days to Come, Waiting for Lefty, They Shall Not Die, Rain from Heaven, Both Your Houses, Here Come the Clowns,* and numerous other works either promised or urged an ideal near-future; only *constructive* criticism was welcome. Thus the leftist Group Theatre, a youthful offshoot of the Theatre Guild, got Paul Green to accord with the general positivism when it launched its career with Green's *The House of Connelly* (1931). A tale of how new blood replaces old in the south (or, how progressivism replaces sterile tradition), Green's script originally ended with the murder of its heroine by two menacing black mammies, imposing the will of the static land on the will of the energetic new breed. At the Group's behest, Green substituted a happy ending, promising a fresh new dynamism. That's how it was.

A weird time. For once, radicals and neutrals both seemed bent on agreeing that the stage was the place to prove that one's brave new world was either likely to happen (radicals) or likely to survive, having happened (everyone else). Lawrence Langner, the head of the Theatre Guild, recalled in his memoirs that "the threat of Hitler's mounting ambitions was constantly before us, and we essayed time after time to produce plays which would publicize the blessings of democracy to an audience skating on the thin ice of financial distress."

Some blamed democracy for that distress in the first place. Clifford Odets, who had pointed his finger at The System so ferociously in *Waiting for Lefty,* did so again in the more fully developed *Awake and Sing!* (1935), another Group Theatre production and a domestic drama of raw vitality. "Awake and sing, ye that dwell in dust," sayeth Isaiah, "for thy dew is as the dew of herbs, and the earth shall cast out the dead." In their Bronx apartment, the Berger family dwells in dust, under pressures for respectability and wealth that they cannot meet. Ruled by an iron matriarch, they resembled no family that had ever been seen in the American family play, treating each other rudely and hating sentimentality. "Here without a dollar you don't look the world in the eye," says Mother Bessie. "Talk from now to next year—this is life in America." The militant left saw *Awake and Sing!*

as another study in their conversion technique, but for the general public such a play offered mainly an artistic alternative—as for instance to the one-joke farces like *The Warrior's Husband* (Katharine Hepburn as an Amazon, her husband as wife) or *Three Men on a Horse* (milquetoast has gift for picking winning horses). By comparison, *Awake and Sing!* was substantial in what it did with place (the Bronx) as character (Jewish immigrants) and with character (the Group Theatre) as real-life enaction. The piece as art almost erased the piece as argument.

True, it was hard to miss the edge of dialectic in the air, though *New Masses* complained that Odets' characters didn't come to accept the Marxist line "out of the understanding of the social forces which have made the Bergers a cursed family." But the Bergers did understand; one character, grandfather Jacob, tells the young hero, "Get out and fight so life shouldn't be printed on dollar bills!"

Awake and Sing! was thrilling theatre. Its exhilarating "struggle for life amidst petty conditions" (Odets' own words) reminded some critics of Sean O'Casey. Others, noting Odets' impatient, fluttering, distracted conversations, invoked Chekhof. But all of them commended the liquid ease of the performance, and the original company—Stella Adler, Morris Carnovsky, Art Smith, and Jules (later John) Garfield—have passed into an insider's legend for their collaborative exactness. At last naturalistic acting was living up to naturalistic writing, and one can say for sure now that the era of the staircase entrance was over.

Truth, in writing and performing, was the obsession of the 1930s. Not every dramatist saw the same truth, however, and even those in relative alignment saw it in contrasting ways. For instance, the humorous complement to *Awake and Sing!*, domestic comedy, showed two very different sides of itself in two classics of the form, Eugene O'Neill's *Ah, Wilderness!* (1933) and George S. Kaufman and Moss Hart's *You Can't Take It with You* (1936).

It was an unencountered O'Neill who wrote *Ah, Wilderness!*, and the novelty of a nostalgic family comedy from the man who had spent the 1920s decimating our nostalgic view of the family with psychological horrors was emphasized in the casting of George M. Cohan as the father. Cohan of the farces, the musicals, the "kangaroo step," the flag-waving—Cohan the *showman*! It was as if the art movement had never happened, as if the O'Neill that we had come to grips with had never existed. Robert Brustein has called *Ah, Wilderness!* "an exercise for the left hand"; a musician would not make that analogy. Left hand pieces are not, as Brustein surely means, half as difficult as two-hand compositions, but twice as difficult, for the left hand must cover the entire keyboard. Still, the point is made: this is O'Neill with one hand tied behind his back. The play is set in Connecticut in 1906, where Nat and Essie Miller are raising a family in a time and space where an automobile ride is an event. No frustration, no furtive sublimation complicates these lives. Husbands work, wives cook and mind the kids, spinster aunts live in, and bachelor uncles with a weakness for liquor are just party tipplers, not alcoholics. Life's sole complication is a seventeen-year-old son who takes his Swinburne and Shaw too seriously, but this too can be dealt with. Everything is containable.

On the other hand, *You Can't Take It with You* is a screwball farce. Many of the decade's plays dealt with disoriented characters—alienated either by epic environmental pressures they don't understand or because they understand and dislike their environment. In *You Can't Take It with You* the screwballs have their world in order; it's everybody else who's disoriented. Throughout the evening, their energetically open, unambitious life is pitted against the tight, pushing straight world, and the straights don't stand a chance, being nothing but Wall Streeters, federal agents, and an internal revenue man. Whereas the screwballs living it up on little or no income at Grandpa Vanderhof's house near Columbia University are liberated and likeable.

They do as they please at Grandpa Vanderhof's. One footles around with a printing press, his wife makes candy and studies ballet, her mother writes plays, two others tinker with explosives, various strays accumulate, and Grandpa, a wry Yankee of the old style, attends Columbia's graduation exercises and keeps pet snakes. They're happy people:

RHEBA: (*the maid*) Finish the second act, Mrs. Sycamore?
PENNY: Oh no, Rheba. I've just got Cynthia entering the monastery.
RHEBA: Monastery? How'd she get there? She was at the El Morocco, wasn't she?
PENNY: Well, she gets tired of the El Morocco, and there's this monastery, so she goes there.
RHEBA: Do they let her in?
PENNY: Yes, I made it Visitors' Day, so of course anybody can come.
RHEBA: Oh.
PENNY: So she arrives on Visitors' Day and—just stays.
RHEBA: All night?
PENNY: Oh, yes. She stays six years.
RHEBA: (*As she goes into the kitchen*) Six years? My, I bet she busts that monastery wide open.
PENNY: (*Half to herself, as she types*) "Six Years Later . . ."

Of all the Kaufman-Hart collaborations, *You Can't Take It with You* proved not only the most immediately successful (two full years in New York) but also the most enduring, the 1965 Phoenix revival doing very nicely all over again and Frank Capra's screen version seconding the efforts of high-school drama clubs to keep the premise alive indefinitely. This is one hit whose popularity is easy to understand. Very much of its time, though not dependent on timely allusions—not, in other words, a semi-satire—this show gave its own reading of Langner's "blessings of democracy," otherwise known as American anti-authoritarian anarchy: do what you want to before it's too late. Grandpa Vanderhof makes the point at the show's end to the Wall Streeter, whose son has suddenly decided to pull out of the business:

> Tony is going through just what you and I did when we were his age. I think . . . you can hear yourself saying the same things to *your* father twenty-five years ago. . . . How many of us would be willing to settle when we're young for what we eventually get? . . . It's only a handful of the lucky ones that can look back and say that they even came close. So . . . before they clean out that closet, Mr. Kirby, I think I'd get in a few good hours on that saxophone.

(It's a telling moment, one to which the whole evening has been working up. But lest the spectator sense so much as a splinter of the soapbox, the authors pull the rug out from under their own Big Moment with more screwball antics—a Russian former Grand Duchess lunges out of the kitchen with an apron tied over her evening dress to ask how many blintzes she should make for dinner.)

Thornton Wilder, too, made this same appeal to the public to enjoy life while you have it in *The Merchant of Yonkers* (1938), adapted from one of Johann Nestroy's Viennese comedies which was in turn a reworking of an English original. (Overdirected by Max Reinhardt with a continental swank too lush for Broadway's taste, the play failed to go over but was successfully revised and restaged in 1955 as *The Matchmaker*.) Wilder was after bigger game as well, and in *Our Town* (1938) he fashioned elements of domestic and Yankee comedy into a white folk play at first sentimental and at length disquieting. Aiming "to find a value above all price for the smallest events in daily life," Wilder took Grover's Corners, New Hampshire, for his miniature and panned back for the long view, building an immensity out of trivia played on a bare stage, the decor mainly comprising a pair of stepladders and some chairs. It was a commonplace of 1938 that

Wilder borrowed his technique from the Chinese theatre; this was frequently repeated by those whose previous acquaintance with Chinese drama consisted of the pagoda number in one of Florenz Ziegfeld's *Follies* revues. Wherever Wilder got the idea for his undecorated stage (which he had already used in several one-act plays), it certainly set off the simplicity of the piece. The story? A patchwork quilt of small-town life. On Wilder's empty stage, Emily Webb falls in love with George Gibbs. A factory whistle blows. Emily asks her mother if she's good-looking. The Stage Manager assembles a profile of Grover's Corners from some of its residents, who address the audience and answer their questions. George and Emily walk home from school together. The church choir rehearses. The town drunk reels home. George and Emily get married . . . and a few years later Emily dies. "We all know that *something* is eternal," the Stage Manager comments. "And it ain't houses and it ain't names, and it ain't earth, and it ain't even the stars . . . everybody knows in their bones that *something* is eternal, and that something has to do with human beings." Sitting on folding chairs with the other dead in the graveyard, Emily elects to relive one day in her life, her twelfth birthday, but the unknowingness of the living appalls her, and she returns to her chair. Now George appears to fling himself at Emily's grave. Gazing down on her sobbing ex-husband, Emily asks her dead mother-in-law, "They don't understand, do they?" "No, dear," answers Mrs. Gibbs. "They don't understand." The Stage Manager reflects on the unending business of life on earth and sends the audience home.

One might want to dismiss *Our Town* as a post-Tarkington small-town sampler, but for all its sentimental appeal, this was no "audience show." Boston hated it, curtailing its tryout from two weeks to one, and the original production didn't make much money, though it ran 336 performances. Militant leftists were very uncomfortable with one moment during the question-and-answer session, when a "belligerent man" asks if anyone in Grover's Corners is "aware of social injustice or industrial inequality." Mr. Webb, editor of the local paper, replies, "I guess we're all hunting like everybody else for a way the diligent and sensible can rise to the top and the lazy and quarrelsome can sink to the bottom." Even sensible theatregoers found something disturbing in the bite of its sentimentality. Something about *Our Town* defeated the very people who should have loved it, who kept *The First Year* open for 760 repetitions back in the 1920s. Frank Craven, *The First Year*'s author and star, played *Our Town*'s Stage Manager (as did Wilder, for two weeks, in an attempt to make a little noise for the slipping property), smoking his pipe, smiling benignly on latecomers, pointing out the production's one concession to spectacle, a pair of trellises: "There's some scenery for people who think they have to have scenery . . . It's a nice town, even though nobody remarkable ever came out of it." One almost expected him to direct the spectators to take out their McGuffey's Readers for the day's installment of the work ethic.

Craven's soothing familiarity wasn't enough to dispel the discomfort aroused in many who saw *Our Town*. And the reason is simple: layered into the offhand serenity of the story is a terrible despair, the helpless *non serviam* of humans who can accept the idea of everlasting continuity but can't face having to believe in it. Wilder's Americans reach out for little things and hold tight, with the vast gape of the universe looming over them and the permanence of death complementing the unkillable fact of having lived. It's a hard play to live up to, for its texture of middle-class serenity hides an undercurrent of worried speculation: where are we headed? In this, Wilder seems no different from Anderson, Sherwood, and other playwrights of the decade—but none of them had tried to ask their "harmful" questions within so "harmless" a context as this. Continuity. Adolescence. Marriage. Death. Continuity. Within these quotidian parameters, *Our Town* (=Our World) built up a universe of little things. For instance, the end of Act I: two teen-agers, brother and sister, in conversation. "I never told you about that letter Jane Crofut got from her minister when she was sick," says the girl. And she recites the address on the envelope: "Jane Crofut; The Crofut Farm; Grover's Corners; Sutton County; New Hampshire; United States of America; Continent of North America; Western Hemisphere; the Earth; the Solar System; the Universe; the Mind of God." The postman, she adds, "brought it just the same." And the Stage Manager ambles on. "That's the end of the First Act, friends," he announces. "You can go and smoke now, those that smoke." And the lights fade on Act I.

One of the few really great American plays and a longtime classic in Europe—although a regular notch in the guns of today's so-called supercritics and the particular *bête noir* of Marxist writers—*Our Town* offered a kind of rebuttal to the earnest awareness of the decade, whether middle-route liberal, anarchist, or Communist, whether S. N. Behrman's shy admission of the totalitarian menace or Clifford Odets' working class ideology. They addressed applied social conditions; Wilder referred to humanity.

This was not, however, a great time for the folk play, which had really had its heyday in the late 1920s and peaked with *The Green Pastures* in 1930. After that, white guilt made a lot of theatre people uneasy about the whole thing. It was as if the (black) folk play, with its dialect study and spirituals, suddenly struck them as another instance of racist oppression. Consequently, the form ground to a halt, except where black companies, who rejoiced in its opportunities for self-expression, mounted their own, usually little-theatre, productions.

A few stragglers hung on in the white folk play. Lynn Riggs won little favor for his look at the vagabond path, *Roadside* (1930)—originally entitled *Borned in Texas*—and for *Green Grow the Lilacs* (1931), beefed up in its Theatre Guild presentation by the insertion of folk songs and renewed twelve years later by Richard Rodgers and Oscar Hammerstein II as *Oklahoma!*, one of the more notable folk musicals. Likewise unsuccessful and comparably typical was E. B. Ginty's *Missouri Legend* (1938), devoted to the last days of Jesse James.

One very successful play about life among the dirt farmers of the Deep South was occasionally taken to be a folk play, but *Tobacco Road* (1933) is anything but. A sloppy reduction of Erskine Caldwell's novel of redneck degradation, Jack Kirkland's script was created for sensation, not folkloring; it had color, but no depth, no line. When it opened, it looked like a long shot, and a closing notice was quickly posted—but the producer had made an agreement with the landlord to clean up the stage upon vacating the theatre, and had so littered it with filth (to convey the Caldwell aura) that he couldn't afford to cart it away. True, he wasn't doing good business. But you never know in the theatre, never; and he certainly couldn't afford to close, not with all the muck on that stage. So he stayed open. For seven-and-a-half years.

Obviously, the more sensational aspects of the show plus its melodramatic "honesty" pushed it over the top; also obviously, not everything in the 1930s that was prominent was important. Many of the decade's best-remembered entries connect this era to others before and after in their perfect, likeable triviality—farces, semi-satire, mystery thrillers, heavy melodrama, and other common coin continued to thrive. No Great Depression inspired, nor marred, the action of, say, *Dinner at Eight* (1932), Kaufman and Ferber's novel conceit which looks in on the lives of the various guests invited to a dressy dinner. And certainly more people *in toto* saw *Dinner at Eight* and the plays of its kind than saw the politically relevant works.

To pick another example, Rachel Crothers, the standout woman playwright of the 1920s, maintained her reputation in the 1930s, always demanding that her subjects pay full coin in topical and psychological development—but never enjoining the political questions so absolute on other stages. Unlike the semi-satires of the Kaufman school, Crothers' comedies needed no wisecrackers—though some, eying her satisfied but hardly hysterical audience, might have observed that wisecrackers were *just* what they needed. Certainly, Crothers' plays are much less well recalled and less frequently revived than Kaufman's.

Susan and God (1937), Crothers' biggest hit, furnishes a test case of the light satirical touch on Broadway, even if it was written by way of comeback after five years' sojourn in Hollywood. As it worked out, *Susan and God's* best feature proved to be neither Crothers' wit nor insight but her star, Gertrude Lawrence, a versatile comedienne, singer, and actress who commuted between London and New York throughout the 1920s, 1930s, and 1940s, sharing her successes with her two publics. No doubt Lawrence's hard-core following regarded *Susan and God* as her latest vehicle for bouts of incandescence, poignance, and caprice, but informed opinion hailed it as one of the era's defter satires: a woman infected with the faddish egotism of the born-again-through-public-confessional Oxford Movement attempts to reform her alcoholic husband and is in the end reformed by him, learning that inner strength, not outward show, yields salvation.

Lawrence's Susan—as, once again, directed by Crothers herself—debunked the essentially romantic woman who thinks she has come upon a logic, eyes magical, head winsomely a-tilt, caressing the stage space with Presence. Lawrence, secretly, was a kind of Susan—Susan, publicly, a kind of Lawrence. The name of this is chemistry; to achieve it, Crothers had to abjure her characteristic middle-class family setting for the house-party set more typical of Barry and Behrman. But then, the American hearthside offered Lawrence no main chance for disclosures of chic (as her unsuitable Amanda Wingfield in the film version of *The Glass Menagerie* made clear). This interest in letting celebrity function as the source of art material sounds more like culturally opportunistic semi-satire than like true character comedy. But can we blame Crothers because Lawrence naturally overpowered anything she appeared in, making it seem as if *she* were the piece?

A more willing orientation to personality is found in Sam and Bella Spewack's *Boy Meets Girl* (1935), which loosely portrayed figures of the media world, Ben Hecht and Charles MacArthur, authors of *The Front Page* and more recently rebellious screenwriters in Hollywood. In *Boy Meets Girl*, Hecht and MacArthur become Benson and Laws, movie scenario writers and irreverent incorrigibles. This was a George Abbott show, and at his breathless direction the chiseling kitsch of the movie factory seemed to scram even as it rushed in; it was *Broadway* without jazz and gangsters. The Boy is a movie extra (titled British nobility, it turns out), the Girl is a studio waitress, unmarried but pregnant. While serving the two writers lunch, she suddenly faints. Reviving, sweetly delirious, she asks, "Did you all get napkins?"

The Spewacks had worked in Hollywood themselves, and took their revenge fabricating the asinine producer, the venal agent, the baby star adored by a nation, the cowboy star as vacant as all outdoors. Of course, the extra got the waitress amid the farcical brouhaha—we got that rule down along time ago: Boy meets girl, boy loses girl, boy gets girl. This was semi-satire then, with a point of view but no real penetration—no penetration intended.

Similarly, Clare Boothe, an Annie Oakley of semi-satirists, blasted her sex with the shotgun in *The Women* (1936) when the scalpel of wit might have revealed an idea. A large all-female cast of cats and kittens plus one good-hearted, deceived, divorced, then reconciled wife kept the season humming. In keeping the men in the story offstage, Boothe did intensify her context for northeastern urban upper-class womanhood, and to disarm her critics, she explained in a preface to the published text that she had limited her survey to "a numerically small group of ladies native to the Park Avenues of America . . . The title, which embraces half the human species, is therefore rather too roomy." Truly, it is; even within Boothe's stated circumscription, her women, with their delicious bitchiness, salon plotting, ambitionless shopping-spree lives, and skirmishes in Reno accord to a type known more to cartoonists than to life. To borrow a line from Trevor Griffiths' recent play, *Comedians*, Boothe's joke hates women.

But the customers didn't think so, and enjoyed as well Boothe's guffaw on Hollywood wheeler-dealing and the southern belle in *Kiss the Boys Goodbye* (1938). Semi-satire is, above all, timely: Boothe built *Kiss the Boys Goodbye* around the much-mooted search for an unknown Southern chick-a-pen to play Scarlett O'Hara in MGM's projected *Gone With the Wind* movie. Boothe's potential Scarlett is Cindy Lou Bethany, all dimples and innocent dogmatism. Speaking to a movie scout, Cindy Lou declares the *Gone With the Wind* tintype, *Kiss the Boys Goodbye*, to be "the finest book America has ever produced," adding that "the *Georgia Star Monthly* book reviewer, Miss Ida Mae Stonewall Jackson, says it's the only unbiased account of the Confederate War ever written." But Cindy Lou's shy of turning starlet: "My daddy says Hollywood is the Abbatoir of Decency and the Outhouse of Civilization." Replies the movie scout, "Daddy sounds like a re-write man."

As many writers noted at the time, Boothe's plays were staged comic strips, chock-full of trendy quips and about as friendly as Cerberus; her announcement that *Kiss the Boys Goodbye* was intended as a slam at Dixie-crat fascism was not seriously entertained. Even Mr. Boothe, Henry Luce, felt driven to shake his head in print over his wife's "satirical melodrama" *Margin for Error* (1939), only half-successful in posing the free world's retort to totalitarianism, though its gruesome onstage murder of a sadistic Nazi (played by Otto Preminger, who also directed) made it much more thriller than polemic and the first financially successful American anti-Nazi play.

A curious quality of semi-satire was its rage, for as absolute pop it was determined to please. Yet an undeniable toughness guided Kaufman, Boothe, and their colleagues in the form; their plays usually included one or more sharp-tongued characters, cynical about life and impatient with the idio-syncratic humanity of those around them—Sylvia, the meanest of *The Women*, or Sheridan Whiteside, the man *Who Came to Dinner*. Even when the semi-satirists adopted domestic comedy, they lacked the droll friendliness that came so naturally to Rachel Crothers. Why? Because they weren't portraying the family; they borrowed it to make jokes.

Broadway in the 1930s was still Broadway, still dedicated to putting on a good show—but, if only because of the artistic revolution of the 1920s, willing to stretch the meaning of the term to encompass a few alternative readings of "good." For example: William Saroyan. No author proves Broad-way's secretly apolitical foundation better than he, though he was launched by the particularly political Group Theatre. A line from his best-known play, *The Time of Your Life*—"No foundation all the way down the line"—applies as easily to Saroyan's sense of dramatic structure as to his often approximating view of the world. He never got used to the discipline and economics of getting a play produced; whimsical, daft, and plotless, his plays dreamed and frolicked in shapes all their own. *My Heart's in the Highlands* and *The Time of Your Life*, both in 1939, set the slow, intimate pace for Saroyan; in both, he drew his characters from life's down-and-outers in wide variety, but depoliticized their social context like a balladeer in a trance. Partyliner Michael Gold, depressed that such fertile territory for agitprop go unworked, suggested that *My Heart's in the Highlands* be retitled "My Art's in the Highlands." And what a chance for the leftist mobilization was thrown away in *The Time of Your Life*, a classic ground-zero of the microcosmic bar play, wherein folks of all sorts hang out and philosophize. Saroyan was into fantasy, not mobilization—though in the odd realistic moment he had some pertinent views to offer, as in this observation from a longshoreman in *The*

Time of Your Life: "I'm a man with too much brawn to be an intellectual, exclusively. I married a small, sensitive, cultured woman so that my kids would be sissies instead of suckers." And a few lines later: "Right now on Telegraph Hill is some punk who is trying to be Shakespeare. Ten years from now he'll be a senator. Or a communist."

Eugene O'Neill also held himself apart from the topical modes of the day. In a deliberate break with his dizzy experimentation of the 1920s, O'Neill had but three works produced in the whole decade. One of them returns to the experimental style of his earlier work, *Days Without End* (1934), in which the protagonist is portrayed by two actors. But this work is virtually non-existent compared to the other two. *Ah, Wilderness!* marked the comic-nostalgic O'Neill; two years earlier, *Mourning Becomes Electra* (1931) ushered in O'Neill's period of maturity, the first of his three master-pieces, followed one to a decade by *The Iceman Cometh* in the 1940s and *Long Day's Journey into Night* in the 1950s.

Like *Ah, Wilderness!*, *Mourning Becomes Electra* is set in an older, almost non-political America, after the movement that had launched the democratic experiment was subsumed in habit and before the new questions about it were raised. A trilogy based on Aeschylus' *Oresteia*, likewise a trilogy (that is, discounting the missing satyric quarter), *Mourning* is per-formed in one night, but it's a long sit. O'Neill's *Homecoming*, *The Hunted*, and *The Haunted* correspond to Aeschylus' *Agamemnon*, *The Libation Bearers*, and *The Eumenides*, updating the action to post–Civil War New England, emphasizing Electra rather than Orestes, and closing the tale in despair rather than deliverance. This is not merely an Americanized *Oresteia*, then. As with such comparable instances of adaptation as Bertolt Brecht's *Edward II* (from Marlowe) or Maxwell Anderson's "Medea and Jason," *The Wingless Victory*, the result is a new work.

In O'Neill's version, General Ezra Mannon (Agamemnon) returns home from war to be murdered by his wife Christine (Clytemnestra), who has been having an affair with the sea captain Adam Brant (Aegisthos), secretly a Mannon family bastard. Brant is murdered in turn by Mannon's son Orin (Orestes), egged on by Mannon's daughter Lavinia (Electra). Like many an O'Neill son, Orin enjoys a profound approach-avoidance relationship with his mother; this Orestes cannot kill Clytemnestra, but she commits suicide, and Orin transfers his mother fixation onto the all-too-willing Lavinia. Now Orin, too, kills himself, shattered by a modern comprehension of guilt that Aeschylus' Orestes didn't have to worry about. In Greek tradition,

Orestes is forgiven, and Electra settles down in domestic vapidity, a fate impossible for O'Neill's tortured son and unrelenting daughter. Mourning becomes her, it seems, as does morbid atonement for the sins of her antecedents—"the guilt for guilt which breeds more guilt," as she phrases it.

Lavinia/Electra is the dynamic center of O'Neill's triptych, not his weak, dominated Orin/Orestes. At the close of the evening, it is she who remains, alone, boarding up the house she will haunt alive, shuttered and apart, the last hateful Mannon. The role was a triumph for Alice Brady, especially in her scenes with Alla Nazimova's Christine, in which she cooed at her mother with an unreachable vileness. Theatre folk, always more responsive to great acting than the public, were floored; some swore you had to see it twice to receive it. Like *Strange Interlude*, *Mourning Becomes Electra* was so long it started early and ceded patrons a dinner intermission for amenity's sake, but who could eat? O'Neill deliberately avoided taking lyrical flights in the work (later, he was to claim that he lacked the poetry to negotiate them), laying a stark, thudding destiny on his public, and though the production was very definitely the Must See of the 1931–32 season, few felt they were paying a debt to art. Art was paying them.

Some ostensive parallels with the Greek theatre were clearly intended. O'Neill used a functional chorus of townspeople to open each of the three parts, and requisitioned a classical-styled facade from designer Robert Edmond Jones for the Mannon residence, a "large building of the Greek temple type that was in vogue in the first half of the nineteenth century. A white wooden portico with six tall columns contrasts with the walls of the house proper, which is of cut gray stone." Early drafts of the text called for masks and interior monologues, but these eventually were dropped for a naturalistic production subject to the conventions of American theatregoing rather than those of the Greek festivals. In his own words, O'Neill was after a "modern psychological approximation of [the] Greek sense of fate . . . which an intelligent audience of today, possessed of no belief in gods or supernatural retribution, could accept and be moved by."

O'Neill's protagonist Lavinia actually comes near to escaping her fate, as contemporary sensibility assumes is possible, by marrying a childhood sweetheart, Peter Niles (Pylades). Moments away from the final curtain, with her father, mother, and brother all dead, she throws herself in Niles' arms:

> I want it now! Can't you be strong, Peter? Can't you be simple and pure? Can't you forget sin and see that all love is beautiful? (*She kisses him*

with desperate passion.) Kiss me! Hold me close! Want me! Want me so much you'd murder anyone to have me! I did that—for you! Take me in this house of the dead and love me! Our love will drive the dead away! It will shame them back into death! (*At the topmost pitch of desperate, frantic abandonment.*) Want me! Take me, Adam!

Adam? The name of her mother's lover, her father's replacement, and, at her own urging, her brother's murder victim? Adam Brant, the skeleton in the Mannon closet, the illegitimate son of a family servant and General Mannon's brother? Instantly, Lavinia realizes that escape is hopeless: "Always the dead between! It's no good trying anymore!" Sending Niles away, Lavinia orders a servant to bar the house to all: "I'll live alone with the dead, and keep their secrets, and let them hound me, until the curse is paid out and the last Mannon is let die!"

Long afterward, playgoers talked of this moment, when Brady stood between the columns of the porch like an icy wraith, pale and unmoving. As the shutters were pulled to with a bang, she pivoted about as if wired by the gods, marched into her tomb, and slammed the door shut. After a moment, the curtain fell. There was a sighing silence followed by a slow, gradually augmented clapping, very heavy and deliberate. A serious play; a serious success. Not till years later did people see the event of this work in performance as a watershed mark in the context of continuity. (The reviews, for whatever it's worth, were the most worshipful ever accorded an American dramatist.) It lends a nice sense of climax to a chapter on American theatre in the 1930s (even though it arrived quite early in the decade), for it reminds us how temporary the American political theatre is. Of all the works produced in the glow of the radical insurgence, not one is much performed today. What are the *surviving* classics of the period (as opposed to the great museum pieces, like *Waiting for Lefty*)?—*Mourning Becomes Electra, Our Town, You Can't Take It with You, The Philadelphia Story, The Little Foxes*. Only the last may be related to the radical stage; of itself—maybe despite itself—it is a universal, not a political, work.

In other words, this major decade of American drama, by quantity of quality the most important decade as of this writing, continued to work out problems of generally artistic character even as it unleashed a new power to confront its audience with incendiary topical material. More positive than in the 1920s, the stage met hard times with possible solutions. Yet it equated hard times with good times in retaining that necessary beauty—call it idealism—without which all topics are so many staged editorials. What is that formula again, the one that the Spewacks proposed as the credo of popular art? Boy Meets Girl:

> Griffith used it. Lubitsch used it. And Eisenstein's coming around to it. Boy meets girl. Boy loses girl. Boy gets girl. The great American fairy tale. Sends the audience back to the relief rolls in a happy frame of mind.

Back to the relief rolls? Maybe there's awareness in that formula after all.

house. Porno and rerun cinema and the Tenderloin have befouled them: moving east to west on the north side of the street, the Republic (now the Victory), the Lyric, the Apollo and Times Square (two auditoriums sharing the same facade and marquee), the Selwyn; on the south side from the same direction, the New Amsterdam, the Harris, the Liberty, the Eltinge (now the Empire), Wallach's (now the Anco), and the American (demolished). Just one block! All, for practical purposes, gone—except the Apollo, reclaimed at the end of the 1970s with its entrance prudently moved to Forty-third Street. Worse yet, the new theatres erected in the bottom floors of skyscrapers tend to be too small and therefore forever dependent on foundation charity or too big, more suitable for Rollerball than for drama.

Another continuity, one as debased as that of the theatres, is that of media coverage, whether as reviews, celebrity interviews, gossip, or newsbreaks on ticket-scalper outrages or Times Square crime. The New York media are ignorant and harmful, yet necessary—watch what happens to theatregoing during a newspaper strike, if you want proof. Some continuities don't ever change: the continuity of the New York-London show trade-off, for example, centuries old, or the continuity of rights to film scripts, which dates far back into the silent era.

What has happened so far is thrilling amplification, but what will follow is contraction: not only fewer theatres but fewer dedicated playwrights, actors, and theatregoers. Movies and then television will cut into the theatre's human resources. But at one time the free flow of an eager public was taken for granted. The public owned the stage as stockholders own a corporation—they didn't run it, but they controlled it. When the theatre took the initiative and began to run itself, the public went along. Nothing deflates Sabina's nostalgia for "plays like we used to have" than the success of *The Skin of Our Teeth* in the early 1940s, for though it was "good entertainment with a message you can take home with you," as she herself demands, it didn't act like one with its loony scene plot and absurdist allegory—it didn't have to, now. There was a continuity of theatregoing, and to those who lived through the thirty years that saw *The Darling of the Gods* turn into *Mourning Becomes Electra*, the theatre had never ceased to be diversion, had never started to be recognition or inspiration. It had been all of them all along; this is what made it a cultural absolute. But it had, at certain points, ceased to be a necessarily popular art—and pop does not treasure its past or reserve a future. Pop is concerned with one thing only: creating immediate revenue.

Ironically, theatre at its most popular, in the 1800s, was not so spendthrift. Then, pop hoarded itself. The earliest American companies were

11

What Has Happened So Far I

BROADWAY SOMETIMES DEFIES and sometimes exalts its traditions. As drama has periodically redefined its purpose in the culture, each new set of moral imperatives moves in on, yet must coexist with, the old sets. Thus, it becomes difficult to speak of "a" purpose in Broadway: a season that features *The American Way* and *The Little Foxes*; *The Philadelphia Story* and *Here Come the Clowns*; *Knickerbocker Holiday* and *The Boys From Syracuse*; a revival of *Lightnin'* and Maurice Evans' *Hamlet*; *Mamba's Daughters* and *The Swing Mikado* and ten weeks of Gilbert and Sullivan by the D'Oyly Carte company, as the 1938–39 season did, is difficult to classify in such terms.

Actually, Broadway is simply giving the paying public what it seems to want; when ticket-buyers tire of something, it dies. Costume melodrama, for instance, in the *Count of Monte Cristo* line, died. The repertory system, for another instance, died. But most of Broadway's program, even going back to its earliest days, has held on in some form. One of its continuities is the theatres themselves, clustering as "Broadway" slowly gravitated up Broadway just as the true New York town moved north. Not so many theatres face onto Broadway as did so in the days of Weber and Fields, and there are fewer in all, so few that each year productions late to organize or amass working capital find all theatres reserved and have to hope that something flops so they can claim the vacant house.

In the last few decades, we have lost many more theatres than we have gained. In the single "block" of Forty-second Street from Seventh to Eighth Avenues stood eleven theatres, only one of which has literally ceased to exist but only one other of which today serves its original purpose as play-

repertory companies, subsisting on a permanent stock of plays, keeping them in trim as they traveled. The notion of opening a new work, running it for as long as it sold tickets, and discarding it for the next new work was unthinkable, partly because the public liked reviewing its pet items from Shakespeare to *Rip Van Winkle* and partly because that public was not big enough to support long runs of anything, new or old.

The long run in one theatre with one cast dates from the late nineteenth century and the centralization of the stage in New York. A public grown sizable enough to sustain long runs and the self-assertion of the playwright replaced the repertory system with the open market, so everybody started to make more money. Suddenly, repertory smelled musty, unsuccessful. And died. The *idea* of repertory, however, lived on in legends of European state-subsidized repertory houses, the so-called national theatres. Rep's advantages were noted: revolving works from night to night protects actors from the lethargy of uttering the same lines over and over till even poetry babbles; the practice of casting one production several times over and switching actors off from night to night intensifies the spontaneity of performances, and, moreover, stimulates versatility—no talent ever shriveled playing Schiller one night, Beckett the next, and Feydeau the following matinée. Best of all, the repertory system keeps plays themselves alive. After all, this is what opera and ballet companies have been doing straight through the 1900s. One doesn't stage *Boris Godunof* or *The Nutcracker* on a one-shot basis and then forget about it forever against the chance of someone's reviving it someday.

If it works for opera and ballet, why not for theatre?, came the question; by the 1930s, repertory felt idealistic and beautiful. And with good reason: the one continuity that Broadway lacks is that of repertory. True, revivals are no rarity; the constant production of Shakespeare, Ibsen, and Chekhof was nothing but revival. But the usage of bringing well-liked or not-liked-enough *American* plays back for repeated viewings—a habit in the early twentieth century—was falling into disuse by the Depression. The expansion of the 1920s, which developed the variety of genre, psychological inquiry, and staging technique to a high level, had also developed a disturbing usefulness in the matter of the literature as a body of work. There was Eugene O'Neill one day—that abruptly—and we had a playwright's theatre. But the public's motto was, "What have you done for me lately?" We were liquidating our past.

We will start to worry about this continuity of literature when the quantity of playwrights drops off and their career patterns reverse that of O'Neill, who wrote better as he went along. (The most respected authors of the post–World War II years—Arthur Miller, Tennessee Williams, William Inge, and Edward Albee—all started strong and then began to dissolve.) With the yearly tally of on-Broadway productions falling steadily from an average of about 250 in the late 1920s to about 35 in the early 1970s, the theatre will have to wonder how useful the free market system is, after all— and might just consider taking an active hand in continuity, keeping its past within reach while negotiating a future.

12

Toward a National Theatre

Contention for, against, and otherwise about an American "national theatre" institution rages evergreen. Critical analysts tell of amazing events on state-sponsored stages in London, East Berlin, or Munich. Theatre people compare their experiences as freelancers in the commercial sector to being on staff with a non-profit organization. The audience has its slant, for it, too, has known the choice of freelancing along The Street or subscribing to a "repertory" theatre.

A lot of theatregoers don't care much one way or another: theatre is theatre. Every American city of any size has at least one resident company and the odd tour. There are classics American and foreign, drama, comedy, musicals, revues, novelties, one-man shows, whatever the season needs. Why arrange it? Art or entertainment, doesn't it just happen?

It does; but while a free market is the ideal production medium for industrial goods, important theatre is not bought off the rack. Or, rather, it is—that's the problem. A cash-and-carry, hit-or-flop economy cannot always deliver a first-rate theatre; the variables of competitive media, career security, public apathy, and the fundamentally destructive pressure of commercial accounting militate against the formidable spiritual and financial investment involved in producing consistently important theatre. Broadway, the land's end of capitalist art, is not always important. Some by-no-means radical theatre people would say it is almost never important.

What is a national theatre? The "national" is misleading—it applies to the state theatre complexes of Europe, where countries as large as France or Austria concentrated their artistic energies on a cultural capital where everyone was and where everything happened, in a climate of artistic vitality. A Comédie-Française in Paris, a Burgtheater in Vienna, evolves out of a national impulse only in the sense that the influential artists—and a sophisticated public—have gravitated to a national nucleus. Once founded, however, a national art institution *becomes* national as a magnet for cultural talent and international attention, as a combination museum and modern exhibition for the national forms. One more thing: it is supported, financially, on the federal, not civic, level. It is a people's theatre, and it is very elite.

No one can reasonably debate the fact that New York is the American cultural capital. There are first-rate theatre companies elsewhere in the country, complete with enthusiastic audiences, but these lack New York's bracing interaction of drama, dance, music, literary, and fine arts worlds plus the major talents in these fields, plus a relatively informed public open to aggression, which is the art dynamic. If there is to be an American federal theatre institution of Western world-class proportion, it is going to be in New York.

What can such an institution provide that the commercial theatre system can't? It provides a permanent occasion for cultivating tradition and defining innovation: repertory. In less romantic terms, a national theatre provides a stable workshop environment dedicated not only to high-quality production but to the training of new talents—actors, directors, writers, designers. This theatre would be more than a succession of plays (new or old), but a company expanded behind and before the scenes by classes, workshops, controversy, communion, principles. Ideally, the public would be stimulated by theatre's public face—penetrating texts, ideas, a versatile acting ensemble, a sense of mission shared. At the same time, the company is stimulated by the sum of all its commingled parts. Everyone learns, everyone teaches. This is not utopian fantasy: theatre *provides* stimulation and *needs* it both.

Unfortunately, setting up and maintaining such an institution is expensive. Even a totally sold-out season in a good-sized theatre would not support a full-time acting pool and administrative and technical staff. Furthermore, philanthropy has so far been shy in underwriting any company not professing mainstream, middle-class ambitions—i.e., the "respectable" Shakespeare-Chekhof-O'Neill revival circuit, the annual farce, the odd touch of Brecht.

We should consider this question now, for at this point in the chronicle, certain alternatives of psychological, poetic, and social drama have set up shop within Broadway's parameters of business-as-usual. How did the organized alternative of a national theatre fare in the decades before World War II? There was the New Theatre, first, with its good intentions but bad man-

agement, its on-and-off star system as opposed to an acting "center," and its poor choice in repertory stock. But second, there was Eva Le Gallienne—and unlike the New people, she knew exactly what she wanted to do: create a permanent home for classic foreign repertory at low prices.

Le Gallienne founded the Civic Repertory Theatre in 1926—a true company, spiritually bound together and working for peanuts to keep admission prices scaled from $1.50 to $.50. Choosing from Shakespeare, Molière, Chekhof, Ibsen, Goldoni, and such, holding over the more successful entries from season to season, staging everything herself and playing lead roles from Juliet to Peter Pan, Le Gallienne hoped to pick up a public not yet initiated into serious drama. By the mid-1920s the theatre district had rumbled north into the west forties, abandoning a lot of older houses south of Thirty-fourth Street, and Le Gallienne and company debouched in an old barn on Fourteenth Street. This was distinctly off-Broadway, but there was star glitter from Alla Nazimova, who graced the bill in a few roles in the Civic's third season, including Madame Ranyefsky in *The Cherry Orchard*.

There is something quixotic in addressing alleged potential theatregoers who, but for the forbidding expense of Broadway ticket prices, are dying for a chance to fill theatres. So far—except within the strictly defined limitations of social theatre, and only in the early 1930s—no one has been able to prove that such a group exists. The people who flocked downtown for Le Gallienne were the same people who flocked uptown for classical fare—they simply got to flock more often at the lower prices. Furthermore, by the late 1920s, Broadway itself was overflowing with classical rep; the actor-manager Walter Hampden was running his own operation in his own theatre, the Theatre Guild was big and getting bigger, and one-time shots at Ibsen and Chekhof were common. For all her vision, Le Gallienne was working a well-nigh glutted market, and in 1932 the pinched budgets of the high Depression brought the Civic down.

Le Gallienne's experience—which she would relive at various times in the following forty years with comparably discouraging results—comprised the first large-scale example of what has recently come to be a standard feature of the non-Broadway adventure, the troupe of actors united by high ideals, a permanent location, and a program of some clarity. Today's Circle Repertory Company and the American Place Theatre, with their insistence on performing new American plays, are really just modern versions of such little groups as the Provincetowners, who launched O'Neill, or the Washington Square Players, who evolved into the Theatre Guild.

Like the Civic Rep, but right on Broadway, the Guild figured that classic theatre meant European theatre—but then what were the American classics in the 1920s? There were none: everything old was over (except *Fashion*, and when it was revived it was camped). Our dependence on European models was nowhere better proved than in the Guild's choice of plays in their early seasons. From their first ventures in 1919, the aforementioned items by St. John Ervine and Jacinto Benavente, the preference ran heavily to foreigners, especially Shaw, who supplied the Guild with much of their cachet with the world premieres of *Heartbreak House, Back to Methuselah*—all of it, on three nights, for Shaw would tolerate no cuts—*Saint Joan, The Apple Cart,* and *Too True To Be Good.*

During the 1920s, the Guild branched out into American art and found places for O'Neill, Behrman, and Sidney Howard (among others). These three were popular authors, commercially successful almost as a rule, and while the Guild never became a blue-chip security, it did find itself inadvertently converted from a countercultural alternative into an establishment house: revered and seldom dangerous. From its little-theatre inception just before World War I, with a firm goal and a tidy base of operations, the Guild exploded into a hit factory. It became a booking agency sprawled from Boston to Chicago (to tour the hits) with a cumbersome "permanent home" on Fifty-second Street (the Guild—now the ANTA—Theatre, designed so inanely that one stepped down so to speak *unto* it, as if into a basement), a dilution of the Guild acting regulars with numerous outsiders (a concomitant of expansion), and what some saw as a faded sense of purpose. "They set the plays out in a show window for as many customers as possible to buy," wrote Harold Clurman, at the time a play reader for the Guild. "They didn't want to say anything through plays, and plays said nothing to them, except that they were amusing in a graceful way or . . . that they were 'art.'" Having made it artistically, the Theatre Guild didn't realize that to continue to make it in the same vein was in effect making it no longer. But this is a cliché of theatre history—everyone blames the Guild for having turned from a little theatre into a big one. Perhaps as a kind of penance, the Guild threw off a revolutionary fledgling, the Group Theatre.

The Group began as an informal rebellion among Guild functionaries and apprentices; led by Clurman, Cheryl Crawford, and Lee Strasberg, they showed every sign of being what the Guild might have been had it started in 1929 instead of 1919. The Guild management gave its protégés a cash grant and the rights to two plays, one of them a reasonably sure thing, and then stood back benignly while the youngsters established a summer workshop in rural Connecticut to develop a set of operational imperatives. Every planet, in science-fiction, calls itself "earth"; every nation calls strangers "foreigners"; Clurman, Crawford, Strasberg, and cohort had been referring to themselves as "the group," and so they incorporated: the Group Theatre.

Of all the companies cited so far—the New, the little theatres, the Guild, and the Civic Rep—the Group shows the most revolutionary alternative to Broadway. Clurman was the philosopher, articulating the principles; Strasberg was the mystic; Crawford wore the business head. The original acting crew included Franchot Tone, Morris Carnovsky, Clifford Odets, Phoebe Brand, Sanford Meisner (all defectors from the Guild), Stella Adler, and Art Smith. Thirty-one people in all spent that first Connecticut summer formulating not only their program as entrepreneurs, but a scientific approach to the mechanics of performing. In classes, rehearsals, symposiums, and bull sessions, from dawn to taps, they communed, classified, and structured. Others had called for a modern realism in the theatre, but it was the Group that instigated the search for the *acting* technique to convey that realism most successfully.

Here was where the controversial Method was devised—the Method associated with Strasberg as mentor and Stanislafsky as inspiration, and with two generations' worth of American acting, though it was not exploited by the media until the 1950s. Stanislafsky's intention was to create an organically naturalistic environment for a character by use of the emotional humanity of the actor playing that character. The actor must not "play" but rather become the character, fusing his personality with a detailed comprehension of the personality of the character. It was as if the actor had read some secret novel version of the play, a four-volume novel in which the character's individual fullness had been revealed as it could never be in the rigorously distilled form of the one-night drama. Before Stanislafsky, the actor (besides learning his lines) kept an ear on vocal embellishment, showed profile, three-quarters, full-face, emoted. Stanislafsky's actors did all that, but only as it served the truth of their portrayals. It was technique, but naturalism was its absolute—not the actor's private naturalism, but the character's.

Stanislafsky would not likely have approved what Strasberg made of his theories, for this Method ended up imposing the actor's personality on the character's, reversing Stanislafsky's terms. While Stanislafsky forced the actor to project himself into an imagined mind and spirit of his subject, Strasberg's students develop their characterization out of their own emotional memories—the "golden box." "Take a minute," they would be told, and they used the space to siphon off an emotional memory and flood a scene with it.

In doing so, though they certainly achieved a riveting theatricality, they could not reach beyond their private world—*its* memories, *its* responses. Instead of playing the various roles assigned them as written by various authors, they re-created themselves.

However flawed, the Method does at least demonstrate the Group's ability to reinvent every aspect of theatre production. This was no mere promise to promote classical drama or a certain style of production. This was a *company*. With no permanent home and on the usual limited funds, they refreshed the repertory, as they did the acting profession, with innovation. Their debut entry, *The House of Connelly* (1931), set the Group off well; Paul Green's script of decadence ceding to new blood in the South drew raves from the critics, who were startled by but generally favorable also about their first view of Strasbergian Methodism.

Basically left-wing in politics but seldom as radical as the workers' theatre, the Group proceeded through the decade, never faltering in their idealism but not all that lucky in their choice of scripts. Unavoidably, their solidarity did at length falter. Some of the Group's premieres are red-letter entries in the annals: *Men in White, Awake and Sing!, Golden Boy, Johnny Johnson, My Heart's in the Highlands.* Many of them are forgotten leftist polemics. This is a permanent problem in theatre, whether commercial or alternative—finding scripts worth producing (regardless of what one sees in the word "worth"). It is especially threatening to a corporate situation like the Group's. A lone producer with nothing to produce is one man out of work; a company idle is another matter. If the New was unfocused, the Civic Rep incessantly classical, and the Theatre Guild "too" successful, the Group was brought down partly because its situation was too collective to go on indefinitely without emotional and spiritual rupture and partly because its anti-commercial taste forbade its renewing the exchequer with those so very useful sure things. Moreover, the Group made serious mistakes in the scripts it accepted and rejected—just after staging William Saroyan's *My Heart's in the Highlands*, the Group turned down his far more successful *The Time of Your Life*; Clurman apparently didn't like it.

Except for the lavishly appointed New Theatre, all these companies struggled against adverse financial conditions. Money, in art, is sometimes incentive but mostly destructive. This is where the government comes in, with a stipend. And this brings us to the first experience in a literally national stage: the Federal Theatre. Money was not its problem—somewhat over forty-six million dollars was spent over the course of its four years, from 1935 to 1939. But economics is not the only pressure cumbering the stage.

The Federal Theatre was one of the four arts projects organized under the New Deal's Works Progress Administration to give employment and vocational sustenance to out-of-work artists. Like similar schemes for musicians, writers, and the fine artists, the Federal Theatre aimed to pull gifted people from the relief rolls, meanwhile stimulating the art-public relationship and keeping trained professionals from getting rusty hacking cabs or hefting trays. To head the Federal Theatre, WPA chief Harry Hopkins chose not a Broadway professional but an experienced administrator from the non-commercial milieu of the little theatre, Hallie Flanagan.

The Federal Theatre proposed to put people to work, not create revenue. In keeping with her training and sympathies, Flanagan appointed other unBroadway people to run the regional Theatre offices. Even her one deputy of practical experience along The Street, Elmer Rice—who headed the New York office—had recently castigated the profit-and-loss system of Broadway production, claiming that it "stifles the creative impulse and drains the free flow of human vitality." A sprawling set-up on a truly national scale made this the first major theatre collective not to hold headquarters in New York—and as for idealistic program, Washington may have seen it as a job corps, but Flanagan saw the chance "to organize and support theatrical enterprises so excellent in nature, so low in cost, and so vital to the communities involved that they will be able to continue after Federal support is withdrawn." Later, she amended to this a statement of folkloristic purpose: "The Federal Theatre at its best was working toward an art in which each region and eventually each state would have its unique, indigenous dramatic expression . . . producing plays of its past and present, in its own rhythm of speech and its native design, in an essentially American pattern."

What loyalties should a national theatre profess? Maintained on public funds, it obviously plays to the general public, but exactly how? By catering to its taste, or uplifting it? By taking it through classic repertory or sponsoring new work? Shall there be cheesy pop or elitist alternatives? In the event, Flanagan and her associates chose the most open road. They did everything: old plays, new plays, foreign and American plays; classics from *King Lear* to *Uncle Tom's Cabin*; pop specials and difficult works such as T. S. Eliot's *Murder in the Cathedral* (which even the Theatre Guild had been afraid to touch); folk plays, tragedies, nutsy farces, musicals, Shaw and O'Neill cycles, plays of social protest, plays in Yiddish and Spanish, children's plays, puppet shows, everything. It sounds great, and in many ways it was. It kept theatre alive in places outside the major cities where it had entirely dissolved (admission was either free or nominal), and helped foster the idea of theatre as an American imperative. If much of its output was amateurish, a surprising amount of mature work was accomplished.

There was much criticism of the project. Commercial producers resented having to compete with the government. Actors Equity noted with horror the hiring of non-professionals (though these were supposedly not eligible for the program). And a number of observers were not pleased by the distinctly Red glow emanating from certain segments of the operation. A high proportion of the radical thespians who had guided the workers' theatre movement had managed to get in on the Federal Theatre, many of them subject to Party direction. To them, the Federal Theatre was both a meal ticket and a platform for propaganda. This same situation obtained in the other federal arts projects, but a Federal theatre, being so public, got much more attention. Any anti-Roosevelt politician looking for a chance to discredit the New Deal had the opportunity waiting.

The Federal Theatre's total output of radical production was small. Flanagan put it at ten percent; most likely, it was even less than that. Most of the agency's activities devolved on trucking low-budget revivals of *Lightnin'* or *The Old Homestead* to high-school auditoriums. Flanagan and her regional directors were not really in a position to screen the many thousands of employees hired by the Theatre, nor monitor the skulduggery going on in the ground-floor levels. On the other hand, Flanagan was no foe of radicalism, and this may well have been the Federal Theatre's tragic flaw. As late as 1934 she had been a contributing editor of *New Theatre*, a Communist publication printed in Moscow, and, when under fire from the House of Representatives' Special Committee for the Investigation of Un-American Propaganda (the HUAC) at the end of the decade, she was less than ingenuous in admitting no Party slant in the Federal Theatre's structure. Asked whether another publication, *New Masses*, wasn't alleged to be Communist, Flanagan replied, "*alleged* to be"—which, as the historian J. C. Furnas has pointed out, "was about like saying that the *Congressional Record* was alleged to be a publication of the U.S. Congress."

The Federal Theatre's radical wing kept the HUAC very busy learning what happens when the government enters the theatre business. A number of new works written for the project by Communists or fellow travelers was the sort of fare that has no business being supported by public money in a free country that wants to stay free—*Battle Hymn* (1936), for example, Michael Gold and Michael Blankfort's corrupt whitewash of John Brown in which that psychopathic terrorist was treated as an idealist ahead of his time; or Marc Blitzstein's Brechtian musical *The Cradle Will Rock* (1937), a frank call to revolution that valiantly withstood Washington's efforts to suppress it at the eleventh hour of its New York premiere, fleeing its pad-locked theatre for a disused house a few blocks up the street. Totalitarian theatre should be financed by totalitarians, not by Americans. (On the other hand, one could argue that as the radical theatre had established itself earlier in the decade in the commercial arena, it had as much right to repre-sentation as *Lightnin'* or *The Old Homestead*.)

There were some extreme attacks on the project, though, involving works that could hardly be called dangerous. These included the fracas over the dramatization of Sinclair Lewis' novel *It Can't Happen Here* (in which it—fascism—does), premiered simultaneously on October 27, 1936, in seventeen cities (taking in three New York productions—one in Yiddish—and an all-black cast in Seattle) and an outcry over a children's show, *The Revolt of the Beavers* (1937), in which political awareness of a Leninist stamp comes to Beaverland. It sounds like a tempest in a mug of cocoa today, but even Brooks Atkinson, generally supportive of the Federal Theatre, felt driven to comment. "Children now unschooled in the technique of revolution," he reported, "now have an opportunity, at government expense, to improve their tender minds . . . Jack and Jill lead the class revolution." Flanagan admitted that it was "very class-conscious."

The most controversial of the agency's endeavors was the "Living News-paper," developed by Elmer Rice's New York outfit to dramatize current events in the Brechtian style of the workers' sketches, but on a much grander scale. With so many people to employ, the Federal Theatre had to come up with something in the genre of spectacle. The Living Newspaper was it: stark narrative passages, impersonation of real-life figures, dance, mime, choral groupings, comic bits and pathetic cameos, speeches and morals, charts, graphs, film clips, light shows, the works. And, of course, relevant subject matter: *Ethiopia** (1936) dealt with Mussolini's imperialist ad-ventures, *Injunction Granted* (1936) with the labor-management war, *Spirochete* (1938) with the fight to control syphilis, "*. . . one-third of a nation . . .*" (1938) with the housing situation (title courtesy of a fireside chat). Flanagan, typically versed in the historical epic of the stage, helped define the Living Newspaper's sources as form: "The Living Newspaper borrows . . . from Aristophanes, from the *commedia dell'arte*, from Shake-spearean soliloquy, from the pantomime of Mei Lan Fang. . . . It still has

---

* *Ethiopia* never opened; the State Department felt its insulting references to Mussolini violated American neutrality on the diplomatic level. However, journalists were allowed to attend *Ethiopia*'s dress rehearsal.

much to learn from the chorus, the camera, the cartoon." She admitted, too, its debt to agitprop, but claimed that "it is as American as Walt Disney, the March of Time, and the Congressional Record."

These highly theatrical items, cooked up so centrally in New York, called a lot of attention to the Federal Theatre; more than anything else, they brought it down. (Although, as part of the emergency measures of the Depression years, the program had Temporary stamped all over its charter). The problem was that most of the Living Newspapers were flagrant propaganda for the New Deal (if not for regimes even farther left): *Triple-A Plowed Under* (1936), purportedly a documentary on American agriculture during the 1930s, was in fact an attack on the Supreme Court for invalidating the Agricultural Adjustment Act, and *Injunction Granted* so craftily manipulated opinion-as-truth that even Flanagan was unnerved. Except for *Spirochete*, not a single Living Newspaper—not even the dully episodic retrospective *1935* (1936)—failed to tackle sociopolitical issues from the leftist angle. Flanagan had all the education and administrative genius required for her job, but she was not politically impartial—nor was her staff— and this is no way to run a Federal Theatre.

A conflict between the Federal Theatre's politics and the HUAC's outrageous cultural ignorance ended in the closing of the entire project in mid-1939. The committee hearings substantiated the Theatre's radical learnings, but dismissed with sneers the ninety-plus percent of its schedule that was literally miscellaneous in derivation. Again, however, this was a relief program—despite Flanagan's optimism about American art—and only those emotionally involved in theatre found it distressing that Congressmen passed judgment on it. Facing the HUAC, Flanagan read from her aforementioned *Theatre Arts* article, the one that described the workers' stage as having "a certain Marlowesque madness." Representative Joseph Starnes of Alabama pricked up his ears and said, "You are quoting from this Marlowe. Is he a Communist?"

The Federal Theatre's four years did not leave much behind, as the program had culled most of its employees from the marginal ranks; when the project was dismantled they went back to whatever they were doing before. And the greater public concerned itself with real life and movies, with the Fed's cheap admissions jacked back up to free-market levels. So the industry settled back into its old habitat, roughly Fortieth to Fiftieth Streets and Sixth to Eighth Avenues in New York. There, we know, there was an attitude toward the theatre; it is one of New York's most admirable qualities. It has the daring, the open-minded approach, the continuity; in a way,

Broadway is our national theatre. It has no direction, no permanent company, no regular repertory, it is artistically irresponsible, and its occasional idealism is constantly humiliated by economics. But it is the American theatre's main stage—even now when off-Broadway and off-off-Broadway and regional theatres across the map have taken over the obligation of mounting new drama. This is a matter of simple demographics: the audience and the communications apparatus are in New York.

Broadway as theatre capital has problems that it shouldn't have. There's no way to "solve" the perennial theatre problems—finding good scripts, filling roles with fully trained and gifted actors, keeping the public engrossed. But has a theatre district ever been so badly located as Broadway is? Granted, most of America's veteran theatres stand in the deteriorated inner cities. But Broadway is amazingly ugly and dangerous—not because of the pornography stores and massage parlors that everyone complains about (and which are almost entirely on Forty-second Street and easily avoidable) but because of the pimps, prostitutes and their johns, derelicts, crazies, and muggers who have made Times Square their hangout. In 1977, when the theatre community held a rally to protest the threatening environment in which they are forced to work, one had to listen between the lines to understand what they were trying to say. Anthony Perkins spoke out against "civil libertarians and first amendment junkies," who, he said, were being "hustled" by the porno bosses in opposing a Times Square cleanup. But the whole event was filmed and edited by the local television news stations to portray actors as puerile troublemakers. By way of "good sportsmanship," they shoved their microphones at the loathsome habitués of Forty-second Street for their opinion of it all, which is like asking a pimp what he thinks of the Mann Act.

The attitude of the civic establishment is helplessness. They know that theatre is strategic to New York's economy, interrelated as it is with the tourist and restaurant trades and commanding an impressive wage equity.* Also, Broadway is essential to the city's cultural prestige. But the politicians know that the American theatre structure is more or less stuck in New York and will have to make do where it is. Leave it alone, they figure. It will survive.

Attitude, and the making of it, is the problem: a constructive attitude toward theatre. Perhaps the biggest hurdle here is the poor quality of theatre criticism in the local and national journals. First-night reviewers wield far

---

* The annual income from theatre and related businesses in New York has been estimated, as of 1980, at five hundred million dollars.

more power now than they did in the Belasco era, when there was no competition from film and television and when a public followed favored actors from role to role like a militant coalition. Reviews, then, were an assistant but not a decisive influence. The modern supercritic with superpower derives from the modern paucity of theatre coverage, the emphasis on non-professional commentary, and the personal ambitions of a few critics to get celebrated on television. Theatre journalism has not only become rotten; it has also dwindled to the point where there is no major magazine in the field.*

If any group could help mold an attitude toward theatre in New York, it is the critics. No natural law decrees that only those who produce art themselves can understand it well enough to report on it—but there is something badly "expedient" about the media's insistence on using pop hacks who have no thespian calling. Some association with the theatre, if on the dilletante level, sparked the writing of persons such as Stark Young, George Jean Nathan, Rosamond Gilder, John Mason Brown, and Percy Hammond† in the 1920s and 1930s.

Theatregoers, even the active ones, are not in a position to test reviewers' fairness for themselves, as they see the shows months after they read the reviews, and thus cannot compare exactly what they read about a show with the show itself. If they were to do so, they would be startled by the inaccuracy of reportage and the lack of consistent premises. This is proved by the seething outrage of theatre people, some of whom can remember a time when criticism was at least reasonable: the time of Brooks Atkinson.

Atkinson's thirty-two-year span as the first-string critic for the New York *Times* offers a prime example of the non-thespian who loves and understands theatre. Atkinson never succumbed to political fashion, never blamed a genre because he disliked its audience, never made his column a vehicle for personal vendetta, self-aggrandizement, or smarmy putdowns—all of which are regular features of the New York critical circle today.

---

* Coverage was once so complete that there were journals of both popular and specialist appeal devoted to the American theatre scene. In the former category were *The Theatre*, with its interviews, editorial articles, and superb critic Arthur Hornblow, Jr.; and *Stage*, ten by fourteen inches and lavishly illustrated. More technical and especially interested in regional theatre was *Theatre Arts*, on the academic side from its inception in 1916 till the late 1940s, when it took over for the defunct *Theatre* and *Stage*. It went out of business in the early 1960s.
† Hammond of the New York *Herald-Tribune* finished his career horribly; his pan of a startlingly African *Macbeth* put on by the Federal Theatre so outraged the actors that some of them held an all-night voodoo in Hammond's honor—and a few days later he was dead of pneumonia.

Starting in 1925, when he inherited a public inured to taking Alexander Woollcott's treacle with a grain of the breakfast salt, Atkinson built up a responsive and even eager readership who trusted him for one reason: he was often right. Fine him if you like for stopping short of real exuberance, but he made the reviewing system work for the theatre and the audience alike. Unlike some of his successors at the later more powerful *Times*, he used his influence as if embarrassed by it, responsibly. He couldn't close a show singlehanded, but he kept a few open. When he was around the profession was respectable.

In the early 1950s, when there were still seven daily newspapers in New York, Atkinson's good work was seconded by Walter Kerr on the *Herald Tribune*. Kerr had the exuberance Atkinson lacked; when Kerr loved a play, that play was *raved*. He was also a veteran of the university theatre and an interesting writer. (His major flaw was a weakness for cheesy musical comedy as opposed to the more artistic musical play, encouraged by an extremely tin ear.) And he, too, won over a ready, thinking, ticket-buying public. The other papers stayed with their yellow-press stooges, but Atkinson and Kerr had the prominence, and between them they kept an attitude going—nobody agreed, yet everyone was talking about, worrying over, analyzing, and attending plays. Theatre mattered, and one of the reasons people thought so is that it obviously mattered so much to Atkinson and Kerr. They were not just reviewing plays; they were attempting to chronicle the continuity—the rise—of an American art.

But Atkinson retired and Kerr's paper folded, and since they vacated the daily columns all the goodwill they had generated was dissipated by those who assumed "leadership" after them. Kerr resurfaced for Sunday pieces in the *Times*, but he had turned finicky and dowdy. Worse yet, the *Times* drama page had lost the credibility that Atkinson had so carefully built up in a series of disastrous successors: Howard Taubman; Stanley Kauffman, a fine critic whose standards were, frankly, too high for Broadway to meet; Clive Barnes, whose destructive regime lasted a decade; Richard Eder, who "guessed wrong" too often and was rudely hustled out (not so rudely as Kauffman, though). But Kerr also has been writing for the *Times* in a supplementary capacity, and lately the first-string spot has passed to the excellent Frank Rich.

The better critics tend to the more thoughtful magazines like the *New Republic* (where Kauffman and then Robert Brustein maintained an excellent theatre column in the 1960s) and usually give up after a few seasons because they find too little worth their attention. Yet Broadway needs criticism, if only as a form of publicity. This is why serious commentators would like to see an American national theatre set up—properly—somewhere: as an antidote to what they see as a lack of important drama on The Street. These better critics want something significant from the stage, in which fun is not necessarily a factor. Not that they're opposed to fun—a good reviewer need only give the various types of theatre the right to meet or fail their own standards, and to help steer the various segments of the public to the kind of theatre it wants. There is room for O'Neill, Kauffman, Odets, *MacBird!*, and *Grease*, and responsible criticism does not measure them all by the same gauge. Truly artistic standards, such as Brustein's, do not belong in the New York *Times*, which is possibly why Brustein turned them down when they offered him Taubman's position in the late 1960s. Of all critics with elitist instincts, only George Jean Nathan, from the 1920s on into the 1950s, was able to retain both his sanity and reputation, and Nathan managed it by turning his entire output into Menckenian satire. He was not the first critic famed for "hating everything," but he was definitely the most pungent stylist of his era, and no phoney: he was the first commentator to recognize and promote the talent of the young and still unknown Eugene O'Neill.

Nathan and his contemporaries were so highly thought of that, when the bad judgment of the Pulitzer drama awards got on Broadway's nerves one of the theatre community actually appealed to the critics to make a competitive award in the name of sanity. Thus was founded the New York Drama Critics Circle, at the instigation of Helen Deutsch, a public relations representative. The last straw, for Deutsch and many others, had been the Pulitzer citation of Zoë Akins' Edith Wharton adaptation, *The Old Maid* (1935), over more worthy endeavors including *The Children's Hour*, *Awake and Sing!*, *Valley Forge*, and *The Petrified Forest*. At the end of the 1935–36 season, the new Critics Circle made its first award, to Maxwell Anderson's *Winterset*—the Pulitzer went to Robert E. Sherwood's more affable *Idiot's Delight*. From then on, the approximate tangent of the two awards led the Critics Circle to cite the more stimulating event, the Pulitzer committee the more successful.

The theatre's connection with the news media has been and remains vital and unpleasant. Awards, suitably publicized, are a surer way of attracting public attention, but press coverage has if nothing else been constant. That is its vitality; its unpleasant side comprises bad reviews, and there have been Episodes as long as there have been critics. The Shuberts, one time in the 1910s, tried to bar the *Times'* Alexander Woollcott from their theatres—

bodily, which can't have been fun—and the *Times* fought back by refusing all Shubert advertisements. In the post–World War II years, Harold Clurman and Elia Kazan bought space in the *Times* to denounce the New York critics, who had recently savaged their production of Maxwell Anderson's *Truckline Café*. Anderson, too, placed an announcement: "Of late years all plays are passed on largely by a sort of Jukes family of journalism who bring to the theatre nothing but their own hopelessness, recklessness, and despair." A year later, there was another skirmish, resulting from bad notices accorded Lillian Hellman's *Another Part of the Forest*.

Will anything ever reconcile these creators and reporters? And will informed criticism ever be able to explain to the public the need for a national theatre institution? The theatre community itself lacks the information on which one might be founded. We have not even developed a recognizable set of national performance styles for our native genres, our domestic comedy, melodrama, folk play, farce, or semi-satire. British thespians know how to revive Restoration comedy or John Osborne; the French are precise with their Racine and Molière and Feydeau; the Germans understand Brecht's "epic theatre." In America, only musical comedy has a certain look and feel that authorize revivals when the original participants are unavailable.

Can we learn from the past? —from the New Theatre's amorphousness, the Civic Rep's choice of fare, the Theatre Guild's love of good text and European-influenced stagecraft, the Group Theatre's technology of *communitas*, the Federal Theatre's politicizing? If a national theatre means federal funding, will we cheer for a pork-barrel theatre rolled by Washington appointees? Politicians don't subsidize anything. We do. It's our tax-patented theatre, if we get one, and please God let it be run by someone without political affiliation, whose only party is art. Consider continuity as we proceed; consider this national theatre.

And take a lesson from Flanagan and Starnes.

13

What Does a Theatre Do in Wartime?

1940–1945

THE PERIOD JUST BEFORE AND DURING active American involvement in World War II emphasized escapism in the theatre. This was not the moral escapism of the old melodramas and romances with their crude idealism, but a more frantic escapism that found its comforts less in battles of good versus evil than in farce, domestic sententia, pathos, nostalgia, and depoliticized "current events." The 1930s had been dangerous; so had the theatre. But in the 1940s, Lefty (who had never actually entered) made his exit. In the interest of a successful war effort, the stage determined not to raise tricky questions; noting the change in the air, Eugene O'Neill kept the finished manuscript of *The Iceman Cometh* on ice to await a postwar public that might better deal with tragedy.

Broadway was not barren of adventure. There were a great many war plays (this was not the case in the last war), some of them quite serious in intent, though none upheld the pacifism of the 1930s in openly opposing American involvement. This was partly simple discretion, and partly a result of Hitler's attacking Russia on June 22, 1941. Because many of the pacifist plays were written by communists or sympathizers, the theme lost its allure during the war years and then became a perilous undertaking in the Cold War era. There was a third reason, however—the major reason for everything that happened to theatre in the early 1940s: daily life had grown so serious that the stage didn't dare put on much that was not comic or sentimental or patriotic.

Star vehicles, as always, were popular: classy plays for the classy actors and fun junk for the "personalities." Ethel Barrymore's career derived some much-needed glow from a British import, Emlyn Williams' *The Corn Is Green* (1940), her first hit in years; and Katharine Cornell's latest production of her ageless Candida in 1942, with a first-rate cast including Raymond Massey, Burgess Meredith, Dudley Digges, and Mildred Natwick, was hailed as the greatest evening of Shaw in Broadway's history. But such were the times that it was thought that any Hollywood star might get by on fame and nerve in scripts of little value. This practice reached a climax in 1945: Mary Astor in *Many Happy Returns* (a boudoir romp), Richard Arlen in *Too Hot for Maneuvers* (sexy fun at a military school), and Gloria Swanson in *A Goose for the Gander* (marital infidelity). The three runs together totaled 23 performances.

On a more adult level, and in line with Lawrence Langner's producing plays depictive of the "blessings of democracy," a number of historical dramas recalled Americans to their glorious past with the presumed intention of keeping them from repeating it. *In Time to Come* (1941) dealt with Woodrow Wilson's vain fight for American participation in a European peacekeeping agency, including a scene of treaty-making in which Clemenceau, Sonino, and Lloyd George intrigued against Wilson like a bunch of old hens, and ending with a reminder that Wilson was right after all. But the strongest impression that one carried away was of European treachery, and one felt it was not Wilson with his League of Nations but Washington with his warning against "entangling alliances" (Jefferson's phrase, by the way) who was right in the first place. More ancient patterns for democratic decisiveness were reviewed in Sidney Kingsley's *The Patriots* (1943), dealing with the standoff between Hamilton's lordly federalism and Jefferson's bourgeois agrarianism. Helen Hayes closed Florence Ryerson and Colin Clements' *Harriet* (1943) as the author of *Uncle Tom's Cabin* giving a pep talk to a mob so they could all break into "The Battle Hymn of the Republic." As for allegorical patriotism, Philip Barry had a disaster with *Liberty Jones* (1941), earnestly political but naive and unnecessary.

One blessing of democracy was the musical, with its populist egotism of informality, sentimentality, and satire. Post-Depression-era experiments in accentuating the naturalism of the form, as in Rodgers and Hart's *Pal Joey* (1940), from John O'Hara's seedy *New Yorker* stories, ceded to studies in Americana and fantasy; undeniably escapist, these often proved the most ambitious artistically. This was the time of Rodgers and Hammerstein's *Oklahoma!* (1943) and *Carousel* (1945): of seeking cultural truths in the idea of homeland. Timely issues were not exactly skirted, but bright colors made them friendly: *Cabin in the Sky* (1940) abstracted an earthy folk poetry for the black subculture; *Bloomer Girl* (1944) tackled the women's movement in the time of the Civil War, and dared to include what was for some a difficult moment in Agnes de Mille's ballet of soldiers leaving wives and mothers behind in wartime.

Cheesily useful musicals distracted the citizenry, ran many months, and then vanished forever—*Follow the Girls* (1944), for instance, an oafish affair set in a nightclub and involving retreads of the baser formal clichés. But daring innovation in modern American dance turned what might have been a conventional musical comedy into a classic reflection of urban hustle in Jerome Robbins' choreography and Leonard Bernstein's music for *On the Town* (1944). Comparable expertise blended fantasy with urban naturalism in Kurt Weill's *One Touch of Venus* (1943), and the war emergency even forced a temporary revival of operetta, led by the radically old-fashioned *Song of Norway* (1944), borrowing the life and music of Edvard Grieg.

The non-comic war plays also dealt with our destiny as a force for democracy, with a modern-dress immediacy. Maxwell Anderson wrote three war plays—*Candle in the Wind* (1941), *The Eve of St. Mark* (1942), and *Storm Operation* (1944)—not omitting the love plot even in the sweatily jingoistic *Storm Operation*, on the North African campaign. John Steinbeck learned how far a theatre can stretch in wartime with the production of his *The Moon Is Down* (1942), based on his novel about the invasion of an unnamed, non-belligerent country. The invaders were obviously Nazis, and Steinbeck's treatment of them was considered ludicrously sympathetic; there was trouble about this. "More sinned against than sinning," Richard Lockridge described Steinbeck's "villains" in the New York *Sun*, and the ensuing controversy made it clear that Steinbeck as playwright was required to use quasi-propagandistic tropes (e.g., invariably ogreish Nazis) that no one would have demanded of Steinbeck as novelist. The stage was still expected to be, at certain times, useful—not independent.

No sympathy for any Nazi confused audiences at Lillian Hellman's *Watch on the Rhine* (1941). Not precisely a war play, *Watch on the Rhine* looked in on the fifth column of underground resistance in its tale of an anti-Nazi German who brings his family to Washington, D.C., where he is menaced by a slimey pro-Nazi Rumanian count. Hellman actually had her hero methodically beat the villain to death on stage; in the charged atmosphere of 1941, most of the public found this invigorating and progressive. It marked a return to the simpler stage of the early 1900s, when *The Deep Purple*'s stalwart "man from the west" simply shot the bad guy, to the public's cheers. Intervening years, however, had brought to the fore authors who tended to discourage such direct routes to justice. Even the apparently simple, in the 1940s, could be devious, and it is notable that, while Hellman staunchly backed every facet of Russian totalitarianism, no matter how vicious, she let the general public accept *Watch on the Rhine* as an "anti-fascist" document. In fact, this so-called anti-fascism is just a preference for one kind of police state over another. It seems astonishing that theatregoers were so easily taken in, for only two years earlier Hellman had been involved in a controversy over whether or not *The Little Foxes* was to play a benefit for Finnish War Relief when Russia attacked Finland. Hellman's star Tallulah Bankhead insisted on playing the benefit; Hellman and her producer Herman Shumlin refused to allow it. Needless to say, Bankhead was not one to shrug the matter away. There was quite some row over it, and it was well publicized that *The Little Foxes* was one of the very few Broadway productions not to play a Finnish benefit. So who are the good guys in the good-versus-evil tales, after all?

This was not a time for complex answers to questions, especially in plays dealing with the war, and melodramas like *Watch on the Rhine* were enjoyed, not debated. Elmer Rice's *Flight to the West* (1940), set aboard a trans-Atlantic clipper with a heterogeneous, *Grand Hotel* sort of cast (German diplomat, Belgian refugee, American oilman, idealistic Jewish man married to a Christian, American pacifist-philosopher-turning-anti-fascist-warrior, and so on) won favor not for Rice's clumsy polemics on the world situation but for his plot twists. Similarly, James Gow and Arnaud D'Usseau's *Tomorrow the World* (1943) attracted attention as a horror story about a little boy indoctrinated by Hitlerism beyond, it appeared, redemption.

World War I had not turned up on stage until some years after it had ended, but the lesson of the 1930s was that Broadway must analyze contemporaneously, not reminisce. The most brutal of the action plays were not to come till the late 1940s, but some aspects of the war experience were investigated on the spot. *Soldier's Wife* (1944) looked at the disorientation of homecoming; *Foxhole in the Parlor* (1945), despite its farcical title, was a rather desperate work, with Montgomery Clift as a pianist demoralized in combat.

Far more popular than these were the sentimental or comic war shows. Two hit farces of 1942, *The Doughgirls* and *Strip for Action*, set the tone for the genre of War Is Fun, set at home instead of overseas and full of bizarre surprises. Joseph Fields wrote most of the laughs in *The Doughgirls* around the overcrowded conditions in Washington, D.C., and the mannish zealotry of a Soviet infantrywoman (played by Arlene Francis). Howard

Lindsay and Russel Crouse's *Strip for Action* covered the production of a burlesque show on an army post in the racy dither of authentic Floogle Street. Though it closed with a serious rendition of "The Caissons Go Rolling Along" by soldiers marching off to imminent battle, the attitude was timeless and silly.

The use of such entertainment was obvious: release. Critics, who normally would have complained, gamely tolerated these pieces for the duration. In *Strip for Action*, a plot of the sort that has outfitted many a movie musical threw strippers, baggy-pants comics, and steaming Army bureaucrats together any old way. It did have energy:

> BILLY: Nutsy, I open with a harem number—what am I going to use for a harem?
> NUTSY: Well, could it be just outside the harem? We got a beautiful drop of a meadow with cows in it.
> BILLY: Listen, I got four [dressing] rooms up there full of cows. What I want is a harem. And another thing: what have we got for an orchestra?
> NUTSY: It's all set. We got musicians. Soldiers.
> BILLY: That's sensational. Eight numbers . . . with the girls dancing to bugle calls!

Higher comedy also tackled the war, in S. N. Behrman's adaptation of Franz Werfel's *Jacobowsky and the Colonel* (1944). Behrman had replaced Clifford Odets on the project, and truly this tale of a supercilious colonel and a resourceful little Jewish man, both Poles racing from Paris to England to escape the marching Reich, called for Behrman's special delicacy, not Odets' bluntness. Louis Calhern made an elegant Colonel Stjerbinsky, Annabella was his winsome amour, and the refugee Jacobowsky was played by a genuine refugee, Oscar Karlweis. Altogether, it was an odd blend of pop fantasy and realism, for its war was almost real. (The war in a work like *The Doughgirls* was merest semi-satiric backdrop.) Furthermore, Karlweis' little hero caught a rare touch of innocent worldliness just right for Behrman. "There are two things a man shouldn't be angry at," he observes—"what he can help and what he can't help." A Jewish Yankee. Still, even this fragile distillation of real-life had to slip in its gags, and Behrman's audience was relieved to giggle at a gullible, lisping Gestapo officer. It was something the pre-war Behrman wouldn't have stooped to.

What low and high comedy could not do about the war, straightforward jingoism could. A few works of no great artistic value affirmed the fact of war, our involvement in it, and our ability to win, and some viewers found these the best of the war plays, the least escapist yet the most thrilling. Irving Berlin appeared with an all-soldier cast in his revue *This Is the Army* (1942), and Moss Hart wrote a saga for the Air Force, *Winged Victory* (1943), also staged with a military cast. Because Berlin had grown out of ragtime, he has always had a bit of Mose the Fireboy about him, and while *This Is the Army* had its share of ballads ("I Left My Heart at the Stage Door Canteen"), it also showed a strong sense of spoof. But *Winged Victory* was almost entirely sentimental, what with the glad tenderness of its inductees, the tremulous arm-punching, the stoicism, the aw's, and the good-guy commanders. Thus, Lieutenant Thompson, to his air corps graduates:

> Fellows, when you first came down to the flying line and I got my first look at you I said to myself, "Are these the jerks that I've got to teach to fly?," and my stomach made an eighty-degree landing and my brain just ground-looped!

Winged Victory turned effortlessly into a movie in 1944; with its huge cast and constant set changes, it was virtually a movie when Hart wrote it.

Clearly, this was no age for diagnoses of the human conditions. Had, say, *Our Town* opened in the early 1940s, it might have become a casualty instead of a classic. Dour drama comes later in the decade—from O'Neill, Arthur Miller, and Tennessee Williams—but the first half of the 1940s launched runs of several years each for the farces *My Sister Eileen* (1940) and *Arsenic and Old Lace* (1941), for the touching domestic chronicle *I Remember Mama* (1944), for the thriller *Angel Street* (1941), for the woozy fantasy *Harvey* (1944); and, of course these were years through which *Life with Father* (1939) unstoppably ran, finally closing late in the decade after setting the record as the longest-running attraction in Broadway's history (a record it continued to hold into the 1970s, when *Fiddler on the Roof* broke it by a mere three weeks; *Grease* then passed *Fiddler* in late 1979). Odd as it sounds, the producer Oscar Serlin tied himself in knots trying to dig up the $35,000 needed to produce *Life with Father*, though the script's source, Clarence Day's stories of growing up in late-Victorian New York, had counted among the *New Yorker*'s most effective fiction pieces and though the play's authors, Lindsay and Crouse, were hardly beginners. Joseph Kesselring's *Arsenic and Old Lace* and Mary Chase's *Harvey*, which broke the three-year mark in their original runs, were also hardship cases when the front money had to be raised.

What was *Life with Father*, anyway? More solidly constructed than

Abie's Irish Rose and better behaved than *Tobacco Road* (its fellow long-run champs), it spent most of the evening simply setting its scene—blustering Father (Lindsay), loveable, illogical Mother (Lindsay's wife Dorothy Stickney), four sons, and a few relations come to visit. The plot, such as it was, concerned Mother's bullying Father into compensating for an infantile oversight and having himself baptized. Somehow, it struck the right note of sitcom universality—though Father is despotic, selfish, and wildly intolerant—lasting into the 1950s in movie and television adaptations. It would be interesting to see how it would do in revival today.

Harvey poses a different case. *Life with Father* was orderly, realistic, and tense with Father's paternalism; *Harvey* was loose and mellow, a vehicle for any aging charmer with the blarney for the lead part of Elwood P. Dowd. Elwood worries everybody because he drinks, but drink doesn't worry Elwood —and, says Chase, isn't that *his* business? Harvey, Elwood's best friend, is a six-foot rabbit, invisible to the audience except for two "let's just see" performances during the Boston tryout (at Chase's insistence). Chase's script upheld the Saroyanesque whimsey left over from the late 1930s, and it was given validity by Josephine Hull as Elwood's dithering sister and by her succession of brothers, starting with Frank Fay, and including James Stewart, Joe E. Brown, Bert Wheeler, Jack Buchanan, and even *Harvey*'s producer, Brock Pemberton.

Arsenic and Old Lace was truly offbeat, a farce about two sweet old ladies deeply into mercy killing. (The original title was *Bodies in Our Cellar*.) "It is a noisy, preposterous, incoherent joy," announced Richard Lockridge in the New York *Sun*. "You wouldn't believe that homicidalmania could be such great fun." Actually, *Arsenic and Old Lace* isn't incoherent. It is busy: the two old women kill only lonely old men, and one of their nephews, who closely resembles and believes himself to be Theodore Roosevelt, takes the corpses for Canal Zone malaria victims and buries them in the cellar while another nephew, a sadistic killer on the lam, turns up after plastic surgery looking and acting like Frankenstein. And so on. The one principal who is not a screwball, a third nephew, is a theatre critic, and the curtain is hardly up before Kesselring gets in a few good ones on the boys along the aisle. "Mortimer hates the theatre," says one of the aunts. "He was so happy writing about real estate, which he knew something about, and then they just made him take this terrible night position . . . But, as he says, the theatre can't last much longer and in the meantime it's a living."

Farce was hot that season, 1940–41. Besides *Arsenic* there was Kaufman and Hart's *George Washington Slept Here* (New Yorkers at loose ends in

Bucks County, with a nasty nephew, a pushy rich uncle, a summer-stock Lothario, and Percy Kilbride's country caretaker, as helpful as a seven-year locust), *Mr. and Mrs. North* (Nick and Nora Charles runoffs letting loose with wisecracks), *My Sister Eileen* (set in Greenwich Village, world's capital of the screwball), plus a revival of the old British warhorse *Charley's Aunt* with José Ferrer. Sated with comic riot, the public turned to the wistful, as in *Johnny Belinda,* the tale of a deaf-mute girl despised by her townsfolk and defended by a doctor who falls in love with her. As the girl, Helen Craig got only one word to say the entire evening, and was very careful how she said it. Her progress in sign language cheered the public as they rotated handkerchiefs and sniffled; the critics hated it, but it was soon happily on its way to Hollywood.

John Van Druten's *I Remember Mama* (1944) represents the middle level of forties sentimentality—note the emphasis on mother, still the key to the American family drama. Mady Christians' sinewy-saintly Norwegian matriarch fighting penury in San Francisco made Van Druten's adaptation of Kathryn Forbes' autobiographical stories far more telling as drama than it should have been. Schooled in Shaw and Shakespeare, Christians disarmed the town despite gaudy high jinks more appropriate to farce (a spinster aunt finally lands a milquetoast suitor) and sodden sentiment (a coyote uncle turns white sheep on his deathbed). Further adapted, the property led the television assimilation of domestic comedy, with Peggy Wood as Mama.

In an age when the theatre massages rather than stimulates, the art of William Saroyan, so brightly lit in *The Time of Your Life,* began to flicker. Acting as his own producer, he kept *The Beautiful People* (1941) open past the 100-performance mark, but this was the last success Saroyan enjoyed (it lost money, but was well-liked by a minority). *Get Away Old Man* (1943), Saroyan's impressions of his adventures in Hollywood (with Richard Widmark as Saroyan) died in two weeks. Whimsey without plot can only go so far in any age. Saroyan thought nothing of raising his curtain on a scene like the one in *The Beautiful People* in which a young boy told an old woman about his sister and her friends the mice—over a thousand of them, it seems, and they adore the girl. "They go all over looking for things for her," says the boy, take it or leave it. *The Beautiful People* may be Saroyan's sweetest play, and it is to theatregoers' credit that so slight a piece lasted more than a week.

Another play, even slighter in tone but far more substantial in character, also won affection in this difficult time, Tennessee Williams' *The Glass Menagerie* (1945). First mounted in Chicago, this touchingly poetic "memory play" tells of a shy girl, her wastrel brother, their pretentious mother, and a "gentleman caller" whom the brother brings home for a date with the girl. The title refers to the girl's collection of glass animals, and emphasizes the play's delicacy. Yet, for a select group of playgoers, this was a blockbuster evening, not only for the work itself but for the production. The onetime Peg O'My Heart Laurette Taylor came out of the years of alcoholic seclusion that followed her husband's death saying, "Well, that was the world's longest wake, wasn't it?"—and suddenly the alleged has-been was etching one of the most fondly admired portraits of the century as the mother. Taylor's Amanda Wingfield, Julie Haydon's daughter, Eddie Dowling's son, Anthony Ross' gentleman caller, Jo Mielziner's design of a rundown apartment and back alley in St. Louis, Paul Bowles' incidental music of remote, imprisoned gaiety, and the stage direction by Dowling and Margo Jones so impressed everyone that the piece itself was not recognized as a prospective classic. No one crowed over the "new playwright in town," as they would in later decades if somebody merely got a play produced, let alone wrote a good one.

Other than *The Glass Menagerie* and one all-time American masterpiece soon to be disclosed, the only major drama of the period was *Native Son* (1941), adapted by Paul Green from Richard Wright's novel about a black man who decides that his only route to freedom in the United States is through violence. As with the gentlemanly Nazis in Steinbeck's *The Moon Is Down,* what was hailed in a novel seemed shocking as a play—not because live action is more *there,* but because literature was allowed to be bold and theatre was supposed to behave. *Native Son* burned with rage at the forces that hunt its outspoken protagonist to destruction—and the black folk play was retired forever. Where playwrights once told tales of dynastic suffering, now they would write of individualists fighting back. Furthermore, Green— an early exponent of the black folk play—was working from a black man's novel, thus overthrowing the custom that blacks act in but do not conceive their own drama. But the pathetically fatalist Green was an absurd choice to dramatize Wright's indignant polemic, and Wright was brought in to edit the script shortly before the opening, though the text had already gone to press in the Green version.

Native Son, staged by Orson Welles with Canada Lee in the lead, was not a play for most tastes. Among those who resisted it were the Urban League, which thought the tragic ending counterproductive to progressivism; the Communist party, protesting Wright's refusal to cater to Soviet blather; and the *Journal-American,* indicting "propaganda that seems nearer to Moscow than Harlem." The first two picketed the theatre briefly. But it was inevitable that history be made with such a play, or the white man's style in the "black folk play" would remain the only black style anyone knew of. As it happens, by 1940 such works were of no interest to anyone; Roark Bradford's *John Henry* sank after a week even with Paul Robeson in the title role, while rumor had it that an amateur group in Harlem did the John Henry legend much greater justice as *Natural Man* a few months earlier.

Canada Lee's performance as *Native Son*'s Bigger Thomas opened a lot of eyes, particularly in the physical presence of his work. It had long been noted that such black actors as came to prominence used their bodies more easily than their white colleagues. But Broadway's directors didn't know how to maneuver them. Except in a very few cases, where the staging evolved out of blacks' instincts (as with Rouben Mamoulian's of *Porgy* or Welles' of *Native Son*—not to mention Welles' radically ethnic *Voodoo Macbeth* for the Federal Theatre), the players were inadvertently kept down. Largely self-trained, black actors often came out of vaudeville and Harlem clubs, which emphasized comic and musical gifts over any others. Everyone was stunned when "the singer" Ethel Waters had a straight-play triumph in DuBose Heyward's *Mamba's Daughters* (1939) after a decade of musicals. Everyone shouldn't have been.

Such *ex post facto* star turns as Waters' and Lee's led to greater racial integration on Broadway. Plays that dealt with interracial romance still stood out in a kind of scandal, as *All God's Chillun Got Wings* had done in 1924; as *Deep Are the Roots* did in 1945. And black playwrights were yet to be heard from. But black acting was coming into renown as a situation of first-class performances by certain persons rather than the quasi-anonymous ensembles that theatregoers associated with the folk play. Sure, everyone raved about Richard Harrison's Lawd in *The Green Pastures*. But could anyone have cited even one other member of the cast by name?

A culmination of sorts was reached in Margaret Webster's production of *Othello* in 1943 with Paul Robeson, José Ferrer, Uta Hagen, and Webster as Emilia. Robeson was an inept Othello—Webster herself eventually admitted that he totally lacked technique and had garnered little savvy from his past stage appearances (mostly in London). But he looked splendid, had the natural sound, and—most importantly—was taking his proper place as a black American star in a starring part. No one at the time could have seen ahead to a day (1964) when a two-character sex comedy, *The Owl and the Pussycat*, could be cast with a white man and a black woman and make no reference to miscegenation. Robeson's Othello, then Canada Lee's Caliban in *The Tempest* two years later, were seen as climactic moments in the first of several necessary evolutions, the stage at which black actors played specifically black (or, as with Caliban, weird) roles usually assigned to whites. More would have to come, but Robeson's Othello, at the time, was big enough. Opening night was as tense as any premiere since Clyde Fitch haunted the premiere of *The City* in 1909. "There is, perhaps," wrote Webster later about that evening, "only one thing which totally distinguishes the stage from its mechanical competitors—the live communication between living actors and a living audience. When the electric spark leaps from the stage to the auditorium, when the pressure mounts till the needle almost runs off the gauge, the theatre could quite easily explode. Bobby [Robert Edmond] Jones said of the *Othello* opening, 'If a cat had walked across the footlights it would have been electrocuted.'"

Of a sort, *Native Son* and the Robeson *Othello* served to remind us of the social theatre of the previous decade, as resistance to racism was one of its themes, and such resistance informed *Native Son* as work and this *Othello* as production. Otherwise, this was not a political time. Still, it does yield one classic in that field, Thornton Wilder's *The Skin of our Teeth* (1942). A kind of epic-absurdist-domestic comedy, *The Skin of Our Teeth* aimed to reassure Americans that man can live through anything. Wilder set aside the chinoiserie, folksy amiability, and drab elegy of *Our Town* for an even kinkier staging, farcical sophistication, and a sermon on survival, wrapped in the history of mankind as it might have been staged by Olsen and Johnson. The scenery doesn't behave, the spectators are constantly hectored or cajoled by one of the characters (who doesn't like or understand the play), and some indisposed actors have to be replaced in the finale by the backstage help. Meanwhile, an average suburban American family suffers through the ice age (as Archimedes, Homer, Moses, and few muses huddle at the living room fireplace singing "Tenting Tonight" while glaciers roll down the street and the theatre ushers pass chairs up from the audience to "save the human race"), the Flood (at an Atlantic City convention of mammals), and war (Father cheers up when he realizes that some of his books are intact).

It is very funny and very crazy, and, besides being perhaps the most significant conquest of formula since the experimental 1920s, it makes its point about survival very smartly. It did excellent business at the height of wartime, receiving official sanction from the Pulitzer Prize Committee and lasting 359 performances despite a flurry of exasperated walkouts. The show did earn a kind of Must See status, but most people were honestly amused by Wilder's script, Elia Kazan's direction, and a very sharp cast including Fredric March and Florence Eldridge as Mr. and Mrs. George Antrobus, the young Montgomery Clift as their son Henry (formerly known as Cain—he has the scar to prove it), Florence Reed as a fortuneteller, and, in the center ring, Tallulah Bankhead as the insouciant maid and harlot, Lily Sabina.

It was Sabina who criticized Wilder's modern style for us earlier in these pages, looking back on the old beautiful stage and its "good entertainment with a message you can take home with you." But Wilder's joke is that *The Skin of Our Teeth* is just that sort of show under its carnival structure, and even recalls the expositions of countless "good" plays by starting the action with Sabina and her dustmop in the parlor, nattering to herself with all the constipated time-and-place setting of the Belasco era:

> Oh, oh, oh! Six o'clock and the master not home yet. Pray God nothing serious has happened to him crossing the Hudson River. If anything happened to him, we would certainly be inconsolable and have to move into a less desirable residence district . . . The whole world's at sixes and at sevens, and why the house hasn't fallen down about our ears long ago is a miracle to me.

So of course one of the walls promptly tilts awry. A bit later it drops away altogether.

The Skin of Our Teeth isn't meant to be profound—as *Our Town* is— but it stands as a flagpin on the map of our dramatic heritage, marking our long overdue arrival in the seriocomic world of modern theatre where we wait for Godot. *Godot* is about not getting there; *Skin* insists that we can. It's an invigorating piece, and should last as long as we do, despite the pall cast on it by José Quintero's incompetent Bicentennial revival. Given that Wilder was an erudite observer of classic theatre, one might propose that *The Skin of Our Teeth* is a comic version of *Our Town*, a satyric comple- ment such as the Greeks often wrote for their tragedies. But *Our Town* is about the hopeless inertia of continuity. *Skin* is about continuity's drive. Said Wilder in the middle of world war a mere thirty years after a war to end wars: we'll make it. It's all cycles, and there's always rebirth, especially in the heritage of the written word. So Wilder ends the action as he began it, with Sabina in her well-made living room. "Oh, oh, oh! Six o'clock and the master not home yet . . ."

14

And What After?

1945-1949

WITH THE WAR OVER, it was time for the theatre to reestablish its militancy, clouded in the effort of affirming the American past and future for the war-time audience. We want perspectives on the American *imagination*—but at the tail end of the first postwar season, 1945–46, a last flourish of "lend-lease" laid some stunning perspective on Broadway in a visit by the Old Vic Company of England. The Old Vic brought no new works over, so there was no comparison to be made with their stock of modern plays as opposed to ours. But the productions themselves—of Chekhof's *Uncle Vanya*, both parts of Shakespeare's *Henry IV*, and a double bill of Sophocles' *Oedipus Rex* and Sheridan's *The Critic*—jolted the unbiased. British acting and production concept were of an embarrassingly high quality—and this was their national theatre company to boot. That they had one at all was reminder of several failed attempts to establish one here, but that theirs was so good humiliated Broadway. Antiquarians ransacked their memories of the Moscow Art Theatre tour twenty-three years before and declared that little or nothing seen here between Stanislafsky and the Old Vic could share their eminence. New-comers sat through Laurence Olivier's juxtaposing of Sheridan's comical Mr. Puff and Sophocles' Oedipus on the same evening and wondered if any American actor could pull that off. Not to mention Ralph Richardson's Falstaff, Vanya, and Tiresias; Margaret Leighton's Yelyena; Joyce Redman's Doll Tearsheet and Sonya; Harry Andrews' Creon; and such tastes of true rep diligence as Leighton and Redman's turning up in *Oedipus* as Jocasta's attendants.

Broadway, by comparison, lacked style. True, the 1947–48 season saw splendid mountings of *Man and Superman* directed by and starring Maurice Evans and Euripides' *Medea* (freely adapted by Robinson Jeffers) with Judith Anderson and John Gielgud, staged by Gielgud. (But note that again the driving energy in both productions was British—Evans, Anderson, Gielgud.) Also true, not everyone thought the Old Vic superior to the home team in style, or in anything else. Some pointed out a distinction not in ability or training, but in idealism—they did great (old) plays all the time and we didn't. George Jean Nathan, always one to see through the emperor's new clothes, spent a long article debunking the Old Vic's alleged excellence of diction, versatility, and ensemble, and likened one of the *Uncle Vanya* portrayals to "Hedda's Tesman as he might be played by George Jessel." Maybe so. Yet the thought crossed many minds that we weren't living up to our potential in theatre. What were the great American performances of the season that culminated in the Old Vic's triumph? There were some striking portrayals: Marlon Brando's overwrought husband in Maxwell Anderson's *Truckline Café*; Spencer Tracy's uncorruptible newspaper editor in Robert E. Sherwood's *The Rugged Path*; Ossie Davis' race-conscious black war hero fighting bigotry back home in Robert Ardrey's *Jeb*; Barbara bel Geddes in another play on American race relations, *Deep Are the Roots*; Judy Holliday's classic dumb blonde Billie Dawn in Garson Kanin's *Born Yesterday*, patenting the voice, walk, and look of the type for all time; Bobby Clark's demented, burlesque Molière in *The Would-Be Gentleman*, a version of *Le Bourgeois Gentilhomme*; and the Lunts in one of their least significant vehicles, Terence Rattigan's *O Mistress Mine* (Alfred, at least, was born Yankee).

But it was not a matter of citing stand-out acting turns; we wanted a sense of inner-directed wholeness from Broadway. So it was gratifying that Eugene O'Neill's *The Iceman Cometh* showed up near the start of the next season in October of 1946. Simply by continuing to produce, O'Neill put us in touch with the young O'Neill of the off-Broadway one-acts, the later O'Neill of experimentation, and the master O'Neill, author of *Mourning Becomes Electra*. Here it was only twenty-six years after *Beyond the Horizon*, and we could count at least one major playwright with a career to parse. Looking back, we commenced looking forward: continuity.

The season had opened with an underpowered revival of *The Front Page* and continued limp with *Hidden Horizons*, a static adaptation of Agatha Christie's *Death on the Nile* (by Christie herself); *The Bees and the Flowers*, an alleged comedy by a pair of Hollywood hacks (sample joke: "He's part Indian"; "Well, for that matter, I'm part Irish." Huh?); *Obsession*, a two-character French play with Eugenie Leontovich and Basil Rathbone, on marital jealousy; *Hear That Trumpet,* about the offstage life of a jazz band; a production of Rostand's *Cyrano de Bergerac* with José Ferrer; and a few stale operettas. Except for *Cyrano,* everything flopped. But one night after *Cyrano,* everything took on a new air by association. The bare fact: O'Neill had emerged after twelve years with a masterpiece. The received fact: Broadway was the sum of parts, and only one part was hoke. Because the other part was O'Neill.

The Iceman Cometh presents a quintessential O'Neill situation, a waterfront saloon in 1912. There, a collection of losers wear out the rest of their lives by rehearsing "pipe dreams"—illusions about what they might have been or had—and drinking themselves into trances. One thing gives their lives structure, the periodic arrival of a hardware salesman, Hickey, who underwrites a binge of drinks and dreaming. Trouble is, Hickey shows up this time not to sponsor illusion but to shatter it. Like someone just off the psychiatrist's couch, Hickey wants to cure everyone, free them all of their hopeless lies about themselves as he has—he claims—freed himself. But, as O'Neill has shown before, hopeless illusions are inescapable. The drunks of Harry Hope's saloon don't want to be cured, cannot be cured—certainly not by Hickey, the sorriest liar of them all because he really lives on his lie. Through imagery, the iceman of the title is seen as death; O'Neill might easily have called his play *Death of a Salesman.* With Hickey led away by the police to pay for the murder of his wife, the barflies fall back into their false nostalgia and never-to-be-implemented future projects, gratefully deluded as before.

This is the silhouette of a deep work, brilliantly organized through verbal repetition in a quasi-symphonic pattern of exposition, development, and (after the "iceman" fingers Hickey for execution) recapitulation. There is much of this repetition, and four long acts; anything this big is fated to be a target for grousing critics. *The Iceman Cometh* has taken a lot of flak, partly from theatre people who find O'Neill clumsy and verbose and partly from critics eager to score elite points. Even at the time, when the very appearance of an ambitious American play had the theatre community eager to see where history would take them next, there were nays. As so often, Mary McCarthy's were the cutest. "This work," she wrote, "gives the assurance that it has been manufactured by a reliable company; it is guaranteed to last two-and-a-half hours longer than any other play, with the exception of the uncut *Hamlet.*" As McCarthy saw it, *The Iceman Cometh* did not expand the context of Broadway as art. Rather, it topped a minor pile called

Broadway as entertainment. "It is attractive positively because of its defects. To audiences accustomed to the oily virtuosity of George Kaufman, George Abbott, Lillian Hellman, Odets, Saroyan, the return of a playwright who— to be frank—cannot write is a solemn and sentimental occasion."

A minority ruling. The 136-performance run, respectable enough for 1946 (if a letdown considering the 426 of *Strange Interlude*), would almost certainly have been longer if the Theatre Guild production had been as first-rate as the script. Legend has exaggerated its flaws. It was not a poor production, but not a great one, and a play as difficult as this needs all the help it can get. O'Neill attended rehearsals, explaining his metaphysics to the eager actors, and the director, Eddie Dowling, was no slouch. Possibly, the Hickey was. Dowling was supposed to play the part, and the Guild had cast the onetime vaudevillian James Barton as Harry Hope, the saloon owner. But it was thought a bit much for Dowling to direct as well as take the lead in so demanding a work, and Barton moved up to the principal part. He had, unquestionably, the right quality—much more so for the gladhanding Hickey than the surly Hope. But vaudeville is not an Eton playing field for O'Neill, and the crucial "stays" of Hickey's persona never quite came off.

There is another problem. The inhabitants of Hope's saloon are written for very strong "character actors"—stronger than what Broadway usually can draft for such parts. A national theatre company would have no problem here: it is a tradition of such organizations that heroic actors too old to play a creditable Hamlet or Peer Gynt move sideways, so to say, into such roles as *The Iceman*'s Larry Slade, a bitter, lapsed radical; Willie Oban, a failed lawyer; Joe Mott, a black who once ran a gambling house; or Piet Wetjoen and Cecil Lewis, opposing veterans of the Boer War. An all-star cast might fit too naturally into separate spotlights and fudge the needed ensemble; ensemble craftsmen will lack the personal immensity.

Another problem is the length: O'Neill's ear for the vernacular had cleared amazingly over the years, but he was still writing loose. Yet this is not as problematic for some spectators as the turgid ideological universality. *The Iceman Cometh* is O'Neill's one major foray into the kind of play that Americans have never fully accepted, that which emphasizes generalized truths over the truth of individual persons and analysis over narration. This universality creeps in early in the show and immediately takes hold; it was O'Neill's way of making the almost surrealistic, *Grand-Hotel* situation sensible, but it is very conscious of its own commentative grandeur. Harry Hope is beautifully drawn, like a true fool's hope alternating between supporting and attacking his clients. Hickey, too, is a finely shaped individual. But the play as a whole is very much a parable, always bigger than itself. Not three minutes after the curtain has gone up, Slade, explaining why he left "the Movement," delivers one of O'Neill's few all-world assessments, one O'Neill himself made privately on occasion:

> I saw men didn't want to be saved from themselves, for that would mean they'd have to give up greed, and they'll never pay that price for liberty. So I said to the world, God bless all here, and may the best man win and die of gluttony! And I took a seat in the grandstand of philosophical detachment to fall asleep observing the cannibals do their death dance.

Staging the German-language premiere in the late 1940s, Eric Bentley despaired of the "rotten fruit of unreality" around "its dramatic core"—the repetitions, the "obvious and unimaginative symbolism." He thought the Guild production too obsequious to O'Neill the Master. Despite the difficulty in encompassing regional dialects and outdated slang in translation, Bentley believes that his *Iceman* production, with some sixty minutes of dialogue pruned away for an unworshipful audience, did better justice to O'Neill than the original mounting—and, incidentally, uncovered the work's hidden quotient of comedy.

A later revival at off-Broadway's Circle-in-the-Square in 1956 was universally hailed as greater than the Guild's: the José Quintero staging with Jason Robards, Jr. This *Iceman* and an *Uncle Vanya* at the Fourth Street Theatre with Franchot Tone, coming just when modern off-Broadway began to attract attention in an important way, were as much news (and history) as they were art, and legend has mythologized the Robards *Iceman* in particular. It was a fine production, certainly, the scroungy theatre blending well with David Hays' set and the three-quarters' arena staging putting the audience virtually in the saloon. Quintero staged the whole text, but his cast made it sound almost natural, repetitions and all. They, too, found the comedy in O'Neill. But Robards was definitely why the show played so well, placing—as James Barton could not—the sour devil in Hickey that lies below the gladhander. Barton played a good guy in ruins; Robards played huge, human doom. It is notable that while this production changed his status from unknown to star-in-the-making, his colleagues remained unknowns: Farrell Pelly played Hope, Conrad Bain played Slade, Larry Robinson played Parritt, William Edmondson played Joe Mott, Phil Pheffer played Ed Mosher, and the others are similarly names of little resonance (though Bain finally earned some fame as one of the regulars on television's *Maude*). Perhaps Quintero hit on the one way of gearing an *Iceman* ensemble by casting

Hickey for the grand style and surrounding him with players of less out-standing gifts.

Productions come and go. It is the text that lives, and Broadway, thespians and public, seemed to understand that in the late 1940s. With the appearance of O'Neill in top form, dismay at Old Vic excellence began to recede. The scripts were coming: a stock of plays. If the original production doesn't work, a later one might bring a piece home; a national theatre is there for just this purpose. Broadway, frankly, doesn't like to give flops a second chance. It leaves the reclamation work to off-Broadway and institutional theatre. Broad-way likes hits.

Broadway must figure itself out, then. Is it a rapacious commercial arena exclusively, or has it room for art on art's terms? And can one work justify a season? But wait: we shall see that O'Neill was not the only master in town.

First, what about the old hands: George Kelly, Maxwell Anderson, Sid-ney Kingsley, Elmer Rice, S.N. Behrman, Philip Barry, Robert E. Sherwood, Lillian Hellman, Clifford Odets—the prominent earnest bylines of the 1930s? Rice, Sherwood, Behrman, and Barry seemed to be running out of juice. With social protest pulled out from under the first two, they floundered for a topic; meanwhile, the social comedy of the second two showed a nerveless glitter. Odets was mostly in Hollywood, reproached by thespians for quitting not only his style-setting working-class drama, but all drama at all. Hellman repeated herself, lamely, in *Another Part of the Forest* (1946), a look at the Hubbard family of *The Little Foxes* one generation earlier, with Patricia Neal playing the younger version of Tallulah Bankhead's Regina.

At least Kelly, Anderson, and Kingsley were in fettle, if not topmost form. Continuing his series of satiric reports on modern American life, Kelly pointed out how a certain betrayed wife (Ina Claire, out of retirement) en-joys portraying her betrayal so enthusiastically that she destroys a salvageable marriage in *The Fatal Weakness* (1946). Anderson turned an interesting trick in *Joan of Lorraine* (1946), a Joan of Arc enactment rehearsed and discussed by the "players" as they perform it; the original run got some mile-age out of the appearance of Ingrid Bergman as The Maid. In a more familiar vein, Anderson came up with another verse play on British royalty, *Anne of the Thousand Days* (1948), Henry VIII (Rex Harrison) and Anne Boleyn (Joyce Redman) reminding the public about British actors and their deftly tripping tongues. Kingsley attempted to retrieve the naturalistic bru-tality of *Dead End* in the more compact *Detective Story* (1949), one taut day of cops, lawbreakers, and their loved ones set in a Manhattan precinct station.

Veteran musical comedy creators were riding out a golden age, continuing to chart the national folk patterns in history, fantasy, sociocultural illustration, and satire. Rodgers and Hammerstein forged ahead in format in *Allegro* (1947), an arraignment of postwar urban superficiality mounted daringly on a bare stage with back projections, while Harold Arlen, Irving Berlin, and Cole Porter each did his best work in, respectively, *St. Louis Woman* (1946), *Annie Get Your Gun* (1946), and *Kiss Me, Kate* (1948). Even Sigmund Romberg sounded fresh in the operetta *Up in Central Park* (1945). Still vitally topical, the musical applied its friendly but earnest focus to postwar homecoming in Harold Rome's revue *Call Me Mister* (1946); to capitalist economics and white racism in *Finian's Rainbow* (1947); and to American marriage in a wild parodistic vaudeville, Kurt Weill and Alan Jay Lerner's *Love Life* (1948).

Continuity was variable, then, but definitely there. At least half of it was the past going on, the other half the future pushing in. It was thought that the war might generate a new crop of playwrights who would write the war plays that couldn't have been produced during the duration—plays of horror, ambiguity, exhaustion, even defeat. And as it happened, four war plays of varying genres did see the light in the late 1940s.

The more serious half of the quartet appeared in the 1945–46 season with the war scarcely over, Harry Brown's *A Sound of Hunting* and Arthur Laurents' *Home of the Brave*. The first told of a platoon sweating out the return of a trapped comrade, the second of a shell-shocked soldier trying to conquer a guilt neurosis. Each made more of a stir among critics than among public, though neither was forbiddingly gruesome. *A Sound of Hunting* proved funny, gripping, and bitter (the trapped soldier, whom none of the others likes anyway, ultimately dies) without reaching for cinema sentiment, though its premise has served many a movie; *Home of the Brave* begged too much sympathy for its protagonist, but the psychodrama-like therapy treatments that bring him around foreshadowed those in *Equus* to a startling degree. (A touch of anti-Semitism caught a lot of attention, but this was peripheral to the play's point.)

Two seasons later came the more apparently "entertaining" half of the quartet, a thriller and a comedy, each graced by movie-star turns in the leads. William Wister Haines' suspenseful *Command Decision* offered Paul Kelly as the harder-than-nails but secretly compassionate general, and Thomas Heggen and Joshua Logan's *Mr. Roberts* had Henry Fonda as the likable Navy lieutenant stuck against his will on a backwatered supply ship.

Command Decision was a straightforward thriller, *Mr. Roberts* a farce with an unhappy ending; neither tested any spectator's assumptions about the war as Steinbeck had in *The Moon Is Down*, and both were received with delight. Haines' play, quite good of its kind, told of an all-out attack on German bases costing incredibly high American casualties. Kelly had come a long way from the giggly adolescent of *Seventeen*, and for *Command Decision* he embodied the all-purpose American titan, sometime westerner, sometime warrior, sometime detective, with a hidden sentimental streak and an unbreakable talent for winning. Unattached to place or person, he rides off into the faraway, his story permanently unfinished. Roberts, in the other play, was a less upfront version of the same type, but his story was, movingly, finished: he dies.

Mr. Roberts was technically Thomas Heggen's brainchild, based on his episodic novel. Logan was only to have directed the author's adaptation, but somewhere along the way he got fledged as a fifty-fifty collaborator and the material suffered a sea-change of prankish whoopee, ensuring great success but a splintered thrust. The courage of Roberts, who desperately wants to transfer from his cushy assignment and help fight the war, got lost in a wash of sitcom fadoodle, what with a tyrannical and thoroughly ridiculous captain, crazy goofings off, and a Katzenjammer crew.

All four—Brown, Laurents, Haines, and Heggen—were new to Broadway, and the newness of their approaches varied inversely with their popular appeal: the less "different," the more profit. Even at that, Brown's play, the most finished of the quartet as sheer writing, was not so much different as brutal. In all, no playwright went so far as to test the system of offensive-defensive war as we had been reading it in the first half of the twentieth century. There was no endorsement of disarmament, no assaults on nuclear power or punitive bombing, on American self-belief or procedure. These were to come later—for now, Broadway dealt with war most intently in patterns of the heroic challenge met (*Command Decision*) or failed (*A Sound of Hunting*).

What of our more enduring forms—farce, the domestic play, and satire? None of them was in good health. It is disturbing to consider that all three conflated more impressively into the one evening of *The Skin of Our Teeth* in 1942 than any one of them impressed on its own throughout the late 1940s. Norman Krasna's *John Loves Mary* (1947) was the farce one expected to see shortly after the war: returning soldier has married his buddy's lost London flame to bring her to America, finds buddy has already married someone else, stalls his own sweetheart, lies, leaps, falls down, groans, runs around . . . you know the rest. It was about as solid as a doughnut hole, and of course it ran a year.

Even the domestic shows that had so brightened Broadway in the previous two decades weren't what they used to be, though Ruth Gordon ingenuously recalled her last days at home before departing for New York and fate in *Years Ago* (1946), with the Marches as her parents. Howard Lindsay and Russel Crouse followed up their *Life with Father* in *Life with Mother* (1948), almost as good but, interestingly, nowhere near as successful. The flow of life with a more resolute mother was tapped in Gertrude Berg's *Me and Molly* (1948), with radio's Goldberg family celebrating the pragmatic affiliation of America's pop media in making this stop on their way to television. As playwright, Berg was a primitive. Still, as with *I Remember Mama*, there was some charm in learning how subcultural ethnics work out the problems of upward mobility, Mama's Katrin with her autobiographical short stories and Molly's Jake with his nervous entry into the management end of the garment business.

Satire and semi-satire trudged their road. The first postwar season brought the much hailed (including a Pulitzer Prize) *State of the Union* (1945), Lindsay and Crouse's look at the pre-nomination campaign of an idealistic industrialist being pushed by certain Republicans as the hope for unseating Harry Truman and the New Deal. ("Is there any difference between the Democrats and the Republicans?" someone asks a Republican politico, who replies, "All the difference in the world—they're in and we're out.") The title is a pun revealing the bimodal format of the script—the state in question is that of both a "reconverting" ex-war-economy nation (political satire) and a marriage on the rocks (marital comedy). The two are tied together in that the presidential possibility is the husband of the wife. Original neither as satire nor boudoir romp, *State of the Union* won its favor because its hero proved too idealistic for the deals and lies of party politics. He withdraws his candidacy, to the cheers of the audience. His wife cheers, too, and all is well.

State of the Union, slim as it was, marked a provisional apex for satire in the late 1940s; this seems not to have been a great era for American wit. As for semi-satire, so much more flexible than real satire because its aim is so much lower, it, too, suffered the blahs. George S. Kaufman's one entry in this period, a collaboration with Edna Ferber called *Bravo!* (1948), stumbled into town after provincial tryouts so disastrous that its doleful five-week run seemed a smash hit by comparison. If even the champion Kaufman could do no better than this, what could we hope for from those who at best learned from and at worst imitated him? His erstwhile partner, Moss Hart, was now on his own (directing as well as writing, in the Kaufman fashion) and should have given us a winner in *Light Up the Sky* (1948). This comedy *à clef* featured copies of Gertrude Lawrence, Billy Rose, Eleanor Holm, and other show people having at each others' throats during tryouts of an avant-garde piece, but theatregoers thought of Kaufman and Ferber's effervescent *The Royal Family* twenty years before and slowly shook their heads. More on the beam, and a big hit, was Garson Kanin's *Born Yesterday* (1946), the one that introduced Judy Holliday's dumb blonde (as a last-minute replacement for Jean Arthur, oddly enough) while blowing razzberries at the anonymous money bosses who buy law in Washington. Or who only attempt to, says Kanin—says semi-satire in general. A pop comedy in which a money boss actually got away with it wouldn't last two weeks on old Broadway.

Tracing the impact of *The Iceman Cometh* must have been an exasperating experience. Broadway had history, but it seemed a shallow one, and continuity appeared to be choking on its own survival—until Tennessee Williams and Arthur Miller turned up. They rose to prominence in the late 1940s, though both had had debuts of sorts earlier on—Williams in the Boston tryout of *Battle of Angels* in 1943 and Miller in a 4-performance flop, *The Man Who Had All the Luck*, in 1944. And, of course, Williams' *The Glass Menagerie* had already happened by this time. But no one had any idea that anything was to follow it, certainly nothing as good as *A Streetcar Named Desire*. It was really in the latter half of the decade that Broadway received Williams and Miller, with a pair of plays each, Williams' *A Streetcar Named Desire* and *Summer and Smoke* and Miller's *All My Sons* and *Death of a Salesman*.

A Streetcar Named Desire (1947) was the pre-eminent romantic triumph of its day, melodrama told in poetry. In a way, it played as a brutal reply to the illusion-loving theatre of the 1930s, for Williams speaks truth to someone whose whole life is a lie, the deluded Blanche duBois. Trouble begins when Saroyan's Lady Beautiful meets the hairy ape: in a raffish corner of New Orleans, Blanche arrives to live with her sister, who has married a rude, ultra-physical man who is nothing but appetites and gut responses, Stanley Kowalski. He thinks Blanche puts on airs, and she thinks Stanley is an animal. They're both right. Ultimately the he-man rapes the fairy queen, sending her off the deep end. "I have always depended on the kindness of strangers," says Blanche to the man in the white coat who, in the last scene, takes her away, a Big Moment of any revival. Like many a heroine of Depression theatre, Blanche is a dreamer, but Stanley is a pragmatist, and in Williams the pragmatists always win.

The Iceman Cometh had a cast full of dreamers, but harkened back to twenties realism; *Streetcar* was conceived with an eye on twenties experimentalism, but avoided entirely that decade's cumbersome avant-garde Mission. It didn't try to convert, or proclaim. Williams just wrote a play with the technique to express a peculiar individuality as if it were universal and even crucial to the audience's experience. The rage of the season and an immediate national treasure (though a terror to bluenoses), it claimed potent ambassadors in its eerie setting, humid with human intensity and atmospheric pictures, in its offstage jazz accompaniment, in Kim Hunter's Stella, Karl Malden's Mitch, and especially in Jessica Tandy's increasingly desperate Blanche, the flirtatious passivity sinking into an almost prudish depravity, and Marlon Brando's Stanley.

Death of a Salesman (1949), too, called up performances of power from Lee J. Cobb and Mildred Dunnock, whose speech at her husband's funeral nightly left the audience mute with embarrassment, the right kind. Miller's salesman, Willy Loman, was seen at the end of a not very successful career, stricken that his steady passes at upward mobility have brought him nowhere. On the hull of domestic drama, Miller erected the rigging of the problem polemic: Loman has played by the rules, plodding at job and hobby, raising a family, looking forward to rewards. But there are none; no longer useful to the firm, Loman gets the axe. The ghost of his dead brother advises him on a final act of atonement for his failure, and Loman races off in his car to die so his insurance policy can pay off as his life could not.

Like *Streetcar*, *Death of a Salesman* won both the Pulitzer and Critics Circle prizes and excited much discussion on its characters, theme, and production. Analysts debated whether or not one could properly term as tragedy this saga of an ordinary bourgeois. The nay-sayers spoke of height and fall, and called Loman no true hero; the answer ran that the stature of a tragic hero is relative to his environment, whether it be the ship of state or a middle-class household.

The whole argument is nonsense and about a hundred years too late. Even leaving out European drama, with its *The Soldiers*, *Woyzeck*, and *The Weavers*, we have seen many tragedies in which the protagonist was an "ordinary" person—*The Adding Machine*, *Porgy*, *Winterset*, *Key Largo*, *Stevedore*, *Golden Boy*, *Native Son*, and several works by O'Neill. How could people so blindly contest the genre of common-man tragedy with O'Neill's own "Death of a Salesman," *The Iceman Cometh*, still fresh in the memory? Moreover, Miller went on to redouble his vindication of simple human tragedy in *The Crucible*, in which the fall of the hero is presented in rigorously noble terms.

The middle- or lower-class settings of *Streetcar* and *Salesman* were no novelty. What was novel about them was their authors' casual use of surreal or quasi-surreal effects in otherwise naturalistic backgrounds. Wilder's defeat of linear space and time in *Our Town* and *The Skin of Our Teeth* stood out when they were new, and meant to. But Williams' bizarre devices for the "playing" of atmosphere and Miller's blending of free-associative dialogue and flashbacks into a realistic plan endorsed the evolution in American playwrighting away from fourth-wall, phoney-real flatness into the more sensitive multi-dimensional arena of modern theatre.

Both *Streetcar* and *Salesman* were directed by Elia Kazan, heir to the art movement of vital acting ensemble, visual thematics (Jo Mielziner designed both shows), conceptual incidental music, superintendent director. This art theatre is not perfect: it seems to want to, yet knows it cannot, contain the exact amount of star performance needed to fill a role without overfilling the whole play. Great roles need great actors, and if both are great enough, Gordon Craig's wholeness is both subverted and improved upon. Tandy and Brando in *Streetcar* and Cobb and Dunnock in *Salesman* were that great. Indeed, Brando's Stanley Kowalski (preserved in Kazan's 1951 film version; Vivien Leigh played Blanche) stands as perhaps the most famous single performance by an American actor in the postwar American theatre. Commentators constantly cite it when identifying an American acting style— even more now when few actors attempt to imitate it than when Brando's meticulous physical pathology was being replayed *ad nauseam* by half his generation. Oddly, when the two works were new, Williams' "Polack" brute was thought to be a theatrical stylization of a first-generation urban ethnic and thus eminently playable, while Miller's average-Joe Salesman was taken as a universal American type, presumably less easy to distinguish via plastique and line. Yet revivals suggest that Stanley is very, very tricky to bring off (especially in confrontation with a strong Blanche, as Jon Voight's underwhelming Stanley proved opposite Faye Dunaway in Los Angeles in 1973), while decent Willy Lomans are almost common.

Miller's *All My Sons* (1947), a condemnation of white-collar crime (committed under the pressure of high-profit-making commerce) and Williams' *Summer and Smoke* (1948), another clash of flesh and spirit, were little siblings to *Salesman* and *Streetcar*. But the similarities were not disturbing, and one had the impression that both writers had a point of view and a style—originality, as O'Neill was original. One could be hopeful about Broadway, too, for if *The Iceman Cometh* had not enjoyed a top-hole staging, Kazan, Mielziner, Brando, Tandy, Cobb, and Dunnock had certainly come through in *Streetcar* and *Salesman*. One thought back to the superbly fragile production that *The Glass Menagerie* had been given. And finally, someone or other raised an important question: could the Old Vic players have presented *Streetcar* and *Salesman* as well as Kazan and his two companies had done? Yes, the British had the stature for classical heroism and the diction for comedy. But wasn't there something lacking that Americans took for granted, something physical in the way Americans carried themselves that the British went without and possibly couldn't even simulate if they tried?

The Old Vic-Broadway controversy opened up all over again, but this time those arguing for the American side had more to work with. And the next time the British landed with their grand manner, we were ready to appreciate without feeling left out. This event, just over the lip of the next decade in January of 1950, was T.S. Eliot's *The Cocktail Party*, with Alec Guinness, Irene Worth, Cathleen Nesbitt, and Robert Flemyng. Obscure and slow, it made a hit with the intelligentsia and attained Must See status, but many were they who were glad that we had Williams and Miller and *they* had Eliot.

15

"Where Is the Man with the Dybbuk?"
Comedy: The 1950s

No ONE HAS ACCOUNTED DEFINITIVELY for the decline of our comic theatre in the 1950s. One could read the signs in the late 1940s: satire was quiescent and farce tired, semi-satire had lost its punch, and comic writers were not producing on a self-renewing basis. Not until 1961, when Neil Simon appeared with *Come Blow Your Horn*, did a steady box-office winner emerge. Worse yet, comedy was losing its impulsiveness and humanity. What now connected back to the domestic comedy shrewdly utilized for social chronicle in *Mary the 3d*, for satire in *The Show Off*, and for cultural reverie in *Ah, Wilderness!*? *Time Out for Ginger* (1952), with its tomboy shocking her suburb by going out for football? Or the banal spatting couple of *Anniversary Waltz* (1954)? Where was the conviction of fantasy? In *Goodbye Charlie* (1959), wherein a merry adulterer is shot by an angry husband and comes back to earth as Lauren Bacall? (It sounds cute; it wasn't.) Is *The Seven-Year Itch* (1952) the best we could do for sex comedy? Low as it was, *The Marriage Go-Round* (1958) brought us lower, with Claudette Colbert, Charles Boyer, and Julie Newmar in two-and-a-half hours of nothing.

Sidney Kingsley tried something new. This master of realistic melodrama suddenly turned up with a farce, *Lunatics and Lovers* (1954), in the style of Damon Runyon. (Shakespeare: "The lunatic, the lover, and the poet are of imagination all compact.") With Buddy Hackett as a somewhat Chaucerian hedonist, Sheila Bond enjoying a bubble bath onstage, Dennis King as a sozzled Irish judge, the usual screwball henchmen, and Frederick Fox's amusing hotel-room set that aligned realism with boozy fancy, *Lunatics and Lovers* seemed a gem of vitality—just what Broadway needed. Kingsley did if nothing else recapture the wiggy esprit of Runyonland, as when the Judge's torrid girlfriend decides to abandon him:

DESIREE: You had your chance and you blew it. You could have made an honest woman of me.
JUDGE: And spoil God's handiwork? Never!

or when Hackett, as Dan Cupid, turns on his fiancée's candid advices:

SABLE: You want me to tell de truth, don't ya?
CUPID: No! Soitenly not! Flatter me! Lie! Lie like hell, but flatter me! Sincere people? Buncha butchers. Dey pin on a pair a homemade wings and hit ya over de head with a meat cleaver—for "your own good." Tree more *sincere* people in dis city, de streets'd be runnin' wit blood.

It was generally agreed that Saroyan had illuminated such characters with far greater sensitivity, though Saroyan's sense of structure could never compare with that of Kingsley, the total professional (who was still staging his plays himself, one of the last playwrights regularly to do so).

Another old-timer tried his hand at farce. For Kingsley it was an innovation; for Thornton Wilder it was the mysterious cobbler finally displaying his last after years of experiment—Wilder had long been a farceur at heart. The play was *The Matchmaker* (1955), a study in precision of genre—four acts, four different sets (dull house, hat shop, restaurant, fun house), gnarled plotting, zesty oddball stereotypes (the miser, the toper, the ardent young lovers, the life-hungry wimp, the dotty spinster), and knockabout craziness with screens, tables, transvestism, and the miser's lost wallet. Always the classicist, Wilder made this a major archeological dig, very lightly revising his old flop *The Merchant of Yonkers*, which in turn had derived from Nestroy, after an English original, *A Day Well Spent*; Wilder also sneaked two little episodes from Molière. Unlike most modern farces, *The Matchmaker* has a lot of heart—risk your security for a little adventure, it advises—and Nestroy specialists have found it perplexing. "Imagine an Austrian Pharmacist," said Wilder, "going to the shelf to draw from a bottle which he knows to contain a stinging corrosive liquid, guaranteed to remove warts and wens; and imagine his surprise when he discovers that it has been filled overnight with a very American birch-bark beer." Nestroy didn't include a Dolly Gallagher Levi, of any nationality, but Wilder makes the matchmaker the center of the event, and Ruth Gordon, perfectly cast for perhaps the sole time in her long career, gave a tremendous performance. The many divas who rotated in the musical version, *Hello, Dolly!*, could only enact flamboyance; Gordon *is* flamboyance. In this genre, one cannot overdo. A one-woman crowd, Gordon, on a scale of one to ten, started the evening at fifty and grew—Atkinson likened her to fresh-cut Hogarth. Tyrone Guthrie directed the production, which—in keeping with the text's international derivation—opened at the Edinburgh Festival, moved to London (with Gordon backed up by Sam Levene, Eileen Herlie, Arthur Hill, and Robert Morse), and then delighted Broadway (Loring Smith replacing Levene). A faithful screen version (with Shirley Booth, Gordon's only peer in the part) that daringly retained Wilder's asides to the audience, contributed to *The Matchmaker*'s potential as an American classic, but *Hello, Dolly!*'s popularity has shoved *The Matchmaker* far to the side.

George S. Kaufman held out, collaborating with Howard Teichmann on *The Solid Gold Cadillac* (1953), on how easily a little old lady can subdue big-business villainy when she is played by Josephine Hull. It had personality —but this was hardly the Kaufman of *You Can't Take It with You* or *Beggar on Horseback*. Like everyone else, Kaufman had mellowed.*

In this vacuum, European imports regularly supplied the resonance that Broadway could not—that of language smartly used. Moreover, such an item as Jean Anouilh's *The Waltz of the Toreadors*, seen here in 1957, kept bringing out the best in British, not American actors, as with—in this case—Ralph Richardson. The same year brought us Anouilh's *Time Remembered* (*Léocadia*), with Helen Hayes, Susan Strasberg, and . . . Richard Burton. And again—same year—an antique of the 1800s, Feydeau's *Hotel Paradiso* (*Free Exchange Hotel*), did give the town a grand exhibition of Bert Lahr's gifts, but the muscle behind the production was Peter Glenville's textual revision and wildly antic clowning from his London staging (originally with Alec Guinness). Similarly, Harold Clurman's direction and Sam Levene's Boss Mangan were the only native contributions to a revival of *Heartbreak House* at the end of the decade, outnumbered by Maurice Evans, Pamela Brown, Alan Webb, Diane Cilento, Diana Wynyard, and Dennis Price. Not only couldn't we write much great comedy, we needed help performing it.

Social comedy had fallen on evil days; but this was not a very social decade. Our best social humorists had made a point of dealing, at least sometimes, with social issues as well as the social life—remember what interesting evolutions were inspired by the rise of fascism in the 1930s. Now, social

---

* Kaufman ended his career as he had begun it, in partnership with Marc Connelly. *Labor Leader*, their projected spoof of Jimmy Hoffa, was aborted at Kaufman's death in 1961.

comedy was society charade. Samuel Taylor covered the Long Island yachting set in *Sabrina Fair* (1953), another Cinderella charmer; Margaret Sullavan was the chauffeur's daughter, Joseph Cotten the prince charming of cut-throat industrial magnate-ism, and Broadway saw that it was good. Taylor consolidated his position with *The Pleasure of His Company* (1958); the evening hung on whether or not Cyril Ritchard would lure his daughter off to Europe on the eve of her wedding. So he did; big deal.

Semi-satire, which renews itself with novel subjects each season, looked back to tenets laid down in Kaufman's day. And looked tired. Edward Chodorov tackled psychoanalysis in *Oh, Men! Oh, Women!* (1954), Harry Kurnitz the concert business in *Once More with Feeling* (1958), Peter De Vries and Joseph Fields suburban child-rearing in *The Tunnel of Love* (1957)—these are the hits, and two days after they closed, who cared, except filmmakers of little ambition? What had happened to the story with a feeling for character with something more up its sleeve than a plastic fist? Super-critics scoff at the endurance of *You Can't Take It with You*, but that work does have spontaneity and point; theatregoers of the 1950s had less to work with, and were beginning to sound like a television laugh track.

There was some worry in the mid-1950s about the influx of television writers to Broadway, just as the 1940s worried over the influx of screen-writers. It seems that the outsiders were going to lower the quality of theatre writing. Actually, old live television was developing new writers for its various anthology series of sixty- and ninety-minute plays. Most of these writers were graduated to Broadway, and many of their better scripts were expanded for the stage. Gore Vidal adapted his videoplay *A Visit to a Small Planet* for The Street in 1957, successfully. Satiric science fiction, *Visit* turned on the earthly adventure of an alien who attempts to start the first nuclear war. ("Isn't hydrogen fun?" he chortles.) Cyril Ritchard as the intruder gave the show most of its energy and a lesson in how to overplay with tact. Oddly, Ritchard's suave mannerism was paired with the grotesquely exaggerated style of Eddie Mayehoff as a bumbling Army general—a characteristic illus-tration of the Broadway that doesn't think its productions through.

A frolic about nuclear holocaust suggests that modern black comedy was coming to Broadway, but it never quite did, being relegated to off-Broadway and at that a decade late. Uptown taste institutionalized midcult obsequies, and perhaps the utterly white comedy *The Teahouse of the August Moon* (1953), John Patrick's loving picture (from Vern Sneider's novel) of Army intransigence (Paul Ford) and Army gentility (John Forsythe) on occupied Okinawa, best typifies the era.

While *Teahouse*'s nimble staging and large, non-English-speaking Oriental cast looked exotic enough, in essence Patrick's script was an American rural comedy. As in a folk play, the "simple" natives knew a lot more about the good life than the figures of authority—ultimately the Occupation must adapt to Okinawa, not the reverse—and they intone their aphorisms like a thousand Yankee villagers before them. David Wayne's Sakini, interpreting the East to the public at the top of the evening, told that there is an explanation for every catastrophe:

> History of Okinawa reveal distinguished record of conquerors. We have honor to be subjugated in fourteenth century by Chinese pirates. In sixteenth century by English missionaries. In eighteenth century by Japanese war lords. And in twentieth century by American marines. Okinawa very fortunate. Culture brought to us . . . not have to leave home for it.

The Teahouse of the August Moon won both the Pulitzer and Critics Circle prizes, and its 1,027 performances—right up with *The Bat*, *My Sister Eileen*, *Mister Roberts*, and *Angel Street*, give or take half a year—place it in the pantheon of champion Broadway hits, all yielding the public a certain satisfaction at curtain fall.

The satisfaction of the star turn, too, was certain, Broadway's oldest continuity. But there were no Barrys, now, to compose sprees for Katharine Hepburn and Tallulah Bankhead, no Behrmans to give the Lunts something to do besides look roguish. (Barry was dead and Behrman off form.) Lynn and Alfred showed up in 1956 as *The Great Sebastians*, a Lindsay and Crouse trifle offering the topical thrill of iron-curtain menace and the novelty of Alfred's dipping into the auditorium in the first scene as the mobile half of a mind-reading act.

Still, star glamor shone notably in these years, with or without help from writers. Audrey Hepburn was discovered in a search for a waif delectable enough to play the lead in *Gigi* (1951), Anita Loos' adaptation of Colette (discovered making a film in Monte Carlo by no less expert an eye than that of Colette herself). Hepburn's overnight sensation made *Gigi* as surely as Mary Martin and Charles Boyer made *Kind Sir* (1953), Shirley Booth made *The Desk Set* (1955), and Rosalind Russell made *Auntie Mame* (1956), the outstanding pop star turn of the decade, though Russell might have shared top billing with her Travis Banton wardrobe. Mame, of course, is the wonderful aunt who raises an orphan in a bohemian Disneyland; Jerome Lawrence and Robert E. Lee's whirlwind reduction of Patrick Dennis' novel tempted women bent on strutting their madcap warmth—Greer Garson and

Beatrice Lillie replacing Russell on Broadway, and Constance Bennett and Sylvia Sidney on national tours. *Auntie Mame* is the *Peter Pan* of the postwar era, almost as fantastic as Barrie's tale. Like uncountable comedy hits, it promised even more Christmas as a musical, bringing forth further gadding about from Angela Lansbury (and, in the film version, Lucille Ball, dimly glimpsed behind gauzes). *Mame* succeeded where the musical adaptation of *The Teahouse of the August Moon*, called *Lovely Ladies, Kind Gentlemen*, flopped: it doesn't always work. But when it does, the musical tends to eclipse the original. *Auntie Mame*, like *The Matchmaker*, will not likely be seen again as a straight play. Shaw and Shakespeare are exceptions to the rule, and *Take Me Along* won't disperse interest in *Ah, Wilderness!*, its source. But who now would revive *Green Grow the Lilacs*?

Speaking of the musical, comedy definitely took the forefront in the 1950s, edging possible successors to *Allegro* out of the picture. Even Rodgers and Hammerstein, after *The King and I* (1951), seemed to lose interest in their own revolution, and elsewhere the scene was dominated by splashy, naturalistic romps: *Guys and Dolls* (1950), *Call Me Madam* (1950), *Wonderful Town* (1953), *The Pajama Game* (1954), *Damn Yankees* (1955), *Lil' Abner* (1956), and so on, each with its bite of political or sociocultural lampoon. More significant work, however entertaining, seemed to make people nervous, and the decade is rich in highly admired flops such as *The Golden Apple* (1954), *Sandhog* (1954), *Candide* (1956), and *Juno* (1959), all of them involving composers of note: respectively, Jerome Moross, Earl Robinson, Leonard Bernstein, and Marc Blitzstein. Ambition was not lacking, but public support for it was; in such a time as this, adaptations rather than original work tend to appease a suspicious public. The biggest hit of the decade, *My Fair Lady* (1956), amounted to a retread of Shaw's *Pygmalion* by the simple insertion of an elegant score and a slight cutting of the text, and it is perhaps typical of the time that when Frank Loesser turned Sidney Howard's *They Knew What They Wanted* into the operatic *The Most Happy Fella* (1956), he carefully pared away the leftist politics of one of the principal characters. The musical, while observing culturally conservative sentimentalism, has long been dominated by liberal politics. But politicians were laying low along The Street these days.

One comedy that should never suffer the détente of musical transformation is Paddy Chayevsky's *The Tenth Man* (1959), an earnest lollipop that displays the commercial theatre's accommodation to the idea of drama. Though Chayevsky is an undeniably commercial writer, *The Tenth Man* is a black comedy of sorts—Broadway black, which means that the tone is not funny-dour but dour lightened by a separate funny (so Broadwayites can shut out the dour and converge upon the funny), and that the action is threatening until the last few minutes. Then, the tone tidies up and the action slips into something comfortable, such as a happy ending.

Ten men are needed as a quorum for particular Jewish religious rites; in a broken-down suburban New York synagogue of aged Orthodox-Jewish widowers who sit around cursing their daughters-in-law, that tenth man can be hard to find. The rite that Chayevsky's script eventually calls for is an exorcism, that of a teenage girl possessed by a dybbuk, the spirit of a dead prostitute of the Kiev ghetto. But it happens that a tenth man dragged in off the street to complete the quorum for morning prayers is a troubled spirit himself, possessed by marital problems, boredom, and northeast-urban gee whiz. At the height of a thrilling (and presumably authentic) exorcism, it is the young man's "dybbuk," not the girl's, that answers the Talmudic summons. The man falls senseless with a terrifying shriek, but minutes later he departs for a new life on the arm of the girl—who is still possessed, still believing herself to be "the whore of Kiev, the companion of sailors." As someone remarks at their exit, "An hour ago he didn't believe in God, now he's exorcising dybbuks." The rejoinder tells us where we are, after two-and-a-half hours of engrossing ethnic drollery and psychoreligious disputation—back on Broadway in the land of Oz: "He still doesn't believe in God. He simply wants to love. And when you stop to think about it, gentlemen, is there any difference?"

Chayevsky, then, had to pay his respects to Broadway's personal dybbuk, boy-meets-girl sentimentality: the love plot. He did manage to cut the sting of prefabricated Jewish levity in his text; even with such ready and able kibitzers as Lou Jacobi, Jack Gilford, Jacob Ben-Ami, and George Voskovec on his hands, his work came off as an American play rather than an ethnic swindle. Held up against *The Seven-Year Itch* and *Oh Men! Oh Women!*, *The Tenth Man* makes a rich noise, as in this snippet of Jacobi's part:

> When I was a boy in Poland, I also heard stories about a man who lived in the next town who was possessed by a dybbuk. I was eight years old, and one day after school my friends and I walked barefoot the six miles to the next town, and we asked everybody, "Where is the man with the dybbuk?" And nobody knew what we were talking about. So I came home and told my mother: "Mama, there is no man with a dybbuk in the next town." And she gave me such a slap across the face that I turned around three times. And she said to me, "Aha! Only eight years old and already an atheist!"

The Tenth Man was criticized for the patness of its love plot, but without it, Broadway might well have passed the show by. In the 1950s, even the late 1950s, modern seriocomedy—such as is far more interested in dybbuks than in romance—hid out off-Broadway. "Where," one can sense the average theatregoer adding, "it belongs." But why is the experimental considered out-of-the-way in New York when it takes the main stages in Europe?

In the hands of such as Eugene Ionesco, Samuel Beckett, and Friedrich Dürrenmatt, modern theatre has loosely derived a new form, neither comedy nor drama exclusively, though at times amusing and at other times profound. Absurdist theatre sees the world through a bifocal lens, trained on the incongruities of comedy, yet in sympathy, of a sort, with man's preposterous ambitions. In *Waiting for Godot*, Beckett's landmark of the modern era (originally composed in French as *En Attendant Godot*), two tramps in nowhereland talk about nothing while waiting for someone named Godot, who never shows up. "Well, shall we go?" asks one of the other. "Yes," is the reply. "Let's go." After a moment, the curtain falls; neither has moved. Neither ever will.

Doubling in on itself, loaded with contradictions and the bizarre, *Waiting for Godot* marks a reinstatement of the pasquinade, a type of anonymous lampoon habitually posted on a mutilated statue in sixteenth-century Rome. The statue had been excavated from classical debris, and was dubbed Pasquino by the Romans, so Pasquino's satires were pasquinades. The pasquinades burlesqued public figures; absurdist theatre gets everybody. Like Pasquino, it is deformed and reclaimed from the past—from the Shakespeare of *King Lear* and *Troilus and Cressida*, for example, and the hollow man of Büchner's *Woyzeck*. Echoes of Western literature stipple Godot as they do T.S. Eliot's casebook of contemporary sensibility, *The Waste Land*. "What are we doing here," offers Vladimir. "*That* is the question." And the answer: "We are waiting for Godot to come . . . or for night to fall. We have kept our appointment. . . . How many people can boast as much?" "Billions," says Estragon.

This funny and baleful look at humanity—this second coming of Pasquino —appeals more to European audiences than to Americans. But non-English-speaking theatre often doesn't travel. Beckett translated *En Attendant Godot* himself, and a few continental authors have succeeded here, but national taste is mysterious. Such American hits as *Merton of the Movies*, *The Show Off*, *The Road to Rome*, *Ah, Wilderness!*, and *Boy Meets Girl* all failed in London—*You Can't Take It with You* lasted only 10 performances! Almost every attempt to produce the work of Jean Giraudoux and Jean Anouilh, two of France's greatest playwrights, has failed here, and of the major new talents of the German-speaking countries we have enjoyed little. We are, in effect, isolated—ironically, as European ideas enriched American drama in the first place.

Certainly, theatregoers snubbed *Waiting for Godot* when it turned up on Broadway in 1956, and the short run would have passed by with scarcely a murmur but for the casting of Bert Lahr as Estragon. Lahr's frantic tramp was one of the great portrayals in living memory, an unnaturally meaningful turn in an ambiguous silhouette of a part. Photographs of Lahr in action, wistfully hugging himself or beaming ecstatically at a carrot, speak volumes on the gut-loftiness of comic acting. The whole cast found the depth in the charade: E.G. Marshall as Vladimir played Lahr's cool foil, while Kurt Kaszner and Alvin Epstein seemed to have entered from another world as the two travelers who divert and terrify the tramps. The production should have caught on as a Must See, but even with Lahr it didn't draw.

Still, *Godot* had to be done, if only to remind some theatregoers that drama had turned modern and the rest of the world had achieved the next plateau: boy meets—actually doesn't—Godot. The Street is determined to hang back; it's scared of dybbuks. Playwrights are going to have to be cagey if they try to put any absurdism—any exciting comedy—over on the butter-and-egg customers of Broadway. That does not bode well for continuity. If Broadway's plan for comedy does not take in more than this cheesy fifties assortment, dramatic comedy could die out altogether. It might just die of survival.

16

Denying the Gas Chambers Drama: The 1950s

IT WORKS WELL FOR THIS CHAPTER that *The Member of the Wedding* ushered in the 1950s on Broadway, for Carson McCullers' adaptation of her novel gives us an updated view of the "audience show." Almost unanimously, informed opinion held that McCullers had failed to assemble her material into a play; yet the general public loved the piece, making a star of the young Julie Harris, a folk heroine of Ethel Waters, and a celebrity of eight-year-old Brandon de Wilde.

If McCullers' script (prepared with Tennessee Williams' advice the previous summer on Cape Cod) is not a play, it is certainly theatre. Her picture of a hoyden with a craving to Belong fitted the short novel better than the stage, for as a story it lacks forward development, but there was great joy here, and much concentration on character to keep the heart engaged. Frankie's older brother is getting married, and the girl is determined to go off with the honeymooners—to cultivate the "we of me," as she repeatedly puts it. For much of the non-action, she wonders and prances in the kitchen she inhabits with Berenice Sadie Brown, the motherly black servant (Waters), and her little cousin from next door, John Henry (de Wilde). These are choice parts and the three actors went to town in them (though de Wilde is said to have lost in diction what he found in cute). Twenty-five at the time, Julie Harris as Frankie launched her decades of enjoying the public's unqualified adoration, and for the great Waters even the big words feel weak. She was one of the most influential talents in the racial integration of the American theatre, spanning the era that began with segregated casts and audiences and ended, more or less, with *The Member of the*

Wedding, with liberation. Consider, then, how much of Broadway in all its contours is an arena of personality (the doer not the deed), hounded by artists but in no way bound to art. What was the hot ticket when *The Member of the Wedding* was new? It was Katharine Hepburn's *As You Like It*, wherein the Forest of Arden seemed to be located just outside of Hartford, Connecticut.

The public did well to single out *The Member of the Wedding*, for it's the kind of show that can easily be passed over. As it was, what saved the production, before word of mouth encouraged good houses, was the critics' raves for Julie Harris. If there's anything the public likes more than a star, it's helping to make one. But this sort of experiment was an easy charity, and generally audiences were holding to the escapism of the war and post-war years. They flocked happily to such events as Margaret Webster's Maurice Evans-Dennis King *The Devil's Disciple* in 1950, a City Center revival moved to Broadway; to Philip Barry's hollow last play, *Second Threshold* (1951), finished by Robert E. Sherwood and produced posthumously; to the murder mysteries *Dial "M" for Murder* (1952, pernicious husband plots wife's demise) and *Witness for the Prosecution* (1954, courtroom chills and the greatest surprise ending ever); and to John Van Druten's *I Am a Camera* (1951), from Christopher Isherwood's stories of decadent Berlin, sparked by Julie Harris' Sally Bowles.

The public was not gambling enough—on unknown writers and actors, on what had *invented* Broadway as art in the 1920s and 1930s: menace. No doubt the high point of old-time theatre was marked by *Anastasia* (1954), Guy Bolton's adaptation of a French play that enjoyed an international success on everyone's nostalgia for formula. A costume show (Russian émigré Berlin, 1926), it dealt with a scheme to pass off as the sole surviving Romanof a girl who may or may not be the real thing. There were Ruritanian gowns and uniforms, *scènes à faire*, romantic tantrums. There was even a Big Moment—several, in fact, for Bolton had been writing for Broadway since *The Rule of Three* in 1914 and didn't lack for experience in cooking up the stew our grandparents savored. A Recognition Scene in Act II between the alleged Anastasia and the tsar's mother was the talk of the season, audiences turning to jelly watching Eugenie Leontovich denounce Viveca Lindfors as a fake, hestitate, start to leave, and then, prompted by one last reminiscent detail from the girl, drop to the floor to scoop her up in her arms. "And please," Leontovich said at her exit, "if it should not be you . . . don't ever tell me." No sooner was she gone than Joseph Anthony and Hurd Hatfield came bounding in, ecstatic that the masquerade had worked. But

the second-act curtain must have its stunner; Lindfors obliged by slumping
to the ground and calling for imperial sisters and brother in flawless Russian.
(Aha! So she *is* Anastasia, after all!) Charles Frohman would have beamed.
At 270 performances, *Anastasia* was no blockbuster, but it made its point.
To progressives it was tinsel; to conservatives it was a rare evening of—
beauty or something. (Off-Broadway had its say on the subject in the spirit
of Weber and Fields in the Phoenix Theatre's *The Littlest Revue*, which
tendered a burlesque of the Recognition Scene set in a Brooklyn candy
store, with Charlotte Rae in Leontovich's role.)

Of course, it is not *Anastasia*'s fault that the progressives couldn't find
much of their kind of drama, but it was somebody's. New playwrights were
not lacking—vital ones were. Critics took heart when works by young authors
seemed to have an air about them, but most of these either failed commercially or weren't important in the first place. Or both. The list includes plays
of minor merit, but nothing that anyone would need to see twice, nothing
to last: N. Richard Nash's *See the Jaguar* (1952), a western mixed with
folkish verse play and introducing James Dean as a sort of human varmint
(good casting); Robert Anderson's *Tea and Sympathy* (1953), with John
Kerr as a wimp suspected of being homosexual, ending with Deborah Kerr's
notorious curtain line as she pulled his hands to her blouse—"Years from
now, when you talk about this . . . and you will . . . be kind"; Michael V.
Gazzo's study of drug addiction, *A Hatful of Rain* (1955), an Actor's Studio
production with Shelley Winters, Anthony Franciosa, and Ben Gazzara
(replaced, when the time came, by Steve McQueen). And William Inge
emerged with four hits in a row, *Come Back, Little Sheba* (1950), *Picnic*
(1953), *Bus Stop* (1955), and *The Dark at the Top of the Stairs* (1957).

Until a spate of flops knocked him off the VIP list in the sixties, Inge
triumphed in the mideastern domestic play. *Bus Stop* was the exception, a
comedy dealing with single people, set in a diner where transients wait for
their connections and a brash cowboy courts and wins a sulky boondocks
"chantoosie." All of Inge is rural but "city"—troubled, as in *Sheba*'s ex-
alcoholic husband who almost kills his wife on a drunken bender; in *Picnic*'s
love-starved spinster schoolteacher aroused by a handsome young drifter; and
in *Dark*'s offstage suicide by a military school cadet crushed by an anti-
Semitic smear at a country-club dance.

Opinion differs over which of the four is Inge's best, but it is certain that
all benefited from strong casting. Shirley Booth was nearly fired during
rehearsals for *Sheba* for her inability to focus her characterization or speak
above a mumble—but under the lights in performance her slatternly Lola,

naively coming on to delivery boys and calling for a runaway dog that will never return, made herself a place in the archives. Kim Stanley, who played a gawky adolescent in *Picnic*, blossomed into a very entertaining Cherie, the Marilyn Monroesque heroine of *Bus Stop*, just two seasons later. *The Dark at the Top of the Stairs*, set in the suburbs of Oklahoma City in the 1920s, has the most opportunities for ensemble casting, and under Elia Kazan's direction in the premiere, Teresa Wright, Pat Hingle, and Eileen Heckert went American native as a spatting couple and the wife's visiting older sister. Getting along without the poetry of Williams or the moral ratiocination of Miller, Inge made that brand-name duo a triumvirate for a while with a little craft and a little flamboyance.

If writers such as Maxwell Anderson, Elmer Rice, Lillian Hellman, and William Saroyan had trouble retaining eminence, Clifford Odets enjoyed a comeback with *The Country Girl* (1950), a look at the struggles of an alcoholic actor. All of the above except Saroyan had been tuned in to social drama back in their youth, but not till the 1960s was the protest play welcomed back. It felt unpleasantly reasonable in the 1950s that Odets had turned from his empathetic instruction of the working class—"Get out and fight so life shouldn't be printed on dollar bills!"—to deal with problems of lesser weight. After *The Country Girl* he affirmed his apolitical stance, borrowing Noah and the Ark for unsocial domestic comedy in *The Flowering Peach* (1954). With Menasha Skulnik playing Noah, it might easily have been called *The Goldbergs Take Up Yachting*.

Most colorful of all in this decade was Tennessee Williams. *The Rose Tattoo* (1951) gave us Maureen Stapleton as an agonizingly sexual Sicilian-American widow (the role written for Anna Magnani, who played it in the film version). Lest Williams be taken for a man of limited genre, he dipped into absurdist symbolism in *Camino Real* (1953), a Latin American fairyland peopled by gypsies and gentles, storm troopers, street cleaners who collect bodies for the city dump, Casanova, Camille, Lord Byron, and Kilroy, an American natural, all belief and bravado, but doomed. An existential vaudeville, *Camino Real* mystified the town, though Elia Kazan was hailed for making a lively show of it. By the 1950s, star directors were winning grapevine reputations as the men "really" responsible for certain plays' successes or distinctive behavior. This set off a controversy that has never died. Helping to start it off, George Jean Nathan commented in his *Camino Real* review, "There is not, nor has there been, a single American dramatist of any genuine worth who has had to depend upon a director to develop that worth . . . This business of magisterial directors posturing as creative geniuses over the bodies of already creative dramatists . . . will make of our stage . . . a circus at the expense of an art."

Kazan was again at the helm of Williams' *Cat on a Hot Tin Roof* (1955), guiding a superlative cast through the story of an ex-athlete on the skids with his wife because she accused his best friend of being a homosexual, precipitating the friend's suicide and the athlete's alcoholism. Barbara bel Geddes hissed and purred as Maggie the Cat; Ben Gazzara exploited his gift for bemused disgust as her husband, Brick; Burl Ives superbly bulled and bullied as Brick's father, Big Daddy; Mildred Dunnock delivered a perfectly silly Big Mama; and Madeline Sherwood and Pat Hingle stole pieces of the show as devious in-laws. It was a thorough exposure of southern rot and, like *The Rose Tattoo*, branded Williams as a specialist in sensuality and degradation. But there is much more to his art than this; his emotional fullness and love of the bizarre tended to obscure his strong sense of concept, made his plays too much fun for the public to think them important.

Catering to that public, or at least to Elia Kazan's view of them, Williams completely redrafted the third act of *Cat on a Hot Tin Roof* for Broadway. Big Daddy is dying and has been lied to, but is confronted with the truth at the very end of Act II and—as originally planned—disappears after that except for an offstage cry. Kazan thought the character too fascinating—the public will want more of him. Also, they will want to love Maggie; she was too much the cat as written, too manipulative. Compromise with pop: this is how melodrama works, even Williams' rather finely spun melodrama. So he rewrote the last act, brought Big Daddy back on, and gilded Maggie. But the original draft is by far the better—bolder, meaner.

Williams' *Sweet Bird of Youth* (1959), also set in the south, had Geraldine Page as a frightened movie star and Paul Newman as her stud pickup, set against a background of political corruption and a horror of time: it passes, murdering beauty. At the close of the piece, about to be mutilated by hit men, Newman, the blackmailing hustler, addressed the audience: "I don't ask for your pity, but just your understanding—not even that—no. Just for your recognition of me in you, and the enemy, time, in us all." *Everybody* was offended.

They were starting to say that Williams was losing his touch, but sneaking into the 1960s we encounter one of his most sound entries, *The Night of the Iguana* (1961), an apparently raucous but at length transcendent look at the playwright's most sympathetic collection of displaced persons, especially in the radiant Hannah Jelkes of Margaret Leighton. Bette Davis made a rare stage appearance as the proprietor of a rundown seaside hotel in Mexico (in 1940), where gather Leighton and her ancient poet grand-father, a defrocked minister, and a captured iguana, fellow creature of these tormented humans bound in limbo and slipping down to hell. Not much happened, exactly, but the talk really drew one on; at the end, the minister freed the iguana and went swimming with Davis, the old poet finished his last opus and died, and Leighton, asking God for a place to rest in, put her head on the old man's shoulder.

Williams typifies postwar American drama (at least through the 1950s) in that he never held his plays answerable to "social conscience." His people are apolitical; with all that sex and liquor to deal with, one doesn't get much time for voting. The pulpits had closed down in the 1950s. At the close of the decade, Pearl Buck and Dore Schary reconvened the theatre of protest to inveigh against nuclear power, but neither Buck's *A Desert Incident* nor Schary's *The Highest Tree* amounted to much in the way of theatre, espe-cially not after Harold Clurman's 1955 staging of Jean Giraudoux' older but so vitally war-banning *The Trojan War Will Not Take Place*, with the usual Briton-dominated cast (and retitled, for reasons best known to the translator, Christopher Fry, *Tiger at the Gates*).

It's odd that the Communist purge of the late 1940s and early 1950s did not inspire much resistant theatre in New York, for the absolute repression of the blacklist that oversaw proceedings on the airways and on film never took hold in the less easily organized and more contemptuous (of organiza-tion) theatre community. True, producers thought of such plays as generally high-risk ventures economically, and a few were written that never got staged. But, on the other hand, virtually all writers of reputation on Broad-way were politically inimical to McCarthyism. Why didn't they use the stage to explain their position?

Some of them, of course, had been scared into silence, and some others had broken with the Party long since and supported the suppression of the hard left, even given the callously scattershot methods of the right, which after all concerned lively-arts people far more than the average citizen, and on a profoundly personal level. (Half one's colleagues were directly involved; the other half might be at any moment.) But considering how daring Broad-way had been in the Depression, how handsomely it had opened up the theatre's social parameters—the Guild, the Group, the workers' theatres—it got terrifically innocent real fast. Why? Possibly, the answer has little to do with McCarthyism. The theatre had been running largely on innocence through the 1940s, and Broadway, when McCarthy ruled, wasn't cowed by the "times." It had deserted the times before they even came about. Social theatre, along with everything else in drama that defined an ideal for life (whether attainable or futile), was moribund.

There were exceptions, some of them financially successful. Sidney Kingsley deserted *verismo* literalism for a study of Soviet terror using flashbacks, cinematic dissolves, and "imaginary" scenes, *Darkness at Noon* (1951), adapted from Arthur Koestler's novel. Broadway admired this thriller, though its picture of an "old revolutionary" taking his own medicine during the show-trial period of the late 1930s (when Stalin systematically eliminated his former comrades) was unremittingly gruesome. Kingsley provided no conflict of heroistic freedom resisting oppression: his hero, Rubashov, is as ruthless, as vicious, as guilty as his torturers. Flashbacks show him in earlier years collaborating with Fascists in Mussolini's Italy to betray a shipbuilder's strike (the Mother Soviet needs those ships) and sending his innocent lover to torture and execution, a compleat son of history. But now it is Stalin's pleasure that Rubashov be made an example in a kind of public burning, and he can come to terms with his fate only if he can believe it a sacrifice needed "for the good of the Party." He knows it is in fact only a dainty fed to Stalin's paranoia. He refuses to confess. Under diabolical torture—emotional as well as physical—he breaks. We last see him in court at the microphone, denouncing himself and demanding to be killed. We see him in prison awaiting execution. And at the very end he is marched into the prison basement as his fellow prisoners thrum a tatoo of fingers on the walls of their cells.

With nothing to "like" in Kingsley's plan, no one but Rubashov's lover (a minor character) to admire, *Darkness at Noon* made for heavy going, but people went. The work was well staged (by Kingsley himself, as always), designed by Frederick Fox to allow maximum fluidity of dissolve from "real" time into imaginary time, and fully developed by Claude Rains as Rubashov, Kim Hunter as his lover, and Jack Palance as a sadistic prison guard turned interrogator, a younger Rubashov. Throughout, the central picture of prison tiers and heaps of prisoners communicating through a code of taps made its accusation not only of the Soviet system but of many of its victims as well. To make history is to suffer history.

It is interesting that Kingsley, so exactly naturalistic in the past, delved into the part-natural, part-fancied format used by Williams and Miller in *A Streetcar Named Desire* and *Death of a Salesman*. In the 1940s, the experiment with time and space was a novelty; in the 1950s, a sign of evolving times; after that, a useful convention. Getting away from the opaquely well made play did not necessitate the building of new theatres, the finding of new audiences, or the training of new actors and playwrights—Kingsley, for instance, was an old hand. All that was needed was an expansion of the "realistic" time and space scheme into a more fluid conception that gave certain plays the right to say more than can be said in a fixed set with a fourth wall made of glass.

Among the few other works that noticed the context of era, Maxwell Anderson's *Barefoot in Athens* (1951) presented Barry Jones and Lotte Lenya as Socrates and Xantippe in a play that could hardly have avoided the issue of free and dissenting speech, but it lasted only 30 performances. However, in 1953 came *The Crucible*, Arthur Miller's treatment of the Salem witch trials of 1692. Once again, Miller brought forth an ordinary citizen to bear the weight of tragedy, but unlike Willy Loman, the defeated bourgeois of *Death of a Salesman*, *The Crucible's* John Proctor is a heroic figure— adversary rather than pitiable, a proud nonconformist brought down not so much through his own weakness (an extramarital affair that sparks a revenge plot) as through his failure to subdue others' evil. (Note that both Loman and Proctor earn one of Miller's favorite guilts, that of the false husband.) The witch-hunting Salem court, asking no more proof of devil worship than a neighbor's accusation, carried certain parallels with the methods of the HUAC, and the McCarthy hearings began a few months after *The Crucible* opened; what could have been more timely? The Communist purge was no witch hunt, since—as many have pointed out in discussing Miller's play—there are no witches but there certainly are Communists. But the drive for political power that infected much of the pietistic anti-communism of the day happened to coincide with what may have been the real motive behind the Salem trials—land greed, vindictiveness, and township politics.

Miller insisted that his piece was not about the times, but a portrait of the corruption of power. He is right. Later viewings (starting with a 1960 off-Broadway revival that was inferior to Jed Harris' Broadway original) have upped the work's rating as sheer theatre. Perhaps the assumption that *The Crucible* was "about" McCarthyism was what held it back at first—its dully good notices preceded a dully respectable 197 performances and red ink when the books were closed. As we have seen throughout the years, the American public is not usually attracted to universalized polemical narrative, and it may be that it took several decades of exposure for *The Crucible* to prove that it is a thrilling piece about a strong man, his strong wife, and a rotten society that destroys them. Now *The Crucible* has taken an honorable place as a piece on human action and is frequently found on the posters when a regional company assembles a season of classics. Overshadowed in its youth by the less apparently argumentative *Death of a Salesman*, it might well prove to be Miller's most enduring work.

History in theatre involves not only artistic and social trends, but economics as well—yet the three are often inseparable. Art and protest sold tickets once; in the 1950s, they failed to. Worse yet, cost-profit feasibility had been altered, and the 125-performance mark no longer meant a profitable run—a bad portent for future *Crucibles*. Perhaps Miller's producer Kermit Bloomgarden kept *The Crucible* open at a loss because it was too important to close; he was also superintending a revival of Hellman's *The Children's Hour* that winter, with Patricia Neal and Kim Hunter, staged by Hellman herself. Nineteen years after its debut, its indictment of character assassination was more apropos than ever, but like *The Crucible* this *Children's Hour* ran half a year and lost money. Enough people showed up each week to cover operating expenses, but not enough to supply a margin of profit.

Broadway's financial tribulations deepen from here on, for the rival entertainment media are going to keep the *Strange Interlude*s and *Winterset*s from doing anything like the business they did in the 1920s and '30s. High risk threatens the better quality drama, not the worse—and one could no longer count on a few philanthropists or gamblers meeting the weekly "nut" by themselves. (In 1926, the Texas oilman Edgar B. Davis kept *The Ladder* going at grievous losses for 789 performances because its theme, reincarnation, was his obsession. Even with *free* admission, each showing of *The Ladder* played to fifteen or twenty people, but Davis could afford it. In the 1950s, not even a Davis could pull off that kind of stunt.)

Producers, authors, and actors were trapped between the public on one hand and cost-accounts on the other—not only those of investors, but of unions as well. Worst of all were the parasite musicians, who are guaranteed a set number of jobs in every Broadway theatre even when the show playing that theatre doesn't call for a note of music. The stagehands are also aficionados of the featherbed; in 1957, their leaders declared that the backstage pinochle table at the virtually setless, black-cast *Waiting for Godot* revival must be garrisoned by seven men instead of the five hired by the producer, thereby forcing the show to close and putting five stagehands on unemployment insurance.

The British lend lease, meanwhile, was entering its most festive period. Once, the English were apt to export things like *The Barretts of Wimpole Street* or *White Cargo* (famous in its day for the jokes that Broadwayites made about Tondelayo, native girl) or something by, with, and about Noel

Coward. Now, in the 1950s, we were lending them our musicals and they were leasing us quality composition and performance. Recalling the Old Vic tour of 1946, theatregoers began to feel, all over again, that no one this side of the Atlantic could rival Margaret Leighton and Eric Portman playing two quite different roles each in Terence Rattigan's double bill *Separate Tables* in 1956 (but wasn't that the year Fredric March and Florence Eldridge astounded with the honesty of their James and Mary Tyrone in *Long Day's Journey into Night?*) or Laurence Olivier abstracting English style, feeling, and destiny as Archie Rice in John Osborne's *The Entertainer* in 1958 (the year the Lunts reopened the old Globe Theatre as the Lunt-Fontanne in Friedrich Dürrenmatt's *The Visit*).

In others words: we had the actors—it was British writing and stage direction that outshone us. This Dürrenmatt play, for example, *The Visit* (which should really translate as *The Old Lady's Visit*), proves how far ahead of us European writers were as of the 1950s. Romantic melodrama in storyline but blunt comedy *noir* in style, *The Visit* follows the return of the richest woman in the world to her shabby Swiss hometown. She left it, half a century before, unmarried, pregnant, friendless, and despised. Now she offers an incredible fortune to her former fellow citizens if they give her justice by killing the man who wronged her. Naturally, the people refuse, but before long they are buying luxuries on credit and looking tense. In the end, they give her what she wants.

Great parts for Fontanne and Lunt, you think; actually, Dürrenmatt wrote the woman as sardonic and passionless and the man as a creep who grows into a tragic figure by refusing to defend himself, by willing his own punishment in a world without logic. His death, at least, will be logical: just. Great parts, yes—but only for actors who don't have to please a following who look to them for glamor and charm. It happens that the pair were at their best in *The Visit* and did Dürrenmatt justice whether the audience liked it or not. But it should be noted that the translation used in this production, by Maurice Valency, is a *version* of the original. Valency disposes of Dürrenmatt's absurdist technique (actors playing trees in a forest scene, for instance), cuts some of his brutality, and almost suggests that the old woman and her quarry are autumnal lovers. No doubt a more faithful rendering* would have been impossible on Broadway in the 1950s; certainly it would not have been the hit that *The Visit* was. But on the other hand

---

* Dürrenmatt worked with Valency on the adaptation, and declared himself pleased with it.

there were some truly chilling moments in the production, directed by Peter Brook as if within a space between genuine absurdist theatre and Luntian romance. A shocked audience nightly wondered what had become of their darling Lynn of the beautiful hands at the last moment of Act I, when the woman first makes her offer to the citizens of Güllen and they reject it out of hand. Their outrage and confusion was something Broadway's theatre-goers could understand, but Fontanne's suave cool was something new. "I can wait," she said.

Few productions stood comparison with that of *The Visit*. In 1958–59, the season in which the Lunts made this startling farewell, those attracted to the Must See had a choice of O'Neill's posthumously produced *A Touch of the Poet* or Archibald MacLeish's retelling of the Book of Job, *J.B.* The O'Neill was longer, so many people hastened to the MacLeish, possibly the most ridiculed serious play in Broadway's recent history. It had been chic to denigrate *Strange Interlude* when it was new—Alexander Woollcott called it "the *Abie's Irish Rose* of the intelligentsia"—but this time virtually every countable opinion was ranged against a work. *J.B.* ran for 364 performances, yet its popularity was shadowy: no one knows anyone who liked it. It was very well staged, however. Placing the action in Boris Aronson's design for a "traveling circus which has been on the roads of the world for a long time" was somebody's very brilliant idea, and a fine cast under Elia Kazan—finest in Christopher Plummer's satanic Mr. Nicholas—was what really sold the tickets.

The O'Neill work, with Eric Portman, Helen Hayes, and Kim Stanley heading an uneven cast, earned a run to rival *J.B.*'s in a far less decorative production. What of the text itself? *A Touch of the Poet* holds an odd place in the canon, being neither altogether admired nor insulted. (The 1977 revival with Jason Robards and Geraldine Fitzgerald didn't decide the matter one way or another.) When new, it carried weight as posthumous O'Neill, as the last of its line, for O'Neill died in 1953 and was from then on the late, in revival or rediscovery. Ironically, he may have enjoyed his first age of unbiased understanding and appreciation at this time, with the Circle-in-the-Square revival of *The Iceman Cometh* in 1956, *Long Day's Journey into Night* and *A Moon for the Misbegotten* a year later, and *A Touch of the Poet* a year after that. This belated looming up of masterwork put the O'Neill oeuvre back into the mainstream of continuity, connecting the increasingly derided New York theatre scene to its better days. Certainly, Broadway seldom looked as good—as important—as it did when *Long Day's Journey into Night* opened; one sensed an extraordinary eagerness in the Helen Hayes Theatre in the moments before the house lights dimmed. Much had been heard of the work (Yale University Press had published the text the previous year), and word of mouth had it that one's most grandiose expectations were to be met. There seemed little doubt that *Long Day's Journey into Night* was O'Neill's best play: the one that finally came to terms with the autobiographical material, the primal concept of self-delusion as the inevitable compromise between one's unconscious drives and the ego's more apparent life-plan, and the thrust of dramatic language.

Confirming along with Raphael, Shakespeare, Monteverdi, Beethoven, Dostoyefsky, and Mann that genius waxes as time passes, O'Neill silenced his long-time detractors with the exorcising self-contempt of this flagrantly personal play. *Long Day's Journey* marks a revolution in O'Neill's style in its spare writing devoid of the dialect, fancy devices, and uncontrolled symbolism of his earlier work; and, most importantly, at last we see the unvarnished characters that furnished, in semi-disguise, the bulk of O'Neill's personas: his father, mother, older brother, and himself. Four acts of self-revelation, attack, and support among the Tyrone family in 1912, the play does indeed take in only one day, keeping action to a minimum but erupting with events of character. As an ocean fog slowly envelops the terrain outside, the four people edge into confrontation with what they are after lifetimes of ruses and charades. The father's quick, easy "great money success" as a one-role actor ruined his career while his petty greed destroyed his dependents. His wife is a helpless morphine addict who drifts through life in a nostalgic trance. His older son James is an alcoholic, whose wild love for his younger brother Edmund comprises as much jealous hatred as tenderness. And Edmund—O'Neill as he sees himself—is a wrecked creature facing tuberculosis. So brutal is this family picture that, though he finished it in 1941, O'Neill wanted it withheld from production until twenty-five years after his death.

Confidence in the proposed American production team (Stockholm hosted the world premiere) seems to have inspired O'Neill's widow to release the script for this Broadway performance: March and Eldridge as the Tyrones, Jason Robards and Bradford Dillman as their sons, under José Quintero's direction. It was, through the strength of the four actors and, perhaps, the thrill of the posthumous event, the only O'Neill Broadway premiere to achieve legendary status as a great staging. There had been great portrayals before—Fontanne's Nina, Louis Wolheim's Yank, George M. Cohan's Nat Miller, Dudley Digges' Harry Hope. But in the matter of all-around ensemble presentation, O'Neill's technique often outraced those of his recreators. The Theatre Guild's *Mourning Becomes Electra* was highly thought of, but the Guild's *Iceman* and aborted *A Moon for the Misbegotten* ran ragged; not till *Long Day's Journey into Night* did an O'Neill Broadway premiere enjoy talent worthy of the material. But then, all the isms of his apprenticeship had at last been retired for a straight evening of persons enacted. These four parts constitute four of the Biggest of the Big Roles in our repertory, though the general public's fear of a heavy evening have prevented the parts from becoming the Cyrano, Prospero, or Mother Courage of the American repertory. Anyway, the world of the Big Role, which nurtured O'Neill and which he helped cultivate, was almost as dead as O'Neill was by then, and the image of continuity one might have sensed faded into one of loss: there was no younger O'Neill, no one that big. *Long Day's Journey into Night* felt thrillingly new, but the tradition that had brought it forth was finished.

Still, one looked for signs that the good old days were passing on great secrets. Off-Broadway's Circle-in-the Square was likened, incorrectly, to the old Provincetown Playhouse; new stars were compared to the greats of the past; and literary or historical endeavors such as Ketti Frings' *Look Homeward, Angel* (1957), after Thomas Wolfe, or Dore Schary's *Sunrise at Campobello* (1958), detailing some moments in the lives of Franklin and Eleanor Roosevelt, Louis Howe, and Al Smith, led many to believe that Broadway was reconnoitering its sense of "class." It was as if a quota of adaptations from the novel and glimpses of historical chronicle assured respectability. On the contrary, these are usually the least satisfactory plays in a given season, the literary jobs cumbersome and the histories sentimental or unfairly biased. People weren't asking for great works, but they seemed dissatisfied with anything that wasn't competent pop, and, in retaliation, writers began to assume that commercial failures that *weren't* pop must be brilliant, too brilliant to succeed. Everyone has his favorites—Jane Bowles' stylish *In the Summer House* (1953), Arthur Laurents' free-associative *A Clearing in the Woods* (1957), in which Kim Stanley met her three earlier selves, or S.N. Behrman's nostalgic *The Cold Wind and the Warm* (1958), which ended in a suicide and depressed people. Whatever the quality of the plays, it was clear that the audience was lowering its standards. It wanted to be diverted—and not by social protest, absurdist existentialism, or too much wit. *Look Homeward, Angel* and *Sunrise at Campobello* were big hits, but they were also, respectively, one touching and one exhilarating domestic play, not significant works of art. Personality helped them along: the discovery of Osgood Perkins' son Anthony in the Wolfe piece and Ralph Bellamy's F.D.R. in *Sunrise* (not to mention Mary Fickett's buck teeth as Eleanor).

Everybody was alerted to be much moved by *The Diary of Anne Frank* (1955) for its subject matter alone. Frances Goodrich and Albert Hackett's reworking of the diary of a young girl who died in a Nazi death camp was, as script, nothing compared with the public's cathartic shock of Remembering —or, more specifically, Forgetting. There surely couldn't be a setting less expedient for the tenets of pop theatre than the garret where two Jewish families hide out from and are eventually discovered by the Nazis in Amsterdam during the war; but did this play inhabit or sweeten this setting? We actually hear the arrival of the storm troopers (the lights black out before they appear), it's true. But a final scene gives us Anne's father, a survivor, reading from her famous diary: "In spite of everything, I still believe that people are really good at heart." Irony? Or scandalous sentimentality?

One day someone may give us the tragedy that Anne Frank's situation deserves; there is heroism in that resistance. But the real tragedy would be a savage and excruciating experience, and wouldn't last a week on Broadway. The psychologist Bruno Bettelheim, himself a survivor of the death camp, analyzed the pop cocoon that protects the audience at *The Diary of Anne Frank*:

> There is good reason why the so successful play ends with Anne stating her belief in the good in all men. What is denied is the importance of accepting the gas chambers as real so that never again will they exist . . . Anne Frank died because her parents could not get themselves to believe in Auschwitz. And her story found wide acclaim because for us, too, it denies implicitly that Auschwitz ever existed. If all men are good, there never was an Auschwitz.

There is evil in the world. If Anne Frank didn't think so, surely her life corrects her. Performances of the Goodrich-Hackett play in Germany have ended not in applause but in mortified silence, and this is the proper response; so is horror, fear, anger. But Germans see the play from a different angle than we do—their memories override the authors' manipulation of Anne's innocent writings. A theatre of conscience should not weep and clap at a performance of *The Diary of Anne Frank*, as Broadway did.

The rage of the 1930s was dead; too bad. We could have used a workers' theatre version of Anne Frank's story—they knew how to present such things. There is nothing wrong with pop in itself, now. But when pop takes over as the sole mode of drama, theatre and public both are degraded. Yet pop was Broadway's tone in the 1950s. A reassurance comparable to that of *The Diary of Anne Frank* was guaranteed audiences by *A Majority of One*

(1959), which offered, sensibly, Gertrude Berg as a Jewish widow and, just as sensibly by Broadway's standards, Sir Cedric Hardwicke as a Japanese widower—object, matrimony. As William Goldman points out in his book *The Season*, casting Sessue Hayakawa opposite Berg would have blown the whole game. With Hardwicke, says Goldman, we knew "that that wasn't really any Pearl Harbor sneak up there on stage pawing our Molly Goldberg."

And the seasons arrived in a flurry of announcements about major projects, many of which would never be implemented or would shutter in a few weeks; and the seasons died in the wails of journalists, calling for new voices, new directions. And new voices were heard, but without the resounding eurekas that had greeted Williams and Miller in the 1940s. Many found Lorraine Hansberry's success with *A Raisin in the Sun* (1959) the most gratifying splash of the era, for there was no racial hype involved in the play's deserved long run. Hansberry told, simply and strongly, of a black Chicago family struggling out of the ghetto into the suburbs, and gave superb opportunities to Sidney Poitier, Ruby Dee, Diana Sands, and especially Claudia McNeil, all superbly taken. Interestingly, it was one of the rare domestic plays to become a big hit in this decade, and stood out all the more in comparison with Miller and Williams in that the former favored soured or defeated families and the latter felt happier with bachelors and spinsters.

Perhaps the best domestic drama of the whole decade—excepting O'Neill —was Morton Wishengrad's *The Rope Dancers* (1957), a gloomy, poetic tragedy of life among New York's Irish poor at the turn of the century. *The Rope Dancers* offered nothing in the way of pop; had Wishengrad's script called for a Japanese, his public would have had to accept Hayakawa. The play depresses right from scene one and never lets up: a tormented little girl with a sixth finger on her left hand suffers from St. Vitus dance and eventually dies, her wastrel father is long on charm but deficient in basic practicalities, and his neurotic wife helplessly punishes their daughter for his adultery, seeing the extra finger as God's punishment.

Melodramatic in plot, *The Rope Dancers* is conceived for vernacular poetry, and the original production (directed by Peter Hall) did Wishengrad justice. It took in a strange collection of elite and popular celebrities—Art Carney played the father, Siobhan McKenna his wife, and Joan Blondell appeared as a slatternly neighbor. Anticipating public apathy to a ferocious evening, most reviewers shied away, sounding boredly respectful—except Brooks Atkinson. His favorable notice almost singlehandedly gave *The Rope*

Dancers a run of 189 performances, drawing on the fund of trust he had amassed over the years.

Wishengrad's text amazes with what it makes of the "little things" of the domestic play, as in McKenna's confrontation of Carney:

> You're a man! What would you know of the thing that tears the belly? (*She thinks of the time.*) I was jealous of the midwife when she washed her. But mine was the first joy of her—mine was the first kiss. I held her in my arms and we slept. (*Unconsciously she rocks her body back and forth and her eyes close. Then the rocking stops and her eyes open wide.*) I wonder if it happens to the others! After the first sleep. You wake up and you hold the child to nurse and you see what you've given birth. Two eyes. A nose. A mouth. Little ears. Fingernails. I kissed the fingernails. (*And her body becomes rigid.*) The finger of God's wrath! (*She remains silent.*) To be a mother is an animal thing. I can't help loving her. But I don't lie to myself that she loves me back.

It was perhaps the most finished writing of the decade.

17

The Great American Playwright

THE DIFFERENCE BETWEEN THE CRITIC (Brustein, Kauffmann, John Lahr) and the reviewer (Barnes, Watt, the *Variety* stringers) is the former's sense of historical perspective. Such thinking is largely based on assessments of the line, point of view, and evolution of specific playwrights, and this perspective began to gather most urgently in the 1950s, when Broadway's consistently aggravated contraction as business and art became the top journalistic issue. Not only was less being done; writers were doing it with less frequency than in the 1930s. It seemed as if a whole generation of semi-satirists, urban naturalists, social wits and protesters, and experimentalists active in the 1930s had dwindled, in the 1950s, into Tennessee Williams, Arthur Miller, and William Inge, joined by Edward Albee in the early 1960s with a passel of one-acts unveiled off-Broadway.

Unfortunately, all four writers failed to hold up with time. By the mid-1960s, it took no critic to note that Williams was relying on slack reprints of early Williams, Miller was producing rarely and without resonance, and Inge had hit a mortifying losing streak. Broadway seemed unable to nurture a writer who would produce quality work at regular intervals.

Then came Albee. He followed the O'Neill route up from one-acts and off-Broadway to full-length works in the big houses, and like O'Neill (and Williams) he was Different. There are hints of Beckett and absurdism, sometimes more than hints, although his first produced play, *The Zoo Story* (1960), is realistic and direct, offering two characters and a bench in Central Park. Peter is harmless and just wants to read his paper; Jerry, a lover and fighter, befriends and harasses Peter and finally gets him to murder him. It sounds right up off-Broadway's alley, and Jerry's role is written so that no actor can fail in it. Yet Albee had trouble getting it staged: its premiere took place in Berlin. But a few months later it turned up at the Province-town Playhouse on a bill with Beckett's *Krapp's Last Tape* and made a fine impression, Albee's nimble candor contrasting precisely with Beckett's weary equivocations.

Now Albee had no trouble getting produced. *The American Dream* (1961) blasted the national self-image, presenting the "dream" as a sterile freak, and mild absurdism kept the show lively. However, some critics found Albee offensive, with his burlesques of the prudish and empathy for the sensualist, with his self-hatred, with his foul language. And the controversy expanded when *Who's Afraid of Virginia Woolf?* (1962), Albee's first evening-long play, appeared on Broadway. Rich in obscenity, word games, and sadomasochistic horror, *Virginia Woolf* is quite funny and quite long, necessitating a special cast to play matinées (Uta Hagen and Arthur Hill led the evening troupe; Kate Reid—later Elaine Stritch—and Shepperd Strudwick led the afternoon cast). The piece covers a boozy, night-long party of two college professors and their wives, pitting vigor against sensitivity and symbolically smashing the American Dream again in the form of the idealized son of the host couple, George and Martha. The son turns out to be imaginary, and so, one infers, is our ideal of George and Martha Wash-ington's America.

Albee was immediately drafted to be the heir presumptive. He had man-aged to ignite our moribund domestic play with taut writing and structure: one set, four actors, virtually no plot, continuous dramatic movement. It diverted, yet stung with investigative report. Broadway's theatregoers met Albee for the first time in *Who's Afraid of Virginia Woolf?*; a few were appalled, but many were thrilled. George and Martha's symbiotic love-and-menace, played out in excessive verbal and even physical abuse, does not typify modern American marital problems, but then American drama doesn't tend to "typify." Even Albee's symbolism felt much less central to the event than his four characters, who were fully drawn, convincing individuals and who in some ways express pertinent views on the ritual solutions some couples might find for problem marriages. (A rumor has followed the work to the effect that the two couples should "really" be played by four men; an insider's joke counters this, claiming that *Virginia Woolf* cast with two homosexual couples is almost as ludicrous as *Virginia Woolf* cast with two straight couples.) Though much less shocking today, in its time *Virginia Woolf* was useful as a transitional work, helping Broadway cope, at long last, with black comedy. And a strong film version and countless revivals here and there have confirmed it as an enduring entry in the American repertory.

But succeeding Albee plays fell into obscurity, fantasy, and sexual radicalism presented in pompous, pseudo-deft English. At first, reviewers and public were patient, loath to lose their new-found propounder of perspective; at first, the obscurity was cute puzzles, the fantasy fun, the sex not overbearing. The word went out: Albee was Experimental. Not crazy experimental, like certain parts of off-Broadway. Experimental: different just enough. At length, however, the balloon burst. The obscurity hid a void of inspiration, the fantasy told nothing, the sex was misogynistic dinge.

The Ballad of the Sad Café (1963), when the glow still burned gold, suggested an interlude between the first big work (*Virginia Woolf*) and the next, at least in those who were glowing. But this lazy adaptation of Carson McCullers' tale of odd love lives in Gothic Dixie was far better acted—by Colleen Dewhurst, Michael Dunn, and Lou Antonio—than written. Albee's southern natives nagged local color at us in empty repetitions and spurious hillbilly argot ("I be partial to collards if they be cooked with sausage"), a narrator emphasized the strange lack of drama in the adaptation, and the climactic fight scene (between Dewhurst and Antonio) just did not play.

Tiny Alice (1964), the glow fading, presented the richest woman in the world buying a lay priest from the church for reasons that were made as unclear as possible. But an intriguing production covered the work's flaws: Irene Worth and John Gielgud (miscast but excellent) in lead roles and William Ritman's main set, a library in Alice's mansion containing an eye-catching scale model of the house (its little windows lit up when the chapel of the mansion burst into flame). Actors and set, by their very weight, lent the evening the substance that the script lacked. *Tiny Alice*, Robert Brustein wrote, "may well turn out to be a huge joke on the American culture industry; then again, it may turn out to be a typical product of that industry." Challenged to explain his "mystery play," Albee demurred, asserting that it was comprehensible as written. To some, it was: comprehensively a camp, pseudo-poetic cartoon with nothing in it but a scale model of a mansion.

Albee declined in critical and popular favor. True, the Pulitzer Prize committee, having registered No Award the season that *Who's Afraid of Virginia Woolf?* was eligible, seemed determined to make up for this with citations for inferior work; and impressionable theatregoers attended Albee feeling arty. But sensible opinion noted that at least Miller and Williams produced a number of first-rate works each before they slipped. Having only *Virginia Woolf*, Albee fell more spectacularly. *Malcolm* (1966), another adaptation, was a disaster from any basis of judgment. And so it went, through *A Delicate Balance* (1966) and *All Over* (1971). By 1976, when Albee staged an impressive revival of *Virginia Woolf* with Colleen Dewhurst and Ben Gazzara, he had handed over five original scripts and three adaptations (plus the rewritten book for the musical *Breakfast at Tiffany's*). The glow was gone. Those who had never contributed to it, who had not let the mania for collecting great American playwrights lead them to lionize a shadowy figure with no interior, were glad to point out that there was still *Virginia Woolf* and the best of the one-acts, *The Zoo Story*. However, there's bitterness in having backed a loser, and the cheap trendmaking reviewers—who are not informed enough to derive their perspective and have to invent it overnight—now blame Albee for their misjudgments as well as his own and run to extremes in their reports on his work. If they see a glimmer, as they did in *Seascape* (1975), they attempt to vindicate their old positions with too much praise all over again; but Albee's most recent failure, *The Lady from Dubuque* (1980), was a critical debacle.

It deserved to be. As so often with Albee, the premise is invitingly theatrical: a mysterious woman (who may or may not be the Angel of Death), accompanied by a mysterious black man, materializes in a house where a young woman (who may or may not be her daughter) is dying while her husband and two other couples are gaming and sparring. But there was nothing more to *The Lady from Dubuque* than this premise, entirely exhausted in a smashing first-act curtain—two hours of pointless and pretentious wordplay (sample line: "Everything is true . . . therefore nothing is true . . . therefore everything is true") for one moment of *frisson*. By an extremely odd coincidence, which escaped almost all the reviewers except Brustein, Irene Worth played not only Albee's Angel of Death, but an exactly similar role, complete with black escort, in Lillian Hellman's *Toys in the Attic* (1960). Not only was Albee repeating his old devices, his main one had already been used, and in a vastly superior play.

The decline of Williams, Miller, and Inge was more saddening than that of Albee, as the three were if nothing else operating on compelling expressive drives: they had something to say. Whether they could continue to say it well is another matter. Inge, first of all, was not of Williams' and Miller's calibre. Second of all, he died (a suicide), and on Broadway you are only as good as your last production. Unlike someone like Philip Barry, who is recalled with friendly neglect, Inge is not only dead, but buried.

Williams and Miller are still alive, but Williams' romantics-versus-pragmatists and Miller's father-son-sibling guilt complexes have not worn well. It was different with O'Neill: he kept writing the same attempted atonement for having grown up bitter in a funhouse until, in *Long Day's Journey into Night,* he got it down perfectly. Williams and Miller ran in the reverse direction. Miller opened up his scene, notoriously, in *After the Fall* (1964), by drawing in highly first-personal terms on his marriage to Marilyn Monroe. But he was back at square one with *The Price* (1968), a heavy-handed slice of leftover Miller realism, talky and immobile. Two middle-aged brothers picked through the property of their late father (and their triangular relationship) while a Jewish appraiser pepped up the text with ethnic boffola. It was not dull, but it went nowhere; confronting the past in this play did not relate to living in the present. Nothing happened. Worse yet was a thick-headed, unfunny comedy, *The Creation of the World and Other Business* (1972). In the daily theatre columns, reviewers tried to shill for Miller, and American drama in general—by then the two were dependents. In the highbrow periodicals, the critics were kind. But not fooled.

Williams' reputation hit even nastier skids than Miller's; since he is so prolific, his disasters accumulate in piles. Actually, his constant production is filled out by revisions of old works, and even before the 12 performances of the two-character *Out Cry* (1973), the closing of *The Red Devil Battery Sign* (1975) during its Boston tryout, and the failures of the autobiographically nostalgic *Vieux Carré* (1977) and *Clothes for a Summer Hotel* (1980), a look at Mr. and Mrs. F. Scott Fitzgerald, Williams had undertaken an unofficial sabbatical from Broadway, lending his tarnished glister to the schedules of second-rate regional companies.

The trendmakers wring their perspective over Williams: what can they do now? It's easier with Miller—he's austere and responsible. Important. Whatever he turns out, at least it'll be good for you, But Williams, from *Streetcar* on, was sexy-poetic, saturnalian, fun. Miller deals with fathers, mothers, and sons, and everyone's a martyr. Williams deals in the one-night stand: everyone's a drifter. He has made turnabouts in genre several times, in the fantastic-symbolic *Camino Real* and the marital comedy *Period of Adjustment,* for instance. But his strongest works depend on two basic types in conflict, the sensitive, alcoholic dreamer and the coarse realist. Sometimes the woman is the dreamer and the man the realist (e.g., *Streetcar* and *Summer and Smoke*). Other times, he dreams and she brings him to earth (*Cat on a Hot Tin Roof* and *Sweet Bird of Youth*). For a variation, in *The Night of the Iguana,* the male dreamer faces off two women, one dreamer and one realist. For another, the entire cast of *Out Cry* were dreamers. And in play after play, in and around the conflict, fears of aging and death career like black angels.

In his vintage, through the early 1960s, Williams was dynamic and imposing. The spell of the quarter in *Streetcar*, the flamboyant miscellany of *Camino Real*, that florid bed that dominated the stage in *Cat on a Hot Tin Roof*, the ninety-seven-year-old poet in *The Night of the Iguana*, the bitchy humor, the shy impersonations of pride or talent or joy in the doomed—that was a whole world. Even at his weakest, Williams fascinates—even in his last-resort attempts to retrench with reprises of the best bits of former successes. He showed bad judgment in 1976 in letting San Francisco's American Conservatory Theatre stage a "work in progress" called *This Is (An Entertainment)*, *Grand Hotel* nestling *Camino Real*; earlier, he combined public persona with author-ego by replacing an actor in the off-Broadway run of his own *Small Craft Warnings* (1972), *Grand Hotel* set in a waterfront bar. Williams is no actor, however. He spliced his own script with bitter ad libs and, at one performance, roared out a side door during intermission to scream "We're giving our hearts to you!" at two members of the audience who were having a row in the aisle. But another replacement on stage that night represented perhaps the most honest piece of casting in all Williams—Candy Darling, a real-life drag queen, playing a woman.

The worst aspect of this media kingmaking is that it has on occasion created such anticipation among theatregoers that new authors found they had to live up to a high reputation before they had earned it. This happened to Preston Jones in 1976 when the three full evenings of *A Texas Trilogy*—*The Last Meeting of the Knights of the White Magnolia*, *Lu Ann Hampton Laverty Oberlander*, and *The Oldest Living Graduate*—arrived in New York from Preston's home state, Texas, by way of the Kennedy Center in Washington, D.C. Jones looked Important. A trilogy, no less; such class. Interviews with him and analyses of his work cropped up everywhere at once, and he made the cover of the *Saturday Review*. He was likened to Williams, to Inge, to Larry McMurtry. His dialect and folkish touch were acclaimed. But the first-night reviewers underrated the plays themselves, they quickly closed, and Jones, as Item, was retired.

The process by which new work is first mounted in regional theatres and then brought to New York became dominant in the 1970s, and this is perhaps the most revolutionary tendency in post–World War II American theatre. Once, Broadway was the cradle of the literature of the stage, but of late it has taken to *reviving* pieces that have presumably proved themselves elsewhere. Worse yet, the journalists' playwright hustle has ignored or hyped new authors, and Broadway started to become the place where new plays come to die

Old plays, too: revivals, which at their best keep an author's style and ideas in perspective, have not been as well staged on Broadway as most new work is; this does nothing for Broadway's perspective as maintainer of a tradition. Thus, merely okay remountings of *A Streetcar Named Desire* and *Cat on a Hot Tin Roof* in the mid-1970s, respectively with Rosemary Harris (succeeded by Lois Nettleton) and Elisabeth Ashley, did not register as they might have—as comparable revivals of British works do, for example, in London. These two Williams revivals were moved to Broadway after originating elsewhere, *Streetcar* at Lincoln Center and *Cat* at Stratford, Connecticut. Why they were so lacking in generical style and so weakly cast (other than in their leading women) is a puzzle, for Williams wrote most of his parts for standard American acting equipment,* and the dynamics of authentic Williams, largely devised by Elia Kazan, are within the living experience of many theatre people. Is this style *already* dead?

William Inge's art, too, may be lost, to judge by a revival of *Picnic* seen on Broadway in 1975. Called *Summer Brave*, this production ventured into Inge's first script, revised when his director Joshua Logan requisitioned a more upbeat ending for the tale of a shiftless vagabond who dallies with and changes the life of a smalltown prom queen virtually overnight. Now, the substance of Inge's world is the false serenity that midwestern life imposes on psychological upheaval—the humdrum moving-right-alongness pasted over blisters. Naturally, Inge saw *Picnic*'s one-day summer jamboree closing with the vagabond off on his way and the girl stuck in her congenital surroundings. But down endings have joined the old domestic comedies in Broadway's oubliette, and at Logan's suggestion Inge sent the girl off on a last-minute elopement with the drifter.

George Jean Nathan once called theatre "what literature does at night," but it isn't by a long shot. First-rate novelists don't have to collaborate the way even first-rate dramatists do, and except for a few strong-willed giants, every playwright given a hearing on Broadway has had to collaborate—with his director, his cast, the reactions of audiences at previews, the opinions of

---

* Marlon Brando's Stanley Kowalski was undoubtedly a novelty, and the southern *traviate* first played by Jessica Tandy, Geraldine Page, and Margaret Leighton belong more to Williams than to tradition. But many of his lead characters and all of his secondary ones, however distinctly drawn, draw on existing thespian types, and after all one of the two or three most essential Williams performances was that of Laurette Taylor, a veteran of the old useful stage, in *The Glass Menagerie*.

the producer and backers. Authors who've worked such different sides of The Street as Tennessee Williams and Jean Kerr had his *Cat on a Hot Tin Roof* and her *Poor Richard* published in both "acting versions" and what they originally had in mind that got subverted along the way for any of a dozen reasons, most of them money. Theatre, all too often, is what literature does in the dark.

As witness this *Summer Brave*, whose failure no doubt finished Inge's reputation forever. It's a "modest" piece; it was modest when it won both the Critics Circle and Pulitzer Prizes for drama and it looks even more modest now. Production, with this play, is everything: a strong cast, from the principals to the bits, and direction that points up the psychological upheaval while playing the outward serenity, letting rawness slowly emerge organically in the action. But Michael Montel's staging was summer tepid, most of the cast terrible, and the all-important hot-under-the-collar mood totally flubbed. Alexis Smith did a jazzy turn as a sex-hungry spinster and Ernest Thompson gave a first-rate, nicely physical performance as the drifter, but this play is not a stars' vehicle, and as the evening ended one could sense the audience thinking, "So this is Inge?"

Broadway thinks increasingly in terms of dollars-and-cents survival. As long as theatres are occupied and people buy tickets, Broadway is doing well—no matter what it is doing. It isn't Broadway that has worried about the great American playwright, then, but all of unBroadway—the better regional companies, like the Arena Stage in Washington, D.C., or the Mark Taper Forum in Los Angeles; certain of New York's off-Broadway organizations, like the American Place Theatre and the Circle Repertory Company; and the off-off-Broadway showcase scene, with its *ad hoc* incorporations of Equity actors and staff working free for experience. Broadway has lost its leadership class—the Mrs. Fiskes, David Belascos, Winthrop Ameses, George Jean Nathans: actors, writers, producers, and critics pushing for history. Who, on Broadway, today, does what they did? There are a few producers around The Street who are willing to back an unknown or semi-known author. But these, too, are *ad hoc* situations, sneaking into town and closing Saturday night. Yet the theatre pageant, as public project, still concentrates on Broadway. The Pulitzer Prize and Critics Circle Awards for the best American play go to unBroadway only when absolutely necessary, and the much publicized Tony Awards are strictly mainline affairs as a rule. Off-Broadway has its "Obie," administered with suitable informality by the *Village Voice*, but these are considered so unimportant that most New York theatre people don't even bother to find out who won. As a result of this paradox—Broadway cannot deal with modern drama but drama doesn't "count" unless Broadway puts it on—the average theatregoer's perspective on American playwrighting cuts off at *The Night of the Iguana, After the Fall,* and Albee.

In the 1930s, when relatively serious theatre was taken for granted, the theatregoer could tell you who was current with no hesitation—O'Neill, Anderson, Odets, Barry, Behrman, Sherwood, Kingsley, and so on. Now, he or she might have some trouble, but patrons of unBroadway can update the list with no trouble—Sam Shepard, Lanford Wilson, Ronald Ribman, Mark Medoff, Robert Patrick, Michael Weller, John Guare, Thomas Babe, John Ford Noonan, Ed Bullins, Steve Tesich, Israel Horowitz, Leonard Melfi, Terrence McNally, and, most recently, David Mamet, Albert Innaurato, Christopher Durang, and Richard Wesley. With Broadway insisting that true theatre is Broadway theatre and the public for true theatre haunting unBroadway, Joseph Papp attempted a détente between the two in projecting his "Booth Theatre Season of New American Plays" for 1975–1976, right in the heart of The Street at Shubert Alley: one play each by Dennis Reardon, Thomas Babe, John Ford Noonan, Miguel Piñero, and Michael Weller.

A full-page announcement in the Sunday *Times* in August of 1975 was headlined "Wanted!" big and bold over a photograph of the five authors posing good-humoredly in Shubert Alley. "The five desperados pictured above are living American playwrights," ran the sidecopy. "And they've been missing from the American scene too long. They are wanted! Alive!"

To underline the mellow daring required of subscribers, the five desperados posed for their photo in countercultural denim, and PR come-ons announced what was to come. Piñero's *The Sun Always Shines for the Cool,* described as "a High Noon confrontation at a Hustlers and Players Bar where loss of pride is worse than death," had an air of *déjà vu* about it after his *Short Eyes,* but in general the five plays offered a promising season. Most important, it was being offered out in plain sight on Forty-fifth Street where everyone could get to it and have no excuse not to give it a try.

Yet as the premiere item, Reardon's *The Leaf People,* neared the end of rehearsals, rumor had it that all was not well at the Booth—that at least two of the four other plays weren't even written, that the project was in Big Trouble. The most disquieting rumors concerned the decorating of Reardon's play by its director Tom O'Horgan, but decorating—that is, theatricalizing—is what O'Horgan gets hired for. Bad luck (a musicians' strike arrested the sellout run of *A Chorus Line,* whose profits were to subsidize the Booth project) shut the whole project down after one week of *The Leaf People.*

The latter, as disclosed, proved an erratically acted but strong and colorful piece about the first white contact with South American savages, any given five minutes of which was worth the entire 1,007-performance run of *Never Too Late*.

Perhaps some will say that an operation like Papp's was never meant to transfer uptown: the theatres are wrong for this type of drama, the public is wrong, and—best reason of all—there seems to be a curse on this sort of thing. You take a play that is doing good business in a small Village theatre, pull it up where people can get to it easily and where a larger house can take in some real money . . . and it suddenly closes. Why? Well, some plays do need the intimate, informal, grungy, or absurd "spaces" of off-Broadway, as opposed to the crustier, more official-feeling showhouses of Broadway. Alternatives to establishment art don't sit right in establishment houses. Too, it is far less expensive (though still no bargain) to keep an off-Broadway show running: the contract, the package of salaries and conditions, is lower. And perhaps there are people who attend off-Broadway theatre who for unknown reasons won't go to see the same show uptown. Such exceptions as *A Chorus Line* and *That Championship Season* never really belonged off-Broadway in the first place (except in that their origins in the Papp Workshop gave them a leeway for improvisational development and preparatory readings not available in the sink-or-swim precincts of commercial Broadway).

The off-Broadway alternative, then, no longer serves as a proving ground for fresh talent or novel forms bound for national acculturation on the country's main stages, as was the rule with the art theatre of the 1920s and the social protest theatre of the 1930s. Now, off-Broadway exists for itself. This is not good; some plays require more leg room, production expense, and acting expertise than off-Broadway can provide, and some plays deserve greater exposure than off-Broadway can afford. It's not an alternative anymore. It's a trap.

The nation's theatregoers should have access to the nation's young playwrights, and access means Broadway—those theatres, that attention and prestige. Again, is there an attitude about playwrights and playwrighting on The Street? Are they *Wanted!* after all? As my final chapter will show, the late 1970s saw an upsurge of new drama on Broadway, much of it successful in financial terms. But there can be no doubt that the artistically questionable Broadway of the 1950s, which made the rise of a separate off-Broadway necessary, has produced two largely non-collaborative environments for American theatre: Broadway and unBroadway. A number of factors will aggravate Broadway's decline as a home for vital theatre: the ill effects of television's dramatic shorthand on the aesthetic instincts of Americans, the emergence of film as the culture's primary artistic situation, the partial abandonment of Broadway by many professionals for more congenial quarters in regional companies, and the bungling non-guidance of the New York journalists. The search for a great American playwright will intensify: the means by which a playwright secures a place in the light will begin to dissolve.

18

What Has Happened So Far II

EXTREMISTS OF ART AND EXTREMISTS OF MASSCULT worked out a treaty in the 1920s, sharing the vigor of sensuality and psychology, and debunking oldtime pop mythologies. The result was our first exciting decade of theatre, one that institutionalized dissent within an established cultural medium. In the 1930s, this dissent hardened, and broke the treaty. The disinherited outsider—the worker—changed the purpose of what drama must do for and if necessary to the culture. But Broadway could not contain this too bitter dissent easily, and its extremism (added to the apolitical nature of wartime theatre) created by reaction the less militant Broadway of the 1940s.

Outsiders had directed the major revolutions in American theatre art in these last few decades, the outsiders of off-Broadway. Avant-garde stagecraft came from the little theatre movement, true realism from the O'Neill of Provincetown, hardline politics from the workers. All three are related (the workers' sketch *Newsboy* may be said to be composed of these three parts in equal measure), and all three did, to various extents, survive on Broadway. But the public was increasingly retreating from them.

Off-Broadway itself was in disrepair. In the late 1940s, it was a chance agglomerate of out-of-the-way theatres rather than a movement. It was classics and revivals and risky ventures in no order. The 1947–48 season, for example: Charles Laughton's translation of Brecht's *Galileo*, with Laughton, in a production first staged in Los Angeles by Joseph Losey; W. H. Auden and Christopher Isherwood's *The Dog Beneath the Skin*, cast including Beatrice Arthur, Gene Saks, Jerry Stiller, and Judith Malina (later one of the co-directors of the Living Theatre); Erwin Piscator's production of Robert Penn Warren's *All the King's Men* (from Warren's novel); a transformation of Gorky's *The Lower Depths* as a black musical called *A Long Way from Home*; O'Neill's *Lazarus Laughed*, an old work which had never been done on Broadway; and Jean-Paul Sartre's unctuously doctrinal attack on life in the American South, *The Respectful Prostitute*, which was moved uptown and made a temporary star out of its principal, Meg Mundy. Clearly, the sense of daring is still there, the ambition to try the untried. But as it passed into the 1950s, off-Broadway was still looking for itself.

At least it was looking; Broadway, these years, was blind. What has happened so far comprises the beginnings of a decline of will on Broadway. Once, it received outcast art. Now, it enforced a ban against it. Not till off-Broadway realized that it was on its own did it find the will to create a new identity for itself—and, in a way, it then took over Broadway's oldest purpose: to find a meaning in character rather than in ideas. Could it be that the art and political revolutions hurt Broadway more than they helped?— that their idealistic and thematic mission overpowered the public? This public is troubled by ideas; not always, but often. The theory of the good show holds story and personality as supreme, and accepts ideas only incidentally. When off-Broadway developed its own formats for the good show, it managed to combine the lure of character with the viewpoint of the outcast.

There was a place, Broadway: a stock of theatres; generations of playwrights, producers, and actors Going On; coherent assumptions about the rightness of beauty, the importance of classics, and the fun of pop; an anxiety about the intensity of the satirist and the dissident but a willingness to tolerate and sometimes encourage them.

No more. Now, the place of American theatre is unchartably diffuse. The new works originate and the brilliant productions are mounted in regional and university theatres, in off-off-Broadway showcases, in workshops closed to the general public or festival workshops in remote places such as the National Playwrights Conference in Waterford, Connecticut (known as the "O'Neill Festival"), where theatre people gather to taste new work, discuss, and revise in pastoral surroundings. There, and in many other places, Broadway is a distant shudder of overdosed glamor. The place that was once Broadway, New York is now Broadway plus off-Broadway plus off-off-Broadway plus the new national Broadway of New Haven and Dallas and Los Angeles. From *Strange Interlude* in the 1920s to *Awake and Sing!* in the 1930s to *The Skin of Our Teeth* in the 1940s, we have traveled out of fantastic realism into realism and on to fantasy. Somewhere along the route, the purpose split and shattered. To find it, we have to expand our view to take in a wild panorama. At the center of it is the rise of modern off-Broadway and its reaffirmation of the individualist ethos in American art.

19

Off-Broadway: "Asking What Is Life Is Like Asking What Is a Carrot— a Carrot Is a Carrot!"

OFF-BROADWAY ITSELF IS ANCIENT, but one can date the rise of *modern* off-Broadway from the 1952 Circle-in-The-Square revival of Tennessee Williams' *Summer and Smoke* with Geraldine Page. The Actors Studio *End as a Man* a year later, the Marc Blitzstein translation of *The Threepenny Opera* (the so-called "Lotte Lenya revival") a year after that, and the Circle-in-the-Square's *The Iceman Cometh* (the "Jason Robards revival") in 1956 consolidated the postwar resurgence. All of off-Broadway had one thing in common, shoestring budgets: low salaries, low profits. This pitiful economy gave off-Broadway a wild diversity, because no project, no matter how bizarre, had much to lose if it failed. The diversity, which took in everything from infantile musicals, camp burlesques, and social polemic to experimental mime, European avant-garde texts, and take-the-money-and-run pornorama, is hard to define. New York fire safety regulations for theatres defined it neatly in the late 1940s, when special exemptions were allowed houses seating fewer than three hundred. Off-Broadway, then, is 299 people or less.

Favorable publicity for *Summer and Smoke* and *The Iceman Cometh* convinced everyone that off-Broadway had been reborn to revive Broadway's old properties in productions superior to the originals. Under José Quintero's direction, Geraldine Page's Alma Winemiller reclaimed Williams' play, shadowed by its quasi-failure uptown in 1948, and Quintero's *Iceman* really did bring that work forward all over again. The show lasted twenty-one months this time around, inspired Carlotta O'Neill to let Quintero stage the New York premiere of *Long Day's Journey into Night*, and inaugurated Jason Robards' reputation as the foremost American O'Neill specialist.

In these early years, modern off-Broadway mainly served as an annex to Broadway, its actors Broadway's hopefuls and its plays Broadway's plays, old flops and hits or new plays that might easily have played to Broadway's public, as for example when Calder Willingham's *End as a Man* moved to a Broadway house on the strength of rave reviews. This picture of brutality at a southern military school faded north of Christopher Street, but it did introduce Ben Gazzara, Pat Hingle, William Smithers, and Mark Richman.

This recycling of old works and discovering of new faces had none of old off-Broadway's sense of revolution, but in 1953 the fire burned again when the Phoenix Theatre took over a 1,200-seat barn on lower Second Avenue (left over from the great days of the Yiddish Theatre) with the idea of reviving the non-Broadway alternative drama company: annual series of international classics and the odd American work (including a few highly audacious operatic musicals, *The Golden Apple* and *Sandhog*). The Phoenix wasn't the only group devoted to non-commercial fare, but it was a big company, working on a contract different from that of the 299-and-under houses, and it won considerable attention by including well-known actors in its roster. The first Phoenix seasons featured such events as *Coriolanus*, staged by John Houseman with Robert Ryan; a *Sea Gull* with Judith Evelyn, Maureen Stapleton, Montgomery Clift, and Kevin McCarthy; a Tyrone Guthrie *Six Characters in Search of an Author*; a Strindberg double bill with Viveca Lindfors; Siobhan McKenna's brilliant, hectic Maid in Shaw's *St. Joan*; Ostrofsky's *Diary of a Scoundrel* with Roddy McDowall, Howard de Silva, Blanche Yurka, Robert Culp, Margaret Hamilton, Doro Merande, Peter Falk in a small role, and a poodle named Lorelei Lee; and Eric Bentley's production of Brecht's *The Good Person of Setzuan*. With an irregular acting base, no stock of productions (each piece opened, ran, closed, and vanished) or repertory schedule, and no stylistic foundation, the Phoenix was no national theatre. But it was surviving, and it was talked about.

As the 1950s continued, off-Broadway began to retrieve its old urge to be Broadway's alternative in all things. Informally, it congealed into a movement for the revelation of not merely new but "difficult" authors, of black drama, of absurdism, and of experimental stagecraft while retaining the revivals and training of raw talent. In the 1959–60 season, the attractions took in O'Neill's *The Great God Brown*, *Lysistrata*, *Peer Gynt* (with Fritz Weaver), and both parts of Shakespeare's *Henry IV*, all at the Phoenix; the extraordinary Living Theatre production of Jack Gelber's *The Connection* (in which a group of drug addicts await, to jazz accompaniment, the arrival of their supplier—the "connection"); Chekhof, Synge, Anouilh, Pirandello,

Ionesco, Schnitzler, John Whiting; revivals of Williams' *Camino Real* and *Orpheus Descending*, Odets' *The Big Knife*, Treadwell's *Machinal*, and *Tobacco Road*; the New York debut of Jean Genet's *The Balcony* at the Circle-in-the-Square; the famous long-running pairing of Beckett's one-man *Krapp's Last Tape* and Albee's two-man *The Zoo Story*; and a number of small-scaled musicals, readings, mime shows, and topical revues. There were ambitious, expensive entries as well as incompetent sketches on little platforms before a mostly invited audience of embarrassed well-wishers. Detractors said Broadway at least meets a minimum level of professionalism. Defenders said off-Broadway has guts.

That it did. Moreover, it began to lose interest in feeding into Broadway. It had developed its own public, its own management echelons, and its way of making intimacy into an aesthetic. Already, there were influences that would prove formative—the Living Theatre, for instance, run by Julian Beck and his wife Judith Malina on a (real) repertory schedule of works dealing with the worldviews of outcasts.

That, of course, is what off-Broadway had always been for. But modern off-Broadway would not state the outcast's case in language Broadway could understand (as Eugene O'Neill and Clifford Odets had done), but would state the true revolutionary art, too revolutionary for Broadway. *Now* we're a movement. Gelber's *The Connection* provided a starting point for such a movement; its drug addicts in their quasi-improvised harangues and trances were there as much to explore artistic innovations first chanced by Alfred Jarry and Pirandello as to portray the subculture of the heroin rider. That the Becks had hit on something purely revolutionary was clear in the horror expressed by reviewers of the major media. Even second-stringers, who should have been ready for off-Broadway to turn on its gyre because they had had to see so much of it, were resentful; they attacked it not as bad theatre but as bad life. Note the studied debunking of the *Times'* off-Broadway man, Louis Calta: "*The Connection* proves to be nothing more than a farrago of dirt, smalltime philosophy, empty talk, and extended runs of 'cool' music . . . Instead of offering the theatregoer the pathos and terror of those sinister activities [i.e., drug addiction], *The Connection* fritters away its theme with inexpert and obvious stunts . . . Mr. Gelber is not exactly going to influence people and make friends."

Pathos and terror, egad? Make *friends*? Dirt, empty talk, and stunts are not errors in Gelber's dramaturgy, but principles of his style—one familiar by then to ambitious off-Broadway theatregoers, who had seen the sudden adaptation of modern European techniques into American drama. Neo-classical parody, farce, interpolated vaudeville, fantasy, the bizarre, experiments in metaphors for contemporary upheaval, alienation, or despair had not yet registered on Broadway—a *Waiting For Godot* there in 1960 would probably have done as badly as the two in 1956 and 1957. But off-Broadway seized all this greedily.

Soon, the outside world began to look in. The media sent in first-stringers to cover certain events, average theatregoers began to chance a trip downtown, and university theatres programmed "off-Broadway" works that might have been unthinkable ten years before. Still, the confusion as to what exactly off-Broadway was scared some customers away: an O'Neill revival was one thing, a perverse improvisation another. Acting crazies threatened to drop all pretense of acting and expose a real-life craziness, perhaps even assault the audience physically. At one point in *The Connection*, an addict screamed abuse at the audience for coming to *The Connection* in the first place: "You like to watch people suffer?"

As off-Broadway expanded, it developed its spin-offs, "coffeehouse theatre" and off-off-Broadway, best defined as a non-Equity off-Broadway on an even smaller budget. In their prime in the early 1960s, such organizations as Phase Two, The Premise, Café Manzini, and Caffe Cino cultivated a following for diverse offerings in tiny spaces. They did everything from political satire to lunatic opera, and they gave a start to numerous talents such as Robert Patrick, whose *Kennedy's Children* grew out of a coffeehouse sketch in 1970 into a full-length play of international reputation. One of *Kennedy's Children*'s characters, an off-off-Broadway actor, recalls the sacerdotally ragbag style of the off-off scene, not exaggerating as much as you'd think:

> One night, before the nine o'clock show, I announced to three N.Y.U. students and a Caribbean astrologer that there would be a brief prologue that evening, and I signaled Corso to put on "Mack the Knife," and then I proceeded to do my two time-steps alternately for fifteen minutes. Biting my tongue. The audience was understandably transfixed . . . Then [the manager] hit me in the face with a pie. I poured ketchup over his head. He slapped me with a raw fish. I tap-danced on his toes. He went on point and pirouetted. The blonde and the amputee . . . came on and went into their dance . . . I countered with every wisecrack I remembered from four million Glenda Farrell musicals. And as luck would have it, a critic from *The Village Voice* was there that night—looking for deaf-mute boys —and he wrote us up that week as the latest thing in Draymah.

This was unBroadway at its most unconstricted. But elsewhere, groups chartered themselves according to specific schemes for technique, politics, genre. Black authors found a ready stage off-Broadway, though most of their work in the 1960s was raw and at times frankly homicidal. LeRoi Jones, who later changed his name to Imamu Amiri Baraka, became prominent for the allegorical *Dutchman* (1964), in which a white slut seduces a bookish, middle-class black on the subway, murders him, disposes of the body, and is last seen starting in with a second black. Baraka's suggestion that white America courts the black race with empty promises and destroys those who demand those promises be kept is a valid point of debate, but the author lost his argument in a double-bill, *The Slave* and *The Toilet* (1965). In *The Toilet*, black adolescents torment a white schoolmate; in *The Slave*, set during an American race war of the future, a black revolutionary reviles a white liberal professor, kills him, terrorizes his wife (the black's ex-wife, and Baraka assures us that she is still madly attracted to him), informs her that he has murdered her two daughters, blows up the house, and leaves the woman mortally wounded. The two plays were not well reasoned as social protest and, at times, not even in English. Let's quote: "Sometimes the place and twist of what we are will push and sting, and what the crust of our stance has become will ring in our ears and shatter that piece of our eyes that is never closed."

Black hostility was in vogue, and now the *Times* was ready. Howard Taubman, who moved to the theatre column from music when Atkinson retired, fawned over Baraka, and another county in the land of off-Broadway was labeled on the map. It was inconvenient that Martin Duberman, a white man, had already put together a vastly telling evening on the black experience called *In White America* (1963), a reading for six actors drawn from documents and connected by Duberman's impartial and yet quite moving historical narrative. But at least we had reached the next plateau in the integration of black art into white American theatre, that revealing black writers in quantity.

To solemnize the event, the Negro Ensemble Company formed in ranks closed against integration, devoting its energy to the production of black plays for all-black casts. Easily the best known of the black troupes, the Ensemble and its distaste for ecumenism recalls the quandary of the workers' groups in the 1930s, who needed to expand their subscription yet could only do so by appealing to the bourgeoisie whom their dogmatic chiefs so resented. The bulk of the theatregoing audience is white; a New York success depends on white appreciation; yet the Negro Ensemble Company despised this appreciation even as it must—to stay alive—woo it. Also torn between the challenge of helping to institute a vital black drama that might exert a national influence and the temptation to hammer at black supremacist racism, the Company tried to meet the one and succumb to the other. For the latter it offered the inane *Ododo* (1970), an alleged history of the black race by Joseph A. Walker, including such curious observations as "Your Mayflower was a fraud: black prisoners of war watched it anchor." For the former, it offered Walker's *The River Niger* (1972), a compelling domestic tragedy, and one of the few off-Broadway shows to transfer successfully to Broadway, when it won a Tony Award for Best Play in 1974.

The racist slant of the black playwrights threatened to become boringly conventionalized, with their constant threats of civil war and symbolic rapings of white women. Likewise mired in routine was the sexual-political stage. This started as a laudable attempt to liberate the theatre of its puritanism, but by the late 1960s it had hooked itself up with radical left-wing politics, the antiwar movement, theories of audience "involvement," and excesses of psychodrama. Its merciless nudity was a stunt, not well used; it thought itself beautiful and free, but acted ugly and bitter. "Love" and "brotherhood" were screamed about, but sex was conveyed, never love. The words, when used, were a drivel. The acting, where attempted, was feeble. Example: the Performing Group's *Dionysus in '69* (1968), an adaptation of Euripides' *The Bacchae* that completely misconstrued the original work, cut away about two-thirds of the words, and filled in between simulated (I hope) orgies with irrelevancies on modern life or confessions of personal hangups. Lengthy, tedious, and ignorant, *Dionysus in '69* was given in an "environment" (a converted garage), theatres as such being considered old-hat on the sexual-political circuit. The Performing Group, directed by Richard Schechner, represented the worst aspect of the "alternative" stage, for the alternative here was that opposed to openness, clarity, literacy, imagination, and everything else that is rated as a positive value by those above the rank of beast. The title, *Dionysus in '69*, was not a hope, but a threat. It meant not "Sexual Liberty Next Year" but "Destruction Next Year."

This is not to debunk the sexual-political thespians in general, for some of this sensationalism grew out of responses to purely artistic questions. The Living Theatre, most notorious and celebrated of the physical troupes of the 1960s, illustrates how "relevance" zapped drama on off-off-Broadway. As organized by the Becks, the Living Theatre rated experimentation in the forms of theatre higher than social commentary. But the one seems to dog the other. *The Connection* and Pirandello's *Tonight We Improvise*, which the Living performed in repertory, offered two different levels of theatre *verité*: Pirandello's dainty game on the reality behind "theatre" and Gelber's flatter game that expunges "theatre" as much as possible.

Such tests of the stage's ability not to reconceive life but to duplicate it led the Living Theatre to Kenneth H. Brown's *The Brig* (1963), a grueling copy of a Marine Corps prison. No story, no "characterization," no Living Newspaper arrangement of facts: just captors and captives. Dangerous stuff. But someone had to do it; "If not I, who?" asked Malina, and how right she was. In 1964 the Internal Revenue Service answered by charging in to claim what it could of Living Theatre bric-à-brac in lieu of tax arrears. But the company refused to be evicted from their home, and pushed past the padlocks to give a last illegal performance of *The Brig* before departing for Europe (the Becks returned briefly to serve jail sentences for impeding federal machinery), the martyrs who got away.

The Becks were far from through. Passing on to the next stage of their quest, they dispensed with prepared text altogether and mounted epics of ferocious mass chanting, semi-nudity, aggressions, and audience "participation." (Actually, those in the hall who responded to invitations to join the play were invariably silenced.) *Dionysus in '69* scrapped two-thirds of Euripides; the Living Theatre dropped the very idea of words as forward or backward motion and just stood there making nasty dada. In *Frankenstein, Antigone, Mysteries and Smaller Pieces,* or *Paradise Now,* the Living Theatre achieved ultimate completion of theatre as non-theatre—and this despite some undeniably engrossing pantomime.* If off-off and off-Broadway were theatres of outcasts, the Becks' troupe supplied its pageant. *Frankenstein's* finale became legendary: bent, scissored, grabbed, clutching, stretched, held bodies wrapped up into one huge mass of limbs that suddenly appeared to be a monster creeping horribly in the direction of the audience. But this sensational effect was not enough to redeem a tedious evening, and the British magazine *Plays and Players'* local man, Alan Brien, reports that at one performance, a wag in the gallery cut through the ovation yelling, "Great! Now make a dog!"

What were these Living Theatre epics about? They seemed to think they were telling of their own resistance to statist oppression; actually, they

---

* Much of off-off-Broadway's physical pageant has been traced to the influence of Jerzy Grotowski, but the Pole and his disciples are precise where his imitators often make a mess. At that, André Gregory's *Alice in Wonderland* (1970), very simply realized by six New York University students, applied Grotowski's dynamics far more effectively than anything like the Living Theatre could.

were about the Living Theatre's own oppressiveness and what the authorities would do when the Living Theatre baited them to act—such as arresting the cast for indecent exposure and disturbing the peace of New Haven during an engagement at the Yale School of Drama in 1968. Robert Brustein, dean of the school, scored the troupe for its "anti-intellectualism, its sensationalism, its sexual obsessiveness, its massacre of language, its noisy attention-getting mechanisms, its indifference to artistry, craft, and skill, its violence, and, above all, its mindless tributes to Love and Togetherness." With its more-alternative-than-thou self-righteousness, it was—Brustein again—"not a vision of human freedom that one took away from *Paradise Now* but rather vague, disturbing memories of the youth rallies in Hitler's Nuremberg."

Far better for off-off-Broadway's fortunes were the groups whose political initiation sought an order in art. Lacking the flesh shows that decoyed the media to the sexual-politicians, the artist-politicians were less well known but, among the cognoscenti, highly prized. Here, too, text was de-emphasized. In some cases, workshop improvisations were eventually "frozen" into a finished piece as much action as words. Group movement was strategic here, as it had been for the workers' theatre. But these radicals of thirty years later were much more fluid in their revolutionary program, urging a cerebral-*cum*-sensual awareness rather than armed uprising. The Leninist thespians of the 1930s read Saint-Simon, Trotsky, and John Reed and were tireless voters; their later counterparts read Artaud and Stanislafsky and hoped the politicians would devour each other.

Such a group was Joseph Chaikin's Open Theatre, founded in 1963. Sympathetic to radical politics, the Open Theatre had no use for propaganda. Indeed, it had organized more to create than perform and at times could not be found even when looked for. Countering the standard premise that a play is 1. written and then 2. staged, the Open Theatre skipped step one, staging through games, abstractions, and variations. The "author" was partly the company, partly a writer who set down a text based on the improvs, and then again the company, improving further on the "script." Action, always, was the primal force in such theatre. One may wonder what kind of artistic integrity is implied in an act of communal manufacture, but the answer is, simply: another kind. The Open Theatre was hailed in 1966 for its technical vision—its elemental mimesis—when two of its projects surfaced in off-Broadway theatres, *America Hurrah* and *Viet Rock*.

In both cases, authors were credited, Jean-Claude van Itallie for *America Hurrah* and Megan Terry for *Viet Rock*. *America Hurrah*, "three views of the U.S.A.," proved a brilliantly satiric indictment of our machine-and-media culture, and perhaps as well of the frightened emptiness of soul that hides in it, mildly complaining about it but needing it as badly as O'Neill's characters need their illusory dreams. The first of van Itallie's three plays, "Interview," reduces job applicants to an absurdist mob under the impersonal rat-a-tat of interviewese and then, moving out into life, shows how everything else has been made impersonal, as in a psychiatrist's "advice" to his patient: "Blah, blah, blah, blah, blah, blah, HOSTILE. Blah, blah, blah, blah, blah, blah, PENIS. Blah, blah, blah, blah, blah, blah, MOTHER. Blah, blah, blah, blah, blah, blah, MONEY." The second play, "TV," pulls an aboutface on the usual mode of satire, which is logical exaggeration to illogical excess; instead, the standard television fare—variety shows, old movies, sitcom, a Spanish lesson, superheroes, the western, commercials, and of course the Vietnam War—is juxtaposed, deadpan, with the humdrum realities of viewers' lives. Ultimately, the humdrum merged with the fantabulous, life's perspective blown away in teletronic fallout. "Motel," the last of the trio, was the most imposing. The acting metaphor in "Interview" was impersonality and in "TV" fantasy. In "Motel" it was violence. As if in Beckett, the only speaking part is a disembodied voice, talking the praise of a motel ("rooms of marble and rooms of cork, all letting forth an avalanche"). As if in Vitrac, the motelkeeper is a huge papier-mâché doll; two guests check in, also papier-mâché grotesques. As if in a Marx Brothers apotheosis, they strip, turn on the television, deface the walls, trash the furniture, and finally demolish the motelkeeper, all to the droning accompaniment of the motel come-on. Hype, sex, rock, and destruction: all one. Building up to "Motel" from "Interview" through "TV" the evening expands in a free-feeling phantasmagoria that, on study, observes a conceptual precision. *America Hurrah* became one of the longest-running non-musical shows in off-Broadway history.

But reviewers who praised it turned against Megan Terry's *Viet Rock*, for unlike *America Hurrah* it ran counter to the gathering sixties vogue for anti-American expression. A synthesis of images relating to war, *Viet Rock* failed to take sides in any specific war; it asserted that war is wrong, therefore all sides are wrong. But New York had been counting on an off-Broadway statement on the Vietnam War, specifically condemning American involvement in it. Terry's arrangement of Open Theatre exercises did not fill the order. Worse yet, she had the arrogance to allude to atrocities committed by the North Vietnamese. Critics who had raved over *America Hurrah* said *Viet Rock* was boring. In fact, the pair were equally representative of the vitality of the workshop approach to composition.

The Open Theatre was very influential, though its montage structure in other hands often degenerated into pretentious ritual, from the Warm-Up of the Cast in Full View of the Public to the Extremely Relevant Procession up the Aisle As One With the Audience. The Open Theatre itself reached such solemn extremes late in its career in *The Serpent* (1970), episodes in the history of murder and another group invention edited by Jean-Claude van Itallie. There, at the start, was the Warm-Up; at the close, the Procession. It was a little much. But in between there were some highly imaginative renderings—the snake in the garden of Eden was played by five people, in wild body language and wordless sounds. One scene, depicting the First Murder, Cain's of Abel, became legendary in theatre circles: as no human in the world has died yet, Cain can't figure out how killing works even as he tries it, pulling at Abel's limbs, then breaking them, watching him to see what effect it has. Abel frantically tries to crawl away, but Cain keeps holding him back, improvising on him until at last he hacks with the flat of his hand at Abel's throat. It sounds too neat to describe it in words; to see it was to learn how pantomime can be all the theatre one needs. The Open Theatre helped free the stage of an unsuspected convention, that of naturalistic verbal artificiality. Pictures *were* more intense than words, it seemed.

In comedy, too, off-Broadway was refreshingly different. Just when farce, satire, and domestic comedy had lost their drive on Broadway, off-Broadway entered an age of absurd burlesque, best typified by Barbara Garson's *MacBird!* (1967), *Macbeth* combined with a spoof of American politics. At times sophomoric and at times wickedly funny (and helped by Stacy Keach's powerful Lyndon Johnson and William Devane's uncanny resemblance to Robert Kennedy as Robert Ken O'Dunc), *MacBird!* shows off-Broadway's tolerance of nonconformist alignments: Garson blasts at everybody of the day, from hippy to hawk. Some were shocked at her apparent suggestion that Lyndon Johnson (via Macbeth) murdered John Kennedy (via Duncan). This was not Garson's message, only a point of departure for a debunking of the political scene, of the tyranny hidden behind the charisma and slogans of the Kennedy-Johnson era, of all government. *MacBird!* is not unlike a comic counterpart to *Gods of the Lightning*. As Peter Brook saw it, Garson's subject was "the mechanism of power . . . this and nothing else."

MacBird! is one kind of comedy; Charles Ludlam is quite another. His style has been dubbed "New York comedy" for its mixture of putdown, paranoia, and know-it-all trivia, but it is more an "off-Broadway, New York" comedy: Ludlam's humor has no connection to what succeeds on Broadway. With his Ridiculous Theatre Company, he has mounted Dumas' *Camille* (taking the title role himself), *Stage Blood* (*Hamlet* as played in Mudville, U.S.A.), and a "fairy tale for the disenchanted" called *The Enchanted Pig*. *Der Ring Gott Farblonjet* (1977) sets the Ludlam tone in its full-length Wagnerian lampoon, constant sense of reductive "production," scabrous puns, literary and showbiz references, sexual tomfoolery, ceaseless camp, extreme length (over three hours), and German-Yiddish title.

Ludlam is as much a part of off-Broadway as any Strindberg revival or anarchic political spoof, and the idea of community in the movement depends somewhat on the outrage that Broadwayites assumably would feel if exposed to his art, or Garson's, or the Living Theatre's. By the late 1960s, certain off-Broadway companies would rather have taken their prize items to European festivals than to Broadway, if invited; and certain companies did exactly that. Off-Broadway is its own ratification now, with its own options on continuity. Broadway sees off-Broadway's people as outcasts; this is correct —because on Broadway, rules are made by money people. Off-Broadway's negligible economics left it in the hands of art people, open to what material and performance can do when set free of convention. Broadway scares too easily. That public wants musicals, thrillers; give them celebrities, lots of color, nuns, kids, and dogs; they say What's for Christmas? and pay extra for charity.

What are off-Broadway's charities?—outcast politics, outcast races, outcast sex, outcast comedy, and technique as absolute truth. Authors and actors, too, are a charity. The list of performers who got their start in modern off-Broadway is very long: Kim Stanley, Colleen Dewhurst, George C. Scott, Nancy Wickwire, Vincent Gardenia, Faye Dunaway, James Earl Jones, Sada Thompson, Anne Meachum, Martin Sheen, Cicely Tyson, Frank Langella, Dustin Hoffman, William Atherton, Meryl Streep, Al Pacino, Richard Gere, Christopher Walken, William Hurt are only a few (not to mention Page, Gazzara, Robards, and Keach). Moreover, off-Broadway became at some point in the recent past a rallying point for all of unBroadway, with its insistent company approach seen as the key to alternative art. From the Equity showcase to the most distant regional stage, the lure of organized fraternity promised the fulfillment of one's profession in a way that the uptown circuit of auditions, featured parts in garbage, and closing notices could not. UnBroadway has many different shapes of company. New Haven has two, the so-called Yale Rep and Arvin Brown's Long Wharf Theatre, both prominent in New York because journalists cover the former and the latter exports its productions. There is the Mark Taper Forum in Los Angeles, run by Gordon Davidson on an enterprising plan that combines old pop classics with better-than-pop new works. The Manhattan Theatre Club, a multi-tiered palace of "spaces" converted from a Slavic community center on East Seventy-third Street, is off-off-Broadway utter typical, offering, as you enter on a given night, a Barry revival on your left, a cabaret revue on your right, a new work by Athol Fugard ahead of you, and anything from Terrence McNally to Mark Medoff on upper floors. Some of these productions are too distinctly by and for outcasts to belong anywhere else, but some others are works that Broadway could and sometimes does produce, picking a show up whole and bringing it downtown. Medoff's wildly literate comedy, *The Wager* (1974), played that route, as did the Fats Waller retrospective, *Ain't Misbehavin'* (1978).

The limited-run, non-profit showcase is a preview for The Business, hoping to impress potential sponsors. Unlike the reading, which is cast but not staged, the showcase is a full production, and has been known to float some big hits. It was a showcase that launched *The Boys in the Band* (1968), Mart Crowley's picture of a male homosexual birthday party, performed in so many places it may rival the Kaufman-Hart repertory in high-school gymnasiums of the future.

Speaking of outcasts. 1968 was about the right time for a straight person's primer on the gay subculture, especially since Crowley's nine characters threatened no one's conception of the "tragedy" of gay life. The party host is a manic-depressive type who turns on his best friends, one couple suffers from the younger man's insistent promiscuity, and the birthday boy is aging, Jewish, and unattractive—which, we learn, are causes of utter despair in the gay world. At the climax, one of the guests, a married man who may or may not be straight, is dared to call the one person he has loved. Crowley cleverly manipulates the scene to suggest that the person he has called is his old college buddy. No: he has phoned his wife. They had quarreled, but they patch it up and he leaves, sober and content. Jean Kerr couldn't have handled it better.

Though it was thought to have enough appeal to be filmed almost exactly as staged (with the original cast), Crowley's play moved uptown from the Playwrights Unit showcase on Vandam Street *not* to Broadway but to a smallish house very far west on Fifty-fifth Street. For once, an unBroadway hit did not risk displeasing the general public, instead finding its own level on a kind of extra-visible off-Broadway. There it ran for years, attracting both Broadwayites and buffs of outcast art thanks to its comforting picture of how miserable homosexuals are, its ensemble of some excellent and some incompetent actors welded into a unit by Robert Moore, and the shock of the gay bite, as in this exchange of a hustler and a camp cut-up:

COWBOY: I lost my grip doing my chin-ups and I fell on my heels and
          twisted my back.
EMORY: You shouldn't wear heels when you do chin-ups.

Gay drama has not distinguished itself on off-Broadway so far, mainly because the most talented gay theatre people have traditionally assimilated themselves into the heterosexual theatre as writers, directors, composers, librettists, and actors. Under pressure to sublimate their drives in parodies of "true" romance, these artists have created an unchartably furtive history —but when the rare honest gay play appeared, it, too, opened on Broadway. Edouard Bourdet's *The Captive* (in the 1920s) and Mordaunt Shairp's *The Green Bay Tree* (in the 1930s) examined the gay sensibility as well as merely presented gay characters, though these were foreign imports, and no American gay work attracted much attention on The Street until Martin Sherman's *Bent* in 1979 (more about *Bent* later).

Still in its infancy, the off-Broadway gay stage shows more variety than point. Bill Solly and Donald Ward's *Boy Meets Boy* (1975) typifies the gay musical in its stupid Cinderella tale, its 1930s setting, and its hollow echoes of antiquated convention. The authors drop their one joke in the opening chorus, recoining the Spewacks' famous Boy Meets Girl trope to exult, "But boy gets boy in the end!" Comparably poor is gay satire, as in Doric Wilson's *The West Street Gang* (1977), set in a waterfront bar (actually premiered in one) and cataloguing the "types" (hustler, aging queen, S and M couple) and a few media figures ("Bnita Aryant") with puerile jokes.

The most popular gay genre is domestic comedy, reflecting the subculture's fascination with coupling patterns and often showing off a smart, fast wit. Robert Patrick's *T-Shirts* (1978) pictures the chance intrusion of an unsophisticated younger man into two older men's sexless friendship, setting off a powerful speech on being unnattractive in a world wired to beauty— powerful, but not smoothly fitted into the play as a whole. Doric Wilson wrote the best of these comedies, *A Perfect Relationship*, rising above *The West Street Gang*'s contrived burlesque for an honest look at the shy, anxious bonding of two riders of the New York bar circuit. Ideology has played a smaller part in the gay theatre movement than it has for blacks and feminists, and there are few documentaries. One exception is *Cornbury*:

The Queen's Governor (1976), presented at Joseph Papp's Public Theatre in high style. William M. Hoffman and Anthony Holland (who also directed) adapted some facts in the life of a Colonial regent into a wildly funny pageant about a dignified transvestite. It was A.J. Kronengold, however, who committed the first gay lowbrow pop hit (not counting *Private Lives*, perhaps), complete with storybook ending. This was the grotesque *Tubstrip* (1973), staged both in the Village and later in a small theatre in the Broadway district. *Tubstrip* was *Grand Hotel* set in a gay bathhouse, with the usual foxhole cohort of hustler, aging queen, S and M couple, and so on; as always, the queen has the best lines. *The Boys in the Band*, too, has its cross-section, but even in its pat conclusions it remains a sturdy and elegant piece. *Tubstrip* is The Wedding of the Painted Doll. There are gay theatre collectives to match those for black, feminist, classic, and experimental drama, and today the collective approach carries the standard for off-Broadway as movement. Some bear the word "repertory" in their titles, mostly because it's there—few of them actually retain a stock of plays in rotation.

One standout instance of true repertory came about when the Association of Producing Artists arrived in New York in 1962. Directed by Ellis Rabb, the company eventually settled down with a permanent acting troupe at a permanent home—on Broadway. This was a fancy endeavor from the start, a generally fine production of Sheridan's *The School for Scandal* with George Grizzard and Clayton Corzatte as the Surface brothers, Rosemary Harris as Lady Teazle, and Nancy Marchand as Lady Sneerwell. The bill went on to include Chekhof, Pirandello, Molière, Ionesco, and some prime American pop—*The Show Off*, *You Can't Take It with You*, and George M. Cohan's *The Tavern*. The A.P.A. shifted its casting, searched for a company style, and even managed to subsume Helen Hayes in its ensemble (though some critics complained that her bit part in the Sheridan and her Mrs. Fisher in *The Show Off* sported halos of self-doting Commitment). Repertory, it seemed, had finally come to Broadway—just when off-Broadway might have pulled it off itself. But then an off-Broadway organization would never have involved the race of actor or type of play featured by the A.P.A. This was too . . . what? *clean* a group, too clearly devised for establishment theatregoing. Not surprisingly, the A.P.A. received the largest take in foundation grants of any company in the vicinity—not surprisingly, said some, because it won't scare anybody. But its traditionalism made it, for a time, not only famous but successful.

When off-Broadway got into a theatre collective, it was on terms such as those that Joseph Papp instituted in 1966 at the Public Theatre, down in the old Astor Library midway between the East and West Villages. Here one found the dangerous theatre of psychopolitical turbulence, restive with countercultural practices in the writing, staging, and casting of plays. A house of several stages, the Public Theatre caught the attention of a wide public—many of whom seldom or never saw anything there—for its constant and various activity: new plays and old, workshops and readings, sharp professionalism and amateurs' erratic stabs, all savoring the tension of the 1960s as a theatre must reflect (Shakespeare, Corneille, Chekhof) and antagonize (Aristophanes, Molière, Ibsen, Shaw) its times. In his succoring of fresh talents, his ability to raise funds, and his dogged gusto for getting it on, stage after stage, Papp was hailed as the most stimulating force in New York theatre.

He had proved his idealism earlier with his mobile theatre units and the New York Shakespeare Festival's free admission performances, launched in the mid-1950s and finally settled down in 1962 in a permanent home in Central Park. What other city boasts free Shakespeare? Eva le Gallienne's Civic Repertory and the City Center for Music and Drama (founded in the 1940s with departments in symphony, theatre, opera, and musical comedy) maintained "popular prices." But they weren't free. The difference to a novice theatregoer between a $1.50 ticket and free admission is more than $1.50: the difference is inertia, not money.

This free Shakespeare was not thrown onstage, either. Given that the first ten years of any collective initiation are bound to be 9/10 trial and 1/10 vindication, the ensemble was notably solid, and several times achieved Shakespearean greatness in what may have been the only attempt in modern theatre history to create an American style for Elizabethan drama. In the summer of 1960, Papp produced a wonderfully aggressive *Henry V* (which he directed himself), an uneven *Measure for Measure* staged by Alan Schneider, and Gerald Freedman's splendid, brawling *The Taming of the Shrew*—Brustein called it "the finest production of a Shakespeare comedy I have ever seen," and he's no pushover. Though George C. Scott played Shylock and Colleen Dewhurst Cleopatra, there were no overt star turns in the early free Shakespeare; over in Stratford, Connecticut, the American Shakespeare Festival brought forth Katharine Hepburn in *Twelfth Night* and *Antony and Cleopatra* that summer to howls of derision from even the more-or-less establishment critics. When Walter Kerr called Stratford "a kind of cultural Howard Johnson's," the Festival press office actually flourished that blurb in its advertisements.

Fighting off constant encroachments from philistine city shoguns (Robert

Moses in particular), Papp at length came to power at about the time that off-Broadway came to its self-knowledge as the inheritor of the culturally purposed stage—of, about, and actively engaged in the destiny of American civilization. As mayor of outcast city, Papp articulated the aims of the movement simply by doing what he did, especially in his emphasis on social relevance and minority ethnocentrism, sometimes at the cost of art. Papp gave black and Hispanic drama every chance to grow, but much of what he chose to present was feeble. Black and Hispanic actors were cast in white-race parts, but diction, among other things, proved a problem, most egregiously in a Shakespeare series launched in 1979 that was so poor that reviewers who traditionally boost minority theatre were appalled. Papp's populist slant is valuable and exciting, but he must learn what the workers' theatre learned, that the stage doesn't get extra credit for populism. On the other hand, a company can fall apart waiting for good scripts to happen along—the Group Theatre, for example.

Papp is not as choosy as the Group was; he wallows in theatre. As a symbol of the off-Broadway spirit—the protest politics, the "community service" approach, the minority-group evangelism, and the workshop where plays are read, discussed, and rewritten—Papp seemed a likely reformer for the troubled Vivian Beaumont complex at Lincoln Center. But his failure to pull a company together marked the end of his honeymoon with the media, and more recent criticism has been more forthright. In *The American Scholar*, Stanley Kauffmann assessed Papp's career in detail, and wrote, "If we disregard the big commercial managements . . . then Papp is the only person who has made a considerable mark in the theatre—in any American or European theatre that I have seen or read about—without extraordinary talent, without exemplary taste, without an esthetic imperative, without intellectual distinction." In the New York *Times*, Charles Marowitz explained Papp's fame in terms of quantity rather than quality: "During his years at the Public Theatre and during [his first] two seasons at Lincoln Center, he has unearthed no major writing talents . . . He is lamentably lacking in judgment. The citation of his successes . . . does not alter this fact. When a producer has as many throws of the dice as Mr. Papp's various outlets provide, his few successful gambles are easily explained by the law of averages."

We'll hear more from off-Broadway in the following pages; for now, consider its purposes. Collectives are its great hope, from the Provincetown Playhouse through the Proletbühne of the Depression to Joseph Papp, Marshall Mason's Circle Rep, and Craig Anderson's Hudson Guild. Always attempting to undo Broadway's freelance instability with the continuity of experimentation, collaboration, and company point-of-view, off-Broadway no longer looks at Broadway much. For its part, Broadway sees off-Broadway as an imitation gone wrong, and thanks God that off-Broadway eventually gave birth to its own "off," the Equity, Broadway-bound showcase. As for the rest of it—the spaced-out coffeehouse spontaneity, the fascist discipline of the Living Theatre, the perverse comix of Charles Ludlam—Broadway would like to remind off-Broadway what Chekhof said to his wife when she asked him, "What is life?"

The title of this chapter bears Chekhof's reply, and it's a sane one in the midst of all the arty jive that off-Broadway occasionally resorts to. Still, better at least to ask the question than to raise your curtain on the same old still life of carrots every time.

20

The Goodbye Audience
The 1960s

THE 1960S WAS A "POLITICAL" TIME, like the 1930s. But in the Depression the issues were clearer and the stage was riding out a momentum of protest art; the issues of the sixties were divisive and the stage half-somnolent, still obedient to the escapist regime that dated back to the World War II years. At first, off-Broadway carried the political ball in drama, sometimes by making touchdowns for unpopular notions—dissent by theme—and sometimes by inventing its own rules for theatre—dissent by style. But by 1964 Broadway was trying to acclimatize its public to what was known as "relevant" theatre. That the bulk of the public did not find it all that relevant could be read in its benign neglect, save when something became a Must See or was simply too good to miss. (Oddly, this was a great decade for controversial cinema; moviegoers doted on *film noir* but refused to commit themselves to black comedy or—worse yet—realistic tragedy. But then movies and theatre in America have always played to two distinct publics.)

The hard-won use of the mainstream theatre as a forum for public debate had been thrown aside. Perhaps it had proved *too* useful, too appropriate in its extremism. People don't like being told that they're doing everything wrong. Playwrights of the 1930s warned that nazism wanted the world, that racism was a convention of American life, that the poor were denied a part in society. Instead of being grateful for the knowledge, many Broadwayites stopped going to those plays. This is one reason why most of the political dramatists either suffered grievous collapse after the 1930s or changed their tunes.

In Europe, the reverse occurred: politics and experimentation were the order of the age by the 1960s (even in opera), and thus much of Broadway's topical theatre consisted of imports. Some of this foreign work won interest by virtue not of topic but of great performances or fine productions: Anthony Quinn's Henry II versus Laurence Olivier's "little Saxon" in Anouilh's *Beckett* (1960), which doubled interest later in the season when Olivier played Henry to Arthur Kennedy's Beckett; Wendy Hiller and John Gielgud sparring, with Henry Jamesian finesse, for the priceless collection of a dead writer's love letters in *The Aspern Papers* (1962), Michael Redgrave's adaptation of James' story, capped by a chilling finale wherein Hiller consigned the letters, gently, lovingly, into the fire; Albert Finney in John Osborne's *Luther* (1963); Nicol Williamson in Osborne's *Inadmissible Evidence* (1965); Alec McCowen dreaming himself to be the second English Pope in Peter Luke's *Hadrian VII* (1969); Maximillian Schell in Osborne's inconclusive portrait of the Viennese double agent Alfred Redl in *A Patriot for Me* (1969), sumptuously designed by Oliver Smith, erratically acted under Peter Glenville's very English direction, and briefly talked about for a drag ball sequence that opened Act II. Openly admitting that serious drama could no longer pay its survival, David Merrick produced *A Patriot for Me* under the aegis of the non-profit Merrick Arts Foundation. Even this emergency measure could only capitalize a show, not maintain it, and the weighty display gave way after 49 performances. On the other hand, a third-rate staging of *Hamlet* (by John Gielgud) in 1964 mobilized an eager clientele for Richard Burton's prince. There's something about an English actor, it seems.

Better yet, bring on an entire English production. In 1965, the Merrick Arts Foundation imported the Royal Shakespeare Company in Peter Brook's brilliantly ugly staging of Peter Weiss' *The Persecution and Assassination of Marat as Performed by the Inmates of Charenton Under the Direction of the Marquis de Sade*. Known as *Marat/Sade*, the German play in Geoffrey Skelton's translation achieved a sensation, more for what it looked like than what it was, for Weiss' text depends on the vicious sensuality, grueling realism, and Brechtian song-and-dance that alienate rather than stimulate most Americans. What attracted them in this case was the unique completeness of the actors' portrayals. Ian Richardson, Patrick Magee, and Glenda Jackson in the three leads were widely hailed, but in fact everyone on stage seemed to have stepped into costume fresh from some real-life asylum. This insane precision made one dizzy, and if Weiss' subject and treatment (the title conveys the plot) were enough to send some patrons scrambling for the exit, the apparent spontaneity with which Brook's company celebrated their

madness felt as irresistible a sight as a bloody car accident. Americans stopped
to watch.

They saw a play imbued with "the Revolution"—nominally the French.
But the bombardment of carmagnole in Richard Peaslee and Adrian Mitchell's
score (the show is virtually a musical) and the company's lunatic cameos
related more to the American sixties than to the French 1790s. Though
Marat/Sade sounded to the uninitiated like Broadway's other imported specials, it comprised one of the decade's first abundantly "relevant" offerings,
a spectacle of anarchy and mob violence. Olivier, Gielgud, and Hiller in
Anouilh and Henry James were one thing, *Marat/Sade* very much something else, brooding and leering and baiting. The sixties had come.

Or, rather, some part of the sixties had turned up on Broadway. Other
foreign plays of a distinctly modern cut preceded and followed *Marat/Sade*
with variable success. Mystery was the motto of Harold Pinter's *The Caretaker* (1961) and *The Homecoming* (1967), both full-length, on-Broadway
evenings and for many theatregoers their first taste of ambiguity in theatre
(there were also several off-Broadway double bills of Pinter one-acts).
Pinter's plot movement was clear, but the action itself dark and quirky.
What was Pinter up to? The adjective "Pinteresque" entered the vocabulary,
and people began to consider that they might be enlightened even as they
were mystified, an important breakthrough in the pop theatregoing heart.
And to top it all, Pinter refused to explain What He Meant, if anything.
Pinter was "useless"—but absorbing. In this, he may have been even more
sixties than *Marat/Sade*, sixties not in commentary but in a raised apolitical
artistic conscience.

Not dissimilar to Pinter's genre of the naturalistically unreal is black
comedy, a kind of compromise between farce and horror, *Godot* without the
music-hall pranks. Here, Broadway proved surprising, rejecting Joe Orton's
very colorful *Entertaining Mr. Sloane* (1965) and *Loot* (1968) but giving a
modest run to Peter Nichols' depressingly honest *A Day in the Death of
Joe Egg* (1968). Orton mainly dealt with the unsavory capers of degraded
humans; Nichols looked in on the parents of a spastic infant and the collapse
of their marriage with an exquisite bitterness, and though *Joe Egg* (as it was
eventually billed, the word "death" being a proved box-office catastrophe)
hardly enjoyed a runaway success, it lasted long enough for Albert Finney to
be replaced by Donal Donnelly.

Many of these British items so intrigued the devoted theatregoer that
they became famous even when they failed to run, and thus "felt" successful.
It seemed logical that *The Royal Hunt of the Sun* (1965) caught on, for

Peter Shaffer's interpretation of the meeting of Pizarro and the Inca Atahuallpa benefited from John Dexter's striking pageant. But Dexter's blunt if no less atmospheric staging of Arnold Wesker's *Chips with Everything* (1963), on the oppressive class system of the R.A.F., suffered months of half-empty houses before packing it in. The Incas had the flair, the music, the misty motion—*Chips* was claustrophobic and hard-drilled. For all that, Wesker's working-class *Roots* (1961) couldn't even find itself on off-Broadway, where protest plays often thrive. Perhaps Wesker's sociology is simply too British for American comprehension.

If British plays and productions became more and more the thing for the intrepid play-seeker, other lands had little effect. Of the French, even Giraudoux and Anouilh are tricky to put over, and the success of *Marat/Sade* is less a German triumph than a British one—Brook held the ace there, not Weiss. And while Bertolt Brecht was making cautious inroads into the repertories of regional theatres, Broadway found him hard to stage well and off-Broadway hard to cast well. The acting talent is there, but only Broadway can afford the more glamorous salaries, and then it can't pull a production together—there appears to be a shortage on style. Brecht's study of Hitler as Chicago gangster, *The Resistible Rise of Arturo Ui*, blew in and out in one week of 1963 even with Christopher Plummer in the lead (five years later, Tyrone Guthrie's Minnesota Theatre Company showed New York a vastly more together staging in repertory with Aeschylus' *Oresteia*), and earlier that same year came what some experts believe to be the definitive disaster in "Broadway Brecht," the Anne Bancroft *Mother Courage and her Children*. Jerome Robbins' direction seemed to preen in its own austerity even as it played Brecht's dialectical ironies for gushing sentiment. In typical Broadway thinking, the work was staged—and accepted—as an "anti-war" play, though Brecht's picture of war is incidental to his main concern, the economic aggression of capitalism. The worst thing about the production was the treatment accorded Bancroft, whose woefully misfired Mother Courage was a fine actress' mistake, not the arrant vanity some people called it—Bancroft, who had won all hearts when she was Discovered as Gittel Mosca in William Gibson's *Two for the Seesaw* and who sustained the find with her moving Annie Sullivan in Gibson's *The Miracle Worker*. A more appropriate director might have drawn from her the performance of her life; as it was, she took more blame than Robbins for the failure, and was touted as the prototypal Broadwayite out of depth in a classic—*Mother Courage* starring Gittel Mosca. Frankly, the spectators at the Bancroft *Mother Courage* acted as poorly as the players; they didn't know what to expect (of an established classic) and didn't know how to deal with what they got.

This lack of understanding also clouded the Broadway production of *Rhinoceros* in 1961, the first broad exposure here for the absurdist Eugène Ionesco. In *Rhinoceros* his structure is orthodox, naturalistic, and colloquial, with a beginning and end in the usual order. But the play is a fantasy. Wild animals appear out of nowhere in a small town, raging through the streets, and it eventually develops that they are former humans, running wild and senseless in bigger and bigger packs. Bystanders evince shock but take no action; indeed, they soon become beasts themselves. Ionesco's favorite hero, the "little man" Bérenger, actually sees his best friend turn into a rhinoceros —while *rationalizing* about his metamorphosis!—and at the close Bérenger stands alone and defiant, the last human. Joseph Anthony's production was a typical first-class New York endeavor, using actors who were then little known outside the Broadway and off-Broadway orbit (Eli Wallach, Anne Jackson, Zero Mostel, Morris Carnovsky, Mike Kellin, Jean Stapleton, Dolph Sweet); a brief controversy attached to producer Leo Kerz' refusal to post the customary critical blurbs did not attract any special attention to the piece. But it was special, an important play in a sane, unfussy staging. It even lasted 240 performances (and lost money), at least partly through the delighted word-of-mouth about Mostel's extraordinary turn as a smug peacock who explodes into a rhinoceros right onstage, the stunt all the more deft in that Mostel used no costume props or make-up.

In Europe, the public got Ionesco's argument. His parable shows how the West sinks into totalitarianism, with all the lily-livered debate and "it's happening; why fight it?" syndrome familiar to resisters of contemporary snake oil. But in New York, in a dull season of little stimulation, those who write about theatre wrote about *Rhinoceros* as a satire on "conformism," degrading an artful thesis into an instant "issue" about as deep as a *Time* magazine cover banner. As they filed *Mother Courage* under the "anti-war" rubric, so did they reduce *Rhinoceros*. The use of the stage as intellectual challenge yielded once again to the beauty of a pop theatre that flatters its public—of course everyone is anti-war; everyone ridicules conformity. But Brecht and Ionesco had other things in mind.

The European stage had outstripped ours. As of the British resurgence in the mid-1950s, the French absurdist avant-garde, and the Germanic obsession with national guilt, European theatre provided much of the topical stimulation in our theatres. Not that the 1960s failed to supply some native ideological input. But American social drama was less substantial and less fully developed—and less successfully supported—than European social drama as produced here at the time.

One unusual characteristic of the topical plays—foreign and American—was their interest in historical documentary. We have met examples of this touchy genre before—interpretations of court cases in the post-Coolidge years, or looks back at our past during World War II, when our future lay in doubt. But never before had there been such a slew of documentaries, ranging from biblical times to virtually the day before the performance. Thomas More, William Shakespeare, Buffalo Bill, Jack Johnson, Joseph Stalin, Pope Pius XII, Winston Churchill, Robert Oppenheimer, Lester Maddox, and other public figures turned up in productions of varying attitude to the record, ranging from the ghastly *Marat/Sade* to the solemn romance of a *Royal Hunt of the Sun*. Even the musical came in on the act in such items as the frivolous *Ben Franklin in Paris* (1964) and the pious *1776* (1969), though the most exacting commentary on history was heard in a British revue, *Oh, What a Lovely War!* (1964), Joan Littlewood's compendium of World War I songs played as mocking music hall.

Most of the American topical entries naturally rose up in the outcast world of off-Broadway; the aforementioned *In White America*, *MacBird!*, *America Hurrah*, *Viet Rock*, and *Dionysus in '69* typify the time's fascination with racism, two-party paranoia, countercultural spoof, anti-war awareness, and radical plastique. On Broadway, things were more dignified and less vital. Early in the decade, the black actor Ossie Davis set one possible tone for Broadway blackness in his *Purlie Victorious* (1961), an amiable lampoon of the Old South concluded by an interminable political harangue. Davis, who wrote himself a dashing title part as a no-account preacher who rises up from jim-crow to jim-dandy, kept the atmosphere comic (not least in Godfrey Cambridge's zesty Uncle Tom spoof as Gitlow) until the militant closing sermon.

Davis' piece helped break the ice for black plays *by* blacks *on* Broadway, and a few years later, just when off-Broadway was winning attention for such forays into black racist vendetta as *Dutchman*, things had opened up somewhat on The Street. Much fanfare attended Bill Manhoff's innocuous two-character sex comedy, *The Owl and the Pussycat* (1964) because black Diana Sands played opposite white Alan Alda in a script that never mentioned race. Pitting Sands against Alda thus suggested that miscegenation, heretofore a subject for tragedy, might be not only fun but unremarkable. (The screen version, aimed at a wide national market, corrected the seasoning by pairing Barbra Streisand with George Segal.) Possibly even more helpful was the casting of a mixed couple in the musical version of Clifford Odets' *Golden Boy* the same year as *The Owl and the Pussycat*, with the part of the boxer reoriented from an Italian in a WASP world to a black in America. Even so, this was not a first for the musical, instances turning up as far back as 1946 in *Beggar's Holiday* and *Jamaica* in 1957. But perhaps it took a sixties climate to publicize the "innovation."

1964 also brought out Broadway's answer to Amiri Baraka in James Baldwin's *Blues for Mister Charlie*. Baldwin handles English better than Baraka, and he once scorned the propaganda that his colleague dotes on, but in *Blues For Mister Charlie* Baldwin came out for the Cause in clumsy agitprop that reduced American racial turmoil to a favorite sixties cliché, whites' sexual envy of blacks. "Why are you always trying to cut off *my* cock? You worried about it?" asks Baldwin's protagonist in his death scene. "Keep your old lady home, you hear? Don't let her near no nigger. She might get to like it. You might get to like it, too." Considering Baldwin's previous career as a homosexual proselytizer, this line of approach seems even more bizarre than Baraka's.

Still, there were those so eager to see the main stages catch up to the times that they raised funds to support *Mister Charlie*'s ailing run—at least, one hopes they had some motive other than aesthetic appreciation of this scrofulous melodrama. Performances were punctuated with bravos and applause for lines of empty racist agitation, and finally, when Diana Sands took one's breath away with a bitterly moving solo scene, one didn't want to applaud. Applause sold cheap at *Mister Charlie*; Sands deserved the acclamation of theatregoers, not of one-party voters. Such was the myopia of the supporters of black theatre in the mid-sixties that black rage was invariably preferred to black talent. While the media kept attention focused on Baraka and Baldwin, the gifted white South African playwright Athol Fugard (whose very pertinent *The Blood Knot* was given in this same initiative year, 1964) was ignored. Not till the decade was almost over, it seems, was the theatre able to deal with blackness as a culture and race relations as an issue. The linchpin here was Howard Sackler's *The Great White Hope* (1968), a look at the white outrage surrounding the black Jack Johnson's ascendancy, just before World War I, to the world heavyweight boxing title, running first to vicious use of the law for persecution and at length to a search for a new white champion to unseat him.

This is a huge play, crowded with folk and flying a panorama from San Francisco to Budapest to Havana, where the climactic fight occurs. Because the work originated at Washington's Arena Stage, it was used to doing without much in the way of sets, and adapted nicely to the Broadway proscenium, deriving its look from the evening-long counterpoint of mob scenes, intimate scenes, and lengthy monologues. Turbulent and moving, Sackler's text sweeps chronicle and personal drama together with amazing consistency; it is notable that while his approach is like that of Baraka and Baldwin—show white oppression, then extrapolate black defiance—his skillful dramaturgy not only erases their work with thrilling dramatic poetry but really deals with the character behind and the reason for the rage. And this is what Americans have always demanded of their theatre: character.

The Great White Hope is a tragedy, showing the fall of a great man (here called Jack Jefferson), and the lead part brought out of James Earl Jones one of the decade's genuinely bravura performances. Jones is sometimes too blustery in Shakespeare, but here he was unerringly subtle, building big in long blocks to a towering finale. A boxer, Jefferson is no brawler—and no "spokesman," for Sackler lets his enforced alienation speak for him. For once, here was a successful analysis of American race relations in a timeless work set in the past that felt wildly current in the 1960s and will never date. It was theatrical in action and epic in concept, roaring and weeping as it pounded to the inevitable bout between a morally destroyed hero and the great white hope, the contest itself only described by onlookers but written and staged so spontaneously that some of the audience actually attempted to peer offstage into the wings to see for themselves. Like any hero, Jefferson brings others down with him when he goes—his sourly wised-up mother, his Jewish manager, and, especially, his white mistress, Ellie, superbly played by Jane Alexander for an inner-directed delicacy of spirit that contrasted with Jefferson's fury in their mutual nonconformity. In a season that cheered the domestic acting turns of Al Pacino (in *Does the Tiger Wear a Necktie?*) and Dustin Hoffman (in *Jimmy Shine*), Jones and Alexander stood pre-eminent, and a great deal must be said for the superior material they had to work with. Sackler's achievement is not only one of overall composition, but of idiomatic writing. Its curtain was unforgettable: mother and lover dead, Jefferson loses the big fight—why? "He beat me, dass all," he tells the reporters. "Ah juss din have it." A gala march breaks out: the new champ is on his way. "Come on Chillun," says Jefferson. "Let 'em pass by!" And the crowd rampages out of the arena, bearing their white hope—our first view of him—on their shoulders like, Sackler directs, "the lifelike wooden saints in Catholic processions." And their hats are screaming in the air as the curtain falls.

Written by a white man, *The Great White Hope* made a breakthrough for black theatre, acclimatizing the public to a better class of racial drama, one in which rage would be explained rather than exploited and—even better —black culture might be explored without the obsessive assaults on Whitey. Just a year after *The Great White Hope* came a noteworthy example, Charles Gordone's *No Place To Be Somebody* (1969). Gordone deals in New York blackness, setting his show in a West Village bar hemmed in by subcultural parameters wider than those of Harlem but not so wide as anything like emergence. Another work rooted in vernacular, *No Place* confused some people and stimulated others with its sometimes fantastic naturalism, but it impressed almost everyone with its individuality.

Other than Joseph Papp's Spanish-language mobile theatre in the ghettos, racial theatre remained almost exclusively black theatre. One exception was Arthur Kopit's *Indians* (1969), a freewheeling vaudeville of skits and monologues, tragedy and satire, on the extermination of the American Indian. Having spent a decade unable to cope with black comedy in any form (*The Beauty Part*, *The Last Analysis*, and *Little Murders* all flopped undeservedly), Broadwayites could not cotton to Kopit's now sincere, now absurdist tone, not even in this period of High Cultural Rebellion. Oddly, they had first met and liked Kopit in the disturbing farce *Oh Dad, Poor Dad, Mamma's Hung You in the Closet and I'm Feeling So Sad* (1962), in which Jo Van Fleet traveled around with a piranha fish, her late husband's coffin (occupied), and her seventeen-year-old baby Austin Pendleton, who murdered his would-be seducer, Barbara Harris. Furthermore, though *Indians'* Broadway production was nowhere near as expert as the Royal Shakespeare production in London the year before, the material itself is quite interesting in its imposition of a Wild West Show on a federal investigation of Indian grievances. Bursting in and out of the inquest are the events of history—the white man's mindless slaughter of the buffalo and the Wounded Knee Massacre, for instance—and binding the evening is the direct address of an emcee, Buffalo Bill himself (a first-rate performance by Stacy Keach). Kopit's reading of history is just, and the parallel with modern American racism pertinent. And if his rationalizing white men grew tiresome finally, his portrayal of the Indians had color and nobility. The play should have run.

Important plays—important in execution or just in intention—often failed in the 1960s. Some of them simply weren't very good, like Joseph Heller's *We Bombed in New Haven* (1968), with an anti-war theme melded on Pirandellian clichés. But because Heller's novel *Catch-22* was one of the documents of the decade, he at least got some attention for his work, and the piece has survived in regional and community theatres. Less celebrated authors suffered fast closings and silence. Paddy Chayevsky's *The Passion of Joseph D.* (1969) lasted only two weeks, though this look at Stalin, Lenin, Krupskaya, and Trotsky from the Revolution to Stalin's takeover proved fascinating theatre. Using the same realist-satirist format that Kopit used for *Indians*, if less hectically, Chayevsky dared paint his icons with their warts and all, earning shameless disparagement from commentators who either don't know the record or choose to ignore it. At one point, Stalin coolly stabs a man for his boots and observes, "When a barefoot fellow tells you he is revolting against tyranny, watch out; he's only after your boots. There you have the class struggle in a nutshell." There was unexpected comedy, too, as when a knock on the door interrupts a secret meeting of the Bolshevik conspirators. Stalin draws his gun and snuffs out the candles. Says Kamenev: "You are being a little *opéra-bouffe*, Stalin, don't you think?"

Modern off-Broadway, as we have seen, finally found itself in the sixties as the theatre of outcast art. But Broadway was in confusion. Looking back on the decade, we find no classic that has survived to fix the time for us, as we certainly can for earlier epochs. What is the essential sixties play, the *Catch-22* of the stage? *One Flew Over the Cuckoo's Nest* (1963), perhaps? Dale Wasserman's adaptation of Ken Kesey's novel touched a vital American nerve in its picture of a bold man's battle against authority in the person of the sadistic head nurse of a mental institution. But it didn't touch that nerve until there was an off-Broadway revival and a film version in the 1970s—the original production ran a mere ten weeks, even with Kirk Douglas in the lead. Similarly, another "sixties" classic, Michael Weller's *Moonchildren*, did not turn up until 1972, in a now-legendary two-week run. *Moonchildren's* partisans claim much for the whimsical universality of its loose tale of college students, some "committed" and one, the protagonist, not. But this is not a major endeavor.

No one writer, it appeared, could place the era in a single work or theme, in any genre. Perhaps the lack of focus is appropriate to the chaotic nature of the period, but too many of the more significant events in theatre kept happening at the edge of the public iris, never in its center. Thus we find a political journalist of the establishment, Theodore H. White, *publishing* his *Caesar at the Rubicon*, a "play about politics," in 1968—not seeing it performed until the beginning of the next decade, at the McCarter Theatre in Princeton. This, one would have thought, must be Broadway's idea of a state-of-the-nation play, just as White is probably the Broadway theatregoer's idea of a historian. But surely something like Rochelle Owens' *Futz* (1967), first performed by Ellen Stewart's off-off-Broadway La MaMa Troupe, spoke more clearly on the era's "politics" in its picture of a farming community outraged by one of its citizens, who has conceived a passion for his pig Amanda. A short play, in vignettes connected by a narrator, *Futz* was both overpraised and overdamned when new; now—crazy dialect, bestiality, and all—it reads with charm and humanity, and its message on the hypocrisy of intrusive "reformers" is evergreen. (Plus, as countercultural wits disarmingly pointed out at the time, the pig at least is female, so the play isn't *that* shocking.) Here, in *Caesar at the Rubicon* and *Futz*, may be seen the situation of topical theatre in the sixties in miniature: a dignified polemic on the power bosses that no one cared to stage, and an undignified parable of the outcast stage that skirted the times' Big Issues entirely.

Perhaps there is no sixties classic. One of the bleaker aspects of the scene was the dearth of enduring dramatists. These were the years when Tennessee Williams and Arthur Miller began to decline, when Edward Albee began strong and almost immediately disintegrated. There were admirable plays but no admirable outputs, no apparent consistency. Even O'Neill looked off-form in two exhumations, the two-character (but virtually a monologue) *Hughie* (1964) and *More Stately Mansions* (1967), the sequel to *A Touch of the Poet* in O'Neill's projected nine-play cycle.

Of course, there were new playwrights, talented and prolific ones. But they were denied the strategic visibility that gives a young career momentum. One factor, obviously, was the dwindling audience for serious drama. Another was the public's failure to catch up to the modern non-realistic stage in which linear time, clear-cut unities of place and action, solidity of tone, and tactful naturalism no longer matter. A further bar, less insidious than these, derives from the expansion of the American theatre scene from the Broadway district to virtually the Western world: with new authors earning their premieres as far afield as Berlin, London, Dallas, Chicago, and the alleys of underground New York; no wonder they could not close in on the regularity that locks a name into the memory. Theatre was too big, too much. Moreover, most of these writers worked extensively in the one-act form. The economic advantage is manifest: little or no decor, small cast, perfect for the compact spaces of off-off-Broadway. (The artistic advantage, from the actors' and director's vantage, is not so great, for they must work out characterizations as fully as if the piece occupied a full evening.) But the American public is conditioned to two-and-a-half-hours of one "story," and doesn't like one-acts.

Occasionally, the right double bill will click. Israel Horovitz won mild prominence for the off-Broadway mounting of *The Indian Wants the Bronx* and *It's Called the Sugar Plum* in 1968. These are two very dissimilar plays. *Sugar Plum* follows the aftermath of a fatal car accident in the quarrel and flirtation of the perpetrator and the victim's fiancée. For much of the play, the public is in doubt as to whether or not it can laugh—but the lines *are* bizarre. At length, it decides it is in on a spoof, and laughs—and then the tone flips around, to wistfully sentimental. *Is* it a comedy? Confused applause at the end is Horovitz' proof that he can manipulate theatrical humor into real-life "humor" with agility. It must have been fun to write, but it's tricky to attend.

The Indian Wants the Bronx attracted by far the greater attention for its blend of comedy and horror. The (east) Indian of the title, who speaks only two or three words of English, is lost in New York late on a chilly night. Two punks appear, playing out a relationship based as strongly on intimidation as affection. We immediately tense in fear for the Indian, and, sure enough, eventually they bring him into their complex sadomasochistic charades. A New York audience particularly responds to the premise, not least because Horovitz used it to compose an intriguing study in neurotic symbiosis.

Both these plays happened to coincide with what most theatregoers like in naturalism—the pretense of real time, place, and persons. But even naturalism can be unnatural nowadays. Simultaneously with Horovitz came Ronald Ribman, perhaps the most praised of the new playwrights of the late 1960s, with *Harry, Noon and Night* (1965), one day in the life of an American dropout in Munich in 1955. This was an oddly engaging event, entertaining but mysteriously incomplete; one felt so much more attracted to Ribman's subsidiary characters that finally one wasn't sure why Harry was in the play at all. Perhaps that was the point. The author reserved his most telling lines for the part of Harry's repulsive, cranky, and inefficiently serious roommate Immanuel (played with all screws loose by Dustin Hoffman); this character virtually carried the play.

Like Horovitz, Ribman came to notice on off-Broadway. The American Place Theatre mounted both *Harry, Noon and Night* and Ribman's *The Journey of the Fifth Horse* (1966), one of the outstanding plays of the decade and a prize study in inventive adaptation. Using Turgyenyef's *The Diary of a Superfluous Man* as a springboard, Ribman devised a complementary tale to tell along with it, balancing Turgyenyef's gentle, generous, shattered loser with a brutal and selfish loser who reads the other man's journal and sees his own nasty existence collaborating with yet combatting it. We survey the two lives in counterpoint, while Ribman's base character mutters imprecations at the fumbling decency of Turgyenyef's. By the 1960s, this kind of non-realism was taken for granted, and Kurt Lundell's excellent layered set allowed for a fluid mingling of the "real world" of Ribman's Zoditch and the "fictional world" of Turgyenyef's Chulkaturin. Similarly, Dustin Hoffman's Zoditch tallied nicely as a reflection-in-reverse of Michael Tolan's Chulkaturin, so that, as the evening wore on, one saw Zoditch's delusions of power mesh with Chulkaturin's tragic honesty about himself. Ribman's writing, wickedly perverse in *Harry, Noon and Night*, here was sensitive, unusually graceful for this rough-talking time; ultimately, he brings us to sympathize as much with the hateful Zoditch as the likeable Chulkaturin, the fifth horse of the title, nowhere needed in a world of already equipped coaches-and-four. Yet he runs along, turning every event into a personal setback: sinking at small talk, challenging a popular officer to a foolish duel, alienating the girl he loves, and finally dying of—losing. At the start of the play, a voice tells of seeing, in the marketplace of Samarkand, a monkey dying in a cage who "grasped my sleeve as if there might be something more to the matter." At the end, as Zoditch rants at the accusing correlation between the diary and his own life, Chulkaturin stretches out his arms to Zoditch. They stare at each other. Zoditch rejects his "other," and the arms fall. In darkness, the voice comes back to tell of passing on through the marketplace, whereupon the monkey's hand fell within his cage, "and there was nothing more to the matter." An extraordinarily finished and poetic piece of work.

Lanford Wilson, another of this young generation, was to achieve wide notice only in the next decade, starting with *The Hot l Baltimore*. His *The Rimers of Eldritch* (1967), premiered at La MaMa, employed a novel structure of small scenes intercut with larger scenes sliced by tiny scenes to bring together the very various residents of a small midwestern town shaken by a murder case. Morsels of the trial chill us throughout the work, but Wilson spends the entire play developing character—the individual characters who in a mass inspirit the town as a unity—and only at the very end shows us what happened. Wilson made it to Broadway, too, as did few of his coevals, in another of the adult plays on race relations that saw the decade to a close, *The Gingham Dog* (and the calico cat, remember?) in 1969. This look at the breakup of the marriage of a white southerner (George Grizzard) and a black girl from Harlem (Diana Sands) lasted only 5 performances; no doubt such experience convinced Wilson to throw his lot in with an off-off-Broadway group that was to become the Circle Repertory Theatre.

It was not unusual for new playwrights to score in one notable event and then either vanish or fail to sustain themselves. For example: William Alfred's *Hogan's Goat* (1965), generally known in Los Angeles as "that thing Faye Dunaway did in New York." Like *The Great White Hope* a verse play that didn't act versey, *Hogan's Goat* looked back to the days when Brooklyn was an Irish city of ward-heelers, priests, good-timers, and scandal. One juicy story involves a man who played stud to a woman named Agnes Hogan (thus the title) when she was the unofficial consort of the tough mayor of Brooklyn, Ned Quinn. Now the man plans to challenge Quinn for the mayor's chair; now also Agnes Hogan lies on her deathbed, and the story sings in the streets. It sounds like melodrama, but Alfred composed an achingly beautiful play, the dancing heft of the Irish-American idiom adding to the force of the play's comedies, deceits, and confrontations. A strong piece, staged by the American Place Theatre, it ran long after Dunaway had departed for the coast. But what has become of Alfred?

Other works by writers with a sure gift for theatre kept no promise of a continuing new career. The longest running serious play of the decade, at 832 performances, was Frank D. Gilroy's *The Subject Was Roses* (1964), a three-character domestic comedy-drama in the old style. This was Gilroy's second New York production—his *Who'll Save the Ploughboy?* (1962) had made some stir off-Broadway—and it was not his last, but Gilroy's own report on the struggle of getting the simple and commercially viable *Roses* onto Broadway may be one reason why he is infrequently heard from. Gilroy at least had that major success. Another domestic comedy-drama, Mary Mercier's *Johnny No-Trump* (1967), lasted one night on Broadway, though the apparent teenage washout Johnny, his disillusioned mother, and his loud-mouthed, intolerant uncle were brought to life in some of the most imaginative dialogue ever used on the quandaries of middle America. A third example of the American domestic genre suffered a third species of the Broadway success-failure problem in that it drooped through a shortish run but was later vindicated in a successful and extremely faithful film version. This was James Goldman's *The Lion in Winter* (1966), staged with Rosemary Harris and Robert Preston in the roles better known through Katharine Hepburn's dazed survivor's elation and Peter O'Toole's rampaging royalism in the movie. Goldman's is not the usual American family: Henry II of England, his sometime wife Eleanor of Aquitaine, his current mistress, his three sons, and the King of France spend Christmas together while Henry chooses a successor. Goldman employs a florid wit that is never, but continually seems to border on being, anachronistic, and detractors called it a modern American soap opera in costume. If it is, it nevertheless offered some of the most intelligent comic English of the decade, with as many quotable lines on loving hatred as there are put-downs in *All About Eve*. Those who appreciated Goldman's writing complained that he had pitched his diction too high above the disintegrating Broadway ear—but virtually the same text triumphed as cinema, drawing on a supposedly less sophisticated audience.

One medium that always knows where it stands is the musical, though it may have trouble trying to rise. The sixties, as era, scarcely touched it, except in a few items of off-Broadway origin. *Camelot* (1960) and *Man of La Mancha* (1965) entered the book of classics in the romantic class, *Hello, Dolly!* (1964), *Funny Girl* (1964), and *Mame* (1966) in brash musical comedy, all reaffirming the American musical's characteristic touches of idealism and fantasy (in the first two) and sentimental naturalism (in the other three). Note that *Dolly*, *Funny Girl*, and *Mame* all owed much of their success to the efforts of their leading women, the freak Carol Channing, the freak-turning-into-glamor-goddess Barbra Streisand, and the gifted-actress-pretending-to-be-a-freak Angela Lansbury.

The musical, in other words, was still either overstating or understating. In comedy and shtick, it could go to extremes in confidence: the public would come along. But in its thematic component, it had to toe the mark. Thus *Camelot* and *Man of La Mancha*, both adaptations of epic novels, won favor for how much they *contradicted* the cynicism of the originals. In adapting *Camelot*'s book from T.H. White's *The Once and Future King*, Alan Jay Lerner followed White's trail through Arthurian democracy in embryo, but failed to follow White's conclusion, in which the noble attempt to let man govern himself fails because man is not fit to do so. Oddly, with White's politics ripped away, *Camelot* struck some people as a suitable paean to the John Kennedy regime, and the term "Camelot" has stuck to it. Cervantes, too, was betrayed: *Man of La Mancha*'s "impossible dream" lushness runs directly counter to the burlesque spirit of *Don Quixote*.

Musical comedy's zest for social commentary, so potent in such works as *Finian's Rainbow* and *The Golden Apple*, was not moribund. It was simply unable to deal with The Issues in ways that would please its public. Stephen Sondheim and Arthur Laurents' *Anyone Can Whistle* (1964) died in one week, quickly passing into cultist memory for its Juvenalian-mode digs at conformity and consumerism, and the ambitious *Mata Hari* (1967), scuttled by poor casting and staging, closed in its Washington tryout. A sad loss: *Mata Hari* was richly topical. Its book-writer Jerome Coopersmith built the love plot around a French intelligence officer's fascination for the ambiguous eroticism of the dancer Mata Hari, which culminates in his destruction of her, presumably because he is unable to tolerate such liberality in a woman. Adult and imposing for its anti-war message in the 1960s, the show might speak more clearly to the feminist 1980s.

Off-Broadway's delightfully surrealistic and also anti-war "opera for actors," *Dynamite Tonite!* (1967) similarly failed to gain a public, and it turned out that *Hair* (1967), the "American tribal love-rock musical," would have to do for a popular topical piece. Originally a product of Joseph Papp's company, *Hair* thrived on Broadway, aimlessly catering to middle Americans' sense of the sixties with fake primitivism, fake rage, and fake joy, all slightly mitigated by the eclectic vitality of Galt MacDermot's music. A braver try was made in *Hallelujah, Baby!* (1967), a chronicle of the American white-black relationship starring Leslie Uggams. Unlike *Hair*, this was a sincere entry with something to say. But if the subject is race relations, could a splashy Broadway musical by Jule Styne, Betty Comden and Adolph Green, and Arthur Laurents say it? If "Broadway" is defined not just by what Broadway does, but also by whom Broadway does it for—the public contract of the native stage—then a big-budget middle-American musical can only deal with topical material on the most flamboyant and non-realistic level. Thus, perhaps the most authentic musical of the decade was none of the above but the one that could be most remote from its time and most honest with its audience—Jerry Bock, Sheldon Harnick, Joseph Stein, and (director) Jerome Robbins' *Fiddler on the Roof* (1964).

One has hopes for comedy, for it, too, is rooted in honesty. It can't have been easy to speak true to the sixties, though, for no matter what side one was on this was a time of despair, of waste and destruction answered by inertia and apathy. But did many even try? Boorish semi-satire and retreaded genre pieces from the 1950s blobbed through the decade on Broadway while off-Broadway struggled to find its several radical comic voices. This was the Neil Simon decade, launching what now stands as financially the most successful single playwrighting career ever. From *Come Blow Your Horn* (1961) to *The Last of the Red-Hot Lovers* (1969), Simon contributed a show a year—six comedies and three musical-comedy books—and quickly gained a steady following among the mass of theatregoers. His idiom is culturally generalized (with little adaptation, his scripts do nicely as films for a national audience), though distinctly Jewish in tone, his plotting thin, and his (non-musical) casts small. The mode is that of farce without farce's construction; one would call Simon's plays character comedies except that he deals less in character than in gags (though this is much less true of Simon today). *Come Blow Your Horn*, an outright farce and Simon's most consistent entry in this decade, upheld ancient values of exposition, development piled on development, sentimental resolution, and surprise boffo curtain. Its characters were familiar types—playboy bachelor, shy younger brother learning to swing, despotic father to whom all unmarried sons are "bums," mother who lives for woe—and if having the playboy fall in love with a Right Girl while the brother grows into a Frankenstein's monster of a playboy is a tired wheeze, Simon made it hum. But thereafter he wrote loose, building whole plays out of vignettes of endless non-development in no real context, no conviction as plays. More and more, Simon depended on gimmicky direction and goons. *The Odd Couple* (1965) took the classic premise of two absolute opposites living together absolutely nowhere; *Plaza Suite* (1968) devolved on the stunt of playing three unconnected one-acters in the same hotel room, each skit yielding changes in identity and make-up in Maureen Stapleton and George C. Scott.

Barefoot in the Park (1963) was prototypal Simon, an empty newlyweds-plus-mother-in-law-plus-weird-neighbor tangle that turned into one of the decade's biggest money-makers at 1530 performances. Here, personality was all, as guided by Mike Nichols and administered by Elizabeth Ashley and Robert Redford, who had already given a nifty display of comic pluck in *Sunday in New York* in 1961, the year that Ashley enjoyed a moderate sensation as Art Carney's college-bound daughter in *Take Her, She's Mine*. When the scripts were as insipid as these (all three), bringing them off comprised casting for charm and directing with the cleaver-sharp pacing that reviewers used to complain of in the days of Abbott and Kaufman and now adored. So alluring was *Barefoot*'s personal chemistry, so efficiently stage-managed, that the show blithely sailed on long after Ashley and Redford had left. Meanwhile, Nichols went on to steer *Luv*, *The Knack*, and *The Odd Couple* to port, and suddenly he was the top kick director in town. And for what? Hollow comedies.

Make no mistake, Simon was funny. So much so that when he attempted to detail a human situation in serious terms, the laughs intruded and definition wobbled. Writing for a public that demands the usefulness that Fitch and Hopwood observed (i.e., people are basically nice and just need to be loved; marriage is sacrosanct; we're all going to make it), Simon's seriousness had no place to go but back where it started from, in jokes. Thus, *The Last of the Red-Hot Lovers* offers another evening of three one-acts, these tied together by the aging restaurateur who, in each of the three, attempts to cheat on his wife. Naturally, he never succeeds—not because of world-irony, but because Simon and his public do not want him to. As the would-be philanderer, James Coco took to walking through his chores at some point in the run, but strong casting bolstered the three women's parts: Linda Lavin (tough and remote), Marcia Rodd (a screwball actress), and Doris Roberts, the only one to test the public's engagement with the premise, as she is of the man's own set and registers the work's only flirtation with genuine suburban sin. The play ends with Coco phoning up for a fourth rendezvous . . . with his wife.

Comparable to Simon was Jean Kerr, though her plays are more fully characterized, romantic moondust cut with literate hip in the manner of the light comedies of the 1930s. Here, too, personality turns the key. The charisma of the central figures in Kerr's smash *Mary, Mary* (1961), Barbara bel Geddes and Barry Nelson, divorced but still in love, celebrated the joy of wit and looks in an East Side Belgravia where divorce doesn't stick. In pop theatre, a *Mary, Mary* in which bel Geddes and Nelson didn't get back together again would be almost unthinkable. (Note, by the way, *Mary, Mary*'s similarity to *The New York Idea* of 1906, sheerly coincidental, but proof of the continuity of the basic pop construction, subclass romantic divorces.) When Kerr matured into a dramatist of some distinction, in *Poor Richard* (1964), she fell athwart of the rules of the mode, and had to repair the romance of a troubled English poet and a sweet, confused, but wise American girl, originally left with an ambiguous parting. When *Poor Richard* opened in New York, the pair were definitely a couple, to the loss of the play's honesty.

Sex comedy thrived; this is old news on Broadway. Some turn on the farcical aspects of seduction (*Under the Yum-Yum Tree*, 1960), some on the farce of aging sex (*Never Too Late*, 1962), and some romanticize (*Butterflies Are Free*, 1969). At least *Butterflies* had a point. Leonard Gershe's script dropped a blind youth afraid of the dark and a rootless girl afraid of commitment into the same living space, teaching him to mature and her to trust, together. It's the same old moral escapism, preaching its beauties to the nation via *Butterflies* on tour, on screen, and on the permanent list in high-school drama clubs.

All of the above comedies are the most recent versions of much-tried propositions. The original and partly original work sought to catch the style of the sixties in vernacular or subject. One of the most gifted of the newer voices, Herb Gardner, seemed most typical of the era because of his love for visionary eccentrics. Like Jules Feiffer, Gardner had surfaced in the 1950s as a cartoonist, but the fifties were not a great day for eccentricity. In the sixties it went down well, and Gardner's crackpot heroes spoke to the enlightened as if offering an alternative to madness. Gardner's *A Thousand Clowns* (1962) offered Jason Robards as a dropout who refers to Manhattan's business district as "Downtown Oz" and Sandy Dennis as a bashful social worker who investigates the welfare of Robards' parentless nephew and ends up spending the night. Whimsey informed Robards' rejection of the square world—he was given to shouting out of his apartment window at odd moments such messages as: "Everybody on stage for the Hawaiian number, please!" The play had muscle, too. In a climactic scene of unnerving honesty, television's Chuckles the Chipmunk comes to Robards' place to ask him to come back as his writer; the job will secure Robards' standing with the Child Welfare Board. But Chuckles (a smart turn by Gene Saks) is as corrupt as the Hollywood jargon he emits. He arrives bearing "Chuckles" hats, a cardboard cutout of himself in Chipmunk outfit, and the sponsor's potato chips, defines humor as "a cloudy, wonderland thing, but simple and clear like the blue, blue sky," and performs a dumb Chuckles routine for the boy. Robards is willing to compromise his sense of self to keep the kid; it's the child who keeps the rebellion afire. Asked his opinion of Chuckles' comedy, he says:

> My simple, child's reaction to what you did is that you are not funny. Funnier than you is even Stuart Slossman my friend who is eleven and puts walnuts in his mouth and makes noises. What is not funny is to call us names and what is mostly not funny is how sad you are that I would feel sorry for you if it wasn't for how dull you are and those are the worst tasting potato chips I ever tasted. And that is my opinion from the blue, blue sky.

Gardner admits that there is no way out for the nonconformist: Big Brother, in the agency of the Child Welfare Board, is watching you. It is a credit to Gardner's sincerity that Robards' capitulation to Society provides resolution to the plot but not release for the protagonist or the audience.

A Thousand Clowns was a hit, but later on Gardner moved into comic tragedy on the same theme, and suffered a terrific commercial failure for a truly brilliant piece, *The Goodbye People* (1968). As before, we admire the nonconformist and his *non serviam* ideology, empathize with the adult waifs who are drawn to him, and pull back from the deputies of the staid world. *The Goodbye People* disclosed a wintry slice of Coney Island, where aged Milton Berle prepares to rally the beach that was by reopening his old hot-dog stand—now, this minute, before time ducks out on him. Earlier, Gardner had identified the enemy in the oily hustle of television; here, it is the humanoid gladhanders of the small business world, the sons of Berle's former contacts, closed to personal appeal ("cold voices, people born for telephones"), but dynamite on the farewells: ". . . all of a sudden, it's happiness, it's sweetness, it's their best number, it's the goodbye people and they're feeling terrific; they got through a whole phone call without promising anything . . ."). With Bob Dishy as a hapless stranger who backs Berle's dream and Brenda Vaccaro as Berle's daughter, *The Goodbye People* kept a tight rein on its material, developing character as a coil of weirdness that at length unwound into a treatise on individuality. A highly unpolitical work in a political time, *The Goodbye People* is contemporary and universal in the way of the best comedy: for all times. (Broadway may never get it; a revival in 1979 with Herschel Bernardi did no better than the original.)

Jules Feiffer has nothing in common with Gardner other than his background in cartoon work and a cynicism about American cultural drift. But together the two have laid the groundwork for the New York School of postwar comedy, typified by neurosis, ineffectuality, *Angst,* and the self-disgust of the wimpy intellectual. But where Gardner favors a fantasy naturalism of an almost poetic vigor, Feiffer works in self-commentative surrealism wherein violence is the popular idiom. His *Little Murders* (1967) opened its fourth wall on a renovated domestic "comedy" at first beset by and at the end joining the homicidal anarchy of the American city. Once, the American stage saw the city as debased by fashion; later, it was glamorous in its fashion. Now, Feiffer helped introduce the new mythology of the barbaric city—the muggings, the obscene phone calls, air and noise pollution, sexual decadence, federal snooping, and a general continuum of brutality that people seem to grow used to and then adopt themselves as "style." George Kelly, the pioneer limner of leathery American women, might have admired Feiffer's heroine Patsy Newquist (though the fans of Barbara Cook, the original Patsy, had trouble adoring in this hard-shelled crab the soubrette who had sung "Here's to Your Illusions" and "Goodnight, My Someone" in musical comedy). But Broadway found *Little Murders* altogether too hard a pleasure to take in. Outcast art, it flopped on The Street only to reassert itself a little later in an off-Broadway revival.

The New York wits were, as a group, highly influential on the national comedy scene from the mid-1960s on, though none of them has the resonance of Gardner or Feiffer at their best. Led by Woody Allen, Murray Schisgal, Bruce Jay Friedman, and a few others, they tend to work best in loose rather than tightly plotted structures, often lose character for The Gag, and center attention on one archetype who might be called the West Side Schlemiel. With his roots in Gardner's Nebbish of the 1950s and the cartoon monologues Feiffer introduced in the *Village Voice*, the West Side Schlemiel is ubiquitous in theatre, film, and fiction. He is the "little man," a victim of other people's aggressiveness, ambition, or thoughtlessness—but where previous little men have cheered us with their imagination or gumption, the Schlemiel is a despicable failure. Chaplin's tramp won out through heart and a kind of inadvertent deviousness; he may lose a battle, but he has—one way or another—fought. Bob Hope's braggart coward, too, managed to stay upright, by outsmarting the tough guys. But the Schlemiel has no initiative, no smarts. Pushed out of line at Zabar's, harassed by civil servants, a failure with women and a disappointment to men, he hopes with a hopeless *Schmerz* and is supposed to enlighten one with his self-deprecating wit. But when he says, as Allen's surrogate does in the film *Annie Hall*, "I'm one of the few males who suffers from [penis envy]," one is less enlightened than disgusted.

Allen is the culture's exponential Schlemiel, though at the end of the 1970s he evolved the character into an alleged winner and sex symbol, one of the more extravagant metamorphoses of the era. In the 1960s, Allen was still active in theatre: he himself enacted his avatar in *Play It Again, Sam* (1969), taking advice from Humphrey Bogart on wooing women, and while he wrote no part for himself in *Don't Drink the Water* (1966)—Anthony Roberts deputized, romanticizing the trope—this tale of a Newark caterer and his family trapped in an American embassy behind the Iron Curtain showed how the Schlemiel's love of the putdown may be applied to married couples as well. This exchange between caterer Walter, wife Marion, and WASP Schlemiel diplomat might easily have been the work of Neil Simon:

WALTER: Am I interested in their missiles and rockets? All I want to do is take some pictures.

MAGEE: I wonder if your photos are valuable.

MARION: He held the camera backwards. They're pictures of his nose.

WALTER: I gotta have my head examined. Every time I listen to you I wind up behind the eightball.

MARION: Here we go again.

WALTER: If you had listened to me, we would've taken a cabana in Atlantic Beach.

MARION: Every year it must be Atlantic Beach. What's the matter, they need you to work the tide?

WALTER: No, we had to go to Europe. Thirty-five hundred dollars for three weeks of uninterrupted diarrhea.

For a national audience, the Jewish tone of the jokes is considered acceptable if the characters don't actually identify themselves as Jewish. Thus, while Kay Medford and Lou Jacobi played Marion and Walter on Broadway for a largely Jewish audience, the film version offered Estelle Parsons and Jackie Gleason. Once, Hollywood bowdlerized New York comedy. Now, it simply reinflects it.

It may well be typical of the mood of the times that a morose loser should prove so endearing to such a broad audience, for there is no question that the Schlemiel's spiel has become one of the most profitable modes in American comedy. It has been overexploited, however. Bruce Jay Friedman's *Scuba Duba* (1967), made up mainly of a suburban American's self-pitying harangue after his wife runs off with a black man, included all sorts of farcical characters who speak exactly as he does, and in Friedman's *Steambath* (1970), virtually everyone on stage is clued into the Jewish jive. We are led to believe that the bath's customers have died and the Puerto Rican attendant is God. One of the several Schlemiels in view defines his generation—"it went by very quickly"—as "Dolph Camili, Dane Clark, Uncle Don, Ducky Medwick, and out." "Sounds like a real bunch of winners," sneers someone. The Schlemiel comes back, "We produced Norman Podhoretz." Now, that much is very funny. But even the attendant, God himself, speaks in the same pattern: "You know what I don't need? Right now? Aggravation." This isn't a worldview, just an argot. And the Schlemiel, more and more, sounds an empty theme on which the ingenious variations have already been heard. Even as soon as 1968, Dustin Hoffman was praised for bringing out of the title role of Murray Schisgal's *Jimmy Shine* the portraiture that the writing lacked—and this was perhaps the most exhaustively observed Schlemiel, composed by one of the experts. Still, he is a strangely adaptable character. In Neil Simon's *The Prisoner of Second Avenue* (1971), the oppressed (drugged, mugged, fired) denizen of the Manhattan high-rise was first played by Peter Falk, then by Art Carney, then by Hector Elizondo—three very different actors—working with the same text. But surely Falk's Schlemiel is not Carney's is not Elizondo's? But surely it is: the city jerk with the Talmudic wail has become a universal American type.

Semi-satire did not hold up well, and provided some of the decade's more spectacular flops (always excepting the musical, which had now reached an apex of flamboyant failure, the one-performance run, launched by the squalid, "million-dollar" *Kelly* in 1965). Once, a novel topic, a few smiling lines, and a star or two meant several months' stay in New York and a reasonably busy tour: salaries and royalties for all concerned. But by the 1960s the average non-musical cost about $135,000 just to open and had to do capacity business to pay off in six months. At these prices, both the inventive and the mediocre could close fast. In the inventive category, one should cite Ronald Alexander's *Nobody Loves an Albatross* (1963), an on-target jab at the lowbrow story mill of television, personified in Robert Preston's con-man series creator. (Alexander had been responsible for one of the 1950's most gaseous domestic comedies, *Time Out for Ginger*; the intervening years, spent in television, certainly sharpened him up.) In the mediocre category one has an embarrassment of choice. Perhaps Gore Vidal's *Weekend* will do, with its ill-focused picture of a Republican presidential contender whose bohemian son suddenly turns up with a black inamorata in tow. Touchingly opened in March of 1968 to take advantage of election-year activity, *Weekend*—like Alexander's deft burlesque—flopped, at least partly because the contender's son, obviously meant to serve as Vidal's mouthpiece, was unbearably flip and self-righteous.

Of quality work in comedy, there was little, though of course many of the brighter wits had moved into what classifiers would think of as serious drama—Lanford Wilson and Ronald Ribman, for example, who can be extremely funny in plays that wouldn't be called "comedies." In an attempt to shatter the commonplace that important American writing is done in fiction, not drama, Saul Bellow wrote a piece of such high quality—of such fastidious clarity of vision—that standard Broadway technique could not pull it off. This was *The Last Analysis* (1964). Bellow pictured an ancient vaudeville comedian staging the crises of his life on closed circuit television for a panel of psychiatric specialists. Farce, quasi-psychodrama, and tragedy at once, it called for a kind of actor American training does not normally produce, a verbal clown, someone *of* burlesque *into* literate theatre. Sam Levene, in the original short-lived production, was badly overparted.

Another sort of verbal clown—out of literacy into burlesque, so to speak—gave what is now thought of as the classic comic performance on Broadway in this decade, as he had done the decade before in *Waiting for Godot*: Bert Lahr. Actually, he gave five performances a night, playing an assortment of roles in S.J. Perelman's *The Beauty Part* (1962), a zany exposure of the commercialism of the American arts scene in a Candide-like picaresque, from painting, publishing, and New York cocktails to film and a televised court session in Los Angeles. Much of it was as droll (and vicious) as anything in its line, as when pulp magazine editrix Hyacinth Beddoes Laffoon proposed a "countrywide golem contest" to beef up sales and terrorized her editorial staff. ("A naked girl tied to a bedpost with a chimpanzee brandishing a whip? No more punch than a seed catalogue!") It's a very certain kind of humor, fleet and lean, related to the sort of nihilistic whimsey the Marx Brothers featured (Perelman helped write two of their films), and while it tends to spill out every which way, digressing in a patchwork, one cannot deny its zest:

> MR. KRUMGOLD: I wouldn't put it past you to hire assassins. . . What about those two truck drivers that stopped me for a light just now? The one wearing mascara looked like a tough customer.
> MRS. KRUMGOLD: Those were Bennington girls.

A newspaper strike combined with the frostbite of Perelman's spoof kept the show from doing well, but it did good, truly, in an age that often lacked an honest sense of humor. With the help of Alice Ghostley and Charlotte Rae, Lahr made that famous step from the sublime to the ridiculous, trying not to be offensive with material that was undeniably hostile to the beliefs of the Broadway public. As smooth eastern plutocrat, cynical agent, right-wing California paranoid, camera-loving judge, and the magazine magnate in drag, Lahr was irresistible—but even he had trouble with Perelman's curtain, saluting a baby basket as "everybody's joy" and then showering the audience with its contents: greenbacks.

Off-Broadway made a better home for assailing corruption in the culture. Elaine May's one-acter *Adaptation* (1969) played contemporary life as a television game show, her contestant pitted against all the trauma of adolescence and maturity on a gigantic board, gaudy with Isolation Squares, Success and Opportunity Cards, a hidden Security Square, and two studio assistants who hum "The Impossible Dream" at ambitious and/or sentimental moments. As a child at a progressive school where freedom marches to Washington are listed in the curriculum, the contestant's idea of a libelous graffito runs to "Phyllis can't make a commitment"; in college he picks an Opportunity card reading, "You make friends with a Negro"; and at the end of the game the emcee tells him, "Remain where you are and die."

As if emphasizing the variety of comic modes off-Broadway has to work in, *Adaptation* played in tandem with Terrence McNally's *Next*, an unsettling look at a mild, middle-aged man undergoing a terrorizing draft physical. Together the pair held out for 707 performances at the Greenwich Mews Theatre, meanwhile upholding the off-Broadway tradition of reprieving or launching reputations: as the harassed and finally (as the worm turns) harassing "draftee" in *Next*, James Coco rose above years of obscurity on and off Broadway to get what are known as "career notices" from the reviewers, while May erased the nervous feelings left by the out-of-town closing of her play *A Matter of Position* (1962) with the *Adaptation* script and her direction of both works. Typically, both Coco and May moved onto bigger stages—Coco to *The Last of the Red-Hot Lovers* and May into cinema. Off-Broadway's value as adversary alternative to Broadway is incalculable— but it remains a way station whose small size and economics cannot consistently support its art.

So the outcast's arena hasn't yet made an effective treaty with the *circi maximi*—which is to say, the arts scene still maintained relatively procultural and countercultural arenas on a segregated basis. Genres, themes, and production aesthetics of the one don't usually mix with those of the other, and it seemed, especially in the sixties, that playwrights were either pro- or counter- and would not be allowed on both teams. Every so often a playwright might attempt to resist this typing—Terrence McNally, for instance. Now thought of as characteristic of the counterculture in its whimsical element, McNally introduced himself—bizarrely, considering his later career—adapting Giles Cooper's adaptation of the younger Dumas' play, *The Lady of the Camellias*. This was Franco Zeffirelli's production starring Susan Strasberg, a sumptuous debacle of 1963. Two years later, and still on Broadway, McNally achieved instant notoriety for his evening of total Baal-worship, *And Things That Go Bump in the Night* (1965), a black domestic comedy laced with rape, murder, transvestism, homosexuality, incest, sadomasochism, and camp humor. On *Broadway*? Eileen Heckart's vicious mother would have disgusted even the new-wave mother-haters of the twenties, and at one of the play's 16 performances a man rushed up to grab at Heckart and beg her to stop the show. The production looked like such a lost cause that the management posted the closing notice and reduced all seats to $1.00. This brought in unexpected hordes of patrons, proving that there were after all potential theatregoers daunted by the stiff tariff, up to $7.50 for a non-musical.

McNally removed to off-Broadway for a while, though his delightfully satiric double-bill *Bad Habits* (1974) attempted, vainly, to move him uptown. Weird sex also found itself more hospitable quarters off-Broadway: not long after *And Things That Go Bump in the Night*, the theatres of the Village donned yet another of the outcast hats as the purveyor of cynical pornothespia, plays produced entirely to turn a profit on representations of debauchery. Among the less well known items, the procedure called for an interminable preview period based on salacious advertising and word-of-mouth; the shows would then close, without having bothered to "open," when business was exhausted. The award for Most Voguish Sleaze goes to the revue *Oh, Calcutta!* (1969), "devised by Kenneth Tynan" out of sketches by such as Samuel Beckett (for repute), John Lennon (for youthful hip), Sam Shepard (for western hip), and Jules Feiffer (for liberal New York paranoia). The title is a smutty French pun ("Oh, quel cul t'as") and the received premise was that satire mixed with frankness about America's favorite taboo would prove salubrious. But the writing as such, despite the eye-opening gaggle of bylines, was mostly poor and the nudity less liberating than titillating. Off-Broadway did run a superb little revolution in freeing the American theatre of unnecessary inhibitions in this time, but the battle was engaged by the Open Theatre, by La MaMa, the American Place, and many others: by dedicated theatre people concerned with new scripts and performing styles, not by fancy pimps. The spectators who frequented *Oh, Calcutta!* and the coeval even more lubricious *Che!* (which promised, but did not apparently deliver, an in-the-flesh copulation between Che Guevara and a nun) were not those in search of theatre art and idea, but those longing for a hot time.

21

Made in England II

IF AMERICAN THEATRE WAS BRITISH in repertory, acting, and production style when it was founded, it evolved its own material and approach so completely that by the 1930s one could always tell the British plays and players apart from everything and -one else: by a certain tightness, more an austerity than a tension. They spoke clean, precise English, which couldn't be said for any number of American players or even plays of that decade— *Waiting for Lefty*, say, or *Boy Meets Girl*. On the other hand, they lacked the intense immediacy of American melodrama, the informality of American farce. The Britons shuddered or ran giddy because genre demanded they do so; the Americans did so because they couldn't help shuddering or because giddy was fun. Then, too, British writers were much less interested— if interested at all—in working in the vernacular patterns that so enlivened the Depression theatre. So while they outdid us in diction, we outstripped them in physicalized realism. (Not to mention our vastly superior popular musical stage, unrivaled anywhere.)

Until the Old Vic visit in 1946, there was little controversy on this matter. Since then, the arguments pro and con British and American acting have raged, and since the 1950s the argument has spread to include British and American playwrighting, since theirs began to flourish just as ours seemed to degenerate. Theatre people maintain fixed opinions as to the quality and desirable amount of American stagings of British plays, whether whole productions should be imported or American casts assembled, and to what extent British stars should be tolerated here. Obviously, when it comes to the limited-run appearances of a superb new work by Harold Pinter with

John Gielgud and Ralph Richardson in Peter Hall's original National Theatre mounting—as was the case with *No Man's Land* (1976)—the public
does not stand on nationalist scruples, and buys up all the tickets, neat. But
Actors Equity looks balefully on such events, and periodically raises squalls
over the hiring of British actors for otherwise American productions, as was
the case with Margaret Leighton and Anthony Quayle for, respectively,
The Little Foxes and *Galileo*, both at Lincoln Center. (The squalls died
quickly: Leighton was a resident alien and Quayle was approved after Rod
Steiger said no.)

Until the end of the 1970s, one could not deny that serious and comic
theatre would have totally disappeared from Broadway for months at a time
but for the importation of British works, for they have something that
contemporary typical Broadway fare did not have—language. Not that
British pop can't be deadly, as *Not Now, Darling* proved in its brief stay
here in 1970, nor that every time an English cast delves into chronicle the
result is *A Man for All Seasons*, as Diana Rigg and Keith Michell proved
in Ronald Millar's *Abelard and Heloise* (1971). But British verbal skills do
wonderful things to the old standby genres. Even sex comedy, in the hands
of Alan Ayckbourn, makes for literate fun, most especially in his trilogy
The Norman Conquests (1975), three evenings' worth of Norman's sexual
essays, viewed successively in the dining room (Norman and his sister-in-
law), the garden (Norman and his wife's sister-in-law), and the living room
(Norman and his wife).

Sex comedy as a genre has totally crashed in America; it has lost the
elegance that the Lunts brought to it and the enlightened banter of Behrman
and Barry; modern sex humorists prefer the coy smut pioneered by Avery
Hopwood—*Cactus Flower* or *Forty Carats*—often with surprisingly gifted
actors in the leads. On Broadway, *The Norman Conquests* was unevenly
cast, but it brought the best out of its best players. Estelle Parsons' hysterical
wife gamed wonderfully with the infatuated detail that real-life cranks bring
to their roles, and as her affable husband, Barry Nelson countered with
understated naturalism—it shouldn't have worked, but it was a scream.
Similarly, Carole Shelley went to town squinting as Norman's "nearsighted
but vain" wife, raging at and forgiving the impossible Norman by turns
and gazing down her nose, frequently, at nothing whatsoever, while Ken
Howard played the drip-next-door with easygoing ordinariness: another neat
match. Note that the production used Broadway regulars rather than a
West End cast; interestingly, a BBC filming of the three plays, screened on
Public Television several times, plays entirely for naturalism rather than

Broadway's naturalism-*cum*-farce and thus turns a very funny show into a dull soap opera. (On the other hand, Ayckbourn's much less vital *Bedroom Farce* [1979] lost almost all its sharpness when—at Equity's behest—Americans replaced most of the original London cast.)

Better, consider Simon Gray's *Butley* (1972), also very funny, but serious as well, covering the last day in the downfall of a brilliant, self-destructive English professor at London University. Alan Bates played into Ben Butley right to the man's many dregs, relishing the ignescent word gaming as can few actors without a heritage of language behind them. Gray's kinky comedy *Wise Child* lasted four nights here in early 1972, yet, a few months later, the more accessible *Butley* had the customers scurrying into line for a rare treat on Broadway—thoroughbred dramatic English. Butley's wife is leaving him, his male lover is leaving him, and there are hints as well that he is about to lose the position he has made such mock of. Gray contracts the wasteful calamity so keenly that his seriocomedy feels like the most natural naturalism:

> JOEY: You spread futility, Ben. It creeps in, like your dirty socks do, into my drawers. Or my clean ones, onto your feet. Or your cigarette butts everywhere. Or your stubble and shaving cream into our razor. Or your voice, booming out nursery rhymes into every corner of this department, it seems to me. Or your—
>
> BUTLEY: Shut up! That's rehearsed.
>
> JOEY: Thousands of times. (*Long pause.*) I'm sorry it had to be today, what with Anne and Tom. I would have waited . . .
>
> BUTLEY: Which shows you have no sense of classical form. We're preserving the unities. The use of messengers has been quite skillful.

Modern British drama had little resonance for Americans before *Look Back in Anger*, but since the mid-1950s London's exports have shamed us in the simple matter of words. And Americans don't necessarily see the best that the West End can offer, for such men as N. F. Simpson, John Mortimer, Henry Livings, and David Mercer aren't exported, and by no means all of Peter Nichols or Harold Pinter is deemed suitable for Broadway. No way around it—their theatre thrives on language, because their best writers aspire to theatre, whereas ours write novels.

Yearly, the British theatre renews itself, not just with new plays or old, but with a concourse of resourceful production and sometimes superb acting. When have Americans mounted Shakespeare to compare with the Peter Brook *King Lear* and *A Midsummer Night's Dream* brought over in recent years? American thespians read Artaud and Kott, cite Stanislafsky and Grotowski, and borrow liberally from anything they've seen, yet too many actors can't get their mouths around the language, too many directors would rather decorate an interpretation or even a mere Look than put the text across, and the public is segmented into those who prefer "traditional" Shakespeare (i.e., in Elizabethan dress, with sets, as at Stratford, Connecticut), those who prefer renovated Shakespeare (as in Ellis Rabb's 1973 Lincoln Center production of *The Merchant of Venice* in modern setting inspired by Antonioni's films with touches of the Fellini *Satyricon*), and those who don't care as long as they get a star turn. The last approach is the oldest one: what manager of the 1800s or early 1900s would have dared a *Richard III* without a ranking Shakespearean in the title role (and obsequiously minor players giving him plenty of celebrity room)? This approach has provided some of America's worst performances in classical repertory, the most recent example being a shockingly sloppy *Richard III* in 1979 starring Al Pacino, filled out by eighth-raters in a variety of accents, and cheered by teenybopper claques.

Charles Frohman's dictum about "the doer, not the deed" still holds— the public cares more for personality than artwork—and this has contributed to the bankrupt state of American acting today. The talent is there, but the training is irregular. Though America now boasts a national plant of resident companies in which a rich practical experience in genres and styles is obtainable, and though acting classes proliferate everywhere, the acting profession remains an improvisation of technique around natural talents and solipsism. In an article on acting in England and America, Robert Brustein wrote in 1973, "The English actor approaches his role as if it were a mask (Olivier, for example, professes to discover the key to his part the moment he finds the right nose), varying his speech, gait, and features to suit the needs of the character. Reflecting his interest in the Self, the American actor usually purveys a single character from role to role, one that is recognizably close to his own personality."

It's no longer compulsory for actors to go to confession three times a year, as it was in Renaissance Italy—it doesn't have to be: American actors confess themselves nightly in their roles. And, of course, the more renowned the actor, the juicier his "portrayal" appears. So no wonder we have had trouble instituting a permanent home for classical repertory: there is doubt that one could collect enough players in one place to fill out the major roles with the necessary ability, and doubt that capable production teams could be assembled. This is the most crushing aspect of the British-American controversy: their brilliance in repertory, as compared to our inability even to compete. And this brings us to the most notorious American "national theatre" project, the Lincoln Center Repertory Company.

Since its first season as an apprentice national stage in 1964–65 (in a temporary home in Washington Square), the Vivian Beaumont Theatre has not tried to be what it hoped to be and failed to be even what it was. Its hopes ran to new and standard repertory American and foreign, an ensemble acting troupe with a company feeling, and, mainly, a lot of respect. Its truth ran to poorish new plays and a bad choice of classics, a grotesque collage of unintegrated acting styles, and near-universal condemnation.

And it wasn't repertory. It was one play after another, one finished forever when the next opened—and no one seemed to like the hall, with its three-quarters thrust stage. Of course, a company needs time to find itself. But when the inauguration is this clumsy, one doesn't want to spend patience. Three administrations failed to make a Lincoln Center idea work—first Robert Whitehead and Elia Kazan of the commercial stage, then Herbert Blau and Jules Irving of regional theatre (the San Francisco Actor's Workshop), then Irving alone. This was supposed to be the alternative to Broadway glitz. What it was was Broadway with a three-quarters thrust stage.

The board of directors handed the complex over to Joseph Papp when they were looking for someone to inaugurate a restitutional fourth regime in 1973. Under Papp, however, Lincoln Center became off-Broadway for the wrong audience. The new chief instituted a policy of mostly new works in the Vivian Beaumont and replaced the experimental series in the little basement theatre, the Forum (renamed the Newhouse), with Shakespeare, one production after another. It was as if the New Theatre of 1909 had been suddenly appropriated by the Provincetown Playhouse; Papp intended to lay a brave new world on a public that had dozed happily through such fare as *Cyrano de Bergerac* (with Robert Symonds); *King Lear* (with Lee J. Cobb); *The Time of Your Life*; *Camino Real* (with Jessica Tandy, Jean-Pierre Aumont, Victor Buono, Sylvia Syms, Susan Tyrrell, and Al Pacino as Kilroy); *The Playboy of the Western World*; a smattering of Brecht (performed with uncomprehending stateliness); and a surprising amount of new material, including the important *In the Matter of J. Robert Oppenheimer*, Heinar Kipphardt's investigation of the atomic scientist's security clearance hearings "freely adapted from the documents"; and the general public's first bewildering taste of Sam Shepard's underground refractions of American mythology, *Operation Sidewinder*.

Not that Papp's Vivian Beaumont seasons were horrifyingly innovative—

merely that they aimed to be. Leaping into his tenure in the fall of 1973, Papp brandished his house playwright of rank, David Rabe, but Rabe's *Boom Boom Room* was a dud, sluggish, vacuous, and—it later turned out— not in finished form. There was a classic (Strindberg's *Dance of Death* with Robert Shaw and Zoë Caldwell in an unpleasantly abbreviated script), a respectable black entry (Ron Milner's *What the Wine Sellers Buy*), and one true taste of outcast brutality, Miguel Piñero's *Short Eyes*, set in a prison and brought in from the Public Theatre to replace a postponed premiere. Though this quartet was representative of what Papp normally produces, the Beaumont audience—the Broadway audience—was disappointed. They had known Papp through his worshipful press, not through his work.

Their introduction to his Shakespeare in the Newhouse belowstairs was shocking. They knew about the free stage in Central Park and the Spanish-language mobile units, but this public is used to Shakespeare in the Stratford, Connecticut, style or the occasional trendy English mounting. Who would go to Papp's Lincoln Center Shakespeare? The Broadway crowd? Probably not more than once—not after seeing the debut production, perhaps the most unanimously lambasted attempt on Shakespeare in New York's history. This was David Schweizer's unconventional but interesting *Troilus and Cressida*, portrayed in American identity symbols, with Achilles a Big Man on Campus and Helen a spangle-eyed Hollywood sex goddess. Granted, this Troilus offered some outlandish performances, but it had excellent ones as well from Christopher Walken, Madeline LeRoux, and Charles Kimbrough.

The Newhouse suffered further setbacks in a conventional but poor *Tempest* and an insufficient *Macbeth*, and the second and last Shakespeare season offered an amazingly incompetent *Midsummer Night's Dream* bearable only for Kathleen Widdoes' Titania. Puck was played as a Puerto Rican janitor, whose "I'll put a girdle round about the earth in forty minutes" read as "I'll get to that drain mañana, Mrs. Smith," as he strolled out of the Athenian forest and into the nearest cantina: the four fairy attendants were entrusted to little children, one precocious pro and three absurd gigglers eye-balling the house for sights of Mom. Upstairs at the Beaumont, Papp's second season proved worse than his first, squeaking through on the basis of a star turn, Liv Ullmann in *A Doll's House*.

It wasn't working. Broadway could not deal with Papp as Papp was (not without Ullmann in tow), and Papp could only be what he is (even with Ullmann)—could not, as Lincoln Center hoped he would, synthesize "national theatre" principles. Railing at audiences for not appreciating new plays or modes of production that were not appreciable in the first place (that is, blaming his public for his having blown the most beautiful opportunity granted an impresario in modern times to raise up a center stage for American theatre; which opportunity Papp blew by raising up the mediocre and the awful through his inability to distinguish Relevance from art), Papp changed his Lincoln Center policy. The Beaumont would house classics and non-toxic new titles; a little later, Papp announced his Booth season ("WANTED!," remember?) for the "difficult" new American works. But even with celebrity leads and amiable entries—Lynn Redgrave and Ruth Gordon in Shaw's *Mrs. Warren's Profession*—the synthesis was not there. Papp had not found the level for institutional theatre; his supervision of traditional fare is as erratic as his discoveries of raw talent.

Papp's later Beaumont seasons ran much better than his first two, and included at least one absolutely first-rate production, Andrei Serban's staging of *The Cherry Orchard* in 1977. As stylish and penetrating a performance as its predecessors under the Herbert Blau-Jules Irving regime were moodless and cursory, this *Cherry Orchard* behaved like a mainstay item in a national repertory: it was very strongly cast; it had line, the tempo and the great moments gathering into a completion; it had a look that helped define it; it had conception; and it breathed, a clinical expanse of white backing a colored riot of life, a comedy.

The Rumanian Serban had made his name in town for radical experiments, such as *The Trojan Women* performed in gibberish, and critics announced that they detected the influence of Artaud and Brook in Serban's work while worrying over whether the performance was suitably Chekhovian, so if nothing else the event was contemporary. With Jean-Claude van Itallie's translation, Santo Loquasto's white walls, glimpsed cherry grove, and Stanislafskyan props, and Serban's precisely disjunct company, the play was Chekhof's again as it hadn't been in the last dozen "respectable" productions. What a collection—Cathryn Damon's merrily dour governess; Max Wright's wheezing clutz of a postal clerk; Dwight Warfield's old valet, a radiant one-man *ancien régime*; Michael Cristofer's student; Raul Julia's bearlike merchant; Marybeth Hurt's dreamy younger daughter; and George Voskovec's gala brother. The most controversial portrait in the gallery was Meryl Streep's maid, unexpectedly slapstick. Streep is a flawless technician, and to see her in action is to realize that some actors do somehow learn their craft, going on to play role after different role not as themselves but as others. An important *Cherry Orchard* does not "star" its Madam Ranyefsky (this was one of the several drawbacks to the Helen Hayes revival of 1950, adapted by Joshua Logan to suit the antebellum South). Yet Irene Worth is a star, and when she plays Ranyefsky one doesn't want to miss a moment of her dance—literally a dance in the play's final moments, when she left home for the last time and cantered lovingly around the rim of the stage apron, feeling the walls as she traveled, once, twice, unbearable, a third time. There was a Big Moment for the modern era!

Despite the excitement generated by Serban's *Cherry Orchard* and Richard Foreman's *Threepenny Opera* of the year before, Papp's Lincoln Center steerage wasn't what his press had led the town—and the press—to expect it should be. In 1977, Papp abandoned Lincoln Center and reconsolidated his empery down at the Public. The Beaumont complex lay dark for two years; in early 1979 its reopening was announced, under an executive committee of directors Woody Allen, Sarah Caldwell, Liviu Ciulei, Robin Phillips, and Ellis Rabb; playwright Edward Albee; and administrators Richmond Crinkley and John S. Samuels, III. This gathering of Names does not bode well.

The American stage has flexibility and a love of adventure. In admiring British polish, we often forget about our own sometimes raw but energetic experiments in mime and motion; it is well to recall as we dote on a Grotowski—who ensures his charisma by limiting his audiences to handfuls who can rave about the exclusivity that favors them—that the Living Theatre has had an extraordinary impact in Europe (Judith Malina and Julian Beck are our Grotowskis, perhaps). True, language, as written and pronounced, remains a formidable problem. But let us not ignore what others consider to be our unique strong points—for example, the physicality, improvisation, and psychological charade that off-Broadway, as far back as the 1910s, exploited as clues to the American theatrical temper. (Was Serban attempting to reconnect with all that when he staged an *Agamemnon* at Lincoln Center in 1977, ripping away the component of language by mixing Aeschylus' Greek with snippets of Edith Hamilton's translation and emphasizing the play as visual and kinetic experience?)

What American actors lack in grace they often balance with ferocity—as witness the meeting of John Barrymore and the Moscow Art Theatre, who happened to cross paths in January of 1924, when the Russians made their famous American tour. Barrymore was known for his opening weeks; thereafter, he would embellish, trying to find some meaning in the inertia of a long run. The producer Arthur Hopkins invited the Muscovites to Barrymore's *Hamlet* when the record-breaking engagement was winding down and Barrymore lost in a frenzy of decoration. "John was particularly anxious to impress them," Hopkins later recalled, "with the result that he played with a hysteria and extravagance that was even exhausting to the spectator. I went back to him after the first scene and begged him to alight. He had no idea that he had been flying."

Barrymore lacked the perspective to control himself, and continued to overdo till the final curtain. There was no way for Hopkins to avoid bringing the Russians backstage, and backstage they trouped—Stanislafsky, Madam Olga Chekhova, and all—embarrassed, eloquently silent. After an endless lull, Chekhova spoke up.

"Tell me," she asked Barrymore, "do you really do this eight times a week?"

22

What Has Happened So Far III

A BACKSTAGE MUSICAL OF 1953, Rodgers and Hammerstein's *Me and Juliet*, devoted one scene to intermission in the lobby, where theatregoers assessed the state of the stage in a song carried half by optimistic enthusiasts and half by gleeful detractors. "The theatre's a thing of the past, tra-la," sang the latter, and "The theatre is passing away, hey-hey."

A very few people were beginning to think so by then, but there was no accord in reasoning why. They blamed economics, artistic effeteness, the remoteness of the new suburban population from the stimulating city centers, and—especially—the competition from other media. Some had reckoned the theatre's doom when sound came to the motion picture; now, some believed that television would do what the talkies failed to. But it was not theatre that television affected but film, forcing a contraction on the movie industry (or conversion to television production) and a brief era of defensive novelties such as 3-D and Cinerama. Strictly in terms of economics, television has not hurt the stage. Granted, fewer plays were being produced after television had been acculturated than before. But the rate of deflation had been steadily building since just before the Depression and was not notably advanced when the home screen went to market.

It may be that television, in that first important decade of the 1950s, actually complemented the stage, for at the time it was awed by drama and tirelessly adapted it for video, invariably live and with often impressive casts. The Hallmark Hall of Fame was especially active here—Julie Harris in *The Lark*, Katharine Cornell and Charles Boyer in *There Shall Be No Night*, Greer Garson, Eileen Heckart, Sidney Blackmer, and E. G. Marshall in *The Little Foxes*, Mary Martin, Helen Hayes, George Abbott, and Florence Reed (in her original role of the Fortune Teller) in *The Skin of Our Teeth*, Maurice Evans and Joan Greenwood in *Man and Superman*, and constant Shakespeare staged by the starring Evans. Who knows what friends the theatre did not make those Sunday afternoons? Later, the Play of the Week did a like service, repeating its programs seven nights running. And of course the numerous dramatic anthology series developed the playwright pool by producing original work conceived expressly for television.

That age has entirely ended. Public television is now the sole producer of drama on the airwaves; except for certain old movies, just about everything else on television is, except for sports telecasts, video dumm. Television's influence is felt not in the numbers of potential theatregoers who stay home, but in those who come to the theatre after assimilating the superficial content, centralized pop concepts, and moronic structural rhythms of the sitcom, the crime thriller, the stooge vaudeville. Lacking irony, ambiguity, surprise, poetry, and breadth, commercial television inculcates indiscriminate vision in the American eye. Television has no quantity: it's always going, and going nowhere. But television has at the same time helped purge the theatre of its more meretricious offerings, which if nothing else clears the fixed number of available stages for more deserving fare. Just as the movies, in the 1920s and '30s, took over some of the more popular genres (crime melodrama, mystery thrillers, and a whole range of sentimental romances), television did likewise in the 1950s and '60s, assuming leadership in moribund domestic comedy and the musical revue. In one sense, television is a repository for the trivial in American art; it has taken some of the "popular" pressure off of the other two drama mediums. Who can deny that—artistically, now—American theatre and film are both more vital in the 1970s than they were in the 1950s, just as the television age began? This is not coincidence. Other factors are involved, true—but something like *Abie's Irish Rose* or *Peg O'My Heart* is seldom attempted in the theatre anymore.

As for Public Television, its effect has yet to be charted: no one is certain who, exactly, watches it. In drama, too, its record is spotty, depending on the BBC to a great degree, though its occasional forays into television film can be excellent, such as its series of adaptations from the American short story—*Verna, U.S.O. Girl,* drawn (by Albert Innaurato) from Paul Gallico and featuring the sharply dovetailed ensemble of Sissy Spacek, William Hurt, Sally Kellerman, and Howard da Silva, is superior to most commercial American film. On the other hand, PBS's transformations of stage plays are seldom superb. O'Neill, as the ranking American dramatist, has dominated the scene—*Ah, Wilderness!*, *Beyond the Horizon*, and *Mourning Becomes Electra* have been done, reasonably well. The first two originated in stage productions in regional theatre, but *Mourning* was filmed especially for television in five hourly segments heavily cut and—one must admit—all the better for cutting. Broadway, too, has made an appearance, in the fine Rosemary Harris-Eva Le Gallienne-Sam Levene-Ellis Rabb revival of *The Royal Family* (a gala event—it felt like the good old Hallmark days). Moreover, via Public Television, the nation has been able to sample the work of far-flung regional companies—the American Conservatory Theatre's definitively lowbrow *The Taming of the Shrew*, so busy with mugging and shoves that the actors seldom bother to pronounce the lines (a handsome Kate from Fredi Olster, however); or *The Time of Your Life* nicely presented by the City Center Acting Company. With *The Taming of the Shrew*, the camera could do little more than stand back and film the staging with close-ups to enliven the view. But this *Time of Your Life* was filmed in all dimensions, the camera roving through Saroyan's bar from group to group, turning a microcosmic but "theatrical" slice of life into a stylized documentary. Little of the wild contemporary experiments have made it to the small screen, but an occasional contemporary script does show up— Lanford Wilson's *The Mound Builders*, for instance, or even Richard Foreman's more exotic *City Archives*, in an authentic performance by his own Ontological-Hysteric Theatre.

The television screen has the potential to invigorate the national attitude toward first-rate dramatic literature, and Public Television knows it. After all, the Hallmark Hall of Fame, Play of the Week, and other such shows in combination formed a kind of national theatre. Too bad the commercial networks have forgotten how to film stage action. Even a faithful resuscitation of some old gem may be sabotaged by "television" procedure—i.e., stippled with countless pulse-killing pauses for the laugh track. A good case in point is the 1979 telecast of *You Can't Take It with You*, complete with its original time, place, and references. With a decent cast (including Art Carney, Jean Stapleton, and Henry Morgan) and a respect of text, this might have been a bright occasion if it hadn't been staged at the crawling tempo of *Welcome Back, Kotter*. Kaufman and Hart call for smarter dynamics.

But Public Television adapts to theatre, doesn't expect theatre to adapt to it. Accordingly, the network planned a historic project: the entire Shakespeare canon of thirty-seven plays as produced jointly by BBC-TV and Time-

Life Television, partly underwritten by American corporations. As the series was to be filmed in Britain (taking in—too rarely—actors such as John Gielgud, Wendy Hiller, Alec McCowen, Celia Johnson, and Derek Jacobi), a small opposition denounced the scheme, chiefly union spokesmen and Joseph Papp. Why isn't this series using American talent? Because Americans generally don't do Shakespeare as well as the British. That simple.

Once the first programs got on the air, however, it was clear that the BBC had not exactly put a better foot forward. The actors had no problem spitting out the poetry, but their portrayals ran from okay to poor, and the stagings, whether as theatre or film, are humdrum. What the BBC Shakespeare will do for the American theatre hunger will be learned in the 1980s; at least one can say that the value for high-school audiences should be immense. In the end, however, television and its low audience targeting inevitably lack the one element that liberated the American stage: challenge. From what was a strictly all-cultural endeavor in the 1800s, the stage gradually learned to test its public's assumptions as well as ratify them, at length giving rise to a succession of countercultural conditions—the art theatre, protest theatre, and so on—all at last coalescing into the off-Broadway "outcast" theatre of the 1960s. We berate Broadway for letting other stages handle all or most of the challenge that keeps art vital—but at least we do have those other stages. Television, even when it dares something like Foreman's *City Archives*, can never run counter to mass culture: television *is* the culture, in its rawest, basest form. It has, flatly, no relation to American drama, and almost certainly never will. Yet, as we head into the 1970s, we must consider that the younger theatregoers represent the generation that was raised on television, and that by the mid-1980s their taste will heavily influence the establishment taste on Broadway. Will they enforce lower standards—or will they raise them in simple delight at the refreshing richness of adult theatre?

23

The Me Decade

IF THE SECOND HALF OF THE 1960s profited from aesthetic and thematic upheaval, the 1970s saw the consolidation of much that this upheaval had revealed. Paradoxically, the 1970s began as the worst of times, loggy but noisy, emptily spectacular yet nearly bankrupt. Broadway was really dying, and off-Broadway suffering the timeless problems of the subterranean attic, admired in theory but ignored in practice. By the close of the 1975–76 season, when the failures are scattered away and the holdouts more or less settled in for the summer, there were—not counting two revivals (*The Royal Family* and *Who's Afraid of Virginia Woolf?*), one British show (*Equus*), and numerous musicals—exactly four plays alive on Broadway: two comedies (*California Suite* and *Same Time, Next Year*), Julie Harris' solo on the life and work of Emily Dickinson, *The Belle of Amherst*, and Milan Stitt's *The Runner Stumbles*, a serious piece on the trial of a priest accused of murdering a nun. Off-Broadway was in slightly better shape, and the bulk of off-off-Broadway on summer vacation. A bleak picture.

All this was to change by the end of the decade, and the main reason for the change was the treaty made between the underground and the mainstream. Of course, this has happened before. But this time the cultural symbolism that separated Broadway (the "true" American stage) from off-Broadway (the experimental stage) and off-off-Broadway (weirdness) and regional theatre (unimportant) was proved to be false. Off-Broadway discovered more than experimented, off-off-Broadway was sane and diverse, regional theatre was extremely crucial; and what was so true about Broadway? As the decade wore on, it became clear that however much new plays aspired to a Broadway production, their real life—their most successful exposure—happened elsewhere. The single most frequently performed new work of the decade never got to Broadway at all: Jerome Lawrence and Robert E. Lee's *The Night Thoreau Spent in Jail* (1970), a potpourri of Thoreau's *mots* and experience centering on his refusal to pay a federal tax to support the war with Mexico and especially popular with university theatres.

Perhaps most importantly, the worst of the sixties innovations—the hostility, illiteracy, and aimless propaganda of the "youth" revolution—disintegrated quickly. The group grope, the black racist harangues, the misinformed exploitation of rock and drugs as essences of social idealism turned out to be fads after all, something that only a few people would applaud more than once. Another piece that was not done on Broadway, Jules Feiffer's *God Bless*, turned up in New Haven, London, and Los Angeles at the very end of the sixties as a kind of farewell to all that in its disgusted look at a takeover of Washington, D.C., by the American Liberation Front. As Barbara Garson had done in *MacBird!*, Feiffer warned the spectator not to be fooled by "reformers": all politicians want power. *God Bless* made many self-professed liberals uncomfortable, not least when Feiffer's revolutionaries speak in a parody of sixties radical cant:

> Words cause cancer! The revolution rejects words! It digs beneath the phoniness of words and comes up with emotion . . . It comes up with joy! Guerilla joy! We pollute the polluters with guerilla joy—we spray it like Mace!

The Me Decade, as Tom Wolfe called it, saw the communications media seeking the utmost in cultural pollution; but in the theatre, amazingly, the 1970s eventually proved energetic, dedicated, playful, and wise. By the end of the decade, it was even making money, and proving what some of the people behind the Federal Theatre had hoped to see happen in the 1930s—that federal tax money, pumped into non-commercial situations (like off-Broadway's companies), is less a contribution than an investment that enhances the scene, introduces new blood into the business, and helps theatre make more theatre.

What makes this decade so engrossing above all is the profusion of new authors. Whether in innovation or in affirmation of tradition, the present junior generation shows vitality, awareness, and point without precedent, even in the industrious 1920s. Some of them, like Lanford Wilson, got started in the 1960s. But it is typical of the times that not till the 1970s did they make a major impression in the national consciousness.

Sam Shepard, one of the best of the younger playwrights, is also the most consistently unBroadway of the lot, in terms of where he is produced, what he does with his pen, and even how he treats the experience of being famous (i.e., by not cooperating with or even showing up for it). The elegantly sleazy, absurdly brilliant rock artist Patti Smith, who coauthored *Cowboy Mouth* with Shepard and played opposite him in its American premiere at the American Place Theatre in 1971, caught Shepard's wild western confrontation of the east in a rare subdued moment:

> Broadway.
> People shouted at him.
> There's something fishy about you boy.
> He didn't care.

And she says, "Sam moved on."

Shepard's voice is so hard to describe, so bafflingly natural, so flat, slangy, unknowing, inspired, and ecstatic that it's more efficient to quote Smith's impression of Shepard than to quote Shepard himself. You have to be there. He is not an absurdist, nor an improviser, though his linear realism seems no more "real" than Pinter's (and he avoids Pinter's irritating constant pauses). Yet Shepard, unlike Pinter, deals with reasonably ordinary people. Of and about the counterculture, he reminds us that what the east calls "hip" is plain vernacular in the west, and he tends to focus on the outcast classes— vagrants, hangers-on, cultural burn-outs, the unemployed. His generation has largely overthrown its elders' dependence on action as structure—the kinetics of story—and in this, Shepard leads his generation. He does indulge in the picturesque, throwing food around or exploding a car (offstage) with someone in it. But he is less interested in unraveling character through action than in unraveling character.

Shepard has made one appearance on a prominent New York stage, at the Vivian Beaumont Theatre in Lincoln Center. This was *Operation Sidewinder* (1970), an expanded essence of Shepard—outlaws and dull citizens; drugs, chance violence, rage, power plays, politics and apolitics; eccentrics and straights; the military on one hand, Indian terrorists on the other, a computer in the form of a huge snake in between them; and commentative use of hard rock (by the Holy Modal Rounders, throbbing between scenes). A kind of linear narrative took the public from a beginning through a middle to an end, but *Operation Sidewinder* is not a story play, and possibly not a theme play, either, at least not in the controversial sense. The format is conversations "around" the plot, edging in and out of the action to create an interior-exterior "other" action that provides the play's real basis. There is a terrible uproar in Shepard, but always on the fringes; his characters are seen trying to flee from it or get to it. But what's happening meanwhile? It's not always easy to pin down. In the brief *Killer's Head* (1975), Richard Gere—the entire cast—considered a deal on a pick-up truck and the quality of certain horses while sitting strapped on an electric chair—the sole piece of decor. When he finished, he was electrocuted.

Most of Shepard's plays turn on unusual versions of familiar occurrences: that is his bizarre naturalism. "It's funny the way the snow is," says a character in *Action* (1975), which shared the bill with *Killer's Head* at the American Place Theatre. And in *The Mad Dog Blues* (1971), a "two-act adventure show," Marlene Dietrich, Mae West, Captain Kidd, and Paul Bunyan take part in a hunt for buried treasure, more or less led by two archetypes of hip, Kosmo and Yahoodi, and all behaving pretty much like treasure hunters, with shifts in allegiance, sell-outs, and incidental panics. The roll of words is artless yet very sharp—but what to quote?; such spontaneity of whimsy and rage does not excerpt.

Not only our everyday, but our national legends proliferate in his work, and it's so engaging as theatre that one wonders why Shepard invariably turns up on unBroadway instead of The Street. Perhaps it's because his plays seldom conform to the preferred two-and-a-half hour length. When Shepard makes a splash, as he did for example in *The Tooth of Crime* (1973), it was not only for an off-Broadway production, but for a piece that had first been seen in London, Vancouver, and upstate New York. A look at an aging rock star, Hoss, challenged by a newcomer, Crow, *The Tooth of Crime* portrayed their show-biz rivalry as a duel of gunfighters, myth on myth, all the while opening up a third level of playspace in an aggressive, Angeleno-drug-rock idiom. Why is such *contemporary* work forced into this provisional exile? In 1979, Shepard won the Pulitzer Prize for a play that most theatregoers hadn't even heard of, *Buried Child*.

Possibly the classic Shepard entry is *Curse of the Starving Class* (1976), a dourly comic look at the collapse of a family in the rural Southwest. Not that it means to be comic, it would seem; but people are sadly funny. These people find a unity in an empty refrigerator, which they continually open and stare into as if hoping for a miracle. It never comes, but at the end of the play, when the refrigerator does fill with food, the degeneration in behavioral norms has overtaken parents and children. When the teenage son attempts to assume his father's patterns in a kind of daze, it is too weird and too late.

Lanford Wilson, last seen here struggling for recognition, has intricated a style as fresh as Shepard's but much less sinister. His aforementioned *The Hot l Baltimore* (1973), a long-run hit at the downtown Circle-in-the-Square, artfully reinstated the *Grand Hotel* cross-section genre of disparate characters interacting in a shared moment in time, in this case in a shabby hotel lobby (the "e" in its electric sign has guttered out) on the day the tenants learn that their haven is shortly due for demolition. Typically, this unremarkable Wilson piece was the one that the general public was alerted to. Mari Gorman and Conchata Ferrell were touted for their spirited acting as a tigress of the vagabond life (Gorman) and an overweight hustler with a nastily exhilarated laugh (Ferrell), uptowners flocked down, and there was even a television series based on the idea, clumsy and shortlived (though it did temporarily preserve Ferrell's sumptuous laugh).

Wilson's plays in general have a broad appeal, even though he usually concentrates on character rather than action; perhaps it's because he draws them with such insight. In *Serenading Louie* (1976), he caught up with two marriages in disarray, letting one living room do for their two different living rooms as they themselves have intertwined their relationships. His most brilliant piece so far is *Fifth of July* (1978); this one is almost all character—very little happens in it that would add up to a plot. But where *Serenading Louie* worked out its marital tangles in terms of four people of settled intimacy and closed their tale in violence, *Fifth of July* brought together a motley lot and held a low ceiling on uproar. In a way, *Fifth of July*'s action has already occurred, years before in a metaphorical fourth when the principals were part of the revolutionary student sixties. The play examines the aftermath: the story is over and what happened then? A great deal, it develops—and Wilson develops it through a lightning storm in language, personality, idealism, and adaptation. *There's* your action. Indeed, there is so much character in *Fifth of July* that Wilson felt bound to produce a spin-off, *Talley's Folly* (1979), to come closer to one of his characters in her youth. No doubt Wilson has profited from the stability of his enduring association with the Circle Repertory Company, for it upholds a high standard of performance, and gives Wilson a showcase other writers cannot count on. *Fifth of July* calls for a Chekhovian ensemble, unobtrusively deft, that is admittedly beyond most American groups, but the performers brought it off, under Marshall Mason's direction, excelling in the simple delivery of who they were. The play's lack of flash is admirable, considering its naturalistic style—but that puts something of a burden on the actors, who are denied both the grand line of tragedy and the showy "improvisation" of New York "method" realism. Perhaps that explains why Nancy Snyder turned in the only really stunning performance—she had the flashy bits as a flakey heiress who applies Marx to her industrial inheritance, sympathy and belief to any-one within reach, and drugs and hysteria to her personal problems. She was very funny complaining about her failure to disappear in the Bermuda Triangle, and very sympathetic, for though she doesn't realize it, everything in her life is a hoax. Snyder was not on hand when the piece was brought to Broadway in Mason's staging in 1980, and a Hollywood notable (Christopher Reeve) replaced the excellent William Hurt in the central role of a legless Vietnam veteran, but the ensemble held up nicely.

Writers who don't have Wilson's Understanding with an important company can be terribly exposed. On the other hand, an early success some-times guarantees one regular productions—though if these ventures don't recut the proportions of success the writer may be urged to disappear, whether his flops stem from script problems or external circumstances such as bad staging or bad reviews. Paul Zindel, for example, is less respected now than he was when his *The Effect of Gamma Rays on Man-in-the-Moon Marigolds* (1970) became a surprise hit off-Broadway for the nearly unbearable pathos of the all-woman household, daughters, mother, and silent, aged boarder in a loving feud. Offered the choice of moving to the larger theatres, Zindel took it, but *And Miss Reardon Drinks a Little* (1971), *The Secret Affairs of Mildred Wild* (1972), and *Ladies of the Alamo* (1977), at 108, 23, and 28 performances respectively, threaten to close his account.

This was not the case in the past, when failures didn't have to lose so much money. Philip Barry suffered constant failures through his career—*White Wings, Here Come the Clowns, Liberty Jones*. Yet, the season after, back he'd come with another play; the support was there. Now Broadway is impatient with failure, even with creators of proved abilities. Off-Broadway always gives another chance, so someone like Lanford Wilson can carve a private continuity for himself as most-favored-playwright at the Circle Rep in a way he couldn't hope to on Broadway. Some writers who dare the jump to Broadway have been tripped unfairly, as Richard Wesley was when *The Last Street Play* was moved from a showcase production on off-off-Broadway to The Street in 1978. Wesley is one of the best of the black playwrights; when he uses race or rage, it is as salients in his conception, not as ends in themselves because he has nothing but them to offer. He *earns* his raves, and on Broadway *The Last Street Play*, renamed *The Mighty Gents*, got them. But the work went out like a candle in the wind. No one bothered to see it.

One missed an evening of polished theatre. Using prototypal figures of the ghetto in northeastern America, Wesley develops characters and verbal images to express the hopelessness of growing older in an environment of fixed zero-growth. Pushing thirty, the gang known to glory as the Mighty Gents are now superannuated punks. What is their next move? Uneducated, unskilled at everything but crime, they can turn pimp or wino—so Wesley shows us in two symbolic characters, the gilded pimp Braxton and the cankerous wino Zeke. Wesley's hero takes a third road, leading his old gang in an assault on Braxton; this, of course, is "the last street play." And for those who are still debating the merits of "common-man" tragedy, this is one for the lists.

It is difficult to know why the public disdained *The Mighty Gents*, good notices and all. Even more difficult is it to know why the public fails to support an already established off-Broadway hit when it is moved to Broadway, which the public very merrily does; it's something of a public specialty. For every exception like *That Championship Season*, there are many more examples like that of David Mamet's *The Water Engine*, which came up from the Public Theatre in 1978 with cheers behind it and apathy, it turned out, ahead—apathy to drama that lacks some flamboyant do-something "visual" (such as the horses in *Equus*) or a *crise de conscience* that can translate into a Must See (such as the rest of *Equus*).

Like Shepard, Mamet is noted for his use of the American vernacular. He is a gifted parodist. His ear for the modern urban idiom distinguished the otherwise lackluster double bill *Duck Variations* (two old men chatting in park) and *Sexual Perversity in Chicago* (shifting partners among the unattached) in 1976, and he went on to set off fey actorese in *A Life in the Theatre* (1977), working-class inarticulateness in *American Buffalo* (1977), and media buoyancy in *Mr. Happiness* (1978). The plays themselves have been getting better, more exuberant, odder. *A Life in the Theatre*, while showing the rise of a younger actor against the leveling-off of an older colleague, balanced dressing-room and rehearsal scenes with pastiche spoofs of genre—no man's land, the lifeboat, the Chekhovian parlor; *American Buffalo* captured a wonderful gloom in its not-all-that-tragic picture of losers planning a theft that never comes off (much credit here to the cast, Kenneth McMillan, Robert Duvall, and John Savage). Oddest of all is *The Revenge of the Space Pandas; or, Binky Ruditch and the Two-Speed Clock* (1977), a wacky put-on in which two children and a pet sheep travel to the distant planet Crestview (asked why it's called Crestview, a panda explains, "Thought it might attract investors").

The Water Engine remains Mamet's most fully conceived piece, and is so tightly constructed that its complex plot does not occupy a full evening. On Broadway, *Mr. Happiness* served as a curtain-raiser: a man at a desk advises correspondents on their personal lives through an antique microphone. Here, Mamet's verbal mimicry is everything—the attitudes, the cultural loyalties, the canned airwave humanism ("We need. We love. We love too much. We love too little . . ."), all beautifully dated. Was it a spoof? The text is ambiguous on point-of-view, and Charles Kimbrough's performance was a tour de force of drab, remote humility. Stimulatingly inconclusive, *Mr. Happiness* proved an effective prelude to *The Water Engine*, whose texture of short, sudden scenes interlocked with verbal leitmotifs demands the utmost in alertness—one must remember everything, for only at the end does the disjunct textural mosaic settle into a complete picture.

The Water Engine is a radio play meant to be staged, dated, like *Mr. Happiness*, to the 1930s. Its premise is simple: an unknown genius who invents an engine that runs on water is captured by a mysterious consortium. Failing to pry his plans out of him, they kill him—but he has passed his secret on to a young boy through a chain letter. The staging is not simple: we see the radio players in operation, sometimes acting into the microphone, and sometimes "becoming" their assigned characters "at" the audience. Throughout, impersonal voices sound mottos, messages, descriptions of the chain letter: "The concrete poetry of Humankind." "All people are connected." "The wonder of the universe at last within our grasp." This is a painful play in that the evil is as real as the wonder—in the overheard jumble of neighbors, strangers, gangsters, and cranks, the inventor cannot elude the money bosses. But he can outwit them.

In praising these dramatists for their command of the native idioms, we should not fail to admire them for what, in the end, they can say through those idioms. This is the great event of the 1970s in the theatre: the penetration of language. Good dramatic writing, after years of punny con games, meaningless pauses, and slobbering poetry, is becoming the norm. Other authors of Mamet's age show a similar drive to make words work, and like him, Shepard, and Wilson, none of them belongs to Broadway. (Shepard is the classic instance of the freelancer, Wilson owes fealty to the Circle Rep, Mamet's base of operations is the St. Nicholas Theatre Company in Chicago.) Mark Medoff, who seems obsessed with manipulation and intimidation, achieved a hit in *When You Comin' Back, Red Ryder?* (1973), with its "nice people" bullied at gunpoint in a diner; the same year, the American Conservatory Theatre in San Francisco presented his more searching version of the same theme in *The Kramer*, about a loser whose marriage and career are smashed by a hot-shot Pygmalion. In both cases, Medoff proves the aggression through dialogue, and really strutted some stuff in *The Wager* (1974), consolidating his attack in the part of an insufferably brilliant college student who uses English scientifically, as a weapon to isolate emotion. Thomas Babe, who writes for Papp at the Public Theatre, excells more diversely: his *Rebel Women* (1976), concerning General Sherman's affair with a southern woman on his march to the sea, employed a delicate mannerism to suggest the period, while *A Prayer for My Daughter* (1977), dealing with cops and killers in a precinct house, found an unusual vernacular all its own, alluding to rather than falling into contemporary urban naturalism.

Of the younger writers, David Rabe, so far, seems the most palatable to Broadway, and remains the only prominent dramatist still working in the social guilt complexes of the 1960s. In this he is exceptional, for one sign of the new vitality is the public's lack of interest in pat moralizing, their refusal to be manipulated by sixties code words. But Rabe may be catching on: his so-called Vietnam trilogy—*The Basic Training of Pavlo Hummel* (1971), *Sticks and Bones* (1971), and *Streamers* (1976)—started off with dull anti-war and anti-American imprecations but ended, in *Streamers*, much more individually.

Rabe's were among the first of the Vietnam plays, with views of readiness and death (*Pavlo*), homecoming (*Sticks and Bones*), and waiting for overseas transport (*Streamers*). Though all three surfaced in non-Broadway houses, *Pavlo Hummel* was revived on Broadway (with Al Pacino) in 1977, *Sticks and Bones* was moved uptown from the Public Theatre, and *Streamers* played in Lincoln Center during Papp's tenure there—technically off-Broadway but patronized by the Broadway audience (and regarded by them as a distillation of their image of "Broadway" as status, professional éclat, and cultural edification). Rabe was, for a time, Papp's fair-haired boy; as such, trend claimed him as the latest post-Albee discovery. But he and Papp suffered an egregious setback when the latter inaugurated his regime at the Beaumont with the former's *Boom Boom Room* (1973), with Madeline Kahn as a go-go dancer in quest of self (and a script). But till then, bets were on Rabe as the next hot playwright. He came off as a lively Arthur Miller, especially in *Sticks and Bones,* a family play (Miller's genre of choice) so heavy with guilt it was like a shriving.

The guilt in question was that related to the Vietnam War, which edged white racism out of the spotlight for a while as the top-okay guilt in American drama. Made notorious when a proposed CBS television showing of the work aroused resistance from segments of the public, *Sticks and Bones* shows the return of a blinded veteran, David, to his American family: Father Ozzie, Mother Harriet, and brother Rickie—the four of them named after the Nelsons, a popular sitcom family of the early 1950s. Rabe's Nelsons are nothing like those of the tv show. Callous and vindictive, they gloat over their alienation from their own son and brother, and eventually arrange his suicide. Throughout, David's Vietnamese love, Zung, hovers around the parlor, visible only to him.

The public and most reviewers accepted *Sticks and Bones* as a fair reflection of America's hypocrisy and viciousness, but a few of the brighter critics smashed through vogue to voice irritation at the self-righteousness of Rabe's hero. A neater justice was unleashed some years later by Christopher Durang, younger than Rabe and possessed of a ferocious gift for satire. In *A American Tragedy,* later called *The Vietnamization of New Jersey* (1977), Durang shredded Rabe's pat set-up. Here, the returning David's Oriental beloved is named Liat (after the Tanganese girl in *South Pacific*), and the family turns up as Ozzie Ann, Harry, and Et. Another booth in the carnival of guilt is knocked over with the addition of a black maid, Hazel (after the cartoon and television character), who lectures the family on white overlordism. As in *Sticks and Bones,* David is blind—but where Rabe plays it for sanctimonious pathos, Durang has him walking into the refrigerator. Liat, too, is blind, and Et extrapolates their condition for us: "The fact that they're blind literally in a way points to the fact that we and the American people are blind figuratively. We suffer, I think, a moral and philosophical blindness."

Durang is a devil.* He has a bright future, but possibly not on Broadway. (*The Vietnamization of New Jersey* was a production of the Yale Rep.) Whatever he touches he uses for enlightenment, but that touch is a raw file. Theatre of anger and guilt we have been taught to "appreciate"—not theatre of absurd wit. In collaboration with Albert Innaurato, one of the few of this

---

* Durang performs as well as writes. With co-author (and wife) Sigourney Weaver, Durang presented a Weill-Brecht spoof, *Das Lusitania Songspiel* (1980).

generation to hold a stage on Broadway, with the likeable domestic farce *Gemini* (1977)—another piece that took the advantage of cheap late-night advertising rates on television and parlayed a minor success into a smash through a clever commercial—Durang reclaimed the old burlesque of Weber and Fields in another Yale premiere, *The Idiots Karamazov* (1974). This is a review of Dostoyefsky somehow involving Anaïs Nin, Djuna Barnes, the mother from *Long Day's Journey Into Night,* and the translator Constance Garnett (known to readers of Modern Library translations of Russian novels) as well as the characters from *The Brothers Karamazof.* Wonderful nonsense pervades: Garnett (Meryl Streep at Yale) first appears in a wheelchair with a doily on her head, introducing herself as the "eminent translatrix from the savage tongues—the Russian, the Lithuanian, the Polish, the Serbo-Croatian—into the hallowed language we are now speaking. French." Then, while Garnett looks on, floundering in her translation and free-associating, the action of Dostoyefsky's novel unfolds in exaggeration and repetition, fondling its own cul-de-sacs or striking off on new lunatic paths. Thus, when Father Zossima and his disciple Alyosha are meditating on life's rich pageant:

> ZOSSIMA: (*takes a jar from his picnic basket*) Do you know what these are, Alyosha?
> ALYOSHA: I believe they're peanuts, Father.
> ZOSSIMA: When Christ washed the feet of his apostles, he did it as an act of humility. Put out your hands.
> (*Alyosha puts forth his hands; Zossima pours peanuts into them.*)
> As an act of humility, I will eat from your hand, Alyosha.
> (*Bends down, eats from Alyosha's hands, looks up*)
> Peeeeeeeeeeeeeeeeeeeeeen-nuuuuuuuuuuuuuuuuuuuuts.
> Peeeeeeeeeeeeeeeeeeeeeeeen-nnuuuuuuuuuuuuuuuuuuuuuuuuuuuts.
> Do you understand, Aloyosha?
> ALYOSHA: I think so, Father.
> (*Zossima pours more peanuts into Alyosha's hands for the blackout.*)

At the conclusion, still wrestling with her translation, Garnett mingles allusions to Dickens, Joyce, Melville, the Bible, and conjugates "the verb Karamazov"—"Karamazov, Karamazas, Karamazat, Karamazamus . . ."—as the lights fade out.

Where *The Vietnamization of New Jersey* is a moralist's satire, *The Idiots Karamazov* is madhouse burlesque. Durang then attempted to combine the approaches in *A History of the American Film,* seen on Broadway in 1978 after productions at Hartford, Los Angeles, and Washington, D.C. It is one of the funniest plays ever staged, but its objective is hard to trace—

is it an exposure of the fantasy behind Hollywood's "realism"? an existential quest? or just a spoof? The work observes a structure, moving chronologically through our film heritage from *Intolerance* (the cradle "endlessly rocking") to *The Exorcist* (a woman screams the familiar obscenities and tries to turn her head around the way Linda Blair's seemed to), and taking James Cagney, Henry Fonda, Bette Davis, and Eve Arden through the clichés of genre—cops-and-robbers, screwball comedy, the western, the spectacular musical—and countless allusions to famous films. Juxtaposing his homages into a kind of history (he includes the HUAC hearings), Durang questions the phoney happiness of Hollywood's "The End" to push, repeatedly, for something more than a retrospective, and, at the conclusion, one is a little puzzled at what it's all supposed to mean. Still, as sheer comedy, *A History of the American Film* is vastly superior to what succeeds on Broadway, and its tiny run there reminds one sadly of George S. Kaufman's prediction about when satire closes.

This little tour through the present ranks is meant as a representative selection rather than a complete parade, for American theatregoing in the 1970s is as frustrating to write about as it is various to take part in—that very variety outreaches any but the most exhaustive analysis. This is an era of newcomers, it turns out, for the veterans did not hold up well, and revivals for the most part lacked power. True, many restagings were successful. An off-Broadway *Moonchildren* in 1973 finally found that play its audience, and Tennessee Williams' *A Streetcar Named Desire* and *Cat on a Hot Tin Roof* both reclaimed their status despite rather ordinary productions. But such popular entries as *Angel Street* and *The Women* foundered, and even O'Neill, always the core of the American repertory, remained beyond Broadway's grasp. Certainly, there was no dearth of interest in reattending *The Great God Brown*, *All God's Chillun Got Wings*, *A Touch of the Poet*, *A Moon for the Misbegotten*, and *Anna Christie*, the last three directed by José Quintero, Broadway's idea of the quintessential O'Neill director, with Jason Robards, Colleen Dewhurst, and Liv Ullmann heading his casts. Certainly. But these were not the totally first-rate stagings we should be getting of our most distinguished playwright. Of them all, only *A Moon For the Misbegotten*, strongly served by Dewhurst, Robards, and Ed Flanders, really held its own, incidentally putting the work itself over as one of interest for the first time in its history.

The older writers did not fare well at all. Tennessee Williams, so often accused of purveying the same scenes over and over, tried the unusual in *Out Cry* (1973), a two-character piece that seems to take place in an insane

asylum, but his characteristic blending of the tender and the sinister—
"Magic is the habit of our existence," the last line runs—did not fill out the
evening. Better and more conventional was an entry in outright autobiography, *Vieux Carré* (1977), recalling Williams' youth in a New Orleans
boarding house peopled by the Williams familiars—the sensual, spinstery
belle, the stud, the eccentric old battleaxe, and so on, sharing pitiful delusions in a hard-truth world. On paper, it sounds like a basic Williams work,
a kind of gloss on his canon, and it may one day assert itself in revival; the
original production was murdered by Arthur Allan Seidelman's abysmal
direction and the embarrassing amateurishness of Richard Alfieri in the
crucial role of Williams' alter ego, called "The Writer."

Other writers fared even less well. William Gibson, for whom great
things were foretold in the 1950s, saw his version of *Golda* (1977) shifting
in out-of-town rewrites into another sort of play altogether, and while bad,
even suspiciously hostile, reviews battled good word-of-mouth, Anne Bancroft—whose portrayal of the Israeli leader provided both the artistic and box-
office reasons for the project in the first place—took sick and the show
collapsed. But at least Gibson was still writing plays; Edward Albee very
nearly wasn't, though a harried Pulitzer committee, with nowhere else to
turn, handed the Prize to *Seascape* (1975), an unintentionally empty meeting between two humans and two lizards on the verge of evolutionary transformation. As late as 1977, *Who's Afraid of Virginia Woolf?* kept Albee
afloat as a Name, at least in the provinces: the Hartford Stage Company
mounted a double-bill of dreadfully pointless one-acts, *Counting the Ways*
and *Listening*, and even wangled Angela Lansbury and William Prince for
the leads.

The main reason for the neglect of new writers was that old devil economics, which was eventually to push ticket prices up to twenty dollars
(sometimes more) a ticket by the end of the decade. Compounding the
problem was Broadway's reliance on the theatre party (charity benefit houses
with notoriously unadventurous tastes in art) and the expense-account crowd,
often out-of-towners looking for flash. These two groups can easily assume
the financial burden of keeping theatre running—but what sort of theatre?

What hurt most was off-Broadway, once the natural home for new
writers, which had simply lost the ability to be cheap. In 1968, it cost $20,000
to stage *The Boys in the Band* (one simple set and nine actors, none at star
salary). Some ten years later its producer Charles Woodward estimated that
would cost $100,000 to do it all over again. With its erstwhile outlet for new
talent inflated away, the New York theatre community institutionalized a

procedure that had come into being during the little theatre days of the early 1900s: the showcase. This is an arrangement by which a play (usually a new one) is mounted on a shoestring budget for a twelve-performance-maximum run during which everybody works for nothing. Literally nothing—except the playwright gets a hearing and the actors and technical staff get exposure. Behind it all lies the not unreasonable hope that money people can be stirred to invest in the project, that some producer will option the play and transfer it, with the better of the original actors, to a lucrative run on union-contract terms. Since this does occasionally happen, and since if nothing else at least plays will be played and actors will act, the showcase caught on in a big way despite off-kilter locations and promotion based almost entirely on the mailing of flyers to friends. The showcase offers a beautiful instance of cooperation and trust in what is generally a crass and even vicious industry. But Actors Equity, which had celebrated the start of the 1970–71 season with an off-Broadway strike that lasted thirty-one days and was settled on the terms a cannibal might make with his dinner, decided to muscle in. That the showcase was made all the more necessary by the 1970 strike settlement was of no concern to Equity. In 1975, it proposed that its members be paid for their part in the showcasing of a play through a percentage of all future earnings of said play.

Playwright Charles Dizenzo made the prize rebuttal in a Swiftian editorial printed in the Sunday theatre pages of the New York *Times*. If actors are to earn an eternal percentage of a play's income for "showcasing" an author, argued Dizenzo, why not the reverse? Give the writer an eternal percentage of the incomes of the actors "showcased" in his play. "We playwrights also welcome another idea proposed by Actors Equity officials: actors who appear in an off-off-Broadway play should have the right to appear in subsequent commercial productions of that play. This seems fair: why should playwrights, directors, and producers have the right to recast a role with a better actor? Why should actors who are good in their roles be treated more favorably than those who are not?" Dizenzo suggested that an actor in a showcase be *forced* to appear in all subsequent productions of the play—"even if he can get a better role in a better play, even if he gets a . . . lead in a movie, even if he'd rather die."

Equity's proposal was squashed, and the showcase has thrived as off-Broadway's off-Broadway.* It is the freelance version of the *company*, the vacation from commercial pressure during which everyone works out of

---

* In 1980 Equity made another assault on the showcase, unresolved as of this writing.

dedication. The company is the archon of the 1970s: a major percentage of the great events of the decade originated in institutions rather than the free market, and for all our smug analysis of the failed "national theatres" in the past, from the New Theatre on up, most serious theatregoers are seeing the results of institutional work whether they know it or not.

For example, what may well be the outstanding play of the decade, Jason Miller's *That Championship Season* (1972), rode Broadway for two years, copping assorted huzzahs and awards of the sort usually reserved for the total upfront mainstream winner of The Street. But Miller's piece first reached the stage at the Public Theatre through a staged reading, a period of revision and rehearsal, and finally A. J. Antoon's famous production of five very different men welded into a resilient ensemble.

A canny indictment of the American teamwork myth, *That Champion-ship Season* takes the form of a reunion of high-school basketball heroes, four veterans of a legendary all-state champion lineup, at their old Coach's house. Miller described these men as "going into their middle age with a sense of terror and defeat . . . The only thing that holds them together is the memory of when they *were* together." As the liquor wears on, dissension grows, until at last it is clear that the celebrated cooperation of this team is a lie; each is rapaciously self-oriented down to the marrow, winner take all. But the Coach is a magician: he melted the original five into an unstoppable combination, and once again, in a bizarre finale, he melts the four survivors into an impregnable unit, ranks closed and nerves frozen in a chilling portrait of hypocritical fraternity.

In its realistic single set, "well-made" structure, and literal time scheme (three acts in a continual movement), *That Championship Season* viewed the strip-mined wasteland of northeastern Pennsylvania in the tradition of the rural debunkers Sherwood Anderson and Sinclair Lewis—their secret horror tales and backroad humor. The vantage is a city like Wilkes-Barre or Scranton, timeless places whose ancient ideals pop theatre would uphold as beautiful and cold-steel art exposes as useless. Miller shreds the camaraderie of these high-school supermen, shows their weaknesses of spirit and flesh. What champions!: one of them has made the wife of another his whore, a third is a confirmed alcoholic ("Do you have a drinking problem, Tom?" "No. No problem. I get all the booze I want"), and each desperately hates and needs the others in a "completion" of glorious youth under the guidance of a Coach like some patriarch out of the Old Testament.

Papp recalls that early on, when *That Championship Season* was tempo-rarily optioned for a Broadway production, Broadway thinking viewed the

Coach as a star part. But as Antoon ultimately staged it downtown, everybody stood out and nobody stood out—a perfect reading of Miller's thesis. His opinion on the lie of democratic concert—winners want to win, solo— was seconded by the Tony awards committee, who blithely nominated one of the cast, Paul Sorvino, for best actor (he lost to Alan Bates for *Butley*) and cited as best supporting actor John Lithgow of *The Changing Room*, another admirable ensemble effort. In truth, any one of Antoon's cast deserved a Tony, and Richard Dysart's tremendous Coach was every bit as special (within the context) as the excellent Sorvino.

But Broadway has never really liked the company idea; Broadway likes stars—the doer, not the deed. Another Public Theatre entry, the musical *A Chorus Line* (1975), depended on a giving, not taking, ensemble in its picture of dancers auditioning for the chorus. But *A Chorus Line* did prove the value of the team effort in composition, so novel in the 1960s, so—we thought—useless. The show was as much edited as written. Under Michael Bennett's direction, the cast improvised psychodrama vignettes on their pasts, on how they came to be dancers. Sifting through the live material, James Kirkwood and Nicholas Dante wrote a book, Edward Kleban the lyrics, Marvin Hamlisch the music. *A Chorus Line* is original, very much so—some of the actors were playing their own or each other's parts. Neorealism comes to the musical. The aura of autobiography proved so compelling that Bennett tacked on a real-life ending to *A Chorus Line*'s love plot by marrying his as-it-were leading lady Donna McKechnie.

The company nurtures art on a patient work-by-work basis. It doesn't just stage plays that commercial producers neglect—it also incubates them in an atelier-like atmosphere, trying them out in stages so the author can perfect his piece. A multi-spaced complex, like Papp's operation or the Manhattan Theatre Club, can afford to proceed on no particular program, picking from New York's acting population in each new audition. Most companies are more compact, with a relatively fixed personnel and the pressure to hand the sole stage over to an important piece every time. By far the most successful such group is the Circle Repertory Company, founded in 1969 by veterans of the café theatre scene, the germ of what was to evolve into the Equity showcase. Led by Marshall Mason as artistic director, Lanford Wilson as what might be called chief playwright, plus actors Tanya Berezin and Rob Thirkield, the Circle began as a workshop to unite the disparate "jobs" of theatre in the fundamental expressionism of live performance: acting. It was something like the Group Theatre in its centralized devotion to thespian rituals, but unlike the Group the Circle did not limit itself to one kind of script. The Circle would do anything worth doing, new or old, and besides maintaining an astonishingly high standard of performance, it also produced more worthwhile scripts than any other comparably sized institution, new or old. Its list of graduates included *The Hot l Baltimore, When You Comin' Back, Red Rider?, Gemini, Knock Knock, Fifth of July,* and its style takes in timely commentary in Albert Innaurato's *Ulysses in Traction* (1977), in which college students and teachers rehearse a play while a ghetto riot explodes outside the building; timeless psychology of friendship and violence among males in Patrick Meyers' *Feedlot* (1977); a simple two-character romance in Edward J. Moore's *The Sea Horse* (1974), beautifully played in its premiere by Conchata Ferrell and the author; *Hamlet* and Schiller's *Mary Stuart* in repertory; and even a musical, *Unsung Cole* (1977), a delightful retrospective of little-known Porter.

In the commercial arena, producers, reviewers, and to a great extent actors, backers, and public tend to think in terms of success or failure; at the Circle, Lanford Wilson once wrote, "the emphasis is on *process.*" There are acting classes, movement classes, readings, twentieth drafts. "We tend to push each other off diving boards." Mason has enriched the American repertory, in ten years, far more than many of Broadway's producers did in their whole lives; but more: he is concerned with the *condition* of performance as the first principle of creation. Wilson recalls writing a short piece for the company to flex character in (the germ, by the way, of *The Hot l Baltimore*): "Conchata Ferrell had marvelous concentration playing the cook in Strindberg's *The Ghost Sonata* and her strength was amazing, but could she be funny? Stephanie Gordon was beautifully elegant, but how would she handle playing a trashy tart?" This was the hope of the seventies: that whatever happened on Broadway, the company idea would nurture new art in dedication to exclusively artistic ideals, letting such variables as commercial success, ideological slant, and community engagement happen as they naturally might happen. The Circle is neither fancy, nor crazy, nor voguish. It lacks the grandeur of Lincoln Center, the screwy rococo of La MaMa, the media coverage of the Public. Yet its "relevance"—because it is not strident but eloquent—far outweighs theirs.

Broadway, by comparison, went slack at first, bolstering its output with British Must Sees, would-be splashy musicals, and stale joke-fests. In every genre, the British seemed to cop the palm—the thriller (*Sleuth*), naturalism (*The Changing Room*), godotism (*Home*), literate comedy (*Travesties*), and farce (*Scapino*, the Young Vic transformation of Molière's *Les Fourberies de Scapin*). This was especially galling in the case of a pop genre like mystery or farce: could American talent not even get *that* much up? Chillers flopped regularly in the early 1970s, with the exception of Robert Marrasco's psychological view into violence in a boy's school, *Child's Play* (1970), and farce languished in such busy but leaden identities as Murray Schisgal's *All Over Town* (1974) and Terrence McNally's *The Ritz* (1975). Schisgal's piece observed the rituals, with slamming doors and screwball episodes; McNally's play sought novelty by imagining the participants in a Mafioso feud holed up in a gay bathhouse. That's one Feydeau never thought of, anyway. But nothing that McNally wrote was as funny as Rita Moreno's personal shtick as Googie Gomez, an ambitious Puerto Rican singer who mistakes the bathhouse clients for, flirtatiously, producers or, violently, minor villains out of her past.

In the musical, this was the decade of revivals, mostly of the less important shows—indeed, their very triviality seemed to be their attraction. Though *Porgy and Bess, Gypsy,* and *The King and I* all reaffirmed their greatness, the general run of things spotlighted works like *No, No, Nanette, Good News, Whoopee,* and *Tip-Toes,* the last two (and others) transferred from the Goodspeed Opera House in Connecticut. This was also the time when producers began to give up on their attempt, launched in the 1960s, to market rock in the musical. Heavy-metal and folk rock did not adapt well to a narrative context, for one thing, and even the more plastic middle-of-the-road sound did not appeal to the theatregoing public except as a novelty. The solution—a blending of rock with diverse other soundscapes from Mozart to ragtime—produced a few hits, such as *Two Gentlemen of Verona* (1971) and the British *Jesus Christ Superstar* (1971), but many flops. One should note that a few scores came through in pure style: *The Wiz* (1975), a black version of L. Frank Baum's *The Wonderful Wizard of Oz,* remained faithful to Motown, and *Grease* (1972), a spoof of the 1950s, re-created antique rock and roll to the last falsetto riff. But the biggest hits were those shows with more traditional scores—the modern-edged *A Chorus Line* and the frankly derivative *Annie* (1977). By the end of the decade, the rock musical was no longer a working issue, and when Andrew Lloyd Webber and Tim Rice, the authors of *Jesus Christ Superstar,* returned to Broadway, it was via the eclectically non-rock *Evita* (1979).

Comedy on Broadway was dominated by the continued popularity of Neil Simon, up to old tricks in *The Sunshine Boys* (1972) and *California Suite* (1976). A touch of sorrow enriched *The Gingerbread Lady* (1970), in which Maureen Stapleton played a faded cabaret singer trying to overcome weaknesses for sex and the bottle, but still the characters all reached for the same gags in the same voice, and there wasn't the slightest suggestion in Simon's script or the production that Stapleton knew a piano from a wok. But Simon clearly was reaching for something, as if, having captured a public for his jokes, he could now capitalize some real drama on their absolutely guaranteed interest. But when he got serious, they sometimes balked; having learned the gags, they wanted nothing but gags. *God's Favorite* (1974), a retelling of the Book of Job, did not go down well, and they spurned also *The Good Doctor* (1973). Easily Simon's best effort, this collection of sketches adapted from Anton Chekhof's stories had an offbeat charm that peaked in "The Drowned Man," in which a derelict offers to entertain a man with an extemporized drowning for three rubles. Horrified, the man complains to a policeman, who says, "Three rubles? What nerve! . . . Why, the other day, right over there, fourteen men acted an entire *shipwreck* for three rubles . . . Yes sir, three kopecks, that's all *I'd* pay for a good drowning." *The Good Doctor* had tenderness, too, as when a father took his nineteen-year-old son to a prostitute for his first sexual adventure. The son is shy and naive. "My God," roars his father, "don't you ever discuss these matters with your young friends?" "Oh yes, all the time," is the reply. "But we get too excited to listen." Just as the boy is about to climb the stairs, his father realizes that his son will descend them a man—will abandon him— and wheedles him out of it: "Plenty of time next year." (*The Good Doctor* was filmed for Public Television, unfortunately in a heavy-handed production inferior to A. J. Antoon's Broadway staging with Christopher Plummer, Barnard Hughes, René Auberjonois, Frances Sternhagen, and Marsha Mason.) A satirical edge has been creeping into Simon's work, giving the gags bite, as in one of *California Suite*'s characters' description of an East Hampton party to benefit striking California farm workers: "There was this teeming mob of women who must have spent a total of twelve thousand dollars on new Gucci pants in order to raise two thousand dollars for the grape pickers . . . Why the hell didn't they just mail in the pants?" A year later, Simon made his following listen to a real play with real people, in the semi-autobiographical *Chapter Two* (1977), the comedy worked in organically rather than plastered on. The 1980s might well be Simon's great decade.

With semi-satire in disrepair, domestic and sex comedy took the lead. Jean Kerr followed up on the further adventures of her archetypes, now quiescent in marriage, in *Finishing Touches* (1973), Barbara bel Geddes now paired with Robert Lansing instead of Barry Nelson. Kerr branched into adultery this trip, but protocol demanded that her people patch it up. The two-principal sex comedy, too, remains conventional, though authors are expected to turn their pieces out in a little novelty. Thus, Bob Randall's *6 Rms Riv Vu* (1972) locked Jane Alexander and Jerry Ohrbach in an apartment to let ("six rooms; river view"), where they met, loved, and parted, being already married elsewhere. Bernard Slade's *Same Time, Next Year* (1975) posed Ellen Burstyn and Charles Grodin as two adulterers who meet at a motel for a yearly fling, seen in the light of changing mores at five-year intervals from 1951 to 1975.

Broadway is the place where comedy reassures, off-Broadway where it threatens. Typical of the latter, then, is John Guare, whose little-known short plays earned him a citation as Most Promising Playwright in *Variety* as the decade began. Then came *The House of Blue Leaves* (1971), with its farcical treatment of anguish, insanity, and murder, the essential Guare. So far, though, he has continued to promise, not building enough of a structure around his assassinations in whimsy. In *Rich and Famous* (1976), he derived much entertainment out of the opening night of a young playwright's first grand opus (Dante, "with a few songs"), piling on the disasters in a succession of vignettes by Anita Gillette and Ron Leibman as, more or less, everybody in the playwright's life, including his characters. But the playwright remained a cartoon and the play absurdist cardboard. Similarly, *The Landscape of the Body* (1977) confused and irritated with its unnecessary mysteries; yet, under this investigation of murder that uncovers a series of murders, all interconnected, there is an original and enticing work of theatre. Guare is a sharp burlesque for sure, but so far only the extremely funny *House of Blue Leaves* and his relaxed and silly lyrics for the *Two Gentlemen of Verona* musical have managed to please the public.

Topically, the 1970s showed not so much new passions as new depth in treating old ones, a willingness to show the sides of an issue—with an "interest," as the British say—rather than to proselytize on a fanatic's bias. One new topic there was, though: woman. Playwrights of both sexes, from committed feminists to curious storytellers, carried the national dialogue on women's rights to the stage with an admirable grace, examining various aspects of the question with moral vigor or high spirits but mainly without the fury that marred other movements in their theatrical transformations. True, off-Broadway pulled off its accustomed militancy in a number of propagandistic pieces whitewashing the career of Emma Goldman—but these disappeared almost as fast as they were mounted. A woman hero did not have to be a terrorist, not in the 1970s. Sympathetic portraits of women attempting to redefine their condition found them as variously as, on one hand, black women in Ntozake Shange's *For Colored Girls Who Have Considered*

Suicide/When the Rainbow Is Enuf (1976), or on another, a politician in a pop piece of interest only for Colleen Dewhurst's performance, *An Almost Perfect Person* (1977).

One of the best of these plays about women accidentally straddled the decade in that its premiere in 1971 was a fast flop but a revival in 1979 briefly found it a public. This was Oliver Hailey's *Father's Day*, a look at what happens to divorced women. There are three of them, plus their ex-husbands—and all the women, it seems, are suffering some version of loneliness while the men have been able to pull their lives together again. And Hailey suggests that, as society stands, this is foreordained: divorce favors the men. It's a very, very funny play, because one of the women flashes that hostile wit that Clare Boothe Luce made popular; but it's a sad play, for this woman more than the others has not been able to come to terms with her husband's rejection. She begs him to return to her. He refuses: she is too damn hard to live with. And he tells her:

> A man who lived next door to us in Cincinnati when I was a kid was arrested for raping a teenager. His wife divorced him. But you know what all the neighbors asked? What was wrong with *Mrs.* Berger, that *Mr.* Berger had to go out and rape a teenager? That's the way it is, honey— Cincinnati, New York, Sioux City—the man wins, the woman loses. That's divorce. That's what's bugging the hell out of you. Because you know they're all wondering what's wrong with you—that you couldn't hold on to me.

Gay drama made slower headway on Broadway, especially as compared to the lively (if flawed) off-Broadway gay stage. John Hopkins' *Find Your Way Home* (1974), a dull British import, ran on the strength of fine work from Michael Moriarty and Jane Alexander. In major work on or off Broadway, gay characters seemed more natural in non-gay plays such as Thomas Babe's *Rebel Women*, Lanford Wilson's *Fifth of July*, or Michael Cristofer's *The Shadow Box* than in plays of specifically gay import. A flurry of "Am I or aren't I?" themes, as in David Rabe's *Streamers* and Albert Innaurato's *Gemini*, tended to obfuscate more than clarify.

On the other hand, rip-off burlesques of the gay theme did not go over well on Broadway. Ron Clark and Sam Bobrick's *Norman, Is That You?* (1970) and Richard T. Johnson and Daniel Hollywood's *All the Girls Came Out To Play* (1972), popular in dinner theatres for their hokey depiction of heterosexuals' bewilderment at homosexuality, utterly bombed—*Norman* even with Lou Jacobi and Maureen Stapleton as gay Norman's parents.

Oddly, this frivolous piece attempted some serious lecture on tolerance, both for Norman's sexuality and his mother's own gathering feminism. But perhaps the most important statement on the whole issue cropped up, in passing, in Terrence McNally's otherwise non-ideological *The Ritz*, spoken by one of the bathhouse patrons:

> I'll tell you something about straight people, and sometimes I think it's the only thing worth knowing about them. They don't like gays. They never have. They never will. Anything else they say is just talk.

The American play (first presented in London) that may prove through its popularity to have made a breakthrough for gay drama on Broadway was Martin Sherman's *Bent* (1979), a second-rate piece—two pieces, really. The first act, picturing the implication, flight, and apprehension of two gay men in Nazi Germany, is a black-comic thriller. The sedentary second act is a protest piece set in a death camp, where the survivor of the pair, an apolitical con man, suffers his first real love affair, non-physically, with a fellow prisoner and dies reveling in what he is rather than attempt to survive in disguise.

Bent is serious, for all its jokes, and was treated respectfully, partly because movie actor Richard Gere played the lead. Theatregoers found it moving, though some reviewers were clearly annoyed that the subject was coming out proudly on Broadway; they prefer tragedies of self-hating, not self-affirming, gays. But while *Bent* presented the Nazi troopers that *The Diary of Anne Frank* did not, it too sentimentalized rather than shocked. Director Robert Allan Ackerman should have studied the Living Theatre's film of their production of *The Brig* and newsreels of what concentration camp inmates looked like; his storm troopers sneered and murdered, but their brutality was ludicrously phoney, and his two principles, Gere and David Dukes, seemed more like victims of a bus-and-truck tour of *The Last Mile* than of the dehumanization of the Nazi death camp. Gere and Dukes were insufficient in heroic roles and most of their colleagues execrable. Two superb performances kept *Bent* intermittently alive, both one-scene bits in the first act: that of Michael Gross as a heterosexual drag entertainer, and that of George Hall as a closeted older gay. Hall played his entire part wrapped in an overcoat, sitting on a bench, and speaking in an undertone; to stand out for so slight a role in a play rich in campies and sadists says as much against Ackerman's flimsiness as for Hall's talent. How can an author lecture the disguised on honesty when his production team is afraid to present his material with convincing realism?

Blacks, a veteran minority by now, had found their emancipation in a black theatre that had learned to take or leave Whitey—and about time, too. There were a few holdouts. Ed Bullins seemed unable to let go of the 1960s in *The Taking of Miss Janie* (1975), one of the last expressions of the old militant's dream of raping white women as a "political act"; worse yet, Bullins' black idiom, though he comes by it naturally, is forced and dull. An ugly episode of a different nature occurred when James Earl Jones appeared in Philip Hayes Dean's one-man play *Paul Robeson* (1978). Just before the work was to open, fifty-six prominent black leaders, including Alvin Ailey, James Baldwin, Julian Bond, and Charles B. Rangel, put their names to a protest in *Variety*, denouncing the play as "a pernicious perversion of the essence of Paul Robeson." Such prior censorship was unique in theatre history, comparable only to the government's attempted closing of *The Cradle Will Rock* in the rocky late days of the Federal Theatre. But in this case it was a group of private individuals who were attempting to close *Paul Robeson*—and under the courageously persistent probing of NBC News' Carl Stokes, it turned out that many of the signers had neither seen nor read the play, and that the real reason for the protest was the rumor (correct) that Dean's script did not deal with Robeson's socialist politics.

Bullins' overpraised work and the *Paul Robeson* controversy, however, were exceptional; in the main, minority group theatre was no longer being patronized by the establishment or manipulated by insiders for propaganda. Minority theatre was going its own way, finding its forms, its materials, its acting pool. Thus, the emergence of a possible first smash hit Mexican-American piece, Luis Valdez' *Zoot Suit* (1979), came to Broadway from a highly successful premiere at Los Angeles' Mark Taper Forum with attendant curiosity but no extra-credit for a race quota. Indeed, it may be that New York reviewers undervalued the piece, a colorful combination of fantasy and documentation on the tense relationship between the Chicanos and almost everyone else in Los Angeles during World War II.

But if drama in general became less severely topical and more humanistic —more turned on to powerful theatre than to vogue-approved agitprop—the political front held to its oath, emphasizing the documentary in such works as *Inquest* (1970), *The Trial of the Catonsville Nine* (1971), *Pueblo* (1971), and *Are You Now Or Have You Ever Been* (1972), all four forms of courtroom drama. The 1960s had developed a phantasmagorically physical stage with incomplete but often mind-bending mime and acrobatics; all that, suddenly, was gone, leaving a host of cheerless zealots of the left, churning out scripts like students fulfilling term projects—some of them, as so often before, doing a certain amount of cheating.

Thus, Donald Freed's *Inquest* (1970), drawn from the Rosenberg trial of 1951, subtitled "a tale of political terror" and purporting to comprise "documented quotation from trial manuscripts and original sources or a reconstruction from actual events," puts a lot of opinion into that "reconstruction." For Freed, the defendants were saints and the prosecution utter devils, and he ignores anything in the record that might mitigate this view, sentimentalizing and simplifying to the point of misrepresentation. How much more effective a documentary was Stanley R. Greenberg's *Pueblo*, honestly reportive and—despite the playwright's sympathy for Commander Lloyd Bucher—deliberately inconclusive, letting the public take its own reading of the case. But *Pueblo* is exceptional in this genre. Since Maxwell Anderson and Harold Hickerson's *Gods of the Lightning*, the purpose of the documentary has been to exhort the public on the question of responsibility, though for *Are You Now or Have You Ever Been*, on the HUAC hearings of the McCarthy years, Eric Bentley simply edited transcripts of the proceedings: the defendants were colorful and eloquent enough to need no arranging. The most popular of this quartet, and the most interesting as theatre, was *The Trial of the Catonsville Nine*, written by one of the Nine, Daniel Berrigan (assisted in a revision by Saul Levitt). Here the exhortation came not out of manipulation of the facts, but out of the defendants' articulate explanation of their action, the seizing and burning of draft records in Catonsville, Maryland, in 1968 to impede the machine of war. It was the fairest form of documentary possible: the truth. The facts were not in doubt at the trial—responsibility was. Not for "the burning of paper instead of children," but for the prosecution of the war and the standing by and having no opinion. The court ruled that this responsibility was not in question, but by taking the case out of the real-life courtroom into its facsimile on stage, Berrigan could restate his questions on guilt to a receptive audience. In its ecstatic, precise moral lines and arguments for fairness, *The Trial of the Catonsville Nine* was a very seventies play (albeit about a very sixties event), and made the rounds of the national theatres throughout the decade.

Indeed, the Vietnam War, unlike previous wars, fired many playwrights to action long before it was over, and continues to do so as the decade ends —another instance of the high level of responsibility the theatre showed in this time. In fact, it is a little unnerving to note how little the *me*ism of the decade affected the stage. For this reason: the culture cannot *use* the theatre as it once could, can't count on it for that old-time beauty of popular flattery. True, Broadway is hardly the center of a full-time operation in adversary dramatics—but then, to paraphrase Mrs. Fiske, Broadway's just a stand. Any discussion of American theatre today takes in the Mark Taper Forum, the Circle Rep, the Manhattan Theatre Club, the Dallas Theatre Center, and La MaMa far more than it does Broadway, and for the obvious reason: they're doing it, and Broadway's reviewing it. 1975 marked a new low in New York, with the sudden collapse of Joseph Papp's idealistic season of new American plays at Broadway's Booth Theatre, with *Seascape* taking the lead in new drama by default, and with Robert Wilson's tiresome, static pageant *A Letter for Queen Victoria* passing itself off as the hot new experiment in theatre. The single best play and best musical both dated back to 1927: the revival of *The Royal Family*, and John Kander, Fred Ebb, and Bob Fosse's adaptation of Maurine Watkins' *Chicago*, drawing on pop tune tropes —from Bert Williams' lamentations to the Jerome Kern "look for the silver lining" ditties—to explode the simplistic façade of pop culture.

A very slight change in the air of 1976 suggested an upswing, however. Though if anything the profit margin fell even further, those who moved fast enough to catch everything before it closed had a real adventure in store. And not everything that failed commercially vanished overnight: one of the few worthy Bicentennial events, *Pacific Overtures*, demonstrated the inevitability of history in the story of the Western rediscovery of Japan, delivered in a cross between the American musical and the Kabuki theatre. With book by John Weidman and score by Stephen Sondheim, a thrilling production and a brilliant, basically all-male cast, the show bewildered the unadventurous and suffered a terrible word-of-mouth, yet held out for half a year. If the idiot rock musical was still vainly attempting to prove its utility—*Rockabye Hamlet* was the latest disaster—this was also the year that New York saw its first major staging of the Brecht-Weill classic *The Three-penny Opera* since the "Lotte Lenya" production of the mid-fifties. (This new one, at Papp's Lincoln Center, claimed that its tone and translation were far more authentic than the somewhat *gemütlich* Lenya show. Actually, as staged by Richard Foreman, Papp's *Threepenny Opera* was more authentically Foreman than Brecht. The point is not who's more Brechtian, but that a masterpiece was available in a stimulating production.)

In drama, two foreign plays, *Ashes* and *Comedians*, and David Rabe's *Streamers* held the forefront, and though this may seem like short weight, the three plays as a group were so different and provocative that to see them all was to experience a kind of season in itself. Too, the talk of a next generation of writers was beginning to settle into prolonged discussion of the development of their styles: Ribman and Horowitz on, respectively, prison and night school in *The Poison Tree* and *The Primary English Class*; Durang, Babe, Shange, Jones, Mamet, and others were produced. More and more, one heard of showcase productions prompting other, more visible productions. One noted with relief that the stage had learned to exploit the television commercial, starting with *The Wiz'* bright little cameo spot, repeated with wicked insistence, of "Ease on Down the Road." One noticed a cheering new back-and-forth between the stage and screen in the acting ranks, badly isolated in the 1960s. Even Broadway comedy, stolidly gag-stuffed for so long, showed an interest in the anarchic farce that once abstracted the native energy and gave rise to such vital modes as Marx Brothers free-for-all and screwball comedy. Two shameless items led the field, Jules Feiffer's *Knock Knock* (which surfaced at the Circle Rep and was moved to Broadway) and Larry Gelbart's *Sly Fox*. This is an odd pairing, one a product of the satiric adversary stage and the other a frankly commercial piece based, very loosely, on Ben Jonson's *Volpone*. But they have much in common. Feiffer's play, too, pays homage to a classic, Beckett's *Waiting for Godot*, and—more importantly —*Knock Knock* and *Sly Fox* both juggle the corny and the brilliant in a comic sweepstakes, a hit-or-miss hysteria. *Knock Knock* had a theme—the urge to action—while *Sly Fox* merely told a sloppy story; but the real joy of both was the extravagant verbal play. Feiffer's word games, tossed around the arrival of Joan of Arc at the isolated domicile of two Schlemiels, share an inspired lunacy with physical games: magical transformations, wishes come true, mayhem, and assorted slapstick. Gelbart's less inventive script depends on bravura type-playing—in Arthur Penn's unruly Broadway staging, George C. Scott's gloating con man, Jack Gilford's senescent miser, Gretchen Wyler's avid tart, Hector Elizondo's abject con man's assistant, and so on. It's ancient, but not tired, as when tart visits miser, supposedly to pawn her baubles, but actually to seduce him. Slowly, she pulls a medallion out of her bosom, urging him to "take a *good* look":

CROUCH: You've got some nice things.
MISS FANCY: Thank you. And what about the jewelry?

That *Sly Fox* was a huge hit and *Knock Knock* did not do well should not depress us: it is a given nowadays that good theatre does not necessarily run long, but does run—and perhaps *Knock Knock* will eventually establish itself in the national repertory as Feiffer's funniest and most provocative play. New York's just a stand.

It had become a grand one by 1977, however, bulging with work: Neil Simon and Charles Ludlum, O'Neill, Molière, and Wedekind, interesting work by Ribman, Mamet, Innaurato, Babe, and Patrick Meyers, and, for once, very little overshadowing by foreigners: Simon Gray's *Otherwise Engaged* (the trials of an almost imperturbable man) and Arnold Wesker's *The Merchant* (a sympathetic look at some of the characters of *The Merchant Of Venice*) hardly represented these two writers at their best, and *The Merchant*'s production, staged for Broadway with an American cast by a *British* team, was a disaster. From another country, Brazil, Roberto Athayde's *Miss Margarida's Way* gave the great Estelle Parsons a dream of a showcase as a viciously authoritarian eighth-grade schoolteacher, the audience her class. Naughty children, she assured them, are sent to the principal's office and never return—but this stylization of fascism couldn't faze Americans, who happily razzed Parsons. (At least, they did downtown at the Public Theatre; when the piece was moved to The Street, spectators were more reserved.)

Another acting triumph came along in a first play by D.L. Coburn, *The Gin Game*, for two players only, and very complete ones: Hume Cronyn, progressively losing control as he blows hand after hand, and Jessica Tandy, reluctant to set off his temper but more reluctant to lose. The town responded to a fine play, stingy with plot to delve into character, typically introduced elsewhere (Hollywood, Louisville, and New Haven) before settling in for a handsome run; to a new writer; and to the thrilling performances by the Cronyns—who, everyone suddenly realized, were riding the crest of two formidable careers too often submerged in second-rate material. Another young writer, the actor Michael Cristofer, emerged with a unique victory: a Broadway hit about the terminally ill, *The Shadow Box*. "Sensitive" and "depressing" become synonyms in discussing a play of this kind—admirers use the former, detractors the latter, and both mean that the author has brought his subject home. He employs three patients—a middle-aged family man, an aged, deluded woman, and a gay intellectual—seen in the context of their domestic situations, and draws out of the dying and the survivors their views on life. Odd that such material should prove so life-affirming.

Affirmation seemed the keynote of the time, where the previous decade had felt destructive or at least amorally burlesque. The public was willing to tolerate and even support such events as *For Colored Girls* . . . , with its touches of man-hating vindictiveness, especially because Oz Scott had staged the piece with a gala abandon. But non-partisan commentators saved their most engaged praise for Marsha W. Norman's *Getting Out*, another but very different view from the woman's side of things. *Getting Out* demonstrated the growing influence of the national stage as initiator: it premiered in Louisville in 1977, traveled to the Mark Taper Forum the next year, and was already being talked about before it finally reached New York, at the Theatre de Lys, in 1979. Norman's play is really outstanding, an investigation of a rehabilitated convict's return to the society. We meet the protagonist as two characters: Arlie, her former violent self, and Arlene, in time present. The two converse, argue, sustain each other, illuminating Arlie's hostility as well as Arlene's painful regeneration—yet there is no socio-emotional blackmail of the audience. Presumably, some of the spectators might leave the theatre hoping they never cross paths with an Arlene; others might alter their views on criminal punishment. But Norman has done her job, filling out her tale with the insight into character and sympathetic fairness we expect of an adult theatre. The 1970s thus provided a consolidation of sixties upheaval: the retention of Issues but the addition of wisdom.

The theatre of the late 1970s so resisted the "me" dynamics of the decade that most media-based campaigns to invent stars were not taken seriously; in fact, making one's own just stardom without the use of movies or television was much harder now than ever before. One could still capitalize on a live appearance to bolster one's cinema legend, yes: but one had to put out, as when Liza Minnelli attempted to shore up a reputation sagging in unattractive films with exhausting stints in musicals, first taking over Gwen Verdon's part in *Chicago* for six weeks and then carrying, virtually by herself, an obnoxious *Chorus-Line*-like biography called *The Act* (1977).

Minnelli was an established star giving back to Broadway's reflected glory far more than she took out, not least in the fact that *Chicago* was failing at the box office and, but for her intervention, would have died early in its run. Other thespians, not yet well established, found the rug slipping out from under them when the publicity mill ground too soon or for the undeserving. Paul Rudd, an actor of severely limited gifts, seemed to be enjoying a vogue when New York's spiffier off-Broadway companies featured him in classic roles from Shakespeare to George Kelly, but Rudd's lack of training could not even get him through contemporary work, let alone the great roles, and even the slower critics looked on askance. Similarly, Joseph Papp attempted to build a following for the composer Elizabeth Swados, using her thinly atmospheric incidental scores as if he had found a new Mozart, and producing with a flourish her amateurish musical revue of angry children, *Runaways* (1978), as if it were a second *Chorus Line*. Surfeited with Swados, New Yorkers neglected her just when she finally earned the right to an all-around hearing, in a flawed but provocative adaptation of Michael Herr's Vietnam impressions ("reportage" doesn't do his prose justice), *Dispatches* (1979). "Stars" weren't being made anymore, not in the theatre; they had to prove themselves. The challenge was not unlike the eye of a needle: even Meryl Streep, whose spectacular technique enables her to span the broadest range of character, knocked around in part after part to, it seemed, the acclaim of the informed few. Not till she turned up in two startlingly dissimilar roles in the films *The Deer Hunter* and *Manhattan* did she achieve the fame she deserves.

Fame has always been a tricky proposition in the theatre. The unshakeable fidelity of a following that adored a Mrs. Fiske or a James O'Neill with little reference to the quality of the plays they performed in dissolved in the 1920s as cinema began to monopolize beauty as the stage began to de-emphasize it. Increasingly thereafter, and never more so than in the 1970s, one never knew how the public might take to their supposed favorites. Moving on to 1978, we find the customers spurning Mary Martin's return to Broadway (with Anthony Quayle) in a two-person Russian comedy, *Do You Turn Somersaults?*, even as they rallied for Henry Fonda (with Jane Alexander) in *First Monday in October* and Jack Lemmon in *Tribute*. And as Fitzgerald, Faulkner, and Bellow learned, a literary reputation means nothing to theatregoers: E. L. Doctorow's *Drinks Before Dinner*, in which a suave dinner party is taken over at gunpoint by one of the guests, won no head start through *Ragtime*—reviewers and public alike judged the play on its merits, and found few. In an interview, Doctorow blamed the failure on the audience's inability to go with the script's "relentlessly verbal" effect, a euphemistic phrase that translates roughly as "ideological and motionless."

In general, 1978 did not sustain 1977's stir of sudden quality in new works and production, but the momentum of the showcase potential kept the theatre world, artists and audience, in a state of curiosity not known since the 1930s. In a mere two or three years, a tired gallery of tableaus and cartoons had been renovated and rehung with contemporary art, and if *Variety* parses the theatre seasons as so many dollars earned, the average theatregoer made a very different sort of assessment: there was an awful lot of good, serious drama. The big foreign hit of 1978, Hugh Leonard's *"Da,"* was a sentimental memoir rather than the once typical Pinter, Gray, or Stoppard, but the big American hit—if only in terms of prestige—was, at long last, a piece by the till now nonchalantly underground Sam Shepard, *Buried Child*. Those reviewers who had been hoping that Shepard would get around to probing the sinister American mythology he often just invokes were disappointed, but that's their problem; the writing was even more finished and enticing than usual for Shepard, the action—another of his washed-out family groupings fringed with violence—as entertaining as anything he has done, and Robert Woodruff's off-Broadway production (similar to that of the San Francisco premiere) what the Italians would call "correct" Shepard. The Pulitzer people, acceding to the inevitable, handed Shepard their Prize, and now the underground, too, had become official.

The musical was doing badly, however. All sorts of things, from homey revivals of silly old romps to determinedly commercial attractions to exciting defeats of convention, fell by the wayside, including 1978's two most intriguing shows—*Working*, a highly collaborative effort on the ecumenism of The Job, and *On The Twentieth Century*, a farce trilling Cy Coleman's finely turned operatic parodies. As 1979 came in and the periodic Stephen Sondheim-Hal Prince show was announced, one sensed a vast doom in store at the box office, but their nasty opera *Sweeney Todd* somehow won an audience despite a misanthropic worldview and some gruesome depictions of rape, throat-cutting, and cannibalism. Adapted from British playwright Christopher Bond's Marxist reading of a bit of folklore about a mass murderer, *Sweeney Todd* melds ideological apocalypse—"We all deserve to die"—on a revenge plot, derving all its thematic data from personal tragedy rather than propaganda. It's an amazing work, with its romantically dark hero paired with a comic sidekick right out of music hall (amazing performances, too, from Len Cariou and Angela Lansbury), and one wonders if the turbulent 1960s could have hosted a piece whose pessimism and protagonism break the most basic rules of "socialist realism."

The 1960s, like certain earlier decades, suffered a kind of vogue—several kinds, really—that both informed and blinded it; the 1970s swing free. The theatre has gathered several ancient awarenesses—those of the star turn, whether as debut, comeback, or simple survival; of flamboyant staging technique; of realism not as a genre but a means toward honesty; of adjustment to economics—with a new one: no rules, no allegiance to faction. The economic adjustment, for example, might have meant the callous neglect of low-paying drama in favor of splash and fadoodle; instead, after several seasons of seeing the serious play become almost extinct on Broadway, theatre people learned how to use the showcase as a tryout, "conducting" drama into port much as O'Neill was first led uptown after establishing himself in the Village.

E.L. Doctorow has accused the public of resisting the theatre of ideas, and this is somewhat true: the 1960s showed us what an American theatre of ideas is—erratic, angry, even irrelevant. We may never raise up an American Brecht: we may not want to. The stage today is mature, literate, and stimulating, but it might be called a theatre of persons as opposed to ideas. Playwrights aren't telling so much anymore; they're showing. In this, they are more like O'Neill and Kaufman than like Anderson and Behrman—they show what certain people do and maybe even how they think, but don't use their people as springboards for an opinion. It's a very human business, suddenly, human in the scope of writers as well as the appeal of the live personalities leased to them for the purposes of performance. (And at that, the appeal of the acting personality is muted, which is why the big stars who once toured the nation in plays have been replaced by movie and television stars.)

A theatre that depends so heavily on writing talent is lucky that, after a long drought, writers are everywhere. Each year discloses more names—1978 brought forward Dick Goldberg, whose *Family Business* examined the relationship of four brothers before and after the death of their father; 1979 introduced Bernard Pomerance (an American who lives in England) with *The Elephant Man*. Episodic and bitterly sentimental, this is one of the few prominent American plays to show some affinity with the Brechtian approach. Historical in setting, cynically matter-of-fact in tone, and using titles as subtextual glosses for each of its short scenes ("Art Is as Nothing to Nature"; "The English Public Will Pay for Him To Be Like Us"; "The Weight of Dreams"), *The Elephant Man* manages to contain the ugliest reality imaginable in a retooled, quasi-stylized reality that protects the public even as it makes them accept the ugliness for what Pomerance says it is: innocence and hope. The Man of the title, horribly misshapen through a rare disorder, is played by a normal-looking actor who scrunches his body slightly; moreover, the character is in a way redeemed through the understanding of an actress, brought in on the case as therapy because who but an actress could face such a grotesque while feigning equanimity? Yes, Pomerance (and his director, Jack Hofsiss, and especially Carole Shelley as the actress) has made the experience easy for the spectator. But the piece is based on truth—there really was an elephant man, one John Merrick.* Knowing this, the spectator makes the necessary adjustment for himself. The eye is shielded, not the mind.

Brecht would not have spared his public so—he never stints on brutality —and more than a few commentators decried the fallacy in dealing with such monstrous alienation while not showing it. But this is to note Pomerance's sentimentality and underestimate his bitterness. Unlike the feeble Nazis in *Bent* (which played concurrently with *The Elephant Man*), the cosmeticized Merrick of Broadway is not an escapist's failed naturalism, but a transcendence of it. Whether in sleazy carnival fairgrounds or in the late-Victorian London hospital that gives him refuge, the elephant man is a display freak— for paying gawkers in the former instance and benign upper-class sponsors in the latter. And for the New York audience. But why turn the aperçu into a sideshow stunt—why show us a monster? Pomerance delivers not Merrick's physical externals (except in a slide-show early on) but the romantic underneath, perhaps to ask us why a man who had a better right than any to be vicious and corrupt is nicer and purer than any in view. This play depends heavily on language: inventively, Pomerance scrapes at his theme even while letting out the line of character, as in this first meeting between the doctor and the actress:

TREVES: [Women] have always shown the greatest fear and loathing of him. While he adores them of course.

MRS. KENDAL: Ah. He is intelligent.

TREVES: I am convinced they are the key to retrieving him from his exclusion. Though, I must warn you, women are not quite real to him —more creatures of his imagination.

MRS. KENDAL: Then he is already like other men, Mr. Treves.

TREVES: So I thought, an actress could help. I mean, unlike most women, you won't give in, you are trained to hide your true feelings and assume others.

MRS. KENDAL: You mean unlike most women I am famous for it, that is really all.

. . .

Shall we try it? Left hand out please. (*Suddenly radiant*) I am *very* pleased to have made your acquaintance Mr. Merrick. I am very

---

* Pomerance, be it said, is writing a play, not a history, and expands chronicle with imagination; the actress, Madge Kendal, took up Merrick's cause but apparently never met him herself.

pleased to have made your acquaintance Mr. Merrick. I am very pleased
to have made your *acquaintance* Mr. Merrick. I am very pleased to
have made *your* acquaintance Mr. Merrick. Yes. That one.

TREVES: By god, they are all splendid. Merrick will be so pleased. It
will be the day he becomes a man like other men.

What *are* men, and women, like? That is the great theme of the time: people,
not precepts. This is one of reasons why off-Broadway has reasserted its
ancient position as supplier of new works to the national theatre—the outcasts matter more, now.

Single works such as *The Elephant Man,* obviously, do not constitute
seasons, and the one fact one must bear in mind in these late 1970s is the
rich variety of theatre. For as new authors joined the lists, the newly established authors sustained or even bettered their quality. 1978 brought out
major New York productions of Durang, Wesley, Wilson, Shepard; 1979
produced more Mamet, Wilson, Weller, Arthur Kopit's moving *Wings*
(another study in the aspiring mind of a physical casualty), and a brace of
comic and semi-comic works by new writers. Admittedly, today's playwrights
don't usually equal the intensity of first success that ushered Arthur Miller,
Tennessee Williams, or Edward Albee into the ranks of the arrived—but
today's playwrights do seem to develop as they write and show no sign of
tapering off. David Rabe rose to *Streamers,* employing three different levels
of idiomatic dialogue—the drunken sergeants, anxious privates, and former
street hood each command a different vernacular context—patterned around
the play's central image of a sky-diver whose chute fails to open. The use of
language is acute, far surpassing the facile guilt marketing of Rabe's two
earlier Vietnam plays. Similarly, Wilson and Mamet respectively grew up to
Fifth of July and *The Water Engine* . . . and so on.

There has been, then, an exuberant resurgence of activity in American
theatre only very lately, and it is too early to take a complete stock of its
strengths and weaknesses. Its problems we know: money. Yet, as Galileo
said, it moves. With production costs and ticket prices at an evil high, there
is still as much to see at any given moment in New York as there was in
the booming 1920s. Moreover, the "road" is back, the national stage, transformed into the immobile regional theatre but connected, as before, to New
York. Only now it sends to as well as receives from, and no longer prefers
reappearances of *Peg O'My Heart* and *The Student Prince* to more ambitious
work. As the 1980s commence, America's various resident theatre companies
show a conservative vitality: Shakespeare is by far the most favored playwright, followed by Tennessee Williams, Noel Coward, Lanford Wilson,

Sam Shepard, Henrik Ibsen, Bertolt Brecht, Edward Albee, Anton Chekhof, Alan Ayckbourne, Eugene O'Neill, George Bernard Shaw, Joe Orton, Tom Stoppard, Arthur Miller, and Samuel Beckett in something like that order, plus special interest in specific new works like *Wings*, *Sly Fox*, and the small revue, *Side by Side by Sondheim*. This is not even to count numerous premieres.

What is most exciting about contemporary theatre is its actually rather graceful acceptance of a new ethic on the condition of theatre. Once, the stage was useful in its affirmation of middle-class homilies and beautiful in its moral escapism. Now, it is useful in enlarging our awareness, in countering the culture; and its beauty, too, confronts with honesty. Having passed much of its sillier traits to sillier mediums, the theatre has gathered in its outcasts with its archetypes, irony with pleasanty, and it can field ideas, too, when it wants to. But its primary concern is in sculpting revelations of human character, in illuminating our understanding of what people are rather than what their system for being might be. As so often elsewhere in our culture, any attempt to impose system, even theoretically in art, is unsuccessful. We do have our classic experiments in universalized description, in which the deed is greater than the doer—*Our Town*, *Waiting for Lefty*, *The Iceman Cometh*. But the American public mainly wants isolated specifics, preferring to draw its own larger conclusions ad lib.

That, at length, is the purpose of our theatre, reaffirmed after decades of trying out other purposes and the consequent retreat from them into an escapism it has only recently broken out of. Who can say how far it may go now? This latest stage has just begun.

For Further Reading

THE CLASSIC COMPREHENSIVE VENERABLE HISTORY is Arthur Hobson Quinn's two-volume set, *A History of the American Drama* (New York: Harper and Brothers, 1923; 1927). Quinn is narrative and comprehensive but he never does pull his epic into perspective and, as a "polite" historian, sometimes frustrates the reader with his omissions. For instance, Quinn reports that the Mrs. Douglass who married the senior Lewis Hallam "had been forced from the stage on account of habits that rendered her unfit to act" and leaves us there, intrigued and left out at once. In his day, Quinn won praise for having made the definitive trek through the generally neglected early years of the American stage. I too have neglected them, finding them more fun than intelligent; readers who want greater detail should make the acquaintance of Quinn's Volume One.

Quinn revised Volume Two halfway through the 1930s, carefully neglecting any mention of the insurgent adversary stage. Luckily, writers have covered this most fascinating decade in depth. The standard work on the protest theatre is Malcolm Goldstein's *The Political Stage* (New York: Oxford University Press, 1974), renowned for its completeness and sturdiness of research. Astonishingly, Goldstein manages to retain his engagement with people and events without ever taking a side, letting the reader contribute to the adventure with his own slant. Narratives by those who were themselves involved in the political theatre lack Goldstein's scholarly precision, but Harold Clurman's *The Fervent Years* (New York: Alfred A. Knopf, 1945) and Jay Williams' *Stage Left* (New York: Charles Scribner's Sons, 1974) carry the savvy of personal witness. Clurman's account is especially inviting, one of the three or four most admired books on American theatre. Nominally a history of the Group Theatre, *The Fervent Years* deals with much of the New York theatre scene in the 1930s, and Clurman has a sharp eye for character. He gives us Clifford Odets exploding out of obscurity into a challenging fame fringed on all sides by Hollywood lotus; John Howard Lawson countering Clurman's underwhelmed opinion of Lawson's working-class *Marching Song* with "Don't you think proletarian plays should be written at this time?" and Clurman's recounter of "Perhaps. But not by you"; and Stella Adler, Clurman's first wife, poking him in bed one morning to say, "Don't sleep like a great man, just sleep."

The post-Depression decades have not found a worthy historian, whether from the establishment or adversary stages. Many readers have made do with the appropriate chapters in full-length histories written by New York drama reviewers. Howard Taubman of the *Times* produced *The Making of the American Theatre* (New York: Coward-McCann, sec. ed., 1967); like Taubman's reviews this is sloppy and worthless. Even worse is Emory Lewis' *Stages* (Englewood Cliffs: Prentice-Hall, 1969), a bid for countercultural vogue that drools over radical entries and pretty much ignores or disdains everything else. In this field of "first-night" historians, Brooks Atkinson's *Broadway* (New York: Macmillan, 1970) is preferred for its many photographs and sensible reporting, though the author's famous probity becomes a bit irritating after a while.

Readers interested in off-Broadway might try Stuart Little's *Off-Broadway: The Prophetic Theatre* (New York: Coward, McCann and Geoghegan, 1972). On the more specifically radical stage of the 1960s and '70s, Judith Malina's *The Enormous Despair* (New York: Random House, 1972), a journal of Malina's peregrinations through America with the Living Theatre from August 1968 to April 1969, is heartily recommended. Malina and her husband Julian Beck stood in the vanguard of the revolutionary theatre in their brief heyday, and she is a superb spectator of the little human events that suggest great public happenings. Moreover, just by being who she is, she pulls together the contradictory drives of the Movement. The paranoia is there: the troupe returns to America just after the 1968 Democratic Convention in Chicago and assumes that the F.B.I. is everywhere. The whimsey is there: one of the group, "flipped out by the American scene," waves her arms and cries, "Evacuate the continent!" The innocence is there: on Merv Griffin's talk show, Malina recounts, "Julian and I talk for more than ten minutes on the beautiful nonviolent anarchist revolution." The hatred and longing for violence is there, too, and Malina knows it. At one point, she writes, "The great question looms: Is our goal destruction or transformation?"

As for the musical, I deliberately skimmed it in these pages, having dealt with it at length in *Better Foot Forward* (New York: The Viking Press, 1976). This is a pleasant but, I must admit, disappointingly superficial book; I hope to revise it one day. Meanwhile, Gerald Bordman's *The American Musical Theatre* (Oxford University Press, 1978) has the advantage of completeness. Bordman goes through the years work by work, missing nothing.

Reference, as opposed to analysis and reading enjoyment, is a problem —no one work does it all. Burns Mantle's *Best Plays* series, launched in 1920, covers each season with introductory essays on the scenes in various cities, digest versions of "best" plays without the slightest taste of theatre in them, and useful appendices that include cast and crew listings for each production. (Two volumes covered 1899–1909 and 1909–1919 as an afterthought.) The Boston firm of Small, Maynard inaugurated the series; in the late 1920s, Dodd, Mead took it over and still issues the yearly volumes, now edited by Otis Guernsey and expanded to cover American regional companies, London and Paris, and, especially, off- and off-off-Broadway. Guernsey's reductions of the scripts capture a sense of theatre better than Mantle's (and those of his successors, John Chapman, Louis Kronenberger, and Henry Hewes) did, though he, like Mantle, doesn't know how to approach the musical libretto. Mantle seldom included one at all, and when he did he tried to treat it like a "regular" play. Guernsey does it in pictures and quotations of lyrics, the musical as song cycle.

In the matter of biographies and critical studies, the litter yields mostly runts, from hackwork to deferentially ghostwritten "autobiographies." Very few of these volumes cast any light on the art; as Mantle did, these authors treat plays as dry text and recall the mere shadow of character. Of the tellers' own tales, the first two volumes of John Houseman's as yet uncompleted life story (New York: Simon and Schuster), *Runthrough* (1972) and *Front and Center* (1980), prove fine reading. Houseman dallied in the arenas of the great, so he knows how to bring them to life. Some theatre people believe he is a second-rater slyly giving himself too much credit, but as sheer reading the books are choice.

Of those who tell others' tales, John Kobler's *Damned in Paradise: The Life of John Barrymore* (New York: Atheneum, 1977) and Tad Mosel and Gertrude Macy's *Leading Lady: The World and Theatre of Katharine Cor-*

nell (Boston: Atlantic Monthly Press, 1978) stand out. Barrymore and Cornell helped lead the crucial transition in acting style from nineteenth-century Big Moment mannerism into the qualified naturalism of the 1910s and '20s, arrestingly honest but still heedful of the Moments. Thus their Broadway is a very historical one, full of revelation on How It Was Done. Mosel and Macy are helpfully intimate with contracts, rehearsals, and the like. But the great Martha Graham, in her brief introduction to their book, tells the most when she recalls Cornell's advice: "Martha, when you exit take everything with you, even the grand piano if there is one on the stage."

For a taste of commercial show business to balance the ideals of Clurman and Malina, try Jerry Stagg's *The Brothers Shubert* (New York: Random House, 1968). George S. Kaufman fits another piece into the puzzle of art as industry, perhaps its most telling piece; again, Malcolm Goldstein supplies the standard work, *George S. Kaufman: His Life, His Theatre* (Oxford University Press, 1979), considering the aesthetics as well as the person, as the title suggests. John Lahr's *Notes on a Cowardly Lion* (Knopf, 1969) occupies a wholly special category, the author's subject being his father. As comedian, Bert Lahr, too, set up a special category, and if most of the plays he appeared in are now forgotten, his persona contributed much to the epistemology of American comedic acting. The book is fine, even essential, reading.

Many critical studies cover the work of one author in one volume, the bulk of attention going to the Miller-Williams-Albee post–World War II Broadway writers. One might do well to pass them all up for O'Neill, whose failures are more interesting than many authors' successes. Two huge works lead the field with a commentative panorama of Life and Work: Barbara and Arthur Gelb's *O'Neill* (New York: Harper and Row, 1960) and Louis Sheaffer's two volumes (Boston: Little, Brown), *Son and Playwright* (1968) and *Son and Artist* (1973). Sheaffer's titles underline the rebellious inheritor in O'Neill, too often discounted by critics looking for more invention than transformation in America's artistic 1920s. Smaller than the Gelbs and Sheaffer but no less able is Travis Bogard's *Contour in Time: The Plays of Eugene O'Neill* (Oxford University Press, 1972).

Collections of theatre journalism—reviews, reminiscences, celebrations, and thinkpieces—stimulate even when the subjects are obsolete works or defunct thespians. Many theatre enthusiasts cite George Oppenheimer's *The Passionate Playgoer* (Viking, 1958), subtitled "a personal scrapbook." Personally, I find Oppenheimer's collection lacking in bite. Typical of his selections are Walter Kerr's *My Fair Lady* review, Edna Ferber on "Glamour,"

Elia Kazan's "Notebook for *A Streetcar Named Desire*" (fascinating), and *Time* magazine's 1949 profile of Cole Porter (obtuse). One may do much better to follow one analyst through a focused train of thought, and a good place to start is with George Jean Nathan. The most probing of critics in the 1920s, '30s, and '40s, Nathan wrote in a rich, cynically witty style, and even the trashiest opus provided him with a platform for some high topical flying. Any of his many books repays investigation, especially his *Theatre Book of the Year* series, annual play-by-play accounts of each season from 1942–43 to 1950–51 (first published by Knopf and now available in reprints from Fairleigh-Dickinson University Press). Still, perhaps the neatest approach to Nathan is through his *Encyclopedia of the Theatre* (Knopf, 1940), filled with exuberant put-downs of the midcult urge in the idea of an American Broadway.

Nathan was contemptuous of the sociopolitical aspect of criticism; more recent analysts welcome it. The collections of Robert Brustein and Stanley Kauffmann, mostly drawn from their *New Republic* pieces, demonstrate how much "awareness" is an inescapable component of aesthetics. Try Kauffmann's *Persons of the Drama* (Harper and Row, 1976) and Brustein's *Seasons of Discontent* (New York: Simon and Schuster, 1965) and *The Third Theatre* (Knopf, 1969). Brustein's "third theatre" describes the youthfully vivacious new theatre typified by *MacBird!* and *America Hurrah*; John Lahr, another advocate of the inventive non-commercial stage, complements Brustein's discussions of the seminal works of this third thespian space with looks into such subjects as street theatre, "The End of the Underground," the Open Theatre, the Performance Group, and Sam Shepard in *Up Against the Fourth Wall* (New York: Grove Press, 1970) and *Astonish Me* (Viking, 1973). Many writers seized upon such items in the late 1960s and early '70s, but I think it is Brustein, Kauffmann, and Lahr, with their curiosity about all kinds of theatre and their wide cultural perspective, who have the most to say. For instance: Kauffmann includes a lengthy disquisition on Verdi, Lahr deals authoritatively with "The American Musical: The Slavery of Escape," and Brustein recalls (in *The Third Theatre*) a stint in New York's moribund Yiddish Theatre that is better than all of *The Passionate Playgoer* put together. Meanwhile, Robert A. Martin has gathered together *The Theater Essays of Arthur Miller* (Viking, 1978), which—like Miller's stage output—is morally inspiriting but loses interest as it proceeds.

Let's close with a miscellany. Bernard Beckerman and Howard Siegman's *On Stage* (New York: Arno Press, 1973) reproduces first-night reports from the *New York Times* from 1920 to 1970 in the original newsprint and fuzzy photos. With its representative selection and prefaces to each decade, the volume was clearly meant to carry historical impact, but its usefulness will depend on the reader's opinion of the critics involved—mainly Brooks Atkinson, but opening with the ludicrous Alexander Woollcott and closing with Clive Barnes. Catharine Hughes' *Plays, Politics, and Polemics* (New York: Drama Book Specialists/Publishers, 1973) is a novelty worth investigating: an unbiased look at plays of bias, all but one (*The Crucible*) dating from the American Vietnam era yet covering—in subjects—a varied itinerary from the extermination of the American Indian to survival in the Nazi death camp. Lastly, let me recommend William Goldman's *The Season* (New York: Harcourt Brace and World, 1969), whose subtitle, "A Candid Look at Broadway," offers a rare instance of publisher's understatement. Goldman goes through the 1967–68 season (by topic rather than by work), dealing, along the way, with the economics of the theatre party, homosexuals, the culture hero, and corruption of all kinds. Candid? The man is brutally honest. Though the persons in Broadway's drama have changed somewhat since 1968, the facts of its life have not, and the book proves as vital and saddening now as it did when new. The chapter on critics, "The Approvers," remains the best supported attack on New York's reviewing system ever mounted.

Index